W9-CAS-962

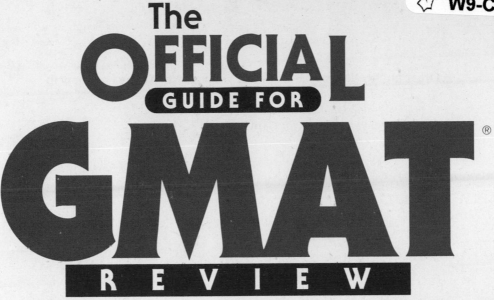

The OFFICIAL GUIDE FOR GMAT® REVIEW

Prepared for the
Graduate Management Admission Council
by Educational Testing Service

Inquiries concerning this publication should be directed to GMAT Program Direction Office, Educational Testing Service, P.O. Box 6106, Princeton, NJ 08541-6106.

Other publications of the Graduate Management Admission Council:
- *The Official Guide to MBA Programs*
- *The Official Guide to Financing Your MBA*
- *The Official Software for GMAT Review*

USA: 0-446-39439-4
CAN: 0-446-39440-8

In association with Warner Books, Inc., a Warner Communications Company

Contents

Graduate Management Admission Council 5

Introduction 8

■ Chapter 1: Description of the Graduate
Management Admission Test 9
Format 9
Content 9
Problem Solving Questions 9
Data Sufficiency Questions 10
Reading Comprehension Questions 10
Critical Reasoning Questions 11
Sentence Correction Questions 11
General Test-Taking Suggestions 12
GMAT: Test Specifications 13
Test Development Process 13

■ Chapter 2: Math Review 15
Arithmetic 15
Algebra 23
Geometry 27
Word Problems 36

■ Chapter 3: Problem Solving 43
Sample Test Section 1 47
Answer Key and Explanatory Material 52
Sample Test Section 2 57
Answer Key and Explanatory Material 62
Sample Test Section 3 66
Answer Key and Explanatory Material 71
Sample Test Section 4 75
Answer Key and Explanatory Material 80
Sample Test Section 5 85
Answer Key and Explanatory Material 91
Sample Test Section 6 95
Answer Key and Explanatory Material 100
Sample Test Section 7 104
Answer Key and Explanatory Material 109
Sample Test Section 8 113
Answer Key and Explanatory Material 118

■ Chapter 4: Data Sufficiency 123
Sample Test Section 1 127
Answer Key and Explanatory Material 132
Sample Test Section 2 137
Answer Key and Explanatory Material 142
Sample Test Section 3 146
Answer Key and Explanatory Material 151
Sample Test Section 4 155
Answer Key and Explanatory Material 161

Contents *continued*

■ **Chapter 5: Reading Comprehension** 167
    Sample Test Section 1 173
    Answer Key and Explanatory Material...................... 179
    Sample Test Section 2 185
    Answer Key and Explanatory Material...................... 191
    Sample Test Section 3 198
    Answer Key and Explanatory Material...................... 204

■ **Chapter 6: Critical Reasoning** 209
    Sample Test Section 1 213
    Answer Key and Explanatory Material...................... 218
    Sample Test Section 2 226
    Answer Key and Explanatory Material...................... 232
    Sample Test Section 3 241
    Answer Key and Explanatory Material...................... 247

■ **Chapter 7: Sentence Correction** 255
    Sample Test Section 1 259
    Answer Key and Explanatory Material...................... 264
    Sample Test Section 2 270
    Answer Key and Explanatory Material...................... 275
    Sample Test Section 3 281
    Answer Key and Explanatory Material...................... 287
    Sample Test Section 4 293
    Answer Key and Explanatory Material...................... 298

■ **Chapter 8: Three Authentic Graduate**
        Management Admission Tests 305
    Form A 309
    Answer Key and Explanatory Material 347
    Form B 383
    Answer Key and Explanatory Material 421
    Form C 459
    Answer Key and Explanatory Material 497

Scoring Information 531

Guidelines for Use of Graduate Management
Admission Test Scores 545

Graduate Management Admission Council

The Graduate Management Admission Council (GMAC) is an organization of graduate business and management schools sharing a common interest in professional management education. The Council provides information to schools and prospective students to help both make reasoned choices in the admission process. It also provides a forum for the exchange of information through research, educational programs, and other services among the broad constituency of individuals and institutions concerned with management education.

The Council has three basic service objectives:

1. to enhance the management education admission process by:

   ■ developing and administering appropriate assessment instruments;

   ■ developing other services and materials related to the selection process;

   ■ informing schools and students about the appropriate use of such instruments and materials;

   ■ providing opportunities for the exchange of information between students and schools.

2. to broaden knowledge about management education by:

   ■ conducting educational research;

   ■ disseminating information about relevant research;

   ■ encouraging the development and exchange of information by professionals in the field.

3. to promote the highest standards of professional practice in the administration of management education programs and related activities by:

   ■ developing appropriate standards of practice;

   ■ offering educational programs and publications to provide essential knowledge, skills, and values;

   ■ providing other opportunities for professional development.

The Council currently contracts with Educational Testing Service (ETS) for development of GMAT test material, administration of the GMAT test, and preparation and distribution of GMAT score reports. The Council also determines policies and procedures for research and development of the GMAT; for publication of materials for students, guidance counselors, and admissions officers; and for nontesting services offered to management schools and applicants.

Member Schools

Arizona State University
College of Business

Babson College
Graduate School of Business

Baruch College
School of Business and Public Administration

Baylor University
Hankamer School of Business

Boston College
The Wallace E. Carroll Graduate School
   of Management

Boston University
School of Management

Bowling Green State University
College of Business Administration

Brigham Young University
Marriott School of Management

California State University, Long Beach
School of Business Administration

California State University, Los Angeles
School of Business and Economics

Carnegie Mellon University
Graduate School of Industrial Administration

Case Western Reserve University
Weatherhead School of Management

Clark Atlanta University
Graduate School of Business Administration

College of William and Mary
Graduate School of Business Administration

Columbia University
Columbia Business School

Cornell University
Johnson Graduate School of Management

Dartmouth College
Amos Tuck School of Business Administration

De Paul University
Graduate School of Business

Duke University
Fuqua School of Business

East Carolina University
School of Business

Emory University
Emory Business School

Florida State University
College of Business

George Mason University
School of Business Administration

Georgetown University
School of Business Administration

Georgia Institute of Technology
College of Management

Georgia Southern University
School of Business

Georgia State University
College of Business Administration

Hofstra University
School of Business

Howard University
School of Business

Indiana University (Bloomington)
Graduate School of Business

Kent State University
Graduate School of Management

Lehigh University
College of Business and Economics

Louisiana Tech University
College of Administration and Business

Marquette University
College of Business Administration

Massachusetts Institute of Technology
Sloan School of Management

Michigan State University
Eli Broad Graduate School of Management

New York University
Leonard N. Stern School of Business

Northeastern University
Graduate School of Business Administration

Northwestern University
J. L. Kellogg Graduate School of Management

The Ohio State University
College of Business

Old Dominion University
Graduate School of Business and Public Administration

Pennsylvania State University
The Smeal College of Business Administration

Purdue University (West Lafayette)
Krannert Graduate School of Management

Rensselaer Polytechnic Institute
School of Management

Rollins College
Roy E. Crummer Graduate School of Business

Rutgers, The State University of New Jersey
Graduate School of Management

San Francisco State University
School of Business

Seton Hall University
W. Paul Stillman School of Business

Southern Methodist University
Edwin L. Cox School of Business

Stanford University
Graduate School of Business

Suffolk University
School of Management

Syracuse University
School of Management

Temple University
School of Business and Management

Texas A&M University
College of Business Administration

Texas Christian University
M. J. Neeley School of Business

Tulane University
A. B. Freeman School of Business

The University of Alabama
Manderson Graduate School of Business

University of Arizona
Karl Eller Graduate School of Management

University at Buffalo (State University of New York)
School of Management

University of California, Berkeley
Walter A. Haas School of Business

University of California, Irvine
Graduate School of Management

University of California, Los Angeles
John E. Anderson Graduate School of Management

University of Chicago
Graduate School of Business

University of Cincinnati
College of Business Administration

University of Colorado at Boulder
Graduate School of Business Administration

University of Connecticut (Storrs)
School of Business Administration

University of Denver
Graduate School of Business

University of Florida
Graduate School of Business

University of Georgia
Graduate School of Business Administration

University of Hawaii at Manoa
College of Business Administration

University of Houston
College of Business Administration

University of Illinois at Chicago
College of Business Administration

University of Illinois at Urbana-Champaign
College of Commerce and Business Administration

University of Iowa
College of Business Administration

The University of Kansas
School of Business

University of Kentucky
College of Business and Economics

University of Maryland
College of Business and Management

University of Miami
School of Business Administration

The University of Michigan (Ann Arbor)
The Michigan Business School

University of Minnesota
Curtis L. Carlson School of Management

University of Missouri—Columbia
College of Business and Public Administration

University of Missouri—St. Louis
School of Business Administration

University of North Carolina at Chapel Hill
Kenan-Flagler Business School

University of Notre Dame
College of Business Administration

University of Oklahoma
College of Business Administration

University of Oregon
Graduate School of Management

University of Pennsylvania
The Wharton School (Graduate Division)

University of Pittsburgh
Joseph M. Katz Graduate School of Business

University of Rhode Island
College of Business Administration

University of Richmond
Richard S. Reynolds Graduate School

University of Rochester
William E. Simon Graduate School of
    Business Administration

University of San Francisco
McLaren College of Business

University of South Carolina
College of Business Administration

University of South Florida
College of Business Administration

University of Southern California
Graduate School of Business Administration

The University of Tennessee, Knoxville
College of Business Administration

University of Texas at Austin
Graduate School of Business

The University of Tulsa
College of Business Administration

University of Utah
David Eccles School of Business

University of Virginia
The Colgate Darden Graduate School of
    Business Administration

University of Washington
Graduate School of Business Administration

University of Wisconsin—Milwaukee
School of Business Administration

Vanderbilt University
Owen Graduate School of Management

Virginia Commonwealth University
School of Business

Virginia Polytechnic Institute and State University
The R. B. Pamplin College of Business

Washington State University
College of Business and Economics

Washington University (St. Louis)
John M. Olin School of Business

Introduction

The Official Guide for GMAT Review has been designed and written by the staff of Educational Testing Service, which prepares the Graduate Management Admission Test used by many graduate schools of business and management as one criterion in considering applications for admission to their graduate programs. This book is intended to be a general guide to the kinds of verbal and mathematical questions likely to appear in the GMAT. All questions used to illustrate the various types of questions are taken from actual editions of the GMAT administered between June 1982 and March 1991.*

The GMAT is not a test of knowledge in specific subjects—for example, it does not test knowledge specifically or uniquely acquired in accounting or economics courses. Rather, it is a test of certain skills and abilities that have been found to contribute to success in graduate programs in business and management. For this reason, it is useful to familiarize yourself with the general types of questions likely to be found in editions of the GMAT and the reasoning skills and problem-solving strategies that these types of questions demand. This book illustrates various types of questions that appear in the GMAT and explains in detail some of the most effective strategies for mastering these questions.

The most efficient and productive way to use this book is to read first through Chapter 1. Each type of question is briefly described, the directions are given, one or two examples are presented, and the skills each question type measures are outlined. You should pay particular attention to the directions for each question type. This is especially important for the Data Sufficiency questions, which have lengthy and complex directions.

Chapters 3-7 provide detailed illustrations and explanations of individual question types. After you read Chapter 1, you will find the most advantageous way to use the book is to choose a chapter on a particular question type, read carefully the introductory material, and then do the sample test sections in that chapter. As you take the sample test sections, follow the directions and time specifications given. When you complete a sample test section, use the answer key that follows it to check your responses. Then review the sample test section carefully, spending as much time as is necessary to familiarize yourself with the range of questions or problems presented in the sample test section.

You may find it useful to read through all of Chapter 2, Math Review, before working through Chapters 3, Problem Solving, and 4, Data Sufficiency, or you may wish to use Chapter 2 as a reference, noting—in Chapters 3 and 4—the suggested sections at the end of each explanation following the first sample test sections as you go along. However, since Chapter 2 is intended to provide you with a comprehensive review of the basic mathematical concepts used in the quantitative sections of the GMAT, you may find it valuable to read through the chapter as a whole.

The introductory material, sample test sections, and answer keys to the sample test sections in Chapter 5, Reading Comprehension, Chapter 6, Critical Reasoning, and Chapter 7, Sentence Correction, should be approached in the way suggested above. The explanatory materials for Reading Comprehension and Critical Reasoning have been written as thorough explanations of the reasoning and problem-solving challenges each question type presents. Demonstrating strategies for successfully meeting these challenges, regardless of the particular content of the questions or problems that appear in a specific edition of the GMAT, is the objective of these explanations.

After you complete the review and practice built in to each chapter you should turn to Chapter 8, which includes three authentic GMAT tests. It will be most helpful in preparing yourself to take the GMAT if you regard the tests in Chapter 8 as facsimiles of the test you will take for scoring. Time yourself on each section, and follow the directions exactly as given.

Following each test reprinted in Chapter 8 is an answer key, information about scoring and score interpretation, and an explanation for every question on that test. Guidelines for the use of GMAT scores are also given.

---

*The material in *The Official Guide for GMAT Review* is intended to familiarize you with the types of questions found on the GMAT. Although the questions on the sample test sections in Chapters 3-7 represent the general nature of the questions on the test, it is possible that a type of question not illustrated by and explained in the *Guide* may appear on the GMAT. It is also possible that material illustrated by and explained in the *Guide* may not appear on the test.

1 Description of the Graduate Management Admission Test

The Graduate Management Admission Test is designed to help graduate schools assess the qualifications of applicants for advanced study in business and management. The test can be used by both schools and students in evaluating verbal and mathematical skills as well as general knowledge and preparation for graduate study. Note, however, that GMAT scores should be considered as only one of several indicators of ability.

Format

The current GMAT test consists entirely of multiple-choice questions, which are divided among seven separately timed sections; the total testing time is about three and a half hours. Each question offers five choices from which the examinee is to select the best answer.

Every form of the test contains one section of trial questions that are needed for pretesting and equating purposes. These questions, however, are not identified, and you should do your best on all questions. The answers to trial questions are not counted in your test score.

Both the Graduate Management Admission Council and Educational Testing Service are aware of the limits of the multiple-choice format, particularly in measuring an applicant's ability to formulate general concepts or to develop detailed supportive or opposing arguments. However, in a national testing program designed for a wide variety of people with different backgrounds, the use of a large number of short, multiple-choice questions has proved to be an effective and reliable way of providing a fair and valid evaluation of specific skills.

Content

It is important to recognize that the GMAT evaluates skills and abilities that develop over relatively long periods of time. Although the sections are basically verbal or mathematical, the complete test provides one method of measuring overall ability. The GMAT does not test specific knowledge obtained in college course work, and it does not seek to measure achievements in any specific areas of study.

The Graduate Management Admission Council recognizes that questions arise concerning techniques for taking standardized examinations such as the GMAT, and it is hoped that the descriptions, sample test sections, and explanations given here, along with the authentic test, will give you a practical familiarity with both the concepts and techniques required by GMAT questions.

The material on the following pages provides a general description and brief discussion of the objectives and techniques for each question type.

Following this general description of the GMAT test are a math review designed to help you review basic mathematical skills useful in the Problem Solving and Data Sufficiency sections of the GMAT and five chapters, one for each question type, that present sample test sections with answer keys and detailed explanations of the specific question types and of all questions and answers from the sample test sections. (The sample test sections are made up of questions that have appeared in the actual GMAT.) Methods of determining the best answer to a particular kind of question as well as explanations of the different kinds of questions appearing in any one section are also presented in these chapters. Chapter 8 contains three authentic GMAT tests. These are followed by answer keys, explanations for each question, and scoring information, which explains how GMAT scores are calculated and how they are interpreted.

Problem Solving Questions

This section of the GMAT is designed to test (1) basic mathematical skills, (2) understanding of elementary mathematical concepts, and (3) the ability to reason quantitatively and to solve quantitative problems. Approximately half the problems in the test are in a mathematical setting; the remainder are based on "real life" situations.

WHAT IS MEASURED

Problem Solving questions test your ability to understand verbal descriptions of situations and to solve problems using arithmetic, elementary algebra, or commonly known concepts of geometry.

The directions for Problem Solving questions read as follows:

Directions: In this section solve each problem, using any available space on the page for scratchwork. Then indicate the best of the answer choices given.

Numbers: All numbers used are real numbers.

Figures: Figures that accompany problems in this section are intended to provide information useful in solving the problems. They are drawn as accurately as possible EXCEPT when it is stated in a specific problem that its figure is not drawn to scale. All figures lie in a plane unless otherwise indicated.

Data Sufficiency Questions

Each of the problems in the Data Sufficiency section of the GMAT consists of a question, often accompanied by some initial information, and two statements, labeled (1) and (2), containing additional information. You must decide whether sufficient information to answer the question is given by either (1) or (2) individually or—if not—by both combined.

These are the directions that you will find for the Data Sufficiency section of the GMAT. Read them carefully.

Directions: Each of the data sufficiency problems below consists of a question and two statements, labeled (1) and (2), in which certain data are given. You have to decide whether the data given in the statements are *sufficient* for answering the question. Using the data given in the statements *plus* your knowledge of mathematics and everyday facts (such as the number of days in July or the meaning of *counterclockwise*), you are to fill in oval

A if statement (1) ALONE is sufficient, but statement (2) alone is not sufficient to answer the question asked;

B if statement (2) ALONE is sufficient, but statement (1) alone is not sufficient to answer the question asked;

C if BOTH statements (1) and (2) TOGETHER are sufficient to answer the question asked, but NEITHER statement ALONE is sufficient;

D if EACH statement ALONE is sufficient to answer the question asked;

E if statements (1) and (2) TOGETHER are NOT sufficient to answer the question asked, and additional data specific to the problem are needed.

Numbers: All numbers used are real numbers.

Figures: A figure in a data sufficiency problem will conform to the information given in the question, but will not necessarily conform to the additional information given in statements (1) and (2).

You may assume that lines shown as straight are straight and that angle measures are greater than zero.

You may assume that the positions of points, angles, regions, etc., exist in the order shown.

All figures lie in a plane unless otherwise indicated.

Example:

In $\triangle PQR$, what is the value of x?

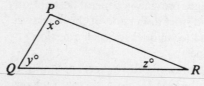

(1) $PQ = PR$
(2) $y = 40$

Explanation: According to statement (1), $PQ = PR$; therefore, $\triangle PQR$ is isosceles and $y = z$. Since $x + y + z = 180$, $x + 2y = 180$. Since statement (1) does not give a value for y, you cannot answer the question using statement (1) by itself. According to statement (2), $y = 40$; therefore, $x + z = 140$. Since statement (2) does not give a value for z, you cannot answer the question using statement (2) by itself. Using both statements together you can find y and z; therefore, you can find x, and the answer to the problem is C.

WHAT IS MEASURED

Data Sufficiency questions are designed to measure your ability to analyze a quantitative problem, to recognize which information is relevant, and to determine at what point there is sufficient information to solve the problem.

Reading Comprehension Questions

The Reading Comprehension section is made up of several reading passages about which you will be asked interpretive, applicative, and inferential questions. The passages are up to 450 words long, and they discuss topics from the social sciences, the physical or biological sciences, and business-related fields such as marketing, economics, and human resource management. Because every Reading Comprehension section includes passages from several different content areas, you will probably be generally familiar with some of the material; however, neither the passages nor the questions assume detailed knowledge of the topics discussed.

WHAT IS MEASURED

Reading Comprehension questions measure your ability to understand, analyze, and apply information and concepts presented in written form. All questions are to be answered on the basis of what is stated or implied in the reading material, and no specific knowledge of the material is required. Reading Comprehension therefore, evaluates your ability to

- understand words and statements in the reading passages (Questions of this type are not vocabulary questions. These questions test your understanding of and ability to use specialized terms as well as your understanding of the English language. You may also find that questions of this type ask about the overall meaning of a passage);

- understand the logical relationships between significant points and concepts in the reading passages (For example, such questions may ask you to determine the strong and weak points of an argument or to evaluate the importance of arguments and ideas in a passage);

- draw inferences from facts and statements in the reading passages (The inference questions will ask you to consider factual statements or information and, on the basis of that information, reach a general conclusion);

- understand and follow the development of quantitative concepts as they are presented in verbal material (This may involve the interpretation of numerical data or the use of simple arithmetic to reach conclusions about material in a passage).

The directions for Reading Comprehension questions read as follows:

Directions: Each passage in this group is followed by questions based on its content. After reading a passage, choose the best answer to each question and fill in the corresponding oval on the answer sheet. Answer all questions following a passage on the basis of what is *stated* or *implied* in that passage.

Critical Reasoning Questions

The Critical Reasoning section of the GMAT is designed to test the reasoning skills involved (1) in making arguments, (2) in evaluating arguments, and (3) in formulating or evaluating a plan of action. Most of the questions are based on a separate argument or set of statements; occasionally, two or three questions are based on the same argument or set of statements. The materials on which questions are based are drawn from a variety of sources. No familiarity with the subject matter of those materials is presupposed.

WHAT IS MEASURED

Critical Reasoning questions are designed to provide one measure of your ability to reason effectively in the areas of

- argument construction (Questions in this category may ask you to recognize such things as the basic structure of an argument; properly drawn conclusions; underlying assumptions; well-supported explanatory hypotheses; parallels between structurally similar arguments);

- argument evaluation (Questions in this category may ask you to analyze a given argument and to recognize such things as factors that would strengthen, or weaken, the given argument; reasoning errors committed in making that argument; aspects of the method by which the argument proceeds);

- formulating and evaluating a plan of action (Questions in this category may ask you to recognize such things as the relative appropriateness, effectiveness, or efficiency of different plans of action; factors that would strengthen, or weaken, the prospects of success for a proposed plan of action; assumptions underlying a proposed plan of action).

The directions for Critical Reasoning questions read as follows:

Directions: For each question in this section, select the best of the answer choices given.

Sentence Correction Questions

Sentence Correction questions ask you which of the five choices best expresses an idea or relationship. The questions will require you to be familiar with the stylistic conventions and grammatical rules of standard written English and to demonstrate your ability to improve incorrect or ineffective expressions.

WHAT IS MEASURED

Sentence Correction questions test two broad aspects of language proficiency:

1. *Correct expression.* A correct sentence is grammatically and structurally sound. It conforms to all the rules of standard written English (for example: noun-verb agreement, noun-pronoun agreement, pronoun consistency, pronoun case, and verb tense sequence). Further, a correct sentence will not have dangling, misplaced, or improperly formed modifiers, will not have unidiomatic or inconsistent expressions, and will not have faults in parallel construction.

2. *Effective expression*. An effective sentence expresses an idea or relationship clearly and concisely as well as grammatically. This does not mean that the choice with the fewest and simplest words is necessarily the best answer. It means that there are no superfluous words or needlessly complicated expressions in the best choice.

In addition, an effective sentence uses proper diction. (Diction refers to the standard dictionary meaning of words and the appropriateness of words in context.) In evaluating the diction of a sentence, you must be able to recognize whether the words are well chosen, accurate, and suitable for the context.

The directions for Sentence Correction questions read as follows:

Directions: In each of the following sentences, some part of the sentence or the entire sentence is underlined. Beneath each sentence you will find five ways of phrasing the underlined part. The first of these repeats the original; the other four are different. If you think the original is better than any of the alternatives, choose answer A; otherwise choose one of the others. Select the best version and fill in the corresponding oval on your answer sheet.

This is a test of correctness and effectiveness of expression. In choosing answers, follow the requirements of standard written English; that is, pay attention to grammar, choice of words, and sentence construction.

Choose the answer that expresses most effectively what is presented in the original sentence; this answer should be clear and exact, without awkwardness, ambiguity, or redundancy.

Examples:
A thunderclap is a complex acoustic signal <u>as a result of</u> rapid expansion of heated air in the path of a lightning flash.

(A) as a result of
(B) caused as a result of
(C) resulting because of the
(D) resulting from the
(E) that results because there is

In choice A, *is a . . . . signal as a result of* is incorrect. It is the thunderclap that results from the expansion; its being a signal is irrelevant. In choice B, it is superfluous to use both *caused* and *result,* and it is also superfluous to use both *result* and *because* in choices C and E. In choice C, *because of* is not the correct preposition to use after *resulting*; *from* is correct and is used in the best answer, D.

<u>Ever since the Civil War, the status of women was</u> a live social issue in this country.

(A) Ever since the Civil War, the status of women was
(B) Since the Civil War, women's status was
(C) Ever since the Civil War, the status of women has been
(D) Even at the time of the Civil War, the status of women has been
(E) From the times of the Civil War, the status of women has been

In choice A, the verb following *women* should be *has been,* not *was,* because *ever since* denotes a period of time continuing from the past into the present. For the same reason, *was* is inappropriately used with *since* in choice B. In choice D, *even at* changes the meaning of the original sentence substantially and does not fit with *has been; was* is correct with *even at.* In choice E, *times* is incorrect; the standard phrase is *from the time of.* C is the best answer.

General Test-Taking Suggestions

1. Although the GMAT stresses accuracy more than speed, it is important to use the allotted time wisely. You will be able to do so if you are familiar with the mechanics of the test and the kinds of materials, questions, and directions in the test. Therefore, become familiar with the formats and requirements of each section of the test.

2. After you become generally familiar with all question types, use the individual chapters on each question type in this book (Chapters 3-7), which include sample test sections and detailed explanations, to prepare yourself for the actual GMAT tests in Chapter 8. When taking the tests, try to follow all the requirements specified in the directions and keep within the

time limits. While these tests are useful for familiarization, they cannot be used to predict your performance on the actual test.

3. Read all test directions carefully. Since many answer sheets give indications that the examinees do not follow directions, this suggestion is particularly important. The directions explain exactly what each section requires in order to answer each question type. If you read hastily, you may miss important instructions and seriously jeopardize your scores.

4. Answer as many questions as possible, but avoid random guessing. Your GMAT scores will be based on the number of questions you answer correctly minus a fraction of the number you answer incorrectly. Therefore, it is unlikely that mere guessing will improve your scores significantly, and it does take time. However, if you have some knowledge of a question and can eliminate at least one of the answer choices as wrong, your chance of getting the best answer is improved, and it will be to your advantage to answer the question. If you know nothing at all about a particular question, it is probably better to skip it. The number of omitted questions will not be subtracted.

5. Take a watch to the examination and be sure to note the time limit for each section. Since each question has the same weight, it is not wise to spend too much time on one question if that causes you to neglect other questions.

6. Make every effort to pace yourself. Work steadily and as rapidly as possible without being careless.

7. A wise practice is to answer the questions you are sure of first. Then, if time permits, go back and attempt the more difficult questions.

8. Read each question carefully and thoroughly. Before answering a question, determine exactly what is being asked. Never skim a question or the possible answers. Skimming may cause you to miss important information or nuances in the question.

9. Do not become upset if you cannot answer a question. A person can do very well without answering every question or finishing every section. No one is expected to get a perfect score.

10. When you take the test, you will mark your answers on a separate answer sheet. As you go through the test, be sure that the number of each answer on the answer sheet matches the corresponding question number in the test book. Your answer sheet may contain space for more answers or questions than there are in the test book. Do not be concerned, but be careful. Indicate each of your answers with a dark mark that completely fills the response position on the answer sheet. Light or partial marks may not be properly read by the scoring machine. Indicate only one response to each question, and erase all unintended marks completely.

GMAT: Test Specifications

All editions of the GMAT are constructed to measure the same skills and meet the same specifications. Thus, each section of the test is constructed according to the same specifications for every edition of the GMAT. These specifications include definite requirements for the number of questions, the points tested by each question, the kinds of questions, and the difficulty of each question.

Because the various editions of the test inevitably differ somewhat in difficulty, they are made equivalent to each other by statistical methods. This equating process makes it possible to assure that all reported scores of a given value denote approximately the same level of ability regardless of the edition being used or of the particular group taking the test at a given time.

Test Development Process

Educational Testing Service professional staff responsible for developing the verbal measures of the GMAT have backgrounds and advanced degrees in the humanities or in measurement. Those responsible for the quantitative portion have advanced degrees in mathematics or related fields.

Standardized procedures have been developed to guide the test-generation process, to assure high-quality test material, to avoid idiosyncratic questions, and to encourage development of test material that is widely appropriate.

An important part of the development of test material is the review process. Each question, as well as any stimulus material on which questions are based, must be reviewed by several independent critics. In appropriate cases, questions are also reviewed by experts outside ETS who can bring fresh perspectives to bear on the questions in terms of actual content or in terms of sensitivity to minority and women's concerns.

After the questions have been reviewed and revised as appropriate, they are assembled into clusters suitable for trial during actual administrations of the GMAT. In this manner, new questions are tried out, under standard testing conditions, by representative samples of GMAT examinees. Questions being tried out do not affect examinees' scores but are themselves evaluated: they are analyzed statistically for usefulness and weaknesses. The questions that perform satisfactorily become part of a pool of questions from which future editions of the GMAT can be assembled; those that do not are rewritten to correct the flaws and tried out again—or discarded.

In preparing those sections of the GMAT that will contribute to the scoring process, the test assembler uses only questions that have been successfully tried out. The test assembler considers not only each question's characteristics but also the relationship of the question to the entire group of questions with respect to the test specifications discussed above. When the test has been assembled, it is reviewed by a second test specialist and by the test development coordinator for the GMAT.

After satisfactory resolution of any points raised in these reviews, the test goes to a test editor. The test editor's review is likely to result in further suggestions for change, and the test assembler must decide how these suggested changes will be handled. If a suggested change yields an editorial improvement, without jeopardizing content integrity, the change is adopted; otherwise, new wording is sought that will meet the dual concerns of content integrity and editorial style. The review process is continued at each stage of test assembly and copy preparation, down to careful scrutiny of the final proof immediately prior to printing.

All reviewers except the editor and proofreader must attempt to answer each question without the help of the answer key. Thus, each reviewer "takes the test," uninfluenced by knowledge of what the question writer or test assembler believed each answer should be. The answer key is certified as official only after at least three reviewers have agreed independently on the best answer for each question.

The extensive, careful procedure described here has been developed over the years to assure that every question in any new edition of the GMAT is appropriate and useful and that the combination of questions that make up the new edition is satisfactory. Nevertheless, the appraisal is not complete until after the new edition has been administered during a national test administration and subjected to a rigorous process of analysis to see whether each question yields the expected result. This further appraisal sometimes reveals that a question is not satisfactory after all; it may prove to be ambiguous, or require information beyond the scope of the test, or be otherwise unsuitable. Answers to such questions are not used in computing scores.

2 Math Review

Although this chapter provides a review of some of the mathematical concepts of arithmetic, algebra, and geometry, it is not intended to be a textbook. You should use this chapter to familiarize yourself with the kinds of topics that are tested in the GMAT. You may wish to consult an arithmetic, algebra, or geometry book for a more detailed discussion of some of the topics.

The topics that are covered in Section A, arithmetic, include:

1. Properties of integers
2. Fractions
3. Decimals
4. Real numbers
5. Positive and negative numbers
6. Ratio and proportion
7. Percents
8. Equivalent forms of a number
9. Powers and roots of numbers
10. Mean
11. Median
12. Mode

The content of Section B, algebra, does not extend beyond what is covered in a first-year high school course. The topics included are:

1. Simplifying algebraic expressions
2. Equations
3. Solving linear equations with one unknown
4. Solving two linear equations with two unknowns
5. Solving factorable quadratic equations
6. Exponents
7. Absolute value
8. Inequalities

Section C, geometry, is limited primarily to measurement and intuitive geometry or spatial visualization. Extensive knowledge of theorems and the ability to construct proofs, skills that are usually developed in a formal geometry course, are not tested. The topics included in this section are:

1. Lines
2. Intersecting lines and angles
3. Perpendicular lines
4. Parallel lines
5. Polygons (convex)
6. Triangles
7. Quadrilaterals
8. Circles
9. Solids
10. Rectangular solids
11. Cylinders
12. Pyramids
13. Coordinate geometry

Section D, word problems, presents examples of and solutions to the following types of word problems:

1. Rate
2. Work
3. Mixture
4. Interest
5. Discount
6. Profit
7. Sets
8. Geometry
9. Measurement
10. Data interpretation

A. Arithmetic

1. INTEGERS

An *integer* is any number in the set $\{\ldots, -3, -2, -1, 0, 1, 2, 3, \ldots\}$. If x and y are integers and $x \neq 0$, x is a *divisor* (*factor*) of y provided that $y = xn$ for some integer n. In this case y is also said to be *divisible* by x or to be a *multiple* of x. For example, 7 is a divisor or factor of 28 since $28 = 7 \cdot 4$, but 6 is not a divisor of 28 since there is no integer n such that $28 = 6n$.

Any integer that is divisible by 2 is an *even integer*; the set of even integers is $\{\ldots -4, -2, 0, 2, 4, 6, 8, \ldots\}$. Integers that are not divisible by 2 are *odd integers*; $\{\ldots -3, -1, 1, 3, 5, \ldots\}$ is the set of odd integers.

If at least one factor of a product of integers is even, then the product is even; otherwise the product is odd. If two integers are both even or both odd, then their sum and their difference are even. Otherwise, their sum and their difference are odd.

A *prime* number is an integer that has exactly two different positive divisors, 1 and itself. For example, 2, 3, 5, 7, 11, and 13 are prime numbers, but 15 is not, since 15 has four different positive divisors, 1, 3, 5, and 15. The number 1 is not a prime number, since it has only one positive divisor.

The numbers $-2, -1, 0, 1, 2, 3, 4, 5$ are *consecutive integers*. Consecutive integers can be represented by $n, n + 1, n + 2, n + 3, \ldots$, where n is an integer. The numbers 0, 2, 4, 6, 8 are *consecutive even integers,* and 1, 3, 5, 7, 9 are *consecutive odd integers.* Consecutive even integers can be represented by $2n$, $2n + 2, 2n + 4, \ldots$, and consecutive odd integers can be represented by $2n + 1$, $2n + 3, 2n + 5, \ldots$, where n is an integer.

Properties of the integer 1. If n is any number, then $1 \cdot n = n$, and for any number $n \neq 0$, $n \cdot \frac{1}{n} = 1$. The number 1 can be expressed in many ways, e.g., $\frac{n}{n} = 1$ for any number $n \neq 0$. Multiplying or dividing an expression by 1, in any form, does not change the value of that expression.

Properties of the integer zero. The integer zero is neither positive nor negative. If n is any number, then $n + 0 = n$ and $n \cdot 0 = 0$. Division by zero is not defined.

2. FRACTIONS

In a fraction $\frac{n}{d}$, n is the *numerator* and d is the *denominator.* The denominator of a fraction can never be zero, because division by zero is not defined.

Two fractions are said to be *equivalent* if they represent the same number. For example, $\frac{4}{8}, \frac{3}{6}$, and $\frac{1}{2}$ are equivalent since all three represent the number $\frac{1}{2}$.

Addition and subtraction of fractions. To add or subtract two fractions with the same denominator, simply perform the required operation with the numerators, leaving the denominators the same. For example, $\frac{3}{5} + \frac{4}{5} = \frac{3+4}{5} = \frac{7}{5}$, and $\frac{5}{7} - \frac{2}{7} = \frac{5-2}{7} = \frac{3}{7}$. If two fractions do not have the same denominator, express them as equivalent fractions with the same denominator. For example, to add $\frac{3}{5}$ and $\frac{4}{7}$, multiply the numerator and denominator of the first fraction by 7 and the numerator and denominator of the second fraction by 5, obtaining $\frac{21}{35}$ and $\frac{20}{35}$, respectively;

$$\frac{21}{35} + \frac{20}{35} = \frac{41}{35}.$$

Also,

$$\frac{2}{3} + \frac{1}{6} = \frac{2}{3} \cdot \frac{2}{2} + \frac{1}{6} = \frac{4}{6} + \frac{1}{6} = \frac{5}{6}.$$

Multiplication and division of fractions. To multiply two fractions, simply multiply the two numerators and multiply the two denominators. For example, $\frac{2}{3} \times \frac{4}{7} = \frac{2 \times 4}{3 \times 7} = \frac{8}{21}$.

To divide by a fraction, invert the divisor (i.e., find its *reciprocal*) and multiply. For example, $\frac{2}{3} \div \frac{4}{7} = \frac{2}{3} \times \frac{7}{4} = \frac{14}{12} = \frac{7}{6}$.

In the problem above, the reciprocal of $\frac{4}{7}$ is $\frac{7}{4}$. In general, the reciprocal of a fraction $\frac{n}{d}$ is $\frac{d}{n}$, where n and d are not zero.

Mixed numbers. A number that consists of a whole number and a fraction, e.g., $7\frac{2}{3}$, is a mixed number. $7\frac{2}{3}$ means $7 + \frac{2}{3}$.

To change a mixed number into a fraction, multiply the whole number by the denominator of the fraction and add this number to the numerator of the fraction; then put the result over the denominator of the fraction. For example,

$$7\frac{2}{3} = \frac{(3 \times 7) + 2}{3} = \frac{23}{3}.$$

3. DECIMALS

In the decimal system, the position of the period or *decimal point* determines the place value of the digits. For example, the digits in the number 7,654.321 have the following place values:

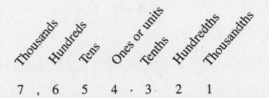

$$7 \quad , \quad 6 \quad 5 \quad 4 \quad \cdot \quad 3 \quad 2 \quad 1$$

Some examples of decimals follow.

$$0.321 = \frac{3}{10} + \frac{2}{100} + \frac{1}{1,000} = \frac{321}{1,000}$$

$$0.0321 = \frac{0}{10} + \frac{3}{100} + \frac{2}{1,000} + \frac{1}{10,000} = \frac{321}{10,000}$$

$$1.56 = 1 + \frac{5}{10} + \frac{6}{100} = \frac{156}{100}$$

Sometimes decimals are expressed as the product of a number with only one digit to the left of the decimal point and a power of 10. For example, 231 may be written as 2.31×10^2 and 0.0231 may be written as 2.31×10^{-2}. The exponent on the 10 indicates the number of places that the decimal point is to be moved in the number that is to be multiplied by a power of 10 in order to obtain the product. The decimal point is moved to the right if the exponent is positive and to the left if the exponent is negative. For example, 20.13×10^3 is equal to 20,130 and 1.91×10^{-4} is equal to 0.000191.

Addition and subtraction of decimals. To add or subtract two decimals, the decimal points of both numbers should be lined up. If one of the numbers has fewer digits to the right of the decimal point than the other, zeros may be inserted to the right of the last digit. For example, to add 17.6512 and 653.27, set up the numbers in a column and add:

$$\begin{array}{r} 17.6512 \\ + 653.2700 \\ \hline 670.9212 \end{array}$$

Likewise, 653.27 minus 17.6512 =

$$\begin{array}{r} 653.2700 \\ - 17.6512 \\ \hline 635.6188 \end{array}$$

Multiplication of decimals. To multiply decimals, multiply the numbers as if they were whole numbers and then insert the decimal point in the product so that the number of digits to the right of the decimal point is equal to the sum of the numbers of digits to the right of the decimal points in the numbers being multiplied. For example:

$$
\begin{array}{r}
2.09 \quad \text{(2 digits to the right)} \\
\times \ \ 1.3 \quad \text{(1 digit to the right)} \\
\hline
627 \\
209 \ \ \ \\
\hline
2.717 \quad \text{(2 + 1 = 3 digits to the right)}
\end{array}
$$

Division of decimals. To divide a number (the dividend) by a decimal (the divisor), move the decimal point of the divisor to the right until the divisor is a whole number. Then move the decimal point of the dividend the same number of places to the right, and divide as you would by a whole number. The decimal point in the quotient will be directly above the decimal point in the new dividend. For example, to divide 698.12 by 12.4:

$$12.4 \,\overline{)698.12}$$

will be replaced by

$$124 \,\overline{)6981.2}$$

and the division would proceed as follows:

$$
\begin{array}{r}
56.3 \\
124 \,\overline{)6981.2} \\
620 \ \ \ \ \\
\hline
781 \ \\
744 \ \\
\hline
372 \\
372 \\
\hline
\end{array}
$$

4. REAL NUMBERS

All *real* numbers correspond to points on the number line and all points on the number line correspond to real numbers. All real numbers except zero are either positive or negative.

On a number line, numbers corresponding to points to the left of zero are negative and numbers corresponding to points to the right of zero are positive. For any two numbers on the number line, the number to the left is less than the number to the right; for example,

$-4 < -3, \frac{1}{2} < \frac{3}{4}$, and $0.05 < 0.12$.

To say that the number n is between 1 and 4 on the number line means that $n > 1$ and $n < 4$; i.e., $1 < n < 4$.

The distance between a number and zero on the number line is called the *absolute value* (magnitude) of the number. Thus 3 and -3 have the same absolute value, 3, since they are both three units from zero. The absolute value of 3 is denoted $|3|$. Examples of absolute values of numbers are

$$|-5| = |5| = 5, \left|-\frac{7}{2}\right| = \frac{7}{2}, \text{ and } |0| = 0.$$

Note that the absolute value of any nonzero number is positive.

5. POSITIVE AND NEGATIVE NUMBERS

Addition and subtraction. To add two numbers that have the same sign, add the absolute values of the numbers and insert the common sign. For example:

$$(-7) + (-9) = -16$$

because

$$(-7) + (-9) = -(|-7| + |-9|) = -(7 + 9) = -16.$$

To add two numbers with different signs, find the positive difference between their absolute values and insert the sign of the number with the greater absolute value. For example,

$$(-13) + 19 = 6$$

because

$$(-13) + 19 = +(|19| - |-13|) = +(19 - 13) = 6.$$

Similarly,

$$-16 + 8 = -8$$

because

$$-16 + 8 = -(|-16| - |8|) = -(16 - 8) = -8.$$

To subtract one number from another, express the difference as a sum and add as indicated above. That is, $a - b = a + (-b)$. For example:

$$(-7) - (5) = -7 + (-5) = -12$$
$$6 - (-4) = 6 + [-(-4)] = 6 + 4 = 10$$
$$-54 - (-23) = -54 + [-(-23)] = -54 + 23$$
$$= -(54 - 23) = -31$$

(Note that for any number n, $-(-n) = n$.)

Multiplication and division. To multiply or divide two numbers with the same sign, multiply or divide their absolute values; thus, the product and quotient are positive. For example:

$$(-13)(-3) = (13)(3) = 39$$
$$(-14) \div (-2) = 14 \div 2 = 7$$

To multiply or divide two numbers with different signs, multiply or divide their absolute values and insert a negative sign; thus, the product and quotient are negative. For example:

$$(13)(-3) = -(13)(3) = -39$$
$$(-14) \div 2 = -(14 \div 2) = -7$$

Some properties of real numbers that are used frequently follow. If x, y, and z are real numbers, then

(1) $x + y = y + x$ and $xy = yx$.

For example, $8 + 3 = 3 + 8 = 11$, and $17 \cdot 5 = 5 \cdot 17 = 85$.

(2) $(x + y) + z = x + (y + z)$ and $(x \cdot y)z = x(y \cdot z)$.

For example, $(7 + 5) + 2 = 7 + (5 + 2) = 7 + (7) = 14$, and $(5 \cdot \sqrt{3})(\sqrt{3}) = 5(\sqrt{3} \cdot \sqrt{3}) = 5 \cdot 3 = 15$.

(3) $x(y + z) = xy + xz$.

For example, $718(36) + 718(64) = 718(36 + 64) = 718(100) = 71{,}800$.

6. RATIO AND PROPORTION

The *ratio* of the number a to the number b (b $\neq$ 0) is $\frac{a}{b}$.

A ratio may be expressed or represented in several ways. For example, the ratio of the number 2 to the number 3 can be written 2 to 3, 2:3, and $\frac{2}{3}$. The order of the terms of a ratio is important. For example, the ratio of the number of months with exactly 30 days to the number with exactly 31 days is $\frac{4}{7}$, not $\frac{7}{4}$.

A *proportion* is a statement that two ratios are equal; for example, $\frac{2}{3} = \frac{8}{12}$ is a proportion. One way to solve a proportion involving an unknown is to cross multiply, obtaining a new equality. For example, to solve for n in the proportion $\frac{2}{3} = \frac{n}{12}$, cross multiply, obtaining $24 = 3n$; then divide both sides by 3, to get $n = 8$.

7. PERCENTS

Percent means per hundred or number out of 100. A percent can be represented as a fraction with a denominator of 100, or as a decimal. For example,

$$37\% = \frac{37}{100} = 0.37.$$

To find a certain percent of a number, multiply the number by the percent expressed as a decimal or fraction. For example:

$$20\% \text{ of } 90 = 0.20 \times 90 = 18$$

or

$$20\% \text{ of } 90 = \frac{20}{100} \times 90 = \frac{1}{5} \times 90 = 18.$$

Percents greater than 100. Percents greater than 100 are represented by numbers greater than 1. For example:

$$300\% = \frac{300}{100} = 3$$

$$250\% \text{ of } 80 = 2.5 \times 80 = 200$$

Percents less than 1. The percent 0.5% means $\frac{1}{2}$ of 1 percent. For example, 0.5% of 12 is equal to $0.005 \times 12 = 0.06$.

Percent change. Often a problem will ask for the percent increase or decrease from one quantity to another quantity. For example, ''If the price of an item increases from \$24 to \$30, what is the percent increase in price?'' To find the percent increase, first find the amount of the increase; then divide this increase by the original amount, and express this quotient as a percent. In the example above, the percent increase would be found in the following way: the amount of the increase is $(30 - 24) = 6$.

Therefore, the percent increase is $\frac{6}{24} = 0.25 = 25\%$.

Likewise, to find the percent decrease (e.g., the price of an item is reduced from $30 to $24), first find the amount of the decrease; then divide this decrease by the original amount, and express this quotient as a percent. In the example above, the amount of decrease is $(30 - 24) = 6$. Therefore, the percent decrease is

$\frac{6}{30} = 0.20 = 20\%$.

Note that the percent increase from 24 to 30 is not the same as the percent decrease from 30 to 24.

In the following example, the increase is greater than 100 percent: If the cost of a certain house in 1983 was 300 percent of its cost in 1970, by what percent did the cost increase?

If n is the cost in 1970, then the percent increase is equal to $\frac{3n - n}{n} = \frac{2n}{n} = 2$, or 200 percent.

8. EQUIVALENT FORMS OF A NUMBER

In solving a particular problem, it may be helpful to convert the given form of a number to a more convenient form.

To convert a fraction to a decimal, divide the numerator by the denominator, e.g., $\frac{3}{4} = 0.75$.

$$
\begin{array}{r}
0.75 \\
4\,\overline{)3.00} \\
\underline{28} \\
20 \\
\underline{20}
\end{array}
$$

To convert a number to a percent, multiply by 100. For example, $0.75 = (0.75 \times 100)\% = 75\%$.

The decimal 0.625 means $\frac{625}{1,000}$ (see page 17). This fraction may be simplified by dividing the numerator and denominator by common factors. For example:

$\frac{625}{1,000} = \frac{5 \cdot \cancel{5} \cdot \cancel{5} \cdot \cancel{5}}{2 \cdot 2 \cdot 2 \cdot \cancel{5} \cdot \cancel{5} \cdot \cancel{5}} = \frac{5}{8}$.

To convert a percent to a decimal, divide by 100; e.g.:

$$24\% = \frac{24}{100} = 0.24.$$

In the following examples, it is helpful to convert from one form of a number to another form.

Of the following, which is LEAST?

(A) 35% (B) $\frac{9}{20}$ (C) 0.42 (D) $\frac{(0.9)(4)}{10}$ (E) $\frac{3}{13}$

These numbers can be compared more easily if they are all converted to decimals:

$35\% = 0.35$

$\dfrac{9}{20} = 0.45$

$0.42 = 0.42$

$\dfrac{(0.9)(4)}{10} = 0.36$

$\dfrac{3}{13} = 0.23$ (to 2 decimal places)

Thus, $\dfrac{3}{13}$ is the least of the numbers.

9. POWERS AND ROOTS OF NUMBERS

When a number k is to be used n times as a factor in a product, it can be expressed as k^n, which means the nth power of k. For example, $2^2 = 2 \times 2 = 4$ and $2^3 = 2 \times 2 \times 2 = 8$ are powers of 2.

Squaring a number that is greater than 1, or raising it to a higher power, results in a larger number; squaring a number between 0 and 1 results in a smaller number. For example:

$3^2 = 9 \qquad\qquad (9 > 3)$

$\left(\dfrac{1}{3}\right)^2 = \dfrac{1}{9} \qquad\qquad \left(\dfrac{1}{9} < \dfrac{1}{3}\right)$

$(0.1)^2 = 0.01 \qquad\qquad (0.01 < 0.1)$

A *square root* of a non-negative number n is a number that when squared is equal to n. Every positive number n has two square roots, one positive and the other negative, but $\sqrt{n}$ denotes the positive number whose square is n. For example, $\sqrt{9}$ denotes 3. The two square roots of 9 are $\sqrt{9} = 3$ and $-\sqrt{9} = -3$.

Every real number r has exactly one real *cube root*, which is the number s such that $s^3 = r$. The real cube root of r is denoted by $\sqrt[3]{r}$. Since $2^3 = 8$, $\sqrt[3]{8} = 2$. Similarly, $\sqrt[3]{-8} = -2$, because $(-2)^3 = -8$.

10. MEAN

The *average (arithmetic mean)* of n values is equal to the sum of the n values divided by n. For example, the average (arithmetic mean) of 9, 6, 5, and 12 is

$\dfrac{9 + 6 + 5 + 12}{4} = 8$.

11. MEDIAN

When an odd number of values are ordered from least to greatest or from greatest to least, the value in the middle is the *median;* i.e., there are equal numbers of values above and below the median. For example, the median of 4, 7, 3, 10, and 8 is 7, since, when ordered from least to greatest (3,4,7,8,10), 7 is the middle value. When there is an even number of values, the median is the average of the two middle values. For example, the median of 5,3,2,10,7, and 8 is $\dfrac{5 + 7}{2} = 6$.

12. MODE

The *mode* of a list of values is the value that occurs most frequently. For example, the mode of 1, 3, 6, 4, 3, and 5 is 3. A list of values may have more than one mode. For example, the list of values 1,2,3,3,3,5,7,10,10,10,20 has two modes, 3 and 10.

B. Algebra

In algebra, a letter such as x or n is used to represent an unknown quantity. For example, suppose Pam has 5 more pencils than Fred. If you let f represent the number of pencils that Fred has, then the number of pencils that Pam has is f + 5.

A combination of letters and mathematical operations, such as f + 5, $\frac{3x^3}{2x - 5}$, and $19x^2 + 6x + 3$, is called an *algebraic expression*.

In the expression 9x − 6, 9x and −6 are *terms* of the expression; 9 is called the *coefficient* of x.

1. SIMPLIFYING ALGEBRAIC EXPRESSIONS

Often when working with algebraic expressions, it is necessary to simplify them by factoring or combining *like* terms. For example, the expression 6x + 5x is equivalent to (6 + 5)x or 11x. In the expression 9x − 3y, 3 is a factor common to both terms: 9x − 3y = 3(3x − y). In the expression $5x^2 + 6y$, there are no like terms and no common factors.

If there are common factors in the numerator and denominator of an expression, they can be divided out, provided that they are not equal to zero.

For example, if x ≠ 3, $\frac{3xy - 9y}{x - 3}$ is equal to $\frac{3y(x - 3)}{x - 3}$; since

$\frac{x - 3}{x - 3}$ is equal to 1, $\frac{3y(x - 3)}{x - 3} = 3y \cdot 1 = 3y$.

To multiply two algebraic expressions, each term of one expression is multiplied by each term of the other expression. For example:

$$(3x - 4)(9y + x) \text{ is equal to } 3x(9y + x) - 4(9y + x) =$$
$$(3x)(9y) + (3x)(x) + (-4)(9y) + (-4)(x) =$$
$$27xy + 3x^2 - 36y - 4x$$

An algebraic expression can be evaluated by substituting values of the unknowns in the expression. For example, if x = 3 and y = −2, $3xy - x^2 + y$ can be evaluated as

$$3(3)(-2) - (3)^2 + (-2) = -18 - 9 - 2 = -29.$$

2. EQUATIONS

A statement that two algebraic expressions are equal is an *equation*. Some examples of equations are

$$5x - 2 = 9$$

and

$$3x + 1 = y - 2.$$

Two equations having the same solution(s) are *equivalent*. For example,

$$2 + x = 3$$

and

$$4 + 2x = 6$$

are equivalent equations, as are

$$3x - y = 6$$

and

$$6x = 2y + 12.$$

3. SOLVING LINEAR EQUATIONS WITH ONE UNKNOWN

To solve a linear equation (i.e., to find the value of the unknown that satisfies the equation) you need to isolate the unknown on one side of the equation. This can be done by performing the same mathematical operations on both sides of the equation.

Remember that if the same number is added to or subtracted from both sides of the equation, this does not change the equality; likewise, multiplying or dividing both sides by the same nonzero number does not change the equality. For example, to solve the equation $\frac{5x - 6}{3} = 4$ for x, you can isolate x using the following steps:

$$\frac{5x - 6}{3} = 4$$
$$5x - 6 = 12 \quad \text{(multiplying by 3)}$$
$$5x = 12 + 6 = 18 \quad \text{(adding 6)}$$
$$x = \frac{18}{5} \quad \text{(dividing by 5)}$$

The solution, $\frac{18}{5}$, can be checked by substituting it in the original equation for x to determine whether it satisfies that equation. For example:

$$\frac{5\left(\frac{18}{5}\right) - 6}{3} = \frac{18 - 6}{3} = \frac{12}{3} = 4$$

Therefore, the value of x obtained above is the solution.

4. SOLVING TWO LINEAR EQUATIONS WITH TWO UNKNOWNS

If you have two linear equations that are not equivalent, you can find any values for the two unknowns that satisfy both equations. One way to solve for the two unknowns is to express one of the unknowns in terms of the other using one of the equations, and then substitute it into the remaining equation to obtain an equation with one unknown. This equation can be solved and the value substituted in one of the equations to find the value of the other unknown. For example, the following two equations can be solved for x and y.

$$(1) \quad 3x + 2y = 11$$
$$(2) \quad x - y = 2$$

In equation (2), $x = 2 + y$. Substitute $2 + y$ in equation (1) for x:

$$3(2 + y) + 2y = 11$$
$$6 + 3y + 2y = 11$$
$$6 + 5y = 11$$
$$5y = 5$$
$$y = 1$$

If $y = 1$, then $x = 2 + 1 = 3$.

Another way to solve for x and y is to solve the two equations simultaneously. The purpose is to eliminate one of the unknowns. This can be done by making the coefficients of one of the unknowns the same (disregarding the sign) in both equations and either adding the equations or subtracting one equation from the other. For example, to solve the equations below simultaneously

$$(1) \quad 6x + 5y = 29$$
$$(2) \quad 4x - 3y = -6$$

multiply equation (1) by 3 and equation (2) by 5 to get

$$18x + 15y = 87$$
$$20x - 15y = -30$$

By adding the two equations you can eliminate y and get $38x = 57$ or $x = \frac{3}{2}$. Then substitute $\frac{3}{2}$ for x in one of the equations to find $y = 4$. These answers can be checked by substituting both values into both of the original equations.

5. SOLVING FACTORABLE QUADRATIC EQUATIONS

An equation that can be put in the standard form

$$ax^2 + bx + c = 0,$$

where a, b, and c are real numbers and $a \neq 0$, is a *quadratic* equation. For example,

$$x^2 + 6x + 5 = 0,$$
$$x^2 - 2x = 0,$$

and

$$x^2 - 4 = 5$$

are quadratic equations. Some quadratic equations can be solved by factoring. For example:

(1) $x^2 + 6x + 5 = 0$
$(x + 5)(x + 1) = 0$
$x + 5 = 0$ or $x + 1 = 0$
$x = -5$ or $x = -1$

(2) $x^2 - 2x = 0$
$x(x - 2) = 0$
$x = 0$ or $x = 2$

(3) $3x^2 - 3 = 8x$
$3x^2 - 8x - 3 = 0$
$(3x + 1)(x - 3) = 0$
$3x + 1 = 0$ or $x - 3 = 0$
$x = -\frac{1}{3}$ or $x = 3$

In general, first put the quadratic equation into the standard form $ax^2 + bx + c = 0$, then factor the left-hand side of the equation, i.e., find two linear expressions whose product is the given quadratic expression. Since the product of the factors is equal to zero, at least one of the factors must be equal to zero. The values found by setting the factors equal to zero are called the *roots* of the equation. These roots can be checked by substituting them into the original equation to determine whether they satisfy the equation.

A quadratic equation has at most two real roots and may have just one or even no real root. For example, the equation $x^2 - 6x + 9 = 0$ can be expressed as $(x - 3)^2 = 0$ or $(x - 3)(x - 3) = 0$; thus the only root is 3.

The equation $x^2 + 1 = 0$ has no real root. Since the square of any real number is greater than or equal to zero, $x^2 + 1$ must be greater than zero.

An expression in the form $a^2 - b^2$ is equal to

$$(a - b)(a + b).$$

For example, if

$$9x^2 - 25 = 0,$$

then

$$(3x - 5)(3x + 5) = 0;$$
$$3x - 5 = 0 \text{ or } 3x + 5 = 0;$$
$$x - \frac{5}{3} \text{ or } x - -\frac{5}{3}.$$

Therefore, the roots are $\frac{5}{3}$ and $-\frac{5}{3}$.

6. EXPONENTS

A positive integer exponent on a number indicates the number of times that number is to be a factor in the product. For example, x^5 means $x \cdot x \cdot x \cdot x \cdot x$; i.e., x is a factor in the product 5 times.

Some rules about exponents are:

Let r, s, x, and y be positive integers.

(1) $(x^r)(x^s) = x^{(r+s)}$; for example $2^2 \cdot 2^3 = 2^{(2+3)} = 2^5 = 32$.

(2) $(x^r)(y^r) = (xy)^r$; for example, $3^3 \cdot 4^3 = 12^3 = 1{,}728$.

(3) $\left(\dfrac{x}{y}\right)^r = \dfrac{x^r}{y^r}$; for example, $\left(\dfrac{2}{3}\right)^3 = \dfrac{2^3}{3^3} = \dfrac{8}{27}$.

(4) $\dfrac{x^r}{x^s} = x^{r-s}$; for example, $\dfrac{4^5}{4^2} = 4^{5-2} = 4^3 = 64$.

(5) $(x^r)^s = x^{rs} = (x^s)^r$; for example, $(x^3)^4 = x^{12} = (x^4)^3$.

(6) $x^{\frac{r}{s}} = \left(x^{\frac{1}{s}}\right)^r = \left(x^r\right)^{\frac{1}{s}} = \sqrt[s]{x^r}$; for example, $8^{\frac{2}{3}} = \left(8^{\frac{1}{3}}\right)^2 = \left(8^2\right)^{\frac{1}{3}} = \sqrt[3]{8^2} = \sqrt[3]{64} = 4$

and $9^{\frac{1}{2}} = \sqrt{9} = 3$.

(7) $x^{-r} = \dfrac{1}{x^r}$; for example, $3^{-2} = \dfrac{1}{3^2} = \dfrac{1}{9}$.

(8) $x^0 = 1$; for example $6^0 = 1$; 0^0 is undefined.

The rules above also apply when r, s, x and y are not integers. Furthermore, the rules also apply when the numbers are negative, except for (5) and (6), which hold in some cases but not others.

7. ABSOLUTE VALUE

The absolute value of x, denoted $|x|$, is defined to be x if $x \geq 0$ and $-x$ if $x < 0$. Note that $\sqrt{x^2}$ denotes the non-negative square root of x^2, that is $\sqrt{x^2} = |x|$.

8. INEQUALITIES

An *inequality* is a statement that uses one of the following symbols:

$\neq$ not equal to

$>$ greater than

$\geq$ greater than or equal to

$<$ less than

$\leq$ less than or equal to

Some examples of inequalities are $5x - 3 < 9$, $6x \geq y$, and $\dfrac{1}{2} < \dfrac{3}{4}$. Solving an inequality is similar to solving an equation; the unknown is isolated on one side of the inequality. Like an equation, the same number can be added to or subtracted from both sides of the inequality or both sides of an inequality can be multiplied or divided by a positive number without changing the truth of the inequality. However, multiplying or dividing an inequality by a negative number reverses the order of the inequality. For example, $6 > 2$, but $(-1)(6) < (-1)(2)$.

To solve the inequality $3x - 2 > 5$ for x, isolate x by using the following steps:

$$3x - 2 > 5$$

$$3x > 7 \text{ (adding 2 to both sides)}$$

$$x > \frac{7}{3} \text{ (dividing both sides by 3)}$$

To solve the inequality $\frac{5x-1}{-2} < 3$ for x, isolate x by using the following steps:

$$\frac{5x-1}{-2} < 3$$

$$5x - 1 > -6 \text{ (multiplying both sides by } -2)$$
$$5x > -5 \text{ (adding 1 to both sides)}$$
$$x > -1 \text{ (dividing both sides by 5)}$$

C. Geometry

1. LINES

In geometry, the word "line" refers to a straight line.

The line above can be referred to as line PQ or line ℓ. The part of the line from P to Q is called a *line segment*. P and Q are the *endpoints* of the segment. The notation PQ is used to denote both the segment and the length of the segment. The intention of the notation can be determined from the context.

2. INTERSECTING LINES AND ANGLES

If two lines intersect, the opposite angles are vertical angles and have the same measure. In the figure

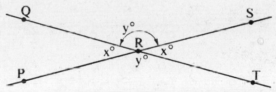

∠PRQ and ∠SRT are vertical angles and ∠QRS and ∠PRT are vertical angles.

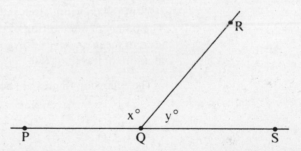

In the figure above, PQS is a straight line, or straight angle, and x + y = 180. ∠PQR and ∠RQS are adjacent angles since they share a common side.

An angle that has a measure of 90° is a *right* angle.

Two angles whose measures sum to 90° are *complementary* angles, and two angles whose measures sum to 180° are *supplementary* angles.

3. PERPENDICULAR LINES

If two lines intersect at right angles, the lines are *perpendicular*. For example:

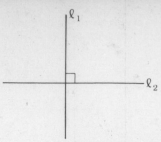

ℓ_1 and ℓ_2 are perpendicular, denoted by $\ell_1 \perp \ell_2$. A right angle symbol in an angle of intersection indicates that the lines are perpendicular.

4. PARALLEL LINES

If two lines that are in the same plane do not intersect, the two lines are *parallel.* In the figure

lines ℓ_1 and ℓ_2 are parallel, denoted by $\ell_1 \parallel \ell_2$. If two parallel lines are intersected by a third line, as shown below, the angle measures are related in the following ways, where $x + y = 180$.

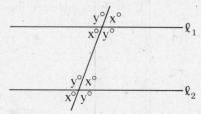

5. POLYGONS (CONVEX)

A *polygon* is a closed plane figure formed by three or more line segments, called the *sides* of the polygon. Each side intersects exactly two other sides at their endpoints. The points of intersection of the sides are *vertices.* The term "polygon" will be used to mean a convex polygon, i.e., a polygon in which each interior angle has a measure of less than 180°.

The following figures are polygons:

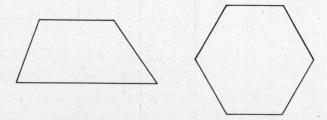

The following figures are not polygons:

-28-

A polygon with three sides is a *triangle*; with four sides, a *quadrilateral*; with five sides, a *pentagon*; and with six sides, a *hexagon*.

The sum of the angle measures of a triangle is 180°. In general, the sum of the angle measures of a polygon with n sides is equal to $(n - 2)180°$. For example, a pentagon has $(5 - 2)180 = (3)180 = 540$ degrees.

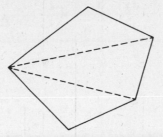

Note that a pentagon can be partitioned into three triangles and therefore the sum of the angle measures can be found by adding the sum of the angle measures of three triangles.

The *perimeter* of a polygon is the sum of the lengths of its sides.

The commonly used phrase ''area of a polygon (or any other plane figure)'' will be used to mean the area of the region enclosed by that figure.

6. TRIANGLES

An *equilateral* triangle has all sides of equal length. All angles of an equilateral triangle have equal measure. An *isosceles* triangle has at least two sides of the same length. If two sides of a triangle have the same length, then the two angles opposite those sides have the same measure. Conversely, if two angles of a triangle have the same measure, then the sides opposite those angles have the same length. In isosceles triangle PQR,

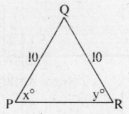

x = y since PQ = QR.

A triangle that has a right angle is a *right* triangle. In a right triangle, the side opposite the right angle is the *hypotenuse*, and the other two sides are the *legs*. An important theorem concerning right triangles is the *Pythagorean theorem*, which states: In a right triangle, the square of the length of the hypotenuse is equal to the sum of the squares of the lengths of the legs.

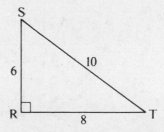

In right $\triangle RST$, $(RS)^2 + (RT)^2 = (ST)^2$. For example, if $RS = 6$ and $RT = 8$, then $ST = 10$, since $6^2 + 8^2 = 36 + 64 = 100 = (ST)^2$ and $ST = \sqrt{100}$. Any triangle in which the lengths of the sides are in the ratio 3:4:5 is a right triangle. In general, if a, b, and c are the lengths of the sides of a triangle and $a^2 + b^2 = c^2$, then the triangle is a right triangle.

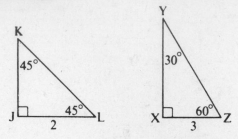

In 45°-45°-90° triangles, the lengths of the sides are in the ratio $1:1:\sqrt{2}$. For example, in $\triangle JKL$, if $JL = 2$, then $JK = 2$, and $KL = 2\sqrt{2}$. In 30°-60°-90° triangles, the lengths of the sides are in the ratio $1:\sqrt{3}:2$. For example, in $\triangle XYZ$, if $XZ = 3$, then $XY = 3\sqrt{3}$, and $YZ = 6$.

Area. The area of a triangle is equal to:

$$\frac{\text{(the length of the altitude)} \times \text{(the length of the base)}}{2}$$

The *altitude* of a triangle is the segment drawn from a vertex perpendicular to the side opposite that vertex. Relative to that vertex and altitude, the opposite side is called the *base*.

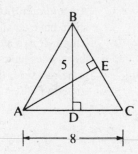

In $\triangle ABC$, BD is the altitude to base AC and AE is the altitude to base BC. The area of $\triangle ABC$ is equal to

$$\frac{BD \times AC}{2} = \frac{5 \times 8}{2} = 20.$$

The area is also equal to $\frac{AE \times BC}{2}$. If $\triangle ABC$ above is isosceles and $AB = BC$, then altitude BD bisects the base; i.e., $AD = DC = 4$. Similarly, any altitude of an equilateral triangle bisects the side to which it is drawn.

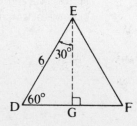

In equilateral triangle DEF, if $DE = 6$, then $DG = 3$, and $EG = 3\sqrt{3}$. The area of $\triangle DEF$ is equal to $\frac{3\sqrt{3} \times 6}{2} = 9\sqrt{3}$.

7. QUADRILATERALS

A polygon with four sides is a *quadrilateral*. A quadrilateral in which both pairs of opposite sides are parallel is a *parallelogram*. The opposite sides of a parallelogram also have equal length.

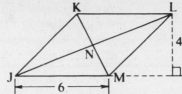

In parallelogram JKLM, JK ∥ LM and JK = LM; KL ∥ JM and KL = JM.

The diagonals of a parallelogram bisect each other (i.e., KN = NM and JN = NL).

The area of a parallelogram is equal to

(the length of the altitude) × (the length of the base).

The area of JKLM is equal to 4 × 6 = 24.

A parallelogram with right angles is a *rectangle,* and a rectangle with all sides of equal length is a *square*.

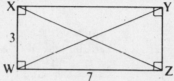

The perimeter of WXYZ = 2(3) + 2(7) = 20 and the area of WXYZ is equal to 3 × 7 = 21. The diagonals of a rectangle are equal; therefore WY = XZ = $\sqrt{9 + 49}$ = $\sqrt{58}$.

Note that a quadrilateral can have two right angles and not be a rectangle. For example, the figures

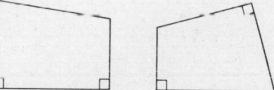

are not rectangles. But, if a quadrilateral has at least three right angles, then it must be a rectangle.

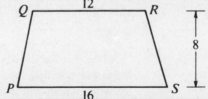

A quadrilateral with two sides that are parallel, as shown above, is a *trapezoid*. The area of trapezoid PQRS may be calculated as follows:

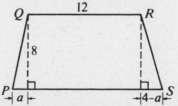

$$\text{Area} = 12 \times 8 + \frac{1}{2}(8a) + \frac{1}{2}(8)(4 - a) = 96 + 16 = 112$$

The area of the trapezoid is also equal to

$$\frac{1}{2}(\text{sum of bases})(\text{height}) = \frac{1}{2}(QR + PS)(8) = \frac{1}{2}(28 \times 8) = 112.$$

-31-

8. CIRCLES

A *circle* is a set of points in a plane that are all located the same distance from a fixed point (the *center* of the circle).

A *chord* of a circle is a line segment that has its endpoints on the circle. A chord that passes through the center of the circle is a *diameter* of the circle. A *radius* of a circle is a segment from the center of the circle to a point on the circle. The words "diameter" and "radius" are also used to refer to the lengths of these segments.

The *circumference* of a circle is the distance around the circle. If r is the radius of the circle, then the circumference is equal to $2\pi r$, where π is approximately $\frac{22}{7}$ or 3.14. The area of a circle of radius r is equal to πr^2.

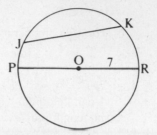

In the circle above, O is the center of the circle and JK and PR are chords. PR is a diameter and OR is a radius. If OR = 7, then the circumference of the circle is $2\pi(7) = 14\pi$ and the area of the circle is $\pi(7)^2 = 49\pi$.

The number of degrees of arc in a circle (or the number of degrees in a complete revolution) is 360.

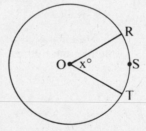

In the circle with center O above, the length of arc RST is $\frac{x}{360}$ of the circumference of the circle; e.g., if x = 60, arc RST has length $\frac{1}{6}$ of the circumference of the circle.

A line that has exactly one point in common with the circle is said to be *tangent* to the circle, and that common point is called the *point of tangency*. A radius or diameter with an endpoint at the point of tangency is perpendicular to the tangent line, and, conversely, a line that is perpendicular to a diameter at one of its endpoints is tangent to the circle at that endpoint.

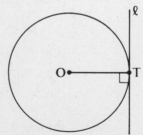

The line ℓ above is tangent to the circle and radius OT is perpendicular to ℓ.

Two different circles that have the same center, as shown below, are *concentric* circles.

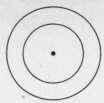

If each vertex of a polygon lies on a circle, then the polygon is *inscribed* in the circle and the circle is *circumscribed* about the polygon. If each side of a polygon is tangent to a circle, then the polygon is *circumscribed* about the circle and the circle is *inscribed* in the polygon.

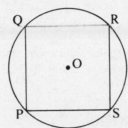 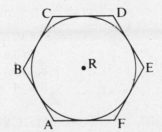

Quadrilateral PQRS is inscribed in circle O and hexagon ABCDEF is circumscribed about circle R.

If a triangle is inscribed in a circle so that one of its sides is a diameter of the circle, then the triangle is a right triangle.

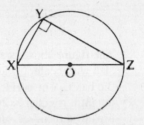

In the circle above, XZ is a diameter and the measure of ∠XYZ = 90°.

9. SOLIDS

The following are examples of three-dimensional figures called *solids:*

Rectangular Cylinder Pyramid Sphere Cone
Solid

10. RECTANGULAR SOLIDS

The *rectangular solid* shown above is formed by six rectangular surfaces. Each rectangular surface is a *face.* Each solid or dotted line segment is an *edge,* and each point at which the edges meet is a *vertex.* A rectangular solid has six faces, twelve edges, and eight vertices. Opposite faces are parallel rectangles that have the same dimensions. A rectangular solid in which all edges are of equal length is a *cube.*

The *surface area* of a rectangular solid is equal to the sum of the areas of all the faces. The *volume* is equal to

$$(\text{length}) \times (\text{width}) \times (\text{height});$$
in other words, (area of base) × (height).

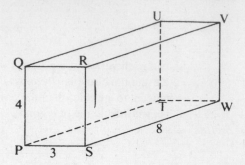

In the rectangular solid above, the dimensions are 3, 4, and 8. The surface area is equal to $2(3 \times 4) + 2(3 \times 8) + 2(4 \times 8) = 136$. The volume is equal to $3 \times 4 \times 8 = 96$.

11. CYLINDERS

The figure above is a right circular *cylinder*. The two bases are circles of the same size with centers O and P, respectively, and altitude (height) OP is perpendicular to the bases. The surface area of a right circular cylinder with a base of radius r and height h is equal to $2(\pi r^2) + 2\pi rh$ (the sum of the areas of the two bases plus the area of the curved surface).

The volume of a cylinder is equal to $\pi r^2 h$, i.e.:

$$(\text{area of base}) \times (\text{height}).$$

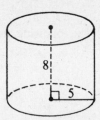

In the cylinder above, the surface area is equal to

$$2(25\pi) + 2\pi(5)(8) = 130\pi,$$

and the volume is equal to

$$25\pi(8) = 200\pi.$$

-34-

12. PYRAMIDS

Another solid with plane surfaces as faces is a *pyramid*. One of the faces (called the base) can be a polygon with any number of edges; the remaining faces are triangles. The figures below are pyramids. The shaded faces are the bases.

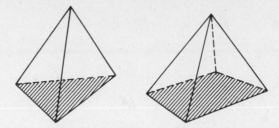

In the pyramid below, PQRS is a square, and the four triangles are the same size. V, the lower endpoint of altitude TV, is the center of the square.

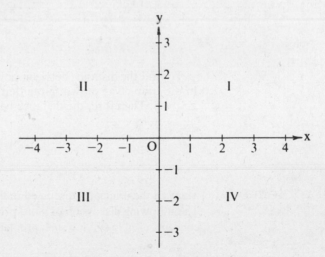

If altitude TV = 12 and VX = $\frac{1}{2}$ PS = 5, then, by the Pythagorean theorem,

TX = $\sqrt{5^2 + 12^2}$ = 13. Since TX = 13, and SX = $\frac{1}{2}$ RS = 5, therefore

TS = $\sqrt{13^2 + 5^2}$ = $\sqrt{194}$.

13. COORDINATE GEOMETRY

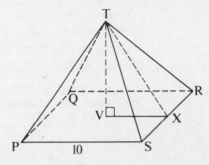

The figure above shows the (rectangular) *coordinate plane*. The horizontal line is called the *x-axis* and the perpendicular vertical line is called the *y-axis*. The point at which these two axes intersect, designated O, is called the *origin*. The axes divide the plane into four quadrants, I, II, III, and IV, as shown.

Each point in the plane has an *x-coordinate* and a *y-coordinate*. A point is identified by an ordered pair (x,y) of numbers in which the x coordinate is the first number and the y-coordinate is the second number.

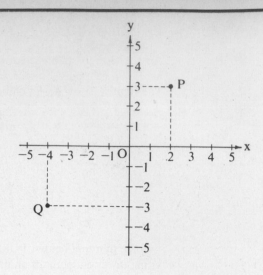

In the graph above, the (x,y) coordinates of point P are (2,3) since P is 2 units to the right of the y-axis (i.e., x = 2) and 3 units above the x-axis (i.e., y = 3). Similarly, the (x,y) coordinates of point Q are $(-4, -3)$. The origin O has coordinates (0,0).

One way to find distance between two points in the coordinate plane is to use the Pythagorean theorem.

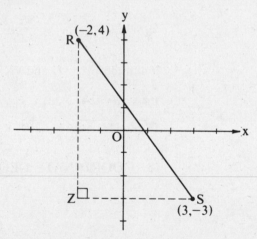

To find the distance between points R and S using the Pythagorean theorem, draw in the triangle as shown. Note that Z has (x,y) coordinates $(-2, -3)$, RZ = 7, and ZS = 5. Therefore, the distance between R and S is equal to:

$$\sqrt{7^2 + 5^2} = \sqrt{74}.$$

D. Word Problems

Many of the principles discussed in this chapter are used to solve word problems. The following discussion of word problems illustrates some of the techniques and concepts used in solving such problems.

1. RATE PROBLEMS

The distance that an object travels is equal to the product of the average speed at which it travels and the amount of time it takes to travel that distance; i.e.,

$$\text{Rate} \times \text{Time} = \text{Distance}.$$

Example 1: If a car travels at an average speed of 70 kilometers per hour for 4 hours, how many kilometers does it travel?

Solution: Since rate × time = distance, simply multiply 70 km/hour × 4 hours. Thus, the car travels 280 kilometers in 4 hours.

To determine the average rate at which an object travels, divide the total distance traveled by the total amount of time.

Example 2: On a 400-mile trip car X traveled half the distance at 40 miles per hour and the other half at 50 miles per hour. What was the average speed of car X?

Solution: First it is necessary to determine the amount of traveling time. During the first 200 miles the car traveled at 40 mph; therefore, it took $\frac{200}{40} = 5$ hours to travel the first 200 miles. During the second 200 miles the car traveled at 50 mph; therefore, it took $\frac{200}{50} = 4$ hours to travel the second 200 miles. Thus, the average speed of car X was $\frac{400}{9} = 44\frac{4}{9}$ mph. Note that the average speed is *not* $\frac{40 + 50}{2} = 45$.

Some of the problems can be solved by using ratios.

Example 3: If 5 shirts cost $44, then, at this rate, what is the cost of 8 shirts?

Solution: If c is the cost of the 8 shirts, then $\frac{5}{44} = \frac{8}{c}$. Cross multiplication results in the equation

$$5c = 8 \times 44 = 352$$
$$c = \frac{352}{5} = 70.40$$

The 8 shirts cost $70.40.

2. WORK PROBLEMS

In a work problem, the rates at which certain persons or machines work alone are usually given, and it is necessary to compute the rate at which they work together (or vice versa).

The basic formula for solving work problems is: $\frac{1}{r} + \frac{1}{s} = \frac{1}{h}$, where r and s are, for example, the number of hours it takes Rae and Sam, respectively, to complete a job when working alone and h is the number of hours it takes Rae and Sam to do the job when working together. The reasoning is that in 1 hour Rae does $\frac{1}{r}$ of the job, Sam does $\frac{1}{s}$ of the job, and Rae and Sam together do $\frac{1}{h}$ of the job.

Example 1: If machine X can produce 1,000 bolts in 4 hours and machine Y can produce 1,000 bolts in 5 hours, in how many hours can machines X and Y, working together at these constant rates, produce 1,000 bolts?

Solution: $\quad \frac{1}{4} + \frac{1}{5} = \frac{1}{h}$

$$\frac{5}{20} + \frac{4}{20} = \frac{1}{h}$$

$$\frac{9}{20} = \frac{1}{h}$$

$$9h = 20$$

$$h = \frac{20}{9} = 2\frac{2}{9} \text{ hours}$$

Working together, machines X and Y can produce 1,000 bolts in $2\frac{2}{9}$ hours.

Example 2: If Art and Rita can do a job in 4 hours when working together at their respective rates and Art can do the job alone in 6 hours, in how many hours can Rita do the job alone?

Solution:
$$\frac{1}{6} + \frac{1}{R} = \frac{1}{4}$$

$$\frac{R + 6}{6R} = \frac{1}{4}$$

$$4R + 24 = 6R$$

$$24 = 2R$$

$$12 = R$$

Working alone, Rita can do the job in 12 hours.

3. MIXTURE PROBLEMS

In mixture problems, substances with different characteristics are combined, and it is necessary to determine the characteristics of the resulting mixture.

Example 1: If 6 pounds of nuts that cost $1.20 per pound are mixed with 2 pounds of nuts that cost $1.60 per pound, what is the cost per pound of the mixture?

Solution: The total cost of the 8 pounds of nuts is

$$6(\$1.20) + 2(\$1.60) = \$10.40.$$

The cost per pound is $\frac{\$10.40}{8} = \$1.30$.

Example 2: How many liters of a solution that is 15 percent salt must be added to 5 liters of a solution that is 8 percent salt so that the resulting solution is 10 percent salt?

Solution: Let n represent the number of liters of the 15% solution. The amount of salt in the 15% solution [0.15n] plus the amount of salt in the 8% solution [(0.08)(5)] must be equal to the amount of salt in the 10% mixture [0.10 (n+5)]. Therefore,

$$0.15n + 0.08(5) = 0.10 (n + 5)$$
$$15n + 40 = 10n + 50$$
$$5n = 10$$
$$n = 2 \text{ liters}$$

Two liters of the 15% salt solution must be added to the 8% solution to obtain the 10% solution.

4. INTEREST PROBLEMS

Interest can be computed in two basic ways. With simple annual interest, the interest is computed on the principal only. If interest is compounded, then interest is computed on the principal as well as on any interest already earned.

Example 1: If $8,000 is invested at 6 percent simple annual interest, how much interest is earned after 3 months?

Solution: Since the annual interest rate is 6%, the interest for 1 year is

(0.06) (8,000) = $480. The interest earned in 3 months is $\frac{3}{12}(480) = \$120$.

Example 2: If $10,000 is invested at 10 percent annual interest, compounded semian-
nually, what is the balance after 1 year?

Solution: The balance after the first 6 months would be
$10,000 + (10,000)(0.05) = 10,500$. The balance after one year would be
$10,500 + (10,500)(0.05) = \$11,025$.

5. DISCOUNT

If a price is discounted by n percent, then the price becomes $(100 - n)$ percent of
the original price.

Example 1: A certain customer paid \$24 for a dress. If that price represented a 25
percent discount on the original price of the dress, what was the original price of
the dress?

Solution: If p is the original price of the dress, then $0.75p$ is the discounted price and
$0.75p = \$24$ or $p = \$32$. The original price of the dress was \$32.

Example 2: The price of an item is discounted by 20 percent and then this reduced
price is discounted by an additional 30 percent. These two discounts are equal to
an overall discount of what percent?

Solution: If p is the original price of the item, then $0.8p$ is the price after the first discount. The price after the second discount is $(0.7)(0.8)p = 0.56p$. This represents
an overall discount of 44 percent $(100 - 56)$.

6. PROFIT

Profit is equal to revenues minus expenses, i.e., selling price minus cost.

Example 1: A certain appliance costs a merchant \$30. At what price should the mer-
chant sell the appliance in order to make a gross profit of 50 percent of the cost of
the appliance?

Solution: If s is the selling price of the appliance, then $s - 30 = (0.5)(30)$ or
$s = \$45$. The merchant should sell the appliance for \$45.

7. SETS

If S is the set of numbers 1, 2, 3, and 4, you can write $S = \{1,2,3,4\}$. Sets can also
be represented by Venn diagrams. That is, the relationship among the members of
sets can be represented by circles.

Example 1: Each of 25 people is enrolled in history, mathematics, or both. If 20 are
enrolled in history and 18 are enrolled in mathematics, how many are enrolled in
both history and mathematics?

Solution: The 25 people can be divided into three sets: those who study history only,
those who study mathematics only, and those who study history and mathematics.
Thus a diagram may be drawn as follows where n is the number of people enrolled
in both courses, 20-n is the number enrolled in history only, and 18-n is the number enrolled in mathematics only.

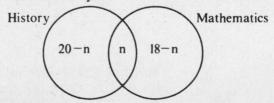

Since there is a total of 25 people, $(20 - n) + n + (18 - n) = 25$, or $n = 13$.
Thirteen people are enrolled in both history and mathematics. Note that
$20 + 18 - 13 = 25$.

Example 2: In a certain production lot, 40 percent of the toys are red and the remaining toys are green. Half of the toys are small and half are large. If 10 percent of the toys are red and small, and 40 toys are green and large, how many of the toys are red and large?

Solution: For this kind of problem, it is helpful to organize the information in a table:

	red	green	
small	10%		50%
large			50%
	40%	60%	100%

The numbers in the table are the percents given. The following percents can be computed on the basis of what is given:

	red	green	
small	10%	40%	50%
large	30%	20%	50%
	40%	60%	100%

Since 20% of the number of toys (n) are green and large, $0.20n = 40$ (40 toys are green and large), or $n = 200$. Therefore, 30% of the 200 toys, or $(0.3)(200) = 60$, are red and large.

8. GEOMETRY PROBLEMS

The following is an example of a word problem involving geometry.

Example 1:

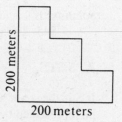

The figure above shows a piece of land. If all angles shown are right angles, what is the perimeter of the piece of land?

Solution: For reference, label the figure as

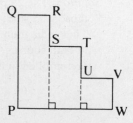

If all the angles are right angles, then QR + ST + UV = PW, and RS + TU + VW = PQ. Hence, the perimeter of the land is
2PW + 2PQ = 2 × 200 + 2 × 200 = 800 meters.

9. MEASUREMENT PROBLEMS

Some questions on the GMAT involve metric units of measure, whereas others involve English units of measure. However, except for units of time, if a question requires conversion from one unit of measure to another, the relationship between those units will be given.

Example 1: A train travels at a constant rate of 25 meters per second. How many kilometers does it travel in 5 minutes? (1 kilometer = 1,000 meters)

Solution: In 1 minute the train travels $(25) \cdot (60)$ = 1,500 meters, so in 5 minutes it travels 7,500 meters. Since 1 kilometer = 1,000 meters, 7,500 meters equals $\frac{7,500}{1,000}$ or 7.5 kilometers.

10. DATA INTERPRETATION

Occasionally a question or set of questions will be based on data provided in a table or graph. Some examples of tables and graphs are given below.

Example 1:

UNITED STATES POPULATION—BY AGE GROUP
(in thousands)

Age	Population
17 years and under	63,376
18-44 years	86,738
45-64 years	43,845
65 years and over	24,054

How many people are 44 years old or younger?

Solution: The figures in the table are given in thousands. The answer in thousands can be obtained by adding 63,376 thousand and 86,738 thousand. The result is 150,114 thousand, which is 150,114,000.

Example 2:

AVERAGE TEMPERATURE AND PRECIPITATION IN CITY X

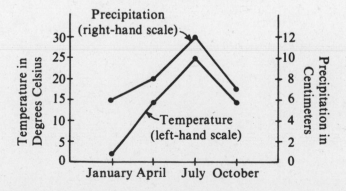

What are the average temperature and precipitation in city X during April?

-41-

Solution: Note that the scale on the left applies to the temperature line graph and the one on the right applies to the precipitation line graph.

According to the graph, during April the average temperature is approximately 14° Celsius and the average precipitation is 8 centimenters.

Example 3:

DISTRIBUTION OF AL'S WEEKLY NET SALARY

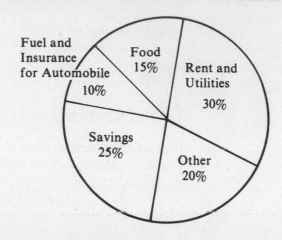

Weekly Net Salary = $350

To how many of the categories listed was at least $80 of Al's weekly net salary allocated?

Solution: In the circle graph the relative sizes of the sectors are proportional to their corresponding values and the sum of the percents given is 100%. $\frac{80}{350}$ is approximately 23%, so at least $80 was allocated to each of 2 categories—Rent and Utilities, and Savings—since their allocations are each greater than 23%.

3 Problem Solving

In these questions you are to solve each problem and select the best of the five answer choices given. The mathematics required to answer the questions does not extend beyond that assumed to be common to the mathematics background of all examinees.

The following pages include test-taking strategies, eight sample test sections (with answer keys), and detailed explanations of every problem on the sample test sections. These explanations present possible problem-solving strategies for the problems.

Test-Taking Strategies for Problem Solving

1. Pacing yourself is very important. Take a watch with you and consult it from time to time. Work as carefully as possible, but do not spend valuable time checking answers or pondering over problems that you find difficult. Make a check mark in your test book next to the troublesome problems or those problems you feel you should double-check. When you have completed the section, go back and spend the remaining time on those difficult problems. Remember, each question has the same weight.

2. Space is available in the test book for scratchwork. Working a problem out in writing may help you avoid errors in solving the problem. If diagrams or figures are not presented, it may help if you draw your own.

3. Read each question carefully to determine what information is given and what is being asked. For word problems, take one step at a time, reading each sentence carefully and translating the information into equations.

4. Before attempting to answer a question, scan the answer choices; otherwise you may waste time putting answers in a form that is not given (for example, putting an answer in the form $\frac{\sqrt{2}}{2}$ when the options are given in the form $\frac{1}{\sqrt{2}}$

or finding the answer in decimal form, such as 0.25,

when the choices are given in fractional form, such as $\frac{1}{4}$).

5. For questions that require approximations, scan the options to get some idea of the required closeness of approximation; otherwise, you may waste time on long computations where a short mental process would serve as well (for example, taking 48 percent of a number instead of half the number).

6. If you cannot solve a problem but you can eliminate some of the options as being unlikely, you should guess. If the options are equally plausible, you should not guess. Remember, a percentage of the wrong answers will be subtracted from the number of right answers to compensate for guessing, but the number of omitted questions will not be subtracted.

When you take the sample test sections, use the answer spaces on pages 45 and 46 to mark your answers.

Answer Spaces for Problem Solving Sample Test Sections

Sample Test Section 1

1 Ⓐ Ⓑ Ⓒ Ⓓ Ⓔ	6 Ⓐ Ⓑ Ⓒ Ⓓ Ⓔ	11 Ⓐ Ⓑ Ⓒ Ⓓ Ⓔ	16 Ⓐ Ⓑ Ⓒ Ⓓ Ⓔ
2 Ⓐ Ⓑ Ⓒ Ⓓ Ⓔ	7 Ⓐ Ⓑ Ⓒ Ⓓ Ⓔ	12 Ⓐ Ⓑ Ⓒ Ⓓ Ⓔ	17 Ⓐ Ⓑ Ⓒ Ⓓ Ⓔ
3 Ⓐ Ⓑ Ⓒ Ⓓ Ⓔ	8 Ⓐ Ⓑ Ⓒ Ⓓ Ⓔ	13 Ⓐ Ⓑ Ⓒ Ⓓ Ⓔ	18 Ⓐ Ⓑ Ⓒ Ⓓ Ⓔ
4 Ⓐ Ⓑ Ⓒ Ⓓ Ⓔ	9 Ⓐ Ⓑ Ⓒ Ⓓ Ⓔ	14 Ⓐ Ⓑ Ⓒ Ⓓ Ⓔ	19 Ⓐ Ⓑ Ⓒ Ⓓ Ⓔ
5 Ⓐ Ⓑ Ⓒ Ⓓ Ⓔ	10 Ⓐ Ⓑ Ⓒ Ⓓ Ⓔ	15 Ⓐ Ⓑ Ⓒ Ⓓ Ⓔ	20 Ⓐ Ⓑ Ⓒ Ⓓ Ⓔ

Sample Test Section 2

1 Ⓐ Ⓑ Ⓒ Ⓓ Ⓔ	6 Ⓐ Ⓑ Ⓒ Ⓓ Ⓔ	11 Ⓐ Ⓑ Ⓒ Ⓓ Ⓔ	16 Ⓐ Ⓑ Ⓒ Ⓓ Ⓔ
2 Ⓐ Ⓑ Ⓒ Ⓓ Ⓔ	7 Ⓐ Ⓑ Ⓒ Ⓓ Ⓔ	12 Ⓐ Ⓑ Ⓒ Ⓓ Ⓔ	17 Ⓐ Ⓑ Ⓒ Ⓓ Ⓔ
3 Ⓐ Ⓑ Ⓒ Ⓓ Ⓔ	8 Ⓐ Ⓑ Ⓒ Ⓓ Ⓔ	13 Ⓐ Ⓑ Ⓒ Ⓓ Ⓔ	18 Ⓐ Ⓑ Ⓒ Ⓓ Ⓔ
4 Ⓐ Ⓑ Ⓒ Ⓓ Ⓔ	9 Ⓐ Ⓑ Ⓒ Ⓓ Ⓔ	14 Ⓐ Ⓑ Ⓒ Ⓓ Ⓔ	19 Ⓐ Ⓑ Ⓒ Ⓓ Ⓔ
5 Ⓐ Ⓑ Ⓒ Ⓓ Ⓔ	10 Ⓐ Ⓑ Ⓒ Ⓓ Ⓔ	15 Ⓐ Ⓑ Ⓒ Ⓓ Ⓔ	20 Ⓐ Ⓑ Ⓒ Ⓓ Ⓔ

Sample Test Section 3

1 Ⓐ Ⓑ Ⓒ Ⓓ Ⓔ	6 Ⓐ Ⓑ Ⓒ Ⓓ Ⓔ	11 Ⓐ Ⓑ Ⓒ Ⓓ Ⓔ	16 Ⓐ Ⓑ Ⓒ Ⓓ Ⓔ
2 Ⓐ Ⓑ Ⓒ Ⓓ Ⓔ	7 Ⓐ Ⓑ Ⓒ Ⓓ Ⓔ	12 Ⓐ Ⓑ Ⓒ Ⓓ Ⓔ	17 Ⓐ Ⓑ Ⓒ Ⓓ Ⓔ
3 Ⓐ Ⓑ Ⓒ Ⓓ Ⓔ	8 Ⓐ Ⓑ Ⓒ Ⓓ Ⓔ	13 Ⓐ Ⓑ Ⓒ Ⓓ Ⓔ	18 Ⓐ Ⓑ Ⓒ Ⓓ Ⓔ
4 Ⓐ Ⓑ Ⓒ Ⓓ Ⓔ	9 Ⓐ Ⓑ Ⓒ Ⓓ Ⓔ	14 Ⓐ Ⓑ Ⓒ Ⓓ Ⓔ	19 Ⓐ Ⓑ Ⓒ Ⓓ Ⓔ
5 Ⓐ Ⓑ Ⓒ Ⓓ Ⓔ	10 Ⓐ Ⓑ Ⓒ Ⓓ Ⓔ	15 Ⓐ Ⓑ Ⓒ Ⓓ Ⓔ	20 Ⓐ Ⓑ Ⓒ Ⓓ Ⓔ

Sample Test Section 4

1 Ⓐ Ⓑ Ⓒ Ⓓ Ⓔ	6 Ⓐ Ⓑ Ⓒ Ⓓ Ⓔ	11 Ⓐ Ⓑ Ⓒ Ⓓ Ⓔ	16 Ⓐ Ⓑ Ⓒ Ⓓ Ⓔ
2 Ⓐ Ⓑ Ⓒ Ⓓ Ⓔ	7 Ⓐ Ⓑ Ⓒ Ⓓ Ⓔ	12 Ⓐ Ⓑ Ⓒ Ⓓ Ⓔ	17 Ⓐ Ⓑ Ⓒ Ⓓ Ⓔ
3 Ⓐ Ⓑ Ⓒ Ⓓ Ⓔ	8 Ⓐ Ⓑ Ⓒ Ⓓ Ⓔ	13 Ⓐ Ⓑ Ⓒ Ⓓ Ⓔ	18 Ⓐ Ⓑ Ⓒ Ⓓ Ⓔ
4 Ⓐ Ⓑ Ⓒ Ⓓ Ⓔ	9 Ⓐ Ⓑ Ⓒ Ⓓ Ⓔ	14 Ⓐ Ⓑ Ⓒ Ⓓ Ⓔ	19 Ⓐ Ⓑ Ⓒ Ⓓ Ⓔ
5 Ⓐ Ⓑ Ⓒ Ⓓ Ⓔ	10 Ⓐ Ⓑ Ⓒ Ⓓ Ⓔ	15 Ⓐ Ⓑ Ⓒ Ⓓ Ⓔ	20 Ⓐ Ⓑ Ⓒ Ⓓ Ⓔ

Sample Test Section 5

1	Ⓐ Ⓑ Ⓒ Ⓓ Ⓔ	6	Ⓐ Ⓑ Ⓒ Ⓓ Ⓔ	11	Ⓐ Ⓑ Ⓒ Ⓓ Ⓔ	16	Ⓐ Ⓑ Ⓒ Ⓓ Ⓔ
2	Ⓐ Ⓑ Ⓒ Ⓓ Ⓔ	7	Ⓐ Ⓑ Ⓒ Ⓓ Ⓔ	12	Ⓐ Ⓑ Ⓒ Ⓓ Ⓔ	17	Ⓐ Ⓑ Ⓒ Ⓓ Ⓔ
3	Ⓐ Ⓑ Ⓒ Ⓓ Ⓔ	8	Ⓐ Ⓑ Ⓒ Ⓓ Ⓔ	13	Ⓐ Ⓑ Ⓒ Ⓓ Ⓔ	18	Ⓐ Ⓑ Ⓒ Ⓓ Ⓔ
4	Ⓐ Ⓑ Ⓒ Ⓓ Ⓔ	9	Ⓐ Ⓑ Ⓒ Ⓓ Ⓔ	14	Ⓐ Ⓑ Ⓒ Ⓓ Ⓔ	19	Ⓐ Ⓑ Ⓒ Ⓓ Ⓔ
5	Ⓐ Ⓑ Ⓒ Ⓓ Ⓔ	10	Ⓐ Ⓑ Ⓒ Ⓓ Ⓔ	15	Ⓐ Ⓑ Ⓒ Ⓓ Ⓔ	20	Ⓐ Ⓑ Ⓒ Ⓓ Ⓔ

Sample Test Section 6

1	Ⓐ Ⓑ Ⓒ Ⓓ Ⓔ	6	Ⓐ Ⓑ Ⓒ Ⓓ Ⓔ	11	Ⓐ Ⓑ Ⓒ Ⓓ Ⓔ	16	Ⓐ Ⓑ Ⓒ Ⓓ Ⓔ
2	Ⓐ Ⓑ Ⓒ Ⓓ Ⓔ	7	Ⓐ Ⓑ Ⓒ Ⓓ Ⓔ	12	Ⓐ Ⓑ Ⓒ Ⓓ Ⓔ	17	Ⓐ Ⓑ Ⓒ Ⓓ Ⓔ
3	Ⓐ Ⓑ Ⓒ Ⓓ Ⓔ	8	Ⓐ Ⓑ Ⓒ Ⓓ Ⓔ	13	Ⓐ Ⓑ Ⓒ Ⓓ Ⓔ	18	Ⓐ Ⓑ Ⓒ Ⓓ Ⓔ
4	Ⓐ Ⓑ Ⓒ Ⓓ Ⓔ	9	Ⓐ Ⓑ Ⓒ Ⓓ Ⓔ	14	Ⓐ Ⓑ Ⓒ Ⓓ Ⓔ	19	Ⓐ Ⓑ Ⓒ Ⓓ Ⓔ
5	Ⓐ Ⓑ Ⓒ Ⓓ Ⓔ	10	Ⓐ Ⓑ Ⓒ Ⓓ Ⓔ	15	Ⓐ Ⓑ Ⓒ Ⓓ Ⓔ	20	Ⓐ Ⓑ Ⓒ Ⓓ Ⓔ

Sample Test Section 7

1	Ⓐ Ⓑ Ⓒ Ⓓ Ⓔ	6	Ⓐ Ⓑ Ⓒ Ⓓ Ⓔ	11	Ⓐ Ⓑ Ⓒ Ⓓ Ⓔ	16	Ⓐ Ⓑ Ⓒ Ⓓ Ⓔ
2	Ⓐ Ⓑ Ⓒ Ⓓ Ⓔ	7	Ⓐ Ⓑ Ⓒ Ⓓ Ⓔ	12	Ⓐ Ⓑ Ⓒ Ⓓ Ⓔ	17	Ⓐ Ⓑ Ⓒ Ⓓ Ⓔ
3	Ⓐ Ⓑ Ⓒ Ⓓ Ⓔ	8	Ⓐ Ⓑ Ⓒ Ⓓ Ⓔ	13	Ⓐ Ⓑ Ⓒ Ⓓ Ⓔ	18	Ⓐ Ⓑ Ⓒ Ⓓ Ⓔ
4	Ⓐ Ⓑ Ⓒ Ⓓ Ⓔ	9	Ⓐ Ⓑ Ⓒ Ⓓ Ⓔ	14	Ⓐ Ⓑ Ⓒ Ⓓ Ⓔ	19	Ⓐ Ⓑ Ⓒ Ⓓ Ⓔ
5	Ⓐ Ⓑ Ⓒ Ⓓ Ⓔ	10	Ⓐ Ⓑ Ⓒ Ⓓ Ⓔ	15	Ⓐ Ⓑ Ⓒ Ⓓ Ⓔ	20	Ⓐ Ⓑ Ⓒ Ⓓ Ⓔ

Sample Test Section 8

1	Ⓐ Ⓑ Ⓒ Ⓓ Ⓔ	6	Ⓐ Ⓑ Ⓒ Ⓓ Ⓔ	11	Ⓐ Ⓑ Ⓒ Ⓓ Ⓔ	16	Ⓐ Ⓑ Ⓒ Ⓓ Ⓔ
2	Ⓐ Ⓑ Ⓒ Ⓓ Ⓔ	7	Ⓐ Ⓑ Ⓒ Ⓓ Ⓔ	12	Ⓐ Ⓑ Ⓒ Ⓓ Ⓔ	17	Ⓐ Ⓑ Ⓒ Ⓓ Ⓔ
3	Ⓐ Ⓑ Ⓒ Ⓓ Ⓔ	8	Ⓐ Ⓑ Ⓒ Ⓓ Ⓔ	13	Ⓐ Ⓑ Ⓒ Ⓓ Ⓔ	18	Ⓐ Ⓑ Ⓒ Ⓓ Ⓔ
4	Ⓐ Ⓑ Ⓒ Ⓓ Ⓔ	9	Ⓐ Ⓑ Ⓒ Ⓓ Ⓔ	14	Ⓐ Ⓑ Ⓒ Ⓓ Ⓔ	19	Ⓐ Ⓑ Ⓒ Ⓓ Ⓔ
5	Ⓐ Ⓑ Ⓒ Ⓓ Ⓔ	10	Ⓐ Ⓑ Ⓒ Ⓓ Ⓔ	15	Ⓐ Ⓑ Ⓒ Ⓓ Ⓔ	20	Ⓐ Ⓑ Ⓒ Ⓓ Ⓔ

PROBLEM SOLVING SAMPLE TEST SECTION 1

30 Minutes
20 Questions

<u>Directions:</u> In this section solve each problem, using any available space on the page for scratchwork. Then indicate the best of the answer choices given.

<u>Numbers:</u> All numbers used are real numbers.

<u>Figures:</u> Figures that accompany problems in this section are intended to provide information useful in solving the problems. They are drawn as accurately as possible EXCEPT when it is stated in a specific problem that its figure is not drawn to scale. All figures lie in a plane unless otherwise indicated.

1. The 180 students in a group are to be seated in rows so that there is an equal number of students in each row. Each of the following could be the number of rows EXCEPT

   (A) 4
   (B) 20
   (C) 30
   (D) 40
   (E) 90

2. A parking garage rents parking spaces for $10 per week or $30 per month. How much does a person save in a year by renting by the month rather than by the week?

   (A) $140   (B) $160   (C) $220

   (D) $240   (E) $260

3. If $y = 5x^2 - 2x$ and $x = 3$, then $y =$

   (A) 24   (B) 27   (C) 39   (D) 51   (E) 219

4. Of the following, which is the best approximation to $\sqrt{0.0026}$?

   (A) 0.05   (B) 0.06   (C) 0.16   (D) 0.5   (E) 0.6

5. At a certain diner, a hamburger and coleslaw cost $3.95, and a hamburger and french fries cost $4.40. If french fries cost twice as much as coleslaw, how much do french fries cost?

   (A) $0.30
   (B) $0.45
   (C) $0.60
   (D) $0.75
   (E) $0.90

GO ON TO THE NEXT PAGE.

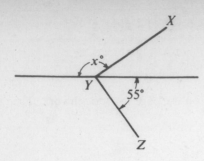

6. If $\angle XYZ$ in the figure above is a right angle, what is the value of x?

(A) 155   (B) 145   (C) 135   (D) 125   (E) 110

7.
$$\dfrac{\left(\dfrac{a}{b}\right)}{c}$$

In the expression above, a, b, and c are different numbers and each is one of the numbers 2, 3, or 5. What is the <u>least</u> possible value of the expression?

(A) $\dfrac{1}{30}$ (B) $\dfrac{2}{15}$ (C) $\dfrac{1}{6}$ (D) $\dfrac{3}{10}$ (E) $\dfrac{5}{6}$

8. A certain culture of bacteria quadruples every hour. If a container with these bacteria was half full at 10:00 a.m., at what time was it one-eighth full?

(A) 9:00 a.m.
(B) 7:00 a.m.
(C) 6:00 a.m.
(D) 4:00 a.m.
(E) 2:00 a.m.

9. Al, Lew, and Karen pooled their funds to buy a gift for a friend. Al contributed \$2 less than $\dfrac{1}{3}$ of the cost of the gift and Lew contributed \$2 more than $\dfrac{1}{4}$ of the cost. If Karen contributed the remaining \$15, what was the cost of the gift?

(A) \$24
(B) \$33
(C) \$36
(D) \$43
(E) \$45

GO ON TO THE NEXT PAGE.

10. What is the total number of integers between 100 and 200 that are divisible by 3 ?

    (A) 33 (B) 32 (C) 31 (D) 30 (E) 29

11. Which of the following inequalities is equivalent to $10 - 2x > 18$?

    (A) $x > -14$
    (B) $x > -4$
    (C) $x > 4$
    (D) $x < 4$
    (E) $x < -4$

12. In 1979 approximately $\frac{1}{3}$ of the 37.3 million airline passengers traveling to or from the United States used Kennedy Airport. If the number of such passengers that used Miami Airport was $\frac{1}{2}$ the number that used Kennedy Airport and 4 times the number that used Logan Airport, approximately how many millions of these passengers used Logan Airport that year?

    (A) 18.6
    (B) 9.3
    (C) 6.2
    (D) 3.1
    (E) 1.6

13. A certain basketball team that has played $\frac{2}{3}$ of its games has a record of 17 wins and 3 losses. What is the greatest number of the remaining games that the team can lose and still win at least $\frac{3}{4}$ of all of its games?

    (A) 7
    (B) 6
    (C) 5
    (D) 4
    (E) 3

14. Dan and Karen, who live 10 miles apart, meet at a café that is directly north of Dan's house and directly east of Karen's house. If the café is 2 miles closer to Dan's house than to Karen's house, how many miles is the café from Karen's house?

    (A) 6
    (B) 7
    (C) 8
    (D) 9
    (E) 10

GO ON TO THE NEXT PAGE.

-49-

15. If n is an integer and $n = \dfrac{2 \cdot 3 \cdot 5 \cdot 7 \cdot 11 \cdot 13}{77k}$,

then which of the following could be the value of k?

(A) 22   (B) 26   (C) 35   (D) 54   (E) 60

16. There were 36,000 hardback copies of a certain novel sold before the paperback version was issued. From the time the first paperback copy was sold until the last copy of the novel was sold, 9 times as many paperback copies as hardback copies were sold. If a total of 441,000 copies of the novel were sold in all, how many paperback copies were sold?

(A)   45,000
(B) 360,000
(C) 364,500
(D) 392,000
(E) 396,900

17. In the formula $w = \dfrac{p}{\sqrt[t]{v}}$, integers p and t are positive constants. If $w = 2$ when $v = 1$ and if $w = \dfrac{1}{2}$ when $v = 64$, then $t =$

(A) 1
(B) 2
(C) 3
(D) 4
(E) 16

18. Last year Mrs. Long received $160 in dividends on her shares of Company X stock, all of which she had held for the entire year. If she had had 12 more shares of the stock last year, she would have received $15 more in total annual dividends. How many shares of the stock did she have last year?

(A) 128
(B) 140
(C) 172
(D) 175
(E) 200

GO ON TO THE NEXT PAGE.

Month	Average Price per Dozen
April	$1.26
May	$1.20
June	$1.08

19. The table above shows the average (arithmetic

mean) price per dozen of the large grade A eggs sold

in a certain store during three successive months. If

$\frac{2}{3}$ as many dozen were sold in April as in May, and

twice as many were sold in June as in April, what

was the average price per dozen of the eggs sold

over the three-month period?

(A) $1.08
(B) $1.10
(C) $1.14
(D) $1.16
(E) $1.18

20. If $y \neq 3$ and $\frac{3x}{y}$ is a prime integer greater than 2,

which of the following must be true?

   I. $x = y$
  II. $y = 1$
 III. x and y are prime integers.

(A) None
(B) I only
(C) II only
(D) III only
(E) I and III

STOP

IF YOU FINISH BEFORE TIME IS CALLED, YOU MAY CHECK YOUR WORK ON THIS SECTION ONLY.
DO NOT TURN TO ANY OTHER SECTION IN THE TEST.

Answer Key for Sample Test Section 1

PROBLEM SOLVING

1. D	11. E
2. B	12. E
3. C	13. D
4. A	14. C
5. E	15. B
6. B	16. C
7. B	17. C
8. A	18. A
9. C	19. D
10. A	20. A

Explanatory Material: Problem Solving

The following discussion is intended to familiarize you with the most efficient and effective approaches to the kinds of problems common to Problem Solving. The questions on the sample tests in this chapter are generally representative of the kinds of problems you will encounter in this section of the GMAT. Remember that it is the problem-solving strategy that is important, not the specific details of a particular problem.

Sample Test Section 1

1. The 180 students in a group are to be seated in rows so that there is an equal number of students in each row. Each of the following could be the number of rows EXCEPT

   (A) 4
   (B) 20
   (C) 30
   (D) 40
   (E) 90

Since there is an equal number of students in each row, it follows that the total number of students, or 180, is a multiple of the number of rows. 180 is a multiple of all of the options except 40. Thus, the best answer is D.

2. A parking garage rents parking spaces for $10 per week or $30 per month. How much does a person save in a year by renting by the month rather than by the week?

   (A) $140   (B) $160   (C) $220
   (D) $240   (E) $260

The yearly cost of renting a parking space on a weekly basis is $10 × 52, or $520.

The yearly cost of renting a parking space on a monthly basis is $30 × 12, or $360.

The amount saved by renting a parking space by the month rather than by the week equals the difference between the two costs, which is ($520 − $360) or $160. Therefore, the best answer is B.

3. If $y = 5x^2 - 2x$ and $x = 3$, then $y =$

   (A) 24   (B) 27   (C) 39   (D) 51   (E) 219

Substituting $x = 3$ in the equation $y = 5x^2 - 2x$ yields $y = 5(3)^2 - 2(3) = 45 - 6 = 39$. Thus, the best answer is C.

4. Of the following, which is the best approximation to $\sqrt{0.0026}$?

   (A) 0.05   (B) 0.06   (C) 0.16   (D) 0.5   (E) 0.6

One way to approximate $\sqrt{.0026}$ is to notice that $.0026 = \dfrac{26}{10^4}$ and 25 (or 5^2) is the perfect square closest to 26.

So $\sqrt{.0026} = \sqrt{\dfrac{26}{10^4}} = \dfrac{\sqrt{26}}{\sqrt{10^4}} = \dfrac{\sqrt{26}}{10^2}$, which is approximately $\dfrac{5}{10^2}$ or 0.05. Thus, the best answer is A.

5. At a certain diner, a hamburger and coleslaw cost $3.95, and a hamburger and french fries cost $4.40. If french fries cost twice as much as coleslaw, how much do french fries cost?

   (A) $0.30
   (B) $0.45
   (C) $0.60
   (D) $0.75
   (E) $0.90

Let h, c, and f denote the cost of a hamburger, coleslaw, and french fries, respectively.
Then,

$$(1)\ h + c = \$3.95$$
$$(2)\ h + f = \$4.40$$
$$(2) - (1)\ f - c = \$0.45$$

Since $f = 2c$, $c = \dfrac{f}{2}$; therefore,

$f - c = f - \dfrac{f}{2} = \dfrac{f}{2} = \$0.45$, and $f = \$0.90$. Thus, the best answer is E.

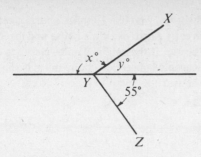

6. If $\angle XYZ$ in the figure above is a right angle, what is the value of x?

   (A) 155   (B) 145   (C) 135   (D) 125   (E) 110

Since $\angle XYZ$ is a right angle, it follows that $y + 55 = 90$, and $y = 35$. Since x and y are the degree measures of supplementary angles, it follows that $x + y = 180$. Therefore, $x = 180 - y = 180 - 35 = 145$. Thus, the best answer is B.

7.
$$\frac{\left(\dfrac{a}{b}\right)}{c}$$

   In the expression above, a, b, and c are different numbers and each is one of the numbers 2, 3, or 5. What is the least possible value of the expression?

   (A) $\dfrac{1}{30}$ (B) $\dfrac{2}{15}$ (C) $\dfrac{1}{6}$ (D) $\dfrac{3}{10}$ (E) $\dfrac{5}{6}$

Note that $\dfrac{\left(\dfrac{a}{b}\right)}{c} = \dfrac{a}{bc}$.

The expression will be least when its numerator is as small as possible and its denominator is as large as possible. Setting $a = 2$, $b = 3$, and $c = 5$ yields $\dfrac{a}{bc} = \dfrac{2}{3(5)} = \dfrac{2}{15}$. Thus, the best answer is B.

8. A certain culture of bacteria quadruples every hour. If a container with these bacteria was half full at 10:00 a.m., at what time was it one-eighth full?

   (A) 9:00 a.m.
   (B) 7:00 a.m.
   (C) 6:00 a.m.
   (D) 4:00 a.m.
   (E) 2:00 a.m.

Since the culture quadruples every hour, it follows that one hour prior to any given time the container was $\dfrac{1}{4}$ as full as it was at the given time. Therefore, if the container was $\dfrac{1}{2}$ full at 10:00 a.m., it was $\dfrac{1}{4}\left(\dfrac{1}{2}\right) = \dfrac{1}{8}$ full at 9:00 a.m. Thus, the best answer is A.

9. Al, Lew, and Karen pooled their funds to buy a gift for a friend. Al contributed \$2 less than $\dfrac{1}{3}$ of the cost of the gift and Lew contributed \$2 more than $\dfrac{1}{4}$ of the cost. If Karen contributed the remaining \$15, what was the cost of the gift?

   (A) \$24
   (B) \$33
   (C) \$36
   (D) \$43
   (E) \$45

Let $C = $ the cost of the gift.

Al's contribution $= \dfrac{1}{3}C - 2$.

Lew's contribution $= \dfrac{1}{4}C + 2$.

Karen's contribution $= 15$.

Total cost of gift $= C = \left(\dfrac{1}{3}C - 2\right) + \left(\dfrac{1}{4}C + 2\right) + 15$.

Thus, $C = \dfrac{7}{12}C + 15$

or $\dfrac{5}{12}C = 15$

or $C = 36$.

Therefore, the best answer is C.

10. What is the total number of integers between 100 and 200 that are divisible by 3?

   (A) 33   (B) 32   (C) 31   (D) 30   (E) 29

The integers between 100 and 200 that are divisible by 3 are $102 (= 3(34))$, $105, \ldots, 198 (= 3(66))$. Thus, the number of integers between 100 and 200 that are divisible by 3 is equal to the number of integers between 34 and 66, inclusive. That is, $66 - 33$ or 33 integers. Thus, the best answer is A.

11. Which of the following inequalities is equivalent to $10 - 2x > 18$?

   (A) $x > -14$
   (B) $x > -4$
   (C) $x > 4$
   (D) $x < 4$
   (E) $x < -4$

$10 - 2x > 18$
$-8 > 2x$
$-4 > x \text{ or } x < -4$

Thus, E is the best answer.

12. In 1979 approximately $\frac{1}{3}$ of the 37.3 million airline passengers traveling to or from the United States used Kennedy Airport. If the number of such passengers that used Miami Airport was $\frac{1}{2}$ the number that used Kennedy Airport and 4 times the number that used Logan Airport, approximately how many millions of these passengers used Logan Airport that year?

(A) 18.6
(B) 9.3
(C) 6.2
(D) 3.1
(E) 1.6

The number of millions of passengers that used Kennedy Airport was approximately $\frac{1}{3}$ (37.3) ≈ 12.4 million. Thus, the number of millions of passengers that used Miami Airport was approximately $\frac{1}{2}$ (12.4) ≈ 6.2 million. This was 4 times the number of millions of passengers that used Logan Airport, so approximately $\frac{1}{4}$ (6.2) ≈ 1.6 million passengers used Logan Airport. Thus, the best answer is E.

13. A certain basketball team that has played $\frac{2}{3}$ of its games has a record of 17 wins and 3 losses. What is the greatest number of the remaining games that the team can lose and still win at least $\frac{3}{4}$ of all of its games?

(A) 7
(B) 6
(C) 5
(D) 4
(E) 3

The total number of games to be played by the team is 30, since 20 games is $\frac{2}{3}$ of the total number to be played. To win at least $\frac{3}{4}$ of all its games, the team must win a whole number of games greater than $\frac{3}{4}$ (30) = $22\frac{1}{2}$. Thus, the least number of games the team must win is 23. This implies that no more than 30 − 23 = 7 games can be lost. Since 3 games have already been lost, it follows that no more than 4 of the remaining games can be lost. Thus, the best answer is D.

14. Dan and Karen, who live 10 miles apart, meet at a café that is directly north of Dan's house and directly east of Karen's house. If the café is 2 miles closer to Dan's house than to Karen's house, how many miles is the café from Karen's house?

(A) 6
(B) 7
(C) 8
(D) 9
(E) 10

Let a = the distance to the café from Karen's house. Then $a - 2$ = the distance to the café from Dan's house. Since the café is north of Dan's house and east of Karen's house, the following figure represents the information given:

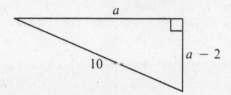

Using the Pythagorean theorem yields
$a^2 + (a - 2)^2 = 10^2$
$a^2 + a^2 - 4a + 4 = 100$
$2a^2 - 4a - 96 = 0$
$2(a^2 - 2a - 48) = 0$
$2(a - 8)(a + 6) = 0$
$a = 8$ or $a = -6$.

Since a represents the distance to the café from Karen's house, it follows that $a = 8$. Thus, the best answer is C.

15. If n is an integer and $n = \dfrac{2 \cdot 3 \cdot 5 \cdot 7 \cdot 11 \cdot 13}{77k}$, then which of the following could be the value of k?

(A) 22   (B) 26   (C) 35   (D) 54   (E) 60

$n = \dfrac{2 \cdot 3 \cdot 5 \cdot 7 \cdot 11 \cdot 13}{77k} = \dfrac{2 \cdot 3 \cdot 5 \cdot 13}{k}$

Since n is an integer, k must be a factor of the numerator $2 \cdot 3 \cdot 5 \cdot 13$. Note that $22 = 2 \cdot 11$, $26 = 2 \cdot 13$, $35 = 5 \cdot 7$, $54 = 2 \cdot 3 \cdot 3 \cdot 3$, and $60 = 2 \cdot 2 \cdot 3 \cdot 5$. Therefore, only 26 is a factor of $2 \cdot 3 \cdot 5 \cdot 13$. Thus, the best answer is B.

16. There were 36,000 hardback copies of a certain novel sold before the paperback version was issued. From the time the first paperback copy was sold until the last copy of the novel was sold, 9 times as many paperback copies as hardback copies were sold. If a total of 441,000 copies of the novel were sold in all, how many paperback copies were sold?

(A) 45,000
(B) 360,000
(C) 364,500
(D) 392,000
(E) 396,900

After the paperback version was issued,
$441,000 - 36,000 = 405,000$ copies of the book were sold, 9 out of 10, or $\frac{9}{10}$, of which were paperback. Thus, $\frac{9}{10}(405,000) = 364,500$ paperback copies were sold, and C is the best answer.

17. In the formula $w = \dfrac{p}{\sqrt[t]{v}}$, integers p and t are positive constants. If $w = 2$ when $v = 1$ and if $w = \dfrac{1}{2}$ when $v = 64$, then $t =$

(A) 1
(B) 2
(C) 3
(D) 4
(E) 16

When $w = 2$ and $v = 1$, the formula yields

$2 = \dfrac{p}{\sqrt[t]{1}}$. Since $\sqrt[t]{1} = 1$ for any t,

this implies that $p = 2$. Thus, when $w = \dfrac{1}{2}$ and $v = 64$, the

formula yields $\dfrac{1}{2} = \dfrac{2}{\sqrt[t]{64}}$.

$\sqrt[t]{64} = 4$
$64 = 4^t$
$t = 3$

Thus, the best answer is C.

18. Last year Mrs. Long received $160 in dividends on her shares of Company X stock, all of which she had held for the entire year. If she had had 12 more shares of the stock last year, she would have received $15 more in total annual dividends. How many shares of the stock did she have last year?

(A) 128
(B) 140
(C) 172
(D) 175
(E) 200

Since 12 shares of stock earned $15 in dividends, it follows that each share of stock earned $1.25 in dividends. To receive $160 in dividends, Mrs. Long must have owned

$\dfrac{160}{1.25} = 128$ shares of stock. Thus, A is the best answer.

Month	Average Price per Dozen
April	$1.26
May	$1.20
June	$1.08

19. The table above shows the average (arithmetic mean) price per dozen of the large grade A eggs sold in a certain store during three successive months. If $\frac{2}{3}$ as many dozen were sold in April as in May, and twice as many were sold in June as in April, what was the average price per dozen of the eggs sold over the three-month period?

(A) $1.08
(B) $1.10
(C) $1.14
(D) $1.16
(E) $1.18

To solve this problem it is convenient to let $A =$ the number of dozens of eggs sold in May and organize the information in a table as shown below:

Month	Number of Dozens of Eggs Sold	Price Paid for Eggs
April	$\frac{2}{3}A$	$1.26\left(\frac{2}{3}A\right)$
May	A	$1.20A$
June	$2\left(\frac{2}{3}A\right)$	$1.08\left[2\left(\frac{2}{3}A\right)\right]$

The average price per dozen of the eggs over the three-month period is thus

$$\dfrac{\$1.26\left(\frac{2}{3}A\right) + \$1.20A + \$1.08\left(2\left(\frac{2}{3}A\right)\right)}{\frac{2}{3}A + A + 2\left(\frac{2}{3}A\right)}$$

$$= \dfrac{\$3.48A}{3A}$$

$$= \$1.16.$$

The best answer is D.

20. If $y \neq 3$ and $\dfrac{3x}{y}$ is a prime integer greater than 2, which of the following must be true?

  I. $x = y$

  II. $y = 1$

  III. x and y are prime integers.

  (A) None
  (B) I only
  (C) II only
  (D) III only
  (E) I and III

One way to approach this problem is to determine whether each of conditions I, II, and III could be false. I is false if $x \neq y$. If $x \neq y$, it follows that $\dfrac{3x}{y}$ would be a prime integer greater than 3, say, 5. $x = 15$ and $y = 9$ satisfy the desired conditions. When $x = 15$ and $y = 9$ it is also true that $y \neq 1$ and x and y are not prime integers. Thus, none of conditions I, II, and III must necessarily be true. Therefore, A is the best answer.

PROBLEM SOLVING SAMPLE TEST SECTION 2

30 Minutes
20 Questions

Directions: In this section solve each problem, using any available space on the page for scratchwork. Then indicate the best of the answer choices given.

Numbers: All numbers used are real numbers.

Figures: Figures that accompany problems in this section are intended to provide information useful in solving the problems. They are drawn as accurately as possible EXCEPT when it is stated in a specific problem that its figure is not drawn to scale. All figures lie in a plane unless otherwise indicated.

1. The market value of a certain machine decreased by 30 percent of its purchase price each year. If the machine was purchased in 1982 for its market value of $8,000, what was its market value two years later?

   (A) $8,000
   (B) $5,600
   (C) $3,200
   (D) $2,400
   (E) $800

2. What percent of 50 is 15 ?

   (A) 30%   (B) 35%   (C) 70%

   (D) 300%   (E) $333\frac{1}{3}$%

3. In a certain diving competition, 5 judges score each dive on a scale from 1 to 10. The point value of the dive is obtained by dropping the highest score and the lowest score and multiplying the sum of the remaining scores by the degree of difficulty. If a dive with a degree of difficulty of 3.2 received scores of 7.5, 8.0, 9.0, 6.0, and 8.5, what was the point value of the dive?

   (A) 68.8   (B) 73.6   (C) 75.2

   (D) 76.8   (E) 81.6

4. If $2x = 3y = 10$, then $12xy =$

   (A) 1,200   (B) 200   (C) 120   (D) 40   (E) 20

GO ON TO THE NEXT PAGE.

-57-

5. If Jack walked 5 miles in 1 hour and 15 minutes, what was his rate of walking in miles per hour?

(A) 4 (B) 4.5 (C) 6 (D) 6.25 (E) 15

6. Of a certain high school graduating class, 75 percent of the students continued their formal education, and 80 percent of those who continued their formal education went to four-year colleges. If 300 students in the class went to four-year colleges, how many students were in the graduating class?

(A) 500 (B) 375 (C) 240 (D) 225 (E) 180

7. What is the least integer greater than $-2 + 0.5$?

(A) -2 (B) -1 (C) 0 (D) 1 (E) 2

8. Which of the following is equivalent to

$\dfrac{2x + 4}{2x^2 + 8x + 8}$ for all values of x for

which both expressions are defined?

(A) $\dfrac{1}{2x^2 + 6}$

(B) $\dfrac{1}{9x + 2}$

(C) $\dfrac{2}{x + 6}$

(D) $\dfrac{1}{x + 4}$

(E) $\dfrac{1}{x + 2}$

GO ON TO THE NEXT PAGE.

9. A certain business printer can print 40 characters per second, which is 4 times as fast as an average printer. If an average printer can print 5 times as fast as an electric typewriter, how many characters per <u>minute</u> can an electric typewriter print?

(A) 2   (B) 32   (C) 50   (D) 120   (E) 600

10. When ticket sales began, Pat was the nth customer in line for a ticket, and customers purchased their tickets at the rate of x customers per minute. Of the following, which best approximates the time, in minutes, that Pat had to wait in line from the moment ticket sales began?

(A) $(n - 1)x$

(B) $n + x - 1$

(C) $\dfrac{n - 1}{x}$

(D) $\dfrac{x}{n - 1}$

(E) $\dfrac{n}{x - 1}$

11. If 6 gallons of gasoline are added to a tank that is already filled to $\dfrac{3}{4}$ of its capacity, the tank is then filled to $\dfrac{9}{10}$ of its capacity. How many gallons does the tank hold?

(A) 20   (B) 24   (C) 36   (D) 40   (E) 60

12. A bus trip of 450 miles would have taken 1 hour less if the average speed S for the trip had been greater by 5 miles per hour. What was the average speed S, in miles per hour, for the trip?

(A) 10   (B) 40   (C) 45   (D) 50   (E) 55

13. 10^3 is how many times $(0.01)^3$?

(A) 10^6 (B) 10^8 (C) 10^9 (D) 10^{12} (E) 10^{18}

GO ON TO THE NEXT PAGE.

14. Which of the following groups of numbers could be the lengths of the sides of a right triangle?

    I. $1, 4, \sqrt{17}$

    II. $4, 7, \sqrt{11}$

    III. $4, 9, 6$

(A) I only
(B) I and II only
(C) I and III only
(D) II and III only
(E) I, II, and III

15. When the stock market opened yesterday, the price of a share of stock X was $10\frac{1}{2}$. When the market closed, the price was $11\frac{1}{4}$. Of the following, which is closest to the percent increase in the price of stock X ?

(A) 0.5%   (B) 1.0%   (C) 6.7%

(D) 7.1%   (E) 7.5%

16. If x and y are integers and xy^2 is a positive odd integer, which of the following must be true?

    I. xy is positive.
    II. xy is odd.
    III. $x + y$ is even.

(A) I only
(B) II only
(C) III only
(D) I and II
(E) II and III

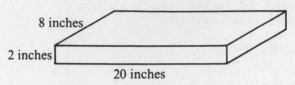

17. The figure above shows the dimensions of a rectangular box that is to be completely wrapped with paper. If a single sheet of paper is to be used without patching, then the dimensions of the paper could be

(A) 17 in by 25 in
(B) 21 in by 24 in
(C) 24 in by 12 in
(D) 24 in by 14 in
(E) 26 in by 14 in

GO ON TO THE NEXT PAGE.

18.
$$x - y = 3$$
$$2x = 2y + 6$$

The system of equations above has how many solutions?

(A) None
(B) Exactly one
(C) Exactly two
(D) Exactly three
(E) Infinitely many

19. If M and N are positive integers that have remainders of 1 and 3, respectively, when divided by 6, which of the following could NOT be a possible value of $M + N$?

(A) 86   (B) 52   (C) 34   (D) 28   (E) 10

20. The R students in a class agree to contribute equally to buy their teacher a birthday present that costs y dollars. If x of the students later fail to contribute their share, which of the following represents the additional number of dollars that each of the remaining students must contribute in order to pay for the present?

(A) $\dfrac{y}{R}$

(B) $\dfrac{y}{R - x}$

(C) $\dfrac{xy}{R - x}$

(D) $\dfrac{xy}{R(R - x)}$

(E) $\dfrac{y}{R(R - x)}$

STOP

IF YOU FINISH BEFORE TIME IS CALLED, YOU MAY CHECK YOUR WORK ON THIS SECTION ONLY.
DO NOT TURN TO ANY OTHER SECTION IN THE TEST.

Answer Key for Sample Test Section 2

PROBLEM SOLVING

1. C	11. D
2. A	12. C
3. D	13. C
4. B	14. A
5. A	15. D
6. A	16. E
7. B	17. B
8. E	18. E
9. D	19. A
10. C	20. D

Explanatory Material: Problem Solving II Sample Test Section 2

1. **The market value of a certain machine decreased by 30 percent of its purchase price each year. If the machine was purchased in 1982 for its market value of $8,000, what was its market value two years later?**

    (A) $8,000
    (B) $5,600
    (C) $3,200
    (D) $2,400
    (E) $800

The market value of the machine decreased by 0.3($8,000) = $2,400 each year. At the end of two years its market value was $8,000 − 2($2,400) = $3,200. Thus, the best answer is C.

2. **What percent of 50 is 15?**

    (A) 30%   (B) 35%   (C) 70%

    (D) 300%   (E) $333\frac{1}{3}$ %

Since $\frac{15}{50} = \frac{30}{100}$, 15 is 30% of 50. Therefore, the best answer is A.

3. **In a certain diving competition, 5 judges score each dive on a scale from 1 to 10. The point value of the dive is obtained by dropping the highest score and the lowest score and multiplying the sum of the remaining scores by the degree of difficulty. If a dive with a degree of difficulty of 3.2 received scores of 7.5, 8.0, 9.0, 6.0, and 8.5, what was the point value of the dive?**

    (A) 68.8   (B) 73.6   (C) 75.2   (D) 76.8   (E) 81.6

The scores remaining after dropping the highest and lowest scores were 7.5, 8.0, and 8.5. Multiplying their sum, which is 24, by a degree of difficulty of 3.2 yields a point value of 76.8. Thus, the best answer is D.

4. **If $2x = 3y = 10$, then $12xy =$**

    (A) 1,200   (B) 200   (C) 120   (D) 40   (E) 20

Solving $2x = 3y = 10$ for x and y yields

$x = 5$ and $y = \frac{10}{3}$. Thus, $12xy = 12(5)\left(\frac{10}{3}\right) = 200$. Therefore, the best answer is B.

An alternative method for solving this problem is:
$12xy = 2(2x)(3y) = 2(10)(10) = 200$. Therefore, the best answer is B.

5. **If Jack walked 5 miles in 1 hour and 15 minutes, what was his rate of walking in miles per hour?**

    (A) 4   (B) 4.5   (C) 6   (D) 6.25   (E) 15

1 hour and 15 minutes = $\frac{5}{4}$ hours. Thus, Jack walked

$\dfrac{5 \text{ miles}}{\frac{5}{4} \text{ hour}} = \dfrac{4 \text{ miles}}{1 \text{ hour}}$.

Therefore, the best answer is A.

6. **Of a certain high school graduating class, 75 percent of the students continued their formal education, and 80 percent of those who continued their formal education went to four-year colleges. If 300 students in the class went to four-year colleges, how many students were in the graduating class?**

    (A) 500   (B) 375   (C) 240   (D) 225   (E) 180

If S is the number of students in the graduating class, it follows that $0.80(0.75S) = 300$. Solving for S yields $S = 500$. Thus, the best answer is A.

7. **What is the least integer greater than $-2 + 0.5$?**

    (A) -2 (B) -1 (C) 0   (D) 1   (E) 2

$-2 + 0.5 = -1.5$. The least integer greater than -1.5 is -1. Therefore, the best answer is B.

8. Which of the following is equivalent to $\dfrac{2x + 4}{2x^2 + 8x + 8}$ for all values of x for which both expressions are defined?

(A) $\dfrac{1}{2x^2 + 6}$

(B) $\dfrac{1}{9x + 2}$

(C) $\dfrac{2}{x + 6}$

(D) $\dfrac{1}{x + 4}$

(E) $\dfrac{1}{x + 2}$

$$\frac{2x + 4}{2x^2 + 8x + 8} = \frac{2(x + 2)}{2(x^2 + 4x + 4)} = \frac{x + 2}{(x + 2)(x + 2)} = \frac{1}{x + 2}$$

Thus, E is the best answer.

9. A certain business printer can print 40 characters per second, which is 4 times as fast as an average printer. If an average printer can print 5 times as fast as an electric typewriter, how many characters per <u>minute</u> can an electric typewriter print?

(A) 2 (B) 32 (C) 50 (D) 120 (E) 600

The business printer can print $40(60) = 2,400$ characters per minute. Thus, an average printer can print $\dfrac{2,400}{4} = 600$ characters per minute and an electric typewriter can print $\dfrac{600}{5} = 120$ characters per minute. The best answer is D.

10. When ticket sales began, Pat was the nth customer in line for a ticket, and customers purchased their tickets at the rate of x customers per minute. Of the following, which best approximates the time, in minutes, that Pat had to wait in line from the moment ticket sales began?

(A) $(n - 1)x$
(B) $n + x - 1$
(C) $\dfrac{n - 1}{x}$
(D) $\dfrac{x}{n - 1}$
(E) $\dfrac{n}{x - 1}$

Since x customers purchased their tickets each minute, it follows that, on the average, it took each customer $\dfrac{1}{x}$ minutes to purchase tickets. Since Pat was the nth customer in line, $n - 1$ customers purchased tickets before Pat. Therefore, Pat waited approximately $(n - 1)\left(\dfrac{1}{x}\right) = \dfrac{n - 1}{x}$ minutes to purchase tickets. Thus, the best answer is C.

11. If 6 gallons of gasoline are added to a tank that is already filled to $\dfrac{3}{4}$ of its capacity, the tank is then filled to $\dfrac{9}{10}$ of its capacity. How many gallons does the tank hold?

(A) 20 (B) 24 (C) 36 (D) 40 (E) 60

If G is the capacity, in gallons, of the tank, it follows that
$$\frac{3}{4} G + 6 = \frac{9}{10} G;$$
$$6 = \left(\frac{9}{10} - \frac{3}{4}\right) G;$$
$$6 = \frac{6}{40} G;$$
$$G = 40.$$
Thus, the best answer is D.

12. A bus trip of 450 miles would have taken 1 hour less if the average speed S for the trip had been greater by 5 miles per hour. What was the average speed S, in miles per hour, for the trip?

(A) 10 (B) 40 (C) 45 (D) 50 (E) 55

If t is the time, in hours, taken for the trip, then $St = 450$ and $(S + 5)(t - 1) = 450$. Solving the first equation for t yields $t = \dfrac{450}{S}$. Substituting for t in the second equation yields

$$(S + 5)\left(\left(\frac{450}{S}\right) - 1\right) = 450;$$
$$450 + \frac{5(450)}{S} - S - 5 = 450;$$
$$\frac{2,250}{S} - S - 5 = 0;$$
$$2,250 - S^2 - 5S = 0;$$
$$S^2 + 5S - 2,250 = 0;$$
$$(S + 50)(S - 45) = 0;$$
$$S = 45.$$

Thus, the best answer is C.

13. 10^3 is how many times $(0.01)^3$?

   (A) 10^6 (B) 10^8 (C) 10^9 (D) 10^{12} (E) 10^{18}

$$\frac{10^3}{(0.01)^3} = \left(\frac{10}{0.01}\right)^3 = (1,000)^3 = (10^3)^3 = 10^9$$

Therefore, the best answer is C.

14. Which of the following groups of numbers could be the lengths of the sides of a right triangle?

   I. $1, 4, \sqrt{17}$

   II. $4, 7, \sqrt{11}$

   III. $4, 9, 6$

   (A) I only
   (B) I and II only
   (C) I and III only
   (D) II and III only
   (E) I, II, and III

If a, b, and c are the lengths of the sides of a right triangle, with c greater than a and b, then $a^2 + b^2 = c^2$. By squaring the numbers in each group (I, II, and III) and arranging them appropriately, it can be verified that only the group of numbers listed in I could be the lengths of the sides of a right triangle.

$$\text{I. } 1^2 + 4^2 = \left(\sqrt{17}\right)^2$$

$$\text{II. } 4^2 + \left(\sqrt{11}\right)^2 \neq 7^2$$

III. $4^2 + 6^2 \neq 9^2$

Thus, the best answer is A.

15. When the stock market opened yesterday, the price of a share of stock X was $10\frac{1}{2}$. When the market closed, the price was $11\frac{1}{4}$. Of the following, which is closest to the percent increase in the price of stock X?

   (A) 0.5%   (B) 1.0%   (C) 6.7%

   (D) 7.1%   (E) 7.5%

The price per share of stock X increased by $\frac{3}{4}$ over the opening price of $10\frac{1}{2}$. The percent increase is thus

$$\frac{\frac{3}{4}}{10\frac{1}{2}} \times 100 = \frac{100}{14}, \text{ which is equal to 7.1 (when rounded to}$$

the nearest tenth). Therefore, the best answer is D.

16. If x and y are integers and xy^3 is a positive odd integer, which of the following must be true?

   I. xy is positive.
   II. xy is odd.
   III. $x + y$ is even.

   (A) I only
   (B) II only
   (C) III only
   (D) I and II
   (E) II and III

Since xy^2 is positive and y^2 must be positive, it follows that x must be positive. Since xy^2 is odd, it follows that both x and y, which are factors of xy^2, must be odd. Thus, x is a positive odd integer and y is an odd integer.

I need not be true, since xy is negative when x is positive and y is negative.

II must be true, since the product of two odd integers must be odd.

III must be true, since the sum of two odd integers must be even.

Therefore, the best answer is E.

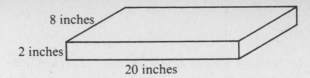

8 inches
2 inches
20 inches

17. The figure above shows the dimensions of a rectangular box that is to be completely wrapped with paper. If a single sheet of paper is to be used without patching, then the dimensions of the paper could be

(A) 17 in by 25 in
(B) 21 in by 24 in
(C) 24 in by 12 in
(D) 24 in by 14 in
(E) 26 in by 14 in

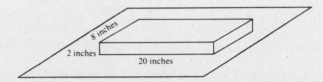

8 inches
2 inches
20 inches

Center the box on the sheet of paper, as shown in the figure above. To cover the box completely, the paper must be wide enough to span the 20-inch width and half of the 2-inch height on each side. Thus, the paper must be at least 22 inches wide. The paper must also be long enough to cover the 8-inch top and bottom and the 2-inch heights on each side. Thus, it must be at least 20 inches long. Therefore, the paper must be at least 20 inches by 22 inches. Note that of the options only 21 inches by 24 inches is bigger than 20 inches by 22 inches. Thus, the best answer is B.

18.
$$x - y = 3$$
$$2x = 2y + 6$$

The system of equations above has how many solutions?

(A) None
(B) Exactly one
(C) Exactly two
(D) Exactly three
(E) Infinitely many

$2x = 2y + 6$
$x = y + 3$ (divide by 2)

$x - y = 3$

Note that this equation is equivalent to the first equation. Therefore, any solution of the first equation is a solution of the second equation. $x - y = 3$ has infinitely many solutions. Therefore, the best answer is E.

19. If M and N are positive integers that have remainders of 1 and 3, respectively, when divided by 6, which of the following could NOT be a possible value of $M + N$?

(A) 86 (B) 52 (C) 34 (D) 28 (E) 10

M can be written as $6q + 1$ and N as $6r + 3$, where q and r are integers. Thus, $M + N = (6q + 1) + (6r + 3) = 6(q + r) + 4$, or $M + N$ has a remainder of 4 when divided by 6. The only option for which this is not true is 86. Thus, the best answer is A.

20. The R students in a class agree to contribute equally to buy their teacher a birthday present that costs y dollars. If x of the students later fail to contribute their share, which of the following represents the additional number of dollars that each of the remaining students must contribute in order to pay for the present?

(A) $\dfrac{y}{R}$

(B) $\dfrac{y}{R - x}$

(C) $\dfrac{xy}{R - x}$

(D) $\dfrac{xy}{R(R - x)}$

(E) $\dfrac{y}{R(R - x)}$

In order to contribute equally to the cost of the y dollar present, each of the R students must contribute $\dfrac{y}{R}$ dollars. The total contribution of the x students who failed to contribute is $x\left(\dfrac{y}{r}\right) = \dfrac{xy}{r}$ dollars, which is the additional amount the other $R - x$ students must contribute as a group. Thus, each of the remaining students must contribute an additional $\dfrac{\frac{xy}{R}}{R - x} = \dfrac{xy}{R(R - x)}$ dollars.

An alternative method for solving this problem is:

The additional amount each of the remaining $R - x$ students must contribute is equal to the difference between the amount they each need to contribute to share the y dollar cost of the present equally among themselves and the amount they each contributed, assuming that all R students would contribute, or
$$\frac{y}{R - x} - \frac{y}{R} = \frac{Ry - (R - x)y}{R(R - x)} = \frac{xy}{R(R - x)}.$$

Therefore, the best answer is D.

Directions: In this section solve each problem, using any available space on the page for scratchwork. Then indicate the best of the answer choices given.

Numbers: All numbers used are real numbers.

Figures: Figures that accompany problems in this section are intended to provide information useful in solving the problems. They are drawn as accurately as possible EXCEPT when it is stated in a specific problem that its figure is not drawn to scale. All figures lie in a plane unless otherwise indicated.

1. $6.09 - 4.693 =$

(A) 1.397 (B) 1.403 (C) 1.407
(D) 1.497 (E) 2.603

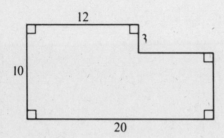

2. What is the area of the region enclosed by the figure above?

(A) 116 (B) 144 (C) 176
(D) 179 (E) 284

3. If $p = 0.2$ and $n = 100$, then $\sqrt{\dfrac{p(1-p)}{n}} =$

(A) $-\sqrt{0.002}$
(B) $\sqrt{0.02} - 0.02$
(C) 0
(D) 0.04
(E) 0.4

4. If each of 4 subsidiaries of Corporation R has been granted a line of credit of $700,000 and each of the other 3 subsidiaries of Corporation R has been granted a line of credit of $112,000, what is the average (arithmetic mean) line of credit granted to a subsidiary of Corporation R?

(A) $1,568,000
(B) $448,000
(C) $406,000
(D) $313,600
(E) $116,000

GO ON TO THE NEXT PAGE.

5. If x is a number such that $x^2 - 3x + 2 = 0$ and $x^2 - x - 2 = 0$, what is the value of x?

(A) -2
(B) -1
(C) 0
(D) 1
(E) 2

6. In traveling from a dormitory to a certain city, a student went $\frac{1}{5}$ of the way by foot, $\frac{2}{3}$ of the way by bus, and the remaining 8 kilometers by car. What is the distance, in kilometers, from the dormitory to the city?

(A) 30   (B) 45   (C) 60   (D) 90   (E) 120

7. A certain elevator has a safe weight limit of 2,000 pounds. What is the greatest possible number of people who can safely ride on the elevator at one time with the average (arithmetic mean) weight of half the riders being 180 pounds and the average weight of the others being 215 pounds?

(A) 7
(B) 8
(C) 9
(D) 10
(E) 11

8. After paying a 10 percent tax on all income over $3,000, a person had a net income of $12,000. What was the income before taxes?

(A) $13,300
(B) $13,000
(C) $12,900
(D) $10,000
(E) $9,000

GO ON TO THE NEXT PAGE.

9. $1 - [2 - (3 - [4 - 5] + 6) + 7] =$

(A) -2 (B) 0 (C) 1 (D) 2 (E) 16

10. The price of a model M camera is $209 and the price of a special lens is $69. When the camera and lens are purchased together, the price is $239. The amount saved by purchasing the camera and lens together is approximately what percent of the total price of the camera and lens when purchased separately?

(A) 14%
(B) 16%
(C) 29%
(D) 33%
(E) 86%

11. If 0.497 mark has the value of one dollar, what is the value to the nearest dollar of 350 marks?

(A) $174 (B) $176 (C) $524
(D) $696 (E) $704

12. A right cylindrical container with radius 2 meters and height 1 meter is filled to capacity with oil. How many empty right cylindrical cans, each with radius $\frac{1}{2}$ meter and height 4 meters, can be filled to capacity with the oil in this container?

(A) 1
(B) 2
(C) 4
(D) 8
(E) 16

13. If a sequence of 8 consecutive odd integers with increasing values has 9 as its 7th term, what is the sum of the terms of the sequence?

(A) 22
(B) 32
(C) 36
(D) 40
(E) 44

GO ON TO THE NEXT PAGE.

14. A rectangular floor is covered by a rug except for a strip p meters wide along each of the four edges. If the floor is m meters by n meters, what is the area of the rug, in square meters?

(A) $mn - p(m + n)$
(B) $mn - 2p(m + n)$
(C) $mn - p^2$
(D) $(m - p)(n - p)$
(E) $(m - 2p)(n - 2p)$

15. Working alone, R can complete a certain kind of job in 9 hours. R and S, working together at their respective rates, can complete one of these jobs in 6 hours. In how many hours can S, working alone, complete one of these jobs?

(A) 18
(B) 12
(C) 9
(D) 6
(E) 3

16. A family made a down payment of $75 and borrowed the balance on a set of encyclopedias that cost $400. The balance with interest was paid in 23 monthly payments of $16 each and a final payment of $9. The amount of interest paid was what percent of the amount borrowed?

(A) 6%
(B) 12%
(C) 14%
(D) 16%
(E) 20%

17. If $x \neq 0$ and $x = \sqrt{4xy - 4y^2}$, then, in terms of y, $x =$

(A) $2y$

(B) y

(C) $\frac{y}{2}$

(D) $\frac{-4y^2}{1 - 4y}$

(E) $-2y$

GO ON TO THE NEXT PAGE.

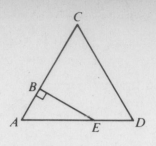

18. Solution Y is 30 percent liquid X and 70 percent water. If 2 kilograms of water evaporate from 8 kilograms of solution Y and 2 kilograms of solution Y are added to the remaining 6 kilograms of liquid, what percent of this new solution is liquid X?

(A) 30%

(B) $33\frac{1}{3}$%

(C) $37\frac{1}{2}$%

(D) 40%

(E) 50%

19. $\dfrac{1}{\dfrac{1}{0.03} + \dfrac{1}{0.37}} =$

(A) 0.004
(B) 0.02775
(C) 2.775
(D) 3.6036
(E) 36.036

20. If each side of $\triangle ACD$ above has length 3 and if AB has length 1, what is the area of region $BCDE$?

(A) $\dfrac{9}{4}$ (B) $\dfrac{7}{4}\sqrt{3}$ (C) $\dfrac{9}{4}\sqrt{3}$

(D) $\dfrac{7}{2}\sqrt{3}$ (E) $6 + \sqrt{3}$

S T O P

IF YOU FINISH BEFORE TIME IS CALLED, YOU MAY CHECK YOUR WORK ON THIS SECTION ONLY.
DO NOT TURN TO ANY OTHER SECTION IN THE TEST.

Answer Key for Sample Test Section 3

PROBLEM SOLVING

1. A	11. E
2. C	12. C
3. D	13. B
4. B	14. E
5. E	15. A
6. C	16. D
7. D	17. A
8. B	18. C
9. D	19. B
10. A	20. B

Explanatory Material:
Problem Solving Sample Test Section 3

1. $6.09 - 4.693 =$

    (A) 1.397 (B) 1.403 (C) 1.407
    (D) 1.497 (E) 2.603

    $$\begin{array}{r} 6.090 \\ -4.693 \\ \hline 1.397 \end{array}$$

Thus, the best answer is A.

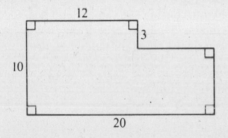

2. What is the area of the region enclosed by the figure above?

    (A) 116 (B) 144 (C) 176
    (D) 179 (E) 284

If a line is drawn dividing the figure into two rectangles, the length of the horizontal segment is $20 - 12 = 8$ and the length of the vertical segment of the smaller rectangle is $10 - 3 = 7$. (See below.)

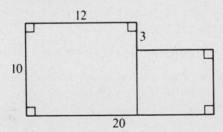

Thus, the area of the region is $(10 \times 12) + (8 \times 7) = 176$. Therefore, the best answer is C.

3. If $p = 0.2$ and $n = 100$, then $\sqrt{\dfrac{p(1-p)}{n}} =$

    (A) $-\sqrt{0.002}$
    (B) $\sqrt{0.0002} - 0.02$
    (C) 0
    (D) 0.04
    (E) 0.4

Substituting for p and n in the radical expression yields:

$$\sqrt{\frac{(0.2)(1-0.2)}{100}} = \sqrt{\frac{(0.2)(0.8)}{100}} = \sqrt{\frac{0.16}{100}} = \frac{0.4}{10} = 0.04$$

Thus, the best answer is D.

4. If each of 4 subsidiaries of Corporation R has been granted a line of credit of \$700,000 and each of the other 3 subsidiaries of Corporation R has been granted a line of credit of \$112,000, what is the average (arithmetic mean) line of credit granted to a subsidiary of Corporation R?

    (A) \$1,568,000
    (B) \$ 448,000
    (C) \$ 406,000
    (D) \$ 313,600
    (E) \$ 116,000

The total amount of credit for the 7 subsidiaries is:

$4(\$700,000) + 3(\$112,000) = \$3,136,000$.

Therefore, the average per subsidiary is $\dfrac{\$3,136,000}{7} =$ \$448,000, and the best answer is B.

5. If x is a number such that $x^2 - 3x + 2 = 0$ and $x^2 - x - 2 = 0$, what is the value of x?

    (A) -2
    (B) -1
    (C)   0
    (D)   1
    (E)   2

Since both polynomials are equal to 0, they are equal to each other. Thus, $x^2 - 3x + 2 = x^2 - x - 2$, $-2x = -4$ and $x = 2$. Therefore, the best answer is E.

6. In traveling from a dormitory to a certain city, a student went $\frac{1}{5}$ of the way by foot, $\frac{2}{3}$ of the way by bus, and the remaining 8 kilometers by car. What is the distance, in kilometers, from the dormitory to the city?

   (A) 30   (B) 45   (C) 60   (D) 90   (E) 120

The student went on foot and by bus $\frac{1}{5} + \frac{2}{3}$ of the way, which is $\frac{3}{15} + \frac{10}{15} = \frac{13}{15}$. Therefore, the student went $1 - \frac{13}{15}$ of the way by car. Since $\frac{2}{15}$ of the distance from the dormitory to the city equals 8 kilometers, the distance equals $\frac{15}{2} \cdot 8 = 60$ kilometers. Thus, the best answer is C.

7. A certain elevator has a safe weight limit of 2,000 pounds. What is the greatest possible number of people who can safely ride on the elevator at one time with the average (arithmetic mean) weight of half the riders being 180 pounds and the average weight of the others being 215 pounds?

   (A) 7
   (B) 8
   (C) 9
   (D) 10
   (E) 11

If n is the greatest number of people who safely ride on the elevator at one time,

$\frac{n}{2}(180)$ is the total weight of half the group

and $\frac{n}{2}(215)$ is the total weight of the other half.

Therefore, $\frac{n}{2}(180) + \frac{n}{2}(215) \le 2,000$

$$180n + 215n \le 4,000$$
$$395n \le 4,000$$
$$n \le 10.2$$

Since n must be an integer, n = 10. Therefore, the best answer is D.

8. After paying a 10 percent tax on all income over $3,000, a person had a net income of $12,000. What was the income before taxes?

   (A) $13,300
   (B) $13,000
   (C) $12,900
   (D) $10,000
   (E) $ 9,000

If x dollars is the income before taxes, then the net income of $12,000 is equal to $3,000 plus the amount left over after the remaining (x − 3,000) dollars is taxed 10 percent, or (0.9)(x − 3,000) dollars. Therefore,

$$3,000 + (0.9)(x - 3,000) = 12,000$$
$$(0.9)(x - 3,000) = 9,000$$
$$0.9x - 2,700 = 9,000$$
$$0.9x = 11,700$$
$$x = \frac{11,700}{0.9} = 13,000$$

Thus, the best answer is B.

9. $1 - [2 - (3 - [4 - 5] + 6) + 7]$

   (A) −2   (B) 0   (C) 1   (D) 2   (E) 16

When removing parentheses and brackets, always remove the innermost parentheses first.

$1 - [2 - (3 - [4 - 5] + 6) + 7] =$
$1 - [2 - (3 - [-1] + 6) + 7] =$
$1 - [2 - (3 + 1 + 6) + 7] =$
$1 - [2 - 10 + 7] =$
$1 - [-1] = 1 + 1 = 2$

Thus, the best answer is D.

10. The price of a model *M* camera is $209 and the price of a special lens is $69. When the camera and lens are purchased together, the price is $239. The amount saved by purchasing the camera and lens together is approximately what percent of the total price of the camera and lens when purchased separately?

    (A) 14%
    (B) 16%
    (C) 29%
    (D) 33%
    (E) 86%

The total price of the camera and lens purchased separately is $209 + $69 = $278. The amount saved by purchasing the two together is $278 − $239 = $39. Therefore, the percent saving is $\frac{$39}{$278}$ or approximately 14%. Thus, the best answer is A.

11. If 0.497 mark has the value of one dollar, what is the value to the nearest dollar of 350 marks?

    (A) $174   (B) $176   (C) $524
      (D) $696   (E) $704

Since 0.497 mark equals one dollar, 350 marks equal $\frac{350}{0.497}$ dollars, or $704, to the nearest dollar. Thus, the best answer is E.

12. A right cylindrical container with radius 2 meters and height 1 meter is filled to capacity with oil. How many empty right cylindrical cans, each with radius $\frac{1}{2}$ meter and height 4 meters, can be filled to capacity with the oil in this container?

(A) 1
(B) 2
(C) 4
(D) 8
(E) 16

The total capacity of the right cylindrical container is $\pi r^2 h = \pi(2)^2(1) = 4\pi$ cubic meters. Each right cylindrical can has a total capacity of $\pi\left(\frac{1}{2}\right)^2(4) = \pi$ cubic meters. Therefore, the container can fill up $\frac{4\pi}{\pi}$, or 4, cans. Thus, the best answer is C.

13. If a sequence of 8 consecutive odd integers with increasing values has 9 as its 7th term, what is the sum of the terms of the sequence?

(A) 22
(B) 32
(C) 36
(D) 40
(E) 44

To derive the terms in the sequences, it is only necessary to write 9 and the six consecutive odd integers less than 9 and the next one greater than 9.

The sequence is: $-3, -1, 1, 3, 5, 7, 9, 11$, and the sum of the terms in the sequence is 32. Thus, the best answer is B.

14. A rectangular floor is covered by a rug except for a strip p meters wide along each of the four edges. If the floor is m meters by n meters, what is the area of the rug, in square meters?

(A) $mn - p(m + n)$
(B) $mn - 2p(m + n)$
(C) $mn - p^2$
(D) $(m - p)(n - p)$
(E) $(m - 2p)(n - 2p)$

It may be helpful to draw a diagram:

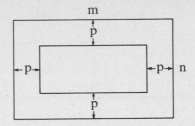

The rug is represented by the inside rectangle with dimensions $m - 2p$ and $n - 2p$. Therefore, its area is $(m - 2p)(n - 2p)$. Thus, the best answer is E.

15. Working alone, R can complete a certain kind of job in 9 hours. R and S, working together at their respective rates, can complete one of these jobs in 6 hours. In how many hours can S, working alone, complete one of these jobs?

(A) 18
(B) 12
(C) 9
(D) 6
(E) 3

If x is the number of hours S needs to complete the job alone, then S can do $\frac{1}{x}$ of the job in one hour. Similarly, R can do $\frac{1}{9}$ of the job in one hour, and R and S, working together, can do $\frac{1}{6}$ of the job in one hour. Therefore, $\frac{1}{x} + \frac{1}{9} = \frac{1}{6}$, and $x = 18$ hours. Thus, the best answer is A.

16. A family made a down payment of $75 and borrowed the balance on a set of encyclopedias that cost $400. The balance with interest was paid in 23 monthly payments of $16 each and a final payment of $9. The amount of interest paid was what percent of the amount borrowed?

(A) 6%
(B) 12%
(C) 14%
(D) 16%
(E) 20%

The family had to borrow $400 − $75 = $325. They paid back 23(16) + $9 = $377. Therefore, they paid $377 − $325 = $52 in interest, which was $\frac{52}{325} = 16\%$ of the amount borrowed. Thus, the best answer is D.

17. If $x \neq 0$ and $x = \sqrt{4xy - 4y^2}$, then in terms of y, $x =$

(A) $2y$

(B) y

(C) $\frac{y}{2}$

(D) $\frac{-4y^2}{1 - 4y}$

(E) $-2y$

The value of x can be expressed in terms of y as follows:

$x = \sqrt{4xy - 4y^2}$
$x^2 = 4xy - 4y^2$
$x^2 - 4xy + 4y^2 = 0$
$(x - 2y)^2 = 0$
$x - 2y = 0$
$x = 2y$

Therefore, the best answer is A.

18. Solution Y is 30 percent liquid X and 70 percent water. If 2 kilograms of water evaporate from 8 kilograms of solution Y and 2 kilograms of solution Y are added to the remaining 6 kilograms of liquid, what percent of this new solution is liquid X?

(A) 30%

(B) $33\frac{1}{3}\%$

(C) $37\frac{1}{2}\%$

(D) 40%

(E) 50%

The original 8 kilograms (kg) of solution Y contains 30%, or 2.4 kg, of liquid X. If 2 kg of water evaporate from the 8 kg, that would leave 6 kg, of which 2.4 kg is liquid X. If 2 kg of solution Y is added to the remaining 6 kg of solution, the resulting 8 kg-solution would contain 2.4 + 0.3(2) kg of liquid X. Therefore, the percent of liquid X in the new solution would be

$\frac{2.4 + 0.6}{8} = \frac{3}{8} = 37\frac{1}{2}\%.$

Thus, the best answer is C.

19. $\dfrac{1}{\dfrac{1}{0.03} + \dfrac{1}{0.37}} =$

(A) 0.004

(B) 0.02775

(C) 2.775

(D) 3.6036

(E) 36.036

The value of the expression can be found as follows:

$\dfrac{1}{\dfrac{1}{0.03} + \dfrac{1}{0.37}} = \dfrac{1}{\dfrac{0.37 + 0.03}{(0.03)(0.37)}} = \dfrac{(0.03)(0.37)}{0.37 + 0.03} = \dfrac{0.0111}{0.4} = 0.02775$

Therefore, the best answer is B.

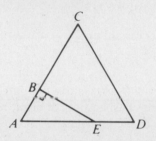

20. If each side of $\triangle ACD$ above has length 3 and if AB has length 1, what is the area of region $BCDE$?

(A) $\frac{9}{4}$ (B) $\frac{7}{4}\sqrt{3}$ (C) $\frac{9}{4}\sqrt{3}$

(D) $\frac{7}{2}\sqrt{3}$ (E) $6 + \sqrt{3}$

The area of region BCDE can be found by subtracting the area of $\triangle$ ABE from the area of $\triangle$ ACD. Since ACD is equilateral, an altitude to its base divides the triangle into two identical right triangles with acute angles of 30 and 60 degrees. Since the hypotenuse of each right triangle is 3 and the base is $\frac{3}{2}$, the altitude must be $\sqrt{3^2 - \left(\frac{3}{2}\right)^2}$ or $\frac{3\sqrt{3}}{2}$, which is also the altitude of $\triangle ACD$. Therefore, the area of $\triangle ACD$ is $\frac{1}{2}(3)\left(\frac{3\sqrt{3}}{2}\right) = \frac{9}{4}\sqrt{3}$. Since right $\triangle ABE$ also has acute angles of 30 and 60 degrees and AB = 1, then AE = 2(1) and BE = $\sqrt{2^2 - 1^2} = \sqrt{3}$. The area of $\triangle ABE$ is $\frac{1}{2}(1)(\sqrt{3}) = \frac{\sqrt{3}}{2}$. Therefore, the area of region BCDE is $\frac{9}{4}\sqrt{3} - \frac{1}{2}(\sqrt{3}) = \frac{7}{4}\sqrt{3}$, and the best answer is B.

PROBLEM SOLVING SAMPLE TEST SECTION 4

30 Minutes
20 Questions

Directions: In this section solve each problem, using any available space on the page for scratchwork. Then indicate the best of the answer choices given.

Numbers: All numbers used are real numbers.

Figures: Figures that accompany problems in this section are intended to provide information useful in solving the problems. They are drawn as accurately as possible EXCEPT when it is stated in a specific problem that its figure is not drawn to scale. All figures lie in a plane unless otherwise indicated.

1. Which of the following is equal to 85 percent of 160?

   (A) 1.88   (B) 13.6   (C) 136
   (D) 188   (E) 13,600

2. The regular hourly wage for an employee of a certain factory is $5.60. If the employee worked 8 hours overtime and earned $1\frac{1}{2}$ times this regular hourly wage for overtime, how much overtime money was earned?

   (A) $67.20
   (B) $55.40
   (C) $50.00
   (D) $44.80
   (E) $12.00

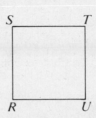

3. Square *RSTU* shown above is rotated in a plane about its center in a clockwise direction the minimum number of degrees necessary for *T* to be in the position where *S* is now shown. The number of degrees through which *RSTU* is rotated is

   (A) 135°   (B) 180°   (C) 225°
   (D) 270°   (E) 315°

GO ON TO THE NEXT PAGE.

BREAKDOWN OF COST TO CONSUMER FOR THE PRODUCTION
OF 6 OUNCES OF FROZEN ORANGE JUICE

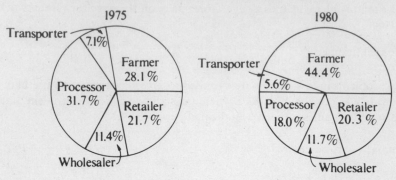

Cost to Consumer: $0.30   Cost to Consumer: $0.70

4. Of the following, which is closest to the increase from 1975 to 1980 in the amount received by the processor in producing 6 ounces of frozen orange juice?

(A) $0.03   (B) $0.05   (C) $0.06
(D) $0.08   (E) $0.13

5. In 1980, approximately what fraction of the cost to the consumer for the production of 6 ounces of frozen orange juice went to the farmer?

(A) $\frac{3}{11}$ (B) $\frac{1}{3}$ (C) $\frac{4}{9}$ (D) $\frac{5}{9}$ (E) $\frac{3}{5}$

GO ON TO THE NEXT PAGE.

6. $\sqrt[4]{496}$ is between

(A) 3 and 4
(B) 4 and 5
(C) 5 and 6
(D) 6 and 7
(E) 7 and 8

7. If $x \neq 0$, $2x = 5y$, and $3z = 7x$, what is the ratio of z to y?

(A) 2 to 21 (B) 3 to 5 (C) 14 to 15
(D) 6 to 5 (E) 35 to 6

8. A grocer purchased a quantity of bananas at 3 pounds for $0.50 and sold the entire quantity at 4 pounds for $1.00. How many pounds did the grocer purchase if the profit from selling the bananas was $10.00?

(A) 40
(B) 60
(C) 90
(D) 120
(E) 240

9. There are between 100 and 110 cards in a collection of cards. If they are counted out 3 at a time, there are 2 left over, but if they are counted out 4 at a time, there is 1 left over. How many cards are in the collection?

(A) 101 (B) 103 (C) 106 (D) 107 (E) 109

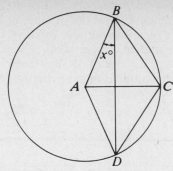

Note: Figure not drawn to scale.

10. If A is the center of the circle shown above and $AB = BC = CD$, what is the value of x?

(A) 15 (B) 30 (C) 45 (D) 60 (E) 75

11. Out of a total of 1,000 employees at a certain corporation, 52 percent are female and 40 percent of these females work in research. If 60 percent of the total number of employees work in research, how many male employees do NOT work in research?

(A) 520
(B) 480
(C) 392
(D) 208
(E) 88

GO ON TO THE NEXT PAGE.

12. An instructor scored a student's test of 50 questions by subtracting 2 times the number of incorrect answers from the number of correct answers. If the student answered all of the questions and received a score of 38, how many questions did that student answer correctly?

(A) 19
(B) 38
(C) 41
(D) 44
(E) 46

13. Which of the following integers does NOT have a divisor greater than 1 that is the square of an integer?

(A) 75
(B) 42
(C) 32
(D) 25
(E) 12

14. There are cogs around the circumference of a wheel and each cog is $\frac{\pi}{16}$ centimeter wide with a space of $\frac{\pi}{16}$ centimeter between consecutive cogs, as shown above. How many cogs of this size, with the same space between any two consecutive cogs, fit on a wheel with diameter 6 centimeters?

(A) 96
(B) 64
(C) 48
(D) 32
(E) 24

GO ON TO THE NEXT PAGE.

15. If $r \odot s = rs + r + s$, then for what value of s is $r \odot s$ equal to r for all values of r?

(A) -1 (B) 0 (C) 1 (D) $\dfrac{1}{r+1}$ (E) r

16. In each production lot for a certain toy, 25 percent of the toys are red and 75 percent of the toys are blue. Half the toys are size A and half are size B. If 10 out of a lot of 100 toys are red and size A, how many of the toys are blue and size B?

(A) 15
(B) 25
(C) 30
(D) 35
(E) 40

17. If $2x + 5y = 8$ and $3x = 2y$, what is the value of $2x + y$?

(A) 4

(B) $\dfrac{70}{19}$

(C) $\dfrac{64}{19}$

(D) $\dfrac{56}{19}$

(E) $\dfrac{40}{19}$

18. A ladder 25 feet long is leaning against a wall that is perpendicular to level ground. The bottom of the ladder is 7 feet from the base of the wall. If the top of the ladder slips down 4 feet, how many feet will the bottom of the ladder slip?

(A) 4
(B) 5
(C) 8
(D) 9
(E) 15

19. What is the least possible product of 4 different integers, each of which has a value between -5 and 10, inclusive?

(A) -5040 (B) -3600 (C) -720
(D) -600 (E) -120

20. If a motorist had driven 1 hour longer on a certain day and at an average rate of 5 miles per hour faster, he would have covered 70 more miles than he actually did. How many more miles would he have covered than he actually did if he had driven 2 hours longer and at an average rate of 10 miles per hour faster on that day?

(A) 100
(B) 120
(C) 140
(D) 150
(E) 160

S T O P

IF YOU FINISH BEFORE TIME IS CALLED, YOU MAY CHECK YOUR WORK ON THIS SECTION ONLY.
DO NOT TURN TO ANY OTHER SECTION IN THE TEST.

Answer Key for Sample Test Section 4

PROBLEM SOLVING

1. C	11. E
2. A	12. E
3. D	13. B
4. A	14. C
5. C	15. B
6. B	16. D
7. E	17. D
8. D	18. C
9. A	19. B
10. B	20. D

Explanatory Material: Problem Solving Sample Test Section 4

1. **Which of the following is equal to 85 percent of 160?**

    (A) 1.88   (B) 13.6   (C) 136
    (D) 188   (E) 13,600

The number equal to 85 percent of 160 can be found by multiplying $160 \times .85 = 136$. Therefore, the best answer is C.

2. **The regular hourly wage for an employee of a certain factory is \$5.60. If the employee worked 8 hours overtime and earned $1\frac{1}{2}$ times this regular hourly wage for overtime, how much overtime money was earned?**

    (A) \$67.20
    (B) \$55.40
    (C) \$50.00
    (D) \$44.80
    (E) \$12.00

The employee would have earned $8 \times \$5.60 = \$44.80$ at the regular rate. For overtime he receives an additional amount equal to half the regular rate, or \$22.40. The total overtime earnings are therefore $\$44.80 + \$22.40 = \$67.20$, so the best answer is A.

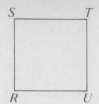

3. **Square *RSTU* shown above is rotated in a plane about its center in a clockwise direction the minimum number of degrees necessary for *T* to be in the position where *S* is now shown. The number of degrees through which *RSTU* is rotated is**

    (A) 135°   (B) 180°   (C) 225°
    (D) 270°   (E) 315°

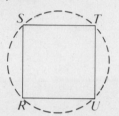

The figure above shows the circle traced by point T as square RSTU rotates about its center. If the square made one complete rotation so that T returned to its original position, the square would have rotated 360 degrees. Since the square rotates clockwise only until point T moves to position S, which is $\frac{3}{4}$ of the way around the circle, the square rotates $\frac{3}{4}$ of 360 or 270 degrees. Thus, the best answer is D.

BREAKDOWN OF COST TO CONSUMER
FOR THE PRODUCTION OF
6 OUNCES OF FROZEN ORANGE JUICE

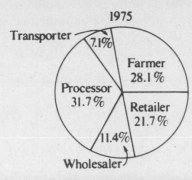

Cost to Consumer: $0.30

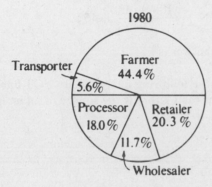

Cost to Consumer: $0.70

4. Of the following, which is closest to the increase from 1975 to 1980 in the amount received by the processor in producing 6 ounces of frozen orange juice?

(A) $0.03 (B) $0.05 (C) $0.06
   (D) $0.08 (E) $0.13

In 1975 the processor received 31.7% of the total $0.30 cost, or approximately $0.10. In 1980 the processor received 18% of the total $0.70 cost, or approximately $0.13. The increase is therefore approximately $0.03. The best answer is therefore A.

5. In 1980, approximately what fraction of the cost to the consumer for the production of 6 ounces of frozen orange juice went to the farmer?

(A) $\frac{3}{11}$ (B) $\frac{1}{3}$ (C) $\frac{4}{9}$ (D) $\frac{5}{9}$ (E) $\frac{3}{5}$

The farmer received 44.4% of the total, which is somewhat less than half. Answers D and E can be eliminated because each exceeds $\frac{1}{2}$. A and B can be eliminated because they are too small: $\frac{3}{11}$ is less than 30% and $\frac{1}{3}$ is about 33%. That C is the best answer can be confirmed by finding the decimal equivalent of $\frac{4}{9}$, which is approximately 0.44.

6. $\sqrt[4]{496}$ is between

(A) 3 and 4
(B) 4 and 5
(C) 5 and 6
(D) 6 and 7
(E) 7 and 8

If x = $\sqrt[4]{496}$, then x^4 = 496. Since 4^4 = 256 and 5^4 = 625, x must be between 4 and 5. Thus, the best answer is B.

7. If $x \neq 0$, $2x = 5y$, and $3z = 7x$, what is the ratio of z to y?

(A) 2 to 21 (B) 3 to 5 (C) 14 to 15
   (D) 6 to 5 (E) 35 to 6

To find the ratio of z to y, it is convenient to express both z and y in terms of x. Thus $z = \frac{7}{3}x$ and $y = \frac{2}{5}x$. Then the ratio of z to y is $\frac{7}{3}x : \frac{2}{5}x = \left(\frac{7}{3}\right)\left(\frac{5}{2}\right) = \frac{35}{6}$. Thus, the best answer is E.

8. A grocer purchased a quantity of bananas at 3 pounds for $0.50 and sold the entire quantity at 4 pounds for $1.00. How many pounds did the grocer purchase if the profit from selling the bananas was $10.00?

(A) 40
(B) 60
(C) 90
(D) 120
(E) 240

Let P represent the number of pounds purchased. Then the grocer's cost is $\left(\frac{0.50}{3}\right)P$ and his revenue is $\left(\frac{1.00}{4}\right)P$. Profit is revenue minus cost, so

$$10 = \left(\frac{1.00}{4}\right)P - \left(\frac{0.50}{3}\right)P$$

$$120 = 3P - 2P = P$$

Thus, the best answer is D.

9. There are between 100 and 110 cards in a collection of cards. If they are counted out 3 at a time, there are 2 left over, but if they are counted out 4 at a time, there is 1 left over. How many cards are in the collection?

(A) 101 (B) 103 (C) 106 (D) 107 (E)109

If the cards are counted three at a time with two left over, the possible totals are 101, 104, or 107. If they are counted four at a time with one left over, the total must be 101, 105, or 109. The only answer that satisfied both conditions is 101, so the best answer is A.

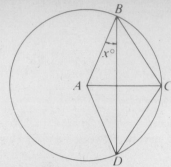

Note: Figure not drawn to scale.

10. If A is the center of the circle shown above and $AB = BC = CD$, what is the value of x?

(A) 15 (B) 30 (C) 45 (D) 60 (E) 75

$AC = AB = AD$, since all are radii of the same circle. Therefore, $AB = BC = CD = AC = AD$, and the triangles ABC and ACD are both equilateral and their angles are all equal to 60°. Because $AB = AD$, $\triangle$ ABD is an isosceles triangle and its base angles are therefore equal. Thus, the measure of $\angle$ ADB is $x°$. The sum of the degree measures of the angles of triangle ABD is $2x + 60 + 60 = 180$, so $x = 30$. The best answer is therefore B.

11. Out of a total of 1,000 employees at a certain corporation, 52 percent are female and 40 percent of these females work in research. If 60 percent of the total number of employees work in research, how many male employees do NOT work in research?

(A) 520
(B) 480
(C) 392
(D) 208
(E) 88

	Total Employees	Research Workers
Female	520	208
Male	480	392
TOTAL	1,000	600

The information presented in the problem is summarized in the table above. Of the 520 females (.52 × 1,000), 208 work in research (.40 × 520 = 208). The number of research workers who are male is 392, since 208 of the 600 (.60 × 1,000) research workers are female. Thus, there are 480 − 392 = 88 males who do not work in research. Therefore, the best answer is E.

12. An instructor scored a student's test of 50 questions by subtracting 2 times the number of incorrect answers from the number of correct answers. If the student answered all of the questions and received a score of 38, how many questions did that student answer correctly?

(A) 19
(B) 38
(C) 41
(D) 44
(E) 46

If N is the number of correct answers, $50 - N$ is the number of incorrect answers. Therefore,

$$N - 2(50 - N) = 38$$
$$3N - 100 = 38$$
$$N = \frac{100 + 38}{3} = 46$$

Thus, the best answer is E.

13. Which of the following integers does NOT have a divisor greater than 1 that is the square of an integer?

(A) 75
(B) 42
(C) 32
(D) 25
(E) 12

Note that $75 = 3 \times 5^2$, $32 = 2 \times 4^2$, $25 = 1 \times 5^2$ and $12 = 3 \times 2^2$. Since $42 = 2 \times 3 \times 7$ and so does not have a divisor greater than 1 that is the square of an integer, the best answer is B.

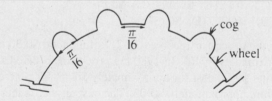

14. There are cogs around the circumference of a wheel and each cog is $\frac{\pi}{16}$ centimeter wide with a space of $\frac{\pi}{16}$ centimeter between consecutive cogs, as shown above. How many cogs of this size, with the same space between any two consecutive cogs, fit on a wheel with diameter 6 centimeters?

(A) 96
(B) 64
(C) 48
(D) 32
(E) 24

The circumference of a circle equals π times the diameter. If the diameter is 6 cm, the circumference is 6π. Each cog, together with a space separating it from the next one, uses

$2 \times \frac{\pi}{16} = \frac{\pi}{8}$ cm. The total number of cogs that would fit is therefore $6\pi \div \left(\frac{\pi}{8}\right) = 6\pi \times \frac{8}{\pi} = 48$. Thus, the best answer is C.

15. If $r \odot s = rs + r + s$, then for what value of s is $r \odot s$ equal to r for all values of r?

(A) -1 (B) 0 (C) 1 (D) $\frac{1}{r+1}$ (E) r

For $r \odot s$ to equal r,
$$rs + r + s = r$$
$$rs + s = 0$$
$$s(r + 1) = 0$$

If s = 0, than s(r + 1) = 0 is true for all values of r. If s ≠ 0, than s(r + 1) = 0 is true only if r = −1. Thus, the best answer is B.

16. In each production lot for a certain toy, 25 percent of the toys are red and 75 percent of the toys are blue. Half the toys are size *A* and half are size *B*. If 10 out of a lot of 100 toys are red and size *A*, how many of the toys are blue and size *B*?

(A) 15
(B) 25
(C) 30
(D) 35
(E) 40

	Total	Size A	Size B
Red	25	10	
Blue	75		
Total	100	50	50

The information presented in the problem is summarized in the table above. If 50 of the toys are size A, and 10 are red, then 40 of the size A toys are blue. If 75 toys are blue, and 40 of these are size A, then 75 − 40 = 35 toys are size B and blue. The best answer is therefore D.

17. If $2x + 5y = 8$ and $3x = 2y$, what is the value of $2x + y$?

(A) 4
(B) $\frac{70}{19}$
(C) $\frac{64}{19}$
(D) $\frac{56}{19}$
(E) $\frac{40}{19}$

Since 3x = 2y, x = $\frac{2y}{3}$. Substituting into the other equation for x yields

$$2\left(\frac{2y}{3}\right) + 5y = 8$$
$$4y + 15y = 24$$
$$19y = 24$$
$$y = \frac{24}{19}$$

Then
$$x = \left(\frac{2}{3}\right)\left(\frac{24}{19}\right) = \frac{16}{19}, \text{ and } 2x + y = 2\left(\frac{16}{19}\right) + \frac{24}{19} = \frac{56}{19}.$$

Thus, the best answer is D.

18. A ladder 25 feet long is leaning against a wall that is perpendicular to level ground. The bottom of the ladder is 7 feet from the base of the wall. If the top of the ladder slips down 4 feet, how many feet will the bottom of the ladder slip?

(A) 4
(B) 5
(C) 8
(D) 9
(E) 15

It may be helpful to draw a figure showing the information given:

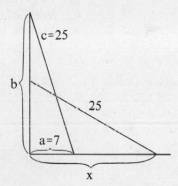

The original height of the top of the ladder can be obtained by the equation $a^2 + b^2 = c^2$ from the Pythagorean theorem. In this case, $7^2 + b^2 = 25^2$, so $b^2 = 625 − 49 = 576$, or b = 24.

After the ladder slips, the hypotenuse of the new triangle is still 25, but the vertical side is now 4 feet shorter, or 20 feet. The new base, x, can be obtained using the same procedure: $20^2 + x^2 = 25^2$, so x = $\sqrt{625 − 400}$ = 15.

Since the bottom of the ladder was originally 7 feet from the wall and is now 15 feet from the wall, it has slipped 8 feet. Therefore, the best answer is C.

19. What is the least possible product of 4 different integers, each of which has a value between -5 and 10, inclusive?

(A) -5040 (B) -3600 (C) -720
(D) -600 (E) -120

The least possible product in this case is the negative product having greatest absolute value, which can be obtained by multiplying $(-5) \times 10 \times 9 \times 8 = -3,600$. Thus, the best answer is B.

20. If a motorist had driven 1 hour longer on a certain day and at an average rate of 5 miles per hour faster, he would have covered 70 more miles than he actually did. How many more miles would he have covered than he actually did if he had driven 2 hours longer and at an average rate of 10 miles per hour faster on that day?

(A) 100
(B) 120
(C) 140
(D) 150
(E) 160

Since distance equals rate times time, $D = rt$, where D, r, and t are the actual distance, rate, and time traveled. If the motorist drives 1 hour longer and at a rate 5 mph faster, the new distance

$$D' = (r + 5)(t + 1) = rt + 70$$
$$rt + 5t + r + 5 = rt + 70$$
$$5t + r - 65$$

If instead he drives 2 hours longer, and at a rate 10 mph faster, the new distance

$$D'' = (r + 10)(t + 2) = rt + 10t + 2r + 20$$
$$= rt + 2(5t + r) + 20.$$

Then

$$D'' - D = rt + 2(5t + r) + 20 - rt$$
$$= 2(65) + 20 = 150.$$

The best answer is therefore D.

PROBLEM SOLVING SAMPLE TEST SECTION 5

30 Minutes
20 Questions

<u>Directions:</u> In this section solve each problem, using any available space on the page for scratchwork. Then indicate the best of the answer choices given.

<u>Numbers:</u> All numbers used are real numbers.

<u>Figures:</u> Figures that accompany problems in this section are intended to provide information useful in solving the problems. They are drawn as accurately as possible EXCEPT when it is stated in a specific problem that its figure is not drawn to scale. All figures lie in a plane unless otherwise indicated.

1. What is the average (arithmetic mean) of the numbers 15, 16, 17, 17, 18, and 19 ?

   (A) 14.2　(B) 16.5　(C) 17　(D) 17.5　(E) 18

2. Kathy bought 4 times as many shares in Company X as Carl, and Carl bought 3 times as many shares in the same company as Tom. Which of the following is the ratio of the number of shares bought by Kathy to the number of shares bought by Tom?

   (A) $\frac{3}{4}$

   (B) $\frac{4}{3}$

   (C) $\frac{3}{1}$

   (D) $\frac{4}{1}$

   (E) $\frac{12}{1}$

3. Of the following, which is closest to $\frac{0.15 \times 495}{9.97}$?

   (A) 7.5　(B) 15　(C) 75　(D) 150　(E) 750

4. A manager has $6,000 budgeted for raises for 4 full-time and 2 part-time employees. Each of the full-time employees receives the same raise, which is twice the raise that each of the part-time employees receives. What is the amount of the raise that each full-time employee receives?

   (A)　$750
   (B)　$1,000
   (C)　$1,200
   (D)　$1,500
   (E)　$3,000

GO ON TO THE NEXT PAGE.

5. $x^2 - \left(\dfrac{x}{2}\right)^2 =$

(A) $x^2 - x$

(B) $\dfrac{x^2}{4}$

(C) $\dfrac{x^2}{2}$

(D) $\dfrac{3x^2}{4}$

(E) $\dfrac{3x^2}{2}$

6. A hospital pharmacy charges $0.40 per fluidram of a certain medicine but allows a discount of 15 percent to Medicare patients. How much should the pharmacy charge a Medicare patient for 3 fluidounces of the medicine? (128 fluidrams = 16 fluidounces)

(A) $9.60
(B) $8.16
(C) $3.20
(D) $2.72
(E) $1.02

7. $(-1)^2 - (-1)^3 =$

(A) -2 (B) -1 (C) 0 (D) 1 (E) 2

8. At a certain bowling alley, it costs $0.50 to rent bowling shoes for the day and $1.25 to bowl 1 game. If a person has $12.80 and must rent shoes, what is the greatest number of complete games that person can bowl in one day?

(A) 7
(B) 8
(C) 9
(D) 10
(E) 11

GO ON TO THE NEXT PAGE.

9. If $\frac{x}{y} = 2$, then $\frac{x - y}{x} =$

(A) -1

(B) $-\frac{1}{2}$

(C) $\frac{1}{2}$

(D) 1

(E) 2

10. If each photocopy of a manuscript costs 4 cents per page, what is the cost, in cents, to reproduce x copies of an x-page manuscript?

(A) $4x$ (B) $16x$ (C) x^2

(D) $4x^2$ (E) $16x^2$

11. Ken left a job paying \$75,000 per year to accept a sales job paying \$45,000 per year plus 15 percent commission. If each of his sales is for \$750, what is the least number of sales he must make per year if he is not to lose money because of the change?

(A) 40
(B) 200
(C) 266
(D) 267
(E) 600

GO ON TO THE NEXT PAGE.

MONTHLY KILOWATT-HOURS

	500	1,000	1,500	2,000
Present	$24.00	$41.00	$57.00	$73.00
Proposed	$26.00	$45.00	$62.00	$79.00

12. The table above shows present rates and proposed rates for electricity for residential customers. For which of the monthly kilowatt-hours shown would the proposed rate be the greatest percent increase over the present rate?

(A) 500
(B) 1,000
(C) 1,500
(D) 2,000
(E) Each of the percent increases is the same.

13. If a, b, and c are three consecutive odd integers such that $10 < a < b < c < 20$ and if b and c are prime numbers, what is the value of $a + b$?

(A) 24
(B) 28
(C) 30
(D) 32
(E) 36

14. Of a group of people surveyed in a political poll, 60 percent said that they would vote for candidate R. Of those who said they would vote for R, 90 percent actually voted for R, and of those who did not say that they would vote for R, 5 percent actually voted for R. What percent of the group voted for R?

(A) 56%
(B) 59%
(C) 62%
(D) 65%
(E) 74%

15. If $r = 1 + \frac{1}{3} + \frac{1}{9} + \frac{1}{27}$ and $s = 1 + \frac{1}{3}r$, then s exceeds r by

(A) $\frac{1}{3}$ (B) $\frac{1}{6}$ (C) $\frac{1}{9}$ (D) $\frac{1}{27}$ (E) $\frac{1}{81}$

GO ON TO THE NEXT PAGE.

16. $\dfrac{0.025 \times \dfrac{15}{2} \times 48}{5 \times 0.0024 \times \dfrac{3}{4}} =$

(A)   0.1
(B)   0.2
(C)   100
(D) 200
(E) 1,000

17. A student responded to all of the 22 questions on a test and received a score of 63.5. If the scores were derived by adding 3.5 points for each correct answer and deducting 1 point for each incorrect answer, how many questions did the student answer <u>incorrectly</u>?

(A) 3   (B) 4   (C) 15   (D) 18   (E) 20

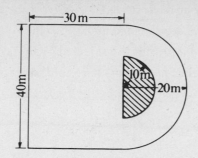

18. The figure above represents a rectangular parking lot that is 30 meters by 40 meters and an attached semicircular driveway that has an outer radius of 20 meters and an inner radius of 10 meters. If the shaded region is <u>not</u> included, what is the area, in square meters, of the lot and driveway?

(A) 1,350π
(B) 1,200 + 400π
(C) 1,200 + 300π
(D) 1,200 + 200π
(E) 1,200 + 150π

GO ON TO THE NEXT PAGE.

-89-

19. One-fifth of the light switches produced by a certain factory are defective. Four-fifths of the defective switches are rejected and $\frac{1}{20}$ of the nondefective switches are rejected by mistake. If all the switches not rejected are sold, what percent of the switches sold by the factory are defective?

(A) 4%
(B) 5%
(C) 6.25%
(D) 11%
(E) 16%

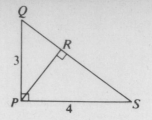

20. In $\triangle PQS$ above, if $PQ = 3$ and $PS = 4$, then $PR =$

(A) $\frac{9}{4}$ (B) $\frac{12}{5}$ (C) $\frac{16}{5}$ (D) $\frac{15}{4}$ (E) $\frac{20}{3}$

STOP

IF YOU FINISH BEFORE TIME IS CALLED, YOU MAY CHECK YOUR WORK ON THIS SECTION ONLY.
DO NOT TURN TO ANY OTHER SECTION IN THE TEST.

Answer Key for Sample Test Section 5

PROBLEM SOLVING

1. C	11. D
2. E	12. B
3. A	13. D
4. C	14. A
5. D	15. E
6. B	16. E
7. E	17. A
8. C	18. E
9. C	19. B
10. D	20. B

Explanatory Material:
Problem Solving Sample Test Section 5

1. What is the average (arithmetic mean) of the numbers 15, 16, 17, 17, 18, and 19?

(A) 14.2 (B) 16.5 (C) 17 (D) 17.5 (E) 18

The "brute force" method of solving this problem is to add the six numbers and divide the sum by 6. However, the same answer can be obtained by inspection, by observing that the mean of the first three numbers is 16 and the mean of the last three numbers is 18. The mean of the original six numbers is equal to the mean of 16 and 18, or 17. Thus, the best answer is C.

2. Kathy bought 4 times as many shares in Company X as Carl, and Carl bought 3 times as many shares in the same company as Tom. Which of the following is the ratio of the number of shares bought by Kathy to the number of shares bought by Tom?

(A) $\frac{3}{4}$

(B) $\frac{4}{3}$

(C) $\frac{3}{1}$

(D) $\frac{4}{1}$

(E) $\frac{12}{1}$

Let K = Kathy's shares, C = Carl's shares, and T = Tom's shares. Then

K = 4C
C = 3T
K = 4(3T) = 12T
$\frac{K}{T} = \frac{12}{1}$

Therefore, E is the best answer.

3. Of the following, which is closest to $\frac{0.15 \times 495}{9.97}$?

(A) 7.5 (B) 15 (C) 75 (D) 150 (E) 750

The value of the expression can be estimated by calculating

$$\frac{0.15 \times 500}{10} = 7.5.$$

Thus, the best answer is A.

4. A manager has $6,000 budgeted for raises for 4 full-time and 2 part-time employees. Each of the full-time employees receives the same raise, which is twice the raise that each of the part-time employees receives. What is the amount of the raise that each full-time employee receives?

(A) $ 750
(B) $1,000
(C) $1,200
(D) $1,500
(E) $3,000

If P is the raise a part-time employee receives, each full-time employee receives 2P. Then the total for the 2 part-time and 4 full-time employees is 2P + 4(2P) = 6,000; so 10P = 6,000 and P = 600. Then each full-time employee receives $1,200, and C is the best answer.

5. $x^2 - \left(\frac{x}{2}\right)^2 =$

(A) $x^2 - x$

(B) $\frac{x^2}{4}$

(C) $\frac{x^2}{2}$

(D) $\frac{3x^2}{4}$

(E) $\frac{3x^2}{2}$

$$x^2 - \left(\frac{x}{2}\right)^2 = x^2 - \frac{x^2}{4} = \frac{4x^2 - x^2}{4} = \frac{3x^2}{4}.$$

Therefore, D is the best answer.

6. A hospital pharmacy charges $0.40 per fluidram of a certain medicine but allows a discount of 15 percent to Medicare patients. How much should the pharmacy charge a Medicare patient for 3 fluidounces of the medicine? (128 fluidrams = 16 fluidounces)

(A) $9.60
(B) $8.16
(C) $3.20
(D) $2.72
(E) $1.02

One fluidounce equals $\frac{128}{16}$ or 8 fluidrams, so 3 fluidounces equal 24 fluidrams. The regular cost would be $0.40 $\times$ 24 = $9.60, and a 15 percent discount ($1.44) would yield a cost to the Medicare patient of $9.60 $-$ $1.44 = $8.16. Thus, the best answer is B.

7. $(-1)^2 - (-1)^3 =$

(A) -2 (B) -1 (C) 0 (D) 1 (E) 2

$(-1)^2 \quad (-1)^3 - (1) - (-1) = 2$. Thus, the best answer is E.

8. At a certain bowling alley, it costs $0.50 to rent bowling shoes for the day and $1.25 to bowl 1 game. If a person has $12.80 and must rent shoes, what is the greatest number of complete games that person can bowl in one day?

(A) 7
(B) 8
(C) 9
(D) 10
(E) 11

The amount the bowler has to spend on games is $12.30 after subtracting the $0.50 to rent shoes. The quotient $\frac{12.30}{1.25}$ is greater than 9 but less than 10, so he can bowl at most 9 games. Thus, the best answer is C.

9. If $\frac{x}{y} = 2$, then $\frac{x-y}{x} =$

(A) -1

(B) $-\frac{1}{2}$

(C) $\frac{1}{2}$

(D) 1

(E) 2

If $\frac{x}{y} = 2$, x = 2y. Then $\frac{x-y}{x} = \frac{2y-y}{2y} = \frac{y}{2y} = \frac{1}{2}$. Thus, the best answer is C.

10. If each photocopy of a manuscript costs 4 cents per page, what is the cost, in cents, to reproduce x copies of an x-page manuscript?

(A) $4x$ (B) $16x$ (C) x^2
(D) $4x^2$ (E) $16x^2$

The total cost is the cost per page times the number of pages per copy times the number of copies, or $4 \cdot x \cdot x = 4x^2$. Thus, the best answer is D.

11. Ken left a job paying $75,000 per year to accept a sales job paying $45,000 per year plus 15 percent commission. If each of his sales is for $750, what is the least number of sales he must make per year if he is not to lose money because of the change?

(A) 40
(B) 200
(C) 266
(D) 267
(E) 600

The difference between Ken's base salary and his previous salary is $30,000. To make up the difference in 15 percent commissions on $750 sales, the number of sales he must make is at least $\frac{30,000}{0.15 \times 750} = 266.67$. Thus, the least (integer) number of sales he must make to avoid losing money is 267, and the best answer is therefore D.

MONTHLY KILOWATT-HOURS

	500	1,000	1,500	2,000
Present	$24.00	$41.00	$57.00	$73.00
Proposed	$26.00	$45.00	$62.00	$79.00

12. The table above shows present rates and proposed rates for electricity for residential customers. For which of the monthly kilowatt-hours shown would the proposed rate be the greatest percent increase over the present rate?

(A) 500
(B) 1,000
(C) 1,500
(D) 2,000
(E) Each of the percent increases is the same.

	500	1,000	1,500	2,000
Percent Change	$\frac{2}{24}$	$\frac{4}{41}$	$\frac{5}{57}$	$\frac{6}{73}$

In order to compare the percent increases for the four rates, it is only necessary to compare the four ratios shown in the table, since they correspond to the percent increases. Since

$$\frac{2}{24} = \frac{1}{12}, \quad \frac{4}{41} > \frac{4}{44}\left(=\frac{1}{11}\right), \quad \frac{5}{57} < \frac{5}{55}\left(=\frac{1}{11}\right), \text{ and}$$

$$\frac{6}{73} < \frac{6}{72}\left(=\frac{1}{12}\right), \text{ the best answer is B.}$$

13. If a, b, and c are three consecutive odd integers such that $10 < a < b < c < 20$ and if b and c are prime numbers, what is the value of $a + b$?

   (A) 24
   (B) 28
   (C) 30
   (D) 32
   (E) 36

The only sets of consecutive odd integers for which $10 < a < b < c < 20$ are $\{11,13,15\}$, $\{13,15,17\}$, and $\{15,17,19\}$. The first two sets are eliminated because b and c must be prime and 15 is not a prime. Therefore, $\{15,17,19\}$ is the only set that meets all the conditions, so a = 15 and b = 17. Then a + b = 32, and the best answer is D.

14. Of a group of people surveyed in a political poll, 60 percent said that they would vote for candidate R. Of those who said they would vote for R, 90 percent actually voted for R, and of those who did not say that they would vote for R, 5 percent actually voted for R. What percent of the group voted for R?

   (A) 56%
   (B) 59%
   (C) 62%
   (D) 65%
   (E) 74%

Of the 60 percent who said they would vote for R, 90 percent (54 percent of the total group) actually did. Of the 40 percent who did not say they would vote for R, 5 percent (2 percent of the total group) actually did. Thus, 54 + 2 = 56 percent of the total group voted for R. The best answer is therefore A.

15. If $r = 1 + \frac{1}{3} + \frac{1}{9} + \frac{1}{27}$ and $s = 1 + \frac{1}{3}r$, then s exceeds r by

   (A) $\frac{1}{3}$ (B) $\frac{1}{6}$ (C) $\frac{1}{9}$ (D) $\frac{1}{27}$ (E) $\frac{1}{81}$

One way to solve this problem is first to compute r by adding the four terms. However, note that each successive term of r is $\frac{1}{3}$ the previous term. Thus,

$$s = 1 + \frac{1}{3}r = 1 + \frac{1}{3} + \frac{1}{9} + \frac{1}{27} + \frac{1}{81} = r + \frac{1}{81},$$

and s exceeds r by $\frac{1}{81}$. Therefore, the best answer is E.

16. $\dfrac{0.025 \times \frac{15}{2} \times 48}{5 \times 0.0024 \times \frac{3}{4}} =$

   (A)   0.1
   (B)   0.2
   (C)   100
   (D)   200
   (E) 1,000

Multiplying both the numerator and denominator by 10,000 yields

$$\frac{250 \times \frac{15}{2} \times 48}{5 \times 24 \times \frac{3}{4}}.$$

Simplifying the numerator and denominator further yields

$$\frac{250 \times 15 \times 24}{5 \times 6 \times 3} = 1,000.$$

Thus, the best answer is E.

17. A student responded to all of the 22 questions on a test and received a score of 63.5. If the scores were derived by adding 3.5 points for each correct answer and deducting 1 point for each incorrect answer, how many questions did the student answer <u>incorrectly</u>?

   (A) 3   (B) 4   (C) 15   (D) 18   (E) 20

If c is the number of correct answers, the number of incorrect answers is $(22 - c)$ and

$$3.5c - 1(22 - c) = 63.5$$
$$3.5c - 22 + c = 63.5$$
$$4.5c = 85.5$$
$$c = 19$$
$$22 - c = 3$$

Thus, the number of incorrect answers is 3 and the best answer is A.

-93-

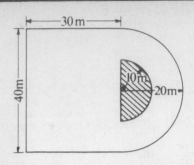

18. The figure above represents a rectangular parking lot that is 30 meters by 40 meters and an attached semi-circular driveway that has an outer radius of 20 meters and an inner radius of 10 meters. If the shaded region is <u>not</u> included, what is the area, in square meters, of the lot and driveway?

(A) $1,350\pi$
(B) $1,200 + 400\pi$
(C) $1,200 + 300\pi$
(D) $1,200 + 200\pi$
(E) $1,200 + 150\pi$

The area of the rectangular section is $30 \times 40 = 1,200$. Since the area of a semicircle is $\frac{1}{2}\pi r^2$, the large semicircular area is $\frac{1}{2} \times \pi \times 20^2 = 200\pi$. The shaded area, also semicircular, is $\frac{1}{2} \times \pi \times 10^2 = 50\pi$. Thus, the total area of the lot, excluding the shaded part, is
$$1,200 + 200\pi - 50\pi = 1,200 + 150\pi.$$
The best answer is therefore E.

19. One-fifth of the light switches produced by a certain factory are defective. Four-fifths of the defective switches are rejected and $\frac{1}{20}$ of the nondefective switches are rejected by mistake. If all the switches not rejected are sold, what percent of the switches sold by the factory are defective?

(A) 4%
(B) 5%
(C) 6.25%
(D) 11%
(E) 16%

The following table describes the condition of each hundred switches the firm makes:

	Rejected	Sold	Total
Nondefective	4	76	80
Defective	16	4	20
Total	20	80	100

If $\frac{4}{5}$ of the defective switches are rejected, 16 are rejected and 4 are sold. If $\frac{1}{20}$ of the 80 nondefective switches are rejected, 4 are rejected and 76 are sold. Thus, a total of 80 switches are sold, of which 4 are defective, or $\frac{4}{80} = 5\%$. Therefore, the best answer is B.

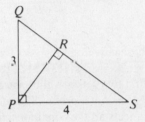

20. In $\triangle PQS$ above, if $PQ = 3$ and $PS = 4$, then $PR =$
(A) $\frac{9}{4}$ (B) $\frac{12}{5}$ (C) $\frac{16}{5}$ (D) $\frac{15}{4}$ (E) $\frac{20}{3}$

By the Pythagorean theorem, $QS = \sqrt{3^2 + 4^2} = 5$. The tedious, but perhaps the most apparent, way to find PR would be to apply the Pythagorean theorem again and solve the equation $3^2 - (QR)^2 = 4^2 - (5 - QR)^2$. A much simpler approach to the problem would be to recognize that, for any triangle with sides of lengths a_1, a_2, and a_3 and corresponding altitudes to those sides with lengths h_1, h_2, and h_3, the area can be expressed as half the product of any side and the altitude to that side. Thus, $a_1 h_1 = a_2 h_2 = a_3 h_3$, and in this particular problem $(PR)(QS) = (3)(4)$, $(PR)5 = 12$, and $PR = \frac{12}{5}$. Therefore, the best answer is B.

PROBLEM SOLVING SAMPLE TEST SECTION 6

30 Minutes
20 Questions

Directions: In this section solve each problem, using any available space on the page for scratchwork. Then indicate the best of the answer choices given.

Numbers: All numbers used are real numbers.

Figures: Figures that accompany problems in this section are intended to provide information useful in solving the problems. They are drawn as accurately as possible EXCEPT when it is stated in a specific problem that its figure is not drawn to scale. All figures lie in a plane unless otherwise indicated.

1. If x is an even integer, which of the following is an odd integer?

   (A) $3x + 2$

   (B) $7x$

   (C) $8x + 5$

   (D) x^2

   (E) x^3

2. On a purchase of $120, a store offered a payment plan consisting of a $20 down payment and 12 monthly payments of $10 each. What percent of the purchase price, to the nearest tenth of a percent, did the customer pay in interest by using this plan?

   (A) 16.7%

   (B) 30%

   (C) 75.8%

   (D) 106.7%

   (E) 107.5%

3. $\frac{5}{4}\left(42 \div \frac{3}{16}\right) =$

   (A) 6.3   (B) 9.8   (C) 179.2

   (D) 224   (E) 280

4. When magnified 1,000 times by an electron microscope, the image of a certain circular piece of tissue has a diameter of 0.5 centimeter. The actual diameter of the tissue, in centimeters, is

   (A) 0.005

   (B) 0.002

   (C) 0.001

   (D) 0.0005

   (E) 0.0002

GO ON TO THE NEXT PAGE.

5. In 1970 there were 8,902 women stockbrokers in the United States. By 1978 the number had increased to 19,947. Approximately what was the percent increase?

(A) 45%

(B) 125%

(C) 145%

(D) 150%

(E) 225%

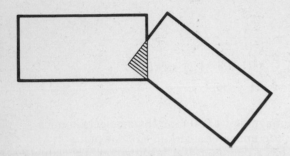

6. In the figure above, two rectangles with the same dimensions overlap to form the shaded region. If each rectangle has perimeter 12 and the shaded region has perimeter 3, what is the total length of the heavy line segments?

(A) 15   (B) 18   (C) 21   (D) 22   (E) 23

7. If one root of the equation $2x^2 + 3x - k = 0$ is 6, what is the value of k?

(A)   90

(B)   42

(C)   18

(D)   10

(E) − 10

8. Bottle R contains 250 capsules and costs $6.25. Bottle T contains 130 capsules and costs $2.99. What is the difference between the cost per capsule for bottle R and the cost per capsule for bottle T?

(A) $0.25

(B) $0.12

(C) $0.05

(D) $0.03

(E) $0.002

GO ON TO THE NEXT PAGE.

9. Trucking transportation rates are x dollars per metric ton per kilometer. How much does it cost, in dollars, to transport one dozen cars, which weigh two metric tons each, n kilometers by truck?

(A) $\frac{x}{12n}$ (B) $\frac{x}{24n}$ (C) $\frac{xn}{24}$

(D) $12xn$ (E) $24xn$

10. For a positive integer n, the number $n!$ is defined to be $n(n-1)(n-2)\ldots(1)$. For example, $4! = 4(3)(2)(1)$. What is the value of $5! - 3!$?

(A) 120

(B) 114

(C) 20

(D) 15

(E)   2

11. A man who died left an estate valued at $111,000. His will stipulated that his estate was to be distributed so that each of his three children received from the estate and his previous gifts, combined, the same total amount. If he had previously given his oldest child $15,000, his middle child $10,000, and his youngest $2,000, how much did the youngest child receive from the estate?

(A) $50,000

(B) $48,000

(C) $46,000

(D) $44,000

(E) $39,000

GO ON TO THE NEXT PAGE.

12. If $y > 0$, which of the following is equal to $\sqrt{48y^3}$?

(A) $4y\sqrt{3y}$

(B) $3y\sqrt{4y}$

(C) $2\sqrt{12y}$

(D) $3\sqrt{8y}$

(E) $16y\sqrt{3y}$

13. The volume of a box with a square base is 54 cubic centimeters. If the height of the box is twice the width of the base, what is the height, in centimeters?

(A) 2

(B) 3

(C) 4

(D) 6

(E) 9

$$q = 3\sqrt{3}$$
$$r = 1 + 2\sqrt{3}$$
$$s = 3 + \sqrt{3}$$

14. If q, r, and s are the numbers shown above, which of the following shows their order from greatest to least?

(A) q, r, s　(B) q, s, r　(C) r, q, s

(D) s, q, r　(E) s, r, q

15. The sum of the interior angles of any polygon with n sides is $180(n - 2)$ degrees. If the sum of the interior angles of polygon P is three times the sum of the interior angles of quadrilateral Q, how many sides does P have?

(A) 6　(B) 8　(C) 10　(D) 12　(E) 14

16. In Company X, 30 percent of the employees live over ten miles from work and 60 percent of the employees who live over ten miles from work are in car pools. If 40 percent of the employees of Company X are in car pools, what percent of the employees of Company X live ten miles or less from work and are in car pools?

(A) 12%

(B) 20%

(C) 22%

(D) 28%

(E) 32%

GO ON TO THE NEXT PAGE.

17. If an organization were to sell n tickets for a theater production, the total revenue from ticket sales would be 20 percent greater than the total costs of the production. If the organization actually sold all but 5 percent of the n tickets, the total revenue from ticket sales was what percent greater than the total costs of the production?

(A) 4%

(B) 10%

(C) 14%

(D) 15%

(E) 18%

18. When the integer n is divided by 6, the remainder is 3. Which of the following is NOT a multiple of 6?

(A) $n - 3$ (B) $n + 3$ (C) $2n$

(D) $3n$ (E) $4n$

19. How many liters of pure alcohol must be added to a 100-liter solution that is 20 percent alcohol in order to produce a solution that is 25 percent alcohol?

(A) $\frac{7}{2}$

(B) 5

(C) $\frac{20}{3}$

(D) 8

(E) $\frac{39}{4}$

20. If 10 persons meet at a reunion and each person shakes hands exactly once with each of the others, what is the total number of handshakes?

(A) $10 \cdot 9 \cdot 8 \cdot 7 \cdot 6 \cdot 5 \cdot 4 \cdot 3 \cdot 2 \cdot 1$

(B) $10 \cdot 10$

(C) $10 \cdot 9$

(D) 45

(E) 36

S T O P

IF YOU FINISH BEFORE TIME IS CALLED, YOU MAY CHECK YOUR WORK ON THIS SECTION ONLY.
DO NOT TURN TO ANY OTHER SECTION IN THE TEST.

Answer Key for Sample Test Section 6

PROBLEM SOLVING

1. C		11. D	
2. A		12. A	
3. E		13. D	
4. D		14. B	
5. B		15. B	
6. C		16. C	
7. A		17. C	
8. E		18. D	
9. E		19. C	
10. B		20. D	

Explanatory Material: Problem Solving Sample Test Section 6

1. **If x is an even integer, which of the following is an odd integer?**

   (A) $3x + 2$
   (B) $7x$
   (C) $8x + 5$
   (D) x^2
   (E) x^3

Since x is an even integer, it contains the factor 2 and any multiple (or power) of x contains the factor 2. Therefore, choices B, D, and E list expressions that must be even. The expression $3x + 2$ is even because it is the sum of two even integers. Since $8x + 5$ is the sum of an even integer and an odd integer, it must be odd, so the best answer is C.

2. **On a purchase of $120, a store offered a payment plan consisting of a $20 down payment and 12 monthly payments of $10 each. What percent of the purchase price, to the nearest tenth of a percent, did the customer pay in interest by using this plan?**

   (A) 16.7%
   (B) 30%
   (C) 75.8%
   (D) 106.7%
   (E) 107.5%

The purchase price was $120, but the customer actually paid a total of $20 + 12($10) = $140. Thus, the interest is equal to the difference $140 − $120 = $20, and the interest as a percent of the purchase price is $\frac{20}{120} = \frac{1}{6} = 16\frac{2}{3}\%$. The best answer is therefore A.

3. $\frac{5}{4}\left(42 \div \frac{3}{16}\right) =$

   (A) 6.3   (B) 9.8   (C) 179.2
   (D) 224   (E) 280

This computation can be done in a number of ways. Perhaps the easiest is: $\frac{5}{4}\left(42 \div \frac{3}{16}\right) = \frac{5}{4}\left(42 \times \frac{16}{3}\right) = \frac{5}{4}(14 \times 16) = 5 \times 14 \times 4 = 20(14) = 280.$
Thus, the best answer is E.

4. **When magnified 1,000 times by an electron microscope, the image of a certain circular piece of tissue has a diameter of 0.5 centimeter. The actual diameter of the tissue, in centimeters, is**

   (A) 0.005
   (B) 0.002
   (C) 0.001
   (D) 0.0005
   (E) 0.0002

Let d be the diameter, in centimeters, of the piece of tissue. Then $1{,}000d = 0.5$, and $d = \frac{0.5}{1000} = \frac{5}{10{,}000} = 0.0005$ cm. Thus, the best answer is D.

5. **In 1970 there were 8,902 women stockbrokers in the United States. By 1978 the number had increased to 19,947. Approximately what was the percent increase?**

   (A) 45%
   (B) 125%
   (C) 145%
   (D) 150%
   (E) 225%

From 1970 to 1978, the number of women stockbrokers increased from approximately 8,900 to 19,900, an increase of a little more than 11,000. Thus, the percent increase is a little more than $\frac{11{,}000}{8{,}900}$, which is approximately $\frac{11}{9}$ or 122.2%. The best answer therefore is B.

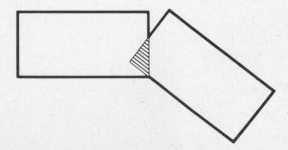

6. **In the figure above, two rectangles with the same dimensions overlap to form the shaded region. If each rectangle has perimeter 12 and the shaded region has perimeter 3, what is the total length of the heavy line segments?**

   (A) 15   (B) 18   (C) 21   (D) 22   (E) 23

The total length of the heavy line segments is equal to the sum of the perimeters of the two rectangles (24) minus the total length of the light line segments forming the shaded region. Since the total length of the light line segments is equal to the perimeter of the shaded region, the heavy line segments have total length $24 - 3 = 21$. The best answer is C.

7. If one root of the equation $2x^2 + 3x - k = 0$ is 6, what is the value of k?

   (A) 90
   (B) 42
   (C) 18
   (D) 10
   (E) -10

If 6 is a root of the equation, then x = 6 must satisfy the equation. Thus, $2(6)^2 + 3(6) - k = 0$, and $k = 2(36) + 18 = 90$. The best answer is A.

8. Bottle *R* contains 250 capsules and costs \$6.25. Bottle *T* contains 130 capsules and costs \$2.99. What is the difference between the cost per capsule for bottle *R* and the cost per capsule for bottle *T*?

   (A) \$0.25
   (B) \$0.12
   (C) \$0.05
   (D) \$0.03
   (E) \$0.002

The cost per capsule in bottle R is $\frac{625}{250} = 2.5$ cents. The cost per capsule in bottle T is $\frac{299}{130} = 2.3$ cents. The difference is $2.5 - 2.3 = 0.2$ cents, or \$0.002, so the best answer is E.

9. Trucking transportation rates are *x* dollars per metric ton per kilometer. How much does it cost, in dollars, to transport one dozen cars, which weigh two metric tons each, *n* kilometers by truck?

   (A) $\frac{x}{12n}$ (B) $\frac{x}{24n}$ (C) $\frac{xn}{24}$

   (D) $12xn$ (E) $24xn$

The total weight of the 12 cars to be transported is $12(2) = 24$ metric tons. Since the cost per kilometer for 1 metric ton is x dollars, the cost per kilometer for 24 metric tons is 24x dollars. If the cost to transport the entire shipment is 24x dollars per kilometer, the cost is 24xn dollars for a distance of n kilometers. The best answer is E.

10. For a positive integer *n*, the number *n*! is defined to be $n(n - 1)(n - 2) \ldots (1)$. For example, $4! = 4(3)(2)(1)$. What is the value of $5! - 3!$?

   (A) 120   (B) 114   (C) 20
   (D) 15   (E) 2

$5! - 3! = 5(4)(3)(2)(1) - (3)(2)(1) = 120 - 6 = 114$. Thus, the best answer is B.

11. A man who died left an estate valued at \$111,000. His will stipulated that his estate was to be distributed so that each of his three children received from the estate and his previous gifts, combined, the same total amount. If he had previously given his oldest child \$15,000, his middle child \$10,000, and his youngest \$2,000, how much did the youngest child receive from the estate?

   (A) \$50,000
   (B) \$48,000
   (C) \$46,000
   (D) \$44,000
   (E) \$39,000

The total value of the estate and the three previous gifts was \$111,000 + \$15,000 + \$10,000 + \$2,000 = \$138,000. Since each child was to receive an equal share of this total, each was to receive $\frac{\$138,000}{3}$, or a total of \$46,000. Therefore, the youngest child, who had previously received only \$2,000 of the \$46,000 share, received \$46,000 − \$2,000 = \$44,000 from the estate, and the best answer is D.

12. If y > 0, which of the following is equal to $\sqrt{48y^3}$?

   (A) $4y\sqrt{3y}$
   (B) $3y\sqrt{4y}$
   (C) $2\sqrt{12y}$
   (D) $3\sqrt{8y}$
   (E) $16y\sqrt{3y}$

To simplify, $\sqrt{48y^3} = (\sqrt{16y^2})(\sqrt{3y}) = 4y\sqrt{3y}$. Thus, the best answer is A.

13. The volume of a box with a square base is 54 cubic centimeters. If the height of the box is twice the width of the base, what is the height, in centimeters?

   (A) 2
   (B) 3
   (C) 4
   (D) 6
   (E) 9

The volume of the box is $x^2 y = 54$, where x is the length of a side of the square base and y is the height of the box. Since $y = 2x$, it follows that $x^2(2x) = 54$, or $x = 3$. Therefore, $y = 2x = 2(3) = 6$ centimeters, and the best answer is D.

$$q = 3\sqrt{3}$$
$$r = 1 + 2\sqrt{3}$$
$$s = 3 + \sqrt{3}$$

14. If q, r, and s are the numbers shown above, which of the following shows their order from greatest to least?

(A) q, r, s (B) q, s, r (C) r, q, s

(D) s, q, r (E) s, r, q

In comparing q, r, and s, it is convenient to subtract $\sqrt{3}$ from each of the numbers and then to compare only the residues Q, R, and S; the order of q, r, and s will be the same as the order of Q, R, and S. Now $Q = 2\sqrt{3}$, $R = 1 + \sqrt{3}$, and $S = 3$. Clearly $Q > R$ since $\sqrt{3} > 1$. Also note that $Q^2 = 12$ and $S^2 = 9$; therefore, $Q > S$. Since Q is greater than either R or S, the answer must be A or B. If 1 is subtracted from both R and S, it can be seen that $S > R$ since $2 > \sqrt{3}$. Therefore $Q > S > R$, and the best answer is B.

15. The sum of the interior angles of any polygon with n sides is $180(n - 2)$ degrees. If the sum of the interior angles of polygon P is three times the sum of the interior angles of quadrilateral Q, how many sides does P have?

(A) 6   (B) 8   (C) 10   (D) 12   (E) 14

The sum of the interior angles of quadrilateral Q is 360 degrees, since Q has 4 sides and $180(4 - 2) = 360$. The sum of the interior angles of polygon P is $3(360) = 1{,}080$ degrees. Now $1{,}080 = 180(n - 2)$ where n is the number of sides polygon P has. When each side of the equation is divided by 180, $6 = n - 2$ and $n = 8$. Thus, the best answer is B.

16. In Company X, 30 percent of the employees live over ten miles from work and 60 percent of the employees who live over ten miles from work are in car pools. If 40 percent of the employees of Company X are in car pools, what percent of the employees of Company X live ten miles or less from work and are in car pools?

(A) 12%
(B) 20%
(C) 22%
(D) 28%
(E) 32%

To solve problems of this type, where the categories are mutually exclusive, it is most convenient to organize the information in a two-dimensional table as shown below:

	10 Miles or Less from Work	More Than 10 Miles from Work	Total
Car Pool		18% (60% of 30%)	40%
No Car Pool			
Total		30%	100%

It is very easy to complete the table by finding the necessary percents to make the totals in each row or column. In this case, since a total of 40 percent of the employees are in car pools and 18 percent live more than 10 miles from work, $40 - 18 = 22\%$ live 10 miles or less from work and are in car pools. Thus, the best answer is C.

17. If an organization were to sell n tickets for a theater production, the total revenue from ticket sales would be 20 percent greater than the total costs of the production. If the organization actually sold all but 5 percent of the n tickets, the total revenue from ticket sales was what percent greater than the total costs of the production?

(A) 4%
(B) 10%
(C) 14%
(D) 15%
(E) 18%

Let p be the price per ticket. Then if n tickets were sold, total revenues would be np. Let c be the total cost of the production. Then, if np is 20 percent greater than c, $np = 1.2c$. Since only 95 percent of the n tickets were sold, $0.95(np) = 0.95(1.2c) = 1.14c$. Therefore, the total revenue from ticket sales was 14 percent greater than the total cost of production. Therefore, the best answer is C.

18. When the integer n is divided by 6, the remainder is 3. Which of the following is NOT a multiple of 6?

(A) $n - 3$ (B) $n + 3$ (C) $2n$

(D) $3n$ (E) $4n$

If the integer n has a remainder of 3 when it is divided by 6, then n is a number of the form $6q + 3$, where q is an integer. Therefore, $6q + 3$ can be substituted for n in each of the expressions listed until an expression is found that is not a multiple of 6 (does not have 6 as a factor). For example:
$n - 3 = (6q + 3) - 3 = 6q$;
$n + 3 = (6q + 3) + 3 = 6q + 6 = 6(q + 1)$;
$2n = 2(6q + 3) = 12q + 6 = 6(2q + 1)$;
$3n = 3(6q + 3) = 18q + 9 = 6(3q + 1) + 3$.
Since the expression given for choice D has a remainder of 3 when divided by 6, it is not a multiple of 6. Therefore, the best answer is D.

19. How many liters of pure alcohol must be added to a 100-liter solution that is 20 percent alcohol in order to produce a solution that is 25 percent alcohol?

(A) $\frac{7}{2}$

(B) 5

(C) $\frac{20}{3}$

(D) 8

(E) $\frac{39}{4}$

If x is the number of liters of alcohol that must be added to a solution that already contains 20 liters of alcohol (20% of 100 liters), then $20 + x$ liters must be 25 percent of the total number of liters in the new solution, which will consist of $100 + x$ liters. Therefore, the equation to be solved is $20 + x = 0.25(100 + x)$. This reduces to $20 + x = 25 + 0.25x$, and $0.75x = 5$. The value of $x = \frac{5}{0.75} = \frac{20}{3}$, and the best answer is C.

20. If 10 persons meet at a reunion and each person shakes hands exactly once with each of the others, what is the total number of handshakes?

(A) $10 \cdot 9 \cdot 8 \cdot 7 \cdot 6 \cdot 5 \cdot 4 \cdot 3 \cdot 2 \cdot 1$
(B) $10 \cdot 10$
(C) $10 \cdot 9$
(D) 45
(E) 36

Each of the 10 persons shakes hands 9 times, once with each of the other 9 people at the reunion. Since there are 10 people, each of whom shakes hands with the other 9 people, it would seem at first that there are 10(9) or 90 handshakes. However, since each handshake was counted twice, once for each of the two people involved, the correct number of handshakes is $\frac{90}{2}$, or 45. Thus, the best answer is D.

PROBLEM SOLVING SAMPLE TEST SECTION 7

Directions: In this section solve each problem, using any available space on the page for scratchwork. Then indicate the best of the answer choices given.

Numbers: All numbers used are real numbers.

Figures: Figures that accompany problems in this section are intended to provide information useful in solving the problems. They are drawn as accurately as possible EXCEPT when it is stated in a specific problem that its figure is not drawn to scale. All figures lie in a plane unless otherwise indicated.

1. At the rate of $7.50 per hour, how many hours must a person work to earn $232.50 ?

   (A) 25   (B) 27   (C) 29   (D) 30   (E) 31

2. Each month for 6 months the amount of money in a benefit fund is doubled. At the end of the 6 months there is a total of $640 in the fund. How much money was in the fund at the end of 3 months?

   (A) $80   (B) $100   (C) $120
   (D) $160   (E) $320

3. $6[-2(6-9)+11-23] =$

   (A) -224 (B) -108 (C) -36
   (D) 24   (E) 79

4. If $\frac{2}{3} \times \frac{3}{5} \times \frac{5}{8} \times \frac{8}{n} = \frac{2}{10}$, then $n =$

   (A) $\frac{1}{10}$ (B) $\frac{1}{5}$ (C) 5   (D) 10   (E) 100

5. If $d = 3.0641$ and $\bar{d}$ is the number obtained by rounding d to the nearest hundredth, then $d - \bar{d} =$

   (A) 0.0001
   (B) 0.0041
   (C) 0.0059
   (D) 0.0141
   (E) 0.0410

GO ON TO THE NEXT PAGE.

6. Mr. Jones drove from Town A to Town B in x hours. On the return trip over the same route, his average speed was twice as fast. Which of the following expresses the total number of driving hours for the round trip?

(A) $\frac{2}{3}x$

(B) $\frac{3}{2}x$

(C) $\frac{5}{3}x$

(D) $2x$

(E) $3x$

7. If 3 is the greatest common divisor of positive integers r and s, what is the greatest common divisor of $2r$ and $2s$?

(A) 2   (B) 3   (C) 4   (D) 6   (E) 12

8. If $x + y = 5$ and $xy = 6$, then $\frac{1}{x} + \frac{1}{y} =$

(A) $\frac{1}{6}$ (B) $\frac{1}{5}$ (C) $\frac{5}{6}$ (D) $\frac{6}{5}$ (E) 5

9. After 5 games, a rugby team had an average of 28 points per game. In order to increase the average by n points, how many points must be scored in a 6th game?

(A) n
(B) $6n$
(C) $28n$
(D) $28 + n$
(E) $28 + 6n$

10. On July 1, 1982, Ms. Fox deposited $10,000 in a new account at the annual interest rate of 12 percent compounded monthly. If no additional deposits or withdrawals were made and if interest was credited on the last day of each month, what was the amount of money in the account on September 1, 1982?

(A) $10,200
(B) $10,201
(C) $11,100
(D) $12,100
(E) $12,544

GO ON TO THE NEXT PAGE.

11. How many prime numbers are less than 25 and greater than 10 ?

(A) Three   (B) Four   (C) Five
(D) Six   (E) Seven

12. Erica has $460 in 5- and 10-dollar bills only. If she has fewer 10- than 5-dollar bills, what is the least possible number of 5-dollar bills she could have?

(A) 32
(B) 30
(C) 29
(D) 28
(E) 27

13. Which of the following is equivalent to the statement that 0.5 is between $\frac{2}{n}$ and $\frac{3}{n}$?

(A) $1 < n < 6$
(B) $2 < n < 3$
(C) $2 < n < 5$
(D) $4 < n < 6$
(E) $n > 10$

14. A corporation with 5,000,000 shares of publicly listed stock reported total earnings of $7.20 per share for the first 9 months of operation. During the final quarter the number of publicly listed shares was increased to 10,000,000 shares, and fourth quarter earnings were reported as $1.25 per share. What are the average annual earnings per share based on the number of shares at the end of the year?

(A) $1.83
(B) $2.43
(C) $4.85
(D) $8.45
(E) $9.70

15. In 1980 the government spent $12 billion for direct cash payments to single parents with dependent children. If this was 2,000 percent of the amount spent in 1956, what was the amount spent in 1956 ? (1 billion = 1,000,000,000)

(A) $6 million
(B) $24 million
(C) $60 million
(D) $240 million
(E) $600 million

GO ON TO THE NEXT PAGE.

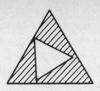

16. The triangles in the figure above are equilateral and the ratio of the length of a side of the larger triangle to the length of a side of the smaller triangle is $\frac{2}{1}$. If the area of the larger triangular region is K, what is the area of the shaded region in terms of K?

(A) $\frac{3}{4}K$ (B) $\frac{2}{3}K$ (C) $\frac{1}{2}K$

(D) $\frac{1}{3}K$ (E) $\frac{1}{4}K$

17. Four cups of milk are to be poured into a 2-cup bottle and a 4-cup bottle. If each bottle is to be filled to the same fraction of its capacity, how many cups of milk should be poured into the 4-cup bottle?

(A) $\frac{2}{3}$

(B) $\frac{7}{3}$

(C) $\frac{5}{2}$

(D) $\frac{8}{3}$

(E) 3

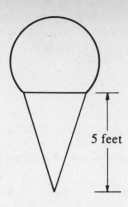

5 feet

18. The outline of a sign for an ice-cream store is made by placing $\frac{3}{4}$ of the circumference of a circle with radius 2 feet on top of an isosceles triangle with height 5 feet, as shown above. What is the perimeter, in feet, of the sign?

(A) $3\pi + 3\sqrt{3}$
(B) $3\pi + 6\sqrt{3}$
(C) $3\pi + 2\sqrt{33}$
(D) $4\pi + 3\sqrt{3}$
(E) $4\pi + 6\sqrt{3}$

GO ON TO THE NEXT PAGE.

19. The sum of the first 100 positive integers is 5,050. What is the sum of the first 200 positive integers?

(A) 10,100
(B) 10,200
(C) 15,050
(D) 20,050
(E) 20,100

20. A merchant purchased a jacket for $60 and then determined a selling price that equalled the purchase price of the jacket plus a markup that was 25 percent of the selling price. During a sale, the merchant discounted the selling price by 20 percent and sold the jacket. What was the merchant's gross profit on this sale?

(A) $0   (B) $3   (C) $4
(D) $12   (E) $15

S T O P

IF YOU FINISH BEFORE TIME IS CALLED, YOU MAY CHECK YOUR WORK ON THIS SECTION ONLY.
DO NOT TURN TO ANY OTHER SECTION IN THE TEST.

Answer Key for Sample Test Section 7

PROBLEM SOLVING

1. E	11. C
2. A	12. A
3. C	13. D
4. D	14. C
5. B	15. E
6. B	16. A
7. D	17. D
8. C	18. B
9. E	19. E
10. B	20. C

Explanatory Material: Problem Solving Sample Test Section 7

1. **At the rate of $7.50 per hour, how many hours must a person work to earn $232.50?**

   (A) 25 (B) 27 (C) 29 (D) 30 (E) 31

If a person earned $232.50 working h hours at $7.50 per hour, then $7.50h = 232.50$, or $h = 232.50/7.50 = 31$. Therefore, the best answer is E.

2. **Each month for 6 months the amount of money in a benefit fund is doubled. At the end of the 6 months there is a total of $640 in the fund. How much money was in the fund at the end of 3 months?**

   (A) $80 (B) $100 (C) $120 (D) $160 (E) $320

Since the fund doubled each of the 6 months, the amount in the fund at the end of month 3 can be found by starting with $640 and successively dividing by 2: month 5 — $320, month 4 — $160, month 3 — $80. Thus, the best answer is A.

3. $6[-2(6 - 9) + 11 - 23] =$

   (A) -224 (B) -108 (C) -36
   (D) 24 (E) 79

$$6[-2(6 - 9) + 11 - 23] = 6[-2(-3) + 11 - 23]$$
$$= 6[6 + 11 - 23]$$
$$= 6[-6]$$
$$= -36.$$

The best answer is C.

4. **If $\frac{2}{3} \times \frac{3}{5} \times \frac{5}{8} \times \frac{8}{n} = \frac{2}{10}$, then $n =$**

   (A) $\frac{1}{10}$ (B) $\frac{1}{5}$ (C) 5 (D) 10 (E) 100

By cancellation of the common factors 3, 5, and 8 in numerator and denominator, the equation reduces to $2/n = 2/10$. Therefore, $n = 10$. The best answer is D.

5. **If $d = 3.0641$ and $\bar{d}$ is the number obtained by rounding d to the nearest hundredth, then $d - \bar{d} =$**

   (A) 0.0001
   (B) 0.0041
   (C) 0.0059
   (D) 0.0141
   (E) 0.0410

Rounding d to the nearest hundredth gives $\bar{d} = 3.06$; thus, $d - \bar{d} = 3.0641 - 3.06 = 0.0041$, and B is the best answer.

6. **Mr. Jones drove from Town A to Town B in x hours. On the return trip over the same route, his average speed was twice as fast. Which of the following expresses the total number of driving hours for the round trip?**

   (A) $\frac{2}{3}x$

   (B) $\frac{3}{2}x$

   (C) $\frac{5}{3}x$

   (D) $2x$

   (E) $3x$

Since the distance traveled equals the product of the average speed and the time traveled, doubling the speed results in halving the time. Therefore, the total number of driving hours for the round trip is $x + x/2 = 3x/2$, and the best answer is B.

7. **If 3 is the greatest common divisor of positive integers r and s, what is the greatest common divisor of $2r$ and $2s$?**

   (A) 2 (B) 3 (C) 4 (D) 6 (E) 12

Since 2 is a factor of both $2r$ and $2s$, it is a common divisor of $2r$ and $2s$. Since the greatest common divisor of r and s is 3, it follows that the greatest common divisor of $2r$ and $2s$ is $(2)(3)$, or 6. Thus, the best answer is D.

8. If $x + y = 5$ and $xy = 6$, then $\frac{1}{x} + \frac{1}{y} =$

(A) $\frac{1}{6}$ (B) $\frac{1}{5}$ (C) $\frac{5}{6}$ (D) $\frac{6}{5}$ (E) 5

Because it is given that $x + y = 5$ and $xy = 6$,
$\frac{1}{x} + \frac{1}{y} = \frac{y}{xy} + \frac{x}{xy} = \frac{y + x}{xy} = \frac{5}{6}$. Therefore, the best answer is C.

9. After 5 games, a rugby team had an average of 28 points per game. In order to increase the average by n points, how many points must be scored in a 6th game?

(A) n
(B) $6n$
(C) $28n$
(D) $28 + n$
(E) $28 + 6n$

The average number of points for 5 games is 28, so the total number of points for the 5 games is $5(28) = 140$. If the team were to score x points in the 6th game, the average for 6 games would be $\frac{140 + x}{6}$. We want this average to be n greater than 28. Therefore,
$$\frac{140 + x}{6} = 28 + n$$
$$140 + x = 168 + 6n$$
$$x = 28 + 6n.$$
Choice E is the best answer.

10. On July 1, 1982, Ms. Fox deposited $10,000 in a new account at the annual interest rate of 12 percent compounded monthly. If no additional deposits or withdrawals were made and if interest was credited on the last day of each month, what was the amount of money in the account on September 1, 1982?

(A) $10,200
(B) $10,201
(C) $11,100
(D) $12,100
(E) $12,544

Since the annual interest rate is 12 percent, the monthly rate is 1 percent. On August 1, 1982, the total amount in the account would be $(1.01)(10,000) = \$10,100$. On September 1, 1982, the total would be $(1.01)(10,100) = \$10,201$, so B is the best answer.

11. How many prime numbers are less than 25 and greater than 10?

(A) Three (B) Four (C) Five
(D) Six (E) Seven

A prime number n cannot have any positive factors other than 1 and n. Therefore, the prime numbers between 10 and 25 are 11, 13, 17, 19, and 23. Since there are five, the best answer is C.

12. Erica has $460 in 5- and 10-dollar bills only. If she has fewer 10- than 5-dollar bills, what is the least possible number of 5-dollar bills she could have?

(A) 32
(B) 30
(C) 29
(D) 28
(E) 27

If Erica has f 5-dollar bills and t 10-dollar bills totaling $460, then $5f + 10t = 460$, or, dividing by 5, $f + 2t = 92$. This equation has many solutions (e.g., $f = 2$, $t = 45$). We want the solution that makes f as small as possible but larger than t (i.e., $f > t$). Since $f > t$, $2f > 2t$ and it follows from the equation that $f + 2f > 92$ or $3f > 92$; and, since f must be even, the least possible value of f is 32. (This solution might also be found through trial and error, using the equation $f + 2t = 92$.) The best answer, therefore, is A.

13. Which of the following is equivalent to the statement that 0.5 is between $\frac{2}{n}$ and $\frac{3}{n}$?

(A) $1 < n < 6$
(B) $2 < n < 3$
(C) $2 < n < 5$
(D) $4 < n < 6$
(E) $n > 10$

The statement "0.5 is between $\frac{2}{n}$ and $\frac{3}{n}$" can be written:
$$\frac{2}{n} < 0.5 < \frac{3}{n}.$$
Since n must be positive, multiplying through the inequality by $2n$ gives
$$(2n)\left(\frac{2}{n}\right) < (2n)(0.5) < (2n)\left(\frac{3}{n}\right), \text{ or } 4 < n < 6.$$
The best answer is D.

14. A corporation with 5,000,000 shares of publicly listed stock reported total earnings of $7.20 per share for the first 9 months of operation. During the final quarter the number of publicly listed shares was increased to 10,000,000 shares, and fourth quarter earnings were reported as $1.25 per share. What are the average annual earnings per share based on the number of shares at the end of the year?

   (A) $1.83
   (B) $2.43
   (C) $4.85
   (D) $8.45
   (E) $9.70

The total earnings for the year were
   $(5,000,000)(7.20) + (10,000,000)(1.25) = \$48,500,000.$

The per-share earnings based on the number of shares at the end of the year are
   $$48,500,000/10,000,000 = \$4.85.$$

Therefore, the best answer is C.

15. In 1980 the government spent $12 billion for direct cash payments to single parents with dependent children. If this was 2,000 percent of the amount spent in 1956, what was the amount spent in 1956? (1 billion = 1,000,000,000)

   (A) $6 million
   (B) $24 million
   (C) $60 million
   (D) $240 million
   (E) $600 million

If x is the amount spent in 1956, then
   $$(2,000\%)x = 12,000,000,000$$
   $$20x = 12,000,000,000$$
   $$x = \$600,000,000.$$
Therefore, E is the best answer.

16. The triangles in the figure above are equilateral and the ratio of the length of a side of the larger triangle to the length of a side of the smaller triangle is $\frac{2}{1}$. If the area of the larger triangular region is K, what is the area of the shaded region in terms of K?

   (A) $\frac{3}{4}K$ (B) $\frac{2}{3}K$ (C) $\frac{1}{2}K$

   (D) $\frac{1}{3}K$ (E) $\frac{1}{4}K$

The area of any triangle is 1/2 the product of the base and the corresponding altitude. Since each dimension of the smaller triangle is 1/2 the corresponding dimension of the larger triangle, the area of the smaller triangle is 1/4 the area of the larger triangle, or $K/4$. Thus, the area of the shaded region is

$$K - \frac{K}{4} = \frac{3K}{4}.$$

The best answer is A.

17. Four cups of milk are to be poured into a 2-cup bottle and a 4-cup bottle. If each bottle is to be filled to the same fraction of its capacity, how many cups of milk should be poured into the 4-cup bottle?

   (A) $\frac{2}{3}$

   (B) $\frac{7}{3}$

   (C) $\frac{5}{2}$

   (D) $\frac{8}{3}$

   (E) 3

Since each bottle is to be filled to the same fraction of its capacity, and since the 4-cup bottle has 2/3 of the total capacity of the two bottles, the 4-cup bottle will get 2/3 of the 4 cups of milk, or

$$\left(\frac{2}{3}\right)(4) = \frac{8}{3}.$$

Or, to use algebraic terms, if x is the number of cups of milk that should be poured into the 4-cup bottle, then $4 - x$ is the number of cups left to be poured into the 2-cup bottle. Because the fraction of milk in a bottle must be the same for both bottles, it follows that

$$\frac{x}{4} = \frac{4-x}{2}.$$

Thus,
$$2x = 16 - 4x$$
$$6x = 16$$
$$x = \frac{16}{6} = \frac{8}{3} \text{ cups.}$$

The best answer is D.

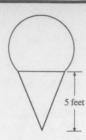

18. The outline of a sign for an ice-cream store is made by placing $\frac{3}{4}$ of the circumference of a circle with radius 2 feet on top of an isosceles triangle with height 5 feet, as shown above. What is the perimeter, in feet, of the sign?

(A) $3\pi + 3\sqrt{3}$
(B) $3\pi + 6\sqrt{3}$
(C) $3\pi + 2\sqrt{33}$
(D) $4\pi + 3\sqrt{3}$
(E) $4\pi + 6\sqrt{3}$

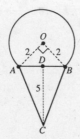

In the figure, O is the center of the partial circle. The measure of $\angle AOB$ is 90° because it cuts off an arc that is 1/4 of the circumference. So, in right $\triangle AOB$,

$$AB = \sqrt{2^2 + 2^2} = \sqrt{8} = 2\sqrt{2}.$$

Therefore, $AD = DB = \frac{1}{2}(AB) = \frac{1}{2}(2\sqrt{2}) = \sqrt{2}$. In right $\triangle CDB$, $BC = \sqrt{5^2 + (\sqrt{2})^2} = \sqrt{27} = 3\sqrt{3}$. Similarly, $AC = 3\sqrt{3}$. The length of the curved line is

$$3/4 \text{ (circumference)} = (3/4)(2\pi r)$$
$$= (3/4)(2\pi)(2)$$
$$= 3\pi.$$

Thus, the perimeter of the sign is

$3\pi + AC + BC = 3\pi + 3\sqrt{3} + 3\sqrt{3} = 3\pi + 6\sqrt{3}$,
and the best answer is B.

19. The sum of the first 100 positive integers is 5,050. What is the sum of the first 200 positive integers?

(A) 10,100
(B) 10,200
(C) 15,050
(D) 20,050
(E) 20,100

Each number in the sequence
$$101, 102, 103, \ldots, 200$$
is 100 larger than the corresponding number in the sequence
$$1, 2, 3, \ldots, 100.$$
Since the sum of the numbers in the latter sequence is 5,050, the sum of the former sequence must be
$$5,050 + 100(100) = 15,050.$$
The sum of the first 200 positive integers is
$$(1 + 2 + 3 + \ldots + 100) + (101 + 102 + 103 + \ldots + 200)$$
$$= 5,050 + 15,050$$
$$= 20,100.$$
Thus, the best answer is E.

20. A merchant purchased a jacket for $60 and then determined a selling price that equalled the purchase price of the jacket plus a markup that was 25 percent of the selling price. During a sale, the merchant discounted the selling price by 20 percent and sold the jacket. What was the merchant's gross profit on this sale?

(A) $0 (B) $3 (C) $4
(D) $12 (E) $15

If the selling price is x dollars, then
$$60 + 0.25x = x$$
$$60 = 0.75x$$
$$80 = x.$$
The merchant sold the jacket for 80 percent of the selling price (due to the 20 percent discount), or
$$(0.8)(\$80) = \$64.$$
Therefore, the merchant's gross profit on the sale was $64 − $60 = $4. The best answer is C.

PROBLEM SOLVING SAMPLE TEST SECTION 8

30 Minutes
20 Questions

Directions: In this section solve each problem, using any available space on the page for scratchwork. Then indicate the best of the answer choices given.

Numbers: All numbers used are real numbers.

Figures: Figures that accompany problems in this section are intended to provide information useful in solving the problems. They are drawn as accurately as possible EXCEPT when it is stated in a specific problem that its figure is not drawn to scale. All figures lie in a plane unless otherwise indicated.

1. A certain club has 237 local branches, one national office, and one social service office. If each local branch has 2 officers, and each of the two other offices has 4 officers, how many officers does the club have altogether?

   (A) 482
   (B) 476
   (C) 474
   (D) 239
   (E) 235

2. An employee is paid a salary of $300 per month and earns a 6 percent commission on all her sales. What must her annual sales be in order for her to have a gross annual salary of exactly $21,600 ?

   (A) $22,896   (B) $26,712   (C) $300,000

   (D) $330,000   (E) $360,000

3. Of the 1,000 students who entered College X as freshmen in September 1979, 112 did not graduate in May 1983. If 962 students graduated in May 1983, how many of the graduates did not enter College X as freshmen in September 1979 ?

   (A) 38
   (B) 74
   (C) 112
   (D) 150
   (E) 188

GO ON TO THE NEXT PAGE.

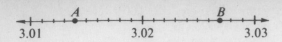

3.01   3.02   3.03

4. On the number line above, what is the length of segment AB?

(A) 13   (B) 1.4   (C) 1.3

(D) 0.13   (E) 0.013

5. Which of the following has a value greater than 1 ?

(A) $\dfrac{2}{\sqrt{3}}$ (B) $\dfrac{\sqrt{2}}{2}$ (C) $\left(\dfrac{3}{4}\right)^2$

(D) $\left(\dfrac{7}{8}\right)^3$ (E) $2\left(\dfrac{3}{7}\right)$

6. If $\dfrac{m^2 + m - 3}{3} = 1$, then m could equal

(A) -1
(B) 0
(C) 1
(D) 2
(E) 3

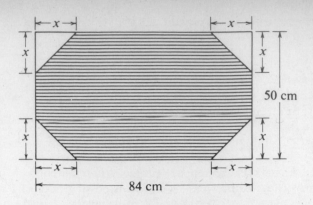

50 cm

84 cm

7. The figure above represents a rectangular desk blotter in a holder with dimensions shown. If $x = 8$ centimeters, what is the area, in square centimeters, of the shaded portion of the blotter?

(A) 4,200
(B) 4,184
(C) 4,124
(D) 4,072
(E) 3,944

GO ON TO THE NEXT PAGE.

8. The number 25 is 2.5 percent of which of the following?

   (A)   10
   (B)   62.5
   (C)   100
   (D)   625
   (E) 1,000

9. Cottages at a resort are rented for half the summer price in each of the 3 spring months and one-third the summer price in each of the 6 fall and winter months. If each cottage brings in a total of $3,861 when rented for each of the 12 months of the year, what is the monthly rent for each of the 3 summer months?

   (A) $297
   (B) $594
   (C) $702
   (D) $858
   (E) $1,782

10. In 1980 John's salary was $15,000 a year and Don's salary was $20,000 a year. If every year thereafter, John receives a raise of $2,450 and Don receives a raise of $2,000, the first year in which John's salary will be more than Don's salary is

   (A) 1987
   (B) 1988
   (C) 1991
   (D) 1992
   (E) 2000

11. Which of the following is equal to $\frac{351}{558}$?

   (A) $\frac{7}{11}$ (B) $\frac{39}{62}$ (C) $\frac{19}{31}$

   (D) $\frac{117}{196}$ (E) $\frac{107}{186}$

GO ON TO THE NEXT PAGE.

12. On a certain airline, the price of a ticket is directly proportional to the number of miles to be traveled. If the ticket for a 900-mile trip on this airline costs \$120, which of the following gives the number of dollars charged for a k-mile trip on this airline?

(A) $\frac{2k}{15}$ (B) $\frac{2}{15k}$ (C) $\frac{15}{2k}$

(D) $\frac{15k}{2}$ (E) $\frac{40k}{3}$

13. If $\frac{n}{41}$ is 1 more than $\frac{m}{41}$, then $n =$

(A) $m - 41$ (B) $m + 1$ (C) $m + 41$

(D) $m + 42$ (E) $41m$

14. A discount of 20 percent on an order of goods followed by a discount of 10 percent amounts to

(A) less than one 15 percent discount
(B) the same as one 15 percent discount
(C) the same as one 30 percent discount
(D) less than a discount of 10 percent followed by a discount of 20 percent
(E) the same as a discount of 10 percent followed by a discount of 20 percent

15. If k is an even integer and p and r are odd integers, which of the following CANNOT be an integer?

(A) $\frac{r}{k}$ (B) $\frac{k}{p}$ (C) $\frac{p}{r}$ (D) $\frac{kp}{r}$ (E) $\frac{kr}{p}$

16. Today Al is 3 times as old as Pat. In 13 years, Al will be one year less than twice as old as Pat will be then. How many years old is Al today?

(A) 12
(B) 33
(C) 36
(D) 42
(E) 49

17. When the integer n is divided by 17, the quotient is x and the remainder is 5. When n is divided by 23, the quotient is y and the remainder is 14. Which of the following is true?

(A) $23x + 17y = 19$
(B) $17x - 23y = 9$
(C) $17x + 23y = 19$
(D) $14x + 5y = 6$
(E) $5x - 14y = -6$

GO ON TO THE NEXT PAGE.

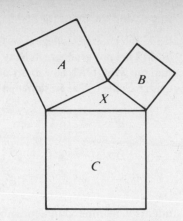

Note: Figure not drawn to scale.

18. In the figure above, three squares and a triangle have areas of A, B, C, and X as shown. If $A = 144$, $B = 81$, and $C = 225$, then $X =$

(A) 150   (B) 144   (C) 80

(D) 54   (E) 36

19. Three types of pencils, J, K, and L, cost $0.05, $0.10, and $0.25 each, respectively. If a box of 32 of these pencils costs a total of $3.40 and if there are twice as many K pencils as L pencils in the box, how many J pencils are in the box?

(A) 6
(B) 12
(C) 14
(D) 18
(E) 20

20. Forty percent of the rats included in an experiment were male rats. If some of the rats died during the experiment and 30 percent of the rats that died were male rats, what was the ratio of the death rate among the male rats to the death rate among the female rats?

(A) $\frac{9}{14}$ (B) $\frac{3}{4}$ (C) $\frac{9}{11}$ (D) $\frac{6}{7}$ (E) $\frac{7}{8}$

S T O P

IF YOU FINISH BEFORE TIME IS CALLED, YOU MAY CHECK YOUR WORK ON THIS SECTION ONLY.
DO NOT TURN TO ANY OTHER SECTION IN THE TEST.

Answer Key for Sample Test Section 8

PROBLEM SOLVING

1.	A	11.	B
2.	C	12.	A
3.	B	13.	C
4.	E	14.	E
5.	A	15.	A
6.	D	16.	C
7.	D	17.	B
8.	E	18.	D
9.	B	19.	C
10.	D	20.	A

Explanatory Material:
Problem Solving Sample Test Section 8

1. A certain club has 237 local branches, one national office, and one social service office. If each local branch has 2 officers, and each of the two other offices has 4 officers, how many officers does the club have altogether?

   (A) 482
   (B) 476
   (C) 474
   (D) 239
   (E) 235

There are 237(2) officers at local branches and 2(4) officers at the other offices, or 474 + 8 = 482 officers altogether. The best answer is A.

2. An employee is paid a salary of $300 per month and earns a 6 percent commission on all her sales. What must her annual sales be in order for her to have a gross annual salary of exactly $21,600?

   (A) $22,896 (B) $26,712 (C) $300,000
       (D) $330,000 (E) $360,000

The gross annual salary of $21,600 includes 300(12), or $3,600, plus 6 percent commission on all sales. Therefore, 21,600 = 3,600 + 0.06s, where s is the amount of sales; 0.06s = 18,000 and s = $300,000. The best answer is C.

3. Of the 1,000 students who entered College X as freshmen in September 1979, 112 did not graduate in May 1983. If 962 students graduate in May 1983, how many of the graduates did not enter College X as freshmen in September 1979?

   (A) 38
   (B) 74
   (C) 112
   (D) 150
   (E) 188

If 112 of the 1,000 students who entered in September 1979 did not graduate in May 1983, then 1,000 − 112 or 888 must have graduated that May. Since a total of 962 students graduated that May, 962 − 888 or 74 did not enter as freshmen in September 1979. The best answer is B.

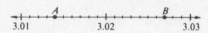

4. On the number line above, what is the length of segment AB?

   (A) 13   (B) 1.4   (C) 1.3
       (D) 0.13   (E) 0.013

Each small interval between consecutive gradations on the segment has length $\frac{0.01}{10} = 0.001$. Therefore, since segment AB consists of 13 small intervals, it has length 13(0.001) = 0.013. The best answer is E.

5. Which of the following has a value greater than 1?

   (A) $\frac{2}{\sqrt{3}}$ (B) $\frac{\sqrt{2}}{2}$ (C) $\left(\frac{3}{4}\right)^2$

   (D) $\left(\frac{7}{8}\right)^3$ (E) $2\left(\frac{3}{7}\right)$

For a ratio to have a value greater than 1, the numerator of the ratio must be greater than the denominator. Since $2 > \sqrt{3}$, choice A gives a number greater than 1 and is, thus, the best answer.

6. If $\dfrac{m^2 + m - 3}{3} = 1$, then m could equal

(A) -1
(B) 0
(C) 1
(D) 2
(E) 3

To solve this equation, it is convenient to multiply both sides of the equation by 3. Then $m^2 + m - 3 = 3$, $m^2 + m - 6 = 0$, and $(m + 3)(m - 2) = 0$. Since one of the factors must be equal to 0, $m = -3$ or $m = 2$. Therefore, the best answer is D.

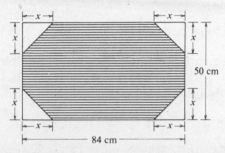

7. The figure above represents a rectangular desk blotter in a holder with dimensions shown. If $x = 8$ centimeters, what is the area, in square centimeters, of the shaded portion of the blotter?

(A) 4,200
(B) 4,184
(C) 4,124
(D) 4,072
(E) 3,944

The area of the entire blotter is $50(84) = 4,200$ square centimeters. The area of each corner is $\dfrac{x^2}{2} = \dfrac{8^2}{2} = 32$. Therefore, the area of the shaded portion is 4,200 minus the areas of the four corners or
$4,200 - 4(32) = 4,200 - 128 = 4,072$. The best answer is D.

8. The number 25 is 2.5 percent of which of the following?

(A) 10
(B) 62.5
(C) 100
(D) 625
(E) 1,000

If 25 is 2.5 percent of a number, then 250 is 25 percent of the number, and $4(250) = 1,000$ is $4(25\%)$ or 100 percent of the number. Another approach is to solve the equation $25 = 0.025n$, where n represents the number. The best answer is E.

9. Cottages at a resort are rented for half the summer price in each of the 3 spring months and one-third the summer price in each of the 6 fall and winter months. If each cottage brings in a total of $3,861 when rented for each of the 12 months of the year, what is the monthly rent for each of the 3 summer months?

(A) $297
(B) $594
(C) $702
(D) $858
(E) $1,782

Let s be the monthly rent for each of the 3 summer months. Then $\dfrac{s}{2}$ is the rent for each of the 3 spring months, and $\dfrac{s}{3}$ is the rent for each of the 6 fall and winter months. Since the total rent for all 12 months is $3,861, the total can be expressed as $3s + 3(\dfrac{s}{2}) + 6(\dfrac{s}{3}) = 3,861$, or
$3s + 1.5s + 2s = 3,861; 6.5s = 3,861$, and $s = \$594$. The best answer is B.

10. In 1980 John's salary was $15,000 a year and Don's salary was $20,000 a year. If every year thereafter, John receives a raise of $2,450 and Don receives a raise of $2,000, the first year in which John's salary will be more than Don's salary is

(A) 1987
(B) 1988
(C) 1991
(D) 1992
(E) 2000

Let n represent the number of years after 1980 until John's salary first exceeds Don's salary. Then
$15,000 + 2,450n > 20,000 + 2,000n$, and $n > 11$. Thus, John's salary will first exceed Don's in the twelfth year after 1980, or $1980 + 12 = 1992$. The best answer is D.

11. Which of the following is equal to $\dfrac{351}{558}$?

(A) $\dfrac{7}{11}$ (B) $\dfrac{39}{62}$ (C) $\dfrac{19}{31}$

(D) $\dfrac{117}{196}$ (E) $\dfrac{107}{186}$

One method of reducing a fraction such as $\dfrac{351}{558}$, where the greatest common factor of the terms may not be apparent, is to test whether any of the first few odd prime numbers, 3, 5, 7, etc., are common factors of the two terms. Since a number is divisible by 3 if the sum of its digits is divisible by 3, 3 is a common factor. Thus, $\dfrac{351}{558} = \dfrac{3 \times 117}{3 \times 186}$. The fraction $\dfrac{117}{186}$ is not one of the options; however, 3 is a common factor of 117 and 186, and so $\dfrac{117}{186} = \dfrac{3 \times 39}{3 \times 62}$. The best answer is B.

12. On a certain airline, the price of a ticket is directly proportional to the number of miles to be traveled. If the ticket for a 900-mile trip on this airline costs $120, which of the following gives the number of dollars charged for a k-mile trip on this airline?

(A) $\dfrac{2k}{15}$ (B) $\dfrac{2}{15k}$ (C) $\dfrac{15}{2k}$

(D) $\dfrac{15k}{2}$ (E) $\dfrac{40k}{3}$

Since the price is directly proportional to the distance and the price of a 900-mile trip is $120, the price per mile is $\dfrac{120}{900}$ or $\dfrac{2}{15}$ dollars, and the price of a k-mile trip is $\dfrac{2k}{15}$ dollars. The best answer is A.

13. If $\dfrac{n}{41}$ is 1 more than $\dfrac{m}{41}$, then $n =$

(A) $m - 41$ (B) $m + 1$ (C) $m + 41$
(D) $m + 42$ (E) $41m$

The statement in the problem is equivalent to the equation $\dfrac{n}{41} = \dfrac{m}{41} + 1$. To solve for n, it is convenient to multiply both sides of the equation by 41, which yields $n = m + 41$. The best answer is C.

14. A discount of 20 percent on an order of goods followed by a discount of 10 percent amounts to

(A) less than one 15 percent discount
(B) the same as one 15 percent discount
(C) the same as one 30 percent discount
(D) less than a discount of 10 percent followed by a discount of 20 percent
(E) the same as a discount of 10 percent followed by a discount of 20 percent

To see the precise effect of successive discounts, let p be the original price of the goods, and then express the price after each successive discount in terms of p. After a 20 percent discount on p, the new price will be $0.8p$. If a second discount, of 10 percent, is taken on $0.8p$, the new price will be $0.9(0.8p) = 0.72p$, which means that the successive discounts are equivalent to a single discount of $(100 - 72)$ or 28 percent. Since $0.9(0.8p) = 0.8(0.9p)$, the total discount is the same regardless of the order in which the two discounts are taken. The best answer is E.

15. If k is an even integer and p and r are odd integers, which of the following CANNOT be an integer?

(A) $\dfrac{r}{k}$ (B) $\dfrac{k}{p}$ (C) $\dfrac{p}{r}$ (D) $\dfrac{kp}{r}$ (E) $\dfrac{kr}{p}$

For a rational number to be equal to an integer, each factor of the denominator must be a factor of the numerator. Since k is an even integer, 2 is a factor of k; 2 is not a factor of any odd number. Thus, choice A cannot be an integer since 2 is a factor of k but not of r. Since the ratio given in A cannot be an integer, it is not necessary to examine the other options. Note, however, that each of the other ratios could be an integer: $\dfrac{k}{p}$ could be an integer if k were an even multiple of p; $\dfrac{p}{r}$ could be an integer if the odd number p were a multiple of r, and similarly, $k(\dfrac{p}{r})$ would be an even multiple of $\dfrac{p}{r}$. By the same reasoning, if r were a multiple of p, $\dfrac{r}{p}$ and $k(\dfrac{r}{p})$ would be integers. Thus, the best answer is A.

16. Today Al is 3 times as old as Pat. In 13 years, Al will be one year less than twice as old as Pat will be then. How many years old is Al today?

(A) 12
(B) 33
(C) 36
(D) 42
(E) 49

If Pat is x years old today, then Al is $3x$ years old. In 13 years, Pat will be $x + 13$ and Al will be $3x + 13$ years old. If these expressions and the information in the problem are used, it follows that $3x + 13 = 2(x + 13) - 1$, and Pat's age is 12. Therefore, Al's age is $3x = 3(12) = 36$. The best answer is C.

17. When the integer n is divided by 17, the quotient is x and the remainder is 5. When n is divided by 23, the quotient is y and the remainder is 14. Which of the following is true?

(A) $23x + 17y = 19$
(B) $17x - 23y = 9$
(C) $17x + 23y = 19$
(D) $14x + 5y = 6$
(E) $5x - 14y = -6$

According to the first sentence, $n = 17x + 5$; similarly, from the second sentence, $n = 23y + 14$. If both expressions are equal to n, then the two expressions are equal to each other, which is to say $17x + 5 = 23y + 14$, or $17x - 23y = 9$. The best answer is B.

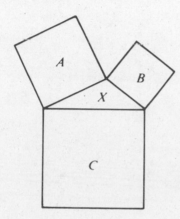

Note: Figure not drawn to scale.

18. In the figure above, three squares and a triangle have areas of A, B, C, and X as shown. If $A = 144$, $B = 81$, and $C = 225$, then $X =$

(A) 150 (B) 144 (C) 80
   (D) 54 (E) 36

Since the sum of the squares of two sides of the triangle is equal to the square of the third side, the triangle must be a right triangle. The sides of the triangle are 12, 9, and 15 (the square roots of the areas of the three squares). The area of the triangle, X, is half the product of the lengths of the two legs, or $(9 \times 12) \div 2 = 54$. The best answer is D.

19. Three types of pencils, J, K, and L, cost $0.05, $0.10, and $0.25 each, respectively. If a box of 32 of these pencils costs a total of $3.40 and if there are twice as many K pencils as L pencils in the box, how many J pencils are in the box?

(A) 6
(B) 12
(C) 14
(D) 18
(E) 20

Let n be the number of type L pencils in the box. Then the number of type K pencils can be denoted by $2n$ and the number of type J pencils can be denoted by $32 - (2n + n)$ or $32 - 3n$. Applying the unit prices, in cents, to these respective quantities yields the equation $25n + 10(2n) + 5(32 - 3n) = 340$; $30n + 160 = 340$, and $n = 6$. Since the number of type J pencils is $32 - 3n$ and $n = 6$, the number is $32 - 3(6) = 14$. The best answer is C.

20. Forty percent of the rats included in an experiment were male rats. If some of the rats died during the experiment and 30 percent of the rats that died were male rats, what was the ratio of the death rate among the male rats to the death rate among the female rats?

(A) $\frac{9}{14}$ (B) $\frac{3}{4}$ (C) $\frac{9}{11}$ (D) $\frac{6}{7}$ (E) $\frac{7}{8}$

If t represents the total number of rats, then $0.4t$ is the number of male rats and $0.6t$ is the number of female rats. If d represents the total number of rats that died, then $0.3d$ is the number of male rats that died and $0.7d$ is the number of female rats that died. The death rate in each of the groups is the ratio of the number in the group that died to the total number in the group. Thus, the death rate among the male rats was $\frac{0.3d}{0.4t}$ and among the female rats was $\frac{0.7d}{0.6t}$, and the ratio of the two death rates was $\dfrac{\frac{0.3d}{0.4t}}{\frac{0.7d}{0.6t}} = \frac{9}{14}$. The best answer is A.

4 Data Sufficiency

In this section of the GMAT, you are to classify each problem according to the five fixed answer choices, rather than find a solution to the problem. Each problem consists of a question and two statements. You are to decide whether the information in each statement alone is sufficient to answer the question or, if neither is, whether the information in the two statements together is sufficient.

The following pages include test-taking strategies, sample test sections (with answer keys), and detailed explanations of every problem from the sample test sections. These explanations present possible problem-solving strategies for the examples.

Test-Taking Strategies for Data Sufficiency

1. Do not waste valuable time solving a problem; you are only to determine whether sufficient information is given to solve the problem. After you have considered statement (1), make a check mark next to (1) if you can determine the answer and a cross mark if you cannot. Be sure to disregard all the information learned from statement (1) while considering statement (2). This is very difficult to do and often results in erroneously choosing answer C when the answer should be B or choosing B when the answer should be C. Suppose statement (2) alone is sufficient. Then a check mark next to (1) indicates that D is the correct answer; a cross mark next to (1) indicates that B is correct. Suppose statement (2) alone is not sufficient. A check mark next to (1) indicates that A is the correct answer; a cross mark next to (1) indicates that you must now consider whether the two statements taken together give sufficient information; if they do, the answer is C; if not, the answer is E.

2. If you determine that the information in statement (1) is sufficient to answer the question, the answer is necessarily either A or D. If you are not sure about statement (1) but you know that statement (2) alone is sufficient, the answer is necessarily either B or D. If neither statement taken alone is sufficient, the answer is either C or E. Thus, if you have doubts about certain portions of the information given but are relatively sure about other portions, you can logically eliminate two or three options and more than double your chances of guessing correctly.

3. Remember that when you are determining whether there is sufficient information to answer a question of the form, "What is the value of y?" the information given must be sufficient to find one and only one value for y. Being able to determine minimum or maximum values or an answer of the form $y = x + 2$ is not sufficient, because such answers constitute a range of values rather than "the value of y."

4. When geometric figures are involved, be very careful not to make unwarranted assumptions based on the figures. A triangle may appear to be isosceles, but can you detect the difference in the lengths of segments 1.8 inches long and 1.85 inches long? Furthermore, the figures are not necessarily drawn to scale; they are generalized figures showing little more than intersecting line segments and the betweenness of points, angles, and regions.

When you take the sample test sections, use the answer spaces on page 125 to mark your answers.

Answer Spaces for Data Sufficiency Sample Test Sections

Sample Test Section 1

1 Ⓐ Ⓑ Ⓒ Ⓓ Ⓔ   8 Ⓐ Ⓑ Ⓒ Ⓓ Ⓔ   15 Ⓐ Ⓑ Ⓒ Ⓓ Ⓔ   22 Ⓐ Ⓑ Ⓒ Ⓓ Ⓔ
2 Ⓐ Ⓑ Ⓒ Ⓓ Ⓔ   9 Ⓐ Ⓑ Ⓒ Ⓓ Ⓔ   16 Ⓐ Ⓑ Ⓒ Ⓓ Ⓔ   23 Ⓐ Ⓑ Ⓒ Ⓓ Ⓔ
3 Ⓐ Ⓑ Ⓒ Ⓓ Ⓔ   10 Ⓐ Ⓑ Ⓒ Ⓓ Ⓔ   17 Ⓐ Ⓑ Ⓒ Ⓓ Ⓔ   24 Ⓐ Ⓑ Ⓒ Ⓓ Ⓔ
4 Ⓐ Ⓑ Ⓒ Ⓓ Ⓔ   11 Ⓐ Ⓑ Ⓒ Ⓓ Ⓔ   18 Ⓐ Ⓑ Ⓒ Ⓓ Ⓔ   25 Ⓐ Ⓑ Ⓒ Ⓓ Ⓔ
5 Ⓐ Ⓑ Ⓒ Ⓓ Ⓔ   12 Ⓐ Ⓑ Ⓒ Ⓓ Ⓔ   19 Ⓐ Ⓑ Ⓒ Ⓓ Ⓔ
6 Ⓐ Ⓑ Ⓒ Ⓓ Ⓔ   13 Ⓐ Ⓑ Ⓒ Ⓓ Ⓔ   20 Ⓐ Ⓑ Ⓒ Ⓓ Ⓔ
7 Ⓐ Ⓑ Ⓒ Ⓓ Ⓔ   14 Ⓐ Ⓑ Ⓒ Ⓓ Ⓔ   21 Ⓐ Ⓑ Ⓒ Ⓓ Ⓔ

Sample Test Section 2

1 Ⓐ Ⓑ Ⓒ Ⓓ Ⓔ   8 Ⓐ Ⓑ Ⓒ Ⓓ Ⓔ   15 Ⓐ Ⓑ Ⓒ Ⓓ Ⓔ   22 Ⓐ Ⓑ Ⓒ Ⓓ Ⓔ
2 Ⓐ Ⓑ Ⓒ Ⓓ Ⓔ   9 Ⓐ Ⓑ Ⓒ Ⓓ Ⓔ   16 Ⓐ Ⓑ Ⓒ Ⓓ Ⓔ   23 Ⓐ Ⓑ Ⓒ Ⓓ Ⓔ
3 Ⓐ Ⓑ Ⓒ Ⓓ Ⓔ   10 Ⓐ Ⓑ Ⓒ Ⓓ Ⓔ   17 Ⓐ Ⓑ Ⓒ Ⓓ Ⓔ   24 Ⓐ Ⓑ Ⓒ Ⓓ Ⓔ
4 Ⓐ Ⓑ Ⓒ Ⓓ Ⓔ   11 Ⓐ Ⓑ Ⓒ Ⓓ Ⓔ   18 Ⓐ Ⓑ Ⓒ Ⓓ Ⓔ   25 Ⓐ Ⓑ Ⓒ Ⓓ Ⓔ
5 Ⓐ Ⓑ Ⓒ Ⓓ Ⓔ   12 Ⓐ Ⓑ Ⓒ Ⓓ Ⓔ   19 Ⓐ Ⓑ Ⓒ Ⓓ Ⓔ
6 Ⓐ Ⓑ Ⓒ Ⓓ Ⓔ   13 Ⓐ Ⓑ Ⓒ Ⓓ Ⓔ   20 Ⓐ Ⓑ Ⓒ Ⓓ Ⓔ
7 Ⓐ Ⓑ Ⓒ Ⓓ Ⓔ   14 Ⓐ Ⓑ Ⓒ Ⓓ Ⓔ   21 Ⓐ Ⓑ Ⓒ Ⓓ Ⓔ

Sample Test Section 3

1 Ⓐ Ⓑ Ⓒ Ⓓ Ⓔ   8 Ⓐ Ⓑ Ⓒ Ⓓ Ⓔ   15 Ⓐ Ⓑ Ⓒ Ⓓ Ⓔ   22 Ⓐ Ⓑ Ⓒ Ⓓ Ⓔ
2 Ⓐ Ⓑ Ⓒ Ⓓ Ⓔ   9 Ⓐ Ⓑ Ⓒ Ⓓ Ⓔ   16 Ⓐ Ⓑ Ⓒ Ⓓ Ⓔ   23 Ⓐ Ⓑ Ⓒ Ⓓ Ⓔ
3 Ⓐ Ⓑ Ⓒ Ⓓ Ⓔ   10 Ⓐ Ⓑ Ⓒ Ⓓ Ⓔ   17 Ⓐ Ⓑ Ⓒ Ⓓ Ⓔ   24 Ⓐ Ⓑ Ⓒ Ⓓ Ⓔ
4 Ⓐ Ⓑ Ⓒ Ⓓ Ⓔ   11 Ⓐ Ⓑ Ⓒ Ⓓ Ⓔ   18 Ⓐ Ⓑ Ⓒ Ⓓ Ⓔ   25 Ⓐ Ⓑ Ⓒ Ⓓ Ⓔ
5 Ⓐ Ⓑ Ⓒ Ⓓ Ⓔ   12 Ⓐ Ⓑ Ⓒ Ⓓ Ⓔ   19 Ⓐ Ⓑ Ⓒ Ⓓ Ⓔ
6 Ⓐ Ⓑ Ⓒ Ⓓ Ⓔ   13 Ⓐ Ⓑ Ⓒ Ⓓ Ⓔ   20 Ⓐ Ⓑ Ⓒ Ⓓ Ⓔ
7 Ⓐ Ⓑ Ⓒ Ⓓ Ⓔ   14 Ⓐ Ⓑ Ⓒ Ⓓ Ⓔ   21 Ⓐ Ⓑ Ⓒ Ⓓ Ⓔ

Sample Test Section 4

1 Ⓐ Ⓑ Ⓒ Ⓓ Ⓔ   8 Ⓐ Ⓑ Ⓒ Ⓓ Ⓔ   15 Ⓐ Ⓑ Ⓒ Ⓓ Ⓔ   22 Ⓐ Ⓑ Ⓒ Ⓓ Ⓔ
2 Ⓐ Ⓑ Ⓒ Ⓓ Ⓔ   9 Ⓐ Ⓑ Ⓒ Ⓓ Ⓔ   16 Ⓐ Ⓑ Ⓒ Ⓓ Ⓔ   23 Ⓐ Ⓑ Ⓒ Ⓓ Ⓔ
3 Ⓐ Ⓑ Ⓒ Ⓓ Ⓔ   10 Ⓐ Ⓑ Ⓒ Ⓓ Ⓔ   17 Ⓐ Ⓑ Ⓒ Ⓓ Ⓔ   24 Ⓐ Ⓑ Ⓒ Ⓓ Ⓔ
4 Ⓐ Ⓑ Ⓒ Ⓓ Ⓔ   11 Ⓐ Ⓑ Ⓒ Ⓓ Ⓔ   18 Ⓐ Ⓑ Ⓒ Ⓓ Ⓔ   25 Ⓐ Ⓑ Ⓒ Ⓓ Ⓔ
5 Ⓐ Ⓑ Ⓒ Ⓓ Ⓔ   12 Ⓐ Ⓑ Ⓒ Ⓓ Ⓔ   19 Ⓐ Ⓑ Ⓒ Ⓓ Ⓔ
6 Ⓐ Ⓑ Ⓒ Ⓓ Ⓔ   13 Ⓐ Ⓑ Ⓒ Ⓓ Ⓔ   20 Ⓐ Ⓑ Ⓒ Ⓓ Ⓔ
7 Ⓐ Ⓑ Ⓒ Ⓓ Ⓔ   14 Ⓐ Ⓑ Ⓒ Ⓓ Ⓔ   21 Ⓐ Ⓑ Ⓒ Ⓓ Ⓔ

DATA SUFFICIENCY SAMPLE TEST SECTION 1

30 Minutes
25 Questions

Directions: Each of the data sufficiency problems below consists of a question and two statements, labeled (1) and (2), in which certain data are given. You have to decide whether the data given in the statements are <u>sufficient</u> for answering the question. Using the data given in the statements <u>plus</u> your knowledge of mathematics and everyday facts (such as the number of days in July or the meaning of <u>counterclockwise</u>), you are to fill in oval

- A if statement (1) ALONE is sufficient, but statement (2) alone is not sufficient to answer the question asked;
- B if statement (2) ALONE is sufficient, but statement (1) alone is not sufficient to answer the question asked;
- C if BOTH statements (1) and (2) TOGETHER are sufficient to answer the question asked, but NEITHER statement ALONE is sufficient;
- D if EACH statement ALONE is sufficient to answer the question asked;
- E if statements (1) and (2) TOGETHER are NOT sufficient to answer the question asked, and additional data specific to the problem are needed.

<u>Numbers:</u> All numbers used are real numbers.

<u>Figures:</u> A figure in a data sufficiency problem will conform to the information given in the question, but will not necessarily conform to the additional information given in statements (1) and (2).

You may assume that lines shown as straight are straight and that angle measures are greater than zero.

You may assume that the positions of points, angles, regions, etc., exist in the order shown.

All figures lie in a plane unless otherwise indicated.

<u>Example:</u>

In $\triangle PQR$, what is the value of x?

(1) $PQ = PR$

(2) $y = 40$

Explanation: According to statement (1), $PQ = PR$; therefore, $\triangle PQR$ is isosceles and $y = z$. Since $x + y + z = 180$, $x + 2y = 180$. Since statement (1) does not give a value for y, you cannot answer the question using statement (1) by itself. According to statement (2), $y = 40$; therefore, $x + z = 140$. Since statement (2) does not give a value for z, you cannot answer the question using statement (2) by itself. Using both statements together, you can find y and z; therefore, you can find x, and the answer to the problem is C.

1. If today the price of an item is $3,600, what was the price of the item exactly 2 years ago?

   (1) The price of the item increased by 10 percent per year during this 2-year period.

   (2) Today the price of the item is 1.21 times its price exactly 2 years ago.

2. By what percent has the price of an overcoat been reduced?

   (1) The original price was $380.

   (2) The original price was $50 more than the reduced price.

GO ON TO THE NEXT PAGE.

A   Statement (1) ALONE is sufficient, but statement (2) alone is not sufficient.
B   Statement (2) ALONE is sufficient, but statement (1) alone is not sufficient.
C   BOTH statements TOGETHER are sufficient, but NEITHER statement ALONE is sufficient.
D   EACH statement ALONE is sufficient.
E   Statements (1) and (2) TOGETHER are NOT sufficient.

3. If the Longfellow Playground is rectangular, what is its width?

   (1) The ratio of its length to its width is 7 to 2.

   (2) The perimeter of the playground is 396 meters.

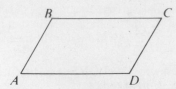

6. In parallelogram $ABCD$ above, what is the measure of $\angle ADC$?

   (1) The measure of $\angle ABC$ is greater than 90°.

   (2) The measure of $\angle BCD$ is 70°.

4. What is the value of $x - 1$?

   (1) $x + 1 = 3$
   (2) $x - 1 < 3$

7. Is x^2 equal to xy?

   (1) $x^2 - y^2 = (x + 5)(y - 5)$
   (2) $x = y$

5. Is William taller than Jane?

   (1) William is taller than Anna.
   (2) Anna is not as tall as Jane.

8. Was 70 the average (arithmetic mean) grade on a class test?

   (1) On the test, half of the class had grades below 70 and half of the class had grades above 70.

   (2) The lowest grade on the test was 45 and the highest grade on the test was 95.

GO ON TO THE NEXT PAGE.

A   Statement (1) ALONE is sufficient, but statement (2) alone is not sufficient.
B   Statement (2) ALONE is sufficient, but statement (1) alone is not sufficient.
C   BOTH statements TOGETHER are sufficient, but NEITHER statement ALONE is sufficient.
D   EACH statement ALONE is sufficient.
E   Statements (1) and (2) TOGETHER are NOT sufficient.

9. What was John's average driving speed in miles per hour during a 15-minute interval?

(1) He drove 10 miles during this interval.

(2) His maximum speed was 50 miles per hour and his minimum speed was 35 miles per hour during this interval.

10. Is $\triangle MNP$ isosceles?

(1) Exactly two of the angles, $\angle M$ and $\angle N$, have the same measure.

(2) $\angle N$ and $\angle P$ do not have the same measure.

11. Is n an integer greater than 4?

(1) $3n$ is a positive integer.

(2) $\frac{n}{3}$ is a positive integer.

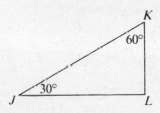

12. In $\triangle JKL$ shown above, what is the length of segment JL?

(1) $JK = 10$
(2) $KL = 5$

13. A coal company can choose to transport coal to one of its customers by railroad or by truck. If the railroad charges by the mile and the trucking company charges by the ton, which means of transporting the coal would cost <u>less</u> than the other?

(1) The railroad charges $5,000 plus $0.01 per mile per railroad car used, and the trucking company charges $3,000 plus $85 per ton.

(2) The customer to whom the coal is to be sent is 195 miles away from the coal company.

14. Is $x - y > r - s$?

(1) $x > r$ and $y < s$.
(2) $y = 2$, $s = 3$, $r = 5$, and $x = 6$.

15. On a certain day it took Bill three times as long to drive from home to work as it took Sue to drive from home to work. How many kilometers did Bill drive from home to work?

(1) Sue drove 10 kilometers from home to work, and the ratio of

$$\frac{\text{distance driven from home to work}}{\text{time to drive from home to work}}$$

was the same for Bill and Sue that day.

(2) The ratio of

$$\frac{\text{distance driven from home to work}}{\text{time to drive from home to work}}$$

for Sue that day was 64 kilometers per hour.

GO ON TO THE NEXT PAGE.

A   Statement (1) ALONE is sufficient, but statement (2) alone is not sufficient.
B   Statement (2) ALONE is sufficient, but statement (1) alone is not sufficient.
C   BOTH statements TOGETHER are sufficient, but NEITHER statement ALONE is sufficient.
D   EACH statement ALONE is sufficient.
E   Statements (1) and (2) TOGETHER are NOT sufficient.

16. The figure above represents the floor of a square foyer with a circular rug partially covering the floor and extending to the outer edges of the floor as shown. What is the area of the foyer that is not covered by the rug?

(1) The area of the foyer is 9 square meters.

(2) The area of the rug is 2.25π square meters.

17. At a certain university, if 50 percent of the people who inquire about admission policies actually submit applications for admission, what percent of those who submit applications for admission enroll in classes at the university?

(1) Fifteen percent of those who submit applications for admission are accepted at the university.

(2) Eighty percent of those who are accepted send a deposit to the university.

18. If x and y are nonzero integers, is $\frac{x}{y}$ an integer?

(1) x is the product of 2 and some other integer.

(2) There is only one pair of positive integers whose product equals y.

19. If x is an integer, what is the value of x?

(1) $\frac{1}{5} < \frac{1}{x+1} < \frac{1}{2}$

(2) $(x-3)(x-4) = 0$

20. Is quadrilateral Q a square?

(1) The sides of Q have the same length.

(2) The diagonals of Q have the same length.

21. If K is a positive integer less than 10 and $N = 4,321 + K$, what is the value of K?

(1) N is divisible by 3.

(2) N is divisible by 7.

GO ON TO THE NEXT PAGE.

A Statement (1) ALONE is sufficient, but statement (2) alone is not sufficient.
B Statement (2) ALONE is sufficient, but statement (1) alone is not sufficient.
C BOTH statements TOGETHER are sufficient, but NEITHER statement ALONE is sufficient.
D EACH statement ALONE is sufficient.
E Statements (1) and (2) TOGETHER are NOT sufficient.

22. A jewelry dealer initially offered a bracelet for sale at an asking price that would give a profit to the dealer of 40 percent of the original cost. What was the original cost of the bracelet?

(1) After reducing this asking price by 10 percent, the jewelry dealer sold the bracelet at a profit of $403.

(2) The jewelry dealer sold the bracelet for $1,953.

23. If n is an integer between 2 and 100 and if n is also the square of an integer, what is the value of n?

(1) n is the cube of an integer.

(2) n is even.

24. Is $x^2 - y^2$ a positive number?

(1) $x - y$ is a positive number.

(2) $x + y$ is a positive number.

25. The surface area of a square tabletop was changed so that one of the dimensions was reduced by 1 inch and the other dimension was increased by 2 inches. What was the surface area before these changes were made?

(1) After the changes were made, the surface area was 70 square inches.

(2) There was a 25 percent increase in one of the dimensions.

S T O P

**IF YOU FINISH BEFORE TIME IS CALLED, YOU MAY CHECK YOUR WORK ON THIS SECTION ONLY.
DO NOT TURN TO ANY OTHER SECTION IN THE TEST.**

Answer Key for Sample Test Section 1

DATA SUFFICIENCY

1. D	14. D
2. C	15. A
3. C	16. D
4. A	17. E
5. E	18. E
6. B	19. C
7. B	20. C
8. E	21. B
9. A	22. A
10. A	23. A
11. E	24. C
12. D	25. D
13. E	

Explanatory Material: Data Sufficiency

The following discussion of Data Sufficiency is intended to familiarize you with the most efficient and effective approaches to the kinds of problems common to Data Sufficiency. The problems on the sample test sections in this chapter are generally representative of the kinds of questions you will encounter in this section of the GMAT. Remember that it is the problem-solving strategy that is important, not the specific details of a particular question.

Sample Test Section 1

1. **If today the price of an item is $3,600, what was the price of the item exactly 2 years ago?**

   (1) **The price of the item increased by 10 percent per year during this 2-year period.**

   (2) **Today the price of the item is 1.21 times its price exactly 2 years ago.**

From (1) it can be determined that if x was the price two years ago, then 110 percent of x, or 1.1x, was the price one year ago, and 1.1(1.1x) = 1.21x is the price today. By solving the equation 1.21x = $3,600, it is possible to find x, the price 2 years ago. Therefore, (1) alone is sufficient to answer the question and the answer must be either A or D. Since (2) gives the same information derived in (1), it also is sufficient by itself to answer the question. Therefore, each statement alone is sufficient to answer the question and the best answer is D.

2. **By what percent has the price of an overcoat been reduced?**

   (1) **The original price was $380.**

   (2) **The original price was $50 more than the reduced price.**

The percent reduction is the ratio of the amount of reduction to the original price. Since (1) gives no information about the amount of reduction, (1) alone is not sufficient to answer the question, and the answer must be B, C, or E. Statement (2) alone gives $50 as the amount of the reduction but gives no information about the original price. Therefore, (2) alone is not sufficient and the answer must be either C or E. Since (1) and (2) together give both pieces of information needed, the percent reduction can be computed. Therefore, the best answer is C.

3. **If the Longfellow Playground is rectangular, what is its width?**

   (1) **The ratio of its length to its width is 7 to 2.**

   (2) **The perimeter of the playground is 396 meters.**

From (1) it can be determined that for some positive number x, the length L of the playground is 7x and the width W is 2x. Since only the ratio $\frac{L}{W} = \frac{7}{2}$ is given, (1) is not sufficient to answer the question and the answer must be B, C, or E. Statement (2) provides the information that the perimeter, or 2L + 2W, is equal to 396, but (2) gives no information about the relationship between L and W. Therefore, (2) alone is not sufficient and the answer must be C or E. From (1) and (2) together, it can be determined that L + W = 7x + 2x = 198. The width can be determined by solving the equation for x. Therefore, the best answer is C.

4. **What is the value of $x - 1$?**

   (1) $x + 1 = 3$

   (2) $x - 1 < 3$

From (1) the value of x, and thus x − 1, can be determined, and the answer must be A or D. Since (2) gives a range rather than a specific value of x, the question cannot be answered from (2); therefore, the best answer is A.

5. **Is William taller than Jane?**

   (1) **William is taller than Anna.**

   (2) **Anna is not as tall as Jane.**

Statement (1) relates William's height to Anna's and (2) relates Jane's height to Anna's. Neither statement relates William's height to Jane's. Therefore, the answer must be either C or E. When (1) and (2) are taken together, it is possible to determine that Anna is the shortest of the three; however, Jane could be either shorter or taller than William. Since the question cannot be answered, the best answer is E.

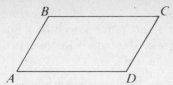

6. In parallelogram *ABCD* above, what is the measure of ∠*ADC*?

   (1) The measure of ∠*ABC* is greater than 90°.

   (2) The measure of ∠*BCD* is 70°.

From (1) it can only be determined that the measure of ∠ADC is greater than 90° since ∠ABC = ∠ADC. Since this information is not sufficient to answer the question, the answer must be B, C, or E. From (2) alone, it can be determined that the measure of ∠ADC is 110° since ∠ADC is a supplement of ∠BCD. Therefore, the best answer is B.

7. Is x^2 equal to *xy*?

   (1) $x^2 - y^2 = (x + 5)(y - 5)$

   (2) $x = y$

If x^2 is equal to *xy*, then either x = 0 or x = y. From (1), if x = −5 or y = 5, then (x + 5)(y − 5) = 0, so $x^2 - y^2 = 0$, and it follows that x = y or x = −y. Thus, (1) would be true whether x = y = 5 or x = −5 and y = 5. Since there are several possibilities, the question cannot be answered from (1) alone, and the answer must be B, C, or E. From (2) alone, it can be determined that $x^2 = xy$ and the best answer is B.

8. Was 70 the average (arithmetic mean) grade on a class test?

   (1) On the test, half of the class had grades below 70 and half of the class had grades above 70.

   (2) The lowest grade on the test was 45 and the highest grade on the test was 95.

Note that the average (arithmetic mean) grade depends on the distribution of the grades. Statement (1) alone is not sufficient since it does not specify how the grades are distributed with respect to 70. Therefore, the answer must be B, C, or E. Obviously (2) is also not sufficient since it only indicates the range of the grades but not their distribution. From (1) and (2) together, the distribution of the grades is not known and so the average cannot be determined. Thus, the best answer is E.

9. What was John's average driving speed in miles per hour during a 15-minute interval?

   (1) He drove 10 miles during this interval.

   (2) His maximum speed was 50 miles per hour and his minimum speed was 35 miles per hour during this interval.

From (1) alone it can be determined that John's average driving speed was 10 miles/0.25 hr = 40 miles per hour. Therefore, the answer is either A or D. Since (2) does not give enough information to determine the total distance driven from which the average driving speed could be derived, the best answer is A.

10. Is △*MNP* isosceles?

   (1) Exactly two of the angles, ∠*M* and ∠*N*, have the same measure.

   (2) ∠*N* and ∠*P* do not have the same measure.

If △MNP has two equal sides, then it is isosceles. If any triangle has two equal angles, the sides opposite the equal angles are also equal. From (1) alone it can be determined that △MNP is isosceles; therefore, the answer must be A or D. From (2) alone, it cannot be determined that △MNP has two equal angles. Therefore, the best answer is A.

11. Is *n* an integer greater than 4?

   (1) 3*n* is a positive integer.

   (2) $\frac{n}{3}$ is a positive integer.

From (1), n could be any positive integer, or even a fraction such as $\frac{1}{3}$. Since the question cannot be answered from (1) alone, the answer must be B, C, or E. From (2) it can be determined that n is a positive multiple of 3, but it cannot be determined whether it is greater or less than 4. Therefore, the answer must be C or E. Since (1) and (2) together do not give any information that precludes n from being 3, it cannot be determined whether n is greater or less than 4 and the best answer is E.

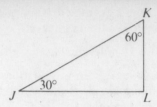

12. In △*JKL* shown above, what is the length of segment *JL*?

    (1) *JK* = 10

    (2) *KL* = 5

From the angle measures given in the figure, JKL is a right triangle and KL = $\frac{1}{2}$JK. From (1) it can be determined that KL = 5 and, by the Pythagorean relationship, that JL = $\sqrt{100 - 25}$. Therefore, the answer is A or D. Similarly, from (2) alone, all sides of the triangle can be found. Therefore, the best answer is D.

13. A coal company can choose to transport coal to one of its customers by railroad or by truck. If the railroad charges by the mile and the trucking company charges by the ton, which means of transporting the coal would cost <u>less</u> than the other?

    (1) The railroad charges $5,000 plus $0.01 per mile per railroad car used, and the trucking company charges $3,000 plus $85 per ton.

    (2) The customer to whom the coal is to be sent is 195 miles away from the coal company.

Although (1) gives detailed information about the rail and truck rates, it gives no information about the weights and distances to which these rates are to be applied. Therefore, the question cannot be answered and the answer must be B, C, or E. Since (2) only gives information about the distance, and (1) and (2) together do not provide information about the tonnage and the number of railroad cars needed, the best answer is E.

14. Is *x* − *y* > *r* − *s*?

    (1) *x* > *r* and *y* < *s*.

    (2) *y* = 2, *s* = 3, *r* = 5, and *x* = 6.

From (1), if x > r and y < s, then −y > −s and x − y > r − s. Since the answer can be determined from (1) alone, the answer must be A or D. From (2), the values of x, y, r, and s can be substituted into the inequality to answer the question. Therefore, the best answer is D.

15. On a certain day it took Bill three times as long to drive from home to work as it took Sue to drive from home to work. How many kilometers did Bill drive from home to work?

    (1) Sue drove 10 kilometers from home to work, and the ratio of

    $\frac{\text{distance driven from home to work}}{\text{time to drive from home to work}}$

    was the same for Bill and Sue that day.

    (2) The ratio of

    $\frac{\text{distance driven from home to work}}{\text{time to drive from home to work}}$

    for Sue that day was 64 kilometers per hour.

From (1) and the information given in the problem, it can be determined that $\frac{\text{Sue's distance}}{\text{Sue's time t}} = \frac{\text{Bill's distance d}}{3t}$ or $\frac{10}{t} = \frac{d}{3t}$ and d = 30 kilometers. Therefore, the answer must be A or D. Since (2) gives no information about Sue's time (from which we could compute Bill's time) and Bill's speed, the question cannot be answered from (2) alone and the best answer is A.

16. The figure above represents the floor of a square foyer with a circular rug partially covering the floor and extending to the outer edges of the floor as shown. What is the area of the foyer floor that is not covered by the rug?

    (1) The area of the foyer is 9 square meters.

    (2) The area of the rug is 2.25π square meters.

From (1), the diameter of the circle is equal to the side of the square, or 3 meters, and the area of the uncovered region is $9 - \pi\left(\frac{3}{2}\right)^2$. Therefore, the answer must be A or D. From (2), the radius of the circle is $\sqrt{2.25} = 1.5$ and the side of the square is 2(1.5) = 3. Therefore, the area of the uncovered region is $3^2 - 2.25\pi$, and the best answer is D.

17. At a certain university, if 50 percent of the people who inquire about admission policies actually submit applications for admission, what percent of those who submit applications for admission enroll in classes at the university?

   (1) Fifteen percent of those who submit applications for admission are accepted at the university.

   (2) Eighty percent of those who are accepted send a deposit to the university.

From (1) and (2) taken together, it can only be determined that $(0.15)(0.8) = 12$ percent of the applicants are accepted and make a deposit. Since neither (1) nor (2) gives information as to what portion of this 12 percent actually enrolls in classes, the best answer is E.

18. If x and y are nonzero integers, is $\frac{x}{y}$ an integer?

   (1) x is the product of 2 and some other integer.

   (2) There is only one pair of positive integers whose product equals y.

From (1), it can be determined that x is an even integer. Since y may, or may not, be a divisor of x, the question cannot be answered from (1) alone and the answer must be B, C, or E. Statement (2) implies that y is a prime number but gives no information about x. Therefore, the answer must be C or E. From (1) and (2) together, x is an even number and y is a prime number. Since y could be the even number 2, in which case $\frac{x}{y}$ would be an integer, or y could be an odd integer, in which case $\frac{x}{y}$ might not be an integer, the best answer is E.

19. If x is an integer, what is the value of x?

   (1) $\frac{1}{5} < \frac{1}{x+1} < \frac{1}{2}$

   (2) $(x - 3)(x - 4) = 0$

From (1) it can be determined that x + 1 = 3 or x + 1 = 4; thus x = 2 or x = 3. From (2) it can be determined that x = 3 or x = 4. Since the precise value of x cannot be determined from either (1) or (2) taken alone, the answer must be C or E. If (1) and (2) are considered together, the only value of x that satisfies both conditions is x = 3. Therefore, the best answer is C.

20. Is quadrilateral Q a square?

   (1) The sides of Q have the same length.

   (2) The diagonals of Q have the same length.

Statement (1) implies that Q is a rhombus that may, or may not, be a square. Therefore, the answer is B, C, or E. Statement (2) alone does not imply that Q is a square since any rectangle or isosceles trapezoid has diagonals of equal length. Therefore, the answer must be C or E. If (1) and (2) are considered together, Q is a rhombus that has diagonals of equal length. Since only a square has both properties, Q is a square and the best answer is C.

21. If K is a positive integer less than 10 and $N = 4,321 + K$, what is the value of K?

   (1) N is divisible by 3.

   (2) N is divisible by 7.

Statement (1) implies that K is one of the integers 2, 5, or 8, since only these values of K will make N divisible by 3. Since the precise value of K cannot be determined from (1), the answer must be B, C, or E. Statement (2) implies that K = 5, since that is the only positive value of K that will make N divisible by 7. Therefore, the best answer is B.

22. A jewelry dealer initially offered a bracelet for sale at an asking price that would give a profit to the dealer of 40 percent of the original cost. What was the original cost of the bracelet?

   (1) After reducing this asking price by 10 percent, the jewelry dealer sold the bracelet at a profit of $403.

   (2) The jewelry dealer sold the bracelet for $1,953.

The problem states that the initial asking price p was equal to 140 percent of the cost c, or p = 1.4c. From (1), the equation 0.9p = c + 403 can be derived. Substituting 1.4c for p and then solving the equation 0.9(1.4c) = c + 403 will yield the cost ($1,550). Therefore, the answer must be A or D. From (2) alone, the cost cannot be related to the selling price. The use of "initially offered" suggests that there was at least one subsequent offer about which (2) gives little useful information. Therefore, the best answer is A.

23. If n is an integer between 2 and 100 and if n is also the square of an integer, what is the value of n?

(1) n is the cube of an integer.

(2) n is even.

The problem is to find which of the integers 4, 9, 16, 25, 36, 49, 64, or 81 is n. Statement (1) implies that n = 64 since 64 is the only one of these squares that is also the cube of an integer. Therefore, the answer must be A or D. From (2) alone, the integer n could be any of the integers 4, 16, 36, or 64. Therefore, the best answer is A.

24. Is $x^2 - y^2$ a positive number?

(1) $x - y$ is a positive number.

(2) $x + y$ is a positive number.

The expression $x^2 - y^2$ is a positive number if, and only if, both of its factors $x + y$ and $x - y$ are positive or both are negative. From (1) alone it cannot be determined whether x + y is positive. For example, if x = −2 and y = −3, then x + y is negative, whereas if x = 3 and y = 2, then x + y is positive. Thus the answer is B, C, or E. Similarly, from (2) it cannot be determined whether x − y is positive, and the answer is C or E. Since both (1) and (2) are needed to establish that the two factors have the same sign, the best answer is C.

25. The surface area of a square tabletop was changed so that one of the dimensions was reduced by 1 inch and the other dimension was increased by 2 inches. What was the surface area before these changes were made?

(1) After the changes were made, the surface area was 70 square inches.

(2) There was a 25 percent increase in one of the dimensions.

From the information in the problem and (1), if s is the length of a side of the square tabletop, then (s − 1)(s + 2) = 70 or $s^2 + s - 72 = 0$. There are two values of s that satisfy this equation, 8 and −9; however, since s cannot be negative in the context of this problem, s = 8. Therefore, the answer must be A or D. From (2) it can be determined that 0.25s = 2 and s = 8. Therefore, the best answer is D.

DATA SUFFICIENCY SAMPLE TEST SECTION 2

30 Minutes

25 Questions

Directions: Each of the data sufficiency problems below consists of a question and two statements, labeled (1) and (2), in which certain data are given. You have to decide whether the data given in the statements are <u>sufficient</u> for answering the question. Using the data given in the statements <u>plus</u> your knowledge of mathematics and everyday facts (such as the number of days in July or the meaning of <u>counterclockwise</u>), you are to fill in oval

- A   if statement (1) ALONE is sufficient, but statement (2) alone is not sufficient to answer the question asked;
- B   if statement (2) ALONE is sufficient, but statement (1) alone is not sufficient to answer the question asked;
- C   if BOTH statements (1) and (2) TOGETHER are sufficient to answer the question asked, but NEITHER statement ALONE is sufficient;
- D   if EACH statement ALONE is sufficient to answer the question asked;
- E   if statements (1) and (2) TOGETHER are NOT sufficient to answer the question asked, and additional data specific to the problem are needed.

Numbers: All numbers used are real numbers.

Figures: A figure in a data sufficiency problem will conform to the information given in the question, but will not necessarily conform to the additional information given in statements (1) and (2).

           You may assume that lines shown as straight are straight and that angle measures are greater than zero.

           You may assume that the positions of points, angles, regions, etc., exist in the order shown.

           All figures lie in a plane unless otherwise indicated.

Example:

In $\triangle PQR$, what is the value of x?

(1) $PQ = PR$

(2) $y = 40$

Explanation: According to statement (1), $PQ = PR$; therefore, $\triangle PQR$ is isosceles and $y = z$. Since $x + y + z = 180$, $x + 2y = 180$. Since statement (1) does not give a value for y, you cannot answer the question using statement (1) by itself. According to statement (2), $y = 40$; therefore, $x + z = 140$. Since statement (2) does not give a value for z, you cannot answer the question using statement (2) by itself. Using both statements together, you can find y and z; therefore, you can find x, and the answer to the problem is C.

GO ON TO THE NEXT PAGE.

A   Statement (1) ALONE is sufficient, but statement (2) alone is not sufficient.
B   Statement (2) ALONE is sufficient, but statement (1) alone is not sufficient.
C   BOTH statements TOGETHER are sufficient, but NEITHER statement ALONE is sufficient.
D   EACH statement ALONE is sufficient.
E   Statements (1) and (2) TOGETHER are NOT sufficient.

1. Who types at a faster rate, John or Bob?

    (1) The difference between their typing rates is 10 words per minute.

    (2) Bob types at a constant rate of 80 words per minute.

2. What is the average distance that automobile D travels on one full tank of gasoline?

    (1) Automobile D averages 8.5 kilometers per liter of gasoline.

    (2) The gasoline tank of automobile D holds exactly 40 liters of gasoline.

3. If l_1, l_2 and l_3 are lines in a plane, is l_1 perpendicular to l_3?

    (1) l_1 is perpendicular to l_2.

    (2) l_2 is perpendicular to l_3.

4. In a certain packinghouse, grapefruit are packed in bags and the bags are packed in cases. How many grapefruit are in each case that is packed?

    (1) The grapefruit are always packed 5 to a bag and the bags are always packed 8 to a case.

    (2) Each case is always 80 percent full.

5. What is the value of x?
    (1) $x + y = 7$
    (2) $x - y = 3 - y$

6. A rectangular floor that is 4 meters wide is to be completely covered with nonoverlapping square tiles, each with side of length 0.25 meter, with no portion of any tile remaining. What is the least number of such tiles that will be required?

    (1) The length of the floor is three times the width.

    (2) The area of the floor is 48 square meters.

GO ON TO THE NEXT PAGE.

A Statement (1) ALONE is sufficient, but statement (2) alone is not sufficient.
B Statement (2) ALONE is sufficient, but statement (1) alone is not sufficient.
C BOTH statements TOGETHER are sufficient, but NEITHER statement ALONE is sufficient.
D EACH statement ALONE is sufficient.
E Statements (1) and (2) TOGETHER are NOT sufficient.

7. If a rope is cut into three pieces of unequal length, what is the length of the shortest of these pieces of rope?

(1) The combined length of the longer two pieces of rope is 12 meters.

(2) The combined length of the shorter two pieces of rope is 11 meters.

8. A certain company paid bonuses of $125 to each of its executive employees and $75 to each of its nonexecutive employees. If 100 of the employees were nonexecutives, how many were executives?

(1) The company has a total of 120 employees.

(2) The total amount that the company paid in bonuses to its employees was $10,000.

9. What fraction of his salary did Mr. Johnson put into savings last week?

(1) Last week Mr. Johnson put $17 into savings.

(2) Last week Mr. Johnson put 5% of his salary into savings.

10. For integers a, b, and c, $\dfrac{a}{b - c} = 1$. What is the value of $\dfrac{b - c}{b}$?

(1) $\dfrac{a}{b} = \dfrac{3}{5}$

(2) a and b have no common factors greater than 1.

11. If the price of a magazine is to be doubled, by what percent will the number of magazines sold decrease?

(1) The current price of the magazine is $1.00.

(2) For every $0.25 of increase in price, the number of magazines sold will decrease by 10 percent of the number sold at the current price.

12. If J, K, L, M, and N are positive integers in ascending order, what is the value of L?

(1) The value of K is 3.

(2) The value of M is 7.

GO ON TO THE NEXT PAGE.

13. If a, b, and c are integers, is the number $3(a + b) + c$ divisible by 3 ?

(1) $a + b$ is divisible by 3.

(2) c is divisible by 3.

14. Each M-type memory unit will increase the base memory capacity of a certain computer by 3 megabytes. What is the base memory capacity, in megabytes, of the computer?

(1) 2 M-type memory units will increase the computer's base memory capacity by 300 percent.

(2) The memory capacity of the computer after 2 M-type memory units are added to the base memory capacity is 1.6 times the memory capacity of the computer after 1 M-type memory unit is added to the base memory capacity.

15. If $xyz \neq 0$, what is the value of $\dfrac{x^5 y^4 z^2}{z^2 y^4 x^2}$?

(1) $x = 1$

(2) $y = 3$

16. What fractional part of the total surface area of cube C is red?

(1) Each of 3 faces of C is exactly $\dfrac{1}{2}$ red.

(2) Each of 3 faces of C is entirely white.

17. If positive integer x is divided by 2, the remainder is 1. What is the remainder when x is divided by 4 ?

(1) $31 < x < 35$

(2) x is a multiple of 3.

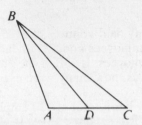

18. In the figure above, D is a point on side AC of $\triangle ABC$. Is $\triangle ABC$ isosceles?

(1) The area of triangular region ABD is equal to the area of triangular region DBC.

(2) $BD \perp AC$ and $AD = DC$

19. If x is an integer, what is the value of x ?

(1) $-2(x + 5) < -1$

(2) $-3x > 9$

GO ON TO THE NEXT PAGE.

-140-

A   Statement (1) ALONE is sufficient, but statement (2) alone is not sufficient.
B   Statement (2) ALONE is sufficient, but statement (1) alone is not sufficient.
C   BOTH statements TOGETHER are sufficient, but NEITHER statement ALONE is sufficient.
D   EACH statement ALONE is sufficient.
E   Statements (1) and (2) TOGETHER are NOT sufficient.

Food	Number of Calories per Kilogram	Number of Grams of Protein per Kilogram
S	2,000	150
T	1,500	90

20. The table above gives the number of calories and grams of protein per kilogram of foods S and T. If a total of 7 kilograms of S and T are combined to make a certain food mixture, how many kilograms of food S are in the mixture?

(1) The mixture has a total of 12,000 calories.

(2) The mixture has a total of 810 grams of protein.

21. If $y \neq 0$ and $y \neq -1$, which is greater,

$\dfrac{x}{y}$ or $\dfrac{x}{y + 1}$?

(1) $x \neq 0$

(2) $x > y$

22. Each person on a committee with 40 members voted for exactly one of 3 candidates, F, G, or H. Did Candidate F receive the most votes from the 40 votes cast?

(1) Candidate F received 11 of the votes.

(2) Candidate H received 14 of the votes.

23. S is a set of integers such that

i) if a is in S, then $-a$ is in S, and
ii) if each of a and b is in S, then ab is in S.

Is -4 in S?

(1) 1 is in S.

(2) 2 is in S.

24. If the area of triangular region RST is 25, what is the perimeter of RST?

(1) The length of one side of RST is $5\sqrt{2}$.

(2) RST is a right isosceles triangle.

25. If x and y are consecutive odd integers, what is the sum of x and y?

(1) The product of x and y is negative.

(2) One of the integers is equal to -1.

S T O P

IF YOU FINISH BEFORE TIME IS CALLED, YOU MAY CHECK YOUR WORK ON THIS SECTION ONLY.
DO NOT TURN TO ANY OTHER SECTION IN THE TEST.

Answer Key for Sample Test Section 2

DATA SUFFICIENCY

1. E	14. D
2. C	15. A
3. C	16. C
4. A	17. A
5. B	18. B
6. D	19. C
7. E	20. D
8. D	21. E
9. B	22. A
10. A	23. B
11. C	24. B
12. E	25. A
13. B	

Explanatory Material:
Data Sufficiency Sample Test Section 2

1. **Who types at a faster rate, John or Bob?**

   (1) **The difference between their typing rates is 10 words per minute.**

   (2) **Bob types at a constant rate of 80 words per minute.**

Statement (1) alone is not sufficient to answer the question since it does not identify who types at the faster rate. Thus, the answer must be B, C, or E. Clearly (2) alone is not sufficient since it provides no information about John's rate. Thus, the answer must be C or E. From (1) and (2) together it can be determined only that John's rate is 70 or 90 words per minute; therefore, the best answer is E.

2. **What is the average distance that automobile D travels on one full tank of gasoline?**

   (1) **Automobile D averages 8.5 kilometers per liter of gasoline.**

   (2) **The gasoline tank of automobile D holds exactly 40 liters of gasoline.**

Statement (1) alone is not sufficient because the capacity of the automobile's gasoline tank is not given. Thus, the answer must be B, C, or E. Statement (2) alone is not sufficient because the average mileage of the automobile is not given. Since (1) and (2) together supply both of these pieces of information, the average distance traveled per tank of gasoline can be determined; thus the best answer is C.

3. **If ℓ_1, ℓ_2 and ℓ_3 are lines in a plane, is ℓ_1 perpendicular to ℓ_3?**

   (1) **ℓ_1 is perpendicular to ℓ_2.**

   (2) **ℓ_2 is perpendicular to ℓ_3.**

Clearly (1) alone and (2) alone are not sufficient to answer the question since neither statement alone gives any information concerning the pair ℓ_1 and ℓ_3. Thus, the answer must be C or E. From (1) and (2) together it can be determined that ℓ_1 and ℓ_3 are parallel rather than perpendicular, since two coplanar lines perpendicular to the same line are parallel. Therefore, the best answer is C.

4. **In a certain packinghouse, grapefruit are packed in bags and the bags are packed in cases. How many grapefruit are in each case that is packed?**

   (1) **The grapefruit are always packed 5 to a bag and the bags are always packed 8 to a case.**

   (2) **Each case is always 80 percent full.**

Statement (1) alone is sufficient since it can be determined from (1) that the grapefruit are packed 40 to a case. Therefore, the answer must be A or D. Clearly (2) alone is not sufficient since it provides no information about how many grapefruit are packed in a case that is 80 percent full. Thus, the best answer is A.

5. **What is the value of x?**

   (1) **$x + y = 7$**

   (2) **$x - y = 3 - y$**

Statement (1) alone is not sufficient since the value of y is not known. Thus, the answer must be B, C, or E. From (2) it can be determined that $x = 3$ after y is added to both sides of the equation. Therefore, the best answer is B.

6. **A rectangular floor that is 4 meters wide is to be completely covered with nonoverlapping square tiles, each with side of length 0.25 meter, with no portion of any tile remaining. What is the least number of such tiles that will be required?**

   (1) **The length of the floor is three times the width.**

   (2) **The area of the floor is 48 square meters.**

From (1) it can be determined that the number of tiles required is $\dfrac{4(3 \cdot 4)}{(0.25)^2}$. Thus, the answer must be A or D. From (2) it can be determined that the number of tiles required is $\dfrac{48}{(0.25)^2}$. Therefore, the best answer is D.

7. If a rope is cut into three pieces of unequal length, what is the length of the shortest of these pieces of rope?

    (1) The combined length of the longer two pieces of rope is 12 meters.

    (2) The combined length of the shorter two pieces of rope is 11 meters.

Let x, y, and z be the lengths of the pieces, $x < y < z$. Statement (1) indicates that $y + z = 12$, and therefore $y < 6$ and $z > 6$. Since (1) alone provides no information about the value of x, the answer must be B, C, or E. Statement (2) indicates that $x + y = 11$, and therefore, $x < 5\frac{1}{2}$ and $y > 5\frac{1}{2}$. Thus, the answer must be C or E. From (1) and (2) together, it can only be determined that $5 < x < 5\frac{1}{2}$, which is a range of values and not a particular value. Therefore, the best answer is E.

8. A certain company paid bonuses of $125 to each of its executive employees and $75 to each of its nonexecutive employees. If 100 of the employees were nonexecutives, how many were executives?

    (1) The company has a total of 120 employees.

    (2) The total amount that the company paid in bonuses to its employees was $10,000.

Let e be the number of executives and n the number of non-executives. From (1) alone it can be determined that $120 = 100 + e$, or $e = 20$. Thus, the answer must be A or D. The information in (2) can be expressed by the equation $10,000 = 75 \cdot 100 + 125e$, which can also be solved for e. Therefore, the best answer is D.

9. What fraction of his salary did Mr. Johnson put into savings last week?

    (1) Last week Mr. Johnson put $17 into savings.

    (2) Last week Mr. Johnson put 5% of his salary into savings.

Clearly (1) alone is not sufficient since Mr. Johnson's salary is not given. Thus, the answer must be B, C, or E. But (2) alone is sufficient since $5\% = \frac{5}{100} = \frac{1}{20}$. Therefore, the best answer is B.

10. For integers a, b, and c, $\frac{a}{b-c} = 1$. What is the value of $\frac{b-c}{b}$?

    (1) $\frac{a}{b} = \frac{3}{5}$

    (2) a and b have no common factors greater than 1.

Note that $a = b - c$, since $\frac{a}{b-c} = 1$; and so $\frac{b-c}{b} = \frac{a}{b}$. Since (1) gives the value of $\frac{a}{b}$, (1) alone is sufficient. Therefore, the answer must be A or D. However, (2) alone is clearly not sufficient since the value of $\frac{a}{b}$ cannot be determined. Thus, the best answer is A.

11. If the price of a magazine is to be doubled, by what percent will the number of magazines sold decrease?

    (1) The current price of the magazine is $1.00.

    (2) For every $0.25 of increase in price, the number of magazines sold will decrease by 10 percent of the number sold at the current price.

From (1) it can be determined that the price of the magazine is to be increased by $1.00, but no information is given as to what effect this price increase will have on sales. Thus, (1) alone is not sufficient, and the answer must be B, C, or E. Statement (2) indicates how sales are affected by price increases of $0.25 increments, but it does not indicate the number of such increments equal to the total increase. Thus, (2) alone is not sufficient, and so the answer must be C or E. From (1) and (2) together, it can be determined that sales will decrease by 40 percent of current sales. Therefore, the best answer is C.

12. If J, K, L, M, and N are positive integers in ascending order, what is the value of L?

    (1) The value of K is 3.
    (2) The value of M is 7.

Note that $J < K < L < M < N$. From (1) it can only be determined that $L \geq 4$. Therefore, (1) alone is not sufficient, and so the answer must be B, C, or E. From (2) it can only be determined that $L \leq 6$; thus (2) alone is also not sufficient. From (1) and (2) together, $4 \leq L \leq 6$, that is $L = 4, 5,$ or 6. But since the precise value of L cannot be determined, the best answer is E.

13. If a, b, and c are integers, is the number $3(a + b) + c$ divisible by 3?

    (1) $a + b$ is divisible by 3.
    (2) c is divisible by 3.

Note that $3(a + b)$ is a multiple of 3 and so is divisible by 3 for any integers a and b. Thus $3(a + b) + c$ will be divisible by 3 if and only if c is divisible by 3. Statement (1) is not sufficient since it gives no information about c. Thus, the answer must be B, C, or E. However, (2) alone is sufficient, in view of the information given above. Therefore, the best answer is B.

14. Each *M*-type memory unit will increase the base memory capacity of a certain computer by 3 megabytes. What is the base memory capacity, in megabytes, of the computer?

(1) 2 *M*-type memory units will increase the computer's base memory capacity by 300 percent.

(2) The memory capacity of the computer after 2 *M*-type memory units are added to the base memory capacity is 1.6 times the memory capacity of the computer after 1 *M*-type memory unit is added to the base memory capacity.

Let c be the base memory capacity of the computer in megabytes. The information given in (1) can be expressed by the equation $6 = 3c$. Therefore (1) alone is sufficient, and the answer must be A or D. The information in (2) can be expressed by the equation $c + 6 = (1.6)(c + 3)$, from which the value of c can again be determined. Thus, (2) alone is also sufficient, and the best answer is D.

15. If $xyz \neq 0$, what is the value of $\frac{x^5 y^4 z^2}{z^2 y^4 x^2}$?

(1) $x = 1$

(2) $y = 3$

Since $xyz \neq 0$, the expression $\frac{x^5 y^4 z^2}{z^2 y^4 x^2}$ is equal to x^3. Now it is easy to see that (1) alone gives the needed information and that (2) is irrelevant. Therefore, the best answer is A.

16. **What fractional part of the total surface area of cube *C* is red?**

(1) Each of 3 faces of *C* is exactly $\frac{1}{2}$ red.

(2) Each of 3 faces of *C* is entirely white.

Neither (1) nor (2), considered separately, gives sufficient information to answer the question since each provides information about only three of the six faces. Therefore, the answer must be C or E. From (1) and (2) together, it can be determined that $\frac{1}{4}$ of the surface area of the cube is red. The best answer is C.

17. **If positive integer *x* is divided by 2, the remainder is 1. What is the remainder when *x* is divided by 4?**

(1) $31 < x < 35$

(2) *x* is a multiple of 3.

Since x has a remainder of 1 when divided by 2, x is an odd integer. From (1), it can be determined that $x = 33$, since 32 and 34 are not odd integers. Therefore, (1) alone is sufficient, and the answer must be A or D. However, (2) alone is not sufficient, since an odd multiple of 3 may have a remainder of either 1 or 3 when divided by 4. For example, $21 = 4(5) + 1$ and $27 = 4(6) + 3$. Thus, the best answer is A.

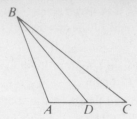

18. **In the figure above, *D* is a point on side *AC* of △*ABC*. Is △*ABC* isosceles?**

(1) The area of triangular region *ABD* is equal to the area of triangular region *DBC*.

(2) $BD \perp AC$ and $AD = DC$

From the fact in (1) that the area of region ABD is equal to the area of region DBC, and the fact that the two triangles have the same altitude from B, it can be determined that $AD = DC$, but not that △ABC is isosceles. Thus, (1) alone is not sufficient, and the answer must be B, C, or E. From (2) it follows that △ABD and △DBC are right triangles. Since $AD = DC$ and BD is a common side, it follows, by the Pythagorean theorem, that $AB = BC$, and so △ABC is isosceles. Thus (2) alone is sufficient, and the best answer is B.

19. **If *x* is an integer, what is the value of *x*?**

(1) $-2(x + 5) < -1$

(2) $-3x > 9$

Clearly (1) alone and (2) alone are insufficient since there is a range of integers for which (1) is true and a range of integers for which (2) is true. Thus, the answer must be C or E. To determine whether the two inequalities, taken together, limit the range sufficiently to determine the value of x, one must solve each inequality. Inequality (1) is equivalent to $x > -4\frac{1}{2}$, and inequality (2) is equivalent to $x < -3$. If x is an integer and $-4\frac{1}{2} < x < -3$, then $x = -4$, and the best answer is C.

Food	Number of Calories per Kilogram	Number of Grams of Protein per Kilogram
S	2,000	150
T	1,500	90

20. **The table above gives the number of calories and grams of protein per kilogram of foods *S* and *T*. If a total of 7 kilograms of *S* and *T* are combined to make a certain food mixture, how many kilograms of food *S* are in the mixture?**

(1) The mixture has a total of 12,000 calories.

(2) The mixture has a total of 810 grams of protein.

Let s equal the number of kilograms of food S in the mixture, and $(7 - s)$ the number of kilograms of food T in the mixture. Then (1) yields the equation

$$2,000s + 1,500(7 - s) = 12,000.$$
Since this equation may be solved for s, (1) alone is sufficient, and the answer must be A or D. Since (2) yields the equation $150s + 90(7 - s) = 810$, which can also be solved for s, the best answer is D.

21. If $y \neq 0$ and $y \neq -1$, which is greater, $\frac{x}{y}$ or $\frac{x}{y + 1}$?

   (1) $x \neq 0$

   (2) $x > y$

In approaching a question such as this, you should remember to consider the possibility of negative values of x and y. Note that $y < y + 1$ for all values of y, so that $\frac{1}{y} > \frac{1}{y + 1}$ for $y > 0$ or for $y < -1$, whereas $\frac{1}{y} < \frac{1}{y + 1}$ for $-1 < y < 0$. Thus, if $x > y > 0$, then $\frac{x}{y} > \frac{x}{y + 1}$, but if $y < x < -1$, then $\frac{x}{y} < \frac{x}{y + 1}$. Therefore, the order relation between $\frac{x}{y}$ and $\frac{x}{y + 1}$ cannot be determined from (1) and (2) together, and the best answer is E.

22. **Each person on a committee with 40 members voted for exactly one of 3 candidates, *F, G,* or *H.* Did Candidate *F* receive the most votes from the 40 votes cast?**

   (1) **Candidate *F* received 11 of the votes.**

   (2) **Candidate *H* received 14 of the votes.**

From (1), it can be determined that F did not receive the most votes since G and H received the remaining 29 votes, and G and H could not both have received less than 11 votes. Thus, from (1) alone it can be determined whether or not F received the most votes, and the answer must be A or D. From (2), it can only be determined that F and G received 26 votes combined; however, F may or may not have received more than 14 votes. Therefore, the best answer is A.

23. *S* is a set of integers such that

   i) if *a* is in *S,* then $-a$ is in *S,* and
   ii) if each of *a* and *b* is in *S,* then *ab* is in *S.*

   Is -4 in *S?*

   (1) 1 is in *S.*

   (2) 2 is in *S.*

From (1) and the definition of *S,* it can only be determined that 1 and -1 are in *S.* Thus, (1) alone is not sufficient, and the answer must be B, C, or E. From (2) and part (i) of the definition of *S,* it can be determined that -2 is in *S.* From (ii), if 2 and -2 are in set *S,* then $2(-2)$ or -4 is also in *S.* Thus, (2) alone is sufficient, and the best answer is B.

24. **If the area of triangular region *RST* is 25, what is the perimeter of *RST*?**

   (1) **The length of one side of *RST* is $5\sqrt{2}$.**

   (2) ***RST* is a right isosceles triangle.**

It may be helpful to draw a figure:

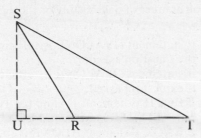

If the length of RT is $5\sqrt{2}$, then it can be determined that the altitude SU from S to side RT has length $5\sqrt{2}$, since $\frac{1}{2}(5\sqrt{2})h = 25$. If this altitude coincides with side SR, then $\triangle RST$ is a right triangle and, by the Pythagorean theorem, the length of the hypotenuse ST may be computed and the perimeter determined. However, as the figure shows, side SR need not be perpendicular to side RT, in which case the perimeter cannot be determined. Therefore, (1) alone is not sufficient and the answer must be B, C, or E. From (2) alone, two sides of the triangle are equal and are perpendicular to each other. If these two sides have length x, then $\frac{1}{2}x^2 = 25$ and $x = 5\sqrt{2}$. Now that the lengths of the legs are known, the hypotenuse can be determined using the Pythagorean theorem, and then the perimeter of the triangle can be computed. Therefore, (2) alone is sufficient, and the best answer is B.

25. **If *x* and *y* are consecutive odd integers, what is the sum of *x* and *y*?**

   (1) **The product of *x* and *y* is negative.**

   (2) **One of the integers is equal to -1.**

If $x < y$, it can be determined from (1) that x is negative and y is positive, since the product of two negative numbers or two positive numbers is positive, whereas the product of a negative number and a positive number is negative. Since x and y are consecutive odd integers, $y - x = 2$, so x cannot be less than -1. Hence $x = -1$ and $y = 1$, and the answer must be A or D. However, (2) alone is not sufficient since it cannot be determined whether $x = -3$ and $y = -1$ or whether $x = -1$ and $y = 1$. Therefore, the best answer is A.

30 Minutes
25 Questions

Directions: Each of the data sufficiency problems below consists of a question and two statements, labeled (1) and (2), in which certain data are given. You have to decide whether the data given in the statements are <u>sufficient</u> for answering the question. Using the data given in the statements <u>plus</u> your knowledge of mathematics and everyday facts (such as the number of days in July or the meaning of <u>counterclockwise</u>), you are to fill in oval

A   if statement (1) ALONE is sufficient, but statement (2) alone is not sufficient to answer the question asked;

B   if statement (2) ALONE is sufficient, but statement (1) alone is not sufficient to answer the question asked;

C   if BOTH statements (1) and (2) TOGETHER are sufficient to answer the question asked, but NEITHER statement ALONE is sufficient;

D   if EACH statement ALONE is sufficient to answer the question asked;

E   if statements (1) and (2) TOGETHER are NOT sufficient to answer the question asked, and additional data specific to the problem are needed.

Numbers: All numbers used are real numbers.

Figures: A figure in a data sufficiency problem will conform to the information given in the question, but will not necessarily conform to the additional information given in statements (1) and (2).

You may assume that lines shown as straight are straight and that angle measures are greater than zero.

You may assume that the positions of points, angles, regions, etc., exist in the order shown.

All figures lie in a plane unless otherwise indicated.

Example:

In $\triangle PQR$, what is the value of x ?

(1) $PQ = PR$

(2) $y = 40$

Explanation: According to statement (1), $PQ = PR$; therefore, $\triangle PQR$ is isosceles and $y = z$. Since $x + y + z = 180$, $x + 2y = 180$. Since statement (1) does not give a value for y, you cannot answer the question using statement (1) by itself. According to statement (2), $y = 40$; therefore, $x + z = 140$. Since statement (2) does not give a value for z, you cannot answer the question using statement (2) by itself. Using both statements together, you can find y and z; therefore, you can find x, and the answer to the problem is C.

1. For a certain bottle and cork, what is the price of the cork?

   (1)   The combined price of the bottle and the cork is 95 cents.

   (2)   The price of the bottle is 75 cents more than the price of the cork.

2. Last year an employee received a gross annual salary of $18,000, which was paid in equal paychecks throughout the year. What was the gross salary received in each of the paychecks?

   (1)   The employee received a total of 24 paychecks during the year.

   (2)   The employee received a paycheck twice a month each month during the year.

GO ON TO THE NEXT PAGE.

A Statement (1) ALONE is sufficient, but statement (2) alone is not sufficient.
B Statement (2) ALONE is sufficient, but statement (1) alone is not sufficient.
C BOTH statements TOGETHER are sufficient, but NEITHER statement ALONE is sufficient.
D EACH statement ALONE is sufficient.
E Statements (1) and (2) TOGETHER are NOT sufficient.

3. What was Bill's average (arithmetic mean) grade for all of his courses?

   (1) His grade in social studies was 75, and his grade in science was 75.

   (2) His grade in mathematics was 95.

4. If $x = 2y$, what is the value of xy?

   (1) $x > y$
   (2) $3x - 2y = 14$

5. A rectangular garden that is 10 feet long and 5 feet wide is to be covered with a layer of mulch 0.5 foot deep. At which store, K or L, will the cost of the necessary amount of mulch be less?

   (1) Store K sells mulch only in bags, each of which costs $7 and contains 6.25 cubic feet of mulch.

   (2) Store L sells mulch only in bags, each of which costs $40 and contains 25 cubic feet of mulch.

6. If $S = \{2, 3, x, y\}$, what is the value of $x + y$?

   (1) x and y are prime numbers.
   (2) 3, x, and y are consecutive odd integers in ascending order.

7. In $\triangle HGM$, what is the length of side HM?

   (1) $HG = 5$
   (2) $GM = 8$

8. Claire paid a total of $1.60 for stamps, some of which cost $0.20 each, and the rest of which cost $0.15 each. How many 20-cent stamps did Claire buy?

   (1) Claire bought exactly 9 stamps.

   (2) The number of 20-cent stamps Claire bought was 1 more than the number of 15-cent stamps she bought.

9. If Ruth began a job and worked continuously until she finished, at what time of day did she finish the job?

   (1) She started the job at 8:15 a.m. and at noon of the same day she had worked exactly half of the time that it took her to do the whole job.

   (2) She was finished exactly $7\frac{1}{2}$ hours after she had started.

GO ON TO THE NEXT PAGE.

A   Statement (1) ALONE is sufficient, but statement (2) alone is not sufficient.
B   Statement (2) ALONE is sufficient, but statement (1) alone is not sufficient.
C   BOTH statements TOGETHER are sufficient, but NEITHER statement ALONE is sufficient.
D   EACH statement ALONE is sufficient.
E   Statements (1) and (2) TOGETHER are NOT sufficient.

10. What is the value of x ?

    (1) $3 + x + y = 14$ and $2x + y = 15$
    (2) $3x + 2y = 12 + 2y$

11. Is x an even integer?

    (1) x is the square of an integer.
    (2) x is the cube of an integer.

12. If John is exactly 4 years older than Bill, how old is John?

    (1) Exactly 9 years ago John was 5 times as old as Bill was then.
    (2) Bill is more than 9 years old.

13. Before play-offs, a certain team had won 80 percent of its games. After play-offs, what percent of all its games had the team won?

    (1) The team competed in 4 play-off games.
    (2) The team won all of its play-off games.

14. If x and y are integers, is $xy + 1$ divisible by 3 ?

    (1) When x is divided by 3, the remainder is 1.
    (2) When y is divided by 9, the remainder is 8.

15. If $x \neq 0$, is $|x| < 1$?

    (1) $x^2 < 1$
    (2) $|x| < \dfrac{1}{x}$

16. The cost to charter a certain airplane is x dollars. If the 25 members of a club chartered the plane and shared the cost equally, what was the cost per member?

    (1) If there had been 5 more members and all 30 had shared the cost equally, the cost per member would have been $40 less.
    (2) The cost per member was 10 percent less than the cost per person on a regularly scheduled flight.

GO ON TO THE NEXT PAGE.

A   Statement (1) ALONE is sufficient, but statement (2) alone is not sufficient.
B   Statement (2) ALONE is sufficient, but statement (1) alone is not sufficient.
C   BOTH statements TOGETHER are sufficient, but NEITHER statement ALONE is sufficient.
D   EACH statement ALONE is sufficient.
E   Statements (1) and (2) TOGETHER are NOT sufficient.

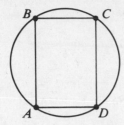

17. Rectangle $ABCD$ is inscribed in a circle as shown above. What is the radius of the circle?

(1) The length of the rectangle is $\sqrt{3}$ and the width of the rectangle is 1.

(2) The length of arc AB is $\frac{1}{3}$ of the circumference of the circle.

18. Bowls X and Y each contained exactly 2 jelly beans, each of which was either red or black. One of the jelly beans in bowl X was exchanged with one of the jelly beans in bowl Y. After the exchange, were both of the jelly beans in bowl X black?

(1) Before the exchange, bowl X contained 2 black jelly beans.

(2) After the exchange, bowl Y contained 1 jelly bean of each color.

19. Does $x + y = 0$?

(1) $xy < 0$
(2) $x^2 = y^2$

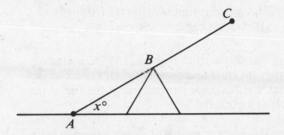

20. In the figure above, line AC represents a seesaw that is touching level ground at point A. If B is the midpoint of AC, how far above the ground is point C ?

(1) $x = 30$
(2) Point B is 5 feet above the ground.

GO ON TO THE NEXT PAGE.

A Statement (1) ALONE is sufficient, but statement (2) alone is not sufficient.
B Statement (2) ALONE is sufficient, but statement (1) alone is not sufficient.
C BOTH statements TOGETHER are sufficient, but NEITHER statement ALONE is sufficient.
D EACH statement ALONE is sufficient.
E Statements (1) and (2) TOGETHER are NOT sufficient.

21. If $\square$ represents a digit in the 7-digit number 3,62$\square$,215, what is the value of $\square$?

   (1) The sum of the 7 digits is equal to 4 times an integer.

   (2) The missing digit is different from any of the other digits in the number.

22. Last Tuesday a trucker paid $155.76, including 10 percent state and federal taxes, for diesel fuel. What was the price per gallon for the fuel if the taxes are excluded?

   (1) The trucker paid $0.118 per gallon in state and federal taxes on the fuel last Tuesday.

   (2) The trucker purchased 120 gallons of the fuel last Tuesday.

23. Is x less than y ?

   (1) $x - y + 1 < 0$
   (2) $x - y - 1 < 0$

24. Is quadrilateral $RSTV$ a rectangle?

   (1) The measure of $\angle RST$ is 90°.
   (2) The measure of $\angle TVR$ is 90°.

25. If b is an integer, is $\sqrt{a^2 + b^2}$ an integer?

   (1) $a^2 + b^2$ is an integer.
   (2) $a^2 - 3b^2 = 0$

S T O P

IF YOU FINISH BEFORE TIME IS CALLED, YOU MAY CHECK YOUR WORK ON THIS SECTION ONLY.
DO NOT TURN TO ANY OTHER SECTION IN THE TEST.

Answer Key for Sample Test Section 3

DATA SUFFICIENCY

1.	C	14.	C
2.	D	15.	D
3.	E	16.	A
4.	B	17.	A
5.	C	18.	E
6.	B	19.	C
7.	E	20.	B
8.	D	21.	C
9.	A	22.	D
10.	D	23.	A
11.	E	24.	E
12.	A	25.	B
13.	E		

Explanatory Material:
Data Sufficiency Sample Test Section 3

1. **For a certain bottle and cork, what is the price of the cork?**

   (1) The combined price of the bottle and the cork is 95 cents.
   (2) The price of the bottle is 75 cents more than the price of the cork.

If b and c denote the costs of the bottle and cork, respectively, then statement (1) yields $b + c = 95$. Since the value of c cannot be determined, statement (1) alone is insufficient to answer the question. Thus, the answer must be B, C, or E. Similarly, statement (2) alone is insufficient since it yields only that $b = c + 75$. However, the value of c can be determined by solving both equations simultaneously; thus, the best answer is C.

2. **Last year an employee received a gross annual salary of $18,000, which was paid in equal paychecks throughout the year. What was the gross salary received in each of the paychecks?**

   (1) The employee received a total of 24 paychecks during the year.
   (2) The employee received a paycheck twice a month each month during the year.

To answer the question it is sufficient to know the number of paychecks received throughout the year, since the answer to the question can be obtained by dividing the gross annual salary by this number. Both statement (1) and statement (2) yield this information. Therefore, the best answer is D.

3. **What was Bill's average (arithmetic mean) grade for all his courses?**

   (1) His grade in social studies was 75, and his grade in science was 75.
   (2) His grade in mathematics was 95.

Statement (1) alone is not sufficient, since it cannot be concluded that social studies and science comprise all of Bill's courses. Therefore, the answer must be B, C, or E. Since from statement (2) it still cannot be concluded that the three courses mentioned comprise all of Bill's courses, the best answer is E.

4. **If $x = 2y$, what is the value of xy?**

   (1) $x > y$
   (2) $3x - 2y = 14$

Statement (1) alone is not sufficient, since there are many pairs of values of x and y such that $x = 2y$ and $x > y$, and these pairs yield different values of xy. Thus, the answer must be B, C, or E. From statement (2) it can be concluded that $2x = 14$ by substituting x for $2y$ in the equation $3x - 2y = 14$, and thus the value of xy can be determined. Therefore, the best answer is B.

5. **A rectangular garden that is 10 feet long and 5 feet wide is to be covered with a layer of mulch 0.5 foot deep. At which store, K or L, will the cost of the necessary amount of mulch be less?**

   (1) Store K sells mulch only in bags, each of which costs $7 and contains 6.25 cubic feet of mulch.
   (2) Store L sells mulch only in bags, each of which costs $40 and contains 25 cubic feet of mulch.

Note that $(10)(5)(0.5) = 25$ cubic feet of mulch is needed. Statement (1) implies that the cost of the necessary amount of mulch at store K will be 4 ($7) = $28, but gives no information about the cost of the mulch at store L. Therefore, the answer must be B, C, or E. Statement (2) implies that the cost of the mulch at store L will be $40, but gives no information about the cost of the mulch at store K. From (1) and (2) together it can be determined that the cost of the mulch will be less at store K than at store L. Thus, the best answer is C.

6. If $S = \{2, 3, x, y\}$, what is the value of $x + y$?

(1) x and y are prime numbers.
(2) 3, x, and y are consecutive odd integers in ascending order.

Statement (1) alone is not sufficient to determine the value of $x + y$, since there are many possible values of x and y that are prime numbers. Thus, the answer must be B, C, or E. Statement (2) implies that $x = 5$ and $y = 7$, and thus $x + y = 12$. Therefore, the best answer is B.

7. In $\triangle HGM$, what is the length of side HM?

(1) $HG = 5$
(2) $GM = 8$

Neither statement (1) alone nor statement (2) alone is sufficient to determine the length of side HM. Thus, the answer must be C or E. However, even together the two statements are not sufficient, because a triangle is not uniquely determined by two of its sides. For instance, the length of side HM will vary between 3 and 13, depending on the size of the angle formed by sides HG and GM. Therefore, the best answer is E.

8. Claire paid a total of $1.60 for stamps, some of which cost $0.20 each, and the rest of which cost $0.15 each. How many 20-cent stamps did Claire buy?

(1) Claire bought exactly 9 stamps.
(2) The number of 20-cent stamps Claire bought was 1 more than the number of 15-cent stamps she bought.

If x and y denote the number of 20-cent stamps and 15-cent stamps, respectively, then $20x + 15y = 160$. Since this equation has two unknowns, another equation in the unknowns is needed to find the value of x. Statement (1) implies that $x + y = 9$, or $y = 9 - x$. Now the equation becomes $20x + 15(9 - x) = 160$, which can be solved for x. Thus the answer is A or D. Statement (2) implies that $x = y + 1$, or $y = x - 1$, and thus the equation $20x + 15(x - 1) = 160$ can be solved for x. The best answer is D.

9. If Ruth began a job and worked continuously until she finished, at what time of day did she finish the job?

(1) She started the job at 8:15 a.m. and at noon of the same day she had worked exactly half of the time that it took her to do the whole job.
(2) She was finished exactly $7\frac{1}{2}$ hours after she had started.

Statement (1) gives the starting time and the time at which she had completed half the job; from this information, it is possible to compute the finishing time. Thus, the answer must be A or D. Statement (2) alone is not sufficient: it gives the total amount of time it took to do the job, but not the starting time. Therefore, the best answer is A.

10. What is the value of x?

(1) $3 + x + y = 14$ and $2x + y = 15$
(2) $3x + 2y = 12 + 2y$

Statement (1) gives two linear equations involving x and y. By inspection it can be determined that the two equations do not represent parallel lines, hence that they have a solution. Therefore, (1) is sufficient, and the answer must be A or D. Statement (2) is equivalent to $3x = 12$, or $x = 4$. Thus, (2) alone is also sufficient, and the best answer is D.

11. Is x an even integer?

(1) x is the square of an integer.
(2) x is the cube of an integer.

Note that any positive integer power of an even integer is even, while any positive integer power of an odd integer is odd. Since it cannot be determined whether x is odd or even by knowing that it is a square or a cube or both, statements (1) and (2), either alone or together, do not give sufficient information. Thus, the best answer is E.

12. If John is exactly 4 years older than Bill, how old is John?

(1) Exactly 9 years ago John was 5 times as old as Bill was then.
(2) Bill is more than 9 years old.

If j and b denote the ages, in years, of John and Bill, respectively, then $j = b + 4$. Statement (1) yields the equation $j - 9 = 5(b - 9)$; substituting $j - 4$ for b in this equation results in an equation in j alone from which the value of j can be determined. Thus, the answer must be A or D. Statement (2) implies only that John is more than 13 years old. Therefore, the best answer is A.

13. Before play-offs, a certain team had won 80 percent of its games. After play-offs, what percent of all its games had the team won?

(1) The team competed in 4 play-off games.
(2) The team won all of its play-off games.

If x denotes the number of games the team played before play-offs, and y and z the number of play-off wins and play-off games, respectively, then the question asks for the value of $\frac{(0.8)x + y}{x + z}$. Statement (1) yields only that $z = 4$. Thus, the value of the ratio cannot be determined, and the answer must be B, C, or E. Statement (2) yields only the value of y, and it is also not sufficient. Since (1) and (2) together do not give the value of x, the value of the ratio, and thus the answer to the question, cannot be determined. Thus, the best answer is E.

14. If x and y are integers, is $xy + 1$ divisible by 3?

    (1) When x is divided by 3, the remainder is 1.
    (2) When y is divided by 9, the remainder is 8.

To determine whether $xy + 1$ is divisible by 3, one must use the given information to see whether the expression $xy + 1$ can be transformed into an expression of the form $3k$, where k is an integer. It should be clear that information is needed about the remainders when both x and y are divided by 3; thus, statements (1) and (2) alone are insufficient, and the answer must be C or E. From the information in both (1) and (2), $x = 3p + 1$ and $y = 9q + 8$, for integers p and q. Substituting these expressions into $xy + 1$, one gets:

$$xy + 1 = (3p + 1)(9q + 8) + 1$$
$$= 27pq + 24p + 9q + 8 + 1,$$

which equals $3(9pq + 8p + 3q + 3)$. Thus, $xy + 1 = 3k$, where k is an integer, and the best answer is C.

15. If $x \neq 0$, is $|x| < 1$?

    (1) $x^2 < 1$
    (2) $|x| < \dfrac{1}{x}$

Note that $|x|$, which denotes the absolute value of x, equals x if $x > 0$ and equals $-x$ if $x < 0$. Thus, $|x| < 1$ if, and only if, $-1 < x < 1$. Since $x^2 < 1$ is equivalent to $-1 < x < 1$, statement (1) alone is sufficient, and the answer must be A or D. Statement (2) implies that $x > 0$, or $|x| = x$; thus, $|x| < 1/|x|$, or $|x|^2 < 1$. Therefore, (2) alone is also sufficient. The best answer is D.

16. The cost to charter a certain airplane is x dollars. If the 25 members of a club chartered the plane and shared the cost equally, what was the cost per member?

    (1) If there had been 5 more members and all 30 had shared the cost equally, the cost per member would have been $40 less.
    (2) The cost per member was 10 percent less than the cost per person on a regularly scheduled flight.

The cost per member can be expressed as $x/25$. Statement (1) yields the equation $\dfrac{x}{30} = \dfrac{x}{25} - 40$, from which the value of x can be determined. Thus, (1) alone is sufficient to determine the value of $\dfrac{x}{25}$, and the answer must be A or D. However, statement (2) alone is not sufficient, because the cost per person on a regularly scheduled flight is not given. Thus, the best answer is A.

17. Rectangle $ABCD$ is inscribed in a circle as shown above. What is the radius of the circle?

    (1) The length of the rectangle is $\sqrt{3}$ and the width of the rectangle is 1.
    (2) The length of arc AB is $\dfrac{1}{3}$ of the circumference of the circle.

Note that the diagonal AC is a diameter of the circle, since $\angle ABC$ is a right angle. From statement (1), the length of AC, which is also the hypotenuse of $\triangle ABC$, can be found by using the Pythagorean theorem. Since AC is a diameter of the circle, the radius is half the length of AC. Therefore, (1) alone is sufficient to answer the question; the answer must be A or D. Statement (2) implies that arc AB has measure 120°, and thus that $\triangle ABC$ is a 30° − 60° − 90° triangle; however, it does not specify the length of any of its sides. Thus, (2) alone is not sufficient; the best answer is A.

18. Bowls X and Y each contained exactly 2 jelly beans, each of which was either red or black. One of the jelly beans in bowl X was exchanged with one of the jelly beans in bowl Y. After the exchange, were both of the jelly beans in bowl X black?

    (1) Before the exchange, bowl X contained 2 black jelly beans.
    (2) After the exchange, bowl Y contained 1 jelly bean of each color.

Statement (1) alone is insufficient to answer the question, since bowl Y may or may not have contained any black jelly beans before the exchange. Therefore, the answer must be B, C, or E. Statement (2) alone is also insufficient, since there is no information about the contents of bowl X. Thus, the answer must be C or E. Together (1) and (2) are insufficient, since there are still two possibilities for the contents of bowl X after the exchange. Thus, the best answer is E.

19. Does $x + y = 0$?

    (1) $xy < 0$
    (2) $x^2 = y^2$

To answer the question, it suffices to determine whether $x = -y$. Statement (1) implies that $x < 0$ and $y > 0$, or that $x > 0$ and $y < 0$; however, it cannot be concluded that $x = -y$. For example, $x = 2$ and $y = -3$ is consistent with statement (1). Thus, (1) alone is not sufficient; the answer must be B, C, or E. Statement (2) implies that $x = y$ or that $x = -y$. Since $y = -y$ only if $y = 0$, it cannot be concluded that $x = -y$. Thus, (2) alone is also insufficient; the answer must be C or E. However, it can be determined from (1) and (2) together that $x = -y$, and therefore the best answer is C.

20. In the figure above, line *AC* represents a seesaw that is touching level ground at point *A*. If *B* is the midpoint of *AC*, how far above the ground is point *C*?

   (1) $x = 30$
   (2) Point *B* is 5 feet above the ground.

It may be helpful to represent *C*'s distance above the ground by drawing in perpendicular segment *CE*, and *B*'s distance above the ground by drawing in perpendicular segment *BD* as shown below:

Note that $\triangle ABD$ and $\triangle ACE$ are similar right triangles, and thus their corresponding sides are in the same proportion. Statement (1) implies that $\triangle ACE$ is a $30° - 60° - 90°$ triangle, and thus the sides are in the ratio $1 : \sqrt{3} : 2$. However, without the length of at least one of the sides, the scale of the drawing cannot be determined. Thus, (1) alone is not sufficient; the answer must be B, C, or E. Statement (2) alone, however, is sufficient to determine that the length of *CE* is 10, since the lengths of the sides of $\triangle ACE$ must be twice the lengths of the corresponding sides of $\triangle ABD$, regardless of the value of *x*. Thus, the best answer is B.

21. If $\square$ represents a digit in the 7-digit number $3,62\square,215$, what is the value of $\square$?

   (1) The sum of the 7 digits is equal to 4 times an integer.
   (2) The missing digit is different from any of the other digits in the number.

The sum of the 7 digits is $19 + \square$. Since $\square$ is one of the integers from 0 to 9, inclusive, the value of $19 + \square$ satisfies $19 \leq 19 + \square \leq 28$. From statement (1), therefore, it can be concluded that $19 + \square$ equals 20, 24, or 28, so $\square$ equals 1, 5, or 9. Thus, (1) alone is not sufficient; the answer must be B, C, or E. Statement (2) implies that $\square$ equals 0, 4, 7, 8, or 9 and, therefore, is not sufficient. However, it can be determined from (1) and (2) together that $\square$ equals 9. Thus, the best answer is C.

22. Last Tuesday a trucker paid $155.76, including 10 percent state and federal taxes, for diesel fuel. What was the price per gallon for the fuel if the taxes are excluded?

   (1) The trucker paid $0.118 per gallon in state and federal taxes on the fuel last Tuesday.
   (2) The trucker purchased 120 gallons of the fuel last Tuesday.

Note that 110 percent of the total price of the fuel was equal to $155.76; so the price of the fuel exclusive of the taxes was $\frac{155.76}{1.1}$. Hence it suffices to determine the number of gallons of fuel purchased. From statement (1), the number of gallons can be determined, since the amount of the taxes is $t = \frac{(0.1)(155.76)}{(1.1)}$; thus, the number of gallons is $\frac{t}{(0.118)}$. Therefore, (1) alone is sufficient, and the answer must be A or D. Statement (2) alone is sufficient since, as was already noted, it suffices to know the number of gallons of fuel. Thus, the best answer is D.

23. Is *x* less than *y*?

   (1) $x - y + 1 < 0$
   (2) $x - y - 1 < 0$

Statement (1) alone is sufficient, as can be seen by adding $y - 1$ to both sides of the inequality: $x < y - 1$. Since $y - 1 < y$ for all values of *y*, $x < y$. Thus, (1) alone is sufficient; the answer must be A or D. Statement (2) implies that $x < y + 1$. Since $x = y$ and $x < y$ are each consistent with (2), statement (2) alone is not sufficient; the best answer is A.

24. Is quadrilateral *RSTV* a rectangle?

   (1) The measure of $\angle RST$ is $90°$.
   (2) The measure of $\angle TVR$ is $90°$.

For *RSTV* to be a rectangle, it is necessary and sufficient that each of the four angles be right angles. Clearly, therefore, neither statement (1) alone nor statement (2) alone is sufficient to determine whether *RSTV* is a rectangle: Given that one of the angles is a right angle does not imply that any of the other three angles are right angles. Therefore, the answer must be C or E. However, it also does not follow that *RSTV* is a rectangle even if a pair of opposite angles are right angles. For example, *RSTV* could look like this:

To understand why this figure is possible, it may be helpful to imagine points *S* and *V* as two points on the circumference of a circle and to draw a diameter RT between points *S* and *V*. Then angles *TVR* and *TSR* will be right angles and the shape of quadrilateral *RSTV* has an infinite number of possibilities, many of which are nonrectangular. The best answer, therefore, is E.

25. If *b* is an integer, is $\sqrt{a^2 + b^2}$ an integer?

   (1) $a^2 + b^2$ is an integer.
   (2) $a^2 - 3b^2 = 0$

Note that for $\sqrt{a^2 + b^2}$ to be an integer, it is necessary and sufficient that $a^2 + b^2$ be the square of an integer. Statement (1) alone is not sufficient, since $a^2 + b^2$ may or may not be the square of an integer: $3^2 + 4^2 = 5^2$, but $2^2 + 3^2 = 13$, which is not the square of an integer. Thus, the answer must be B, C, or E. From statement (2) it can be concluded that $a^2 = 3b^2$ or that $a^2 + b^2 = 4b^2 = (2b)^2$. Therefore, (2) alone is sufficient; the best answer is B.

DATA SUFFICIENCY SAMPLE TEST SECTION 4

Directions: Each of the data sufficiency problems below consists of a question and two statements, labeled (1) and (2), in which certain data are given. You have to decide whether the data given in the statements are <u>sufficient</u> for answering the question. Using the data given in the statements <u>plus</u> your knowledge of mathematics and everyday facts (such as the number of days in July or the meaning of <u>counterclockwise</u>), you are to fill in oval

    A   if statement (1) ALONE is sufficient, but statement (2) alone is not sufficient to answer the question asked;

    B   if statement (2) ALONE is sufficient, but statement (1) alone is not sufficient to answer the question asked;

    C   if BOTH statements (1) and (2) TOGETHER are sufficient to answer the question asked, but NEITHER statement ALONE is sufficient;

    D   if EACH statement ALONE is sufficient to answer the question asked;

    E   if statements (1) and (2) TOGETHER are NOT sufficient to answer the question asked, and additional data specific to the problem are needed.

Numbers: All numbers used are real numbers.

Figures: A figure in a data sufficiency problem will conform to the information given in the question, but will not necessarily conform to the additional information given in statements (1) and (2).

You may assume that lines shown as straight are straight and that angle measures are greater than zero.

You may assume that the positions of points, angles, regions, etc., exist in the order shown.

All figures lie in a plane unless otherwise indicated.

Example:

In $\triangle PQR$, what is the value of x?

(1) $PQ = PR$

(2) $y = 40$

Explanation: According to statement (1), $PQ = PR$; therefore, $\triangle PQR$ is isosceles and $y = z$. Since $x + y + z = 180$, $x + 2y = 180$. Since statement (1) does not give a value for y, you cannot answer the question using statement (1) by itself. According to statement (2), $y = 40$; therefore, $x + z = 140$. Since statement (2) does not give a value for z, you cannot answer the question using statement (2) by itself. Using both statements together, you can find y and z; therefore, you can find x, and the answer to the problem is C.

GO ON TO THE NEXT PAGE.

A   Statement (1) ALONE is sufficient, but statement (2) alone is not sufficient.
B   Statement (2) ALONE is sufficient, but statement (1) alone is not sufficient.
C   BOTH statements TOGETHER are sufficient, but NEITHER statement ALONE is sufficient.
D   EACH statement ALONE is sufficient.
E   Statements (1) and (2) TOGETHER are NOT sufficient.

1. What is the value of x ?

   (1) x is negative.
   (2) $2x = -4$

2. Did United States carriers use more than 10 billion gallons of jet fuel during 1983 ?

   (1) United States carriers paid a total of $9.4 billion for the jet fuel used in 1983.
   (2) United States carriers paid an average (arithmetic mean) of $0.90 per gallon for the jet fuel used in 1983.

3. In Country S, if 60 percent of the women aged 18 and over are in the labor force, how many million women are in the labor force?
   (1) In Country S, women comprise 45 percent of the labor force.
   (2) In Country S, there are no women under 18 years of age in the labor force.

4. If x and y are different positive numbers, is z between x and y?

   (1) $z > 0$
   (2) $z < y$

5. What percent of 16 is m ?

   (1) m is 5 percent of 10.
   (2) 400 percent of m is 2.

6. Kay put 12 cards on a table, some faceup and the rest facedown. How many were put facedown?

   (1) Kay put an even number of the cards faceup.
   (2) Kay put twice as many of the cards faceup as she put facedown.

7. Is $\triangle RST$ a right triangle?

   (1) The degree measure of $\angle R$ is twice the degree measure of $\angle T$.
   (2) The degree measure of $\angle T$ is 30.

8. If x is a positive number, is x greater than 1 ?

   (1) $1 > \dfrac{1}{x}$
   (2) $-\dfrac{1}{x} > -1$

GO ON TO THE NEXT PAGE.

A   Statement (1) ALONE is sufficient, but statement (2) alone is not sufficient.
B   Statement (2) ALONE is sufficient, but statement (1) alone is not sufficient.
C   BOTH statements TOGETHER are sufficient, but NEITHER statement ALONE is sufficient.
D   EACH statement ALONE is sufficient.
E   Statements (1) and (2) TOGETHER are NOT sufficient.

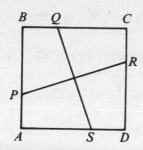

9. The figure above shows four pieces of tile that have been glued together to form a square tile $ABCD$. Is $PR = QS$?

    (1) $BQ = CR = DS = AP$

    (2) The perimeter of $ABCD$ is 16.

10. How old is Jim?

    (1) Eight years ago Jim was half as old as he is now.

    (2) Four years from now Jim will be twice as old as he was six years ago.

11. What is the value of x?

    (1) When x is multiplied by 8, the result is between 50 and 60.

    (2) When x is doubled, the result is between 10 and 15.

12. At a certain state university last term, there were p students each of whom paid either the full tuition of x dollars or half the full tuition. What percent of the tuition paid by the p students last term was tuition from students who paid the full tuition?

    (1) Of the p students, 20 percent paid the full tuition.

    (2) The p students paid a total of $91.2 million for tuition last term.

GO ON TO THE NEXT PAGE.

A Statement (1) ALONE is sufficient, but statement (2) alone is not sufficient.
B Statement (2) ALONE is sufficient, but statement (1) alone is not sufficient.
C BOTH statements TOGETHER are sufficient, but NEITHER statement ALONE is sufficient.
D EACH statement ALONE is sufficient.
E Statements (1) and (2) TOGETHER are NOT sufficient.

13. If a bottle is to be selected at random from a certain collection of bottles, what is the probability that the bottle will be defective?

   (1) The ratio of the number of bottles in the collection that are defective to the number that are not defective is $3:500$.

   (2) The collection contains 3,521 bottles.

14. If a grocery shopper received $0.25 off the original price of a certain product by using a coupon, what was the original price of the product?

   (1) The shopper received a 20 percent discount by using the coupon.

   (2) The original price was 25 percent higher than the price the shopper paid by using the coupon.

15. What was Casey's total score for eighteen holes of golf?

   (1) Casey's score for the first nine holes was 13 less than his score for the last nine holes.

   (2) Twice Casey's score for the last nine holes was 58 more than his score for the first nine holes.

16. What is the rate, in cubic feet per minute, at which water is flowing into a certain rectangular tank?

   (1) The height of the water in the tank is increasing at the rate of 2 feet per minute.

   (2) The capacity of the tank is 216 cubic feet.

17. Is the positive integer n equal to the square of an integer?

   (1) For every prime number p, if p is a divisor of n, then so is p^2.

   (2) $\sqrt{n}$ is an integer.

18. What is the volume of a certain cube?

   (1) The sum of the areas of the faces of the cube is 54.

   (2) The greatest possible distance between two points on the cube is $3\sqrt{3}$.

19. What is the value of $k^2 - k$?

   (1) The value of $k - \frac{1}{k}$ is 1.

   (2) The value of $2k - 1$ is $\sqrt{5}$.

GO ON TO THE NEXT PAGE.

A Statement (1) ALONE is sufficient, but statement (2) alone is not sufficient.
B Statement (2) ALONE is sufficient, but statement (1) alone is not sufficient.
C BOTH statements TOGETHER are sufficient, but NEITHER statement ALONE is sufficient.
D EACH statement ALONE is sufficient.
E Statements (1) and (2) TOGETHER are NOT sufficient.

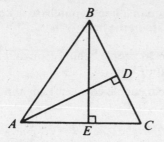

20. In the figure above, what is the product of the lengths of AD and BC?

    (1) The product of the lengths of AC and BE is 60.

    (2) The length of BC is 8.

21. At a business association conference, the registration fee for members of the association was $20 and the registration fee for nonmembers was $25. If the total receipts from registration were $5,500, did more members than nonmembers pay the registration fee?

    (1) Registration receipts from members were $500 greater than receipts from nonmembers.

    (2) A total of 250 people paid the registration fee.

22. If x and y are positive integers and x is a multiple of y, is $y = 2$?

    (1) $y \neq 1$

    (2) $x + 2$ is a multiple of y.

23. What is the value of n?

    (1) $n(n - 1)(n - 2) = 0$

    (2) $n^2 + n - 6 = 0$

GO ON TO THE NEXT PAGE.

A   Statement (1) ALONE is sufficient, but statement (2) alone is not sufficient.
B   Statement (2) ALONE is sufficient, but statement (1) alone is not sufficient.
C   BOTH statements TOGETHER are sufficient, but NEITHER statement ALONE is sufficient.
D   EACH statement ALONE is sufficient.
E   Statements (1) and (2) TOGETHER are NOT sufficient.

24. If x and y are integers between 10 and 99, inclusive, is $\dfrac{x - y}{9}$ an integer?

   (1) x and y have the same two digits, but in reverse order.

   (2) The tens' digit of x is 2 more than the units' digit, and the tens' digit of y is 2 less than the units' digit.

25. Pam and Ed are in a line to purchase tickets. How many people are in the line?

   (1) There are 20 people behind Pam and 20 people in front of Ed.

   (2) There are 5 people between Pam and Ed.

STOP

**IF YOU FINISH BEFORE TIME IS CALLED, YOU MAY CHECK YOUR WORK ON THIS SECTION ONLY.
DO NOT TURN TO ANY OTHER SECTION IN THE TEST.**

Answer Key for Sample Test Section 4

DATA SUFFICIENCY

1. B	14. D
2. C	15. C
3. E	16. E
4. E	17. B
5. D	18. D
6. B	19. D
7. C	20. A
8. D	21. D
9. A	22. C
10. D	23. C
11. E	24. A
12. A	25. E
13. A	

Explanatory Material: Data Sufficiency Sample Test Section 4

1. What is the value of x?

(1) x is negative.
(2) $2x = -4$

Statement (1) alone is clearly not sufficient to determine the value of x, since there are infinitely many negative numbers. Thus, the answer must be B, C, or E. Statement (2) implies that $x = -2$, since $2(-2) = -4$. Therefore, the best answer is B.

2. Did United States carriers use more than 10 billion gallons of jet fuel during 1983?

(1) United States carriers paid a total of $9.4 billion for the jet fuel used in 1983.
(2) United States carriers paid an average (arithmetic mean) of $0.90 per gallon for the jet fuel used in 1983.

The total amount paid for the jet fuel used, t, is equal to the number of gallons used, n, multiplied by the average price per gallon, p. In order to calculate n, the values of both t and p must be known. Statement (1) says only that $t = 9.4$ and statement (2) says only that $p = \$0.90$. Thus, both (1) and (2) together, but neither alone, are sufficient to determine the value of n. The best answer is C.

3. In Country S, if 60 percent of the women aged 18 and over are in the labor force, how many million women are in the labor force?

(1) In Country S, women comprise 45 percent of the labor force.
(2) In Country S, there are no women under 18 years of age in the labor force.

Statement (1) is not sufficient, since the size of the labor force is not specified. Therefore, the answer must be B, C, or E. From statement (2), together with the fact given in the question, it follows only that the female labor force comprises 60 percent of the women aged 18 and over, and the answer must be C or E. Since statements (1) and (2) together do not provide any actual numbers to which the percents given could be applied, the best answer is E.

4. If x and y are different positive numbers, is z between x and y?

(1) $z > 0$
(2) $z < y$

From statement (1) it follows that z is positive but not that z is between x and y. Thus, the answer must be B, C, or E. Statement (2) alone is also not sufficient, because it is not known whether or not $x < z$. Thus, the answer must be C or E. Since $0 < x < z < y$ or $0 < z < x < y$ or $0 < z < y < x$ are all consistent with (1) and (2), the best answer is E.

5. What percent of 16 is m?

(1) m is 5 percent of 10.
(2) 400 percent of m is 2.

The question can be answered if the value of m is known. According to statement (1), $m = \dfrac{5}{100}(10) = 0.5$. Therefore, $m = \left(\dfrac{0.5}{16}\right) \times 100\%$ of 16, and the answer must be A or D.

According to statement (2), $4m = 2$, or $m = \dfrac{1}{2}$, and again m as a percent of 16 can be determined. Thus, the best answer is D.

6. Kay put 12 cards on a table, some faceup and the rest facedown. How many were put facedown?

   (1) Kay put an even number of the cards faceup.
   (2) Kay put twice as many of the cards faceup as she put facedown.

If x denotes the number of cards that were put facedown, it follows from statement (1) that x could be 2, 4, 6, 8, 10, or 12. Thus statement (1) alone is not sufficient, and the answer must be B, C, or E. From statement (2) it can be determined that $2x + x = 3x = 12$, or $x = 4$. Therefore, statement (2) alone is sufficient, and the best answer is B.

7. Is $\triangle RST$ a right triangle?

   (1) The degree measure of $\angle R$ is twice the degree measure of $\angle T$.
   (2) The degree measure of $\angle T$ is 30.

Let r, s, and t denote the degree measures of angles R, S, and T, respectively. Then $r + s + t = 180$. From statement (1) it follows that $r = 2t$, and thus $3t + s = 180$. Since infinitely many values of t can satisfy this equation, and $s = 90$ only if $t = 30$, statement (1) alone is not sufficient. Therefore, the answer must be B, C, or E. Clearly, statement (2) alone is not sufficient, and the answer must be C or E. Since $3t + s = 180$ and $t = 30$ together imply that $s = 90$, the best response is C.

8. If x is a positive number, is x greater than 1?

   (1) $1 > \dfrac{1}{x}$

   (2) $-\dfrac{1}{x} > -1$

Multiplying both sides of an inequality by a positive number does not change the order of the inequality, whereas multiplying both sides by a negative number reverses its order. In statement (1), multiplying both sides of $1 > \dfrac{1}{x}$ by x, which is given to be positive, yields $x > 1$. Therefore, statement (1) is sufficient, and the answer must be A or D. In statement (2), multiplying both sides of $-\dfrac{1}{x} > -1$ by -1 yields $\dfrac{1}{x} < 1$, which is the same as statement (1). Therefore, the best answer is D.

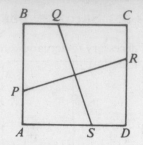

9. The figure above shows four pieces of tile that have been glued together to form a square tile $ABCD$. Is $PR = QS$?

   (1) $BQ = CR = DS = AP$
   (2) The perimeter of $ABCD$ is 16.

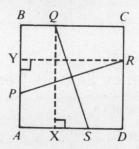

In the figure above, $QX \perp AD$ and $RY \perp AB$. Therefore, $AX = BQ$ and $BY = CR$. From statement (1) and the fact that $AB = AD$, it follows that $XS = YP$. Since $QX = YR$, it follows by the Pythagorean theorem that $PR = QS$. Thus, statement (1) is sufficient, and the answer must be A or D. Note that the reasoning above assumes that neither points S and X nor points P and Y coincide. However, if both pairs of points do coincide, then $PR = QS$ = the length of a side of the square, and (1) alone is sufficient in this case also. Since statement (2) is clearly not sufficient, the best answer is A.

   Another solution is to observe that from statement (1) it follows that quadrilateral $BQSA$ is congruent to quadrilateral $CRPB$. Thus, since corresponding parts of congruent figures are equal, it follows that $PR = QS$.

10. How old is Jim?

    (1) Eight years ago Jim was half as old as he is now.
    (2) Four years from now Jim will be twice as old as he was six years ago.

Let j denote Jim's age. It follows from statement (1) that $j - 8 = \dfrac{j}{2}$, or $j = 16$. Thus, statement (1) alone is sufficient, and the answer must be A or D. From statement (2) it follows that $j + 4 = 2(j - 6)$, which has the solution $j = 16$. (Note that it is not necessary to actually solve the equation for the value of j.) Therefore, the best answer is D.

11. What is the value of x?

   (1) When x is multiplied by 8, the result is between 50 and 60.

   (2) When x is doubled, the result is between 10 and 15.

Statement (1) implies that $50 < 8x < 60$, or $6\frac{1}{4} < x < 7\frac{1}{2}$. Since it is not specified that x is an integer, x can be any real number in this interval and not just 7. Thus, statement (1) is not sufficient, and the answer must be B, C, or E. Statement (2) implies that $10 < 2x < 15$, or $5 < x < 7\frac{1}{2}$, which again determines a range of possible values. Therefore, the answer must be C or E. Since statements (1) and (2) together imply only that $6\frac{1}{4} < x < 7\frac{1}{2}$, the best answer is E.

12. At a certain state university last term, there were p students each of whom paid either the full tuition of x dollars or half the full tuition. What percent of the tuition paid by the p students last term was tuition from students who paid the full tuition?

   (1) Of the p students, 20 percent paid the full tuition.

   (2) The p students paid a total of $91.2 million for tuition last term.

From statement (1) it follows that the tuition from students who paid the full tuition, F, was $0.2px$ dollars and the tuition from students who paid half the full tuition, H, was $0.8p\left(\frac{x}{2}\right) = 0.4px$ dollars. Thus,

$$\frac{F}{F + H} = \frac{0.2px}{0.2px + 0.4px} = \frac{1}{3}, \text{ or } 33\frac{1}{3}\%, \text{ and the answer}$$

must be A or D. Clearly, statement (2) alone is not sufficient, since the amount of tuition paid by students who paid the full tuition would also need to be known. Therefore, the best answer is A.

13. If a bottle is to be selected at random from a certain collection of bottles, what is the probability that the bottle will be defective?

   (1) The ratio of the number of bottles in the collection that are defective to the number that are not defective is 3 : 500.

   (2) The collection contains 3,521 bottles.

The probability that the bottle will be defective is the ratio of the number of defective bottles to the total number of bottles in the collection. From statement (1) it follows that, for some integer k, the number of defective bottles is $3k$ and the number of bottles that are not defective is $500k$. Thus, the probability in question is $\frac{3k}{503k} = \frac{3}{503}$. Statement (1) is sufficient, and the answer must be A or D. However, statement (2) alone is not sufficient, since the number of defective bottles or the number of nondefective bottles would also need to be known. Therefore, the best answer is A.

14. If a grocery shopper received $0.25 off the original price of a certain product by using a coupon, what was the original price of the product?

   (1) The shopper received a 20 percent discount by using the coupon.

   (2) The original price was 25 percent higher than the price the shopper paid by using the coupon.

From statement (1) it follows that the discount of $0.25 was 20 percent, or $\frac{1}{5}$, of the original price. Thus, the original price was $5($0.25$) = 1.25. Statement (1) is sufficient, and the answer must be A or D. From statement (2) it follows that the original price was 125 percent, or $\frac{5}{4}$, of the discounted price; in other words, the discounted price was $\frac{4}{5}$, or 80 percent, of the original price. Since this is a discount of 20 percent, it again follows that the original price was $1.25. Therefore, statement (2) is also sufficient and the best answer is D.

15. What was Casey's total score for eighteen holes of golf?

   (1) Casey's score for the first nine holes was 13 less than his score for the last nine holes.

   (2) Twice Casey's score for the last nine holes was 58 more than his score for the first nine holes.

If f and g denote Casey's score for the first nine holes and for the last nine holes, respectively, then the question asks for the value of $f + g$. Statement (1) implies that $f = g - 13$, or $f + g = 2g - 13$. Since the value of g is unknown, statement (1) is not sufficient, and the answer must be B, C, or E. Statement (2) implies that $2g = f + 58$, or $f + g = 3g - 58$. Again, the total score $f + g$ cannot be determined, and the answer must be C or E. From (1) and (2) together, it follows that the values of f and g, and thus the value of $f + g$, can be determined. Therefore, the best answer is C.

16. **What is the rate, in cubic feet per minute, at which water is flowing into a certain rectangular tank?**

(1) The height of the water in the tank is increasing at the rate of 2 feet per minute.
(2) The capacity of the tank is 216 cubic feet.

The desired rate can be calculated by multiplying the rate at which the height of the water increases, in feet per minute, by the surface area of the water in square feet. Statement (1) is, therefore, not sufficient, since the surface area of the water is not specified. Thus, the answer is B, C, or E. Clearly statement (2) is not sufficient, since it gives no information about either the flow of water into the tank or the surface area of the water in the tank. For example, the tank could have height 6 feet and water surface area 36 square feet, or height 3 feet and water surface area 72 square feet. Since neither statement (1) nor statement (2) gives any information about the surface area of the water in the tank, the best answer is E.

17. **Is the positive integer n equal to the square of an integer?**

(1) For every prime number p, if p is a divisor of n, then so is p^2.
(2) $\sqrt{n}$ is an integer.

Statement (1) is not sufficient since, for example, both $n = 2^2 = 4$, which is the square of an integer, and $n = 2^3 = 8$, which is not, satisfy the given conditions. Thus, the answer must be B, C, or E. From statement (2) it follows that $\sqrt{n} = r$, for some positive integer r, or that $n = r^2$. Therefore, statement (2) is sufficient and the best answer is B.

18. **What is the volume of a certain cube?**

(1) The sum of the areas of the faces of the cube is 54.
(2) The greatest possible distance between two points on the cube is $3\sqrt{3}$.

Since the volume of a cube is determined by the length of an edge, if the length of an edge can be determined, the question can be answered. If the surface area of the cube is known, the area of one face, and thus the length of an edge, can be determined. Furthermore, if the greatest possible distance between two points on the cube (i.e., the "space" diagonal) is known, the length of an edge of the cube can be found. Therefore, both statements (1) and (2) alone are sufficient, and the best answer is D.

19. **What is the value of $k^2 - k$?**

(1) The value of $k - \dfrac{1}{k}$ is 1.
(2) The value of $2k - 1$ is $\sqrt{5}$.

Statement (1) implies that $k - \dfrac{1}{k} = 1$. If both sides of the equation are multiplied by k, the result is $k^2 - 1 = k$, or $k^2 - k = 1$. Thus, statement (1) is sufficient, and the answer must be A or D. Statement (2) implies that $2k - 1 = \sqrt{5}$, from which the value of k, and thus the value of $k^2 - k$, can be determined. Therefore, statement (2) alone is also sufficient, and the best answer is D.

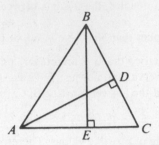

20. **In the figure above, what is the product of the lengths of AD and BC?**

(1) The product of the lengths of AC and BE is 60.
(2) The length of BC is 8.

The area of a triangle equals half the product of the length of a side and the length of the altitude to that side. Thus, in the figure $\dfrac{1}{2}(AC)(BE) = \dfrac{1}{2}(AD)(BC)$, or $(AC)(BE) = (AD)(BC)$. Statement (1) yields $(AC)(BE) = 60$, and the answer must be A or D. Statement (2) is clearly not sufficient, since the length of AD is not specified. Therefore, the best answer is A.

21. **At a business association conference, the registration fee for members of the association was $20 and the registration fee for nonmembers was $25. If the total receipts from registration were $5,500, did more members than nonmembers pay the registration fee?**

(1) Registration receipts from members were $500 greater than receipts from nonmembers.
(2) A total of 250 people paid the registration fee.

If m and n denote the number of members and nonmembers, respectively, the information given in the question can be expressed by the equation $20m + 25n = 5,500$. Since the information in statement (1) is given by $20m = 25n + 500$, the two equations can be solved for m and n. ($m = 150$ and $n = 100$, but it is not necessary to actually determine these values.) Thus, statement (1) is sufficient, and the answer must be A or D. Statement (2) yields $m + n = 250$. Again, this equation together with the equation $20m + 25n = 5,500$ can be solved for m and n. Thus, it can also be determined from statement (2) whether or not $m > n$. Therefore, the best answer is D.

22. If x and y are positive integers and x is a multiple of y, is $y = 2$?

    (1) $y \neq 1$
    (2) $x + 2$ is a multiple of y.

Since x is a multiple of y, there is an integer n such that $x = ny$. Statement (1) is clearly not sufficient. For example, $x = 4$, $y = 2$ and $x = 9$, $y = 3$ both satisfy the information given in the question. Thus, the answer must be B, C, or E. From statement (2) it follows that $x + 2 = my$ for some integer m. Since $x = ny$, $ny + 2 = my$ or $2 = (m - n)y$. Since y is positive, it follows that $y = 1$ or 2. Note that two values for y are determined, and not a unique value. Thus, statement (2) is not sufficient, and the answer must be C or E. From (1) and (2) together it can be concluded that $y = 2$. Therefore, the best answer is C.

23. What is the value of n?

    (1) $n(n - 1)(n - 2) = 0$
    (2) $n^2 + n - 6 = 0$

From statement (1) it follows that $n = 0$, 1, or 2. Since a unique value of n is not determined, statement (1) is not sufficient, and the answer must be B, C, or E. In statement (2), since $n^2 + n - 6 = (n + 3)(n - 2)$, it follows that $n = -3$ or 2, and statement (2) also is not sufficient. The only value of n that satisfies both statements (1) and (2) is $n = 2$. Therefore, the best answer is C.

24. If x and y are integers between 10 and 99, inclusive, is $\dfrac{x - y}{9}$ an integer?

    (1) x and y have the same two digits, but in reverse order.
    (2) The tens' digit of x is 2 more than the units' digit, and the tens' digit of y is 2 less than the units' digit.

From statement (1) it follows that
$$x = (M)(10) + N$$
$$y = (N)(10) + M,$$
where M and N are each digits from 1 to 9, inclusive. Subtracting the bottom equation from the top equation, it follows that $x - y = (M - N)10 + (N - M)$, or
$$x - y = (M - N)10 - (M - N). \text{ Thus,}$$
$$x - y = (10 - 1)(M - N) = 9(M - N),$$
and $\dfrac{x - y}{9} = M - N$, which is an integer. Thus, statement (1) is sufficient, and the answer must be A or D. Statement (2) is not sufficient. For example, if $x = 53$ and $y = 35$, then $x - y = 18$, which is divisible by 9; however, if $x = 53$ and $y = 46$, then $x - y = 7$, which is not divisible by 9. Therefore, the best answer is A.

25. Pam and Ed are in a line to purchase tickets. How many people are in the line?

    (1) There are 20 people behind Pam and 20 people in front of Ed.
    (2) There are 5 people between Pam and Ed.

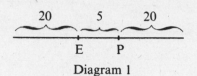

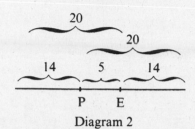

Diagram 1

Diagram 2

Note that either Pam is behind Ed in the line (see Diagram 1 above), or Ed is behind Pam (see Diagram 2 above). Clearly, neither statement alone is sufficient, and the answer must be C or E. As the diagrams indicate, statements (1) and (2) together are sufficient to determine the number of people in the line only if it is specified whether Pam is behind or ahead of Ed in the line. In the first case, there must be 47 people in the line, including Pam and Ed; in the second case, there must be 35 people in the line. Therefore, the best answer is E.

5 Reading Comprehension

There are six kinds of Reading Comprehension questions, each of which tests a different reading skill. The following pages include descriptions of the various question types, test-taking strategies, sample test sections (with answer keys), and detailed explanations of every question on the sample test sections. The explanations further illustrate the ways in which Reading Comprehension questions evaluate basic reading skills.

Reading Comprehension questions include:

1. **Questions that ask about the main idea of a passage**
   Each Reading Comprehension passage in the GMAT is a unified whole—that is, the individual sentences and paragraphs support and develop one main idea or central point. Sometimes you will be told the central point in the passage itself, and sometimes it will be necessary for you to determine the central point from the overall organization or development of the passage. You may be asked in this kind of question to recognize a correct restatement, or paraphrase, of the main idea of a passage; to identify the author's primary purpose, or objective, in writing the passage; or to assign a title that summarizes briefly and pointedly the main idea developed in the passage.

2. **Questions that ask about the supporting ideas presented in a passage**
   These questions measure your ability to comprehend the supporting ideas in a passage and to differentiate those supporting ideas from the main idea. The questions also measure your ability to differentiate ideas that are *explicitly stated* in a passage from ideas that are *implied* by the author but are not explicitly stated. You may be asked about facts cited in a passage, or about the specific content of arguments presented by the author in support of his or her views, or about descriptive details used to support or elaborate on the main idea. Whereas questions about the main idea ask you to determine the meaning of a passage *as a whole,* questions about supporting ideas ask you to determine the meanings of individual sentences and paragraphs that *contribute* to the meaning of the passage as a whole. One way to think about these questions is to see them as questions asking for the main point of *one small part* of the passage.

3. **Questions that ask for inferences based on information presented in a passage**
   These questions ask about ideas that are not explicitly stated in a passage but are *strongly implied* by the author. Unlike questions about supporting details, which ask about information that is directly stated in a passage, inference questions ask about ideas or meanings that must be inferred from information that is directly stated. Authors can make their points in indirect ways, suggesting ideas without actually stating them. These questions measure your ability to infer an author's intended meaning in parts of a passage where the meaning is only suggested. The questions do not ask about meanings or implications that are remote from the passage but about meanings that are developed indirectly or implications specifically suggested by the author. To answer these questions, you may have to carry statements made by the author one step beyond their literal meanings, or recognize the *opposite* of a statement made by the author, or identify the intended meaning of a word used figuratively in a passage. If a passage explicitly states an effect, for example, you may be asked to infer its cause. If the author compares two phenomena, you may be asked to infer the basis for the comparison. You may be asked to infer the characteristics of an old policy from an explicit description of a new one. When you read a passage, therefore, you should concentrate not only on the explicit meaning of the author's words, but also on the more subtle meaning implied by those words.

4. **Questions that ask how information given in a passage can be applied to a context outside the passage itself**

These questions measure your ability to discern the relationships between situations or ideas presented by the author and other situations or ideas that might parallel those in the passage. In this kind of question, you may be asked to identify a hypothetical situation that is comparable to a situation presented in the passage, or to select an example that is similar to an example provided in the passage, or to apply ideas given in the passage to a situation not mentioned by the author, or to recognize ideas that the author would probably agree or disagree with on the basis of statements made in the passage. Unlike inference questions, these questions use ideas or situations *not* taken from the passage. Ideas and situations given in a question are *like* those given in the passage, and they parallel ideas and situations given in the passage. Therefore, to answer the question, you must do more than recall what you read. You must recognize the essential attributes of ideas and situations presented in the passage when they appear in different words and in an entirely new context.

5. **Questions that ask about the logical structure of a passage**

These questions ask you to analyze and evaluate the organization and the logic of a passage. They may ask how a passage is constructed: for instance, does it define, does it compare or contrast, does it present a new idea, does it refute an idea. They may also ask how the author persuades readers to accept his or her assertions, or about the reason behind the author's use of any particular supporting detail. You may also be asked to identify assumptions that the author is making, to assess the strengths and weaknesses of the author's arguments, or to recognize appropriate counterarguments. These questions measure your ability not only to comprehend a passage but to evaluate it critically. However, it is important for you to realize that these questions do not rely on any kind of formal logic, nor do they require that you be familiar with specific terms of logic or argumentation. You can answer these questions using only the information in the passage and careful reasoning.

6. **Questions that ask about the style and tone of a passage**

These questions ask about the language of a passage and about the ideas in a passage that may be expressed through its language. You may be asked to deduce the author's attitude toward an idea, a fact, or a situation from the words that he or she uses to describe it. You may also be asked to select a word that accurately describes the tone of a passage—for instance, ''critical,'' ''questioning,'' ''objective,'' or ''enthusiastic.'' To answer this type of question, you will have to consider the language of the passage as a whole: it takes more than one pointed critical word to make the tone of an entire passage ''critical.'' Sometimes, these questions ask what audience the passage was probably intended for or what type of publication it probably appeared in. Style and tone questions may apply to one small part of the passage or to the passage as a whole. To answer them, you must ask yourself what meanings are contained in the words of a passage beyond their literal meanings. Were such words selected because of their emotional content, or because of their suggestiveness, or because a particular audience would expect to hear them? Remember, these questions measure your ability to discern meaning expressed by the author through his or her choice of words.

Test-Taking Strategies for Reading Comprehension

1. You should not expect to be completely familiar with any of the material presented in Reading Comprehension passages. You may find some passages easier to understand than others, but all passages are designed to present a challenge. If you have some familiarity with the material being presented in a passage, do not let this knowledge influence your choice of answers to the questions. Answer all questions on the basis of what is *stated or implied* in the passage itself.

2. Since the questions require specific and detailed understanding of the material in a passage, analyze each passage carefully the first time you read it. Even if you read at a relatively slow rate, you should be able to read the passages in about 6 minutes and will have about 24 minutes left for answering the questions. You should, of course, be sure to allow sufficient time to work on each passage and its questions. There are other ways of approaching Reading Comprehension passages: some test-takers prefer to skim the passages the first time through or even to read the questions before reading the passages. You should choose the method most suitable for you.

3. Underlining parts of a passage may be helpful to you. Focus on key words and phrases and try to follow exactly the development of separate ideas. In the margins, note where each important idea, argument, or set of related facts begins. Make every effort to avoid losing the sense of what is being discussed. If you become lost, you will have to go back over the material, and that wastes time. Keep the following in mind:

   - Note how each fact relates to an idea or an argument.
   - Note where the passage moves from one idea to the next.
   - Separate main ideas from supporting ideas.
   - Determine what conclusions are reached and why.

4. Read the questions carefully, making certain that you understand what is being asked. An answer choice may be incorrect, even though it accurately restates information given in the passage, if it does not answer the question. If you need to, refer back to the passage for clarification.

5. Read all the choices carefully. Never assume that you have selected the best answer without first reading all the choices.

6. Select the choice that best answers the question in terms of the information given in the passage. Do not rely on outside knowledge of the material for answering the questions.

7. Remember that understanding, not speed, is the critical factor in reading comprehension.

When you take the sample test sections, use the answer spaces on page 171 to mark your answers.

Answer Spaces for Reading Comprehension Sample Test Sections

Sample Test Section 1

1 A B C D E	8 A B C D E	15 A B C D E	22 A B C D E
2 A B C D E	9 A B C D E	16 A B C D E	23 A B C D E
3 A B C D E	10 A B C D E	17 A B C D E	24 A B C D E
4 A B C D E	11 A B C D E	18 A B C D E	25 A B C D E
5 A B C D E	12 A B C D E	19 A B C D E	
6 A B C D E	13 A B C D E	20 A B C D E	
7 A B C D E	14 A B C D E	21 A B C D E	

Sample Test Section 2

1 A B C D E	8 A B C D E	15 A B C D E	22 A B C D E
2 A B C D E	9 A B C D E	16 A B C D E	23 A B C D E
3 A B C D E	10 A B C D E	17 A B C D E	24 A B C D E
4 A B C D E	11 A B C D E	18 A B C D E	25 A B C D E
5 A B C D E	12 A B C D E	19 A B C D E	
6 A B C D E	13 A B C D E	20 A B C D E	
7 A B C D E	14 A B C D E	21 A B C D E	

Sample Test Section 3

1 A B C D E	8 A B C D E	15 A B C D E	22 A B C D E
2 A B C D E	9 A B C D E	16 A B C D E	23 A B C D E
3 A B C D E	10 A B C D E	17 A B C D E	24 A B C D E
4 A B C D E	11 A B C D E	18 A B C D E	25 A B C D E
5 A B C D E	12 A B C D E	19 A B C D E	
6 A B C D E	13 A B C D E	20 A B C D E	
7 A B C D E	14 A B C D E	21 A B C D E	

30 Minutes
25 Questions

Directions: Each passage in this group is followed by questions based on its content. After reading a passage, choose the best answer to each question and fill in the corresponding oval on the answer sheet. Answer all questions following a passage on the basis of what is stated or implied in that passage.

(This passage was written in 1978.)

Recent years have brought minority-owned businesses in the United States unprecedented opportunities—as well as new and significant risks. Civil rights activists have long argued that one of (5) the principal reasons why Blacks, Hispanics, and other minority groups have difficulty establishing themselves in business is that they lack access to the sizable orders and subcontracts that are generated by large companies. Now Congress, in appar- (10) ent agreement, has required by law that businesses awarded federal contracts of more than $500,000 do their best to find minority subcontractors and record their efforts to do so on forms filed with the government. Indeed, some federal and local agen- (15) cies have gone so far as to set specific percentage goals for apportioning parts of public works contracts to minority enterprises.

Corporate response appears to have been substantial. According to figures collected in 1977, (20) the total of corporate contracts with minority businesses rose from $77 million in 1972 to $1.1 billion in 1977. The projected total of corporate contracts with minority businesses for the early 1980's is estimated to be over $3 billion per year with no (25) letup anticipated in the next decade.

Promising as it is for minority businesses, this increased patronage poses dangers for them, too. First, minority firms risk expanding too fast and overextending themselves financially, since most (30) are small concerns and, unlike large businesses, they often need to make substantial investments in new plants, staff, equipment, and the like in order to perform work subcontracted to them. If, thereafter, their subcontracts are for some reason (35) reduced, such firms can face potentially crippling fixed expenses. The world of corporate purchasing can be frustrating for small entrepreneurs who get requests for elaborate formal estimates and bids. Both consume valuable time and resources, and a (40) small company's efforts must soon result in orders, or both the morale and the financial health of the business will suffer.

A second risk is that White-owned companies may seek to cash in on the increasing apportion- (45) ments through formation of joint ventures with minority-owned concerns. Of course, in many instances there are legitimate reasons for joint ventures; clearly, White and minority enterprises can team up to acquire business that neither could (50) acquire alone. But civil rights groups and minority business owners have complained to Congress about minorities being set up as "fronts" with White back-

ing, rather than being accepted as full partners in legitimate joint ventures.
(55) Third, a minority enterprise that secures the business of one large corporate customer often runs the danger of becoming—and remaining—dependent. Even in the best of circumstances, fierce competition from larger, more established companies (60) makes it difficult for small concerns to broaden their customer bases; when such firms have nearly guaranteed orders from a single corporate benefactor, they may truly have to struggle against complacency arising from their current success.

1. The primary purpose of the passage is to

(A) present a commonplace idea and its inaccuracies
(B) describe a situation and its potential drawbacks
(C) propose a temporary solution to a problem
(D) analyze a frequent source of disagreement
(E) explore the implications of a finding

2. The passage supplies information that would answer which of the following questions?

(A) What federal agencies have set percentage goals for the use of minority-owned businesses in public works contracts?
(B) To which government agencies must businesses awarded federal contracts report their efforts to find minority subcontractors?
(C) How widespread is the use of minority-owned concerns as "fronts" by White backers seeking to obtain subcontracts?
(D) How many more minority-owned businesses were there in 1977 than in 1972?
(E) What is one set of conditions under which a small business might find itself financially overextended?

GO ON TO THE NEXT PAGE.

3. According to the passage, civil rights activists maintain that one disadvantage under which minority-owned businesses have traditionally had to labor is that they have

(A) been especially vulnerable to governmental mismanagement of the economy
(B) been denied bank loans at rates comparable to those afforded larger competitors
(C) not had sufficient opportunity to secure business created by large corporations
(D) not been able to advertise in those media that reach large numbers of potential customers
(E) not had adequate representation in the centers of government power

4. The passage suggests that the failure of a large business to have its bids for subcontracts result quickly in orders might cause it to

(A) experience frustration but not serious financial harm
(B) face potentially crippling fixed expenses
(C) have to record its efforts on forms filed with the government
(D) increase its spending with minority subcontractors
(E) revise its procedure for making bids for federal contracts and subcontracts

5. The author implies that a minority-owned concern that does the greater part of its business with one large corporate customer should

(A) avoid competition with larger, more established concerns by not expanding
(B) concentrate on securing even more business from that corporation
(C) try to expand its customer base to avoid becoming dependent on the corporation
(D) pass on some of the work to be done for the corporation to other minority-owned concerns
(E) use its influence with the corporation to promote subcontracting with other minority concerns

6. It can be inferred from the passage that, compared with the requirements of law, the percentage goals set by "some federal and local agencies" (lines 14-15) are

(A) more popular with large corporations
(B) more specific
(C) less controversial
(D) less expensive to enforce
(E) easier to comply with

7. Which of the following, if true, would most weaken the author's assertion that, in the 1970's, corporate response to federal requirements (lines 18-19) was substantial?

(A) Corporate contracts with minority-owned businesses totaled $2 billion in 1979.
(B) Between 1970 and 1972, corporate contracts with minority-owned businesses declined by 25 percent.
(C) The figures collected in 1977 underrepresented the extent of corporate contracts with minority-owned businesses.
(D) The estimate of corporate spending with minority-owned businesses in 1980 is approximately $10 million too high.
(E) The $1.1 billion represented the same percentage of total corporate spending in 1977 as did $77 million in 1972.

8. The author would most likely agree with which of the following statements about corporate response to working with minority subcontractors?

(A) Annoyed by the proliferation of "front" organizations, corporations are likely to reduce their efforts to work with minority-owned subcontractors in the near future.
(B) Although corporations showed considerable interest in working with minority businesses in the 1970's, their aversion to government paperwork made them reluctant to pursue many government contracts.
(C) The significant response of corporations in the 1970's is likely to be sustained and conceivably be increased throughout the 1980's.
(D) Although corporations are eager to cooperate with minority-owned businesses, a shortage of capital in the 1970's made substantial response impossible.
(E) The enormous corporate response has all but eliminated the dangers of overexpansion that used to plague small minority-owned businesses.

GO ON TO THE NEXT PAGE.

Woodrow Wilson was referring to the liberal idea of the economic market when he said that the free enterprise system is the most efficient economic system. Maximum freedom means
(5) maximum productiveness; our "openness" is to be the measure of our stability. Fascination with this ideal has made Americans defy the "Old World" categories of settled possessiveness *versus* unsettling deprivation, the cupidity of retention
(10) *versus* the cupidity of seizure, a "status quo" defended or attacked. The United States, it was believed, had no *status quo ante*. Our only "station" was the turning of a stationary wheel, spinning faster and faster. We did not base our
(15) system on property but opportunity—which meant we based it not on stability but on mobility. The more things changed, that is, the more rapidly the wheel turned, the steadier we would be. The conventional picture of class politics is
(20) composed of the Haves, who want a stability to keep what they have, and the Have-Nots, who want a touch of instability and change in which to scramble for the things they have not. But Americans imagined a condition in which spec-
(25) ulators, self-makers, runners are always using the new opportunities given by our land. These economic leaders (front-runners) would thus be mainly agents of change. The nonstarters were considered the ones who wanted stability, a
(30) strong referee to give them some position in the race, a regulative hand to calm manic speculation; an authority that can call things to a halt, begin things again from compensatorily staggered "starting lines."
(35)   "Reform" in America has been sterile because it can imagine no change except through the extension of this metaphor of a race, wider inclusion of competitors, "a piece of the action," as it were, for the disenfranchised. There is no
(40) attempt to call off the race. Since our only stability is change, America seems not to honor the quiet work that achieves social interdependence and stability. There is, in our legends, no heroism of the office clerk, no stable industrial work
(45) force of the people who actually make the system work. There is no pride in being an employee (Wilson asked for a return to the time when everyone was an employer). There has been no boasting about our social workers—they are
(50) merely signs of the system's failure, of opportunity denied or not taken, of things to be eliminated. We have no pride in our growing interdependence, in the fact that our system can serve others, that we are able to help those in
(55) need; empty boasts from the past make us ashamed of our present achievements, make us

try to forget or deny them, move away from them. There is no honor but in the Wonderland race we must all run, all trying to win, none
(60) winning in the end (for there is no end).

9. The primary purpose of the passage is to

(A) criticize the inflexibility of American economic mythology
(B) contrast "Old World" and "New World" economic ideologies
(C) challenge the integrity of traditional political leaders
(D) champion those Americans whom the author deems to be neglected
(E) suggest a substitute for the traditional metaphor of a race

10. According to the passage, "Old World" values were based on

(A) ability
(B) property
(C) family connections
(D) guild hierarchies
(E) education

11. In the context of the author's discussion of regulating change, which of the following could be most probably regarded as a "strong referee" (line 30) in the United States?

(A) A school principal
(B) A political theorist
(C) A federal court judge
(D) A social worker
(E) A government inspector

12. The author sets off the word " 'Reform' " (line 35) with quotation marks in order to

(A) emphasize its departure from the concept of settled possessiveness
(B) show his support for a systematic program of change
(C) underscore the flexibility and even amorphousness of United States society
(D) indicate that the term was one of Wilson's favorites
(E) assert that reform in the United States has not been fundamental

GO ON TO THE NEXT PAGE.

13. It can be inferred from the passage that the author most probably thinks that giving the disenfranchised " 'a piece of the action' " (line 38) is

   (A) a compassionate, if misdirected, legislative measure
   (B) an example of Americans' resistance to profound social change
   (C) an innovative program for genuine social reform
   (D) a monument to the efforts of industrial reformers
   (E) a surprisingly "Old World" remedy for social ills

14. Which of the following metaphors could the author most appropriately use to summarize his own assessment of the American economic system (lines 35-60)?

   (A) A windmill
   (B) A waterfall
   (C) A treadmill
   (D) A gyroscope
   (E) A bellows

15. It can be inferred from the passage that Woodrow Wilson's ideas about the economic market

   (A) encouraged those who "make the system work" (lines 45-46)
   (B) perpetuated traditional legends about America
   (C) revealed the prejudices of a man born wealthy
   (D) foreshadowed the stock market crash of 1929
   (E) began a tradition of presidential proclamations on economics

16. The passage contains information that would answer which of the following questions?

   I. What techniques have industrialists used to manipulate a free market?
   II. In what ways are "New World" and "Old World" economic policies similar?
   III. Has economic policy in the United States tended to reward independent action?

   (A) I only
   (B) II only
   (C) III only
   (D) I and II only
   (E) II and III only

17. Which of the following best expresses the author's main point?

   (A) Americans' pride in their jobs continues to give them stamina today.
   (B) The absence of a *status quo ante* has undermined United States economic structure.
   (C) The free enterprise system has been only a useless concept in the United States.
   (D) The myth of the American free enterprise system is seriously flawed.
   (E) Fascination with the ideal of "openness" has made Americans a progressive people.

GO ON TO THE NEXT PAGE.

-176-

No very satisfactory account of the mechanism that caused the formation of the ocean basins has yet been given. The traditional view supposes that the upper mantle of the earth behaves as a

(5) liquid when it is subjected to small forces for long periods and that differences in temperature under oceans and continents are sufficient to produce convection in the mantle of the earth with rising convection currents under the mid-

(10) ocean ridges and sinking currents under the continents. Theoretically, this convection would carry the continental plates along as though they were on a conveyor belt and would provide the forces needed to produce the split that occurs

(15) along the ridge. This view may be correct; it has the advantage that the currents are driven by temperature differences that themselves depend on the position of the continents. Such a back-coupling, in which the position of the moving

(20) plate has an impact on the forces that move it, could produce complicated and varying motions.

On the other hand, the theory is implausible because convection does not normally occur along lines, and it certainly does not occur along

(25) lines broken by frequent offsets or changes in direction, as the ridge is. Also it is difficult to see how the theory applies to the plate between the Mid-Atlantic Ridge and the ridge in the Indian Ocean. This plate is growing on both sides, and

(30) since there is no intermediate trench, the two ridges must be moving apart. It would be odd if the rising convection currents kept exact pace with them. An alternative theory is that the sinking part of the plate, which is denser than the

(35) hotter surrounding mantle, pulls the rest of the plate after it. Again it is difficult to see how this applies to the ridge in the South Atlantic, where neither the African nor the American plate has a sinking part.

(40) Another possibility is that the sinking plate cools the neighboring mantle and produces convection currents that move the plates. This last theory is attractive because it gives some hope of explaining the enclosed seas, such as the Sea of

(45) Japan. These seas have a typical oceanic floor, except that the floor is overlaid by several kilometers of sediment. Their floors have probably been sinking for long periods. It seems possible that a sinking current of cooled mantle material

(50) on the upper side of the plate might be the cause of such deep basins. The enclosed seas are an important feature of the earth's surface and seriously require explanation because, in addition to the enclosed seas that are developing at

(55) present behind island arcs, there are a number of older ones of possibly similar origin, such as the Gulf of Mexico, the Black Sea, and perhaps the North Sea.

18. According to the traditional view of the origin of the ocean basins, which of the following is sufficient to move the continental plates?

(A) Increases in sedimentation on ocean floors
(B) Spreading of ocean trenches
(C) Movement of mid-ocean ridges
(D) Sinking of ocean basins
(E) Differences in temperature under oceans and continents

19. It can be inferred from the passage that, of the following, the deepest sediments would be found in the

(A) Indian Ocean
(B) Black Sea
(C) Mid-Atlantic
(D) South Atlantic
(E) Pacific

20. The author refers to a "conveyor belt" in line 13 in order to

(A) illustrate the effects of convection in the mantle
(B) show how temperature differences depend on the positions of the continents
(C) demonstrate the linear nature of the Mid-Atlantic Ridge
(D) describe the complicated motions made possible by back-coupling
(E) account for the rising currents under certain mid-ocean ridges

21. The author regards the traditional view of the origin of the oceans with

(A) slight apprehension
(B) absolute indifference
(C) indignant anger
(D) complete disbelief
(E) guarded skepticism

GO ON TO THE NEXT PAGE.

22. According to the passage, which of the following are separated by a plate that is growing on both sides?

(A) The Pacific Ocean and the Sea of Japan
(B) The South Atlantic Ridge and the North Sea Ridge
(C) The Gulf of Mexico and the South Atlantic Ridge
(D) The Mid-Atlantic Ridge and the Indian Ocean Ridge
(E) The Black Sea and the Sea of Japan

23. Which of the following, if it could be demonstrated, would most support the traditional view of ocean formation?

(A) Convection usually occurs along lines.
(B) The upper mantle behaves as a dense solid.
(C) Sedimentation occurs at a constant rate.
(D) Sinking plates cool the mantle.
(E) Island arcs surround enclosed seas.

24. According to the passage, the floor of the Black Sea can best be compared to a

(A) rapidly moving conveyor belt
(B) slowly settling foundation
(C) rapidly expanding balloon
(D) violently erupting volcano
(E) slowly eroding mountain

25. Which of the following titles would best describe the content of the passage?

(A) A Description of the Oceans of the World
(B) Several Theories of Ocean Basin Formation
(C) The Traditional View of the Oceans
(D) Convection and Ocean Currents
(E) Temperature Differences Among the Oceans of the World

S T O P

IF YOU FINISH BEFORE TIME IS CALLED, YOU MAY CHECK YOUR WORK ON THIS SECTION ONLY.
DO NOT TURN TO ANY OTHER SECTION IN THE TEST.

Answer Key for Sample Test Section 1

READING COMPREHENSION

1. B	14. C
2. E	15. B
3. C	16. C
4. A	17. D
5. C	18. E
6. B	19. B
7. E	20. A
8. C	21. E
9. A	22. D
10. B	23. A
11. C	24. B
12. E	25. B
13. B	

Explanatory Material: Reading Comprehension

The following discussion of Reading Comprehension is intended to familiarize you with the most efficient and effective approaches to the kinds of problems common to Reading Comprehension. The particular questions on the sample test sections in this chapter are generally representative of the kinds of questions you will encounter in this section of the GMAT. Remember that it is the problem-solving strategy that is important, not the specific details of a particular question.

Sample Test Section 1

1. The primary purpose of the passage is to

    (A) present a commonplace idea and its inaccuracies
    (B) describe a situation and its potential drawbacks
    (C) propose a temporary solution to a problem
    (D) analyze a frequent source of disagreement
    (E) explore the implications of a finding

The best answer is B. The author begins by describing in the first two paragraphs the new opportunities for minority-owned businesses in the United States engendered by changes in federal law. The author then goes on in the last three paragraphs to point out three specific risks for minority-owned businesses posed by the new federal laws. Thus a situation is described and the drawbacks that it might entail are suggested.

2. The passage supplies information that would answer which of the following questions?

    (A) What federal agencies have set percentage goals for the use of minority-owned businesses in public works contracts?
    (B) To which government agencies must businesses awarded federal contracts report their efforts to find minority subcontractors?
    (C) How widespread is the use of minority-owned concerns as "fronts" by White backers seeking to obtain subcontracts?
    (D) How many more minority-owned businesses were there in 1977 than in 1972?
    (E) What is one set of conditions under which a small business might find itself financially overextended?

The best answer is E. Choices A and B can be eliminated because the passage mentions only "some federal and local agencies" (lines 14-15), not any specific ones. C and D can be eliminated because no specific data are provided about minority-owned firms except in the area of the value of their corporate contracts. Only E is clearly answered by the passage; the author describes in lines 33-36 the possibility of a reduction in subcontracts leaving a small business that had just expanded (lines 28-33) financially overextended.

3. According to the passage, civil rights activists maintain that one disadvantage under which minority-owned businesses have traditionally had to labor is that they have

    (A) been especially vulnerable to governmental mismanagement of the economy
    (B) been denied bank loans at rates comparable to those afforded larger competitors
    (C) not had sufficient opportunity to secure business created by large corporations
    (D) not been able to advertise in those media that reach large numbers of potential customers
    (E) not had adequate representation in the centers of government power

The best answer is C because lines 4-9 state that civil rights activists have long argued that a problem for members of minority groups who are attempting to establish businesses has been that minority groups "lack access to the sizable orders and subcontracts that are generated by large companies."

4. The passage suggests that the failure of a large business to have its bids for subcontracts result quickly in orders might cause it to

(A) experience frustration but not serious financial harm
(B) face potentially crippling fixed expenses
(C) have to record its efforts on forms filed with the government
(D) increase its spending with minority subcontractors
(E) revise its procedure for making bids for federal contracts and subcontracts

The best answer is A. In lines 28-36 the author points out that small businesses might have to make substantial new investments to meet the demands of a large subcontract, and that small businesses could thus "face potentially crippling fixed expenses." Large businesses, the author suggests in line 30, would not have to make such investments, and therefore would not face serious financial consequences. In lines 39-42 the author notes that if a company is small, it must get orders quickly, or "the financial health of the business will suffer." Thus, although any firm would suffer if it did not receive orders for subcontracts quickly, only small firms facing large fixed expenses would experience serious financial harm. Large firms do not face or can handle these expenses.

5. The author implies that a minority-owned concern that does the greater part of its business with one large corporate customer should

(A) avoid competition with larger, more established concerns by not expanding
(B) concentrate on securing even more business from that corporation
(C) try to expand its customer base to avoid becoming dependent on the corporation
(D) pass on some of the work to be done for the corporation to other minority-owned concerns
(E) use its influence with the corporation to promote subcontracting with other minority concerns

The best answer is C. The passage states in lines 55-57 that becoming dependent on one large corporate customer constitutes a "danger" for a minority enterprise. It is then noted in lines 58-64 that it is "difficult for small concerns to broaden their customer bases" even at the best of times, but that it is important that they "struggle against complacency." Thus, the author implies that a minority firm should attempt to escape the danger of dependency on a single corporate customer, and that in order to do so such a firm must try to expand its customer base.

6. It can be inferred from the passage that, compared with the requirements of law, the percentage goals set by "some federal and local agencies" (lines 14-15) are

(A) more popular with large corporations
(B) more specific
(C) less controversial
(D) less expensive to enforce
(E) easier to comply with

The best answer is B. Lines 9-14 state that the law mandates that businesses simply "do their best" to use minority subcontractors and report their efforts to the federal government. In contrast, the author notes in lines 14-17 that some federal and local agencies have gone much further, "so far as to set specific percentage goals." Thus, it can be inferred that the author considers the percentage goals of the federal and local agencies to be more specific than the more general requirements of federal law.

7. Which of the following, if true, would most weaken the author's assertion that, in the 1970's, corporate response to federal requirements (lines 18-19) was substantial?

(A) Corporate contracts with minority-owned businesses totaled $2 billion in 1979.
(B) Between 1970 and 1972, corporate contracts with minority-owned businesses declined by 25 percent.
(C) The figures collected in 1977 underrepresented the extent of corporate contracts with minority-owned businesses.
(D) The estimate of corporate spending with minority-owned businesses in 1980 is approximately $10 million too high.
(E) The $1.1 billion represented the same percentage of total corporate spending in 1977 as did $77 million in 1972.

The best answer is E. The author's assertion that, in the 1970's, the corporate response to federal requirements was substantial rests on the fact that "corporate contracts with minority businesses rose from $77 million in 1972 to $1.1 billion in 1977" (lines 20-22). The author's claim that such a rise indicates a substantial corporate response to federal requirements would be weakened if other factors were at work. Such a condition is presented only in choice E, where it is stated that the percentage of corporate spending remained constant; this implies that the increased dollar amount allocated to minority businesses was due simply to general economic growth, and that minority businesses proportionally gained nothing during those years.

8. The author would most likely agree with which of the following statements about corporate response to working with minority subcontractors?

(A) Annoyed by the proliferation of "front" organizations, corporations are likely to reduce their efforts to work with minority-owned subcontractors in the near future.

(B) Although corporations showed considerable interest in working with minority businesses in the 1970's, their aversion to government paperwork made them reluctant to pursue many government contracts.

(C) The significant response of corporations in the 1970's is likely to be sustained and conceivably be increased throughout the 1980's.

(D) Although corporations are eager to cooperate with minority-owned businesses, a shortage of capital in the 1970's made substantial response impossible.

(E) The enormous corporate response has all but eliminated the dangers of overexpansion that used to plague small minority-owned businesses.

The best answer is C, because the author states in lines 22-25 that "no letup [is] anticipated" in the projected total of corporate contracts with minority businesses throughout the next decade. There is no support in the passage for any of the other choices.

9. The primary purpose of the passage is to

(A) criticize the inflexibility of American economic mythology

(B) contrast "Old World" and "New World" economic ideologies

(C) challenge the integrity of traditional political leaders

(D) champion those Americans whom the author deems to be neglected

(E) suggest a substitute for the traditional metaphor of a race

The best answer is A. The passage is structured so that the first paragraph sets out the basic issue to be explored—the nature of the dominant economic mythology in America—and the second paragraph provides the actual purpose of the passage—the presentation of a sharp critique of this mythology. In particular, lines 35-60 describe this mythology as resulting in sterile reform, not permitting change in the race metaphor, not honoring quiet work or social work or interdependence, and not valuing present achievements. Choice B is incorrect because the passage focuses mainly on the "New World" ideologies; C is incorrect because no one's integrity is challenged; D is only a supporting point; and E does not appear in the passage.

10. According to the passage, "Old World" values were based on

(A) ability
(B) property
(C) family connections
(D) guild hierarchies
(E) education

The best answer is B. In lines 6-11, "the 'Old World' categories of settled possessiveness" and "the cupidity of retention" are contrasted with the American categories of "unsettling deprivation" and "the cupidity of seizure." This contrast is continued in lines 14-17: "We did not base our system on property but opportunity." All of these references state or imply that property was the basis for "Old World" values.

11. In the context of the author's discussion of regulating change, which of the following could be most probably regarded as a "strong referee" (line 30) in the United States?

(A) A school principal
(B) A political theorist
(C) A federal court judge
(D) A social worker
(E) A government inspector

The best answer is C. Lines 31-34 describe the "strong referee" mentioned in the question as "a regulative hand to calm manic speculation; an authority that can call things to a halt, begin things again from compensatorily staggered 'starting lines.' " Of the choices, only C has sufficient and appropriate authority to satisfy this description.

12. The author sets off the word " 'Reform' " (line 35) with quotation marks in order to

(A) emphasize its departure from the concept of settled possessiveness

(B) show his support for a systematic program of change

(C) underscore the flexibility and even amorphousness of United States society

(D) indicate that the term was one of Wilson's favorites

(E) assert that reform in the United States has not been fundamental

The best answer is E. Lines 35-39 assert that "reform" has been "sterile because it can imagine no change" except in the terms already described by the passage. Since it is the entire thrust of the second paragraph that the race metaphor is the problem, "reform" that accepts this metaphor can in no way solve the underlying problem. The author signals this point by setting the word "reform" off with quotation marks.

13. It can be inferred from the passage that the author most probably thinks that giving the disenfranchised " 'a piece of the action' " (line 38) is

(A) a compassionate, if misdirected, legislative measure
(B) an example of Americans' resistance to profound social change
(C) an innovative program for genuine social reform
(D) a monument to the efforts of industrial reformers
(E) a surprisingly "Old World" remedy for social ills

The best answer is B. The author implies, in lines 35-39, that Americans will not permit fundamental reform (i.e., social change); they will permit only sterile "reform," such as giving the disenfranchised "a piece of the action." Thus, giving the disenfranchised "a piece of the action" is, for the author, an example of Americans' resistance to profound social change.

14. Which of the following metaphors could the author most appropriately use to summarize his own assessment of the American economic system (lines 35-60)?

(A) A windmill
(B) A waterfall
(C) A treadmill
(D) A gyroscope
(E) A bellows

The best answer is C. The author states in lines 58-60 that "There is no honor but in the Wonderland race we must all run, all trying to win, none winning in the end (for there is no end)." Of the choices given, only a treadmill fits this description of people running without end.

15. It can be inferred from the passage that Woodrow Wilson's ideas about the economic market

(A) encouraged those who "make the system work" (lines 45-46)
(B) perpetuated traditional legends about America
(C) revealed the prejudices of a man born wealthy
(D) foreshadowed the stock market crash of 1929
(E) began a tradition of presidential proclamations on economics

The best answer is B. Woodrow Wilson's ideas about the economic market are mentioned in lines 1-4 and lines 47-48. Both appear in contexts that imply that Wilson's ideas are consistent with the "legends" (line 43) that Americans have traditionally held about their economic system. This is especially evident in lines 46-48, where it is noted that Wilson called specifically for "a return to the time when everyone was an employer," which corresponds to the legend that "There is no pride in being an employee." In articulating ideas such as these, Wilson was perpetuating traditional legends about America.

16. The passage contains information that would answer which of the following questions?

   I. What techniques have industrialists used to manipulate a free market?
   II. In what ways are "New World" and "Old World" economic policies similar?
   III. Has economic policy in the United States tended to reward independent action?

(A) I only
(B) II only
(C) III only
(D) I and II only
(E) II and III only

The best answer is C. Question I can be eliminated because the passage never mentions specific techniques of manipulation. Question II can be eliminated because the passage discusses only differences between the "Old World" and the American economic systems, not similarities. Question III can be answered on the basis of information contained in the passage. Lines 40-43 indicate that America is a land of change where "work that achieves social interdependence and stability" is not honored. What is honored is that which promotes constant change, the work of speculators, self-makers, and runners who consistently respond to new opportunities (lines 24-28). Thus those who are rewarded by the American economic system, according to the passage, are those who act independently.

17. Which of the following best expresses the author's main point?

(A) Americans' pride in their jobs continues to give them stamina today.
(B) The absence of a *status quo ante* has undermined United States economic structure.
(C) The free enterprise system has been only a useless concept in the United States.
(D) The myth of the American free enterprise system is seriously flawed.
(E) Fascination with the ideal of "openness" has made Americans a progressive people.

The best answer is D. The first paragraph compares Americans' ideas concerning their own economic system with "Old World" beliefs and provides a basis for criticism of the American view in the second paragraph. Thus, the main point of the passage is that the "myth" described in the first paragraph is "seriously flawed," as shown in the second paragraph. Choice A does not describe a point made in the passage. Choice B inaccurately states a point made in the passage. Choice C is an overstatement and does not articulate the idea of "myth" as it is developed in the first paragraph. Choice E does not convey the criticism that is the concern of the second paragraph.

18. According to the traditional view of the origin of the ocean basins, which of the following is sufficient to move the continental plates?

    (A) Increases in sedimentation on ocean floors
    (B) Spreading of ocean trenches
    (C) Movement of mid-ocean ridges
    (D) Sinking of ocean basins
    (E) Differences in temperature under oceans and continents

The best answer is E. The traditional view of the origin of the ocean basins is described in lines 3-21. Lines 6-7 state that, according to the traditional view, "differences in temperature under oceans and continents are sufficient to produce convection in the mantle of the earth." Lines 11-13 state that, according to the traditional view, "this convection would carry the continental plates along as though they were on a conveyor belt." Thus, it can be inferred that the temperature differences are sufficient to move the continental plates, according to the traditional view.

19. It can be inferred from the passage that, of the following, the deepest sediments would be found in the

    (A) Indian Ocean
    (B) Black Sea
    (C) Mid-Atlantic
    (D) South Atlantic
    (E) Pacific

The best answer is B. Lines 42-58 discuss the enclosed seas, describing them in lines 45-47 as having "a typical oceanic floor, except that the floor is overlaid by several kilometers of sediment." From this it can be inferred that seas that are not enclosed do not have deep sediments on their floors. Of the choices, only the Black Sea is mentioned in the passage as an enclosed sea (lines 51-57). Therefore, it can be inferred that, of the five choices, the Black Sea has the deepest sediments.

20. The author refers to a "conveyor belt" in line 13 in order to

    (A) illustrate the effects of convection in the mantle
    (B) show how temperature differences depend on the positions of the continents
    (C) demonstrate the linear nature of the Mid-Atlantic Ridge
    (D) describe the complicated motions made possible by back-coupling
    (E) account for the rising currents under certain mid-ocean ridges

The best answer is A because "as though they were on a conveyor belt" in lines 12-13 refers to the manner in which convection in the mantle carries the continental plates along. The "conveyor belt" image enables the author to illustrate the effects of convection.

21. The author regards the traditional view of the origin of the oceans with

    (A) slight apprehension
    (B) absolute indifference
    (C) indignant anger
    (D) complete disbelief
    (E) guarded skepticism

The best answer is E. Throughout the passage, the author refers to the traditional view of the origin of the oceans in terms that indicate a cautious and doubtful but not totally disbelieving attitude. Lines 1-3 state, "No very satisfactory account of the mechanism that caused the formation of the ocean basins has yet been given." Line 15 says, "This view may be correct." Lines 22-23 say, "On the other hand, the theory is implausible because. . . ." Lines 26-27 add, "Also it is difficult to see how. . . ." Line 31 says, "It would be odd if. . . ." Taken together, these references convey an attitude of guarded skepticism, though not complete disbelief, toward the traditional view.

22. According to the passage, which of the following are separated by a plate that is growing on both sides?

    (A) The Pacific Ocean and the Sea of Japan
    (B) The South Atlantic Ridge and the North Sea Ridge
    (C) The Gulf of Mexico and the South Atlantic Ridge
    (D) The Mid-Atlantic Ridge and the Indian Ocean Ridge
    (E) The Black Sea and the Sea of Japan

The best answer is D because lines 27-29 mention "the plate between the Mid-Atlantic Ridge and the ridge in the Indian Ocean," and line 29 then refers to it, stating, "This plate is growing on both sides."

23. Which of the following, if it could be demonstrated, would most support the traditional view of ocean formation?

    (A) Convection usually occurs along lines.
    (B) The upper mantle behaves as a dense solid.
    (C) Sedimentation occurs at a constant rate.
    (D) Sinking plates cool the mantle.
    (E) Island arcs surround enclosed seas.

The best answer is A. If it could be demonstrated that convection usually occurs along lines, the objection to the traditional view that is stated in lines 22-24 would be removed, and the traditional view's assumptions about the way in which convection occurs would be supported. The other choices either contradict the traditional view (and thus would weaken it) or are irrelevant to it.

24. According to the passage, the floor of the Black Sea can best be compared to a

(A) rapidly moving conveyor belt
(B) slowly settling foundation
(C) rapidly expanding balloon
(D) violently erupting volcano
(E) slowly eroding mountain

The best answer is B. Lines 53-57 indicate that the Black Sea is an enclosed sea, and lines 47-48 state that the floors of enclosed seas "have probably been sinking for long periods." Thus it can be inferred that the floor of the Black Sea has been slowly settling. Since the floor of an ocean supports water in the same general way that the foundation of a building supports a building, the floor of the Black Sea can be compared to a slowly settling foundation. The passage provides no support for the comparisons in the other choices.

25. Which of the following titles would best describe the content of the passage?

(A) A Description of the Oceans of the World
(B) Several Theories of Ocean Basin Formation
(C) The Traditional View of the Oceans
(D) Convection and Ocean Currents
(E) Temperature Differences Among the Oceans of the World

The best answer is B. The passage discusses three theories of ocean basin formation—the "traditional view" in lines 1-33, an "alternative theory" in lines 33-39, and a third theory in lines 42-58. These theories are the focus of the passage and constitute its entire content. Therefore, B is an excellent description of the content of the passage. Choice A is incorrect because the passage describes only a few oceans of the world and then only peripherally. Choice C is too narrow, leaving out two of the theories. Choices D and E refer to only small portions of the passage's content.

30 Minutes
25 Questions

Directions: Each passage in this group is followed by questions based on its content. After reading a passage, choose the best answer to each question and fill in the corresponding oval on the answer sheet. Answer all questions following a passage on the basis of what is stated or implied in that passage.

The fossil remains of the first flying vertebrates, the pterosaurs, have intrigued paleontologists for more than two centuries. How such large creatures, which weighed in some cases as much as a piloted hang-glider and had wingspans from 8 to 12 meters, solved the problems of powered flight, and exactly what these creatures were—reptiles or birds—are among the questions scientists have puzzled over.

Perhaps the least controversial assertion about the pterosaurs is that they were reptiles. Their skulls, pelvises, and hind feet are reptilian. The anatomy of their wings suggests that they did not evolve into the class of birds. In pterosaurs a greatly elongated fourth finger of each forelimb supported a winglike membrane. The other fingers were short and reptilian, with sharp claws. In birds the second finger is the principal strut of the wing, which consists primarily of feathers. If the pterosaurs walked on all fours, the three short fingers may have been employed for grasping. When a pterosaur walked or remained stationary, the fourth finger, and with it the wing, could only turn upward in an extended inverted V-shape along each side of the animal's body.

The pterosaurs resembled both birds and bats in their overall structure and proportions. This is not surprising because the design of any flying vertebrate is subject to aerodynamic constraints. Both the pterosaurs and the birds have hollow bones, a feature that represents a savings in weight. In the birds, however, these bones are reinforced more massively by internal struts.

Although scales typically cover reptiles, the pterosaurs probably had hairy coats. T.H. Huxley reasoned that flying vertebrates must have been warm-blooded because flying implies a high rate of metabolism, which in turn implies a high internal temperature. Huxley speculated that a coat of hair would insulate against loss of body heat and might streamline the body to reduce drag in flight. The recent discovery of a pterosaur specimen covered in long, dense, and relatively thick hairlike fossil material was the first clear evidence that his reasoning was correct.

Efforts to explain how the pterosaurs became airborne have led to suggestions that they launched themselves by jumping from cliffs, by dropping from trees, or even by rising into light winds from the crests of waves. Each hypothesis has its difficulties. The first wrongly assumes that the pterosaurs' hind feet resembled a bat's and could serve as hooks by which the animal could hang in preparation for flight. The second hypothesis seems unlikely because large pterosaurs could not have landed in trees without damaging their wings. The third calls for high waves to channel updrafts. The wind that made such waves however, might have been too strong for the pterosaurs to control their flight once airborne.

1. It can be inferred from the passage that scientists now generally agree that the

(A) enormous wingspan of the pterosaurs enabled them to fly great distances
(B) structure of the skeleton of the pterosaurs suggests a close evolutionary relationship to bats
(C) fossil remains of the pterosaurs reveal how they solved the problem of powered flight
(D) pterosaurs were reptiles
(E) pterosaurs walked on all fours

2. The author views the idea that the pterosaurs became airborne by rising into light winds created by waves as

(A) revolutionary
(B) unlikely
(C) unassailable
(D) probable
(E) outdated

3. According to the passage, the skeleton of a pterosaur can be distinguished from that of a bird by the

(A) size of its wingspan
(B) presence of hollow spaces in its bones
(C) anatomic origin of its wing strut
(D) presence of hooklike projections on its hind feet
(E) location of the shoulder joint joining the wing to its body

GO ON TO THE NEXT PAGE.

4. The ideas attributed to T.H. Huxley in the passage suggest that he would most likely agree with which of the following statements?

   (A) An animal's brain size has little bearing on its ability to master complex behaviors.
   (B) An animal's appearance is often influenced by environmental requirements and physical capabilities.
   (C) Animals within a given family group are unlikely to change their appearance dramatically over a period of time.
   (D) The origin of flight in vertebrates was an accidental development rather than the outcome of specialization or adaptation.
   (E) The pterosaurs should be classified as birds, not reptiles.

5. It can be inferred from the passage that which of the following is characteristic of the pterosaurs?

   (A) They were unable to fold their wings when not in use.
   (B) They hung upside down from branches as bats do before flight.
   (C) They flew in order to capture prey.
   (D) They were an early stage in the evolution of the birds.
   (E) They lived primarily in a forestlike habitat.

6. Which of the following best describes the organization of the last paragraph of the passage?

   (A) New evidence is introduced to support a traditional point of view.
   (B) Three explanations for a phenomenon are presented, and each is disputed by means of specific information.
   (C) Three hypotheses are outlined, and evidence supporting each is given.
   (D) Recent discoveries are described, and their implications for future study are projected.
   (E) A summary of the material in the preceding paragraphs is presented, and conclusions are drawn.

7. It can be inferred from the passage that some scientists believe that pterosaurs

   (A) lived near large bodies of water
   (B) had sharp teeth for tearing food
   (C) were attacked and eaten by larger reptiles
   (D) had longer tails than many birds
   (E) consumed twice their weight daily to maintain their body temperature

GO ON TO THE NEXT PAGE.

How many really suffer as a result of labor market problems? This is one of the most critical yet contentious social policy questions. In many ways, our social statistics exaggerate the degree of hard-
(5) ship. Unemployment does not have the same dire consequences today as it did in the 1930's when most of the unemployed were primary breadwinners, when income and earnings were usually much closer to the margin of subsistence, and when there
(10) were no countervailing social programs for those failing in the labor market. Increasing affluence, the rise of families with more than one wage earner, the growing predominance of secondary earners among the unemployed, and improved social welfare pro-
(15) tection have unquestionably mitigated the consequences of joblessness. Earnings and income data also overstate the dimensions of hardship. Among the millions with hourly earnings at or below the minimum wage level, the overwhelming majority
(20) are from multiple-earner, relatively affluent families. Most of those counted by the poverty statistics are elderly or handicapped or have family responsibilities which keep them out of the labor force, so the poverty statistics are by no means an
(25) accurate indicator of labor market pathologies.

Yet there are also many ways our social statistics underestimate the degree of labor-market-related hardship. The unemployment counts exclude the millions of fully employed workers whose wages are
(30) so low that their families remain in poverty. Low wages and repeated or prolonged unemployment frequently interact to undermine the capacity for self-support. Since the number experiencing jobless-ness at some time during the year is several times
(35) the number unemployed in any month, those who suffer as a result of forced idleness can equal or exceed average annual unemployment, even though only a minority of the jobless in any month really suffer. For every person counted in the monthly
(40) unemployment tallies, there is another working part-time because of the inability to find full-time work, or else outside the labor force but wanting a job. Finally, income transfers in our country have always focused on the elderly, disabled, and depen-
(45) dent, neglecting the needs of the working poor, so that the dramatic expansion of cash and in-kind transfers does not necessarily mean that those failing in the labor market are adequately protected.

As a result of such contradictory evidence, it is
(50) uncertain whether those suffering seriously as a result of labor market problems number in the hundreds of thousands or the tens of millions, and, hence, whether high levels of joblessness can be tolerated or must be countered by job creation and
(55) economic stimulus. There is only one area of agreement in this debate—that the existing poverty, employment, and earnings statistics are inadequate for one of their primary applications, measuring the consequences of labor market problems.

8. Which of the following is the principal topic of the passage?

(A) What causes labor market pathologies that result in suffering
(B) Why income measures are imprecise in measuring degrees of poverty
(C) Which of the currently used statistical procedures are the best for estimating the incidence of hardship that is due to unemployment
(D) Where the areas of agreement are among poverty, employment, and earnings figures
(E) How social statistics give an unclear picture of the degree of hardship caused by low wages and insufficient employment opportunities

9. The author uses "labor market problems" in lines 1-2 to refer to which of the following?

(A) The overall causes of poverty
(B) Deficiencies in the training of the work force
(C) Trade relationships among producers of goods
(D) Shortages of jobs providing adequate income
(E) Strikes and inadequate supplies of labor

10. The author contrasts the 1930's with the present in order to show that

(A) more people were unemployed in the 1930's
(B) unemployment now has less severe effects
(C) social programs are more needed now
(D) there now is a greater proportion of elderly and handicapped people among those in poverty
(E) poverty has increased since the 1930's

GO ON TO THE NEXT PAGE.

11. Which of the following proposals best responds to the issues raised by the author?

   (A) Innovative programs using multiple approaches should be set up to reduce the level of unemployment.
   (B) A compromise should be found between the positions of those who view joblessness as an evil greater than economic control and those who hold the opposite view.
   (C) New statistical indices should be developed to measure the degree to which unemployment and inadequately paid employment cause suffering.
   (D) Consideration should be given to the ways in which statistics can act as partial causes of the phenomena that they purport to measure.
   (E) The labor force should be restructured so that it corresponds to the range of job vacancies.

12. The author's purpose in citing those who are repeatedly unemployed during a twelve-month period is most probably to show that

   (A) there are several factors that cause the payment of low wages to some members of the labor force
   (B) unemployment statistics can underestimate the hardship resulting from joblessness
   (C) recurrent inadequacies in the labor market can exist and can cause hardships for individual workers
   (D) a majority of those who are jobless at any one time do not suffer severe hardship
   (E) there are fewer individuals who are without jobs at some time during a year than would be expected on the basis of monthly unemployment figures

13. The author states that the mitigating effect of social programs involving income transfers on the income level of low-income people is often not felt by

   (A) the employed poor
   (B) dependent children in single-earner families
   (C) workers who become disabled
   (D) retired workers
   (E) full-time workers who become unemployed

14. According to the passage, one factor that causes unemployment and earnings figures to overpredict the amount of economic hardship is the

   (A) recurrence of periods of unemployment for a group of low-wage workers
   (B) possibility that earnings may be received from more than one job per worker
   (C) fact that unemployment counts do not include those who work for low wages and remain poor
   (D) establishment of a system of record-keeping that makes it possible to compile poverty statistics
   (E) prevalence, among low-wage workers and the unemployed, of members of families in which others are employed

15. The conclusion stated in lines 33-39 about the number of people who suffer as a result of forced idleness depends primarily on the point that

   (A) in times of high unemployment, there are some people who do not remain unemployed for long
   (B) the capacity for self-support depends on receiving moderate-to-high wages
   (C) those in forced idleness include, besides the unemployed, both underemployed part-time workers and those not actively seeking work
   (D) at different times during the year, different people are unemployed
   (E) many of those who are affected by unemployment are dependents of unemployed workers

16. Which of the following, if true, is the best criticism of the author's argument concerning why poverty statistics cannot properly be used to show the effects of problems in the labor market?

   (A) A short-term increase in the number of those in poverty can indicate a shortage of jobs, because the basic number of those unable to accept employment remains approximately constant.
   (B) For those who are in poverty as a result of joblessness, there are social programs available that provide a minimum standard of living.
   (C) Poverty statistics do not consistently agree with earnings statistics, when each is taken as a measure of hardship resulting from unemployment.
   (D) The elderly and handicapped categories include many who previously were employed in the labor market.
   (E) Since the labor market is global in nature, poor workers in one country are competing with poor workers in another with respect to the level of wages and the existence of jobs.

GO ON TO THE NEXT PAGE.

In the eighteenth century, Japan's feudal overlords, from the shogun to the humblest samurai, found themselves under financial stress. In part, this stress can be attributed to (5) the overlords' failure to adjust to a rapidly expanding economy, but the stress was also due to factors beyond the overlords' control. Concentration of the samurai in castle-towns had acted as a stimulus to trade. Commercial efficiency, in (10) turn, had put temptations in the way of buyers. Since most samurai had been reduced to idleness by years of peace, encouraged to engage in scholarship and martial exercises or to perform administrative tasks that took little time, it is (15) not surprising that their tastes and habits grew expensive. Overlords' income, despite the increase in rice production among their tenant farmers, failed to keep pace with their expenses. Although shortfalls in overlords' income re- (20) sulted almost as much from laxity among their tax collectors (the nearly inevitable outcome of hereditary officeholding) as from their higher standards of living, a misfortune like a fire or flood, bringing an increase in expenses or a drop (25) in revenue, could put a domain in debt to the city rice-brokers who handled its finances. Once in debt, neither the individual samurai nor the shogun himself found it easy to recover.

It was difficult for individual samurai over- (30) lords to increase their income because the amount of rice that farmers could be made to pay in taxes was not unlimited, and since the income of Japan's central government consisted in part of taxes collected by the shogun from his (35) huge domain, the government too was constrained. Therefore, the Tokugawa shoguns began to look to other sources for revenue. Cash profits from government-owned mines were already on the decline because the most (40) easily worked deposits of silver and gold had been exhausted, although debasement of the coinage had compensated for the loss. Opening up new farmland was a possibility, but most of what was suitable had already been exploited (45) and further reclamation was technically unfeasible. Direct taxation of the samurai themselves would be politically dangerous. This left the shoguns only commerce as a potential source of government income.

(50) Most of the country's wealth, or so it seemed, was finding its way into the hands of city mer- chants. It appeared reasonable that they should contribute part of that revenue to ease the shogun's burden of financing the state. A means (55) of obtaining such revenue was soon found by levying forced loans, known as *goyo-kin;* although these were not taxes in the strict sense, since they were irregular in timing and arbitrary in amount, they were high in yield. Unfortunate- (60) ly, they pushed up prices. Thus, regrettably, the Tokugawa shoguns' search for solvency for the government made it increasingly difficult for individual Japanese who lived on fixed stipends to make ends meet.

17. The passage is most probably an excerpt from

   (A) an economic history of Japan
   (B) the memoirs of a samurai warrior
   (C) a modern novel about eighteenth-century Japan
   (D) an essay contrasting Japanese feudalism with its Western counterpart
   (E) an introduction to a collection of Japanese folktales

18. Which of the following financial situations is most analogous to the financial situation in which Japan's Tokugawa shoguns found themselves in the eighteenth century?

   (A) A small business borrows heavily to invest in new equipment, but is able to pay off its debt early when it is awarded a lucrative government contract.
   (B) Fire destroys a small business, but insurance covers the cost of rebuilding.
   (C) A small business is turned down for a loan at a local bank because the owners have no credit history.
   (D) A small business has to struggle to meet operating expenses when its profits decrease.
   (E) A small business is able to cut back sharply on spending through greater commercial efficiency and thereby compensate for a loss of revenue.

GO ON TO THE NEXT PAGE.

19. Which of the following best describes the attitude of the author toward the samurai discussed in lines 11-16?

(A) Warmly approving
(B) Mildly sympathetic
(C) Bitterly disappointed
(D) Harshly disdainful
(E) Profoundly shocked

20. According to the passage, the major reason for the financial problems experienced by Japan's feudal overlords in the eighteenth century was that

(A) spending had outdistanced income
(B) trade had fallen off
(C) profits from mining had declined
(D) the coinage had been sharply debased
(E) the samurai had concentrated in castle-towns

21. The passage implies that individual samurai did not find it easy to recover from debt for which of the following reasons?

(A) Agricultural production had increased.
(B) Taxes were irregular in timing and arbitrary in amount.
(C) The Japanese government had failed to adjust to the needs of a changing economy.
(D) The domains of samurai overlords were becoming smaller and poorer as government revenues increased.
(E) There was a limit to the amount in taxes that farmers could be made to pay.

22. The passage suggests that, in eighteenth-century Japan, the office of tax collector

(A) was a source of personal profit to the officeholder
(B) was regarded with derision by many Japanese
(C) remained within families
(D) existed only in castle-towns
(E) took up most of the officeholder's time

23. Which of the following could best be substituted for the word "This" in line 47 without changing the meaning of the passage?

(A) The search of Japan's Tokugawa shoguns for solvency
(B) The importance of commerce in feudal Japan
(C) The unfairness of the tax structure in eighteenth-century Japan
(D) The difficulty of increasing government income by other means
(E) The difficulty experienced by both individual samurai and the shogun himself in extricating themselves from debt

24. The passage implies that which of the following was the primary reason why the Tokugawa shoguns turned to city merchants for help in financing the state?

(A) A series of costly wars had depleted the national treasury.
(B) Most of the country's wealth appeared to be in city merchants' hands.
(C) Japan had suffered a series of economic reversals due to natural disasters such as floods.
(D) The merchants were already heavily indebted to the shoguns.
(E) Further reclamation of land would not have been economically advantageous.

25. According to the passage, the actions of the Tokugawa shoguns in their search for solvency for the government were regrettable because those actions

(A) raised the cost of living by pushing up prices
(B) resulted in the exhaustion of the most easily worked deposits of silver and gold
(C) were far lower in yield than had originally been anticipated
(D) did not succeed in reducing government spending
(E) acted as a deterrent to trade

STOP

**IF YOU FINISH BEFORE TIME IS CALLED, YOU MAY CHECK YOUR WORK ON THIS SECTION ONLY.
DO NOT TURN TO ANY OTHER SECTION IN THE TEST.**

Answer Key for Sample Test Section 2

READING COMPREHENSION

1. D	14. E
2. B	15. D
3. C	16. A
4. B	17. A
5. A	18. D
6. B	19. B
7. A	20. A
8. E	21. E
9. D	22. C
10. B	23. D
11. C	24. B
12. B	25. A
13. A	

Explanatory Material: Reading Comprehension Sample Test Section 2

1. It can be inferred from the passage that scientists now generally agree that the

   (A) enormous wingspan of the pterosaurs enabled them to fly great distances
   (B) structure of the skeleton of the pterosaurs suggests a close evolutionary relationship to bats
   (C) fossil remains of the pterosaurs reveal how they solved the problem of powered flight
   (D) pterosaurs were reptiles
   (E) pterosaurs walked on all fours

The best answer is D. In the first paragraph, the author observes that for more than two centuries paleontologists have been puzzled by the question of whether pterosaurs are birds or reptiles. Lines 9-10 state that the assertion that the pterosaurs were reptiles is "perhaps the least controversial" of those that paleontologists have made about them. The author then cites evidence to support the classification of the pterosaurs as reptiles. In lines 11-13, the author observes that the skulls, pelvises, and feet of the pterosaurs are "reptilian," and that the "anatomy of their wings suggests that they did not evolve into the class of birds." Lines 13-16 elaborate on this difference in wing structure, noting that in pterosaurs it is the "greatly elongated fourth finger of each forelimb"—and in birds "the second finger"—that provides principle support for the wing. It can thus be inferred that at present scientists generally agree that pterosaurs were reptiles.

2. The author views the idea that the pterosaurs became airborne by rising into light winds created by waves as

   (A) revolutionary
   (B) unlikely
   (C) unassailable
   (D) probable
   (E) outdated

The best answer is B. In the last paragraph of the passage, the author observes that each of three hypotheses concerning how pterosaurs became airborne "has its difficulties." In relation to the third hypothesis—the suggestion that pterosaurs became airborne "by rising into light winds from the crests of waves"—the author further observes that such waves would have to be high in order to "channel updrafts" and that wind that made waves as high as these "might have been too strong for the pterosaurs to control their flight once airborne."

3. According to the passage, the skeleton of a pterosaur can be distinguished from that of a bird by the

   (A) size of its wingspan
   (B) presence of hollow spaces in its bones
   (C) anatomic origin of its wing strut
   (D) presence of hooklike projections on its hind feet
   (E) location of the shoulder joint joining the wing to its body

The best answer is C. Choices A and E are incorrect because the passage states that the "pterosaurs resembled both birds and bats in their overall structure and proportions" (lines 24-25). Choice D can be eliminated because, in the last paragraph of the passage, the author notes that it is wrongly assumed that the "pterosaurs' hind feet. . .could serve as hooks by which the animal could hang in preparation for flight" (lines 47-49). Lines 27-28 state that the bones of both pterosaurs and birds are hollow, making B an incorrect choice. Choice C is correct because, in lines 13-17, the author observes that the anatomical structure of the pterosaur differs from that of birds in that the fourth, rather than the second, finger of each forelimb provided the major support for the pterosaur's "winglike membrane."

4. The ideas attributed to T. H. Huxley in the passage suggest that he would most likely agree with which of the following statements?

(A) An animal's brain size has little bearing on its ability to master complex behaviors.
(B) An animal's appearance is often influenced by environmental requirements and physical capabilities.
(C) Animals within a given family group are unlikely to change their appearance dramatically over a period of time.
(D) The origin of flight in vertebrates was an accidental development rather than the outcome of specialization or adaptation.
(E) The pterosaurs should be classified as birds, not reptiles.

The best answer is B. According to the second paragraph of the passage, Huxley theorized that the pterosaurs had to have been warm-blooded in order to maintain the high rate of metabolism and high internal temperature necessitated by their flight, and that an external coat of hair would have helped the pterosaurs to maintain their relatively high internal body temperature in addition to streamlining the body "to reduce drag in flight." It can thus be concluded that Huxley would agree with the assertion that "An animal's appearance is often influenced by environmental requirements and physical capabilities."

5. It can be inferred from the passage that which of the following is characteristic of the pterosaurs?

(A) They were unable to fold their wings when not in use.
(B) They hung upside down from branches as bats do before flight.
(C) They flew in order to capture prey.
(D) They were an early stage in the evolution of the birds.
(E) They lived primarily in a forestlike habitat.

The best answer is A. Lines 19-23 state that when it was walking or remaining stationary, the pterosaur could only turn its wings "upward in an extended inverted V-shape" along the sides of its body. Since most winged creatures' wings fold horizontally close to the body, it can therefore be inferred that pterosaurs could not fold their wings when they were not being used.

6. Which of the following best describes the organization of the last paragraph of the passage?

(A) New evidence is introduced to support a traditional point of view.
(B) Three explanations for a phenomenon are presented, and each is disputed by means of specific information.
(C) Three hypotheses are outlined, and evidence supporting each is given.
(D) Recent discoveries are described, and their implications for future study are projected.
(E) A summary of the material in the preceding paragraphs is presented, and conclusions are drawn.

The best answer is B. The question requires you to examine the organization of the last paragraph as a whole. Choice B is the best answer because, in the last paragraph, the author presents three explanations of how pterosaurs became airborne and provides specific information that undermines each of them. The author disputes the first explanation—that pterosaurs "launched themselves by jumping from cliffs"—by noting that pterosaurs could not use their hind feet to "hang in preparation for flight." The author disputes the second explanation—that pterosaurs became airborne "by dropping from trees"—with the assertion that "pterosaurs could not have landed in trees without damaging their wings." The author undermines the third explanation—that pterosaurs launched themselves "by rising into light winds from the crests of waves"—by observing that the winds that generated such waves "might have been too strong for the pterosaurs to control their flight once airborne."

7. It can be inferred from the passage that some scientists believe that pterosaurs

(A) lived near large bodies of water
(B) had sharp teeth for tearing food
(C) were attacked and eaten by larger reptiles
(D) had longer tails than many birds
(E) consumed twice their weight daily to maintain their body temperature

The best answer is A. In the last paragraph, the author observes that some scientists have argued that pterosaurs launched themselves "by rising into light winds from the crests of waves." If this explanation of how pterosaurs became airborne were true, it would be reasonable to conclude that pterosaurs must have lived in the vicinity of bodies of water large enough to create such waves; otherwise, according to this theory, pterosaurs would never have been able to use their capacity to fly. Thus, it is reasonable to infer that at least some scientists believe that pterosaurs "lived near large bodies of water."

8. Which of the following is the principal topic of the passage?

(A) What causes labor market pathologies that result in suffering
(B) Why income measures are imprecise in measuring degrees of poverty
(C) Which of the currently used statistical procedures are the best for estimating the incidence of hardship that is due to unemployment
(D) Where the areas of agreement are among poverty, employment, and earnings figures
(E) How social statistics give an unclear picture of the degree of hardship caused by low wages and insufficient employment opportunities

The best answer is E. The author begins the passage with a question about the degree of hardship caused by labor market problems. The first paragraph is devoted to an exploration of the ways in which social statistics may exaggerate such hardship. Paragraph two explores the ways in which the same social statistics may underestimate such hardship. The final paragraph acknowledges the contradictory nature of the evidence available from social statistics that report the degree of hardship caused by labor market problems. None of the topics mentioned in A, B, C, and D are examined in the passage.

9. The author uses "labor market problems" in lines 1-2 to refer to which of the following?

   (A) The overall causes of poverty
   (B) Deficiencies in the training of the work force
   (C) Trade relationships among producers of goods
   (D) Shortages of jobs providing adequate income
   (E) Strikes and inadequate supplies of labor

The best answer is D. This question asks you to determine what the author means by a particular phrase used in the opening sentence of the passage. To answer the question, you must connect that opening sentence with the rest of the passage. The first paragraph discusses the labor market problems connected with unemployment and earnings; the second paragraph also discusses unemployment and earnings. The concluding paragraph mentions "poverty, employment, and earnings statistics" (lines 56-57) in connection with "labor market problems" (line 59). Thus, the author uses the phrase cited in the question to refer to "shortages of jobs providing adequate income," the topic mentioned in D. In its discussion of "labor market problems," the passage does not refer to the topics mentioned in the other choices.

10. The author contrasts the 1930's with the present in order to show that

   (A) more people were unemployed in the 1930's
   (B) unemployment now has less severe effects
   (C) social programs are more needed now
   (D) there now is a greater proportion of elderly and handicapped people among those in poverty
   (E) poverty has increased since the 1930's

The best answer is B. To answer this question, you must first find the author's statement contrasting the 1930's with the present. This contrast is contained in the sentence in lines 5-11: "Unemployment does not have the same dire consequences today as it did in the 1930's. . . ." The rest of the sentence supports this opening assertion with specific contrasting details. None of the topics mentioned in the other options are mentioned in the passage in connection with the 1930's.

11. Which of the following proposals best responds to the issues raised by the author?

   (A) Innovative programs using multiple approaches should be set up to reduce the level of unemployment.
   (B) A compromise should be found between the positions of those who view joblessness as an evil greater than economic control and those who hold the opposite view.
   (C) New statistical indices should be developed to measure the degree to which unemployment and inadequately paid employment cause suffering.
   (D) Consideration should be given to the ways in which statistics can act as partial causes of the phenomena that they purport to measure.
   (E) The labor force should be restructured so that it corresponds to the range of job vacancies.

The best answer is C. This question requires you to evaluate the choices in light of the passage as a whole. Thus, in choosing the answer, you must keep in mind what issues are central to the passage. The passage begins with a question that raises the issue of the accuracy of the statistical information available. In the first paragraph, the author details the ways in which social statistics exaggerate the hardship created by labor market problems. Then, in the second paragraph, the author discusses the ways in which these same statistics underestimate these hardships. In the last sentence of the passage, the author says, ". . .existing poverty, employment, and earnings statistics are inadequate for one of their primary applications. . . ." Thus, the issues raised by the passage are all connected with the adequacy of the social statistics used to measure the hardship caused by labor market problems. Only the proposal mentioned in C suggests the need for the improvement of social statistics.

12. The author's purpose in citing those who are repeatedly unemployed during a twelve-month period is most probably to show that

   (A) there are several factors that cause the payment of low wages to some members of the labor force
   (B) unemployment statistics can underestimate the hardship resulting from joblessness
   (C) recurrent inadequacies in the labor market can exist and can cause hardships for individual workers
   (D) a majority of those who are jobless at any one time do not suffer severe hardship
   (E) there are fewer individuals who are without jobs at some time during a year than would be expected on the basis of monthly unemployment figures

The best answer is B. This question asks you to identify the purpose of a particular statement in the passage. First, you must locate the statement mentioned in the question. In lines 30-32, the author mentions "Low wages and repeated or prolonged unemployment. . . ." To determine the purpose of this citation, you must look at the context in which it appears, the paragraph as a whole. The paragraph begins by asserting that "social statistics underestimate the degree of labor-market-related hardship" (lines 26-28). The first piece of evidence cited to support this assertion is the mention of "millions of fully employed workers whose wages are so low that their families remain in poverty" (lines 29-30). The second piece of evidence is the mention, in the next sentence, of those workers who experience repeated unemployment.

13. The author states that the mitigating effect of social programs involving income transfers on the income level of low-income people is often not felt by

    (A) the employed poor
    (B) dependent children in single-earner families
    (C) workers who become disabled
    (D) retired workers
    (E) full-time workers who become unemployed

The best answer is A. This question asks you to choose the option that would, in combination with the given statement, restate a point the author makes in the passage. To answer the question, you must locate in the passage the author's statements about the subject mentioned in the question, "the mitigating effect of social programs involving income transfers on the income level of low-income people. . . ." Income transfers are mentioned only once in the passage, in lines 43-48, and in that sentence the author clearly states that such transfers have ". . .neglect[ed] the needs of the working poor. . ." (line 45). Those individuals mentioned in B, C, and D are specifically cited in this sentence as beneficiaries of income transfers, while those individuals mentioned in E are not included in the author's discussion of income transfers.

14. According to the passage, one factor that causes unemployment and earnings figures to overpredict the amount of economic hardship is the

    (A) recurrence of periods of unemployment for a group of low-wage workers
    (B) possibility that earnings may be received from more than one job per worker
    (C) fact that unemployment counts do not include those who work for low wages and remain poor
    (D) establishment of a system of record-keeping that makes it possible to compile poverty statistics
    (E) prevalence, among low-wage workers and the unemployed, of members of families in which others are employed

The best answer is E. This question asks you to identify one factor mentioned in the passage as a cause for overprediction of economic hardship. The first paragraph of the pas-

sage asserts, in lines 3-5, that the degree of economic hardship reflected in social statistics is exaggerated in many ways. The rest of the first paragraph supports this assertion by citing various factors that lead to the exaggeration, or overprediction. Only choice E restates one of the factors mentioned in the first paragraph. Choices A and C mention factors cited in the second paragraph of the passage as support for the assertion that social statistics *underpredict* economic hardship. Choices B and D state factors not mentioned in the passage.

15. The conclusion stated in lines 33-39 about the number of people who suffer as a result of forced idleness depends primarily on the point that

    (A) in times of high unemployment, there are some people who do not remain unemployed for long
    (B) the capacity for self-support depends on receiving moderate-to-high wages
    (C) those in forced idleness include, besides the unemployed, both underemployed part-time workers and those not actively seeking work
    (D) at different times during the year, different people are unemployed
    (E) many of those who are affected by unemployment are dependents of unemployed workers

The best answer is D. To answer the question, you must first look at the conclusion cited in the question (lines 33-39 of the passage). This conclusion is stated in the context of the second paragraph, which begins by asserting that "social statistics underestimate the degree of labor-market-related hardship" (lines 26-28). In lines 33-39, the author suggests that the average annual unemployment rate, which is presented as one example of potentially problematic social statistics, does not measure the total number of people who are unemployed at some time during the year. The total number of people unemployed at some time is much larger than the average annual unemployment rate would indicate. The author uses this fact to draw a conclusion—"those who suffer as a result of forced idleness can equal or exceed average annual unemployment" (lines 35-37)—that supports the assertion at the beginning of the second paragraph. This conclusion depends on the point stated in choice D.

16. **Which of the following, if true, is the best criticism of the author's argument concerning why poverty statistics cannot properly be used to show the effects of problems in the labor market?**

(A) A short-term increase in the number of those in poverty can indicate a shortage of jobs, because the basic number of those unable to accept employment remains approximately constant.

(B) For those who are in poverty as a result of joblessness, there are social programs available that provide a minimum standard of living.

(C) Poverty statistics do not consistently agree with earnings statistics, when each is taken as a measure of hardship resulting from unemployment.

(D) The elderly and handicapped categories include many who previously were employed in the labor market.

(E) Since the labor market is global in nature, poor workers in one country are competing with poor workers in another with respect to the level of wages and the existence of jobs.

The best answer is A. To answer this question, you must first identify the author's argument concerning poverty statistics. Such statistics are mentioned in lines 21-25, where the author argues that they include people who are kept out of the labor force for reasons other than fluctuations in the labor market itself. Thus, according to the author, poverty statistics do not accurately reflect labor market problems. The best criticism of such an argument would be to show that poverty statistics do, in fact, reflect fluctuations in the labor market. Choice A provides such a criticism, by pointing out that the author's account of poverty statistics could still leave room for change in the statistics that does reflect labor market problems. None of the points mentioned in the other choices address the author's argument about the inadequacies of poverty statistics.

17. **The passage is most probably an excerpt from**

(A) an economic history of Japan
(B) the memoirs of a samurai warrior
(C) a modern novel about eighteenth-century Japan
(D) an essay contrasting Japanese feudalism with its Western counterpart
(E) an introduction to a collection of Japanese folktales

The best answer is A. This question requires you to make two judgments: what is the general nature of the style and content of the passage and in what kind of publication would a passage of that nature appear? The passage is a somewhat technical discussion of the economic situation of a certain class of eighteenth-century Japanese, focusing on an analysis of then prevalent economic practices and trends. Thus, an economic history of Japan (choice A) is certainly a probable source for such material. Although any of the works in the other choices could conceivably contain such material, it is not probable, and there is no internal evidence to suggest that this excerpt could be appropriately placed in the types of works listed in choices B, C, D, or E.

18. **Which of the following financial situations is most analogous to the financial situation in which Japan's Tokugawa shoguns found themselves in the eighteenth century?**

(A) A small business borrows heavily to invest in new equipment, but is able to pay off its debt early when it is awarded a lucrative government contract.

(B) Fire destroys a small business, but insurance covers the cost of rebuilding.

(C) A small business is turned down for a loan at a local bank because the owners have no credit history.

(D) A small business has to struggle to meet operating expenses when its profits decrease.

(E) A small business is able to cut back sharply on spending through greater commercial efficiency and thereby compensate for a loss of revenue.

The best answer is D. In order to answer this question you must first determine what were the essential elements of the shoguns' financial situation and then decide which of the choices presents a situation with the same basic elements. Lines 16-18 indicate that the overlords' income failed to keep pace with their expenses. Lines 19-26 describe some of the reasons expenses rose while income declined. Choice D is the only choice that contains these two critical elements. With the exception of E, the other choices describe situations in which one of the elements is analogous to critical elements in the shoguns' situation, but the other is not. Choice E is not analogous in either of its elements.

19. **Which of the following best describes the attitude of the author toward the samurai discussed in lines 11-16?**

(A) Warmly approving
(B) Mildly sympathetic
(C) Bitterly disappointed
(D) Harshly disdainful
(E) Profoundly shocked

The best answer is B. This question asks about the attitude of the author toward a particular group as that attitude is revealed in the language of the passage. To answer this question, you should first re-examine the lines cited. The samurai are described as idle and given to expensive pursuits. The author, however, does not dismiss them; rather, it is implied that their idleness is not totally a matter of choice: they were "reduced to idleness," (line 11) and their response seems to the author "not surprising." Thus, the author's attitude can be described as "mildly sympathetic."

20. According to the passage, the major reason for the financial problems experienced by Japan's feudal overlords in the eighteenth century was that

(A) spending had outdistanced income
(B) trade had fallen off
(C) profits from mining had declined
(D) the coinage had been sharply debased
(E) the samurai had concentrated in castle-towns

The best answer is A. This question requires you to identify the major reason stated in the passage for the problems of the feudal overlords. To answer the question, it is necessary to distinguish between the major reason and the factors that contributed to, but alone do not completely account for, the problem. Lines 16-18 state that the overlords' income "failed to keep pace with their expenses." The rest of the paragraph goes on to explain the various factors that contributed to the problem. Notice that choices C, D, and E are discussed in the passage as factors influencing the economic situation; they are not, however, the major reason for the problems of the overlords.

21. The passage implies that individual samurai did not find it easy to recover from debt for which of the following reasons?

(A) Agricultural production had increased.
(B) Taxes were irregular in timing and arbitrary in amount.
(C) The Japanese government had failed to adjust to the needs of a changing economy.
(D) The domains of samurai overlords were becoming smaller and poorer as government revenues increased.
(E) There was a limit to the amount in taxes that farmers could be made to pay.

The best answer is E. This question asks you to identify the reason that individual samurai, once they had become indebted, could not extricate themselves from debt. Lines 16-18 suggest that individual samurai drew their income from rice production among tenant farmers, and lines 30-32 indicate that this income could not be increased indefinitely. Thus, it can be concluded that the samurai could not raise enough money to recover from debt because they could not increase the income derived from tenant farms. Choice E is a statement of this idea.

22. The passage suggests that, in eighteenth-century Japan, the office of tax collector

(A) was a source of personal profit to the officeholder
(B) was regarded with derision by many Japanese
(C) remained within families
(D) existed only in castle-towns
(E) took up most of the officeholder's time

The best answer is C. This question asks for a specific supporting detail presented in the passage. To answer the question, it is necessary to locate the reference in the passage to the office of tax collector. Lines 21-22 contain a parenthetical reference to the office of tax collector. It is indicated there that the office of tax collector is hereditary. Choice C presents a paraphrase of this idea: the office "remained within families." There is no evidence to support any of the statements made in the other choices.

23. Which of the following could best be substituted for the word "This" in line 47 without changing the meaning of the passage?

(A) The search of Japan's Tokugawa shoguns for solvency
(B) The importance of commerce in feudal Japan
(C) The unfairness of the tax structure in eighteenth-century Japan
(D) The difficulty of increasing government income by other means
(E) The difficulty experienced by both individual samurai and the shogun himself in extricating themselves from debt

The best answer is D. This question requires you to determine the referent of the pronoun "This" in line 47. You should first reread the paragraph containing the sentence, and decide what "This" refers to. The paragraph discusses ways in which the Tokugawa shogun and the government attempted to increase revenues and explains why each of the attempts fell short of solving the problem. The pronoun "This" in line 47 introduces a sentence that draws a conclusion based on the fact that most means of increasing government revenue had been exhausted; "This" can only refer to the difficulty they experienced. Choice D contains a phrase that conveys this idea and that can be substituted for the pronoun "This" without altering the meaning of the sentence.

24. The passage implies that which of the following was the primary reason why the Tokugawa shoguns turned to city merchants for help in financing the state?

(A) A series of costly wars had depleted the national treasury.
(B) Most of the country's wealth appeared to be in city merchants' hands.
(C) Japan had suffered a series of economic reversals due to natural disasters such as floods.
(D) The merchants were already heavily indebted to the shoguns.
(E) Further reclamation of land would not have been economically advantageous.

The best answer is B. This question requires you to identify the major reason why the Tokugawa shoguns began to require city merchants to contribute to the state revenues. The second paragraph indicates that the shoguns had exhausted most sources of revenue for the government. Lines 50-54 indicate that the shoguns believed that city merchants had acquired most of the country's wealth. Because of that belief, they deemed it "reasonable" to turn to the city merchants. Thus, choice B is the best answer.

25. According to the passage, the actions of the Tokugawa shoguns in their search for solvency for the government were regrettable because those actions

    (A) raised the cost of living by pushing up prices
    (B) resulted in the exhaustion of the most easily worked deposits of silver and gold
    (C) were far lower in yield than had originally been anticipated
    (D) did not succeed in reducing government spending
    (E) acted as a deterrent to trade

The best answer is A. To answer this question, you must determine why the author of the passage judges the actions of the shoguns as "regrettable," a judgment rendered in the conclusion of the passage. The passage indicates that the forced loans demanded of city merchants by the shoguns (lines 54-60) had the ultimate effect of driving up prices. The next sentence discusses the effects of the rise in prices on the cost of living, an effect that the author finds unfortunate ("Thus, regrettably," line 60). Therefore, choice A is the best answer.

30 Minutes
25 Questions

<u>Directions</u>: Each passage in this group is followed by questions based on its content. After reading a passage, choose the best answer to each question and fill in the corresponding oval on the answer sheet. Answer all questions following a passage on the basis of what is <u>stated</u> or <u>implied</u> in that passage.

Between the eighth and eleventh centuries A.D., the Byzantine Empire staged an almost unparalleled economic and cultural revival, a recovery that is all the
Line more striking because it followed a long period of severe
(5) internal decline. By the early eighth century, the empire had lost roughly two-thirds of the territory it had possessed in the year 600, and its remaining area was being raided by Arabs and Bulgarians, who at times threatened to take Constantinople and extinguish the
(10) empire altogether. The wealth of the state and its subjects was greatly diminished, and artistic and literary production had virtually ceased. By the early eleventh century, however, the empire had regained almost half of its lost possessions, its new frontiers were secure, and its
(15) influence extended far beyond its borders. The economy had recovered, the treasury was full, and art and schol- arship had advanced.

To consider the Byzantine military, cultural, and economic advances as differentiated aspects of a single
(20) phenomenon is reasonable. After all, these three forms of progress have gone together in a number of states and civilizations. Rome under Augustus and fifth-century Athens provide the most obvious examples in antiquity. Moreover, an examination of the apparent sequential
(25) connections among military, economic, and cultural forms of progress might help explain the dynamics of historical change.

The common explanation of these apparent connec- tions in the case of Byzantium would run like this:
(30) when the empire had turned back enemy raids on its own territory and had begun to raid and conquer enemy territory, Byzantine resources naturally expanded and more money became available to patronize art and liter- ature. Therefore, Byzantine military achievements led to
(35) economic advances, which in turn led to cultural revival.

No doubt this hypothetical pattern did apply at times during the course of the recovery. Yet it is not clear that military advances invariably came first, economic advances second, and intellectual advances third. In the
(40) 860's the Byzantine Empire began to recover from Arab incursions so that by 872 the military balance with the Abbasid Caliphate had been permanently altered in the empire's favor. The beginning of the empire's economic revival, however, can be placed between 810 and 830.
(45) Finally, the Byzantine revival of learning appears to have begun even earlier. A number of notable scholars and writers appeared by 788 and, by the last decade of the eighth century, a cultural revival was in full bloom, a revival that lasted until the fall of Constantinople in
(50) 1453. Thus the commonly expected order of military

revival followed by economic and then by cultural recovery was reversed in Byzantium. In fact, the revival of Byzantine learning may itself have influenced the subsequent economic and military expansion.

1. Which of the following best states the central idea of the passage?

(A) The Byzantine Empire was a unique case in which the usual order of military and economic revival preceding cultural revival was reversed.

(B) The economic, cultural, and military revival in the Byzantine Empire between the eighth and eleventh centuries was similar in its order to the sequence of revivals in Augustan Rome and fifth-century Athens.

(C) After 810 Byzantine economic recovery spurred a military and, later, cultural expansion that lasted until 1453.

(D) The eighth-century revival of Byzantine learning is an inexplicable phenomenon, and its economic and military precursors have yet to be discovered.

(E) The revival of the Byzantine Empire between the eighth and eleventh centuries shows cultural rebirth preceding economic and mili- tary revival, the reverse of the commonly accepted order of progress.

2. The primary purpose of the second paragraph is which of the following?

(A) To establish the uniqueness of the Byzantine revival

(B) To show that Augustan Rome and fifth-century Athens are examples of cultural, economic, and military expansion against which all subsequent cases must be measured

(C) To suggest that cultural, economic, and military advances have tended to be closely interre- lated in different societies

(D) To argue that, while the revivals of Augustan Rome and fifth-century Athens were similar, they are unrelated to other historical exam- ples

(E) To indicate that, wherever possible, historians should seek to make comparisons with the earliest chronological examples of revival

GO ON TO THE NEXT PAGE.

3. It can be inferred from the passage that by the eleventh century the Byzantine military forces

   (A) had reached their peak and begun to decline
   (B) had eliminated the Bulgarian army
   (C) were comparable in size to the army of Rome under Augustus
   (D) were strong enough to withstand the Abbasid Caliphate's military forces
   (E) had achieved control of Byzantine governmental structures

4. It can be inferred from the passage that the Byzantine Empire sustained significant territorial losses

   (A) in 600
   (B) during the seventh century
   (C) a century after the cultural achievements of the Byzantine Empire had been lost
   (D) soon after the revival of Byzantine learning
   (E) in the century after 873

5. In the third paragraph, the author most probably provides an explanation of the apparent connections among economic, military, and cultural development in order to

   (A) suggest that the process of revival in Byzantium accords with this model
   (B) set up an order of events that is then shown to be not generally applicable to the case of Byzantium
   (C) cast aspersions on traditional historical scholarship about Byzantium
   (D) suggest that Byzantium represents a case for which no historical precedent exists
   (E) argue that military conquest is the paramount element in the growth of empires

6. Which of the following does the author mention as crucial evidence concerning the manner in which the Byzantine revival began?

   (A) The Byzantine military revival of the 860's led to economic and cultural advances.
   (B) The Byzantine cultural revival lasted until 1453.
   (C) The Byzantine economic recovery began in the 900's.
   (D) The revival of Byzantine learning began toward the end of the eighth century.
   (E) By the early eleventh century the Byzantine Empire had regained much of its lost territory.

7. According to the author, "The common explanation" (line 28) of connections between economic, military, and cultural development is

   (A) revolutionary and too new to have been applied to the history of the Byzantine Empire
   (B) reasonable, but an antiquated theory of the nature of progress
   (C) not applicable to the Byzantine revival as a whole, but does perhaps accurately describe limited periods during the revival
   (D) equally applicable to the Byzantine case as a whole and to the history of military, economic, and cultural advances in ancient Greece and Rome
   (E) essentially not helpful, because military, economic, and cultural advances are part of a single phenomenon

GO ON TO THE NEXT PAGE.

Virtually everything astronomers know about objects outside the solar system is based on the detection of photons—quanta of electromagnetic radiation. Yet there is another form of radiation that permeates the universe: neutrinos. With (as its name implies) no electric charge, and negligible mass, the neutrino interacts with other particles so rarely that a neutrino can cross the entire universe, even traversing substantial aggregations of matter, without being absorbed or even deflected. Neutrinos can thus escape from regions of space where light and other kinds of electromagnetic radiation are blocked by matter. Furthermore, neutrinos carry with them information about the site and circumstances of their production; therefore, the detection of cosmic neutrinos could provide new information about a wide variety of cosmic phenomena and about the history of the universe.

But how can scientists detect a particle that interacts so infrequently with other matter? Twenty-five years passed between Pauli's hypothesis that the neutrino existed and its actual detection; since then virtually all research with neutrinos has been with neutrinos created artificially in large particle accelerators.and studied under neutrino microscopes. But a neutrino telescope, capable of detecting cosmic neutrinos, is difficult to construct. No apparatus can detect neutrinos unless it is extremely massive, because great mass is synonymous with huge numbers of nucleons (neutrons and protons), and the more massive the detector, the greater the probability of one of its nucleon's reacting with a neutrino. In addition, the apparatus must be sufficiently shielded from the interfering effects of other particles.

Fortunately, a group of astrophysicists has proposed a means of detecting cosmic neutrinos by harnessing the mass of the ocean. Named DUMAND, for Deep Underwater Muon and Neutrino Detector, the project calls for placing an array of light sensors at a depth of five kilometers under the ocean surface. The detecting medium is the seawater itself: when a neutrino interacts with a particle in an atom of seawater, the result is a cascade of electrically charged particles and a flash of light that can be detected by the sensors. The five kilometers of seawater above the sensors will shield them from the interfering effects of other high-energy particles raining down through the atmosphere.

The strongest motivation for the DUMAND project is that it will exploit an important source of information about the universe. The extension of astronomy from visible light to radio waves to x-rays and gamma rays never failed to lead to the discovery of unusual objects such as radio galaxies, quasars, and pulsars. Each of these discoveries came as a surprise. Neutrino astronomy will doubtless bring its own share of surprises.

8. Which of the following titles best summarizes the passage as a whole?

(A) At the Threshold of Neutrino Astronomy
(B) Neutrinos and the History of the Universe
(C) The Creation and Study of Neutrinos
(D) The DUMAND System and How It Works
(E) The Properties of the Neutrino

9. With which of the following statements regarding neutrino astronomy would the author be most likely to agree?

(A) Neutrino astronomy will supersede all present forms of astronomy.
(B) Neutrino astronomy will be abandoned if the DUMAND project fails.
(C) Neutrino astronomy can be expected to lead to major breakthroughs in astronomy.
(D) Neutrino astronomy will disclose phenomena that will be more surprising than past discoveries.
(E) Neutrino astronomy will always be characterized by a large time lag between hypothesis and experimental confirmation.

10. In the last paragraph, the author describes the development of astronomy in order to

(A) suggest that the potential findings of neutrino astronomy can be seen as part of a series of astronomical successes
(B) illustrate the role of surprise in scientific discovery
(C) demonstrate the effectiveness of the DUMAND apparatus in detecting neutrinos
(D) name some cosmic phenomena that neutrino astronomy will illuminate
(E) contrast the motivation of earlier astronomers with that of the astrophysicists working on the DUMAND project

11. According to the passage, one advantage that neutrinos have for studies in astronomy is that they

(A) have been detected for the last twenty-five years
(B) possess a variable electric charge
(C) are usually extremely massive
(D) carry information about their history with them
(E) are very similar to other electromagnetic particles

GO ON TO THE NEXT PAGE.

12. According to the passage, the primary use of the apparatus mentioned in lines 24-32 would be to

   (A) increase the mass of a neutrino
   (B) interpret the information neutrinos carry with them
   (C) study the internal structure of a neutrino
   (D) see neutrinos in distant regions of space
   (E) detect the presence of cosmic neutrinos

13. The passage states that interactions between neutrinos and other matter are

   (A) rare
   (B) artificial
   (C) undetectable
   (D) unpredictable
   (E) hazardous

14. The passage mentions which of the following as a reason that neutrinos are hard to detect?

   (A) Their pervasiveness in the universe
   (B) Their ability to escape from different regions of space
   (C) Their inability to penetrate dense matter
   (D) The similarity of their structure to that of nucleons
   (E) The infrequency of their interaction with other matter

15. According to the passage, the interaction of a neutrino with other matter can produce

   (A) particles that are neutral and massive
   (B) a form of radiation that permeates the universe
   (C) inaccurate information about the site and circumstances of the neutrino's production
   (D) charged particles and light
   (E) a situation in which light and other forms of electromagnetic radiation are blocked

16. According to the passage, one of the methods used to establish the properties of neutrinos was

   (A) detection of photons
   (B) observation of the interaction of neutrinos with gamma rays
   (C) observation of neutrinos that were artificially created
   (D) measurement of neutrinos that interacted with particles of seawater
   (E) experiments with electromagnetic radiation

GO ON TO THE NEXT PAGE.

Most economists in the United States seem captivated by the spell of the free market. Consequently, nothing seems good or normal that does not accord with the requirements of the free market.
(5) A price that is determined by the seller or, for that matter, established by anyone other than the aggregate of consumers seems pernicious. Accordingly, it requires a major act of will to think of price-fixing (the determination of prices by the
(10) seller) as both "normal" and having a valuable economic function. In fact, price-fixing is normal in all industrialized societies because the industrial system itself provides, as an effortless consequence of its own development, the price-fixing
(15) that it requires. Modern industrial planning requires and rewards great size. Hence, a comparatively small number of large firms will be competing for the same group of consumers. That each large firm will act with consideration of
(20) its own needs and thus avoid selling its products for more than its competitors charge is commonly recognized by advocates of free-market economic theories. But each large firm will also act with full consideration of the needs that it has in
(25) common with the other large firms competing for the same customers. Each large firm will thus avoid significant price-cutting, because price-cutting would be prejudicial to the common interest in a stable demand for products. Most economists
(30) do not see price-fixing when it occurs because they expect it to be brought about by a number of explicit agreements among large firms; it is not.

Moreover, those economists who argue that allowing the free market to operate without inter-
(35) ference is the most efficient method of establishing prices have not considered the economies of non-socialist countries other than the United States. These economies employ intentional price-fixing, usually in an overt fashion. Formal price-fixing
(40) by cartel and informal price-fixing by agreements covering the members of an industry are common-place. Were there something peculiarly efficient about the free market and inefficient about price-fixing, the countries that have avoided the first
(45) and used the second would have suffered drastically in their economic development. There is no indication that they have.

Socialist industry also works within a frame-work of controlled prices. In the early 1970's,
(50) the Soviet Union began to give firms and industries some of the flexibility in adjusting prices that a more informal evolution has accorded the capitalist system. Economists in the United States have hailed the change as a return to the free market.
(55) But Soviet firms are no more subject to prices established by a free market over which they exercise little influence than are capitalist firms; rather, Soviet firms have been given the power to fix prices.

17. The primary purpose of the passage is to

(A) refute the theory that the free market plays a useful role in the development of industrialized societies
(B) suggest methods by which economists and members of the government of the United States can recognize and combat price-fixing by large firms
(C) show that in industrialized societies price-fixing and the operation of the free market are not only compatible but also mutually beneficial
(D) explain the various ways in which industrialized societies can fix prices in order to stabilize the free market
(E) argue that price-fixing, in one form or another, is an inevitable part of and benefit to the economy of any industrialized society

18. The passage provides information that would answer which of the following questions about price-fixing?

I. What are some of the ways in which prices can be fixed?
II. For what products is price-fixing likely to be more profitable than the operation of the free market?
III. Is price-fixing more common in socialist industrialized societies or in nonsocialist industrialized societies?

(A) I only
(B) III only
(C) I and II only
(D) II and III only
(E) I, II, and III

GO ON TO THE NEXT PAGE.

19. The author's attitude toward "Most economists in the United States" (line 1) can best be described as

(A) spiteful and envious
(B) scornful and denunciatory
(C) critical and condescending
(D) ambivalent but deferential
(E) uncertain but interested

20. It can be inferred from the author's argument that a price fixed by the seller "seems pernicious" (line 7) because

(A) people do not have confidence in large firms
(B) people do not expect the government to regulate prices
(C) most economists believe that consumers as a group should determine prices
(D) most economists associate fixed prices with communist and socialist economies
(E) most economists believe that no one group should determine prices

21. The suggestion in the passage that price-fixing in industrialized societies is normal arises from the author's statement that price-fixing is

(A) a profitable result of economic development
(B) an inevitable result of the industrial system
(C) the result of a number of carefully organized decisions
(D) a phenomenon common to industrialized and nonindustrialized societies
(E) a phenomenon best achieved cooperatively by government and industry

22. According to the author, price-fixing in nonsocialist countries is often

(A) accidental but productive
(B) illegal but useful
(C) legal and innovative
(D) traditional and rigid
(E) intentional and widespread

23. According to the author, what is the result of the Soviet Union's change in economic policy in the 1970's?

(A) Soviet firms show greater profit.
(B) Soviet firms have less control over the free market.
(C) Soviet firms are able to adjust to technological advances.
(D) Soviet firms have some authority to fix prices.
(E) Soviet firms are more responsive to the free market.

24. With which of the following statements regarding the behavior of large firms in industrialized societies would the author be most likely to agree?

(A) The directors of large firms will continue to anticipate the demand for products.
(B) The directors of large firms are less interested in achieving a predictable level of profit than in achieving a large profit.
(C) The directors of large firms will strive to reduce the costs of their products.
(D) Many directors of large firms believe that the government should establish the prices that will be charged for products.
(E) Many directors of large firms believe that the price charged for products is likely to increase annually.

25. In the passage, the author is primarily concerned with

(A) predicting the consequences of a practice
(B) criticizing a point of view
(C) calling attention to recent discoveries
(D) proposing a topic for research
(E) summarizing conflicting opinions

STOP

**IF YOU FINISH BEFORE TIME IS CALLED, YOU MAY CHECK YOUR WORK ON THIS SECTION ONLY.
DO NOT TURN TO ANY OTHER SECTION IN THE TEST.**

Answer Key for Sample Test Section 3

READING COMPREHENSION

1. E	14. E
2. C	15. D
3. D	16. C
4. B	17. E
5. B	18. A
6. D	19. C
7. C	20. C
8. A	21. B
9. C	22. E
10. A	23. D
11. D	24. A
12. E	25. B
13. A	

Explanatory Material: Reading Comprehension Sample Test Section 3

1. **Which of the following best states the central idea of the passage?**

   (A) The Byzantine Empire was a unique case in which the usual order of military and economic revival preceding cultural revival was reversed.

   (B) The economic, cultural, and military revival in the Byzantine Empire between the eighth and eleventh centuries was similar in its order to the sequence of revivals in Augustan Rome and fifth-century Athens.

   (C) After 810 Byzantine economic recovery spurred a military and, later, cultural expansion that lasted until 1453.

   (D) The eight-century revival of Byzantine learning is an inexplicable phenomenon, and its economic and military precursors have yet to be discovered.

   (E) The revival of the Byzantine Empire between the eighth and eleventh centuries shows cultural rebirth preceding economic and military revival, the reverse of the commonly accepted order of progress.

The best answer is E. The passage examines the revival of the Byzantine Empire between the eighth and eleventh centuries A.D., and evidence suggesting how the revival occurred is discussed. The author acknowledges in the second paragraph that "sequential connections among military, economic, and cultural forms of progress" have in the past helped to explain historical changes. It is further granted, in the third paragraph, that one usually expects military revival first, leading to economic revival, which, in turn, leads to cultural revival. The last paragraph points out, however, that in the Byzantine Empire a cultural revival preceded both economic revival and military revival. Choice E summarizes these points. There is no evidence that the Byzantine Empire is a "unique case"; thus, choice A is not correct. Choices B, C, and D are not statements supported by information in the passage.

2. **The primary purpose of the second paragraph is which of the following?**

   (A) To establish the uniqueness of the Byzantine revival

   (B) To show that Augustan Rome and fifth-century Athens are examples of cultural, economic, and military expansion against which all subsequent cases must be measured

   (C) To suggest that cultural, economic, and military advances have tended to be closely interrelated in different societies

   (D) To argue that, while the revivals of Augustan Rome and fifth-century Athens were similar, they are unrelated to other historical examples

   (E) To indicate that, wherever possible, historians should seek to make comparisons with the earliest chronological examples of revival

The best answer is C. In the second paragraph, the author suggests a way to analyze the Byzantine revival—i.e., by suggesting factors that have explained "the dynamics of historical change" in other societies. The passage indicates that these factors—cultural, military, and economic advances—have "gone together in a number of states and civilizations." The other answer choices do not accurately reflect either the purpose or the content of the second paragraph.

3. **It can be inferred from the passage that by the eleventh century the Byzantine military forces**

   (A) had reached their peak and begun to decline

   (B) had eliminated the Bulgarian army

   (C) were comparable in size to the army of Rome under Augustus

   (D) were strong enough to withstand the Abbasid Caliphate's military forces

   (E) had achieved control of Byzantine governmental structures

The best answer is D. This question requires you to select a statement that must be true given the information in the passage. According to the passage, by the eleventh century, the Byzantine Empire was militarily secure (lines 12-14). In lines 41-43, it is stated that "by 872 the military balance with the Abbasid Caliphate had been permanently altered in the empire's favor." This information allows the conclusion stated in Choice D. There is no information in the passage that supports the other choices.

4. **It can be inferred from the passage that the Byzantine Empire sustained significant territorial losses**

   (A) in 600

   (B) during the seventh century

   (C) a century after the cultural achievements of the Byzantine Empire had been lost

   (D) soon after the revival of Byzantine learning

   (E) in the century after 873

The best answer is B. The passage indicates that "By the early eighth century, the empire had lost roughly two-thirds of the territory it had possessed in the year 600" (lines 5-7). Thus, it can be inferred that territorial losses occurred between 600 and the early 700's, i.e., during the seventh century, as is stated in choice B.

5. In the third paragraph, the author most probably provides an explanation of the apparent connections among economic, military, and cultural development in order to

   (A) suggest that the process of revival in Byzantium accords with this model
   (B) set up an order of events that is then shown to be not generally applicable to the case of Byzantium
   (C) cast aspersions on traditional historical scholarship about Byzantium
   (D) suggest that Byzantium represents a case for which no historical precedent exists
   (E) argue that military conquest is the paramount element in the growth of empires

The best answer is B. The main purpose of the passage is to establish and explain the sequence in which the Byzantine revival occurred. The author examines an order of events that might be used to explain the growth of the Byzantine Empire. The author then shows that the Byzantine revival did not actually adhere to this pattern.

6. Which of the following does the author mention as crucial evidence concerning the manner in which the Byzantine revival began?

   (A) The Byzantine military revival of the 860's led to economic and cultural advances.
   (B) The Byzantine cultural revival lasted until 1453.
   (C) The Byzantine economic recovery began in the 900's.
   (D) The revival of Byzantine learning began toward the end of the eighth century.
   (E) By the early eleventh century the Byzantine Empire had regained much of its lost territory.

The best answer is D. An important point made by the author is that the sequence of events that led to the recovery of the Byzantine Empire did not begin with military achievements, but with a cultural revival (lines 45-48). An important piece of evidence supporting this assertion is the revival of learning, which began before 788. Choice D restates this evidence.

7. According to the author, "The common explanation" (line 28) of connections between economic, military, and cultural development is

   (A) revolutionary and too new to have been applied to the history of the Byzantine Empire
   (B) reasonable, but an antiquated theory of the nature of progress
   (C) not applicable to the Byzantine revival as a whole, but does perhaps accurately describe limited periods during the revival
   (D) equally applicable to the Byzantine case as a whole and to the history of military, economic, and cultural advances in ancient Greece and Rome
   (E) essentially not helpful, because military, economic, and cultural advances are part of a single phenomenon

The best answer is C. The author states that the "common explanation," which is referred to as a "hypothetical pattern" in line 36, did probably "apply at times during the course of the recovery." But the paragraph then indicates that another sequence of events characterized the Byzantine revival as a whole.

8. Which of the following titles best summarizes the passage as a whole?

   (A) At the Threshold of Neutrino Astronomy
   (B) Neutrinos and the History of the Universe
   (C) The Creation and Study of Neutrinos
   (D) The DUMAND System and How It Works
   (E) The Properties of the Neutrino

The best answer is A. The passage describes how the study of neutrinos could be useful (lines 12-17) and discusses efforts that are being made to detect neutrinos. These are developments that have led astronomy to a point at which knowledge about the universe can be increased by detecting neutrinos, that is, to the threshold of neutrino astronomy. In the last sentence, the author suggests that neutrino astronomy will become a reality.

The titles given in C, D, and E summarize only portions of the passage. The title given in B describes a topic too broad to be a summary of the passage.

9. With which of the following statements regarding neutrino astronomy would the author be most likely to agree?

(A) Neutrino astronomy will supersede all present forms of astronomy.
(B) Neutrino astronomy will be abandoned if the DUMAND project fails.
(C) Neutrino astronomy can be expected to lead to major breakthroughs in astronomy.
(D) Neutrino astronomy will disclose phenomena that will be more surprising than past discoveries.
(E) Neutrino astronomy will always be characterized by a large time lag between hypothesis and experimental confirmation.

The best answer is C. In lines 14-17, the author mentions new information about a wide variety of cosmic phenomena and about the history of the universe as advances in knowledge that could be derived from the detection of cosmic neutrinos. There is no evidence in the passage to indicate that the author would agree with the statements in choice A, B, D, or E.

10. In the last paragraph, the author describes the development of astronomy in order to

(A) suggest that the potential findings of neutrino astronomy can be seen as part of a series of astronomical successes
(B) illustrate the role of surprise in scientific discovery
(C) demonstrate the effectiveness of the DUMAND apparatus in detecting neutrinos
(D) name some cosmic phenomena that neutrino astronomy will illuminate
(E) contrast the motivation of earlier astronomers with that of the astrophysicists working on the DUMAND project

The best answer is A. In the last paragraph, the author mentions that each of several extensions of astronomy led to important and surprising discoveries or successes. The statement that "Neutrino astronomy will doubtless bring its own share of surprises" (lines 52-53) ties neutrino astronomy to this series of successes.

11. According to the passage, one advantage that neutrinos have for studies in astronomy is that they

(A) have been detected for the last twenty-five years
(B) possess a variable electric charge
(C) are usually extremely massive
(D) carry information about their history with them
(E) are very similar to other electromagnetic particles

The best answer is D. The answer to this question can be found in lines 12-17 of the passage, which state that "neutrinos carry with them information about the site and circumstances of their production" (that is, about their history) and so "could provide new information about a wide variety of cosmic phenomena and about the history of the universe."

12. According to the passage, the primary use of the apparatus mentioned in lines 24-32 would be to

(A) increase the mass of a neutrino
(B) interpret the information neutrinos carry with them
(C) study the internal structure of a neutrino
(D) see neutrinos in distant regions of space
(E) detect the presence of cosmic neutrinos

The best answer is E, since the apparatus mentioned in lines 24-32 is "capable of detecting cosmic neutrinos" (line 25). D is not correct because, in order to be detected, the cosmic neutrinos must encounter the apparatus; therefore, the purpose of the apparatus is not to simply "see neutrinos in distant regions of space." There is no indication in the passage that the apparatus would analyze or operate on neutrinos as suggested in choices A, B, and C.

13. The passage states that interactions between neutrinos and other matter are

(A) rare
(B) artificial
(C) undetectable
(D) unpredictable
(E) hazardous

The best answer is A. Lines 6-9 state that neutrinos can cross the entire universe without interacting with other particles of matter. Thus, these interactions can correctly be described as "rare."

B is not the best answer because, although neutrinos can be artificially created, their interactions with other matter are not artificial. Although interactions between neutrinos and other matter are difficult to detect, they are not undetectable, as stated in C. The passage does not state that interactions between neutrinos and other matter are unpredictable or hazardous (D and E).

14. The passage mentions which of the following as a reason that neutrinos are hard to detect?

(A) Their pervasiveness in the universe
(B) Their ability to escape from different regions of space
(C) Their inability to penetrate dense matter
(D) The similarity of their structure to that of nucleons
(E) The infrequency of their interaction with other matter

The best answer is E. Lines 5-9 describe the infrequency of the interactions of neutrinos with other matter. The question in lines 18-19, "how can scientists detect a particle that interacts so infrequently with other matter?" implies that the infrequent interaction of neutrinos with other matter makes detection of the neutrinos difficult.

15. According to the passage, the interaction of a neutrino with other matter can produce

(A) particles that are neutral and massive
(B) a form of radiation that permeates the universe
(C) inaccurate information about the site and circumstances of the neutrino's production
(D) charged particles and light
(E) a situation in which light and other forms of electromagnetic radiation are blocked

The best answer is D. Lines 39-42 describe the result of an interaction of a neutrino with other matter (a particle in an atom of seawater) as "a cascade of electrically charged particles and a flash of light."

16. According to the passage, one of the methods used to establish the properties of neutrinos was

(A) detection of photons
(B) observation of the interaction of neutrinos with gamma rays
(C) observation of neutrinos that were artifically created
(D) measurement of neutrinos that interacted with particles of seawater
(E) experiments with electromagnetic radiation

The best answer is C. According to the second paragraph of the passage, since neutrinos were first detected, most neutrino research has been done with artificially created neutrinos.

17. The primary purpose of the passage is to

(A) refute the theory that the free market plays a useful role in the development of industrialized societies
(B) suggest methods by which economists and members of the government of the United States can recognize and combat price-fixing by large firms
(C) show that in industrialized societies price-fixing and the operation of the free market are not only compatible but also mutually beneficial
(D) explain the various ways in which industrialized societies can fix prices in order to stabilize the free market
(E) argue that price-fixing, in one form or another, is an inevitable part of and benefit to the economy of any industrialized society

The best answer is E. The author contends in lines 7-15 that price-fixing is normal and beneficial in industrialized societies. The author proceeds to support this assertion with descriptions of various forms of price-fixing in various kinds of industrialized societies (lines 23-29, 36-42, and 48-59).

Moreover, in lines 42-47, in the context of a discussion of nonsocialist countries other than the United States, the author indirectly restates the argument in favor of price-fixing.

18. The passage provides information that would answer which of the following questions about price-fixing?

I. What are some of the ways in which prices can be fixed?
II. For what products is price-fixing likely to be more profitable than the operation of the free market?
III. Is price-fixing more common in socialist industrialized societies or in nonsocialist industrialized societies?

(A) I only
(B) III only
(C) I and II only
(D) II and III only
(E) I, II, and III

This question asks whether one or more of the questions identified by Roman numerals can be answered on the basis of the information given in the passage. In questions of this kind, each part identified by a Roman numeral must be considered individually. Question I can be answered by information in lines 26-27, 31-32, 38-42, and 50-53 of the passage, which mention some different ways of fixing prices. Questions II and III cannot be answered from information provided by the passage. The best answer, therefore, is A (I only).

19. The author's attitude toward "Most economists in the United States" (line 1) can best be described as

(A) spiteful and envious
(B) scornful and denunciatory
(C) critical and condescending
(D) ambivalent but deferential
(E) uncertain but interested

The best answer is C. Determining the author's attitude toward a topic requires locating all references to the topic in the passage and considering both the literal meanings and the connotations of the words used concerning the topic. Thus, the author refers to "most economists" or "economists in the United States" or "those economists" in lines 1-2, 29-32, 33-37, and 53-54. The author describes them as "captivated by the spell of the free market," as failing to see price-fixing when it occurs, as failing to consider the economies of nonsocialist countries other than the United States, and as mistakenly "hailing" price-fixing in the Soviet Union as a return to the free market. The choice that best describes these references is "critical and condescending."

20. It can be inferred from the author's argument that a price fixed by the seller "seems pernicious" (line 7) because

(A) people do not have confidence in large firms
(B) people do not expect the government to regulate prices
(C) most economists believe that consumers as a group should determine prices
(D) most economists associate fixed prices with communist and socialist economies
(E) most economists believe that no one group should determine prices

The best answer is C. Lines 1-7 allow one to infer that it is to "Most economists" (line 1) that a price fixed by the seller "seems pernicious," and that these economists consider price-fixing pernicious because they believe that only the "aggregate of consumers" (line 7) should establish prices.

21. The suggestion in the passage that price-fixing in industrialized societies is normal arises from the author's statement that price-fixing is

(A) a profitable result of economic development
(B) an inevitable result of the industrial system
(C) the result of a number of carefully organized decisions
(D) a phenomenon common to industrialized and nonindustrialized societies
(E) a phenomenon best achieved cooperatively by government and industry

The best answer is B, based on lines 11-15, which state that price-fixing is normal in all industrialized societies because the industrial system provides price-fixing "as an effortless consequence of its own development."

22. According to the author, price-fixing in nonsocialistic countries is often

(A) accidental but productive
(B) illegal but useful
(C) legal and innovative
(D) traditional and rigid
(E) intentional and widespread

The best answer is E, based on lines 38 ("intentional price-fixing") and 41-42 ("commonplace").

23. According to the author, what is the result of the Soviet Union's change in economic policy in the 1970's?

(A) Soviet firms show greater profit.
(B) Soviet firms have less control over the free market.
(C) Soviet firms are able to adjust to technological advances.
(D) Soviet firms have some authority to fix prices.
(E) Soviet firms are more responsive to the free market.

The best answer is D. In lines 49-53, the author states that, in the early 1970's, the Soviet Union gave firms some "flexibility in adjusting prices." In lines 58-59, the author states that what these firms have in fact been given is "the power to fix prices." Thus, the result of the Soviet Union's change in economic policy in the 1970's is choice D, "Soviet firms have some authority to fix prices."

24. With which of the following statements regarding the behavior of large firms in industrialized societies would the author be most likely to agree?

(A) The directors of large firms will continue to anticipate the demand for products.
(B) The directors of large firms are less interested in achieving a predictable level of profit than in achieving a large profit.
(C) The directors of large firms will strive to reduce the costs of their products.
(D) Many directors of large firms believe that the government should establish the prices that will be charged for products.
(E) Many directors of large firms believe that the price charged for products is likely to increase annually.

The best answer is A. The author discusses the behavior of large firms in industrialized societies in lines 15-29. In lines 26-29, the author refers to the firms' "common interest in a stable demand for products." It can be inferred from these references that the author believes that the directors of large firms currently anticipate the demand for products. Since the author describes price-fixing as an ongoing phenomenon (lines 11-29), it can be inferred that the author would be likely to agree that the large firms' directors will also continue to anticipate the demand for products.

25. In the passage, the author is primarily concerned with

(A) predicting the consequences of a practice
(B) criticizing a point of view
(C) calling attention to recent discoveries
(D) proposing a topic for research
(E) summarizing conflicting opinions

The best answer is B. Throughout the passage, the author criticizes the point of view of "most economists in the United States"—those who believe that the free market is best and that price-fixing is pernicious. Thus, the first paragraph argues that price-fixing is normal and valuable in all industrialized countries. The second paragraph argues that the experience of nonsocialist countries other than the United States provides no support for the point of view of these economists. The third paragraph argues that these economists are wrong in thinking that the Soviet Union has moved toward a free market. Thus, it can be inferred that the author's primary concern is to criticize this point of view.

6 Critical Reasoning

In these questions, you are to analyze the situation on which each question is based, and then select the answer choice that is the most appropriate response to the question. No specialized knowledge of any particular field is required for answering the questions, and no knowledge of the terminology and of the conventions of formal logic is presupposed. The sample Critical Reasoning test sections that begin on page 213 provide good illustrations of the variety of topics that may be covered, of the kinds of questions that may be asked, and of the level of analysis that will generally be required.

Test-Taking Strategies for Critical Reasoning

1. The set of statements on which a question is based should be read very carefully with close attention to such matters as (1) what is put forward as factual information, (2) what is not said but necessarily follows from what is said, (3) what is claimed to follow from facts that have been put forward, and (4) how well substantiated are any claims to the effect that a particular conclusion follows from the facts that have been put forward. In reading arguments, it is important to attend to the soundness of the reasoning employed; it is not necessary to make a judgment of the actual truth of anything that is put forward as factual information.

2. If a question is based on an argument, be careful to identify clearly which part of the argument is its conclusion. The conclusion does not necessarily come at the end of the text of the argument; it may come somewhere in the middle, or it may even come at the beginning. Be alert to clues in the text that one of the statements made is not simply asserted but is said to follow logically from another statement or other statements in the text.

3. It is important to determine exactly what the question is asking; in fact, you might find it helpful to read the question first, before reading the material on which it is based. For example, an argument may appear to have an obvious flaw, and you may expect to be asked to detect that flaw; but the question may actually ask you to recognize the one among the answer choices that does NOT describe a weakness of the argument.

4. Read all the answer choices carefully. You should not assume that a given answer is the best answer without first reading all the choices.

When you take the sample test sections, use the answer spaces on page 211 to mark your answers.

Answer Spaces for Critical Reasoning Sample Test Sections

Sample Test Section 1

1 Ⓐ Ⓑ Ⓒ Ⓓ Ⓔ   6 Ⓐ Ⓑ Ⓒ Ⓓ Ⓔ   11 Ⓐ Ⓑ Ⓒ Ⓓ Ⓔ   16 Ⓐ Ⓑ Ⓒ Ⓓ Ⓔ
2 Ⓐ Ⓑ Ⓒ Ⓓ Ⓔ   7 Ⓐ Ⓑ Ⓒ Ⓓ Ⓔ   12 Ⓐ Ⓑ Ⓒ Ⓓ Ⓔ   17 Ⓐ Ⓑ Ⓒ Ⓓ Ⓔ
3 Ⓐ Ⓑ Ⓒ Ⓓ Ⓔ   8 Ⓐ Ⓑ Ⓒ Ⓓ Ⓔ   13 Ⓐ Ⓑ Ⓒ Ⓓ Ⓔ   18 Ⓐ Ⓑ Ⓒ Ⓓ Ⓔ
4 Ⓐ Ⓑ Ⓒ Ⓓ Ⓔ   9 Ⓐ Ⓑ Ⓒ Ⓓ Ⓔ   14 Ⓐ Ⓑ Ⓒ Ⓓ Ⓔ   19 Ⓐ Ⓑ Ⓒ Ⓓ Ⓔ
5 Ⓐ Ⓑ Ⓒ Ⓓ Ⓔ   10 Ⓐ Ⓑ Ⓒ Ⓓ Ⓔ   15 Ⓐ Ⓑ Ⓒ Ⓓ Ⓔ   20 Ⓐ Ⓑ Ⓒ Ⓓ Ⓔ

Sample Test Section 2

1 Ⓐ Ⓑ Ⓒ Ⓓ Ⓔ   6 Ⓐ Ⓑ Ⓒ Ⓓ Ⓔ   11 Ⓐ Ⓑ Ⓒ Ⓓ Ⓔ   16 Ⓐ Ⓑ Ⓒ Ⓓ Ⓔ
2 Ⓐ Ⓑ Ⓒ Ⓓ Ⓔ   7 Ⓐ Ⓑ Ⓒ Ⓓ Ⓔ   12 Ⓐ Ⓑ Ⓒ Ⓓ Ⓔ   17 Ⓐ Ⓑ Ⓒ Ⓓ Ⓔ
3 Ⓐ Ⓑ Ⓒ Ⓓ Ⓔ   8 Ⓐ Ⓑ Ⓒ Ⓓ Ⓔ   13 Ⓐ Ⓑ Ⓒ Ⓓ Ⓔ   18 Ⓐ Ⓑ Ⓒ Ⓓ Ⓔ
4 Ⓐ Ⓑ Ⓒ Ⓓ Ⓔ   9 Ⓐ Ⓑ Ⓒ Ⓓ Ⓔ   14 Ⓐ Ⓑ Ⓒ Ⓓ Ⓔ   19 Ⓐ Ⓑ Ⓒ Ⓓ Ⓔ
5 Ⓐ Ⓑ Ⓒ Ⓓ Ⓔ   10 Ⓐ Ⓑ Ⓒ Ⓓ Ⓔ   15 Ⓐ Ⓑ Ⓒ Ⓓ Ⓔ   20 Ⓐ Ⓑ Ⓒ Ⓓ Ⓔ

Sample Test Section 3

1 Ⓐ Ⓑ Ⓒ Ⓓ Ⓔ   6 Ⓐ Ⓑ Ⓒ Ⓓ Ⓔ   11 Ⓐ Ⓑ Ⓒ Ⓓ Ⓔ   16 Ⓐ Ⓑ Ⓒ Ⓓ Ⓔ
2 Ⓐ Ⓑ Ⓒ Ⓓ Ⓔ   7 Ⓐ Ⓑ Ⓒ Ⓓ Ⓔ   12 Ⓐ Ⓑ Ⓒ Ⓓ Ⓔ   17 Ⓐ Ⓑ Ⓒ Ⓓ Ⓔ
3 Ⓐ Ⓑ Ⓒ Ⓓ Ⓒ   8 Ⓐ Ⓑ Ⓒ Ⓓ Ⓔ   13 Ⓐ Ⓑ Ⓒ Ⓓ Ⓔ   18 Ⓐ Ⓑ Ⓒ Ⓓ Ⓔ
4 Ⓐ Ⓑ Ⓒ Ⓓ Ⓔ   9 Ⓐ Ⓑ Ⓒ Ⓓ Ⓔ   14 Ⓐ Ⓑ Ⓒ Ⓓ Ⓔ   19 Ⓐ Ⓑ Ⓒ Ⓓ Ⓔ
5 Ⓐ Ⓑ Ⓒ Ⓓ Ⓔ   10 Ⓐ Ⓑ Ⓒ Ⓓ Ⓔ   15 Ⓐ Ⓑ Ⓒ Ⓓ Ⓔ   20 Ⓐ Ⓑ Ⓒ Ⓓ Ⓔ

<u>Directions</u>: For each question in this section, select the best of the answer choices given.

1. Nearly one in three subscribers to *Financial Forecaster* is a millionaire, and over half are in top management. Shouldn't you subscribe to *Financial Forecaster* now?

   A reader who is neither a millionaire nor in top management would be most likely to act in accordance with the advertisement's suggestion if he or she drew which of the following questionable conclusions invited by the advertisement?

   (A) Among finance-related periodicals, *Financial Forecaster* provides the most detailed financial information.
   (B) Top managers cannot do their jobs properly without reading *Financial Forecaster*.
   (C) The advertisement is placed where those who will be likely to read it are millionaires.
   (D) The subscribers mentioned were helped to become millionaires or join top management by reading *Financial Forecaster*.
   (E) Only those who will in fact become millionaires, or at least top managers, will read the advertisement.

Questions 2-3 are based on the following.

Contrary to the charges made by some of its opponents, the provisions of the new deficit-reduction law for indiscriminate cuts in the federal budget are justified. Opponents should remember that the New Deal pulled this country out of great economic troubles even though some of its programs were later found to be unconstitutional.

2. The author's method of attacking the charges of certain opponents of the new deficit-reduction law is to

   (A) attack the character of the opponents rather than their claim
   (B) imply an analogy between the law and some New Deal programs
   (C) point out that the opponents' claims imply a dilemma
   (D) show that the opponents' reasoning leads to an absurd conclusion
   (E) show that the New Deal also called for indiscriminate cuts in the federal budget

3. The opponents could effectively defend their position against the author's strategy by pointing out that

   (A) the expertise of those opposing the law is outstanding
   (B) the lack of justification for the new law does not imply that those who drew it up were either inept or immoral
   (C) the practical application of the new law will not entail indiscriminate budget cuts
   (D) economic troubles present at the time of the New Deal were equal in severity to those that have led to the present law
   (E) the fact that certain flawed programs or laws have improved the economy does not prove that every such program can do so

4. In Millington, a city of 50,000 people, Mercedes Pedrosa, a realtor, calculated that a family with Millington's median family income, $28,000 a year, could afford to buy Millington's median-priced $77,000 house. This calculation was based on an 11.2 percent mortgage interest rate and on the realtor's assumption that a family could only afford to pay up to 25 percent of its income for housing.

   Which of the following corrections of a figure appearing in the passage above, if it were the only correction that needed to be made, would yield a new calculation showing that even incomes below the median family income would enable families in Millington to afford Millington's median-priced house?

   (A) Millington's total population was 45,000 people.
   (B) Millington's median annual family income was $27,000.
   (C) Millington's median-priced house cost $80,000.
   (D) The rate at which people in Millington had to pay mortgage interest was only 10 percent.
   (E) Families in Millington could only afford to pay up to 22 percent of their annual income for housing.

5. Psychological research indicates that college hockey and football players are more quickly moved to hostility and aggression than are college athletes in noncontact sports such as swimming. But the researchers' conclusion—that contact sports encourage and teach participants to be hostile and aggressive—is untenable. The football and hockey players were probably more hostile and aggressive to start with than the swimmers.

Which of the following, if true, would most strengthen the conclusion drawn by the psychological researchers?

(A) The football and hockey players became more hostile and aggressive during the season and remained so during the off-season, whereas there was no increase in aggressiveness among the swimmers.

(B) The football and hockey players, but not the swimmers, were aware at the start of the experiment that they were being tested for aggressiveness.

(C) The same psychological research indicated that the football and hockey players had a great respect for cooperation and team play, whereas the swimmers were most concerned with excelling as individual competitors.

(D) The research studies were designed to include no college athletes who participated in both contact and noncontact sports.

(E) Throughout the United States, more incidents of fan violence occur at baseball games than occur at hockey or football games.

6. Ross: The profitability of Company X, restored to private ownership five years ago, is clear evidence that businesses will always fare better under private than under public ownership.

Julia: Wrong. A close look at the records shows that X has been profitable since the appointment of a first-class manager, which happened while X was still in the public sector.

Which of the following best describes the weak point in Ross's claim on which Julia's response focuses?

(A) The evidence Ross cites comes from only a single observed case, that of Company X.

(B) The profitability of Company X might be only temporary.

(C) Ross's statement leaves open the possibility that the cause he cites came after the effect he attributes to it.

(D) No mention is made of companies that are partly government owned and partly privately owned.

(E) No exact figures are given for the current profits of Company X.

7. Stronger patent laws are needed to protect inventions from being pirated. With that protection, manufacturers would be encouraged to invest in the development of new products and technologies. Such investment frequently results in an increase in a manufacturer's productivity.

Which of the following conclusions can most properly be drawn from the information above?

(A) Stronger patent laws tend to benefit financial institutions as well as manufacturers.

(B) Increased productivity in manufacturing is likely to be accompanied by the creation of more manufacturing jobs.

(C) Manufacturers will decrease investment in the development of new products and technologies unless there are stronger patent laws.

(D) The weakness of current patent laws has been a cause of economic recession.

(E) Stronger patent laws would stimulate improvements in productivity for many manufacturers.

8. Which of the following best completes the passage below?

At large amusement parks, live shows are used very deliberately to influence crowd movements. Lunchtime performances relieve the pressure on a park's restaurants. Evening performances have a rather different purpose: to encourage visitors to stay for supper. Behind this surface divergence in immediate purpose there is the unified underlying goal of _ _ _ _ _ _ _.

(A) keeping the lines at the various rides short by drawing off part of the crowd

(B) enhancing revenue by attracting people who come only for the live shows and then leave the park

(C) avoiding as far as possible traffic jams caused by visitors entering or leaving the park

(D) encouraging as many people as possible to come to the park in order to eat at the restaurants

(E) utilizing the restaurants at optimal levels for as much of the day as possible

9. James weighs more than Kelly.
Luis weighs more than Mark.
Mark weighs less than Ned.
Kelly and Ned are exactly the same weight.

If the information above is true, which of the following must also be true?

(A) Luis weighs more than Ned.
(B) Luis weighs more than James.
(C) Kelly weighs less than Luis.
(D) James weighs more than Mark.
(E) Kelly weighs less than Mark.

Partly because of bad weather, but also partly because some major pepper growers have switched to high-priced cocoa, world production of pepper has been running well below worldwide sales for three years. Pepper is consequently in relatively short supply. The price of pepper has soared in response: it now equals that of cocoa.

10. Which of the following can be inferred from the passage?

    (A) Pepper is a profitable crop only if it is grown on a large scale.
    (B) World consumption of pepper has been unusually high for three years.
    (C) World production of pepper will return to previous levels once normal weather returns.
    (D) Surplus stocks of pepper have been reduced in the past three years.
    (E) The profits that the growers of pepper have made in the past three years have been unprecedented.

11. Some observers have concluded that the rise in the price of pepper means that the switch by some growers from pepper to cocoa left those growers no better off than if none of them had switched; this conclusion, however, is unwarranted because it can be inferred to be likely that

    (A) those growers could not have foreseen how high the price of pepper would go
    (B) the initial cost involved in switching from pepper to cocoa is substantial
    (C) supplies of pepper would not be as low as they are if those growers had not switched crops
    (D) cocoa crops are as susceptible to being reduced by bad weather as are pepper crops
    (E) as more growers turn to growing cocoa, cocoa supplies will increase and the price of cocoa will fall precipitously

12. Using computer techniques, researchers analyze layers of paint that lie buried beneath the surface layers of old paintings. They claim, for example, that additional mountainous scenery once appeared in Leonardo da Vinci's *Mona Lisa*, which was later painted over. Skeptics reply to these claims, however, that X-ray examinations of the *Mona Lisa* do not show hidden mountains.

Which of the following, if true, would tend most to weaken the force of the skeptics' objections?

    (A) There is no written or anecdotal record that Leonardo da Vinci ever painted over major areas of his *Mona Lisa*.
    (B) Painters of da Vinci's time commonly created images of mountainous scenery in the backgrounds of portraits like the *Mona Lisa*.
    (C) No one knows for certain what parts of the *Mona Lisa* may have been painted by da Vinci's assistants rather than by da Vinci himself.
    (D) Infrared photography of the *Mona Lisa* has revealed no trace of hidden mountainous scenery.
    (E) Analysis relying on X-rays only has the capacity to detect lead-based white pigments in layers of paint beneath a painting's surface layers.

13. While Governor Verdant has been in office, the state's budget has increased by an average of 6 percent each year. While the previous governor was in office, the state's budget increased by an average of $11\frac{1}{2}$ percent each year. Obviously, the austere budgets during Governor Verdant's term have caused the slowdown in the growth in state spending.

Which of the following, if true, would most seriously weaken the conclusion drawn above?

    (A) The rate of inflation in the state averaged 10 percent each year during the previous governor's term in office and 3 percent each year during Verdant's term.
    (B) Both federal and state income tax rates have been lowered considerably during Verdant's term in office.
    (C) In each year of Verdant's term in office, the state's budget has shown some increase in spending over the previous year.
    (D) During Verdant's term in office, the state has either discontinued or begun to charge private citizens for numerous services that the state offered free to citizens during the previous governor's term.
    (E) During the previous governor's term in office, the state introduced several so-called "austerity" budgets intended to reduce the growth in state spending.

14. Federal agricultural programs aimed at benefiting one group whose livelihood depends on farming often end up harming another such group.

Which of the following statements provides support for the claim above?

   I. An effort to help feed-grain producers resulted in higher prices for their crops, but the higher prices decreased the profits of livestock producers.
   II. In order to reduce crop surpluses and increase prices, growers of certain crops were paid to leave a portion of their land idle, but the reduction was not achieved because improvements in efficiency resulted in higher production on the land in use.
   III. Many farm workers were put out of work when a program meant to raise the price of grain provided grain growers with an incentive to reduce production by giving them surplus grain from government reserves.

   (A) I, but not II and not III
   (B) II, but not I and not III
   (C) I and III, but not II
   (D) II and III, but not I
   (E) I, II, and III

15. Technological education is worsening. People between eighteen and twenty-four, who are just emerging from their formal education, are more likely to be technologically illiterate than somewhat older adults. And yet, issues for public referenda will increasingly involve aspects of technology.

Which of the following conclusions can be properly drawn from the statements above?

   (A) If all young people are to make informed decisions on public referenda, many of them must learn more about technology.
   (B) Thorough studies of technological issues and innovations should be made a required part of the public and private school curriculum.
   (C) It should be suggested that prospective voters attend applied science courses in order to acquire a minimal competency in technical matters.
   (D) If young people are not to be overly influenced by famous technocrats, they must increase their knowledge of pure science.
   (E) On public referenda issues, young people tend to confuse real or probable technologies with impossible ideals.

16. In a political system with only two major parties, the entrance of a third-party candidate into an election race damages the chances of only one of the two major candidates. The third-party candidate always attracts some of the voters who might otherwise have voted for one of the two major candidates, but not voters who support the other candidate. Since a third-party candidacy affects the two major candidates unequally, for reasons neither of them has any control over, the practice is unfair and should not be allowed.

If the factual information in the passage above is true, which of the following can be most reliably inferred from it?

   (A) If the political platform of the third party is a compromise position between that of the two major parties, the third party will draw its voters equally from the two major parties.
   (B) If, before the emergence of a third party, voters were divided equally between the two major parties, neither of the major parties is likely to capture much more than one-half of the vote.
   (C) A third-party candidate will not capture the votes of new voters who have never voted for candidates of either of the two major parties.
   (D) The political stance of a third party will be more radical than that of either of the two major parties.
   (E) The founders of a third party are likely to be a coalition consisting of former leaders of the two major parties.

17. Companies considering new cost-cutting manufacturing processes often compare the projected results of making the investment against the alternative of not making the investment with costs, selling prices, and share of market remaining constant.

Which of the following, assuming that each is a realistic possibility, constitutes the most serious disadvantage for companies of using the method above for evaluating the financial benefit of new manufacturing processes?

   (A) The costs of materials required by the new process might not be known with certainty.
   (B) In several years interest rates might go down, reducing the interest costs of borrowing money to pay for the investment.
   (C) Some cost-cutting processes might require such expensive investments that there would be no net gain for many years, until the investment was paid for by savings in the manufacturing process.
   (D) Competitors that do invest in a new process might reduce their selling prices and thus take market share away from companies that do not.
   (E) The period of year chosen for averaging out the cost of the investment might be somewhat longer or shorter, thus affecting the result.

18. There are far fewer children available for adoption than there are people who want to adopt. Two million couples are currently waiting to adopt, but in 1982, the last year for which figures exist, there were only some 50,000 adoptions.

Which of the following statements, if true, most strengthens the author's claim that there are far fewer children available for adoption than there are people who want to adopt?

(A) The number of couples waiting to adopt has increased significantly in the last decade.

(B) The number of adoptions in the current year is greater than the number of adoptions in any preceding year.

(C) The number of adoptions in a year is approximately equal to the number of children available for adoption in that period.

(D) People who seek to adopt children often go through a long process of interviews and investigation by adoption agencies.

(E) People who seek to adopt children generally make very good parents.

Questions 19-20 are based on the following.

Archaeologists seeking the location of a legendary siege and destruction of a city are excavating in several possible places, including a middle and a lower layer of a large mound. The bottom of the middle layer contains some pieces of pottery of type 3, known to be from a later period than the time of the destruction of the city, but the lower layer does not.

19. Which of the following hypotheses is best supported by the evidence above?

(A) The lower layer contains the remains of the city where the siege took place.

(B) The legend confuses stories from two different historical periods.

(C) The middle layer does not represent the period of the siege.

(D) The siege lasted for a long time before the city was destroyed.

(E) The pottery of type 3 was imported to the city by traders.

20. The force of the evidence cited above is most seriously weakened if which of the following is true?

(A) Gerbils, small animals long native to the area, dig large burrows into which objects can fall when the burrows collapse.

(B) Pottery of types 1 and 2, found in the lower level, was used in the cities from which, according to the legend, the besieging forces came.

(C) Several pieces of stone from a lower-layer wall have been found incorporated into the remains of a building in the middle layer.

(D) Both the middle and the lower layer show evidence of large-scale destruction of habitations by fire.

(E) Bronze axheads of a type used at the time of the siege were found in the lower level of excavation.

S T O P

IF YOU FINISH BEFORE TIME IS CALLED, YOU MAY CHECK YOUR WORK ON THIS SECTION ONLY. DO NOT TURN TO ANY OTHER SECTION IN THE TEST.

Answer Key for Sample Test Section 1

CRITICAL REASONING

1. D	11. C
2. B	12. E
3. E	13. A
4. D	14. C
5. A	15. A
6. C	16. B
7. E	17. D
8. E	18. C
9. D	19. C
10. D	20. A

Explanatory Material: Critical Reasoning Sample Test Section 1

The following discussion of Critical Reasoning is intended to illustrate the variety of ways Critical Reasoning questions may be approached, and to give you an indication of the degree of precision and depth of reasoning that solving these problems will typically require. The particular questions in the sample test sections in this chapter are generally representative of the kinds of questions you will encounter in this section of the GMAT. Remember that the subject matter of a particular question is less important than the reasoning task you are asked to perform.

1. Nearly one in three subscribers to *Financial Forecaster* is a millionaire, and over half are in top management. Shouldn't you subscribe to *Financial Forecaster* now?

   A reader who is neither a millionaire nor in top management would be most likely to act in accordance with the advertisement's suggestion if he or she drew which of the following questionable conclusions invited by the advertisement?

   (A) Among finance-related periodicals, *Financial Forecaster* provides the most detailed financial information.
   (B) Top managers cannot do their jobs properly without reading *Financial Forecaster*.
   (C) The advertisement is placed where those who will be likely to read it are millionaires.
   (D) The subscribers mentioned were helped to become millionaires or join top management by reading *Financial Forecaster*.
   (E) Only those who will in fact become millionaires, or at least top managers, will read the advertisement.

The advertisement presents statistics about the representation of millionaires and top managers among *Financial Forecaster's* subscribers and suggests that these statistics might induce the reader to subscribe. A nonsubscriber who is neither a millionaire nor in top management would have a good reason to subscribe if that nonsubscriber thought that D was true and further thought, "If it worked for them, why not for me?" Therefore, D is the best answer.

Choice A is inappropriate because the advertisement does not touch on the contents of the magazine. For the nonsubscriber who is not in top management, B is not a reason to subscribe now. Someone who concluded C would probably feel that the advertisement was not addressed to nonmillionaires. The advertisement associates being a millionaire or top manager with being a subscriber, but not with being a reader of the advertisement, as E suggests.

Questions 2-3 are based on the following.

Contrary to the charges made by some of its opponents, the provisions of the new deficit-reduction law for indiscriminate cuts in the federal budget are justified. Opponents should remember that the New Deal pulled this country out of great economic troubles even though some of its programs were later found to be unconstitutional.

2. The author's method of attacking the charges of certain opponents of the new deficit-reduction law is to

   (A) attack the character of the opponents rather than their claim
   (B) imply an analogy between the law and some New Deal programs
   (C) point out that the opponents' claims imply a dilemma
   (D) show that the opponents' reasoning leads to an absurd conclusion
   (E) show that the New Deal also called for indiscriminate cuts in the federal budget

The author cites certain New Deal programs as a relevant precedent for certain highly desirable ends justifying the use of controversial means. The New Deal programs and the new deficit-reduction law are treated as analogous inasmuch as they are the controversial means in the two situations. Therefore, B is the best answer.

Choice A is inappropriate because the author takes issue with what the opponents say, not with their character. The author claims that the opponents are wrong, not that their position leads to a choice between two equally unsatisfactory alternatives, as C implies. The author attempts to show that the opponents' position is wrong, not, as D states, that it is absurd. Choice E adds information not given by the author, who does not indicate what was found unconstitutional in the New Deal programs.

3. The opponents could effectively defend their position against the author's strategy by pointing out that

(A) the expertise of those opposing the law is outstanding
(B) the lack of justification for the new law does not imply that those who drew it up were either inept or immoral
(C) the practical application of the new law will not entail indiscriminate budget cuts
(D) economic troubles present at the time of the New Deal were equal in severity to those that have led to the present law
(E) the fact that certain flawed programs or laws have improved the economy does not prove that every such program can do so

Choice E is an instance of a basic defense against any loose argument by analogy: the mere fact that two situations share one set of characteristics—here, an economic goal and the use of controversial means to achieve that goal—does not mean that they will automatically share other characteristics—here, effectiveness in reaching the objective. Therefore, E is the best answer.

Choices A and B suggest that the disagreement between author and opponents deserves to be taken seriously, but neither addresses the specific merits of the author's argument. Both C and D seem to favor the author's, not the opponents', side of the argument—C by suggesting judicious implemetation of the new law and D by suggesting that the circumstances that engendered New Deal programs are analogous and thus New Deal programs are an appropriate precedent.

4. In Millington, a city of 50,000 people, Mercedes Pedrosa, a realtor, calculated that a family with Millington's median family income, $28,000 a year, could afford to buy Millington's median-priced $77,000 house. This calculation was based on an 11.2 percent mortgage interest rate and on the realtor's assumption that a family could only afford to pay up to 25 percent of its income for housing.

Which of the following corrections of a figure appearing in the passage above, if it were the only correction that needed to be made, would yield a new calculation showing that even incomes below the median family income would enable families in Millington to afford Millington's median-priced house?

(A) Millington's total population was 45,000 people.
(B) Millington's median annual family income was $27,000.
(C) Millington's median-priced house cost $80,000.
(D) The rate at which people in Millington had to pay mortgage interest was only 10 percent.
(E) Families in Millington could only afford to pay up to 22 percent of their annual income for housing.

A given monthly mortgage payment can pay off a higher mortgage if the rate of mortgage interest is lower. Thus, if correction D were made, a family with the median family income could afford a more expensive house than the median-priced house, and median-priced houses would come within the reach of lower-than-median family incomes. Therefore, D is the best answer.

If A is the only correction, none of the figures entering into Pedrosa's calculations change. Both B and E imply a reduced ability to pay on the part of the median-income family, which would put the median-priced house out of its reach. Choice C implies large mortgage payments without any improvement in ability to pay.

5. Psychological research indicates that college hockey and football players are more quickly moved to hostility and aggression than are college athletes in noncontact sports such as swimming. But the researchers' conclusion—that contact sports encourage and teach participants to be hostile and aggressive—is untenable. The football and hockey players were probably more hostile and aggressive to start with than the swimmers.

Which of the following, if true, would most strengthen the conclusion drawn by the psychological researchers?

(A) The football and hockey players became more hostile and aggressive during the season and remained so during the off-season, whereas there was no increase in aggressiveness among the swimmers.
(B) The football and hockey players, but not the swimmers, were aware at the start of the experiment that they were being tested for aggressiveness.
(C) The same psychological research indicated that the football and hockey players had a great respect for cooperation and team play, whereas the swimmers were most concerned with excelling as individual competitors.
(D) The research studies were designed to include no college athletes who participated in both contact and noncontact sports.
(E) Throughout the United States, more incidents of fan violence occur at baseball games than occur at hockey or football games.

Choice A strengthens the psychologists' conclusion by citing facts that their conclusion can help account for while the opposing view cannot. Therefore, A is the best answer.

The differential awareness among experimental subjects suggested in B is a serious design flaw that tends to invalidate the experimental results and any conclusions drawn from them. Based on the available information, C has no bearing on the conclusion being examined. Choice D is an element of good experimental design that increases the likelihood that the experimental data were sound but not the likelihood that the correct conclusion was drawn from them. Choice E makes a statement about spectators that has no direct relevance to the psychological states of athletes participating in the games.

6. **Ross:** The profitability of Company X, restored to private ownership five years ago, is clear evidence that businesses will always fare better under private than under public ownership.

   Julia: Wrong. A close look at the records shows that X has been profitable since the appointment of a first-class manager, which happened while X was still in the public sector.

   Which of the following best describes the weak point in Ross's claim on which Julia's response focuses?

   (A) The evidence Ross cites comes from only a single observed case, that of Company X.
   (B) The profitability of Company X might be only temporary.
   (C) Ross's statement leaves open the possibility that the cause he cites came after the effect he attributes to it.
   (D) No mention is made of companies that are partly government owned and partly privately owned.
   (E) No exact figures are given for the current profits of Company X.

Ross cites the fact that X is profitable under the current private ownership as evidence that this type of ownership is causally related to a company's ability to show a profit. But Ross neglects to establish specifically that X had failed to be profitable under its previous, public ownership. Julia's response focuses on this omission on Ross's part. Therefore, C is the best answer.

Ross overgeneralizes, as A says, but Julia does not react to that. The condition cited by Ross as evidence might not be stable, as B suggests, but Julia does not take up this point. Those companies with mixed ownership mentioned in D would not clearly bear on Ross's conclusion. Julia's response ignores the size of current profits, the issue mentioned in E; it concentrates on when the return to profitability occurred.

7. Stronger patent laws are needed to protect inventions from being pirated. With that protection, manufacturers would be encouraged to invest in the development of new products and technologies. Such investment frequently results in an increase in a manufacturer's productivity.

   Which of the following conclusions can most properly be drawn from the information above?

   (A) Stronger patent laws tend to benefit financial institutions as well as manufacturers.
   (B) Increased productivity in manufacturing is likely to be accompanied by the creation of more manufacturing jobs.
   (C) Manufacturers will decrease investment in the development of new products and technologies unless there are stronger patent laws.
   (D) The weakness of current patent laws has been a cause of economic recession.
   (E) Stronger patent laws would stimulate improvements in productivity for many manufacturers.

Stronger patent laws increase protection; protection encourages investment; investment often raises productivity. Thus, stronger patent laws initiate a chain of events that often culminates in improved productivity. Choice E expresses that and is, therefore, the best answer.

Choice A is inappropriate because the role, if any, that financial institutions would play in investments is left open. The increased productivity mentioned in B may mean fewer hours of labor for a given level of output, and may thus threaten jobs. Investments of the sort described in C may already be at the lowest possible level. The passage gives no indication that there has been an economic recession as D suggests; hence, there is no attempt to isolate the causes of economic recessions.

8. Which of the following best completes the passage below?

   At large amusement parks, live shows are used very deliberately to influence crowd movements. Lunchtime performances relieve the pressure on a park's restaurants. Evening performances have a rather different purpose: to encourage visitors to stay for supper. Behind this surface divergence in immediate purpose there is the unified underlying goal of _ _ _ _ _ _ _ .

   (A) keeping the lines at the various rides short by drawing off part of the crowd
   (B) enhancing revenue by attracting people who come only for the live shows and then leave the park
   (C) avoiding as far as possible traffic jams caused by visitors entering or leaving the park
   (D) encouraging as many people as possible to come to the park in order to eat at the restaurants
   (E) utilizing the restaurants at optimal levels for as much of the day as possible

Lunchtime performances keep people away from the restaurants at the restaurants' busiest time, presumably causing restaurant patrons to have lunch either early or late, when they can be accommodated better. Evening performances can be inferred to bring customers to the restaurants at a time when business there is slack. The effect is to spread out business in the restaurants and bring the level of business more in line with capacity. Therefore, E is the best answer.

Choice A is inappropriate because the lines at rides are not mentioned as a consideration. Live shows are said to be aimed at people already in the park, making B inaccurate. Choice C is inadequate: evening performances might actually create traffic jams if everyone leaves at their conclusion. Choice D is incompatible with the stated purpose of lunchtime performances.

9. James weighs more than Kelly.
Luis weighs more than Mark.
Mark weighs less than Ned.
Kelly and Ned are exactly the same weight.

If the information above is true, which of the following must also be true?

(A) Luis weighs more than Ned.
(B) Luis weighs more than James.
(C) Kelly weighs less than Luis.
(D) James weighs more than Mark.
(E) Kelly weighs less than Mark.

Since Mark weighs less than Ned, and since Ned weighs the same as Kelly, Mark also weighs less than Kelly. Since James weighs more than Kelly, James must also weigh more than Mark. Therefore, D is the best answer.

A, B, and C might be true, but none of them can be inferred to be true, since not enough information is given about Luis's weight in relation to the weight of the others. Choice E can be inferred to be false from the information given.

Questions 10-11 are based on the following.

Partly because of bad weather, but also partly because some major pepper growers have switched to high-priced cocoa, world production of pepper has been running well below worldwide sales for three years. Pepper is consequently in relatively short supply. The price of pepper has soared in response: it now equals that of cocoa.

10. Which of the following can be inferred from the passage?

(A) Pepper is a profitable crop only if it is grown on a large scale.
(B) World consumption of pepper has been unusually high for three years.
(C) World production of pepper will return to previous levels once normal weather returns.
(D) Surplus stocks of pepper have been reduced in the past three years.
(E) The profits that the growers of pepper have made in the past three years have been unprecedented.

If more pepper was sold than was produced, some sales must have come from surplus stocks, and those stocks must have dropped during the three-year period in question. Therefore, D is the best answer.

Choice A is inappropriate because the information in the passage is consistent with pepper being a profitable crop if grown on a modest scale. The passage provides no figures on which to base estimates of the world consumption of pepper, such as those made in B. Choice C is inconsistent with the information in the passage that states that world production will not return to previous levels unless either the pepper acreage lost to cocoa is replaced or the reduced remaining acreage is made more productive. No clear inferences can be made about growers' profits in the last three, or any earlier, years; consequently, E is inappropriate.

11. Some observers have concluded that the rise in the price of pepper means that the switch by some growers from pepper to cocoa left those growers no better off than if none of them had switched; this conclusion, however, is unwarranted because it can be inferred to be likely that

(A) those growers could not have foreseen how high the price of pepper would go
(B) the initial cost involved in switching from pepper to cocoa is substantial
(C) supplies of pepper would not be as low as they are if those growers had not switched crops
(D) cocoa crops are as susceptible to being reduced by bad weather as are pepper crops
(E) as more growers turn to growing cocoa, cocoa supplies will increase and the price of cocoa will fall precipitously

Choice C can be inferred to be likely: it requires only the assumption that those growers, if they had not switched crops, would have continued to grow pepper. But if supplies of pepper were not as low as they are, the price of pepper would not have risen enough to equal the price of cocoa, and the growers in question would not have done as well, financially, as they actually did as a result of switching to cocoa. Therefore, C is the best answer.

The better foresight mentioned in A might have kept the growers from doing what they did, but it is irrelevant to the outcome of what they did do. Choices B, D, and E are not inferrable and do not bear on the role of the rise in the price of pepper in affecting the financial consequences of the switch in crops.

12. Using computer techniques, researchers analyze layers of paint that lie buried beneath the surface layers of old paintings. They claim, for example, that additional mountainous scenery once appeared in Leonardo da Vinci's *Mona Lisa,* which was later painted over. Skeptics reply to these claims, however, that X-ray examinations of the *Mona Lisa* do not show hidden mountains.

Which of the following, if true, would tend most to weaken the force of the skeptics' objections?

(A) There is no written or anecdotal record that Leonardo da Vinci ever painted over major areas of his *Mona Lisa.*
(B) Painters of da Vinci's time commonly created images of mountainous scenery in the backgrounds of portraits like the *Mona Lisa.*
(C) No one knows for certain what parts of the *Mona Lisa* may have been painted by da Vinci's assistants rather than by da Vinci himself.
(D) Infrared photography of the *Mona Lisa* has revealed no trace of hidden mountainous scenery.
(E) Analysis relying on X-rays only has the capacity to detect lead-based white pigments in layers of paint beneath a painting's surface layers.

Even assuming that lead-based white pigments were in fact used in painting the *Mona Lisa,* it is not clear, without further argument, that mountainous scenery, if it had been painted, would contain white pigments in such a configuration that the presence of mountainous scenery could be deduced. Thus, the skeptics' evidence might have no force. Therefore, E is the best answer.

The fact cited in A does not bear on whether mountainous scenery was ever present; it merely suggests that, if someone painted over any mountainous scenery, it was not da Vinci. The skeptics base their case on a physical examination of the *Mona Lisa.* Unless it is shown that their method yields inconclusive results, counterevidence derived from general artistic conventions, such as that mentioned in B, has no force. The information in C does not help determine what was in the painting. The statement in D strengthens the skeptics' case, or is irrelevant if infrared photography does not reveal deeper layers of paint.

13. While Governor Verdant has been in office, the state's budget has increased by an average of 6 percent each year. While the previous governor was in office, the state's budget increased by an average of $11\frac{1}{2}$ percent each year. Obviously, the austere budgets during Governor Verdant's term have caused the slowdown in the growth in state spending.

    Which of the following, if true, would most seriously weaken the conclusion drawn above?

    (A) The rate of inflation in the state averaged 10 percent each year during the previous governor's term in office and 3 percent each year during Verdant's term.
    (B) Both federal and state income tax rates have been lowered considerably during Verdant's term in office.
    (C) In each year of Verdant's term in office, the state's budget has shown some increase in spending over the previous year.
    (D) During Verdant's term in office, the state has either discontinued or begun to charge private citizens for numerous services that the state offered free to citizens during the previous governor's term.
    (E) During the previous governor's term in office, the state introduced several so-called "austerity" budgets intended to reduce the growth in state spending.

If inflation is, say 5 percent, then an amount of $105 at the end of a year has the same "real value" (purchasing power) as an amount of $100 at the beginning of that year. Given this, the figures in A show that "real" spending has increased by more under Verdant than under Verdant's predecessor. Therefore, A is the best answer.

Choice B deals with the sources of government income, not with government spending. The accuracy of the 6-percent figure given in the argument and on which the argument rests is not called into question, so C does not weaken the conclusion. Choice D tends to strengthen, rather than weaken, the position that Verdant's budgets have been austere. Choice E is inappropriate because the conclusion is based on actual figures, not descriptive phrases and avowed goals.

14. Federal agricultural programs aimed at benefiting one group whose livelihood depends on farming often end up harming another such group.

    Which of the following statements provides support for the claim above?

    I. An effort to help feed-grain producers resulted in higher prices for their crops, but the higher prices decreased the profits of livestock producers.
    II. In order to reduce crop surpluses and increase prices, growers of certain crops were paid to leave a portion of their land idle, but the reduction was not achieved because improvements in efficiency resulted in higher production on the land in use.
    III. Many farm workers were put out of work when a program meant to raise the price of grain provided grain growers with an incentive to reduce production by giving them surplus grain from government reserves.

    (A) I, but not II and not III
    (B) II, but not I and not III
    (C) I and III, but not II
    (D) II and III, but not I
    (E) I, II, and III

Any specific agricultural program that is designed to benefit one group whose livelihood depends on farming but also harms another such group provides support for the claim made here. Statement I describes such a case: feed-grain producers were intended to benefit, but livestock producers' interests were hurt. Statement III also describes such a case: grain growers were meant to benefit, but farm workers were adversely affected. Statement II does not describe a relevantly similar case: growers of certain crops were meant to benefit, but the hoped-for benefit did not materialize; yet there is no indication of any harm coming to another group making its living from farming. Therefore, C is the best answer.

15. Technological education is worsening. People between eighteen and twenty-four, who are just emerging from their formal education, are more likely to be technologically illiterate than somewhat older adults. And yet, issues for public referenda will increasingly involve aspects of technology.

Which of the following conclusions can be properly drawn from the statements above?

(A) If all young people are to make informed decisions on public referenda, many of them must learn more about technology.

(B) Thorough studies of technological issues and innovations should be made a required part of the public and private school curriculum.

(C) It should be suggested that prospective voters attend applied science courses in order to acquire a minimal competency in technical matters.

(D) If young people are not to be overly influenced by famous technocrats, they must increase their knowledge of pure science.

(E) On public referenda issues, young people tend to confuse real or probable technologies with impossible ideals.

The technologically illiterate among the young people cannot make informed decisions about technological issues that are increasingly a part of referenda. Informed decisions require knowledge. Therefore, choice A can be inferred and is the best answer.

Choices B, C, and D are inappropriate because while the passage presents a problem and allows the general outlines of a solution to be inferred, specific solutions such as those presented in B and C go beyond what can be inferred, as do recommendations like D that address potential problems that are not touched on in the passage. Choice E is too specific: the passage supports the conclusion that some young people will be unable to make informed decisions, but it suggests nothing about the kinds of errors young people might make.

16. In a political system with only two major parties, the entrance of a third-party candidate into an election race damages the chances of only one of the two major candidates. The third-party candidate always attracts some of the voters who might otherwise have voted for one of the two major candidates, but not voters who support the other candidate. Since a third-party candidacy affects the two major candidates unequally, for reasons neither of them has any control over, the practice is unfair and should not be allowed.

If the factual information in the passage above is true, which of the following can be most reliably inferred from it?

(A) If the political platform of the third party is a compromise position between that of the two major parties, the third party will draw its voters equally from the two major parties.

(B) If, before the emergence of a third party, voters were divided equally between the two major parties, neither of the major parties is likely to capture much more than one-half of the vote.

(C) A third-party candidate will not capture the votes of new voters who have never voted for candidates of either of the two major parties.

(D) The political stance of a third party will be more radical than that of either of the two major parties.

(E) The founders of a third party are likely to be a coalition consisting of former leaders of the two major parties.

If, as B hypothesizes, the electorate is split evenly between two parties, and if then a third-party candidate attracts votes from only one of the two parties, even the party that loses no votes to the third party is unlikely to capture more than one-half of the votes. Therefore, B is the best answer. best answer.

Choice A is inappropriate because it contradicts information given in the passage, while C goes beyond the passage, which does not exclude new voters from those "who might otherwise have voted for one of the two major candidates." The information given in the passage is not specific enough to make the inferences about the politics, or the founding, of the third party, as suggested in D and E.

17. Companies considering new cost-cutting manufacturing processes often compare the projected results of making the investment against the alternative of not making the investment with costs, selling prices, and share of market remaining constant.

Which of the following, assuming that each is a realistic possibility, constitutes the most serious disadvantage for companies of using the method above for evaluating the financial benefit of new manufacturing processes?

(A) The costs of materials required by the new process might not be known with certainty.

(B) In several years interest rates might go down, reducing the interest costs of borrowing money to pay for the investment.

(C) Some cost-cutting processes might require such expensive investments that there would be no net gain for many years, until the investment was paid for by savings in the manufacturing process.

(D) Competitors that do invest in a new process might reduce their selling prices and thus take market share away from companies that do not.

(E) The period of year chosen for averaging out the cost of the investment might be somewhat longer or shorter, thus affecting the result.

The method of evaluation described assumes that D will not happen. If D did happen, the method would systematically tend to value the noninvestment option too highly. Since D is said to be entirely possible, it represents a disadvantage of the method described. Therefore, D is the best answer.

Since the cost mentioned in A has to be estimated no matter what method of evaluation is chosen, A cannot be a disadvantage of one method relative to another. The factor mentioned in B may affect the timing of the investment, but the method described can accommodate alternative investment dates. The payback of the investment is a feature that the method described can presumably accommodate, and thus C is not appropriate. Evaluating the investment option inevitably involves uncertainty, but this is not a function of the method used, as E suggests it is.

18. There are far fewer children available for adoption than there are people who want to adopt. Two million couples are currently waiting to adopt, but in 1982, the last year for which figures exist, there were only some 50,000 adoptions.

Which of the following statements, if true, most strengthens the author's claim that there are far fewer children available for adoption than there are people who want to adopt?

(A) The number of couples waiting to adopt has increased significantly in the last decade.

(B) The number of adoptions in the current year is greater than the number of adoptions in any preceding year.

(C) The number of adoptions in a year is approximately equal to the number of children available for adoption in that period.

(D) People who seek to adopt children often go through a long process of interviews and investigation by adoption agencies.

(E) People who seek to adopt children generally make very good parents.

The evidence the author presents is weak because it is unclear how the number of adoptions in a year is related to the number of children available for adoption. Choice C settles that question in a way that strengthens the author's claim. The only remaining point of uncertainty is whether the 1982 figures are representative. Choices A, B, and D are all compatible with a situation in which there are as many children available for adoption as there are people wanting to adopt, but only a small fraction of the children available get adopted in any given year. The quality of parenting mentioned in E is irrelevant to any of the numbers cited. Thus, C is the only choice that clearly strengthens the author's claim and is, therefore, the best answer.

Archaeologists seeking the location of a legendary siege and destruction of a city are excavating in several possible places, including a middle and a lower layer of a large mound. The bottom of the middle layer contains some pieces of pottery of type 3, known to be from a later period than the time of the destruction of the city, but the lower layer does not.

19. Which of the following hypotheses is best supported by the evidence above?

(A) The lower layer contains the remains of the city where the siege took place.
(B) The legend confuses stories from two different historical periods.
(C) The middle layer does not represent the period of the siege.
(D) The siege lasted for a long time before the city was destroyed.
(E) The pottery of type 3 was imported to the city by traders.

If the city was destroyed before any pottery of type 3 was made, the hypothesis that the middle layer represents a period later than that of the siege is strongly supported. The major assumptions on which this hypothesis rests are only that lower layers represent earlier time periods and that objects from a later period did not become embedded in some unusual way in layers representing earlier periods. Hypothesis A is not strongly supported since the large mound may just be the wrong place to look. The evidence as described reveals nothing about any particular siege or episode of destruction; so neither hypothesis B nor D is supported. Hypothesis E is unsupported because the city of the legend is known to have been destroyed before type-3 pottery was first made. On balance, then, the best answer is C.

20. The force of the evidence cited above is most seriously weakened if which of the following is true?

(A) Gerbils, small animals long native to the area, dig large burrows into which objects can fall when the burrows collapse.
(B) Pottery of types 1 and 2, found in the lower level, was used in the cities from which, according to the legend, the besieging forces came.
(C) Several pieces of stone from a lower-layer wall have been found incorporated into the remains of a building in the middle layer.
(D) Both the middle and the lower layer show evidence of large-scale destruction of habitations by fire.
(E) Bronze axheads of a type used at the time of the siege were found in the lower level of excavation.

Choice A provides a way for an object from a higher, thus more recent, layer to get into a lower, older layer. If the lower layer is dated by such an object, that layer's age will be underestimated. Choice A suggests that it is possible that the type-3 pottery ended up in an older layer than is chronologically appropriate. The evidence cited leaves open what B and E suggest: that the lower layer represents the period of the siege. B and E are thus not contrary to the evidence cited. Choice C shows that materials from an earlier period may be reused in a later period. The question raised by the evidence cited, however, is whether materials from a later period can end up in a layer that dates from an earlier period. D is additional evidence of a neutral kind. Therefore, A is the best answer.

CRITICAL REASONING SAMPLE TEST SECTION 2

30 Minutes
20 Questions

Directions: For each question in this section, select the best of the answer choices given.

1. After the national speed limit of 55 miles per hour was imposed in 1974, the number of deaths per mile driven on a highway fell abruptly as a result. Since then, however, the average speed of vehicles on highways has risen, but the number of deaths per mile driven on a highway has continued to fall.

Which of the following conclusions can be properly drawn from the statements above?

(A) The speed limit alone is probably not responsible for the continued reduction in highway deaths in the years after 1974.
(B) People have been driving less since 1974.
(C) Driver-education courses have been more effective since 1974 in teaching drivers to drive safely.
(D) In recent years highway patrols have been less effective in catching drivers who speed.
(E) The change in the speed limit cannot be responsible for the abrupt decline in highway deaths in 1974.

2. Neighboring landholders: Air pollution from the giant aluminum refinery that has been built next to our land is killing our plants.

Company spokesperson: The refinery is not to blame, since our study shows that the damage is due to insects and fungi.

Which of the following, if true, most seriously weakens the conclusion drawn by the company spokesperson?

(A) The study did not measure the quantity of pollutants emitted into the surrounding air by the aluminum refinery.
(B) The neighboring landholders have made no change in the way they take care of their plants.
(C) Air pollution from the refinery has changed the chemical balance in the plants' environment, allowing the harmful insects and fungi to thrive.
(D) Pollutants that are invisible and odorless are emitted into the surrounding air by the refinery.
(E) The various species of insects and fungi mentioned in the study have been occasionally found in the locality during the past hundred years.

3. Sales taxes tend to be regressive, affecting poor people more severely than wealthy people. When all purchases of consumer goods are taxed at a fixed percentage of the purchase price, poor people pay a larger proportion of their income in sales taxes than wealthy people do.

It can be correctly inferred on the basis of the statements above that which of the following is true?

(A) Poor people constitute a larger proportion of the taxpaying population than wealthy people do.
(B) Poor people spend a larger proportion of their income on purchases of consumer goods than wealthy people do.
(C) Wealthy people pay, on average, a larger amount of sales taxes than poor people do.
(D) The total amount spent by all poor people on purchases of consumer goods exceeds the total amount spent by all wealthy people on consumer goods.
(E) The average purchase price of consumer goods bought by wealthy people is higher than that of consumer goods bought by poor people.

GO ON TO THE NEXT PAGE.

4. Reviewing historical data, medical researchers in California found that counties with the largest number of television sets per capita have had the lowest incidence of a serious brain disease, mosquito-borne encephalitis. The researchers have concluded that people in these counties stay indoors more and thus avoid exposure to the disease.

The researchers' conclusion would be most strengthened if which of the following were true?

(A) Programs designed to control the size of disease-bearing mosquito populations have not affected the incidence of mosquito-borne encephalitis.

(B) The occupations of county residents affect their risk of exposure to mosquito-borne encephalitis more than does television-watching.

(C) The incidence of mosquito-borne encephalitis in counties with the largest number of television sets per capita is likely to decrease even further.

(D) The more time people in a county spend outdoors, the greater their awareness of the dangers of mosquito-borne encephalitis.

(E) The more television sets there are per capita in a county, the more time the average county resident spends watching television.

5. The city's public transportation system should be removed from the jurisdiction of the municipal government, which finds it politically impossible either to raise fares or to institute cost-saving reductions in service. If public transportation were handled by a private firm, profits would be vigorously pursued, thereby eliminating the necessity for covering operating costs with government funds.

The statements above best support the conclusion that

(A) the private firms that would handle public transportation would have experience in the transportation industry

(B) political considerations would not prevent private firms from ensuring that revenues cover operating costs

(C) private firms would receive government funding if it were needed to cover operating costs

(D) the public would approve the cost-cutting actions taken by the private firm

(E) the municipal government would not be resigned to accumulating merely enough income to cover costs

6. To entice customers away from competitors, Red Label supermarkets have begun offering discounts on home appliances to customers who spend $50 or more on any shopping trip to Red Label. Red Label executives claim that the discount program has been a huge success, since cash register receipts of $50 or more are up thirty percent since the beginning of the program.

Which of the following, if true, most seriously weakens the claim of the Red Label executives?

(A) Most people who switched to Red Label after the program began spend more than $50 each time they shop at Red Label.

(B) Most people whose average grocery bill is less than $50 would not be persuaded to spend more by any discount program.

(C) Most people who received discounts on home appliances through Red Label's program will shop at Red Label after the program ends.

(D) Since the beginning of the discount program, most of the people who spend $50 or more at Red Label are people who have never before shopped there and whose average grocery bill has always been higher than $50.

(E) Almost all of the people who have begun spending $50 or more at Red Label since the discount program began are longtime customers who have increased the average amount of their shopping bills by making fewer trips.

7. Throughout the 1950's, there were increases in the numbers of dead birds found in agricultural areas after pesticide sprayings. Pesticide manufacturers claimed that the publicity given to bird deaths stimulated volunteers to look for dead birds, and that the increase in numbers reported was attributable to the increase in the number of people looking.

Which of the following statements, if true, would help to refute the claim of the pesticide manufacturers?

(A) The publicity given to bird deaths was largely regional and never reached national proportions.

(B) Pesticide sprayings were timed to coincide with various phases of the life cycles of the insects they destroyed.

(C) No provision was made to ensure that a dead bird would not be reported by more than one observer.

(D) Initial increases in bird deaths had been noticed by agricultural workers long before any publicity had been given to the matter.

(E) Dead birds of the same species as those found in agricultural areas had been found along coastal areas where no farming took place.

GO ON TO THE NEXT PAGE.

8. Teenagers are often priced out of the labor market by the government-mandated minimum-wage level because employers cannot afford to pay that much for extra help. Therefore, if Congress institutes a subminimum wage, a new lower legal wage for teenagers, the teenage unemployment rate, which has been rising since 1960, will no longer increase.

Which of the following, if true, would most weaken the argument above?

(A) Since 1960 the teenage unemployment rate has risen when the minimum wage has risen.
(B) Since 1960 the teenage unemployment rate has risen even when the minimum wage remained constant.
(C) Employers often hire extra help during holiday and warm weather seasons.
(D) The teenage unemployment rate rose more quickly in the 1970's than it did in the 1960's.
(E) The teenage unemployment rate has occasionally declined in the years since 1960.

9. Which of the following best completes the passage below?

The computer industry's estimate that it loses millions of dollars when users illegally copy programs without paying for them is greatly exaggerated. Most of the illegal copying is done by people with no serious interest in the programs. Thus, the loss to the industry is much smaller than estimated because

(A) many users who illegally copy programs never find any use for them
(B) most of the illegally copied programs would not be purchased even if purchasing them were the only way to obtain them
(C) even if the computer industry received all the revenue it claims to be losing, it would still be experiencing financial difficulties
(D) the total market value of all illegal copies is low in comparison to the total revenue of the computer industry
(E) the number of programs that are frequently copied illegally is low in comparison to the number of programs available for sale

10. This year the New Hampshire Division of Company X set a new record for annual sales by that division. This record is especially surprising since the New Hampshire Division has the smallest potential market and the lowest sales of any of Company X's divisions.

Which of the following identifies a flaw in the logical coherence of the statement above?

(A) If overall sales for Company X were sharply reduced, the New Hampshire Division's new sales record is irrelevant to the company's prosperity.
(B) Since the division is competing against its own record, the comparison of its sales record with that of other divisions is irrelevant.
(C) If this is the first year that the New Hampshire Division has been last in sales among Company X's divisions, the new record is not surprising at all.
(D) If overall sales for Company X were greater than usual, it is not surprising that the New Hampshire Division was last in sales.
(E) Since the New Hampshire Division has the smallest potential market, it is not surprising that it had the lowest sales.

11. Statement of a United States copper mining company: Import quotas should be imposed on the less expensive copper mined outside the country to maintain the price of copper in this country; otherwise, our companies will not be able to stay in business.

Response of a United States copper wire manufacturer: United States wire and cable manufacturers purchase about 70 percent of the copper mined in the United States. If the copper prices we pay are not at the international level, our sales will drop, and then the demand for United States copper will go down.

If the factual information presented by both companies is accurate, the best assessment of the logical relationship between the two arguments is that the wire manufacturer's argument

(A) is self-serving and irrelevant to the proposal of the mining company
(B) is circular, presupposing what it seeks to prove about the proposal of the mining company
(C) shows that the proposal of the mining company would have a negative effect on the mining company's own business
(D) fails to give a reason why the proposal of the mining company should not be put into effect to alleviate the concern of the mining company for staying in business
(E) establishes that even the mining company's business will prosper if the mining company's proposal is rejected

GO ON TO THE NEXT PAGE.

12. Y has been believed to cause Z. A new report, noting that Y and Z are often observed to be preceded by X, suggests that X, not Y, may be the cause of Z.

Which of the following further observations would best support the new report's suggestion?

(A) In cases where X occurs but Y does not, X is usually followed by Z.
(B) In cases where X occurs, followed by Y, Y is usually followed by Z.
(C) In cases where Y occurs but X does not, Y is usually followed by Z.
(D) In cases where Y occurs but Z does not, Y is usually preceded by X.
(E) In cases where Z occurs, it is usually preceded by X and Y.

13. Mr. Primm: If hospitals were private enterprises, dependent on profits for their survival, there would be no teaching hospitals, because of the intrinsically high cost of running such hospitals.

Ms. Nakai: I disagree. The medical challenges provided by teaching hospitals attract the very best physicians. This, in turn, enables those hospitals to concentrate on nonroutine cases.

Which of the following, if true, would most strengthen Ms. Nakai's attempt to refute Mr. Primm's claim?

(A) Doctors at teaching hospitals command high salaries.
(B) Sophisticated, nonroutine medical care commands a high price.
(C) Existing teaching hospitals derive some revenue from public subsidies.
(D) The patient mortality rate at teaching hospitals is high.
(E) The modern trend among physicians is to become highly specialized.

14. A recent survey of all auto accident victims in Dole County found that, of the severely injured drivers and front-seat passengers, 80 percent were not wearing seat belts at the time of their accidents. This indicates that, by wearing seat belts, drivers and front-seat passengers can greatly reduce their risk of being severely injured if they are in an auto accident.

The conclusion above is not properly drawn unless which of the following is true?

(A) Of all the drivers and front-seat passengers in the survey, more than 20 percent were wearing seat belts at the time of their accidents.
(B) Considerably more than 20 percent of drivers and front-seat passengers in Dole County always wear seat belts when traveling by car.
(C) More drivers and front-seat passengers in the survey than rear-seat passengers were very severely injured.
(D) More than half of the drivers and front-seat passengers in the survey were not wearing seat belts at the time of their accidents.
(E) Most of the auto accidents reported to police in Dole County do not involve any serious injury.

15. Six months or so after getting a video recorder, many early buyers apparently lost interest in obtaining videos to watch on it. The trade of businesses selling and renting videos is still buoyant, because the number of homes with video recorders is still growing. But clearly, once the market for video recorders is saturated, businesses distributing videos face hard times.

Which of the following, if true, would most seriously weaken the conclusion above?

(A) The market for video recorders would not be considered saturated until there was one in 80 percent of homes.
(B) Among the items handled by video distributors are many films specifically produced as video features.
(C) Few of the early buyers of video recorders raised any complaints about performance aspects of the new product.
(D) The early buyers of a novel product are always people who are quick to acquire novelties, but also often as quick to tire of them.
(E) In a shrinking market, competition always intensifies and marginal businesses fail.

GO ON TO THE NEXT PAGE.

16. Advertiser: The revenue that newspapers and magazines earn by publishing advertisements allows publishers to keep the prices per copy of their publications much lower than would otherwise be possible. Therefore, consumers benefit economically from advertising.

Consumer: But who pays for the advertising that pays for low-priced newspapers and magazines? We consumers do, because advertisers pass along advertising costs to us through the higher prices they charge for their products.

Which of the following best describes how the consumer counters the advertiser's argument?

(A) By alleging something that, if true, would weaken the plausibility of the advertiser's conclusion
(B) By questioning the truth of the purportedly factual statement on which the advertiser's conclusion is based
(C) By offering an interpretation of the advertiser's opening statement that, if accurate, shows that there is an implicit contradiction in it
(D) By pointing out that the advertiser's point of view is biased
(E) By arguing that the advertiser too narrowly restricts the discussion to the effects of advertising that are economic

17. Mr. Lawson: We should adopt a national family policy that includes legislation requiring employers to provide paid parental leave and establishing government-sponsored day care. Such laws would decrease the stress levels of employees who have responsibility for small children. Thus, such laws would lead to happier, better-adjusted families.

Which of the following, if true, would most strengthen the conclusion above?

(A) An employee's high stress level can be a cause of unhappiness and poor adjustment for his or her family.
(B) People who have responsibility for small children and who work outside the home have higher stress levels than those who do not.
(C) The goal of a national family policy is to lower the stress levels of parents.
(D) Any national family policy that is adopted would include legislation requiring employers to provide paid parental leave and establishing government-sponsored day care.
(E) Most children who have been cared for in day-care centers are happy and well adjusted.

18. Lark Manufacturing Company initiated a voluntary Quality Circles program for machine operators. Independent surveys of employee attitudes indicated that the machine operators participating in the program were less satisfied with their work situations after two years of the program's existence than they were at the program's start. Obviously, any workers who participate in a Quality Circles program will, as a result, become less satisfied with their jobs.

Each of the following, if true, would weaken the conclusion drawn above EXCEPT:

(A) The second survey occurred during a period of recession when rumors of cutbacks and layoffs at Lark Manufacturing were plentiful.
(B) The surveys also showed that those Lark machine operators who neither participated in Quality Circles nor knew anyone who did so reported the same degree of lessened satisfaction with their work situations as did the Lark machine operators who participated in Quality Circles.
(C) While participating in Quality Circles at Lark Manufacturing, machine operators exhibited two of the primary indicators of improved job satisfaction: increased productivity and decreased absenteeism.
(D) Several workers at Lark Manufacturing who had participated in Quality Circles while employed at other companies reported that, while participating in Quality Circles in their previous companies, their work satisfaction had increased.
(E) The machine operators who participated in Quality Circles reported that, when the program started, they felt that participation might improve their work situations.

GO ON TO THE NEXT PAGE.

Questions 19-20 are based on the following.

Blood banks will shortly start to screen all donors for NANB hepatitis. Although the new screening tests are estimated to disqualify up to 5 percent of all prospective blood donors, they will still miss two-thirds of donors carrying NANB hepatitis. Therefore, about 10 percent of actual donors will still supply NANB-contaminated blood.

19. The argument above depends on which of the following assumptions?

   (A) Donors carrying NANB hepatitis do not, in a large percentage of cases, carry other infections for which reliable screening tests are routinely performed.
   (B) Donors carrying NANB hepatitis do not, in a large percentage of cases, develop the disease themselves at any point.
   (C) The estimate of the number of donors who would be disqualified by tests for NANB hepatitis is an underestimate.
   (D) The incidence of NANB hepatitis is lower among the potential blood donors than it is in the population at large.
   (E) The donors who will still supply NANB-contaminated blood will donate blood at the average frequency for all donors.

20. Which of the following inferences about the consequences of instituting the new tests is best supported by the passage above?

   (A) The incidence of new cases of NANB hepatitis is likely to go up by 10 percent.
   (B) Donations made by patients specifically for their own use are likely to become less frequent.
   (C) The demand for blood from blood banks is likely to fluctuate more strongly.
   (D) The blood supplies available from blood banks are likely to go down.
   (E) The number of prospective first-time donors is likely to go up by 5 percent.

STOP

IF YOU FINISH BEFORE TIME IS CALLED, YOU MAY CHECK YOUR WORK ON THIS SECTION ONLY. DO NOT TURN TO ANY OTHER SECTION IN THE TEST.

Answer Key for Sample Test Section 2
CRITICAL REASONING

1. A	11. C
2. C	12. A
3. B	13. B
4. E	14. A
5. B	15. D
6. E	16. A
7. D	17. A
8. B	18. E
9. B	19. A
10. B	20. D

Explanatory Material: Critical Reasoning Sample Test Section 2

1. After the national speed limit of 55 miles per hour was imposed in 1974, the number of deaths per mile driven on a highway fell abruptly as a result. Since then, however, the average speed of vehicles on highways has risen, but the number of deaths per mile driven on a highway has continued to fall.

   Which of the following conclusions can be properly drawn from the statements above?

   (A) The speed limit alone is probably not responsible for the continued reduction in highway deaths in the years after 1974.
   (B) People have been driving less since 1974.
   (C) Driver-education courses have been more effective since 1974 in teaching drivers to drive safely.
   (D) In recent years highway patrols have been less effective in catching drivers who speed.
   (E) The change in the speed limit cannot be responsible for the abrupt decline in highway deaths in 1974.

Choices B and C cannot be inferred, because the denial of each is compatible with the given statements. Similarly with D—the rise in average speeds might occur despite relatively greater success by patrols in catching speeders—and with E—the possibility is left open that the abrupt decline *was* due to the new speed limit.

Any effect the speed limit may have had on the fatality rate probably came about through the effect that imposing the speed limit had on average highway speeds. These, however, have since risen even though the speed limit is unchanged. It is thus highly unlikely that the continuing decrease in the fatality rate stems from the speed limit alone. Therefore, A, which expresses this inference, is the best answer.

2. Neighboring landholders: Air pollution from the giant aluminum refinery that has been built next to our land is killing our plants.

   Company spokesperson: The refinery is not to blame, since our study shows that the damage is due to insects and fungi.

   Which of the following, if true, most seriously weakens the conclusion drawn by the company spokesperson?

   (A) The study did not measure the quantity of pollutants emitted into the surrounding air by the aluminum refinery.
   (B) The neighboring landholders have made no change in the way they take care of their plants.
   (C) Air pollution from the refinery has changed the chemical balance in the plants' environment, allowing the harmful insects and fungi to thrive.
   (D) Pollutants that are invisible and odorless are emitted into the surrounding air by the refinery.
   (E) The various species of insects and fungi mentioned in the study have been occasionally found in the locality during the past hundred years.

The company spokesperson's defense is essentially that pollution does not directly kill the plants. Choice C, however, establishes that the immediate causes—insects and fungi—are abundant *because* of the pollution. Since blame can properly attach to the initial link in a causal chain, C strongly suggests that the refinery can be blamed, contrary to the spokesperson's conclusion. Therefore, C is the best answer.

Neither A nor D weakens the spokesperson's conclusion, since quantity and specific characteristics of the pollution are irrelevant unless a connection between pollution and damaged vegetation can be established. Choices B and E each eliminate potential causes—changed plant-care practices and newly imported harmful organisms not yet subject to natural controls—but neither specifically points to pollution as the culprit.

3. Sales taxes tend to be regressive, affecting poor people more severely than wealthy people. When all purchases of consumer goods are taxed at a fixed percentage of the purchase price, poor people pay a larger proportion of their income in sales taxes than wealthy people do.

It can be correctly inferred on the basis of the statements above that which of the following is true?

(A) Poor people constitute a larger proportion of the taxpaying population than wealthy people do.

(B) Poor people spend a larger proportion of their income on purchases of consumer goods than wealthy people do.

(C) Wealthy people pay, on average, a larger amount of sales taxes than poor people do.

(D) The total amount spent by all poor people on purchases of consumer goods exceeds the total amount spent by all wealthy people on consumer goods.

(E) The average purchase price of consumer goods bought by wealthy people is higher than that of consumer goods bought by poor people.

If sales tax is a higher proportion of poor people's income than of rich people's, then the total of taxable purchases must be too, because, with the tax rate equal for everyone, taxes are directly proportional to purchase totals. Therefore, B is the best answer.

Choice A cannot be inferred: none of the information given bears on group size. Choices C and E cannot be inferred because it is not inconsistent with the passage that wealthy people's purchases of consumer goods, as well as price paid per consumer product, should be on average no higher than poor people's. Since the total amount mentioned in D is the product of average amount times number of people in each group, and since it cannot be inferred that one group exceeds the other either in size or in average amount, D is not inferable.

4. Reviewing historical data, medical researchers in California found that counties with the largest number of television sets per capita have had the lowest incidence of a serious brain disease, mosquito-borne encephalitis. The researchers have concluded that people in these counties stay indoors more and thus avoid exposure to the disease.

The researchers' conclusion would be most strengthened if which of the following were true?

(A) Programs designed to control the size of disease-bearing mosquito populations have not affected the incidence of mosquito-borne encephalitis.

(B) The occupations of county residents affect their risk of exposure to mosquito-borne encephalitis more than does television-watching.

(C) The incidence of mosquito-borne encephalitis in counties with the largest number of television sets per capita is likely to decrease even further.

(D) The more time people in a county spend outdoors, the greater their awareness of the dangers of mosquito-borne encephalitis.

(E) The more television sets there are per capita in a county, the more time the average county resident spends watching television.

The researchers' conclusion is particularly vulnerable to the objection that unwatched television sets, no matter how numerous they are, do not keep people indoors. Choice E addresses this potential objection in a way favorable to the researchers' position: the more sets per capita, the more time spent watching and thus spent, most likely, indoors. Therefore, E is the best answer.

Neither A nor B strengthens appreciably: A does not, because ineffective control programs do not bear on different counties differently, and B does not, because nothing is said about how low-risk occupations are distributed across counties. C and D most probably weaken the conclusion: C by suggesting some unidentified cause possibly unrelated to television sets, and D because greater awareness might help compensate for greater exposure.

5. The city's public transportation system should be removed from the jurisdiction of the municipal government, which finds it politically impossible either to raise fares or to institute cost-saving reductions in service. If public transportation were handled by a private firm, profits would be vigorously pursued, thereby eliminating the necessity for covering operating costs with government funds.

The statements above best support the conclusion that

(A) the private firms that would handle public transportation would have experience in the transportation industry

(B) political considerations would not prevent private firms from ensuring that revenues cover operating costs

(C) private firms would receive government funding if it were needed to cover operating costs

(D) the public would approve the cost-cutting actions taken by the private firm

(E) the municipal government would not be resigned to accumulating merely enough income to cover costs

Since the necessity for covering operating costs with government funds is said to be eliminable through a transfer of the system to a private operator, that operator must be able to make enough profit to stay in business. Choice B is well supported because it attributes to private firms a level of freedom from political considerations that must be reached for profits to be made. Therefore, B is the best answer.

Choice A is unsupported: the private firm may not even exist yet. Because the basic point is to eliminate government subsidies, C is not supported, since it contemplates continuing subsidies; neither is E supported, since breaking even would in fact do away with the need for subsidies. The public's reaction is not raised as a concern, so D is unsupported.

6. To entice customers away from competitors, Red Label supermarkets have begun offering discounts on home appliances to customers who spend $50 or more on any shopping trip to Red Label. Red Label executives claim that the discount program has been a huge success, since cash register receipts of $50 or more are up thirty percent since the beginning of the program.

Which of the following, if true, most seriously weakens the claim of the Red Label executives?

(A) Most people who switched to Red Label after the program began spend more than $50 each time they shop at Red Label.

(B) Most people whose average grocery bill is less than $50 would not be persuaded to spend more by any discount program.

(C) Most people who received discounts on home appliances through Red Label's program will shop at Red Label after the program ends.

(D) Since the beginning of the discount program, most of the people who spend $50 or more at Red Label are people who have never before shopped there and whose average grocery bill has always been higher than $50.

(E) Almost all of the people who have begun spending $50 or more at Red Label since the discount program began are longtime customers who have increased the average amount of their shopping bills by making fewer trips.

The discount program is not a success unless people who would otherwise do their shopping elsewhere shop at Red Label, thanks to the program. Red Label's executives claim success because of the increase in certain receipts they cite. Choice E, however, establishes that this increase comes almost entirely from longtime Red Label customers. The executives' claim of success is thereby seriously weakened. Therefore, E is the best answer.

Choices A and D strengthen the executives' claim, since each suggests that the program actually brought Red Label new customers. The people mentioned in B—not particularly addressed by the program—are essentially irrelevant to its success. What C describes is as compatible with success as with failure of the program.

7. Throughout the 1950's, there were increases in the numbers of dead birds found in agricultural areas after pesticide sprayings. Pesticide manufacturers claimed that the publicity given to bird deaths stimulated volunteers to look for dead birds, and that the increase in numbers reported was attributable to the increase in the number of people looking.

Which of the following statements, if true, would help to refute the claim of the pesticide manufacturers?

(A) The publicity given to bird deaths was largely regional and never reached national proportions.
(B) Pesticide sprayings were timed to coincide with various phases of the life cycles of the insects they destroyed.
(C) No provision was made to ensure that a dead bird would not be reported by more than one observer.
(D) Initial increases in bird deaths had been noticed by agricultural workers long before any publicity had been given to the matter.
(E) Dead birds of the same species as those found in agricultural areas had been found along coastal areas where no farming took place.

Choice D establishes that some increases in bird deaths preceded the publicity given to bird deaths, and thus raises the presumption, contrary to the pesticide manufacturers' claim, that there were genuine increases in the number of bird deaths. Therefore, D is the best answer.

Since the manufacturers' claim might be about the consequences of regional publicity, A does nothing to refute it. Choice B is entirely compatible with the manufacturers' claim. Choice C suggests a way that relatively few volunteers could generate reports of misleadingly large numbers of dead birds. This is, on balance, favorable to the manufacturers' case. Concerning E, it cannot be determined whether the information it provides is even relevant.

8. Teenagers are often priced out of the labor market by the government-mandated minimum-wage level because employers cannot afford to pay that much for extra help. Therefore, if Congress institutes a subminimum wage, a new lower legal wage for teenagers, the teenage unemployment rate, which has been rising since 1960, will no longer increase.

Which of the following, if true, would most weaken the argument above?

(A) Since 1960 the teenage unemployment rate has risen when the minimum wage has risen.
(B) Since 1960 the teenage unemployment rate has risen even when the minimum wage remained constant.
(C) Employers often hire extra help during holiday and warm weather seasons.
(D) The teenage unemployment rate rose more quickly in the 1970's than it did in the 1960's.
(E) The teenage unemployment rate has occasionally declined in the years since 1960.

Choice B suggests that there are economic forces pushing up the teenage unemployment rate that are not directly related to the minimum-wage level. This casts doubt on any prediction, such as the one in the passage, that appears to treat wage level as the sole determinant of the unemployment rate. Therefore, B is the best answer.

Choice A relates wage level and unemployment rate in the same way as the passage, thus strengthening the conclusion. Choice C suggests that care must be taken to distinguish seasonal fluctuations from general trends, but there is no indication that the argument neglects this distinction. Since neither D nor E relates changes in unemployment rate to prevailing wage levels, it cannot be determined how either bears on the argument.

9. Which of the following best completes the passage below?

The computer industry's estimate that it loses millions of dollars when users illegally copy programs without paying for them is greatly exaggerated. Most of the illegal copying is done by people with no serious interest in the programs. Thus, the loss to the industry is much smaller than estimated because

(A) many users who illegally copy programs never find any use for them
(B) most of the illegally copied programs would not be purchased even if purchasing them were the only way to obtain them
(C) even if the computer industry received all the revenue it claims to be losing, it would still be experiencing financial difficulties
(D) the total market value of the illegal copies is low in comparison to the total revenue of the computer industry
(E) the number of programs that are frequently copied illegally is low in comparison to the number of programs available for sale

The computer industry is presented in the passage as basing its loss estimate on the estimated number of illegal copies made of programs, and on the difference between the profit the industry derives from illegal copies (zero dollars) and the profit it would have realized from program sales if programs could not have been illegally copied. If this loss estimate is too high, the reason might be that the number of illegal copies was overestimated, and/or that the assumption is false that each illegal copy represents a program that would have been sold if there were no copying, and/or that the profit per extra program imagined sold was overestimated. Only B expresses one of these possible reasons, and is thus the best answer.

10. This year the New Hampshire Division of Company X set a new record for annual sales by that division. This record is especially surprising since the New Hampshire Division has the smallest potential market and the lowest sales of any of Company X's divisions.

Which of the following identifies a flaw in the logical coherence of the statement above?

(A) If overall sales for Company X were sharply reduced, the New Hampshire Division's new sales record is irrelevant to the company's prosperity.

(B) Since the division is competing against its own record, the comparison of its sales record with that of other divisions is irrelevant.

(C) If this is the first year that the New Hampshire Division has been last in sales among Company X's divisions, the new record is not surprising at all.

(D) If overall sales for Company X were greater than usual, it is not surprising that the New Hampshire Division was last in sales.

(E) Since the New Hampshire Division has the smallest potential market, it is not surprising that it had the lowest sales.

Surprise is appropriate when something happens that one had reasonably expected would not happen. It is not reasonable to expect that a division of a company cannot have higher sales than it ever had before if the only basis for that expectation is the fact that the division is relatively small. Thus, the passage fails to cohere because it posits surprise where there should be none, and B best expresses why there should be none.

The other choices range from statements that seem quite accurate (e.g., E) to statements that seem highly dubious (e.g., C), but they all fail to address the flaw in the logical coherence of the passage.

11. Statement of a United States copper mining company: Import quotas should be imposed on the less expensive copper mined outside the country to maintain the price of copper in this country; otherwise, our companies will not be able to stay in business.

Response of a United States copper wire manufacturer: United States wire and cable manufacturers purchase about 70 percent of the copper mined in the United States. If the copper prices we pay are not at the international level, our sales will drop, and then the demand for United States copper will go down.

If the factual information presented by both companies is accurate, the best assessment of the logical relationship between the two arguments is that the wire manufacturer's argument

(A) is self-serving and irrelevant to the proposal of the mining company

(B) is circular, presupposing what it seeks to prove about the proposal of the mining company

(C) shows that the proposal of the mining company would have a negative effect on the mining company's own business

(D) fails to give a reason why the proposal of the mining company should not be put into effect to alleviate the concern of the mining company for staying in business

(E) establishes that even the mining company's business will prosper if the mining company's proposal is rejected

If demand for United States copper goes down, as the wire manufacturer predicts, then a given copper mining company may either cut prices, trying to maintain sales, or lose sales, trying to maintain prices, or cut prices *and* lose sales. In each case, there is a negative effect on the mining company's business as a foreseeable consequence of implementing its own proposal. Therefore, C is the best answer.

The assessment given in C shows that the wire manufacturer's argument is relevant—contrary to A—and that the manufacturer does give reasons against the mining company's proposal—contrary to D. There is no evidence here of circularity—contrary to B—and nothing to suggest that the mining company has misanalyzed the implications of current business conditions—contrary to E.

12. Y has been believed to cause Z. A new report, noting that Y and Z are often observed to be preceded by X, suggests that X, not Y, may be the cause of Z.

Which of the following further observations would best support the new report's suggestion?

(A) In cases where X occurs but Y does not, X is usually followed by Z.

(B) In cases where X occurs, followed by Y, Y is usually followed by Z.

(C) In cases where Y occurs but X does not, Y is usually followed by Z.

(D) In cases where Y occurs but Z does not, Y is usually preceded by X.

(E) In cases where Z occurs, it is usually preceded by X and Y.

The speculation that X rather than Y may be the cause of Z would be considerably strengthened if one or both of two circumstances were discovered to prevail: in cases where Y occurs but X does not, Z generally does not occur (or, better still, never occurs), and in cases where X occurs but Y does not, Z generally (or, better still, always) occurs after X has occurred. Choice A states the second of these circumstances and is, therefore, the best answer.

Choices B and E offer no information that would help one choose between the original belief and the current speculation. Choice C supports the original belief. Choice D casts some doubt on both the original belief and the current speculation.

13. Mr. Primm: If hospitals were private enterprises, dependent on profits for their survival, there would be no teaching hospitals, because of the intrinsically high cost of running such hospitals.

Ms. Nakai: I disagree. The medical challenges provided by teaching hospitals attract the very best physicians. This, in turn, enables those hospitals to concentrate on nonroutine cases.

Which of the following, if true, would most strengthen Ms. Nakai's attempt to refute Mr. Primm's claim?

(A) Doctors at teaching hospitals command high salaries.

(B) Sophisticated, nonroutine medical care commands a high price.

(C) Existing teaching hospitals derive some revenue from public subsidies.

(D) The patient mortality rate at teaching hospitals is high.

(E) The modern trend among physicians is to become highly specialized.

Ms. Nakai's attempted rebuttal seems to confirm Mr. Primm's point that teaching hospitals are expensive to run since "the very best physicians" and "nonroutine cases" both sound costly. But if B is true, high charges to patients might compensate for the high expenses. Choice B makes Ms. Nakai's challenge more effective, and it is thus the best answer.

Choice A supports Mr. Primm's position concerning high costs. Public subsidies, mentioned in C, suggest that Mr. Primm is correct in his doubts about the profitability of private teaching hospitals. Since high mortality rates are not plausibly related to greater profitability, D does not strengthen Ms. Nakai's case. The impact of E, if any, on Ms. Nakai's position cannot be gauged on the basis of the information given.

14. A recent survey of all auto accident victims in Dole County found that, of the severely injured drivers and front-seat passengers, 80 percent were not wearing seat belts at the time of their accidents. This indicates that, by wearing seat belts, drivers and front-seat passengers can greatly reduce their risk of being severely injured if they are in an auto accident.

The conclusion above is not properly drawn unless which of the following is true?

(A) Of all the drivers and front-seat passengers in the survey, more than 20 percent were wearing seat belts at the time of their accidents.

(B) Considerably more than 20 percent of drivers and front-seat passengers in Dole County always wear seat belts when traveling by car.

(C) More drivers and front-seat passengers in the survey than rear-seat passengers were very severely injured.

(D) More than half of the drivers and front-seat passengers in the survey were not wearing seat belts at the time of their accidents.

(E) Most of the auto accidents reported to police in Dole County do not involve any serious injury.

The survey results support the conclusion drawn only if those wearing seat belts are a smaller proportion of the severely injured than they are of all those covered by the survey. Choice A expresses this precondition and is thus the best answer.

Since the conclusion might be properly drawn even if it were true that no one in Dole County wears seat belts 100 percent of the time, B can be eliminated. Choice C draws a comparison with rear-seat passengers that is irrelevant to the conclusion. Choice D can be ruled out because the smaller the proportion of those not wearing seat belts among the total survey population, the better the conclusion is supported. Since the conclusion might be properly drawn even if most of the accidents referred to in E did involve serious injuries, E can also be ruled out.

15. Six months or so after getting a video recorder, many early buyers apparently lost interest in obtaining videos to watch on it. The trade of businesses selling and renting videos is still buoyant, because the number of homes with video recorders is still growing. But clearly, once the market for video recorders is saturated, businesses distributing videos face hard times.

Which of the following, if true, would most seriously weaken the conclusion above?

(A) The market for video recorders would not be considered saturated until there was one in 80 percent of homes.

(B) Among the items handled by video distributors are many films specifically produced as video features.

(C) Few of the early buyers of video recorders raised any complaints about performance aspects of the new product.

(D) The early buyers of a novel product are always people who are quick to acquire novelties, but also often as quick to tire of them.

(E) In a shrinking market, competition always intensifies and marginal businesses fail.

The argument treats early buyers as typical. If they are, it can reasonably be predicted that the demand for videos will sharply decline soon after the market for video recorders has become saturated. But D raises the distinct possibility that early buyers may be unusual in precisely the respect on which the prediction depends: rapid loss of interest in videos. Therefore, D is the best answer.

Choice A is not a good answer since nothing rules out saturation so defined. Choices B and C, on balance, make the early buyers' loss of interest seem surprising, but give no hint that it is not a real phenomenon. Choice E points out an unfortunate consequence of the conclusion but raises no doubt about its truth.

16. Advertiser: The revenue that newspapers and magazines earn by publishing advertisements allows publishers to keep the prices per copy of their publications much lower than would otherwise be possible. Therefore, consumers benefit economically from advertising.

Consumer: But who pays for the advertising that pays for low-priced newspapers and magazines? We consumers do, because advertisers pass along advertising costs to us through the higher prices they charge for their products.

Which of the following best describes how the consumer counters the advertiser's argument?

(A) By alleging something that, if true, would weaken the plausibility of the advertiser's conclusion

(B) By questioning the truth of the purportedly factual statement on which the advertiser's conclusion is based

(C) By offering an interpretation of the advertiser's opening statement that, if accurate, shows that there is an implicit contradiction in it

(D) By pointing out that the advertiser's point of view is biased

(E) By arguing that the advertiser too narrowly restricts the discussion to the effects of advertising that are economic

The advertiser says that consumers benefit because of the low prices for newspapers and magazines that advertising makes possible. The consumer counters that advertising hurts consumers by driving up the prices of products being advertised. The consumer's claim, if true, means that quite possibly consumers will not enjoy any financial net benefit from advertising. Choice A accurately describes this and is, therefore, the best answer.

The consumer does question the advertiser's conclusion, but neither disputes the claim it is based on nor offers to reinterpret it; thus, B and C are incorrect. Although the consumer argues that the advertiser overlooked an important fact, there is no allegation of bias or of the excessive narrowness of purely economic concerns, contrary to D and E, respectively.

17. Mr. Lawson: We should adopt a national family policy that includes legislation requiring employers to provide paid parental leave and establishing government-sponsored day care. Such laws would decrease the stress levels of employees who have responsibility for small children. Thus, such laws would lead to happier, better-adjusted families.

Which of the following, if true, would most strengthen the conclusion above?

(A) An employee's high stress level can be a cause of unhappiness and poor adjustment for his or her family.

(B) People who have responsiblity for small children and who work outside the home have higher stress levels than those who do not.

(C) The goal of a national family policy is to lower the stress levels of parents.

(D) Any national family policy that is adopted would include legislation requiring employers to provide paid parental leave and establishing government-sponsored day care.

(E) Most children who have been cared for in day care centers are happy and well adjusted.

Mr. Lawson bases his case on the claim that certain laws would lead to happier, better-adjusted families. He fails to substantiate that claim, however, since he does not relate stress reduction causally to families' greater happiness. Choice A suggests such a causal connection. It thereby strengthens the basis for Mr. Lawson's conclusion, and is, therefore, the best answer.

Choice B establishes instances of relatively high levels of stress but in no way suggests that families would be happier or better adjusted without those stress levels. Choices C and D suggest that Mr. Lawson knows what a family policy aims to accomplish and how, but not that it would be good to have one. Choice E does not comment on whether parental stress levels were significant in influencing the situation.

18. Lark Manufacturing Company initiated a voluntary Quality Circles program for machine operators. Independent surveys of employee attitudes indicated that the machine operators participating in the program were less satisfied with their work situations after two years of the program's existence than they were at the program's start. Obviously, any workers who participate in a Quality Circles program will, as a result, become less satisfied with their jobs.

Each of the following, if true, would weaken the conclusion draw above EXCEPT:

(A) The second survey occurred during a period of recession when rumors of cutbacks and layoffs at Lark Manufacturing were plentiful.

(B) The surveys also showed that those Lark machine operators who neither participated in Quality Circles nor knew anyone who did so reported the same degree of lessened satisfaction with their work situations as did the Lark machine operators who participated in Quality Circles.

(C) While participating in Quality Circles at Lark Manufacturing, machine operators exhibited two of the primary indicators of improved job satisfaction: increased productivity and decreased absenteeism.

(D) Several workers at Lark Manufacturing who had participated in Quality Circles while employed at other companies reported that, while participating in Quality Circles in their previous companies, their work satisfaction had increased.

(E) The machine operators who participated in Quality Circles reported that, when the program started, they felt that participation might improve their work situations.

The task is to find the answer choice that would *not* weaken the stated conclusion. Choices A and B both weaken the conclusion, since each describes a situation in which it is likely that the reduced level of satisfaction stems from causes other than participation in the Quality Circles program. Choice C weakens because it indicates that there are objective measures of job satisfaction that contradict the workers' self-reports. Choice D weakens by providing relevant hearsay evidence that directly contradicts the conclusion.

Choice E, however, does not weaken the conclusion: the workers seem to have had neither overly high expectations that were bound to be disappointed nor any self-fulfilling expectations of failure. Therefore, E is the best answer.

Blood banks will shortly start to screen all donors for NANB hepatitis. Although the new screening tests are estimated to disqualify up to 5 percent of all prospective blood donors, they will still miss two-thirds of donors carrying NANB hepatitis. Therefore, about 10 percent of actual donors will still supply NANB-contaminated blood.

19. The argument above depends on which of the following assumptions?

   (A) Donors carrying NANB hepatitis do not, in a large percentage of cases, carry other infections for which reliable screening tests are routinely performed.

   (B) Donors carrying NANB hepatitis do not, in a large perentage of cases, develop the disease themselves at any point.

   (C) The estimate of the number of donors who would be disqualified by tests for NANB hepatitis is an underestimate.

   (D) The incidence of NANB hepatitis is lower among the potential blood donors than it is in the population at large.

   (E) The donors who will still supply NANB-contaminated blood will donate blood at the average frequency for all donors.

Contrary to C, the argument proceeds as if the figures used were essentially accurate. Choice D is irrelevant because the argument is concerned only with the threat of NANB contamination posed by donors, and ignores the population at large. Choice E is incorrect because the argument focuses on quantitative information about donors, not donations, so nothing is assumed about relative frequencies of donations. Choice B is also incorrect: the argument may hold even if B is false, provided there is a rough balance between carriers developing the disease and newly infected carriers.

However, if a large proportion of carriers of NANB hepatitis were eliminated by other screening tests, the 10 percent figure would be significantly too high, and the conclusion incorrect. Choice A is thus assumed.

20. Which of the following inferences about the consequences of instituting the new tests is best supported by the passage above?

   (A) The incidence of new cases of NANB hepatitis is likely to go up by 10 percent.

   (B) Donations made by patients specifically for their own use are likely to become less frequent.

   (C) The demand for blood from blood banks is likely to fluctuate more strongly.

   (D) The blood supplies available from blood banks are likely to go down.

   (E) The number of prospective first-time donors is likely to go up by 5 percent.

The passage claims that there are new screening tests that will eliminate up to 5 percent of prospective donors. The most likely consequence is that there will be less blood donated overall, and thus less blood going to blood banks. Therefore, D is the best answer.

Choice A is unsupported: the incidence of any new cases of NANB hepatitis from contaminated blood should go down, not up. Since nothing is said about donations for the donors' own use, no inferences about such donations receive any support; this rules out B. Choice C can also be eliminated, since the argument is not concerned with the demand for donated blood. The argument does not consider the issue of first-time donors separately; thus E remains unsupported.

CRITICAL REASONING SAMPLE TEST SECTION 3

30 minutes

20 Questions

Directions: For each question in this section, select the best of the answer choices given.

1. Child's World, a chain of toy stores, has relied on a "supermarket concept" of computerized inventory control and customer self-service to eliminate the category of sales clerks from its force of employees. It now plans to employ the same concept in selling children's clothes.

The plan of Child's World assumes that

(A) supermarkets will not also be selling children's clothes in the same manner
(B) personal service by sales personnel is not required for selling children's clothes successfully
(C) the same kind of computers will be used in inventory control for both clothes and toys at Child's World
(D) a self-service plan cannot be employed without computerized inventory control
(E) sales clerks are the only employees of Child's World who could be assigned tasks related to inventory control

2. Continuous indoor fluorescent light benefits the health of hamsters with inherited heart disease. A group of them exposed to continuous fluorescent light survived twenty-five percent longer than a similar group exposed instead to equal periods of indoor fluorescent light and of darkness.

The method of the research described above is most likely to be applicable in addressing which of the following questions?

(A) Can industrial workers who need to see their work do so better by sunlight or by fluorescent light?
(B) Can hospital lighting be improved to promote the recovery of patients?
(C) How do deep-sea fish survive in total darkness?
(D) What are the inherited illnesses to which hamsters are subject?
(E) Are there plants that require specific periods of darkness in order to bloom?

3. Millions of identical copies of a plant can be produced using new tissue-culture and cloning techniques.

If plant propagation by such methods in laboratories proves economical, each of the following, if true, represents a benefit of the new techniques to farmers EXCEPT:

(A) The techniques allow the development of superior strains to take place more rapidly, requiring fewer generations of plants grown to maturity.
(B) It is less difficult to care for plants that will grow at rates that do not vary widely.
(C) Plant diseases and pests, once they take hold, spread more rapidly among genetically uniform plants than among those with genetic variations.
(D) Mechanical harvesting of crops is less difficult if plants are more uniform in size.
(E) Special genetic traits can more easily be introduced into plant strains with the use of the new techniques.

4. Which of the following best completes the passage below?

Sales campaigns aimed at the faltering personal computer market have strongly emphasized ease of use, called user-friendliness. This emphasis is oddly premature and irrelevant in the eyes of most potential buyers, who are trying to address the logically prior issue of whether -------.

(A) user-friendliness also implies that owners can service their own computers
(B) personal computers cost more the more user-friendly they are
(C) currently available models are user-friendly enough to suit them
(D) the people promoting personal computers use them in their own homes
(E) they have enough sensible uses for a personal computer to justify the expense of buying one

GO ON TO THE NEXT PAGE.

5. A weapons-smuggling incident recently took place in country Y. We all know that Y is a closed society. So Y's government must have known about the weapons.

Which of the following is an assumption that would make the conclusion above logically correct?

(A) If a government knows about a particular weapons-smuggling incident, it must have intended to use the weapons for its own purposes.

(B) If a government claims that it knew nothing about a particular weapons-smuggling incident, it must have known everything about it.

(C) If a government does not permit weapons to enter a country, it is a closed society.

(D) If a country is a closed society, its government has a large contingent of armed guards patrolling its borders.

(E) If a country is a closed society, its government has knowledge about everything that occurs in the country.

6. Banning cigarette advertisements in the mass media will not reduce the number of young people who smoke. They know that cigarettes exist and they know how to get them. They do not need the advertisements to supply that information.

The above argument would be most weakened if which of the following were true?

(A) Seeing or hearing an advertisement for a product tends to increase people's desire for that product.

(B) Banning cigarette advertisements in the mass media will cause an increase in advertisements in places where cigarettes are sold.

(C) Advertisements in the mass media have been an exceedingly large part of the expenditures of the tobacco companies.

(D) Those who oppose cigarette use have advertised against it in the mass media ever since cigarettes were found to be harmful.

(E) Older people tend to be less influenced by mass-media advertisements than younger people tend to be.

7. People tend to estimate the likelihood of an event's occurrence according to its salience; that is, according to how strongly and how often it comes to their attention.

By placement and headlines, newspapers emphasize stories about local crime over stories about crime elsewhere and about many other major events.

It can be concluded on the basis of the statements above that, if they are true, which of the following is most probably also true?

(A) The language used in newspaper headlines about local crime is inflammatory and fails to respect the rights of suspects.

(B) The coverage of international events in newspapers is neglected in favor of the coverage of local events.

(C) Readers of local news in newspapers tend to overestimate the amount of crime in their own localities relative to the amount of crime in other places.

(D) None of the events concerning other people that are reported in newspapers is so salient in people's minds as their own personal experiences.

(E) The press is the news medium that focuses people's attention most strongly on local crimes.

8. By analyzing the garbage of a large number of average-sized households, a group of modern urban anthropologists has found that a household discards less food the more standardized—made up of canned and prepackaged foods—its diet is. The more standardized a household's diet is, however, the greater the quantities of fresh produce the household throws away.

Which of the following can be properly inferred from the passage?

(A) An increasing number of households rely on a highly standardized diet.

(B) The less standardized a household's diet is, the more nonfood waste the household discards.

(C) The less standardized a household's diet is, the smaller is the proportion of fresh produce in the household's food waste.

(D) The less standardized a household's diet is, the more canned and prepackaged foods the household discards as waste.

(E) The more fresh produce a household buys, the more fresh produce it throws away.

GO ON TO THE NEXT PAGE.

Questions 9-10 are based on the following.

In the past, teachers, bank tellers, and secretaries were predominantly men; these occupations slipped in pay and status when they became largely occupied by women. Therefore, if women become the majority in currently male-dominated professions like accounting, law, and medicine, the income and prestige of these professions will also drop.

9. The argument above is based on

(A) another argument that contains circular reasoning
(B) an attempt to refute a generalization by means of an exceptional case
(C) an analogy between the past and the future
(D) an appeal to popular beliefs and values
(E) an attack on the character of the opposition

10. Which of the following, if true, would most likely be part of the evidence used to refute the conclusion above?

(A) Accountants, lawyers, and physicians attained their current relatively high levels of income and prestige at about the same time that the pay and status of teachers, bank tellers, and secretaries slipped.
(B) When large numbers of men join a female-dominated occupation, such as airline flight attendant, the status and pay of the occupation tend to increase.
(C) The demand for teachers and secretaries has increased significantly in recent years, while the demand for bank tellers has remained relatively stable.
(D) If present trends in the awarding of law degrees to women continue, it will be at least two decades before the majority of lawyers are women.
(E) The pay and status of female accountants, lawyers, and physicians today are governed by significantly different economic and sociological forces than were the pay and status of female teachers, bank tellers, and secretaries in the past.

11. An electric-power company gained greater profits and provided electricity to consumers at lower rates per unit of electricity by building larger-capacity more efficient plants and by stimulating greater use of electricity within its area. To continue these financial trends, the company planned to replace an old plant by a plant with triple the capacity of its largest plant.

The company's plan as described above assumed each of the following EXCEPT:

(A) Demand for electricity within the company's area of service would increase in the future.
(B) Expenses would not rise beyond the level that could be compensated for by efficiency or volume of operation, or both.
(C) The planned plant would be sufficiently reliable in service to contribute a net financial benefit to the company as a whole.
(D) Safety measures to be instituted for the new plant would be the same as those for the plant it would replace.
(E) The tripling of capacity would not result in insuperable technological obstacles to efficiency.

GO ON TO THE NEXT PAGE.

Questions 12-13 are based on the following.

Meteorologists say that if only they could design an accurate mathematical model of the atmosphere with all its complexities, they could forecast the weather with real precision. But this is an idle boast, immune to any evaluation, for any inadequate weather forecast would obviously be blamed on imperfections in the model.

12. Which of the following, if true, could best be used as a basis for arguing against the author's position that the meteorologists' claim cannot be evaluated?

   (A) Certain unusual configurations of data can serve as the basis for precise weather forecasts even though the exact causal mechanisms are not understood.
   (B) Most significant gains in the accuracy of the relevant mathematical models are accompanied by clear gains in the precision of weather forecasts.
   (C) Mathematical models of the meteorological aftermath of such catastrophic events as volcanic eruptions are beginning to be constructed.
   (D) Modern weather forecasts for as much as a full day ahead are broadly correct about 80 percent of the time.
   (E) Meteorologists readily concede that the accurate mathematical model they are talking about is not now in their power to construct.

13. Which of the following, if true, would cast the most serious doubt on the meteorologists' boast, aside from the doubt expressed in the passage above?

   (A) The amount of energy that the Earth receives from the Sun is monitored closely and is known not to be constant.
   (B) Volcanic eruptions, the combustion of fossil fuels, and several other processes that also cannot be quantified with any accuracy are known to have a significant and continuing impact on the constitution of the atmosphere.
   (C) As current models of the atmosphere are improved, even small increments in complexity will mean large increases in the number of computers required for the representation of the models.
   (D) Frequent and accurate data about the atmosphere collected at a large number of points both on and above the ground are a prerequisite for the construction of a good model of the atmosphere.
   (E) With existing models of the atmosphere, large-scale weather patterns can be predicted with greater accuracy than can relatively local weather patterns.

14. Of the countries that were the world's twenty largest exporters in 1953, four had the same share of total world exports in 1984 as in 1953. These countries can therefore serve as models for those countries that wish to keep their share of the global export trade stable over the years.

Which of the following, if true, casts the most serious doubt on the suitability of those four countries as models in the sense described?

   (A) Many countries wish to increase their share of world export trade, not just keep it stable.
   (B) Many countries are less concerned with exports alone than with the balance between exports and imports.
   (C) With respect to the mix of products each exports, the four countries are very different from each other.
   (D) Of the four countries, two had a much larger, and two had a much smaller, share of total world exports in 1970 than in 1984.
   (E) The exports of the four countries range from 15 percent to 75 percent of the total national output.

GO ON TO THE NEXT PAGE.

Questions 15-16 are based on the following.

In the United States, the Postal Service has a monopoly on first-class mail, but much of what is sent first class could be transmitted electronically. Electronic transmittal operators argue that if the Postal Service were to offer electronic transmission, it would have an unfair advantage, since its electronic transmission service could be subsidized from the profits of the monopoly.

15. Which of the following, if each is true, would allay the electronic transmittal operators' fears of unfair competition?

   (A) If the Postal Service were to offer electronic transmission, it could not make a profit on first-class mail.
   (B) If the Postal Service were to offer electronic transmission, it would have a monopoly on that kind of service.
   (C) Much of the material that is now sent by first-class mail could be delivered much faster by special package couriers, but is not sent that way because of cost.
   (D) There is no economy of scale in electronic transmission—that is, the cost per transaction does not go down as more pieces of information are transmitted.
   (E) Electronic transmission will never be cost-effective for material not sent by first-class mail such as newspapers and bulk mail.

16. Which of the following questions can be answered on the basis of the information in the passage above?

   (A) Is the Postal Service as efficient as privately owned electric transmission services?
   (B) If private operators were allowed to operate first-class mail services, would they choose to do so?
   (C) Do the electronic transmittal operators believe that the Postal Service makes a profit on first-class mail?
   (D) Is the Postal Service prohibited from offering electronic transmission services?
   (E) Is the Postal Service expected to have a monopoly on electronic transmission?

17. Lists of hospitals have been compiled showing which hospitals have patient death rates exceeding the national average. The data have been adjusted to allow for differences in the ages of patients.

Each of the following, if true, provides a good logical ground for hospitals to object to interpreting rank on these lists as one of the indices of the quality of hospital care EXCEPT:

   (A) Rank order might indicate insignificant differences, rather than large differences, in numbers of patient deaths.
   (B) Hospitals that keep patients longer are likely to have higher death rates than those that discharge patients earlier but do not record deaths of patients at home after discharge.
   (C) Patients who are very old on admission to a hospital are less likely than younger patients to survive the same types of illnesses or surgical procedures.
   (D) Some hospitals serve a larger proportion of low-income patients, who tend to be more seriously ill when admitted to a hospital.
   (E) For-profit hospitals sometimes do not provide intensive-care units and other expensive services for very sick patients but refer or transfer such patients to other hospitals.

18. Teresa: Manned spaceflight does not have a future, since it cannot compete economically with other means of accomplishing the objectives of spaceflight.

   Edward: No mode of human transportation has a better record of reliability: two accidents in twenty five years. Thus manned spaceflight definitely has a positive future.

Which of the following is the best logical evaluation of Edward's argument as a response to Teresa's argument?

   (A) It cites evidence that, if true, tends to disprove the evidence cited by Teresa in drawing her conclusion.
   (B) It indicates a logical gap in the support that Teresa offers for her conclusion.
   (C) It raises a consideration that outweighs the argument Teresa makes.
   (D) It does not meet Teresa's point because it assumes that there is no serious impediment to transporting people into space, but this was the issue raised by Teresa.
   (E) It fails to respond to Teresa's argument because it does not address the fundamental issue of whether space activities should have priority over other claims on the national budget.

GO ON TO THE NEXT PAGE.

19. Black Americans are, on the whole, about twice as likely as White Americans to develop high blood pressure. This likelihood also holds for westernized Black Africans when compared to White Africans. Researchers have hypothesized that this predisposition in westernized Blacks may reflect an interaction between western high-salt diets and genes that adapted to an environmental scarcity of salt.

Which of the following statements about present-day, westernized Black Africans, if true, would most tend to confirm the researchers' hypothesis?

(A) The blood pressures of those descended from peoples situated throughout their history in Senegal and Gambia, where salt was always available, are low.

(B) The unusually high salt consumption in certain areas of Africa represents a serious health problem.

(C) Because of their blood pressure levels, most White Africans have markedly decreased their salt consumption.

(D) Blood pressures are low among the Yoruba, who, throughout their history, have been situated far inland from sources of sea salt and far south of Saharan salt mines.

(E) No significant differences in salt metabolism have been found between those peoples who have had salt available throughout their history and those who have not.

20. The following proposal to amend the bylaws of an organization was circulated to its members for comment.

When more than one nominee is to be named for an office, prospective nominees must consent to nomination and before giving such consent must be told who the other nominees will be.

Which of the following comments concerning the logic of the proposal is accurate if it cannot be known who the actual nominees are until prospective nominees have given their consent to be nominated?

(A) The proposal would make it possible for each of several nominees for an office to be aware of who all of the other nominees are.

(B) The proposal would widen the choice available to those choosing among the nominees.

(C) If there are several prospective nominees, the proposal would deny the last nominee equal treatment with the first.

(D) The proposal would enable a prospective nominee to withdraw from competition with a specific person without making that withdrawal known.

(E) If there is more than one prospective nominee, the proposal would make it impossible for anyone to become a nominee.

STOP

IF YOU FINISH BEFORE TIME IS CALLED, YOU MAY CHECK YOUR WORK ON THIS SECTION ONLY. DO NOT TURN TO ANY OTHER SECTION IN THE TEST.

Answer Key for Sample Test Section 3

CRITICAL REASONING

1.	B	11.	D
2.	B	12.	B
3.	C	13.	B
4.	E	14.	D
5.	E	15.	A
6.	A	16.	C
7.	C	17.	C
8.	C	18.	D
9.	C	19.	A
10.	E	20.	E

Explanatory Material:
Critical Reasoning
Sample Test Section 3

1. Child's World, a chain of toy stores, has relied on a "supermarket concept" of computerized inventory control and customer self-service to eliminate the category of sales clerks from its force of employees. It now plans to employ the same concept in selling children's clothes.

   The plan of Child's World assumes that

   (A) supermarkets will not also be selling children's clothes in the same manner
   (B) personal service by sales personnel is not required for selling children's clothes successfully
   (C) the same kind of computers will be used in inventory control for both clothes and toys at Child's World
   (D) a self-service plan cannot be employed without computerized inventory control
   (E) sales clerks are the only employees of Child's World who could be assigned tasks related to inventory control

If B were false, eliminating the sales personnel for children's clothes would be an economic mistake. Since the plan is presumably regarded as laying out an economically desirable course of action, the truth of B must be assumed.

   If A were false, Child's World might nevertheless be successful in competition with supermarkets; thus A is not assumed. Neither is C: if inventory control for children's clothes really was more sensibly computerized using a different kind of computer, the plan itself would remain unaffected. Choice D is also not assumed: Child's World may plan to combine self-service and computerized inventory control because it is cost-effective, not because there are no alternatives. Finally, E is not assumed, especially not for computerized inventory control.

2. Continuous indoor fluorescent light benefits the health of hamsters with inherited heart disease. A group of them exposed to continuous fluorescent light survived twenty-five percent longer than a similar group exposed instead to equal periods of indoor fluorescent light and of darkness.

   The method of the research described above is most likely to be applicable in addressing which of the following questions?

   (A) Can industrial workers who need to see their work do so better by sunlight or by fluorescent light?
   (B) Can hospital lighting be improved to promote the recovery of patients?
   (C) How do deep-sea fish survive in total darkness?
   (D) What are the inherited illnesses to which hamsters are subject?
   (E) Are there plants that require specific periods of darkness in order to bloom?

The variable controlled in the research is the length of exposure to artificial light. This aspect of the research also applies to patients in a hospital. The statistical aspect of the method—the collection of quantitative results about the entire group of subjects—is likewise applicable. Therefore, B is the best of the choices.

   Choice A involves exposure to different kinds of light, not different lengths of exposure. The method of differential exposure to light is unpromising in the case of C, where total darkness is a given, and the method is not germane in the case of D. Choice E can be eliminated because the statistical aspect of the method is inapplicable: the only information of concern here is presence or absence of blooms.

3. Millions of identical copies of a plant can be produced using new tissue-culture and cloning techniques.

   If plant propagation by such methods in laboratories proves economical, each of the following, if true, represents a benefit of the new techniques to farmers EXCEPT:

   (A) The techniques allow the development of superior strains to take place more rapidly, requiring fewer generations of plants grown to maturity.
   (B) It is less difficult to care for plants that will grow at rates that do not vary widely.
   (C) Plant diseases and pests, once they take hold, spread more rapidly among genetically uniform plants than among those with genetic variations.
   (D) Mechanical harvesting of crops is less difficult if plants are more uniform in size.
   (E) Special genetic traits can more easily be introduced into plant strains with the use of the new techniques.

From the perspective of C, genetic variability is more highly valued than genetic uniformity. But the new techniques, while making it easy to achieve previously unattainable uniformity, are not described as providing any means of achieving variability. Therefore, C does not represent or imply a benefit to farmers, and is thus the best answer.

Because identical copies, given similar growing conditions, will not differ appreciably in either growth rate or size attained by harvest time, both B and D represent benefits to farmers. Choice A suggests the benefit of having superior strains available earlier than would otherwise be possible, and E suggests the benefit of being able to obtain strains that are superior in specific, predesignated ways.

4. Which of the following best completes the passage below?

   Sales campaigns aimed at the faltering personal computer market have strongly emphasized ease of use, called user-friendliness. This emphasis is oddly premature and irrelevant in the eyes of most potential buyers, who are trying to address the logically prior issue of whether ------.

   (A) user-friendliness also implies that owners can service their own computers
   (B) personal computers cost more the more user-friendly they are
   (C) currently available models are user-friendly enough to suit them
   (D) the people promoting personal computers use them in their own homes
   (E) they have enough sensible uses for a personal computer to justify the expense of buying one

The question raised in A is closely related to user-friendliness: it explores potential further implications of user-friendliness. The issue raised by B also concerns user-friendliness: is it an advantageous feature that buyers pay for? Choice C presupposes user-friendliness as a criterion for purchasing decisions. The issue mentioned in D is not logically prior to user-friendliness, though D may be a way of probing promotional claims, including claims about user-friendliness.

Choice E, however, depicts potential buyers as asking themselves whether buying a computer at all makes sense for them. As long as their answer might still be "no," questions of user-friendliness, which bear on the choice from among competing models, are indeed premature. Therefore, E is the best answer.

5. A weapons-smuggling incident recently took place in country Y. We all know that Y is a closed society. So Y's government must have known about the weapons.

   Which of the following is an assumption that would make the conclusion above logically correct?

   (A) If a government knows about a particular weapons-smuggling incident, it must have intended to use the weapons for its own purposes.
   (B) If a government claims that it knew nothing about a particular weapons-smuggling incident, it must have known everything about it.
   (C) If a government does not permit weapons to enter a country, it is a closed society.
   (D) If a country is a closed society, its government has a large contingent of armed guards patrolling its borders.
   (E) If a country is a closed society, its government has knowledge about everything that occurs in the country.

Choice E is the best answer. If E is true, country Y's government must have known about the weapons, even if they were coming into Y from abroad (rather than being smuggled out of Y), as soon as they had crossed Y's border.

Choice A draws out implications of the conclusion but leaves the conclusion itself inadequately supported. The assumption in B is insufficient to establish the conclusion as correctly drawn: no information about claims by Y's government is given. The prospect offered by C—being able to tell whether Y is closed—is of no consequence: Y is known to be closed. The patrols mentioned in D make it likely, but not deductively certain, that Y's government found out about the weapons.

6. Banning cigarette advertisements in the mass media will not reduce the number of young people who smoke. They know that cigarettes exist and they know how to get them. They do not need the advertisements to supply that information.

   The above argument would be most weakened if which of the following were true?

   (A) Seeing or hearing an advertisement for a product tends to increase people's desire for that product.
   (B) Banning cigarette advertisements in the mass media will cause an increase in advertisements in places where cigarettes are sold.
   (C) Advertisements in the mass media have been an exceedingly large part of the expenditures of the tobacco companies.
   (D) Those who oppose cigarette use have advertised against it in the mass media ever since cigarettes were found to be harmful.
   (E) Older people tend to be less influenced by mass-media advertisements than younger people tend to be.

The possibility that A raises is that, in the case of some young nonsmokers, cigarette advertising increases their desire for cigarettes just enough to make the difference between their continuing to be nonsmokers and their taking up smoking, thus affecting the numbers of young smokers. Therefore, A is the best answer.

Both B and C leave open the possibility that advertising affects only smokers' choice of cigarette brands, and not who smokes and who does not. Similarly, the relevance of D has not been established: the effects of anti-cigarette advertising are no more settled than are the effects of pro-cigarette advertising. Choice E presupposes that advertising does influence people but leaves unspecified the nature of this influence.

7. People tend to estimate the likelihood of an event's occurrence according to its salience; that is, according to how strongly and how often it comes to their attention.

By placement and headlines, newspapers emphasize stories about local crime over stories about crime elsewhere and about many other major events.

It can be concluded on the basis of the statements above that, if they are true, which of the following is most probably also true?

(A) The language used in newspaper headlines about local crime is inflammatory and fails to respect the rights of suspects.
(B) The coverage of international events in newspapers is neglected in favor of the coverage of local events.
(C) Readers of local news in newspapers tend to overestimate the amount of crime in their own localities relative to the amount of crime in other places.
(D) None of the events concerning other people that are reported in newspapers is so salient in people's minds as their own personal experiences.
(E) The press is the news medium that focuses people's attention most strongly on local crimes.

The fact that newspapers emphasize local crime coverage relative to coverage of crimes elsewhere means that readers will be more likely to be aware of local crime, or will be aware of it more strongly; in short, local crime will be more salient. Consequently, local crime will be judged to be relatively more likely to occur, though it may actually be no more frequent. The best answer, therefore, is C.

The information given neither suggests emphasis by questionable means—contrary to A—nor suggests special relative emphasis on *all* local events—contrary to B. Choices D and E can be eliminated: it is entirely possible that people's personal experiences are unremarkable, and that other news media highlight local crime even more than newspapers do.

8. By analyzing the garbage of a large number of average-sized households, a group of modern urban anthropologists has found that a household discards less food the more standardized—made up of canned and prepackaged foods—its diet is. The more standardized a household's diet is, however, the greater the quantities of fresh produce the household throws away.

Which of the following can be properly inferred from the passage?

(A) An increasing number of households rely on a highly standardized diet.
(B) The less standardized a household's diet is, the more nonfood waste the household discards.
(C) The less standardized a household's diet is, the smaller is the proportion of fresh produce in the household's food waste.
(D) The less standardized a household's diet is, the more canned and prepackaged foods the household discards as waste.
(E) The more fresh produce a household buys, the more fresh produce it throws away.

If households with more standardized diets discard less food overall, but more fresh produce, than do households with less standardized diets, then fresh produce will be a greater proportion of total food waste in households with more standardized diets, and a smaller proportion in those with less standardized diets. Choice C correctly reflects this relationship and is, therefore, the best answer.

Choices A and B can be ruled out because the passage makes no claims about numbers of households or nonfood waste. Since many foods are neither fresh produce nor canned or prepackaged, D cannot be inferred. The passage provides no basis for relating amount of produce purchased to amount discarded, because in different households different amounts may be consumed. Thus, E is incorrect.

Questions 9-10 are based on the following.

In the past, teachers, bank tellers, and secretaries were predominantly men; these occupations slipped in pay and status when they became largely occupied by women. Therefore, if women become the majority in currently male-dominated professions like accounting, law, and medicine, the income and prestige of these professions will also drop.

9. The argument above is based on

    (A) another argument that contains circular reasoning
    (B) an attempt to refute a generalization by means of an exceptional case
    (C) an analogy between the past and the future
    (D) an appeal to popular beliefs and values
    (E) an attack on the character of the opposition

The argument assumes that, in relevant respects, the future will be like the past. Those relevant respects are the levels of pay and prestige associated with occupations that are occupied at one stage mostly by men and, at a later stage, mostly by women. Therefore, C is the best answer.

Choice A is incorrect because there is no indication that the argument is based on another argument. Neither is there any suggestion that the argument depends on a refutation, so B is also incorrect. The argument does not mention any popular beliefs or values, nor can one infer that it tacitly appeals to any; thus, D is unsupported. The argument is presented as though it had no opponents, so E cannot be correct.

10. Which of the following, if true, would most likely be part of the evidence used to refute the conclusion above?

    (A) Accountants, lawyers, and physicians attained their current relatively high levels of income and prestige at about the same time that the pay and status of teachers, bank tellers, and secretaries slipped.
    (B) When large numbers of men join a female-dominated occupation, such as airline flight attendant, the status and pay of the occupation tend to increase.
    (C) The demand for teachers and secretaries has increased significantly in recent years, while the demand for bank tellers has remained relatively stable.
    (D) If present trends in the awarding of law degrees to women continue, it will be at least two decades before the majority of lawyers are women.
    (E) The pay and status of female accountants, lawyers, and physicians today are governed by significantly different economic and sociological forces than were the pay and status of female teachers, bank tellers, and secretaries in the past.

The argument relies on continuity between past and present with regard to the phenomena being considered. Choice E strongly suggests that such continuity cannot be relied on, and would thus be useful evidence in refuting the conclusion. Therefore, E is the best answer.

The argument says nothing about gains in pay or status; thus, it is unaffected by the coincidence described in A. Choice B is most probably evidence for, not against, the conclusion, since it associates higher pay and status with larger numbers of men employed. Choice C focuses on changes in total numbers employed rather than changes in the male/female ratio and is thus irrelevant. Choice D only bears on when the prediction may become testable, not on whether it is correct.

11. An electric-power company gained greater profits and provided electricity to consumers at lower rates per unit of electricity by building larger-capacity, more efficient plants and by stimulating greater use of electricity within its area. To continue these financial trends, the company planned to replace an old plant by a plant with triple the capacity of its largest plant.

    The company's plan as described above assumed each of the following EXCEPT:

    (A) Demand for electricity within the company's area of service would increase in the future.
    (B) Expenses would not rise beyond the level that could be compensated for by efficiency or volume of operation, or both.
    (C) The planned plant would be sufficiently reliable in service to contribute a net financial benefit to the company as a whole.
    (D) Safety measures to be instituted for the new plant would be the same as those for the plant it would replace.
    (E) The tripling of capacity would not result in insuperable technological obstacles to efficiency.

Choice A is assumed, because the added capacity is financially worthless unless there is a market for extra output. Choice B is assumed, because if expenses rose beyond the level described, it would not be possible to increase profits while reducing unit rates. Choice C is assumed, because a new investment will increase overall profits only if it contributes a net financial benefit. Finally, E is assumed, since rising profits combined with lower unit rates are impossible unless unit costs decrease, i.e., unless efficiency improves.

Choice D, however, is not assumed. There is no reason to think that changes in safety measures would be bound to jeopardize the company's plan.

Questions 12-13 are based on the following.

Meteorologists say that if only they could design an accurate mathematical model of the atmosphere with all its complexities, they could forecast the weather with real precision. But this is an idle boast, immune to any evaluation, for any inadequate weather forecast would obviously be blamed on imperfections in the model.

12. Which of the following, if true, could best be used as a basis for arguing against the author's position that the meteorologists' claim cannot be evaluated?

   (A) Certain unusual configurations of data can serve as the basis for precise weather forecasts even though the exact causal mechanisms are not understood.
   (B) Most significant gains in the accuracy of the relevant mathematical models are accompanied by clear gains in the precision of weather forecasts.
   (C) Mathematical models of the meteorological aftermath of such catastrophic events as volcanic eruptions are beginning to be constructed.
   (D) Modern weather forecasts for as much as a full day ahead are broadly correct about 80 percent of the time.
   (E) Meteorologists readily concede that the accurate mathematical model they are talking about is not now in their power to construct.

The author does not presuppose that precise weather forecasts based on imperfect understanding cannot ever occur, so A cannot be used to argue against the author. Choice C, which says nothing about the quality of the models or their effect on the precision of the weather forecasts, also provides no material for a counterargument. The author's position is consistent with D. The concession described in E is already tacitly conveyed in the author's report of the meteorologists' claim.

However, B can be used to argue that the claim is not impossible to evaluate but actually somewhat plausible, because B indicates that there is a strong correlation between increasing perfection of the model and increasingly accurate forecasts. Therefore, B is the best answer.

13. Which of the following, if true, would cast the most serious doubt on the meteorologists' boast, aside from the doubt expressed in the passage above?

   (A) The amount of energy that the Earth receives from the Sun is monitored closely and is known not to be constant.
   (B) Volcanic eruptions, the combustion of fossil fuels, and several other processes that also cannot be quantified with any accuracy are known to have a significant and continuing impact on the constitution of the atmosphere.
   (C) As current models of the atmosphere are improved, even small increments in complexity will mean large increases in the number of computers required for the representation of the models.
   (D) Frequent and accurate data about the atmosphere collected at a large number of points both on and above the ground are a prerequisite for the construction of a good model of the atmosphere.
   (E) With existing models of the atmosphere, large-scale weather patterns can be predicted with greater accuracy than can relatively local weather patterns.

A mathematical model, a system of postulates, data, and inferences, cannot be accurate unless its components are accurate. Choice B strongly indicates that a model of the atmosphere will be inaccurate in at least one respect: the data. This source of inaccuracy known in advance means that meteorologists know that their claim is likely to remain unverifiable, and the characterization of their boast as idle is thus supported, in a way different from the way the author supports it. Therefore, B is the best choice.

Choice A describes an activity and a piece of information that, on balance, favor accuracy in forecasting. Choices C and D both state prerequisites, but do not suggest that those cannot be met. Choice E only refers to the present state of affairs, with no obvious bearing on the meteorologists' claim.

14. Of the countries that were the world's twenty largest exporters in 1953, four had the same share of total world exports in 1984 as in 1953. These countries can therefore serve as models for those countries that wish to keep their share of the global export trade stable over the years.

Which of the following, if true, casts the most serious doubt on the suitability of those four countries as models in the sense described?

(A) Many countries wish to increase their share of world export trade, not just keep it stable.
(B) Many countries are less concerned with exports alone than with the balance between exports and imports.
(C) With respect to the mix of products each exports, the four countries are very different from each other.
(D) Of the four countries, two had a much larger, and two had a much smaller, share of total world exports in 1970 than in 1984.
(E) The exports of the four countries range from 15 percent to 75 percent of the total national output.

Choice D establishes that the four countries cannot have maintained a stable share of total world exports from 1953 through 1984. There is no reason to suppose that 1970 was an exceptional year, so D suggests that the four countries are not good models in the sense described. Therefore, D is the best answer.

Choices A and B are concerned with countries that would not particularly wish for a constant share of world exports, and are thus irrelevant to the question posed. Choices C and E indicate that the proposed models are rather varied. Variety would be a desirable property of the models—countries could select the models most like themselves as the ones to emulate—and thus casts no doubt on their suitability.

Questions 15-16 are based on the following.

In the United States, the Postal Service has a monopoly on first-class mail, but much of what is sent first class could be transmitted electronically. Electronic transmittal operators argue that if the Postal Service were to offer electronic transmission, it would have an unfair advantage, since its electronic transmission service could be subsidized from the profits of the monopoly.

15. Which of the following, if each is true, would allay the electronic transmittal operators' fears of unfair competition?

(A) If the Postal Service were to offer electronic transmission, it could not make a profit on first-class mail.
(B) If the Postal Service were to offer electronic transmission, it would have a monopoly on that kind of service.
(C) Much of the material that is now sent by first-class mail could be delivered much faster by special package couriers, but is not sent that way because of cost.
(D) There is no economy of scale in electronic transmission—that is, the cost per transaction does not go down as more pieces of information are transmitted.
(E) Electronic transmission will never be cost-effective for material not sent by first-class mail such as newspapers and bulk mail.

The fears of unfair competition are based on the speculation that the Postal Service could use profits from its monopoly on first-class mail to subsidize its electronic transmission service. Choice A states that there would be no such profit if the Postal Service had an electronic transmission service; thus, the fears are unfounded. Therefore, A is the best answer.

Choice B, rather than allaying fears, probably expresses the private operators' worst fears. The issues raised by C—the importance of relative cost—and by D—absence of economies of scale—are side issues. Choice E cannot allay private operators' fears, because what those operators fear is specifically unfair competition in the electronic transmission of materials otherwise sent by first-class mail.

16. Which of the following questions can be answered on the basis of the information in the passage above?

(A) Is the Postal Service as efficient as privately owned electric transmission services?
(B) If private operators were allowed to operate first-class mail services, would they choose to do so?
(C) Do the electronic transmittal operators believe that the Postal Service makes a profit on first-class mail?
(D) Is the Postal Service prohibited from offering electronic transmission services?
(E) Is the Postal Service expected to have a monopoly on electronic transmission?

The answer to the question in C is yes, for the operators could not reasonably make their argument unless they believed that first-class mail was profitable. Therefore, C is the best of the choices.

Since private operators might worry about an unfair advantage regardless of how the Postal Service's efficiency compares to their own, the question in A cannot be answered. Neither can the question in B: the Postal Service, highly experienced with first-class mail, might enjoy advantages that prevent newcomers from competing effectively. Since the current unavailability of electronic transmissions through the Postal Service may be a matter either of choice or of law, D poses an unanswerable question, as does E, since a large enough unfair advantage might confer a monopoly.

17. Lists of hospitals have been compiled showing which hospitals have patient death rates exceeding the national average. The data have been adjusted to allow for differences in the ages of patients.

Each of the following, if true, provides a good logical ground for hospitals to object to interpreting rank on these lists as one of the indices of the quality of hospital care EXCEPT:

(A) Rank order might indicate insignificant differences, rather than large differences, in numbers of patient deaths.
(B) Hospitals that keep patients longer are likely to have higher death rates than those that discharge patients earlier but do not record deaths of patients at home after discharge.
(C) Patients who are very old on admission to a hospital are less likely than younger patients to survive the same types of illnesses or surgical procedures.
(D) Some hospitals serve a larger proportion of low-income patients, who tend to be more seriously ill when admitted to a hospital.
(E) For-profit hospitals sometimes do not provide intensive-care units and other expensive services for very sick patients but refer or transfer such patients to other hospitals.

Choice A supports an objection based on the possibility that even seemingly large differences in rank may have rather small differences in death rates associated with them. Choices B, D, and E all support objections because they describe circumstances not related to quality of hospital care that distort the death rates for some hospitals relative to those for others. These circumstances are hospitals' discharge policies, patients' economic circumstances, and the range of medical services offered, respectively.

On the other hand, C, as stated, supports no objection, because any substantial differences among hospitals with regard to the age profile of their patient populations will have been allowed for. That is the express purpose of the data adjustment mentioned. Therefore, C is the best answer.

18. Teresa: Manned spaceflight does not have a future, since it cannot compete economically with other means of accomplishing the objectives of spaceflight.

Edward: No mode of human transportation has a better record of reliability: two accidents in twenty-five years. Thus manned spaceflight definitely has a positive future.

Which of the following is the best logical evaluation of Edward's argument as a response to Teresa's argument?

(A) It cites evidence that, if true, tends to disprove the evidence cited by Teresa in drawing her conclusion.
(B) It indicates a logical gap in the support that Teresa offers for her conclusion.
(C) It raises a consideration that outweighs the argument Teresa makes.
(D) It does not meet Teresa's point because it assumes that there is no serious impediment to transporting people into space, but this was the issue raised by Teresa.
(E) It fails to respond to Teresa's argument because it does not address the fundamental issue of whether space activities should have priority over other claims on the national budget.

Teresa evaluates manned spaceflight as a means of accomplishing the objectives of spaceflight, finds it excessively costly, and predicts its demise. Edward makes the opposite prediction, on the basis of the safety record of manned spaceflight as a mode of human transportation. Edward ignores the issue Teresa raises: that manned spaceflight is an economically unjustifiable instance of human transportation. Therefore, D is the best answer.

Nothing in Edward's evidence suggests that Teresa's evidence is false or her conclusion ill-supported, so A and B are incorrect. Because Teresa evidently favors unmanned spaceflight, Edward's concern with human safety is irrelevant, and C can be eliminated. Regarding the "fundamental issue" described in E, neither Teresa nor Edward seems to question the availability of funds for space activities.

19. Black Americans are, on the whole, about twice as likely as White Americans to develop high blood pressure. This likelihood also holds for westernized Black Africans when compared to White Africans. Researchers have hypothesized that this predisposition in westernized Blacks may reflect an interaction between western high-salt diets and genes that adapted to an environmental scarcity of salt.

Which of the following statements about present-day, westernized Black Africans, if true, would most tend to confirm the researchers' hypothesis?

(A) The blood pressures of those descended from peoples situated throughout their history in Senegal and Gambia, where salt was always available, are low.
(B) The unusually high salt consumption in certain areas of Africa represents a serious health problem.
(C) Because of their blood pressure levels, most White Africans have markedly decreased their salt consumption.
(D) Blood pressures are low among the Yoruba, who, throughout their history, have been situated far inland from sources of sea salt and far south of Saharan salt mines.
(E) No significant differences in salt metabolism have been found between those peoples who have had salt available throughout their history and those who have not.

Choice A describes a situation in which one of the interacting factors is present, but the second—genes adapted to an environmental scarcity of salt—is not. If the result were nonetheless high blood pressure, then the second explanatory factor, and thus the hypothesis, would be called into question. In actual fact, low blood pressure is reported. The hypothesis has thus withstood potentially disconfirming evidence, and this circumstance tends to confirm it. The best answer, therefore, is A.

Both B and C are compatible with any explanation that relates high blood pressure to high salt intake, and thus have no special bearing on the current hypothesis. Both D and E are unexpected, given the hypothesis, and so tend to disconfirm rather than confirm it.

20. The following proposal to amend the bylaws of an organization was circulated to its members for comment.

When more than one nominee is to be named for an office, prospective nominees must consent to nomination and before giving such consent must be told who the other nominees will be.

Which of the following comments concerning the logic of the proposal is accurate if it cannot be known who the actual nominees are until prospective nominees have given their consent to be nominated?

(A) The proposal would make it possible for each of several nominees for an office to be aware of who all of the other nominees are.
(B) The proposal would widen the choice available to those choosing among the nominees.
(C) If there are several prospective nominees, the proposal would deny the last nominee equal treatment with the first.
(D) The proposal would enable a prospective nominee to withdraw from competition with a specific person without making that withdrawal known.
(E) If there is more than one prospective nominee, the proposal would make it impossible for anyone to become a nominee.

Suppose that there were to be two nominees. Neither of them can consent to being nominated unless the other one has already so consented. But this, in effect, means that neither can consent to being nominated. Thus, neither can be nominated, and it is impossible to have two nominees. Analogous arguments would show that having more than two nominees is likewise impossible. Therefore, E is the best answer.

The impossibility of having two or more nominees means that A makes a false assumption, B makes a wrong prediction, and C describes an impossible scenario, so none of them accurately comments on the logic of the proposal. Nor does D: if the sort of withdrawal it describes were currently prohibited, the proposal would not change the situation.

7 Sentence Correction

Sample Sentence Correction test sections begin on page 259; answers to the questions follow the test sections. After the answers are explanations for all of the questions. These explanations address types of grammatical and syntactical problems you are likely to encounter in the Sentence Correction section of the GMAT.

Study Suggestions

1. One way to gain familiarity with the basic conventions of standard written English is to read material that reflects standard usage. Suitable material will usually be found in good magazines and nonfiction books, editorials in outstanding newspapers, and the collections of essays used by many college and university writing courses.

2. A general review of basic rules of grammar and practice with writing exercises are also ways of studying for the Sentence Correction section. If you have papers that have been carefully evaluated for grammatical errors, it may be helpful to review the comments and corrections.

Test-Taking Strategies for Sentence Correction

1. Read the entire sentence carefully. Try to understand the specific idea or relationship that the sentence should express.

2. Since the part of the sentence that *may* be incorrect is underlined, concentrate on evaluating the underlined part for errors and possible corrections before reading the answer choices.

3. Read each answer choice carefully. Choice A always repeats the underlined portion of the original sentence. Choose A if you think that the sentence is best as it stands, but only after examining all of the other choices.

4. Try to determine how well each choice corrects whatever you consider wrong with the original sentence.

5. Make sure that you evaluate the sentence and the choices in terms of general clarity, grammatical and idiomatic usage, economy and precision of language, and appropriateness of diction.

6. Read the whole sentence, substituting the choice that you prefer for the underlined part. A choice may be wrong because it does not fit grammatically or structurally with the rest of the sentence. Remember that some sentences will require no corrections. The answer to such sentences should be A.

When you take the sample test sections, use the answer spaces on page 257 to mark your answers.

Answer Spaces for Sentence Correction Sample Test Sections

Sample Test Section 1

1 Ⓐ Ⓑ Ⓒ Ⓓ Ⓔ	8 Ⓐ Ⓑ Ⓒ Ⓓ Ⓔ	15 Ⓐ Ⓑ Ⓒ Ⓓ Ⓔ	22 Ⓐ Ⓑ Ⓒ Ⓓ Ⓔ
2 Ⓐ Ⓑ Ⓒ Ⓓ Ⓔ	9 Ⓐ Ⓑ Ⓒ Ⓓ Ⓔ	16 Ⓐ Ⓑ Ⓒ Ⓓ Ⓔ	23 Ⓐ Ⓑ Ⓒ Ⓓ Ⓔ
3 Ⓐ Ⓑ Ⓒ Ⓓ Ⓔ	10 Ⓐ Ⓑ Ⓒ Ⓓ Ⓔ	17 Ⓐ Ⓑ Ⓒ Ⓓ Ⓔ	24 Ⓐ Ⓑ Ⓒ Ⓓ Ⓔ
4 Ⓐ Ⓑ Ⓒ Ⓓ Ⓔ	11 Ⓐ Ⓑ Ⓒ Ⓓ Ⓔ	18 Ⓐ Ⓑ Ⓒ Ⓓ Ⓔ	25 Ⓐ Ⓑ Ⓒ Ⓓ Ⓔ
5 Ⓐ Ⓑ Ⓒ Ⓓ Ⓔ	12 Ⓐ Ⓑ Ⓒ Ⓓ Ⓔ	19 Ⓐ Ⓑ Ⓒ Ⓓ Ⓔ	
6 Ⓐ Ⓑ Ⓒ Ⓓ Ⓔ	13 Ⓐ Ⓑ Ⓒ Ⓓ Ⓔ	20 Ⓐ Ⓑ Ⓒ Ⓓ Ⓔ	
7 Ⓐ Ⓑ Ⓒ Ⓓ Ⓔ	14 Ⓐ Ⓑ Ⓒ Ⓓ Ⓔ	21 Ⓐ Ⓑ Ⓒ Ⓓ Ⓔ	

Sample Test Section 2

1 Ⓐ Ⓑ Ⓒ Ⓓ Ⓔ	8 Ⓐ Ⓑ Ⓒ Ⓓ Ⓔ	15 Ⓐ Ⓑ Ⓒ Ⓓ Ⓔ	22 Ⓐ Ⓑ Ⓒ Ⓓ Ⓔ
2 Ⓐ Ⓑ Ⓒ Ⓓ Ⓔ	9 Ⓐ Ⓑ Ⓒ Ⓓ Ⓔ	16 Ⓐ Ⓑ Ⓒ Ⓓ Ⓔ	23 Ⓐ Ⓑ Ⓒ Ⓓ Ⓔ
3 Ⓐ Ⓑ Ⓒ Ⓓ Ⓔ	10 Ⓐ Ⓑ Ⓒ Ⓓ Ⓔ	17 Ⓐ Ⓑ Ⓒ Ⓓ Ⓔ	24 Ⓐ Ⓑ Ⓒ Ⓓ Ⓔ
4 Ⓐ Ⓑ Ⓒ Ⓓ Ⓔ	11 Ⓐ Ⓑ Ⓒ Ⓓ Ⓔ	18 Ⓐ Ⓑ Ⓒ Ⓓ Ⓔ	25 Ⓐ Ⓑ Ⓒ Ⓓ Ⓔ
5 Ⓐ Ⓑ Ⓒ Ⓓ Ⓔ	12 Ⓐ Ⓑ Ⓒ Ⓓ Ⓔ	19 Ⓐ Ⓑ Ⓒ Ⓓ Ⓔ	
6 Ⓐ Ⓑ Ⓒ Ⓓ Ⓔ	13 Ⓐ Ⓑ Ⓒ Ⓓ Ⓔ	20 Ⓐ Ⓑ Ⓒ Ⓓ Ⓔ	
7 Ⓐ Ⓑ Ⓒ Ⓓ Ⓔ	14 Ⓐ Ⓑ Ⓒ Ⓓ Ⓔ	21 Ⓐ Ⓑ Ⓒ Ⓓ Ⓔ	

Sample Test Section 3

1 Ⓐ Ⓑ Ⓒ Ⓓ Ⓔ	8 Ⓐ Ⓑ Ⓒ Ⓓ Ⓔ	15 Ⓐ Ⓑ Ⓒ Ⓓ Ⓔ	22 Ⓐ Ⓑ Ⓒ Ⓓ Ⓔ
2 Ⓐ Ⓑ Ⓒ Ⓓ Ⓔ	9 Ⓐ Ⓑ Ⓒ Ⓓ Ⓔ	16 Ⓐ Ⓑ Ⓒ Ⓓ Ⓔ	23 Ⓐ Ⓑ Ⓒ Ⓓ Ⓔ
3 Ⓐ Ⓑ Ⓒ Ⓓ Ⓔ	10 Ⓐ Ⓑ Ⓒ Ⓓ Ⓔ	17 Ⓐ Ⓑ Ⓒ Ⓓ Ⓔ	24 Ⓐ Ⓑ Ⓒ Ⓓ Ⓔ
4 Ⓐ Ⓑ Ⓒ Ⓓ Ⓔ	11 Ⓐ Ⓑ Ⓒ Ⓓ Ⓔ	18 Ⓐ Ⓑ Ⓒ Ⓓ Ⓔ	25 Ⓐ Ⓑ Ⓒ Ⓓ Ⓔ
5 Ⓐ Ⓑ Ⓒ Ⓓ Ⓔ	12 Ⓐ Ⓑ Ⓒ Ⓓ Ⓔ	19 Ⓐ Ⓑ Ⓒ Ⓓ Ⓔ	
6 Ⓐ Ⓑ Ⓒ Ⓓ Ⓔ	13 Ⓐ Ⓑ Ⓒ Ⓓ Ⓔ	20 Ⓐ Ⓑ Ⓒ Ⓓ Ⓔ	
7 Ⓐ Ⓑ Ⓒ Ⓓ Ⓔ	14 Ⓐ Ⓑ Ⓒ Ⓓ Ⓔ	21 Ⓐ Ⓑ Ⓒ Ⓓ Ⓔ	

Sample Test Section 4

1 Ⓐ Ⓑ Ⓒ Ⓓ Ⓔ	8 Ⓐ Ⓑ Ⓒ Ⓓ Ⓔ	15 Ⓐ Ⓑ Ⓒ Ⓓ Ⓔ	22 Ⓐ Ⓑ Ⓒ Ⓓ Ⓔ
2 Ⓐ Ⓑ Ⓒ Ⓓ Ⓔ	9 Ⓐ Ⓑ Ⓒ Ⓓ Ⓔ	16 Ⓐ Ⓑ Ⓒ Ⓓ Ⓔ	23 Ⓐ Ⓑ Ⓒ Ⓓ Ⓔ
3 Ⓐ Ⓑ Ⓒ Ⓓ Ⓔ	10 Ⓐ Ⓑ Ⓒ Ⓓ Ⓔ	17 Ⓐ Ⓑ Ⓒ Ⓓ Ⓔ	24 Ⓐ Ⓑ Ⓒ Ⓓ Ⓔ
4 Ⓐ Ⓑ Ⓒ Ⓓ Ⓔ	11 Ⓐ Ⓑ Ⓒ Ⓓ Ⓔ	18 Ⓐ Ⓑ Ⓒ Ⓓ Ⓔ	25 Ⓐ Ⓑ Ⓒ Ⓓ Ⓔ
5 Ⓐ Ⓑ Ⓒ Ⓓ Ⓔ	12 Ⓐ Ⓑ Ⓒ Ⓓ Ⓔ	19 Ⓐ Ⓑ Ⓒ Ⓓ Ⓔ	
6 Ⓐ Ⓑ Ⓒ Ⓓ Ⓔ	13 Ⓐ Ⓑ Ⓒ Ⓓ Ⓔ	20 Ⓐ Ⓑ Ⓒ Ⓓ Ⓔ	
7 Ⓐ Ⓑ Ⓒ Ⓓ Ⓔ	14 Ⓐ Ⓑ Ⓒ Ⓓ Ⓔ	21 Ⓐ Ⓑ Ⓒ Ⓓ Ⓔ	

SENTENCE CORRECTION SAMPLE TEST SECTION 1

30 Minutes
25 Questions

<u>Directions:</u> In each of the following sentences, some part of the sentence or the entire sentence is underlined. Beneath each sentence you will find five ways of phrasing the underlined part. The first of these repeats the original; the other four are different. If you think the original is better than any of the alternatives, choose answer A; otherwise choose one of the others. Select the best version and fill in the corresponding oval on your answer sheet.

This is a test of correctness and effectiveness of expression. In choosing answers, follow the requirements of standard written English; that is, pay attention to grammar, choice of words, and sentence construction. Choose the answer that expresses most effectively what is presented in the original sentence; this answer should be clear and exact, without awkwardness, ambiguity, or redundancy.

1. Researchers at Cornell University have demonstrated that homing pigeons can sense changes in the earth's magnetic field, see light waves that people cannot see, detect low-frequency sounds from miles away, <u>sense changes in air pressure, and can identify familiar odors</u>.

   (A) sense changes in air pressure, and can identify familiar odors
   (B) can sense changes in air pressure, and can identify familiar odors
   (C) sense changes in air pressure, and identify familiar odors
   (D) air pressure changes can be sensed, and familiar odors identified
   (E) air pressure changes are sensed, and familiar odors identified

2. In ancient times, Nubia was the principal corridor <u>where there were cultural influences transmitted</u> between Black Africa and the Mediterranean basin.

   (A) where there were cultural influences transmitted
   (B) through which cultural influences were transmitted
   (C) where there was a transmission of cultural influences
   (D) for the transmitting of cultural influences
   (E) which was transmitting cultural influences

3. It is a special feature of cell aggregation in the developing nervous system that in most regions of the brain the cells not only adhere <u>to one another and also adopt</u> some preferential orientation.

   (A) to one another and also adopt
   (B) one to the other, and also they adopt
   (C) one to the other, but also adopting
   (D) to one another but also adopt
   (E) to each other, also adopting

4. Among the reasons for the decline of New England agriculture in the last three decades were the high cost of land, the pressure of housing and commercial development, and <u>basing a marketing and distribution system on importing produce from Florida and California</u>.

   (A) basing a marketing and distribution system on importing produce from Florida and California
   (B) basing a marketing and distribution system on the imported produce of Florida and California
   (C) basing a system of marketing and distribution on the import of produce from Florida and California
   (D) a marketing and distribution system based on importing produce from Florida and California
   (E) a marketing and distribution system importing produce from Florida and California as its base

GO ON TO THE NEXT PAGE.

5. <u>Like Byron</u> at Missolonghi, Jack London was slowly killed by the mistakes of the medical men who treated him.

   (A) Like Byron
   (B) Like Byron's death
   (C) Just as Byron died
   (D) Similar to Byron
   (E) As did Byron

6. One of every two new businesses <u>fail</u> within two years.

   (A) fail
   (B) fails
   (C) should fail
   (D) may have failed
   (E) has failed

7. Even today, a century after Pasteur developed the first vaccine, rabies almost always kills <u>its victims unless inoculated</u> in the earliest stages of the disease.

   (A) its victims unless inoculated
   (B) its victims unless they are inoculated
   (C) its victims unless inoculation is done
   (D) the victims unless there is an inoculation
   (E) the victims unless inoculated

8. <u>In a period of time when women typically have</u> had a narrow range of choices, Mary Baker Eddy became a distinguished writer and the founder, architect, and builder of a growing church.

   (A) In a period of time when women typically have
   (B) During a time in which typically women have
   (C) Typically, during a time when women
   (D) At a time when women typically
   (E) Typically in a time in which women

9. As the price of gasoline rises, <u>which makes substituting alcohol distilled from cereal grain attractive</u>, the prices of bread and livestock feed are sure to increase.

   (A) which makes substituting alcohol distilled from cereal grain attractive
   (B) which makes substituting the distillation of alcohol from cereal grain attractive
   (C) which makes distilling alcohol from cereal grain an attractive substitute
   (D) making an attractive substitution of alcohol distilled from cereal grain
   (E) making alcohol distilled from cereal grain an attractive substitute

10. Climatic shifts are <u>so gradual as to be indistinguishable</u> at first from ordinary fluctuations in the weather.

    (A) so gradual as to be indistinguishable
    (B) so gradual they can be indistinguishable
    (C) so gradual that they are unable to be distinguished
    (D) gradual enough not to be distinguishable
    (E) gradual enough so that one cannot distinguish them

11. Although <u>the lesser cornstalk borer is widely distributed, control of them is</u> necessary only in the South.

    (A) the lesser cornstalk borer is widely distributed, control of them is
    (B) widely distributed, measures to control the lesser cornstalk borer are
    (C) widely distributed, lesser cornstalk borer control is
    (D) the lesser cornstalk borer is widely distributed, measures to control it are
    (E) it is widely distributed, control of the lesser cornstalk borer is

GO ON TO THE NEXT PAGE.

12. Traveling the back roads of Hungary, in 1905 Béla Bartók and Zoltán Kodály began their pioneering work in ethnomusicology, and they were armed only with an Edison phonograph and insatiable curiosity.

(A) Traveling the back roads of Hungary, in 1905 Béla Bartók and Zoltán Kodály began their pioneering work in ethnomusicology, and they were armed only

(B) In 1905, Béla Bartók and Zoltán Kodály, traveling the back roads of Hungary, began their pioneering work in ethnomusicology, and they were only armed

(C) In 1905 Béla Bartók and Zoltán Kodály began their pioneering work in ethnomusicology, traveling the back roads of Hungary armed only

(D) Having traveled the back roads of Hungary, in 1905 Béla Bartók and Zoltán Kodály began their pioneering work in ethnomusicology; they were only armed

(E) Béla Bartók and Zoltán Kodály, in 1905 began their pioneering work in ethnomusicology, traveling the back roads of Hungary, arming themselves only

13. It is as difficult to prevent crimes against property as those that are against a person.

(A) those that are against a
(B) those against a
(C) it is against a
(D) preventing those against a
(E) it is to prevent those against a

14. Unlike the acid smoke of cigarettes, pipe tobacco, cured by age-old methods, yields an alkaline smoke too irritating to be drawn into the lungs.

(A) Unlike the acid smoke of cigarettes, pipe tobacco, cured by age-old methods, yields an alkaline smoke

(B) Unlike the acid smoke of cigarettes, pipe tobacco is cured by age-old methods, yielding an alkaline smoke

(C) Unlike cigarette tobacco, which yields an acid smoke, pipe tobacco, cured by age-old methods, yields an alkaline smoke

(D) Differing from cigarettes' acid smoke, pipe tobacco's alkaline smoke, cured by age-old methods, is

(E) The alkaline smoke of pipe tobacco differs from cigarettes' acid smoke in that it is cured by age-old methods and is

15. Joplin's faith in his opera "Tremonisha" was unshakeable; in 1911 he published the score at his own expense and decided on staging it himself.

(A) on staging it himself
(B) that he himself would do the staging
(C) to do the staging of the work by himself
(D) that he himself would stage it
(E) to stage the work himself

16. Los Angeles has a higher number of family dwellings per capita than any large city.

(A) a higher number of family dwellings per capita than any large city
(B) higher numbers of family dwellings per capita than any other large city
(C) a higher number of family dwellings per capita than does any other large city
(D) higher numbers of family dwellings per capita than do other large cities
(E) a high per capita number of family dwellings, more than does any other large city

GO ON TO THE NEXT PAGE.

17. During the nineteenth century Emily Eden and Fanny Parks journeyed throughout India, sketching and keeping journals forming the basis of news reports about the princely states where they had visited.

    (A) forming the basis of news reports about the princely states where they had
    (B) that were forming the basis of news reports about the princely states
    (C) to form the basis of news reports about the princely states which they have
    (D) which had formed the basis of news reports about the princely states where they had
    (E) that formed the basis of news reports about the princely states they

18. School integration plans that involve busing between suburban and central-city areas have contributed, according to a recent study, to significant increases in housing integration, which, in turn, reduces any future need for busing.

    (A) significant increases in housing integration, which, in turn, reduces
    (B) significant integration increases in housing, which, in turn, reduces
    (C) increase housing integration significantly, which, in turn, reduces
    (D) increase housing integration significantly, in turn reducing
    (E) significantly increase housing integration, which, in turn, reduce

19. The commission acknowledged that no amount of money or staff members can ensure the safety of people who live in the vicinity of a nuclear plant, but it approved the installation because it believed that all reasonable precautions had been taken.

    (A) no amount of money or staff members
    (B) neither vast amounts of money nor staff members
    (C) neither vast amounts of money nor numbers of staff members
    (D) neither vast amounts of money nor a large staff
    (E) no matter how large the staff or how vast the amount of money

20. Sartre believed each individual is responsible to choose one course of action over another one, that it is the choice that gives value to the act, and that nothing that is not acted upon has value.

    (A) each individual is responsible to choose one course of action over another one
    (B) that each individual is responsible for choosing one course of action over another
    (C) that each individual is responsible, choosing one course of action over another
    (D) that each individual is responsible to choose one course of action over the other
    (E) each individual is responsible for choosing one course of action over other ones

21. While the owner of a condominium apartment has free and clear title to the dwelling, owners of cooperative apartments have shares in a corporation that owns a building and leases apartments to them.

    (Λ) While the owner of a condominium apartment has free and clear title to the dwelling,
    (B) The owner of a condominium apartment has free and clear title to the dwelling, but
    (C) Whereas owners of condominium apartments have free and clear title to their dwellings,
    (D) An owner of a condominium apartment has free and clear title to the dwelling, whereas
    (E) Condominium apartment owners have a title to their dwelling that is free and clear, while

GO ON TO THE NEXT PAGE.

22. Although <u>films about the American West depict coyotes as solitary animals howling mournfully on the tops of distant hills</u>, in reality these gregarious creatures live in stable groups that occupy the same territory for long periods.

(A) films about the American West depict coyotes as solitary animals howling mournfully on the tops of distant hills

(B) in films about the American West coyotes are depicted to be solitary animals that howl mournfully on the tops of distant hills

(C) coyotes are depicted as solitary animals howling mournfully on the tops of distant hills in films about the American West

(D) films about the American West depict coyotes as if they were solitary, mournfully howling animals on the tops of distant hills

(E) films about the American West depict coyotes to be solitary and mournfully howling animals on the tops of distant hills

23. In 1980 the United States exported <u>twice as much of its national output of goods as they had</u> in 1970.

(A) twice as much of its national output of goods as they had

(B) double the amount of their national output of goods as they did

(C) twice as much of its national output of goods as it did

(D) double the amount of its national output of goods as it has

(E) twice as much of their national output of goods as they had

24. <u>Even though its per capita food supply hardly increased during</u> two decades, stringent rationing and planned distribution have allowed the People's Republic of China to ensure nutritional levels of 2,000 calories per person per day for its population.

(A) Even though its per capita food supply hardly increased during

(B) Even though its per capita food supply has hardly increased in

(C) Despite its per capita food supply hardly increasing over

(D) Despite there being hardly any increase in its per capita food supply during

(E) Although there is hardly any increase in per capita food supply for

25. Few people realize that the chance of accidental injury or death <u>may be as great or greater in the "safety" of their own homes than</u> in a plane or on the road.

(A) may be as great or greater in the "safety" of their own homes than

(B) is at least as great or greater in the "safety" of their own homes than

(C) might be so great or greater in the "safety" of their own home as

(D) may be at least as great in the "safety" of their own homes as

(E) can be at least so great in the "safety" of their own home as

STOP

IF YOU FINISH BEFORE TIME IS CALLED, YOU MAY CHECK YOUR WORK ON THIS SECTION ONLY.
DO NOT TURN TO ANY OTHER SECTION IN THE TEST.

Answer Key for Sample Test Section 1
SENTENCE CORRECTION

1.	C	14.	C
2.	B	15.	E
3.	D	16.	C
4.	D	17.	E
5.	A	18.	A
6.	B	19.	D
7.	B	20.	B
8.	D	21.	C
9.	E	22.	A
10.	A	23.	C
11.	D	24.	B
12.	C	25.	D
13.	E		

Explanatory Material: Sentence Correction Sample Test Section 1

1. **Researchers at Cornell University have demonstrated that homing pigeons can sense changes in the earth's magnetic field, see light waves that people cannot see, detect low-frequency sounds from miles away, sense changes in air pressure, and can identify familiar odors.**

   (A) sense changes in air pressure, and can identify familiar odors
   (B) can sense changes in air pressure, and can identify familiar odors
   (C) sense changes in air pressure, and identify familiar odors
   (D) air pressure changes can be sensed, and familiar odors identified
   (E) air pressure changes are sensed, and familiar odors identified

This question requires you to choose an answer that completes a series of parallel verbs. Choice A is incorrect because the *can* before *identify* breaks a parallel sequence of verbs that complete the *can* in line 2: A states, *homing pigeons can sense, . . . see, . . . detect, . . . sense, . . . and can identify.* Choice B makes the problem worse by adding *can* before two verbs so that both are nonparallel. Choice C is best. Choices D and E wrongly substitute independent clauses for the verb phrases in C that continue the parallel construction.

2. **In ancient times, Nubia was the principal corridor where there were cultural influences transmitted between Black Africa and the Mediterranean basin.**

   (A) where there were cultural influences transmitted
   (B) through which cultural influences were transmitted
   (C) where there was a transmission of cultural influences
   (D) for the transmitting of cultural influences
   (E) which was transmitting cultural influences

Choice A is imprecise and unidiomatic. In choice B, the best answer, *through which* suggests the movement or passage of cultural influences between the ends of the corridor and so provides a clearer description of Nubia's role in the ancient world. Choice C, like A, is unidiomatic and needlessly indirect; D is awkward and imprecise. In choice E, *which* refers to *corridor*, thereby suggesting somewhat imprecisely that the corridor itself, not the civilizations it connected, *was transmitting cultural influences*. Also, *transmitted* is preferable to *transmitting* in a description of past events.

3. **It is a special feature of cell aggregation in the developing nervous system that in most regions of the brain the cells not only adhere to one another and also adopt some preferential orientation.**

   (A) to one another and also adopt
   (B) one to the other, and also they adopt
   (C) one to the other, but also adopting
   (D) to one another but also adopt
   (E) to each other, also adopting

Choices A and B are incorrect because *and* should be *but* to conform to the idiomatic construction *not only but also*. Choice B can be faulted for including *they* where there should be only *adopt* to form a parallel with *adhere*. Moreover, *the other* in B is inappropriate because many more than two brain cells are being discussed. Choice C contains *the other* and has *adopting* in place of *adopt,* the verb form parallel to *adhere*. Choice D is best. In choice E, *adopting* is again wrong and *each other* is less appropriate than *one another* for referring to a multitude of cells.

4. **Among the reasons for the decline of New England agriculture in the last three decades were the high cost of land, the pressure of housing and commercial development, and basing a marketing and distribution system on importing produce from Florida and California.**

   (A) basing a marketing and distribution system on importing produce from Florida and California
   (B) basing a marketing and distribution system on the imported produce of Florida and California
   (C) basing a system of marketing and distribution on the import of produce from Florida and California
   (D) a marketing and distribution system based on importing produce from Florida and California
   (E) a marketing and distribution system importing produce from Florida and California as its base

Choices A, B, and C can be faulted for putting a verb phrase, *basing . . .*, where a noun phrase is needed to continue the list of parallel elements that begins with *the high cost of land, the pressure of housing. . . .* Also, *the imported produce* in B suggests that the system is based on the produce itself rather than on the practice of importing produce. In C, *the import of produce* is unidiomatic. D, the best choice, presents a noun phrase (*. . . a marketing and distribution system*) that completes the list of parallel elements and refers to the act of *importing produce*. E also supplies the noun phrase but states illogically that the system imports produce *as its base*.

5. <u>Like Byron</u> at Missolonghi, Jack London was slowly killed by the mistakes of the medical men who treated him.

   (A) Like Byron
   (B) Like Byron's death
   (C) Just as Byron died
   (D) Similar to Byron
   (E) As did Byron

Choice A, the best answer, correctly compares two persons, Byron and Jack London. Choice B illogically compares Byron's death to London. Choice C does not compare one person to another and could be read as saying *Just at the time that Byron died*. Choice D misstates the idea: the point is not that London was *similar to Byron* but that he was like Byron in the manner of his death. In choice E, *did* cannot grammatically be substituted for *was* in the phrase *was slowly killed*.

6. One of every two new businesses <u>fail</u> within two years.

   (A) fail
   (B) fails
   (C) should fail
   (D) may have failed
   (E) has failed

Choice A is wrong because the verb *fail* does not agree in number with *One,* the subject of the sentence; *businesses* is not the subject of the sentence but the object of the preposition *of*. In choice C, *should fail* is inappropriate for a statement of fact and carries the unintended suggestion of *ought to fail*. In choices D and E, *may have failed* and *has failed* wrongly refer to a completed action rather than an ongoing condition. Choice B is best.

7. Even today, a century after Pasteur developed the first vaccine, rabies almost always kills <u>its victims unless inoculated</u> in the earliest stages of the disease.

   (A) its victims unless inoculated
   (B) its victims unless they are inoculated
   (C) its victims unless inoculation is done
   (D) the victims unless there is an inoculation
   (E) the victims unless inoculated

Choices A and E illogically suggest that rabies rather than the victims of rabies should be inoculated in the earliest stages of the disease. Choice B is best: it is logical, clear, and more precise than C and D, which do not specify who or what is being inoculated.

8. <u>In a period of time when women typically have</u> had a narrow range of choices, Mary Baker Eddy became a distinguished writer and the founder, architect, and builder of a growing church.

   (A) In a period of time when women typically have
   (B) During a time in which typically women have
   (C) Typically, during a time when women
   (D) At a time when women typically
   (E) Typically in a time in which women

Choices A and B are wrong because *have had* in the resulting sentence does not correspond to *became;* a simple *had* is needed to match *became* in referring to past events. Choice C drops the erroneous *have*, but *Typically* is misplaced so that it modifies the main clause; in other words, C says that it was typical for Mary Baker Eddy to become distinguished, not that it was typical for women to have a narrow range of choices. Choice E suffers from the same confusion. D is the best answer.

9. As the price of gasoline rises, <u>which makes substituting alcohol distilled from cereal grain attractive</u>, the prices of bread and livestock feed are sure to increase.

   (A) which makes substituting alcohol distilled from cereal grain attractive
   (B) which makes substituting the distillation of alcohol from cereal grain attractive
   (C) which makes distilling alcohol from cereal grain an attractive substitute
   (D) making an attractive substitution of alcohol distilled from cereal grain
   (E) making alcohol distilled from cereal grain an attractive substitute

Choices A, B, and C are faulty because the pronoun *which* refers loosely to the whole clause rather than to some noun. The original sentence is intended to say that alcohol is an attractive substitute for gasoline, but the understood phrase *for gasoline* cannot be inserted anywhere in A without producing an awkward construction. Both B and C are illogically worded: the *distillation of alcohol,* not the alcohol itself, is substituted for gasoline in B, as the act of *distilling alcohol* is in C. Choice D is unidiomatic and suggests that the rising price of gasoline is what makes the substitution. Choice E is the best for this question.

10. Climatic shifts are so gradual as to be indistinguishable at first from ordinary fluctuations in the weather.

    (A) so gradual as to be indistinguishable
    (B) so gradual they can be indistinguishable
    (C) so gradual that they are unable to be distinguished
    (D) gradual enough not to be distinguishable
    (E) gradual enough so that one cannot distinguish them

Choice A, the best answer, presents the idiomatic form (*some things) are so X as to be Y.* Choices B, C, D, and E can be faulted for not using this form. In addition, C confusedly refers to the climatic shifts themselves as being *unable* when it is really people who are unable at first to distinguish climatic shifts.

11. Although the lesser cornstalk borer is widely distributed, control of them is necessary only in the South.

    (A) the lesser cornstalk borer is widely distributed, control of them is
    (B) widely distributed, measures to control the lesser cornstalk borer are
    (C) widely distributed, lesser cornstalk borer control is
    (D) the lesser cornstalk borer is widely distributed, measures to control it are
    (E) it is widely distributed, control of the lesser cornstalk borer is

Choice A is incorrect because the plural pronoun *them* does not agree in number with its singular noun referent, *the lesser cornstalk borer.* Choice B wrongly states that *measures* are widely distributed, not that *the cornstalk borer* is. Similarly, C and E assert that *control* is widely distributed. Choice D is the best answer.

12. Traveling the back roads of Hungary, in 1905 Béla Bartók and Zoltán Kodály began their pioneering work in ethnomusicology, and they were armed only with an Edison phonograph and insatiable curiosity.

    (A) Traveling the back roads of Hungary, in 1905 Béla Bartók and Zoltán Kodály began their pioneering work in ethnomusicology, and they were armed only
    (B) In 1905, Béla Bartók and Zoltán Kodály, traveling the back roads of Hungary, began their pioneering work in ethnomusicology, and they were only armed
    (C) In 1905 Béla Bartók and Zoltán Kodály began their pioneering work in ethnomusicology, traveling the back roads of Hungary armed only
    (D) Having traveled the back roads of Hungary, in 1905 Béla Bartók and Zoltán Kodály began their pioneering work in ethnomusicology; they were only armed
    (E) Béla Bartók and Zoltán Kodály, in 1905 began their pioneering work in ethnomusicology, traveling the back roads of Hungary, arming themselves only

Choices A and B are wordy and imprecise: the phrasing suggests that Bartók and Kodály were already *traveling the back roads of Hungary* when they began their pioneering work, not that they traveled the back roads in order to conduct such work. Moreover, *and* suggests in both cases that they were armed with a phonograph *in addition* to being on the road, rather than *while* they were on the road, and *only* in B is misplaced before the verb *armed.* In choice D, *Having traveled . . .* suggests that the two had finished traveling before they began their work in ethnomusicology, and *only* is again misplaced. Choice E is wordy and awkwardly constructed. Choice C is best.

13. It is as difficult to prevent crimes against property as those that are against a person.

    (A) those that are against a
    (B) those against a
    (C) it is against a
    (D) preventing those against a
    (E) it is to prevent those against a

This sentence compares two actions, preventing *crimes against property* and preventing *crimes against a person,* in terms of difficulty. These actions should be described in grammatically parallel structures. Consequently, choices A, B, and D are faulty because they fail to parallel the first clause, which has *it* as a subject and *is* as a verb. Choice C contains *it is* but lacks *to prevent those,* words needed to complete the required clause and identify the other action in the comparison. Choice E is best: all of the elements necessary to describe the second action are presented in a form that is both idiomatic and grammatically parallel to the description of the first action.

14. Unlike the acid smoke of cigarettes, pipe tobacco, cured by age-old methods, yields an alkaline smoke too irritating to be drawn into the lungs.

   (A) Unlike the acid smoke of cigarettes, pipe tobacco, cured by age-old methods, yields an alkaline smoke
   (B) Unlike the acid smoke of cigarettes, pipe tobacco is cured by age-old methods, yielding an alkaline smoke
   (C) Unlike cigarette tobacco, which yields an acid smoke, pipe tobacco, cured by age-old methods, yields an alkaline smoke
   (D) Differing from cigarettes' acid smoke, pipe tobacco's alkaline smoke, cured by age-old methods, is
   (E) The alkaline smoke of pipe tobacco differs from cigarettes' acid smoke in that it is cured by age-old methods and is

Choices A and B illogically compare *the acid smoke of cigarettes* with *pipe tobacco,* not with the *smoke* from pipe tobacco. B is also faulty for making the curing methods rather than the nature of the smoke the basis of comparison. Choice C is best, for it compares cigarette tobacco with pipe tobacco in terms of the type of smoke each produces. Choices D and E garble the intended meaning by saying that the *smoke* of pipe tobacco is *cured by age-old methods.* Moreover, the phrasing is less compact and idiomatic than *Unlike* is for expressing a contrast.

15. Joplin's faith in his opera "Tremonisha" was unshakeable; in 1911 he published the score at his own expense and decided on staging it himself.

   (A) on staging it himself
   (B) that he himself would do the staging
   (C) to do the staging of the work by himself
   (D) that he himself would stage it
   (E) to stage the work himself

Choice A is poorly worded: *it* refers to *the score,* not to the opera itself, and *decided on staging it* is unidiomatic. Choice B does not specify what it was that Joplin decided to stage. Choice C is unidiomatic and needlessly wordy. Because the pronoun reference of *it* is faulty, choice D, like choice A, confuses staging the score with staging the work. Choice E is best.

16. Los Angeles has a higher number of family dwellings per capita than any large city.

   (A) a higher number of family dwellings per capita than any large city
   (B) higher numbers of family dwellings per capita than any other large city
   (C) a higher number of family dwellings per capita than does any other large city
   (D) higher numbers of family dwellings per capita than do other large cities
   (E) a high per capita number of family dwellings, more than does any other large city

Choice A is illogical because it implies that Los Angeles is not a large city. Choice B emends this problem by specifying *any other large city,* but the plural *numbers* is incorrect in that there is only a single number of such dwellings. Choice C is best. The plural *numbers* is again wrong in choice D, which in addition fails to establish that Los Angeles exceeds *all* other large cities in family dwellings per capita. Choice E is wordy and very awkward.

17. During the nineteenth century Emily Eden and Fanny Parks journeyed throughout India, sketching and keeping journals forming the basis of news reports about the princely states where they had visited.

   (A) forming the basis of news reports about the princely states where they had
   (B) that were forming the basis of news reports about the princely states
   (C) to form the basis of news reports about the princely states which they have
   (D) which had formed the basis of news reports about the princely states where they had
   (E) that formed the basis of news reports about the princely states they

In choice A it is not immediately clear whether *forming* modifies *journals* or parallels *sketching and keeping.* Also, *where they had visited* is wordy and inappropriate for a simple reference to past events. Choice B does not establish who visited the *princely states,* and *that were forming* should be *that formed.* Choice C is unclear because *to form* could be read as either *in order to form* or *so as to form,* and the present perfect *have visited* does not agree with the past tense *journeyed.* In choice D, as in choice A, *where they had* is faulty, and *had formed* suggests that the journals and news reports existed before the journey. E is best for this question.

18. School integration plans that involve busing between suburban and central-city areas have contributed, according to a recent study, to <u>significant increases in housing integration, which, in turn, reduces</u> any future need for busing.

    (A) significant increases in housing integration, which, in turn, reduces
    (B) significant integration increases in housing, which, in turn, reduces
    (C) increase housing integration significantly, which, in turn, reduces
    (D) increase housing integration significantly, in turn reducing
    (E) significantly increase housing integration, which, in turn, reduce

Choice A is best. In choice B, the phrase *integration increases in housing* is unidiomatic and imprecise: *integration* cannot modify *increases,* and the increases are not in *housing* but rather in *housing integration.* Choices C, D, and E entail the ungrammatical construction *have contributed. . .to increase.* Moreover, it is not clear whether *which* in C and *reducing* in D refer to *housing integration* or the *increase* in housing integration. In choice E, *which* clearly refers to *housing integration,* making the plural verb *reduce* incorrect.

19. The commission acknowledged that <u>no amount of money or staff members</u> can ensure the safety of people who live in the vicinity of a nuclear plant, but it approved the installation because it believed that all reasonable precautions had been taken.

    (A) no amount of money or staff members
    (B) neither vast amounts of money nor staff members
    (C) neither vast amounts of money nor numbers of staff members
    (D) neither vast amounts of money nor a large staff
    (E) no matter how large the staff or how vast the amount of money

In choice A, *amount of. . .staff members* is incorrect; *amount* properly refers to an undifferentiated mass, as in the case of *money.* Choice B does not make clear whether *vast amounts* is supposed to describe *money* only or *money* and *staff members,* and in choice C it is not certain whether *vast* modifies *amounts* only or *amounts* and *numbers.* Choice D is best. Choice E cannot fit grammatically into the original sentence because it supplies no noun that can function as a subject for the verb *can.*

20. Sartre believed <u>each individual is responsible to choose one course of action over another one,</u> that it is the choice that gives value to the act, and that nothing that is not acted upon has value.

    (A) each individual is responsible to choose one course of action over another one
    (B) that each individual is responsible for choosing one course of action over another
    (C) that each individual is responsible, choosing one course of action over another
    (D) that each individual is responsible to choose one course of action over the other
    (E) each individual is responsible for choosing one course of action over other ones

Choice A is faulty because *that* is needed after *believed* to make the clause parallel with the two *that. . .* clauses following it. Also, the idiomatic expression is *responsible for choosing* rather than *responsible to choose,* and *one* is superfluous. Choice B is best. Choice C distorts the intended meaning because it says, in effect, only that individuals are responsible and that they choose a course of action, not that they are *responsible for choosing* such a course. In choice D, *responsible to choose* is unidiomatic and *the other* wrongly suggests that there is some particular alternative under discussion. Choice E lacks the necessary *that,* and *other ones* is less precise than *another.*

21. <u>While the owner of a condominium apartment has free and clear title to the dwelling,</u> owners of cooperative apartments have shares in a corporation that owns a building and leases apartments to them.

    (A) While the owner of a condominium apartment has free and clear title to the dwelling,
    (B) The owner of a condominium apartment has free and clear title to the dwelling, but
    (C) Whereas owners of condominium apartments have free and clear title to their dwellings,
    (D) An owner of a condominium apartment has free and clear title to the dwelling, whereas
    (E) Condominium apartment owners have a title to their dwelling that is free and clear, while

Choices A, B, and D can be faulted for comparing a single *owner of a condominium* with *owners of cooperative apartments.* In choice C, the best answer, the nouns agree in number. Nouns also agree in choice E, but one cannot tell whether the *title* or the *dwelling* is said to be *free and clear.*

22. Although films about the American West depict coyotes as solitary animals howling mournfully on the tops of distant hills, in reality these gregarious creatures live in stable groups that occupy the same territory for long periods.

(A) films about the American West depict coyotes as solitary animals howling mournfully on the tops of distant hills

(B) in films about the American West coyotes are depicted to be solitary animals that howl mournfully on the tops of distant hills

(C) coyotes are depicted as solitary animals howling mournfully on the tops of distant hills in films about the American West

(D) films about the American West depict coyotes as if they were solitary, mournfully howling animals on the tops of distant hills

(E) films about the American West depict coyotes to be solitary and mournfully howling animals on the tops of distant hills

Choice A is best. In choice B, *depicted to be* is unidiomatic. The phrase *in films about the American West* is misplaced in choice C so that one cannot tell whether it indicates where the distant hills are, where the animals howl, or where coyotes are depicted as solitary creatures; the phrase should appear next to the word it is meant to modify. Choice D is wordy and awkward, and choice E contains the faulty *depict. . .to be*.

23. In 1980 the United States exported twice as much of its national output of goods as they had in 1970.

(A) twice as much of its national output of goods as they had

(B) double the amount of their national output of goods as they did

(C) twice as much of its national output of goods as it did

(D) double the amount of its national output of goods as it has

(E) twice as much of their national output of goods as they had

Choice A is incorrect because the plural pronoun *they* does not agree with its singular noun referent, *the United States,* and because *had* cannot substitute for *exported.* In choice B, *double the amount* is a less idiomatic form of comparison than *twice as much;* also, the plural pronouns *their* and *they* are incorrect. Choice C is best: the form of the comparison is idiomatic, the pronouns agree with the noun referent, and *did* — the simple past tense of *do* — can substitute for *exported.* Choice D contains *double the amount* as well as *has* for *exported,* and choice E is faulty because of *their* and *they had.*

24. Even though its per capita food supply hardly increased during two decades, stringent rationing and planned distribution have allowed the People's Republic of China to ensure nutritional levels of 2,000 calories per person per day for its population.

(A) Even though its per capita food supply hardly increased during

(B) Even though its per capita food supply has hardly increased in

(C) Despite its per capita food supply hardly increasing over

(D) Despite there being hardly any increase in its per capita food supply during

(E) Although there is hardly any increase in per capita food supply for

In choice A, the simple past tense *hardly increased* does not match the present perfect *have allowed;* consequently, it seems that two different time periods are being discussed. In B, the best choice, *has hardly increased* parallels *have allowed* to indicate that the events described took place at the same time. Also *in* is the best word here for making a comparison between the beginning and the end of the twenty-year period. Choices C and D are awkward and unidiomatic, and choice E fails to specify *where* there was no increase in per capita food supply.

25. Few people realize that the chance of accidental injury or death may be as great or greater in the "safety" of their own homes than in a plane or on the road.

(A) may be as great or greater in the "safety" of their own homes than

(B) is at least as great or greater in the "safety" of their own homes than

(C) might be so great or greater in the "safety" of their own home as

(D) may be at least as great in the "safety" of their own homes as

(E) can be at least so great in the "safety" of their own home as

In choices A and B, *as great or greater. . .than* is incorrect: *greater* takes *than,* but *as great* must be completed by *as.* The statement in B is also redundant in that the notion of *greater* is contained in *at least as great,* and *may be* would be better than *is* for expressing a distinct possibility. In choice C, *might* expresses too much doubt, *so* in place of *as* is unidiomatic, *home* should be *homes* to agree with *people,* and *greater. . .as* is erroneous. Choice D is best. In choice E, *so* and *home* are faulty.

SENTENCE CORRECTION SAMPLE TEST SECTION 2

30 Minutes
25 Questions

Directions: In each of the following sentences, some part of the sentence or the entire sentence is underlined. Beneath each sentence you will find five ways of phrasing the underlined part. The first of these repeats the original; the other four are different. If you think the original is better than any of the alternatives, choose answer A; otherwise choose one of the others. Select the best version and fill in the corresponding oval on your answer sheet.

This is a test of correctness and effectiveness of expression. In choosing answers, follow the requirements of standard written English; that is, pay attention to grammar, choice of words, and sentence construction. Choose the answer that expresses most effectively what is presented in the original sentence; this answer should be clear and exact, without awkwardness, ambiguity, or redundancy.

1. A fire in an enclosed space burns with the aid of reflected radiation that preheats the fuel, making ignition much easier and flames spreading more quickly.

   (A) flames spreading
   (B) flame spreads
   (C) flames are caused to spread
   (D) causing flames to spread
   (E) causing spreading of the flames

2. Roy Wilkins was among the last of a generation of civil rights activists who led the nation through decades of change so profound many young Americans are not able to imagine, even less to remember, what segregation was like.

   (A) so profound many young Americans are not able to imagine, even less to remember
   (B) so profound that many young Americans cannot imagine, much less remember
   (C) so profound many young Americans cannot imagine nor even less remember
   (D) of such profundity many young Americans cannot imagine, even less can they remember
   (E) of such profundity that many young Americans are not able to imagine, much less to remember

3. The residents' opposition to the spraying program has rekindled an old debate among those who oppose the use of pesticides and those who feel that the pesticides are necessary to save the trees.

   (A) among those who oppose the use of pesticides and
   (B) between those who oppose the use of pesticides and
   (C) among those opposing the use of pesticides with
   (D) between those who oppose the use of pesticides with
   (E) among those opposing the use of pesticides and

4. In cold-water habitats, certain invertebrates and fish convert starches into complex carbohydrates called glycerols, in effect manufacturing its own antifreeze.

   (A) in effect manufacturing its own antifreeze
   (B) effectively manufacturing antifreeze of its own
   (C) in effect manufacturing their own antifreeze
   (D) so that they manufacture their own antifreeze
   (E) thus the manufacture of its own antifreeze

5. Slips of the tongue do not necessarily reveal concealed beliefs or intentions but rather are the result from the competition between various processing mechanisms in the brain.

   (A) but rather are the result from
   (B) and instead are the result from
   (C) being rather the result of
   (D) and rather result from
   (E) but rather result from

6. The new contract forbids a strike by the transportation union.

   (A) forbids a strike by the transportation union
   (B) forbids the transportation union from striking
   (C) forbids that there be a strike by the transportation union
   (D) will forbid the transportation union from striking
   (E) will forbid that the transportation union strikes

GO ON TO THE NEXT PAGE.

7. Monitoring heart patients' exercise, as well as athletes exercising, is now done by small transmitters broadcasting physiological measurements to nearby recording machines.

   (A) Monitoring heart patients' exercise, as well as athletes exercising, is now done by small transmitters broadcasting physiological measurements to nearby recording machines.
   (B) Monitoring the exercise of heart patients, as well as athletes exercising, is now done by small transmitters broadcasting physiological measurements to nearby recording machines.
   (C) Small transmitters broadcasting physiological measurements to nearby recording machines are now used to monitor the exercise of both heart patients and athletes.
   (D) Broadcasting physiological measurements to nearby recording machines, small transmitters are now used to monitor heart patients' exercise, as well as athletes exercising.
   (E) Both athletes exercising and heart patients' exercise are now monitored by small transmitters broadcasting physiological measurements to nearby recording machines.

8. The commission has directed advertisers to restrict the use of the word "natural" to foods that do not contain color or flavor additives, chemical preservatives, or nothing that has been synthesized.

   (A) or nothing that has been
   (B) nor anything that was
   (C) and nothing that is
   (D) or anything that has been
   (E) and anything

9. Bringing the Ford Motor Company back from the verge of bankruptcy shortly after the Second World War was a special governmentally sanctioned price increase during a period of wage and price controls.

   (A) Bringing the Ford Motor Company back from the verge of bankruptcy shortly after the Second World War was a special governmentally sanctioned price increase during a period of wage and price controls.
   (B) What brought the Ford Motor Company back from the verge of bankruptcy shortly after the Second World War was a special price increase that the government sanctioned during a period of wage and price controls.
   (C) That which brought the Ford Motor Company back from the verge of bankruptcy shortly after the Second World War was a special governmentally sanctioned price increase during a period of wage and price controls.
   (D) What has brought the Ford Motor Company back from the verge of bankruptcy shortly after the Second World War was a special price increase that the government sanctioned during a period of wages and price controls.
   (E) To bring the Ford Motor Company back from the verge of bankruptcy shortly after the Second World War, there was a special price increase during a period of wages and price controls that government sanctioned.

10. Like Haydn, Schubert wrote a great deal for the stage, but he is remembered principally for his chamber and concert-hall music.

    (A) Like Haydn, Schubert
    (B) Like Haydn, Schubert also
    (C) As has Haydn, Schubert
    (D) As did Haydn, Schubert also
    (E) As Haydn did, Schubert also

GO ON TO THE NEXT PAGE.

11. Charlotte Perkins Gilman, a late nineteenth-century feminist, called for urban apartment houses <u>including child-care facilities and clustered suburban houses including communal eating and social facilities</u>.

(A) including child-care facilities and clustered suburban houses including communal eating and social facilities
(B) that included child-care facilities, and for clustered suburban houses to include communal eating and social facilities
(C) with child-care facilities included and for clustered suburban houses to include communal eating and social facilities
(D) that included child-care facilities and for clustered suburban houses with communal eating and social facilities
(E) to include child-care facilities and for clustered suburban houses with communal eating and social facilities included

12. The odds are about 4 to 1 against surviving a takeover offer, and many business consultants therefore advise <u>that a company's first line of defense in eluding offers like these be to even refuse</u> to take calls from likely corporate raiders.

(A) that a company's first line of defense in eluding offers like these be to even refuse
(B) that a company's first line of defense in eluding such offers be to refuse even
(C) a company defending itself against offers of this kind that, as a first line of defense, they should even refuse
(D) companies which are defending themselves against such an offer that, as a first line of defense, they should even refuse
(E) that the first line of defense for a company who is eluding offers like these is the refusal even

13. <u>Japan received huge sums of capital from the United States after the Second World War, using it to help build</u> a modern industrial system.

(A) Japan received huge sums of capital from the United States after the Second World War, using it to help build
(B) Japan received huge sums of capital from the United States after the Second World War and used it to help in building
(C) Japan used the huge sums of capital it received from the United States after the Second World War to help build
(D) Japan's huge sums of capital received from the United States after the Second World War were used to help it in building
(E) Receiving huge sums of capital from the United States after the Second World War, Japan used it to help build

14. Although one link in the chain was <u>demonstrated to be weak, but not sufficiently so to require</u> the recall of the automobile.

(A) demonstrated to be weak, but not sufficiently so to require
(B) demonstrated as weak, but it was not sufficiently so that it required
(C) demonstrably weak, but not sufficiently so to require
(D) demonstrably weak, it was not so weak as to require
(E) demonstrably weak, it was not weak enough that it required

15. Although the Supreme Court ruled as long ago as 1880 that Blacks could not be excluded outright from jury service, nearly a century of case-by-case adjudication <u>has been necessary to develop and enforce the principle that all juries must be</u> drawn from "a fair cross section of the community."

(A) has been necessary to develop and enforce the principle that all juries must be
(B) was necessary for developing and enforcing the principle of all juries being
(C) was to be necessary in developing and enforcing the principle of all juries to be
(D) is necessary to develop and enforce the principle that all juries must be
(E) will be necessary for developing and enforcing the principle of all juries being

16. <u>The modernization program for the steel mill will cost approximately 51 million dollars, which it is hoped can be completed in the late 1980's.</u>

(A) The modernization program for the steel mill will cost approximately 51 million dollars, which it is hoped can be completed in the late 1980's.
(B) The modernization program for the steel mill, hopefully completed in the late 1980's, will cost approximately 51 million dollars.
(C) Modernizing the steel mill, hopefully to be completed in the late 1980's, will cost approximately 51 million dollars.
(D) The program for modernizing the steel mill, which can, it is hoped, be completed in the late 1980's and cost approximately 51 million dollars.
(E) Modernizing the steel mill, a program that can, it is hoped, be completed in the late 1980's, will cost approximately 51 million dollars.

GO ON TO THE NEXT PAGE.

17. Camus broke with Sartre in a bitter dispute over the nature of Stalinism.

    (A) in a bitter dispute over
    (B) over bitterly disputing
    (C) after there was a bitter dispute over
    (D) after having bitterly disputed about
    (E) over a bitter dispute about

18. Nowhere in Prakta is the influence of modern European architecture more apparent than their government buildings.

    (A) more apparent than their
    (B) so apparent as their
    (C) more apparent than in its
    (D) so apparent than in their
    (E) as apparent as it is in its

19. Federal legislation establishing a fund for the cleanup of sites damaged by toxic chemicals permits compensating state governments for damage to their natural resources but does not allow claims for injury to people.

    (A) compensating state governments for damage to
    (B) compensating state governments for the damaging of
    (C) giving state governments compensation for damaging
    (D) giving compensation to state governments for the damage of
    (E) the giving of compensation to state governments for damaging

20. The lawyer for the defense charged that she suspected the police of having illegally taped her confidential conversations with her client and then used the information obtained to find evidence supporting their murder charges.

    (A) used the information obtained to find evidence supporting
    (B) used such information as they obtained to find evidence supporting
    (C) used the information they had obtained to find evidence that would support
    (D) of using the information they had obtained to find evidence that would support
    (E) of using such information as they obtained to find evidence that would be supportive of

21. According to surveys by the National Institute on Drug Abuse, about 20 percent of young adults used cocaine in 1979, doubling those reported in the 1977 survey.

    (A) doubling those reported in the 1977 survey
    (B) to double the number the 1977 survey reported
    (C) twice those the 1977 survey reported
    (D) twice as much as those reported in the 1977 survey
    (E) twice the number reported in the 1977 survey

GO ON TO THE NEXT PAGE

22. Inflation has made many Americans reevaluate their assumptions about the future; they still expect to live better than their parents have, but not so well as they once thought they could.

(A) they still expect to live better than their parents have
(B) they still expect to live better than their parents did
(C) they still expect to live better than their parents had
(D) still expecting to live better than their parents had
(E) still expecting to live better than did their parents

23. Europeans have long known that eating quail sometimes makes the eater ill, but only recently has it been established that the illness is caused by a toxin present in the quail's body only under certain conditions.

(A) Europeans have long known that eating quail sometimes makes
(B) Europeans have long known quail eating is sometimes able to make
(C) Eating quail has long been known to Europeans to sometimes make
(D) It has long been known to Europeans that quail eating will sometimes make
(E) It has long been known to Europeans that quail, when it is eaten, has sometimes made

24. The caterpillar of the geometrid moth strikes when special tactile hairs on its body are disturbed, after capturing its prey, holds the victim so that it cannot escape.

(A) strikes when special tactile hairs on its body are disturbed,
(B) striking when special tactile hairs on its body are disturbed, but
(C) which strikes when special tactile hairs on its body are disturbed,
(D) which, striking when special tactile hairs on its body are disturbed,
(E) strikes when special tactile hairs on its body are disturbed and,

25. In assessing the problems faced by rural migrant workers, the question of whether they are better off materially than the urban working poor is irrelevant.

(A) In assessing the problems faced by rural migrant workers, the question of whether they are better off materially than the urban working poor is irrelevant.
(B) The question of whether the rural migrant worker is better off materially than the urban working poor is irrelevant in assessing the problems that they face.
(C) A question that is irrelevant in assessing the problems that rural migrant workers face is whether they are better off materially than the urban working poor.
(D) In an assessment of the problems faced by rural migrant workers, the question of whether they are better off materially than the urban working poor is irrelevant.
(E) The question of whether the rural migrant worker is better off materially than the urban working poor is irrelevant in an assessment of the problems that they face.

S T O P

IF YOU FINISH BEFORE TIME IS CALLED, YOU MAY CHECK YOUR WORK ON THIS SECTION ONLY.
DO NOT TURN TO ANY OTHER SECTION IN THE TEST.

Answer Key for Sample Test Section 2

SENTENCE CORRECTION

1. D	14. D
2. B	15. A
3. B	16. E
4. C	17. A
5. E	18. C
6. A	19. A
7. C	20. D
8. D	21. E
9. B	22. B
10. A	23. A
11. D	24. E
12. B	25. D
13. C	

Explanatory Material: Sentence Correction Sample Test Section 2

1. A fire in an enclosed space burns with the aid of re-flected radiation that preheats the fuel, making igni-tion much easier and <u>flames spreading</u> more quickly.

   (A) flames spreading
   (B) flame spreads
   (C) flames caused to spread
   (D) causing flames to spread
   (E) causing spreading of the flames

Choices A, B, and C are incorrect because a present particip-ial (or "—ing") verb must precede *flames* to form a structure parallel to the phrase *making ignition much easier.* . . .
Choice D is best. Choice E is wordy, unidiomatic, and also awkward in that *spreading,* although used here as a noun, appears at first to be another present participle that could be modified by *more quickly.*

2. Roy Wilkins was among the last of a generation of civil rights activists who led the nation through dec-ades of change <u>so profound many young Americans are not able to imagine, even less to remember,</u> what segregation was like.

   (A) so profound many young Americans are not able to imagine, even less to remember
   (B) so profound that many young Americans cannot imagine, much less remember
   (C) so profound many young Americans cannot imagine nor even less remember
   (D) of such profundity many young Americans can-not imagine, even less can they remember
   (E) of such profundity that many young Americans are not able to imagine, much less to remember

Choice A can be faulted for omitting *that* after *profound;* the idiomatic form of the expression is "*so X that Y.*" Also, *much less remember* is more idiomatic than *even less to re-member,* and *cannot imagine* is more concise than *are not able to imagine.* Choice B is best. Choice C lacks *that* after *profound,* and *nor* is incorrectly used to join verbs modified by *cannot.* In choice D, *of such profundity* is wordy, *that* is missing, and *even less can they remember* is not an idiomatic way to complete *cannot imagine.* In choice E, *of such profun-dity* and *are not able to imagine* are wordy, and the *to* in *to remember* is unnecessary.

3. The residents' opposition to the spraying program has rekindled an old debate <u>among those who oppose the use of pesticides and</u> those who feel that the pesticides are necessary to save the trees.

   (A) among those who oppose the use of pesticides and
   (B) between those who oppose the use of pesticides and
   (C) among those opposing the use of pesticides with
   (D) between those who oppose the use of pesticides with
   (E) among those opposing the use of pesticides and

Choices A, C, and E can be faulted for using *among* in place of *between* to refer to two factions. Choices C and D incor-rectly use *with* in place of *and.* Also, *those opposing* in choices C and E is not parallel with *those who feel.* Choice B is best.

4. In cold-water habitats, certain invertebrates and fish convert starches into complex carbohydrates called glycerols, <u>in effect manufacturing its own antifreeze.</u>

   (A) in effect manufacturing its own antifreeze
   (B) effectively manufacturing antifreeze of its own
   (C) in effect manufacturing their own antifreeze
   (D) so that they manufacture their own antifreeze
   (E) thus the manufacture of its own antifreeze

Choices A and B are incorrect because the pronoun *its* does not agree in number with *invertebrates and fish,* the noun referents. B also distorts the intended meaning of the sen-tence by making a statement about how effectively the inver-tebrates and fish manufacture their own antifreeze. Choice C is best. In D and E, *so that they manufacture* and *thus the manufacture* do not form logical connections with the rest of the sentence, and *its* in E is incorrect.

5. Slips of the tongue do not necessarily reveal concealed beliefs or intentions <u>but rather are the result from</u> the competition between various processing mechanisms in the brain.

   (A) but rather are the result from
   (B) and instead are the result from
   (C) being rather the result of
   (D) and rather result from
   (E) but rather result from

Choices A and B are incorrect because *are the result from* is unidiomatic; *result from* or *are the result of* are the idiomatic forms. Choices B, C, and D are faulty because *but* is needed to complete the construction *do not reveal but (verb)*. E is the best answer.

6. The new contract <u>forbids a strike by the transportation union</u>.

(A) forbids a strike by the transportation union
(B) forbids the transportation union from striking
(C) forbids that there be a strike by the transportation union
(D) will forbid the transportation union from striking
(E) will forbid that the transportation union strikes

Choice A is best. B, C, D, and E are unidiomatic: a form of the verb *forbid* may be completed by a noun, as in *forbids a strike,* or by a noun and an infinitive, as in *forbids the union to strike.*

7. <u>Monitoring heart patients' exercise, as well as athletes exercising, is now done by small transmitters broadcasting physiological measurements to nearby recording machines</u>.

(A) Monitoring heart patients' exercise, as well as athletes exercising, is now done by small transmitters broadcasting physiological measurements to nearby recording machines.
(B) Monitoring the exercise of heart patients, as well as athletes exercising, is now done by small transmitters broadcasting physiological measurements to nearby recording machines.
(C) Small transmitters broadcasting physiological measurements to nearby recording machines are now used to monitor the exercise of both heart patients and athletes.
(D) Broadcasting physiological measurements to nearby recording machines, small transmitters are now used to monitor heart patients' exercise, as well as athletes exercising.
(E) Both athletes exercising and heart patients' exercise are now monitored by small transmitters broadcasting physiological measurements to nearby recording machines.

Choices A, B, D, and E incorrectly compare *heart patients' exercise* and *athletes* who are *exercising,* not *patients' exercise* and *athletes' exercise,* a more logical pairing. Choice C, which clarifies the comparison, is best.

8. The commission has directed advertisers to restrict the use of the word "natural" to foods that do not contain color or flavor additives, chemical preservatives, <u>or nothing that has been</u> synthesized.

(A) or nothing that has been
(B) nor anything that was
(C) and nothing that is
(D) or anything that has been
(E) and anything

Choices A, B, and C are faulty because the *not* in *do not contain* makes the negatives *nothing* and *nor* unidiomatic. Choice D is best. In E, *and* fails to indicate that *anything. . .* is an all-inclusive term, not another separate item in the list *additives, . . . preservatives. . . .*

9. <u>Bringing the Ford Motor Company back from the verge of bankruptcy shortly after the Second World War was a special governmentally sanctioned price increase during a period of wage and price controls</u>.

(A) Bringing the Ford Motor Company back from the verge of bankruptcy shortly after the Second World War was a special governmentally sanctioned price increase during a period of wage and price controls.
(B) What brought the Ford Motor Company back from the verge of bankruptcy shortly after the Second World War was a special price increase that the government sanctioned during a period of wage and price controls.
(C) That which brought the Ford Motor Company back from the verge of bankruptcy shortly after the Second World War was a special governmentally sanctioned price increase during a period of wage and price controls.
(D) What has brought the Ford Motor Company back from the verge of bankruptcy shortly after the Second World War was a special price increase that the government sanctioned during a period of wages and price controls.
(E) To bring the Ford Motor Company back from the verge of bankruptcy shortly after the Second World War, there was a special price increase during a period of wages and price controls that government sanctioned.

Choice A, awkward and imprecise, leaves one confused about what it was that happened *during a period of wage and price controls*—the revitalization of the Ford Motor Company or the sanctioning of a price increase. B, the best answer, clarifies the matter by making *during. . .* modify *the government sanctioned.* Choice C, wordy and awkward, suffers from the same imprecision as choice A. The present perfect *has brought* in D is inappropriate for action completed well in the past, and *wages,* which should modify *control,* is not idiomatic. In choice E, *wages* is again wrong, and E, contrary to intent, suggests that the government sanctioned a *period of . . . controls* rather than *a special price increase.*

10. Like Haydn, Schubert wrote a great deal for the stage, but he is remembered principally for his chamber and concert-hall music.

    (A) Like Haydn, Schubert
    (B) Like Haydn, Schubert also
    (C) As has Haydn, Schubert
    (D) As did Haydn, Schubert also
    (E) As Haydn did, Schubert also

Choice A is best. In B, *also* is redundant after *Like,* which establishes the similarity between Haydn and Schubert. *As* in choices C, D, and E is not idiomatic in a comparison of persons; *has* in C wrongly suggests that the action was recently completed; and *also* in D and E is superfluous.

11. Charlotte Perkins Gilman, a late nineteenth-century feminist, called for urban apartment houses including child-care facilities and clustered suburban houses including communal eating and social facilities.

    (A) including child-care facilities and clustered suburban houses including communal eating and social facilities
    (B) that included child-care facilities, and for clustered suburban houses to include communal eating and social facilities
    (C) with child-care facilities included and for clustered suburban houses to include communal eating and social facilities
    (D) that included child-care facilities and for clustered suburban houses with communal eating and social facilities
    (E) to include child-care facilities and for clustered suburban houses with communal eating and social facilities included

The function and meaning of the *including* . . . phrases are unclear in choice A: for example, it is hard to tell whether Gilman called for urban apartment houses that included child-care facilities or whether such facilities represent one variety of the urban apartment houses she wanted built. Choice B resolves the ambiguity concerning *child-care facilities,* but *called for . . . houses to include . . . facilities* is unidiomatic in B and C. Choice D is best. In E, *to include* is again faulty.

12. The odds are about 4 to 1 against surviving a take-over offer, and many business consultants therefore advise that a company's first line of defense in eluding offers like these be to even refuse to take calls from likely corporate raiders.

    (A) that a company's first line of defense in eluding offers like these be to even refuse
    (B) that a company's first line of defense in eluding such offers be to refuse even
    (C) a company defending itself against offers of this kind that, as a first line of defense, they should even refuse
    (D) companies which are defending themselves against such an offer that, as a first line of defense, they should even refuse
    (E) that the first line of defense for a company who is eluding offers like these is the refusal even

Choice A is awkward and poorly phrased: *these* has no plural noun to which it can refer, and *even* should be placed immediately before *to take calls,* the phrase it modifies. Choice B is best. In C, the plural *they* does not agree with the singular *company, even* is misplaced, and *advise . . . that . . . they should* is unidiomatic. D has the plural *companies* but retains the other flaws of C. In E, *who* in place of *that* is an inappropriate pronoun for *company, these* does not agree with the singular *offer,* and *is the refusal* should be *be to refuse.*

13. Japan received huge sums of capital from the United States after the Second World War, using it to help build a modern industrial system.

    (A) Japan received huge sums of capital from the United States after the Second World War, using it to help build
    (B) Japan received huge sums of capital from the United States after the Second World War and used it to help in building
    (C) Japan used the huge sums of capital it received from the United States after the Second World War to help build
    (D) Japan's huge sums of capital received from the United States after the Second World War were used to help it in building
    (E) Receiving huge sums of capital from the United States after the Second World War, Japan used it to help build

Choice A can be faulted because *it*, a singular pronoun, does not agree with *sums of capital*; also, *using* does not establish a logical time sequence in which Japan first received and then used the capital from the United States. In B, *it* is again wrong, and *to help in building* is less compact and idiomatic than *to help build*. Choice C is best. In D, *to help it in building* is flawed, and *it* has no free noun as its referent since *Japan's* is a possessive modifier of *sums*. In E, *it* is again without a singular noun referent, and *Receiving huge sums . . ., Japan used . . .* does not make clear the sequence of events.

14. Although one link in the chain was <u>demonstrated to be weak, but not sufficiently so to require</u> the recall of the automobile.

   (A) demonstrated to be weak, but not sufficiently so to require
   (B) demonstrated as weak, but it was not sufficiently so that it required
   (C) demonstrably weak, but not sufficiently so to require
   (D) demonstrably weak, it was not so weak as to require
   (E) demonstrably weak, it was not weak enough that it required

Choices A and C entail ungrammatical constructions because they do not produce a sentence that has a main clause with a subject and a verb. In choice B, *demonstrated as weak* is un-idiomatic; also in choices B and C *Although* and *but* should not be used together because only one is needed to express the relationship between the ideas. Choice D is best. Choice E is less concise and idiomatic than D; moreover, it is impre-cise to say that *one link in the chain* (the referent of *it*) actu-ally *required the recall.*

15. Although the Supreme Court ruled as long ago as 1880 that Blacks could not be excluded outright from jury service, nearly a century of case-by-case adjudi-cation <u>has been necessary to develop and enforce the principle that all juries must be</u> drawn from "a fair cross section of the community."

   (A) has been necessary to develop and enforce the principle that all juries must be
   (B) was necessary for developing and enforcing the principle of all juries being
   (C) was to be necessary in developing and enforcing the principle of all juries to be
   (D) is necessary to develop and enforce the principle that juries must be
   (E) will be necessary for developing and enforcing the principle of all juries being

Choice A is best: *has been* appropriately refers to recently completed action. In B, *was* does not indicate that the action is recent. Also, *necessary for developing . . .* is less idiom-atic than *necessary to develop . . .*, and *principle of all juries being* is less direct than *principle that all juries must be*. The *to be* infinitives make choice C incorrect. The present tense *is* in D and the future tense *will be* in E make these choices faulty.

16. <u>The modernization program for the steel mill will cost approximately 51 million dollars, which it is hoped can be completed in the late 1980's.</u>

   (A) The modernization program for the steel mill will cost approximately 51 million dollars, which it is hoped can be completed in the late 1980's.
   (B) The modernization program for the steel mill, hopefully completed in the late 1980's will cost approximately 51 million dollars.
   (C) Modernizing the steel mill, hopefully to be com-pleted in the late 1980's will cost approximately 51 million dollars.
   (D) The program for modernizing the steel mill, which can, it is hoped, be completed in the late 1980's and cost approximately 51 million dollars.
   (E) Modernizing the steel mill, a program that can, it is hoped, be completed in the late 1980's, will cost approximately 51 million dollars.

Choice A can be faulted because *which* grammatically refers to *51 million dollars,* the nearest noun phrase. At any rate, it is not clear in choices A, B, C, or D whether the moderniza-tion program or the steel mill is supposed to be completed in the late 1980's. In B and C, the use of *hopefully* for *it is hoped* still meets with strong and widespread objection from many editors, lexicographers, and authors of usage hand-books. Aside from having an ambiguous *which*, D contains no independent clause and so cannot stand as a sentence. Choice E is the best answer.

17. Camus broke with Sartre <u>in a bitter dispute over</u> the nature of Stalinism.

   (A) in a bitter dispute over
   (B) over bitterly disputing
   (C) after there was a bitter dispute over
   (D) after having bitterly disputed about
   (E) over a bitter dispute about

Choice A is best. In B, *over* is misused: it should appear immediately before the issue in dispute (i.e., *the nature of Stalinism*). Choice C, wordy and imprecise, does not specify who was involved in the dispute. In D and E, *dispute(d) about* is less direct and idiomatic than *dispute(d) over*. Also, D is needlessly wordy and *over* is misused in E.

18. Nowhere in Prakta is the influence of modern European architecture <u>more apparent than their</u> government buildings.

   (A) more apparent than their
   (B) so apparent as their
   (C) more apparent than in its
   (D) so apparent than in their
   (E) as apparent as it is in its

Choice A is incorrect because *in* must appear after *than* and because the plural pronoun *their* does not agree in number with the singular noun *Prakta*. B also lacks *in* and misuses *their*. Choice C is best. In D, *so...than* in place of *more... than* is unidiomatic, and *their* is again wrong. Choice E is confusing because *it* refers to *architecture* whereas *its* refers to *Prakta*.

19. Federal legislation establishing a fund for the cleanup of sites damaged by toxic chemicals permits <u>compensating state governments for damage to</u> their natural resources but does not allow claims for injury to people.

   (A) compensating state governments for damage to
   (B) compensating state governments for the damaging of
   (C) giving state governments compensation for damaging
   (D) giving compensation to state governments for the damage of
   (E) the giving of compensation to state governments for damaging

Choice A is best. Choices B, C, and E could be read as saying that state governments can be compensated for damaging their own natural resources. The phrasing in C, D, and E is needlessly wordy, and *for the damage of* in D is unidiomatic.

20. The lawyer for the defense charged that she suspected the police of having illegally taped her confidential conversations with her client and then <u>used the information obtained to find evidence supporting</u> their murder charges.

   (A) used the information obtained to find evidence supporting
   (B) used such information as they obtained to find evidence supporting
   (C) used the information they had obtained to find evidence that would support
   (D) of using the information they had obtained to find evidence that would support
   (E) of using such information as they obtained to find evidence that would be supportive of

Choices A, B, and C are incorrect because *then* must be followed by a construction that parallels *of having* in line 2 — that is, by *of* and a present participial, or "-ing," verb form. Choice D is best. Choice E is very wordy, awkward, and indirect.

21. According to surveys by the National Institute on Drug Abuse, about 20 percent of young adults used cocaine in 1979, <u>doubling those reported in the 1977 survey</u>.

   (A) doubling those reported in the 1977 survey
   (B) to double the number the 1977 survey reported
   (C) twice those the 1977 survey reported
   (D) twice as much as those reported in the 1977 survey
   (E) twice the number reported in the 1977 survey

Choice A is phrased illogically in that it says the young adults in the 1979 survey somehow doubled the people in the 1977 survey, not that the *number* of young adults using cocaine doubled. The infinitive *to double*, used unidiomatically in B, carries the sense of *in order to double*. Again in choice C, *twice the number* would be preferable to *twice those (people)*. It is not clear in choice D whether *twice as much* . . . refers to the number of young adults using cocaine in 1979 or the amount of cocaine they used. Choice E is best.

22. Inflation has made many Americans reevaluate their assumptions about the future; <u>they still expect to live better than their parents have</u>, but not so well as they once thought they could.

   (A) they still expect to live better than their parents have
   (B) they still expect to live better than their parents did
   (C) they still expect to live better than their parents had
   (D) still expecting to live better than their parents had
   (E) still expecting to live better than did their parents

Choice A is incorrect because *have* cannot function as the auxiliary of *live*; i.e., *have live* is ungrammatical. Choice B, which substitutes *did* for *have*, is correct and logically places the parents' action in the past. In C and D, *had* places the parents' action in the past but is wrong as an auxiliary, just as *have* is in A. Choices D and E are faulty because neither is the independent clause that is needed to complete a grammatical sentence.

23. Europeans have long known that eating quail sometimes makes the eater ill, but only recently has it been
established that the illness is caused by a toxin present
in the quail's body only under certain conditions.

(A) Europeans have long known that eating quail
sometimes makes

(B) Europeans have long known quail eating is sometimes able to make

(C) Eating quail has long been known to Europeans
to sometimes make

(D) It has long been known to Europeans that quail
eating will sometimes make

(E) It has long been known to Europeans that quail,
when it is eaten, has sometimes made

Choice A is best. Choice B is awkward: *that* is preferable
after *known* to introduce the clause describing what
Europeans have long known, and *quail eating is . . . able* is
unidiomatic. Choices C, D, and E are also awkward; moreover, *will. . .make* in D and *has. . .made* in E are inappropriate to describe a condition that holds true in the present as
well as in the future or the past.

24. The caterpillar of the geometrid moth strikes when
special tactile hairs on its body are disturbed, after
capturing its prey, holds the victim so that it cannot
escape.

(A) strikes when special tactile hairs on its body are
disturbed,

(B) striking when special tactile hairs on its body are
disturbed, but

(C) which strikes when special tactile hairs on its
body are disturbed,

(D) which, striking when special tactile hairs on its
body are disturbed,

(E) strikes when special tactile hairs on its body are
disturbed and,

Choice A is incorrect because it provides no word or construction that can form a grammatical link with the remainder
of the sentence. By substituting *striking* for *strikes,* choice B
improperly removes the verb form that is needed with *caterpillar*, the grammatical subject, to make a complete sentence.
C is awkward and also ambiguous because it is not immediately clear whether *which* is meant to refer to *caterpillar* or
moth. In D, *which* is again ambiguous, and with *striking* in
place of *strikes*, *which* takes *holds* as its verb, leaving no verb
for the subject of the sentence. Choice E is best: *and* links the
verbs *strikes* and *holds* to form a compound verb for the subject, *caterpillar*.

25. In assessing the problems faced by rural migrant
workers, the question of whether they are better off
materially than the urban working poor is irrelevant.

(A) In assessing the problems faced by rural migrant
workers, the question of whether they are better
off materially than the urban working poor is
irrelevant.

(B) The question of whether the rural migrant
worker is better off materially than the urban
working poor is irrelevant in assessing the problems that they face.

(C) A question that is irrelevant in assessing the
problems that rural migrant workers face is
whether they are better off materially than the
urban working poor.

(D) In an assessment of the problems faced by rural
migrant workers, the question of whether they
are better off materially than the urban working
poor is irrelevant.

(E) The question of whether the rural migrant
worker is better off materially than the urban
working poor is irrelevant in an assessment of the
problems that they face.

Choice A presents a dangling modifier because nothing mentioned in the sentence can perform the action of *assessing the
problems faced by rural migrant workers*. Choice A states
illogically that *the question* is assessing these problems. In B,
the plural pronoun *they* cannot refer as intended to the singular *rural migrant worker*. C is awkward and ambiguous:
again, the *question* is not *assessing the problems*, and *irrelevant in assessing* could be taken to mean either that the act
of assessing the problems is irrelevant or that the question
described is irrelevant in an assessment of the problems.
Choice D is best. Lack of agreement between *worker* and
they makes E wrong.

SENTENCE CORRECTION SAMPLE TEST SECTION 3

30 Minutes
25 Questions

<u>Directions:</u> In each of the following sentences, some part of the sentence or the entire sentence is underlined. Beneath each sentence you will find five ways of phrasing the underlined part. The first of these repeats the original; the other four are different. If you think the original is better than any of the alternatives, choose answer A; otherwise choose one of the others. Select the best version and fill in the corresponding oval on your answer sheet.

This is a test of correctness and effectiveness of expression. In choosing answers, follow the requirements of standard written English; that is, pay attention to grammar, choice of words, and sentence construction. Choose the answer that expresses most effectively what is presented in the original sentence; this answer should be clear and exact, without awkwardness, ambiguity, or redundancy.

1. The sale of government surplus machinery <u>will begin at 9 a.m. and continue until the supply lasts.</u>

   (A) will begin at 9 a.m. and continue until the supply lasts
   (B) begins at 9 a.m., continuing until the supply lasts
   (C) will begin at 9 a.m. and, until the supply lasts, will continue
   (D) begins at 9 a.m. and, as long as the supply may last, it continues
   (E) will begin at 9 a.m. and continue as long as the supply lasts

2. In England the well-dressed <u>gentleman of the eighteenth century protected their clothing while having their wig powdered by poking their head</u> through a device that resembled the stocks.

   (A) gentleman of the eighteenth century protected their clothing while having their wig powdered by poking their head
   (B) gentleman of the eighteenth century protected his clothing while having his wig powdered by poking his head
   (C) gentleman of the eighteenth century protected their clothing while having their wigs powdered by poking their heads
   (D) gentlemen of the eighteenth century protected his clothing while having his wig powdered by poking his head
   (E) gentlemen of the eighteenth century protected their clothing while having his wig powdered by poking his head

3. <u>Reared apart from each other, a recent United States study showed striking similarities in identical twins, including many idiosyncrasies of behavior.</u>

   (A) Reared apart from each other, a recent United States study showed striking similarities in identical twins, including many idiosyncrasies of behavior.
   (B) Reared apart from each other, striking similarities between identical twins that include many idiosyncrasies of behavior were shown in a recent United States study.
   (C) A recent United States study showed striking similarities in identical twins reared apart from each other that include many idiosyncrasies of behavior.
   (D) According to a recent United States study, identical twins reared apart from each other showed striking similarities, including many idiosyncrasies of behavior.
   (E) According to a recent United States study, identical twins showed striking similarities reared apart from each other, including many idiosyncrasies of behavior.

GO ON TO THE NEXT PAGE.

4. Developing nations in various parts of the world have amassed $700 billion in debts; at stake, should a significant number of these debts be repudiated, is the solvency of some of the world's largest multinational banks.

    (A) should a significant number of these debts be repudiated, is
    (B) should a significant number of these debts be repudiated, are
    (C) should they repudiate a significant number of these debts, are
    (D) if there is a repudiation of a significant number of these debts, would be
    (E) if a significant number of these debts will be repudiated, is

5. South Korea has witnessed the world's most dramatic growth of Christian congregations; church membership is expanding by 6.6 percent a year, fully two-thirds of the growth coming from conversions rather than the population increasing.

    (A) coming from conversions rather than the population increasing
    (B) coming from conversions rather than increases in the population
    (C) coming from conversions instead of the population's increasing
    (D) is from conversions instead of population increases
    (E) is from conversions rather than increasing the population

6. There is ample evidence, derived from the lore of traditional folk medicine, that naturally occurring antibiotics are usually able to be modified to make them a more effective drug.

    (A) are usually able to be modified to make them a more effective drug
    (B) are usually able to be modified to make them more effective drugs
    (C) are usually able to be modified, which makes them more effective drugs
    (D) can usually be modified to make them a more effective drug
    (E) can usually be modified to make them more effective drugs

7. Many investors base their choice between bonds and stocks on comparing bond yields to the dividends available on common stocks.

    (A) between bonds and stocks on comparing bond yields to
    (B) among bonds and stocks on comparisons of bond yields to
    (C) between bonds and stocks on comparisons of bond yields with
    (D) among bonds and stocks on comparing bond yields and
    (E) between bonds and stocks on comparing bond yields with

GO ON TO THE NEXT PAGE.

8. Some of the tenth-century stave churches of Norway are still standing, demonstrating that with sound design and maintenance, wooden buildings can last indefinitely.

(A) standing, demonstrating that with sound design and maintenance, wooden buildings can last indefinitely

(B) standing, demonstrating how wooden buildings, when they have sound design and maintenance, can last indefinitely

(C) standing; they demonstrate if a wooden building has sound design and maintenance it can last indefinitely

(D) standing, and they demonstrate wooden buildings can last indefinitely when there is sound design and maintenance

(E) standing, and they demonstrate how a wooden building can last indefinitely when it has sound design and maintenance

9. In the United States, trade unions encountered far more intense opposition against their struggle for social legitimacy than the organized labor movements of most other democratic nations.

(A) against their struggle for social legitimacy than

(B) in their struggle for social legitimacy than did

(C) against their struggle for social legitimacy as

(D) in their struggle for social legitimacy as did

(E) when they struggled for social legitimacy than has

10. For many people, household labor remains demanding even if able to afford household appliances their grandparents would find a miracle.

(A) even if able to afford household appliances their grandparents would find a miracle

(B) despite being able to afford household appliances their grandparents would find a miracle

(C) even if they can afford household appliances their grandparents would have found miraculous

(D) although they could afford household appliances their grandparents would find miraculous

(E) even if they are able to afford household appliances which would have been a miracle to their grandparents

11. In the most common procedure for harvesting forage crops such as alfalfa, as much as 20 percent of the leaf and small-stem material, which is the most nutritious of all the parts of the plant, shattered and fell to the ground.

(A) which is the most nutritious of all the parts of the plant, shattered and fell

(B) the most nutritious of all parts of the plant, shatter and fall

(C) the parts of the plant which were most nutritious, will shatter and fall

(D) the most nutritious parts of the plant, shatters and falls

(E) parts of the plant which are the most nutritious, have shattered and fallen

GO ON TO THE NEXT PAGE.

12. To ensure consistently high quality in its merchandise, the chain of retail stores became involved in every aspect of <u>their suppliers' operations, dictating not only the number of stitches and the width of the hem in every garment as well as</u> the profit margins of those suppliers.

(A) their suppliers' operations, dictating not only the number of stitches and the width of the hem in every garment as well as

(B) its suppliers' operations, dictating not only the number of stitches and the width of the hem in every garment as well as

(C) their suppliers' operations, dictating not only the number of stitches and the width of the hem in every garment but also

(D) its suppliers' operations, dictating not only the number of stitches and the width of the hem in every garment but also

(E) their suppliers' operations, dictating the number of stitches, the width of the hem in every garment, and

13. The medieval scholar made almost no attempt to investigate the anatomy of plants, their mechanisms of growth, <u>nor the ways where each was related to the other.</u>

(A) nor the ways where each was related to the other

(B) nor how each was related to some other

(C) or the way where one is related to the next

(D) or the ways in which they are related to one another

(E) or the ways that each related to some other

14. Originally published in 1950, *Some Tame Gazelle* was Barbara Pym's first novel, but it <u>does not read like an apprentice work.</u>

(A) does not read like an apprentice work

(B) seems not to read as an apprentice work

(C) does not seem to read as an apprentice work would

(D) does not read like an apprentice work does

(E) reads unlike an apprentice work

15. By installing special electric pumps, <u>farmers' houses could be heated by the warmth from cows' milk, according to one agricultural engineer.</u>

(A) farmers' houses could be heated by the warmth from cows' milk, according to one agricultural engineer

(B) the warmth from cows' milk could be used by farmers to heat their houses, according to one agricultural engineer

(C) one agricultural engineer reports that farmers could use the warmth from cows' milk to heat their houses

(D) farmers, according to one agricultural engineer, could use the warmth from cows' milk to heat their houses

(E) one agricultural engineer reports that farmers' houses could be heated by the warmth from cows' milk

16. In the traditional Japanese household, most clothing could be packed <u>flatly, and so it was not necessary to have elaborate closet facilities.</u>

(A) flatly, and so it was not necessary to have elaborate closet facilities

(B) flat, and so elaborate closet facilities were unnecessary

(C) flatly, and so there was no necessity for elaborate closet facilities

(D) flat, there being no necessity for elaborate closet facilities

(E) flatly, as no elaborate closet facilities were necessary

GO ON TO THE NEXT PAGE.

17. The unskilled workers at the Allenby plant realized that their hourly rate of $4.11 to $4.75 was better than <u>many nearby factory wages</u>.

    (A) many nearby factory wages
    (B) many wages in nearby factories
    (C) what are offered by many nearby factories
    (D) it is in many nearby factories
    (E) that offered by many nearby factories

18. Since 1970 the number of Blacks elected to state and federal offices in the United States <u>has multiplied nearly four times</u>.

    (A) has multiplied nearly four times
    (B) has almost quadrupled
    (C) has almost multiplied by four
    (D) is almost four times as great
    (E) is nearly fourfold what it was

19. India is a country with at least fifty major regional languages, <u>of whom fourteen have official recognition</u>.

    (A) of whom fourteen have official recognition
    (B) fourteen that have official recognition
    (C) fourteen of which are officially recognized
    (D) fourteen that are officially recognized
    (E) among whom fourteen have official recognition

20. Wind resistance created by opening windows while driving results in a fuel penalty <u>as great or greater than is incurred by using air conditioning</u>.

    (A) as great or greater than is incurred by using air conditioning
    (B) that is as great or greater than is incurred using air conditioning
    (C) as great as or greater than that of using air conditioning
    (D) at least as great as air conditioning's
    (E) at least as great as that incurred by using air conditioning

21. At the time of the Mexican agrarian revolution, the most radical faction, that of Zapata and his followers, proposed a return to communal ownership of <u>land, to what had been a pre-Columbian form of ownership respected by the Spaniards</u>.

    (A) land, to what had been a pre-Columbian form of ownership respected by the Spaniards
    (B) land, a form of ownership of the pre-Columbians and respected by the Spaniards
    (C) land, respected by the Spaniards and a pre-Columbian form of ownership
    (D) land in which a pre-Columbian form of ownership was respected by the Spaniards
    (E) land that had been a pre-Columbian form of ownership respected by the Spaniards

GO ON TO THE NEXT PAGE.

22. Even though Béla Bartók's music has proved less popular than Igor Stravinsky's and less influential than Arnold Schönberg's, it is no less important.

(A) Stravinsky's and less influential than Arnold Schönberg's, it
(B) Stravinsky's and less influential than Arnold Schönberg's, he
(C) Stravinsky's is and less influential than Arnold Schönberg's is, it
(D) Stravinsky and not as influential as Arnold Schönberg, he
(E) Stravinsky and not as influential as Arnold Schönberg, it

23. According to United States Air Force officials, a cannon shooting dead chickens at airplanes has proved helpful to demonstrate what kind of damage can result when jets fly into a flock of large birds.

(A) shooting dead chickens at airplanes has proved helpful to demonstrate
(B) shooting dead chickens at airplanes has proved itself helpful as a demonstration of
(C) shooting dead chickens at airplanes proves itself helpful as demonstrating
(D) that shoots dead chickens at airplanes proves itself helpful to demonstrate
(E) that shoots dead chickens at airplanes has proved helpful in demonstrating

24. In his eagerness to find a city worthy of Priam, the German archaeologist Schliemann cut through Troy and uncovered a civilization a thousand years older as was the city Homer's heroes knew.

(A) older as was the city Homer's heroes knew
(B) more ancient than the city known to Homer's heroes
(C) older than was the city known to Homer's heroes
(D) more ancient of a city than Homer's heroes knew
(E) older of a city than was the one known to Homer's heroes

25. To speak habitually of the "truly needy" is gradually instilling the notion that many of those who are just called "needy" actually have adequate resources; such a conclusion is unwarranted.

(A) To speak habitually of the "truly needy" is gradually instilling the notion
(B) To speak habitually of the "truly needy" is instilling the notion gradually
(C) To speak habitually of the "truly needy" is gradually to instill the notion
(D) Speaking habitually of the "truly needy" is to instill the gradual notion
(E) Speaking habitually of the "truly needy" is instilling the gradual notion

S T O P

IF YOU FINISH BEFORE TIME IS CALLED, YOU MAY CHECK YOUR WORK ON THIS SECTION ONLY.
DO NOT TURN TO ANY OTHER SECTION IN THE TEST.

Answer Key for Sample Test Section 3
SENTENCE CORRECTION

1.	E	14.	A
2.	B	15.	D
3.	D	16.	B
4.	A	17.	E
5.	B	18.	B
6.	E	19.	C
7.	C	20.	E
8.	A	21.	A
9.	B	22.	A
10.	C	23.	E
11.	D	24.	B
12.	D	25.	C
13.	D		

Explanatory Material: Sentence Correction Sample Test Section 3

1. The sale of government surplus machinery **will begin at 9 a.m. and continue until the supply lasts.**

   (A) will begin at 9 a.m. and continue until the supply lasts
   (B) begins at 9 a.m., continuing until the supply lasts
   (C) will begin at 9 a.m. and, until the supply lasts, will continue
   (D) begins at 9 a.m. and, as long as the supply may last, it continues
   (E) will begin at 9 a.m. and continue as long as the supply lasts

In A, B, and C, the phrase *until the supply lasts* is illogical. *Until* means "up to but not beyond a certain time"; it could indicate the time at which the sale will end, but not the condition (*the supply lasts*) that allows it to continue. Choices D and E correctly use *as long as* rather than *until,* but, in addition to being awkward, D contains errors in its verb forms. The use of *may last* to suggest a possibility is inappropriate, since the supply will last for a certain period of time. Also, the present tense *continues* fails to indicate that the sale will continue beyond 9 a.m. In E, the best choice, *will* refers both to *begin* and *continue.*

2. In England the well-dressed <u>gentleman of the eighteenth century protected their clothing while having their wig powdered by poking their head</u> through a device that resembled the stocks.

   (A) gentleman of the eighteenth century protected their clothing while having their wig powdered by poking their head
   (B) gentleman of the eighteenth century protected his clothing while having his wig powdered by poking his head
   (C) gentleman of the eighteenth century protected their clothing while having their wigs powdered by poking their heads
   (D) gentlemen of the eighteenth century protected his clothing while having his wig powdered by poking his head
   (E) gentlemen of the eighteenth century protected their clothing while having his wig powdered by poking his head

In A, C, D, and E, pronouns do not agree with the nouns to which they refer. In A and C, the plural *their* refers incorrectly to the singular *gentleman,* while in D and E, the singular *his* refers incorrectly to the plural *gentlemen.* Only in B do all the pronouns agree with all the nouns. Choice B is the best answer.

3. <u>Reared apart from each other, a recent United States study showed striking similarities in identical twins, including many idiosyncrasies of behavior.</u>

   (A) Reared apart from each other, a recent United States study showed striking similarities in identical twins, including many idiosyncrasies of behavior.
   (B) Reared apart from each other, striking similarities between identical twins that include many idiosyncrasies of behavior were shown in a recent United States study.
   (C) A recent United States study showed striking similarities in identical twins reared apart from each other that include many idiosyncrasies of behavior.
   (D) According to a recent United States study, identical twins reared apart from each other showed striking similarities, including many idiosyncrasies of behavior.
   (E) According to a recent United States study, identical twins showed striking similarities reared apart from each other, including many idiosyncrasies of behavior.

Choices A, B, C, and E all contain errors of modification. The phrase *reared apart from each other* is intended to describe the twins, but grammatically it modifies the nearest noun phrase. Thus, in A, it illogically describes *a recent study,* and, in B and E, it illogically describes *striking similarities.* In C, the adjective clause *that include many idiosyncrasies of behavior* is awkwardly and confusingly separated from its antecedent, *similarities.* Only D, the best choice, presents a logical and clear statement.

4. Developing nations in various parts of the world have amassed $700 billion in debts; at stake, <u>should a significant number of these debts be repudiated, is</u> the solvency of some of the world's largest multinational banks.

(A) should a significant number of these debts be repudiated, is
(B) should a significant number of these debts be repudiated, are
(C) should they repudiate a significant number of these debts, are
(D) if there is a repudiation of a significant number of these debts, would be
(E) if a significant number of these debts will be repudiated, is

Choice A correctly presents both the singular verb (*is*) for the singular subject (*solvency*) and the subjunctive verb form for a situation that might happen but has not yet happened (*should a significant number. . .be repudiated*). Choices B and C mistakenly pair the plural verb (*are*) with the singular subject (*solvency*), and the pronoun reference in C is awkward because other plural nouns intrude between *they* and its antecedent, *nations*. In D, the use of the conditional (*if there is. . .would be*) is incorrect: since the solvency of the banks *is* at stake, it is incorrect to state that the solvency *would be* at stake. Choice E wrongly uses the future tense (*will be repudiated*) to indicate what is, in the context of the sentence, merely a possibility.

5. South Korea has witnessed the world's most dramatic growth of Christian congregations; church membership is expanding by 6.6 percent a year, fully two-thirds of the growth <u>coming from conversions rather than the population increasing</u>.

(A) coming from conversions rather than the population increasing
(B) coming from conversions rather than increases in the population
(C) coming from conversions instead of the population's increasing
(D) is from conversions instead of population increases
(E) is from conversions rather than increasing the population

The terms of the contrast established by the underlined portion of the sentence (from x rather than y) are equivalent in kind and importance, and should therefore be presented in parallel grammatical form. In this sentence, the object of the preposition *from* is a simple noun, *conversions*. To maintain parallelism, *conversions* should be matched with another simple noun rather than the participle (*increasing*) that appears in A, C, and E. The presence of the verb *is* in D and E results in comma splices, and therefore run-on sentences, because the comma after *year* is not alone sufficient to join two independent clauses. Choice B, the best choice, correctly uses a participle, *coming*, in a subordinate construction, and also matches *conversions* with the noun *increases*.

6. There is ample evidence, derived from the lore of traditional folk medicine, that naturally occurring antibiotics <u>are usually able to be modified to make them a more effective drug</u>.

(A) are usually able to be modified to make them a more effective drug
(B) are usually able to be modified to make them more effective drugs
(C) are usually able to be modified, which makes them more effective drugs
(D) can usually be modified to make them a more effective drug
(E) can usually be modified to make them more effective drugs

Choices A, B, and C unidiomatically describe the antibiotics as having abilities; in A, moreover, *a. . .drug* does not agree in number with *them* (meaning *antibiotics*). In C, the word *which* refers awkwardly and imprecisely to the action denoted by an entire clause. Choice D correctly states that the antibiotics *can. . .be modified*, but *drug* does not agree in number with *antibiotics* and *them*. Choice E is the best answer for this question.

7. Many investors base their choice <u>between bonds and stocks on comparing bond yields to</u> the dividends available on common stocks.

(A) between bonds and stocks on comparing bond yields to
(B) among bonds and stocks on comparisons of bond yields to
(C) between bonds and stocks on comparisons of bond yields with
(D) among bonds and stocks on comparing bond yields and
(E) between bonds and stocks on comparing bond yields with

Choice C is the best answer. Choosing A, D, or E produces the phrase *base their choice. . .on comparing*, which is unidiomatic and imprecise; *on comparisons* correctly completes the construction begun by *base their choice*. The use of *among* in B and D is also incorrect; *among* is used with three or more things, but the investors have only two options— bonds and stocks. Choice C uses the appropriate preposition, *between*, to refer to the investors' options, and also uses the appropriate preposition, *with*, to describe the comparison the investors make: "to compare x *to* y" is to stress the similarities of x and y, but "to compare x *with* y" is to stress their differences.

8. Some of the tenth-century stave churches of Norway are still <u>standing, demonstrating that with sound design and maintenance, wooden buildings can last indefinitely</u>.

(A) standing, demonstrating that with sound design and maintenance, wooden buildings can last indefinitely
(B) standing, demonstrating how wooden buildings, when they have sound design and maintenance, can last indefinitely
(C) standing; they demonstrate if a wooden building has sound design and maintenance it can last indefinitely
(D) standing, and they demonstrate wooden buildings can last indefinitely when there is sound design and maintenance
(E) standing, and they demonstrate how a wooden building can last indefinitely when it has sound design and maintenance

Choice A is best. In B and E, the use of *how* is unidiomatic: the fact that the churches are standing demonstrates *that* such buildings can last, not *how* they can last. Choices B, C, and E state awkwardly that buildings can "have" *maintenance*. In D, the wording of the clause *when there is sound design and maintenance* is especially vague. In C and E, the shift from the plural *churches* and *they* to the singular *building* and *it* is distracting and unnecessary.

9. In the United States, trade unions encountered far more intense opposition <u>against their struggle for social legitimacy than</u> the organized labor movements of most other democratic nations.

(A) against their struggle for social legitimacy than
(B) in their struggle for social legitimacy than did
(C) against their struggle for social legitimacy as
(D) in their struggle for social legitimacy as did
(E) when they struggled for social legitimacy than has

In A and C, *against* is awkward and redundant because the idea of the resistance met by the trade unions is already established by the phrase *encountered. . .opposition*. Additionally, the failure in A and C to include *did* makes the comparisons in those choices incomplete, allowing the misreading that trade unions in the United States encountered the organized labor movements of other nations. Choices C and D both incorrectly use *more. . .as* to make a comparison; the idiomatic form of this expression is "more x than y." Choice B is best, both idiomatic and unambiguous. Choice E is awkward, and the singular verb *has* does not agree with the plural subject of the clause, *labor movements*.

10. For many people, household labor remains demanding <u>even if able to afford household appliances their grandparents would find a miracle</u>.

(A) even if able to afford household appliances their grandparents would find a miracle
(B) despite being able to afford household appliances their grandparents would find a miracle
(C) even if they can afford household appliances their grandparents would have found miraculous
(D) although they could afford household appliances their grandparents would find miraculous
(E) even if they are able to afford household appliances which would have been a miracle to their grandparents

Choices A and B are imprecise because they do not say who is able to afford appliances. In fact, the wording of B suggests that it is *household labor* that can afford them. In D, *although* is less precise than *even if* in stating the relationship between the ideas that household labor is demanding and that people can afford household appliances. Also, in A, B, and D, the verb used with *grandparents* must show past action for the sentence to make sense: *would find* is therefore incorrect. The wordy and awkward choice E needlessly switches noun number from the plural *appliances* to the singular *a miracle*. Choice C is the best answer.

11. In the most common procedure for harvesting forage crops such as alfalfa, as much as 20 percent of the leaf and small-stem material, <u>which is the most nutritious of all the parts of the plant, shattered and fell</u> to the ground.

(A) which is the most nutritious of all the parts of the plant, shattered and fell
(B) the most nutritious of all parts of the plant, shatter and fall
(C) the parts of the plant which were most nutritious, will shatter and fall
(D) the most nutritious parts of the plant, shatters and falls
(E) parts of the plant which are the most nutritious, have shattered and fallen

Making a factual statement about a regularly repeated occurrence—in this case, the harvesting of crops—requires conjugated verbs in the simple present tense. Choice A uses the past (*shattered and fell*), C the future (*will shatter and fall*), and E the past perfect (*have shattered and fallen*). Choice B uses the present, but the verbs *shatter and fall* do not agree in number with the singular subject, *20 percent*. Choice A contains an additional error of agreement (*the leaf and small-stem material. . .is*), and C contains an additional error of tense (*were most nutritious*). Only D, the best answer, matches the subject with verbs appropriate in tense and number: *as much as 20 percent. . .shatters and falls*. D is also the most concise choice.

12. To ensure consistently high quality in its merchandise, the chain of retail stores became involved in every aspect of <u>their suppliers' operations, dictating not only the number of stitches and the width of the hem in every garment as well as</u> the profit margins of those suppliers.

   (A) their suppliers' operations, dictating not only the number of stitches and the width of the hem in every garment as well as
   (B) its suppliers' operations, dictating not only the number of stitches and the width of the hem in every garment as well as
   (C) their suppliers' operations, dictating not only the number of stitches and the width of the hem in every garment but also
   (D) its suppliers' operations, dictating not only the number of stitches and the width of the hem in every garment but also
   (E) their suppliers' operations, dictating the number of stitches, the width of the hem in every garment, and

In A, C, and E, the pronoun (*their*) does not agree in number with the noun (*chain*) to which it refers. Choices A and B do not properly complete the construction beginning with *not only:* the correct version of the sentence should contain the phrase *not only. . .but also*. The best choice for this question is D.

13. The medieval scholar made almost no attempt to investigate the anatomy of plants, their mechanisms of growth, <u>nor the ways where each was related to the other</u>.

   (A) nor the ways where each was related to the other
   (B) nor how each was related to some other
   (C) or the way where one is related to the next
   (D) or the ways in which they are related to one another
   (E) or the ways that each related to some other

Choice D is the best answer. Choices A and B incorrectly use the conjunction *nor* to connect elements in an expression that begins with *no*. Since *no* negates all of the activities listed, the correct form in this sentence is "no attempt to investigate x, y, *or* z." Choices A, B, and E inappropriately use the past tense; although the scholar's studies were conducted in the past, the relatedness of the plants is a condition that continues into the present and should be described in the present tense. Finally, all the choices except D are awkward and unidiomatic, and they shift unnecessarily from a plural noun (*plants*) to a singular pronoun (*each* in A, B, and E, and *one* in C).

14. Originally published in 1950, *Some Tame Gazelle* was Barbara Pym's first novel, but it <u>does not read like an apprentice work</u>.

   (A) does not read like an apprentice work
   (B) seems not to read as an apprentice work
   (C) does not seem to read as an apprentice work would
   (D) does not read like an apprentice work does
   (E) reads unlike an apprentice work

Choice A is best, for it uses the comparative preposition *like* properly in stating a comparison between *it* (Pym's first novel) and *an apprentice work*. In B, *as* inappropriately suggests the meaning, "in the capacity of an apprentice work." Choices C and D wrongly attribute the act of reading to the book itself rather than to the reader. The use of *unlike* in E is unidiomatic: *unlike* can negate only the noun phrase *apprentice work*, but *not* is needed to negate the condition expressed by the verb phrase *read like an apprentice work*.

15. By installing special electric pumps, <u>farmers' houses could be heated by the warmth from cows' milk, according to one agricultural engineer</u>.

   (A) farmers' houses could be heated by the warmth from cows' milk, according to one agricultural engineer
   (B) the warmth from cows' milk could be used by farmers to heat their houses, according to one agricultural engineer
   (C) one agricultural engineer reports that farmers could use the warmth from cows' milk to heat their houses
   (D) farmers, according to one agricultural engineer, could use the warmth from cows' milk to heat their houses
   (E) one agricultural engineer reports that farmers' houses could be heated by the warmth from cows' milk

The introductory phrase *By installing special electric pumps* modifies the subject of the sentence—who or what installs the pumps. For clarity, this subject should be the noun closest to the modifier. None of the subjects in A, B, C, or E is the intended subject of the modifier: A illogically suggests that *farmers' houses* install the pumps; B suggests that *the warmth from cows milk* installs the pumps; C and E falsely attribute this action to the agricultural engineer. Logically, the farmers would install the pumps. Only D, the best answer, makes this clear by using *farmers* as the subject of the sentence and positioning it immediately after the modifier.

16. In the traditional Japanese household, most clothing could be packed <u>flatly, and so it was not necessary to have elaborate closet facilities</u>.

   (A) flatly, and so it was not necessary to have elaborate closet facilities
   (B) flat, and so elaborate closet facilities were unnecessary
   (C) flatly, and so there was no necessity for elaborate closet facilities
   (D) flat, there being no necessity for elaborate closet facilities
   (E) flatly, as no elaborate closet facilities were necessary

The best answer will begin with an adjective (*flat*) to describe the noun (*clothing*); A, C, and E begin with an adverb (*flatly*) that describes the act of packing rather than the arrangement of the clothing. Choices D and E do not correctly state the cause-and-effect relationship between the way in which clothes are packed and the need for closet facilities, suggesting instead that clothes are packed flat because closets are not necessary. Choice B, which contains both the adjective *flat* and the appropriate statement of cause-and-effect, *and so*, is the best answer.

-290-

17. The unskilled workers at the Allenby plant realized that their hourly rate of $4.11 to $4.75 was better than <u>many nearby factory wages</u>.

(A) many nearby factory wages
(B) many wages in nearby factories
(C) what are offered by many nearby factories
(D) it is in many nearby factories
(E) that offered by many nearby factories

To be clear and logical, comparisons should be made between like items. Choices A and B, however, compare an hourly rate of pay not with another rate, but with actual *wages*. These choices are also imprecise in that *many* modifies *wages* rather than *factories*. In C, *what* is imprecise as a substitute for *hourly rate,* and in D *it* refers illogically to the Allenby workers' rate, which cannot be said to be *in. . .nearby factories*. Both choices illogically shift from the past tense in one part of the comparison to the present tense in the other part; C compounds this error by using a plural rather than a singular verb. Choice E is best because it uses the correct pronoun, *that,* and does not introduce inconsistencies of tense.

18. Since 1970 the number of Blacks elected to state and federal offices in the United States <u>has multiplied nearly four times</u>.

(A) has multiplied nearly four times
(B) has almost quadrupled
(C) has almost multiplied by four
(D) is almost four times as great
(E) is nearly fourfold what it was

The best choice for this sentence will be the one that most accurately and idiomatically conveys the information that a number is now nearly four times greater than it was in 1970. Choice A inaccurately speaks of the number as having *multiplied nearly four times*; this phrase does not express the intended meaning, that the number has been multiplied by a factor of nearly four. Choice C speaks of the number as having *almost multiplied*. D does not complete the comparison by specifying what the number is *almost four times as great* as. In E, the present tense *is* cannot describe action that has occurred over a period of years; also, *what it was* is redundant because the starting point for the comparison is established by the phrase *Since 1970*. Choice B is the best answer for this question.

19. India is a country with at least fifty major regional languages, <u>of whom fourteen have official recognition</u>.

(A) of whom fourteen have official recognition
(B) fourteen that have official recognition
(C) fourteen of which are officially recognized
(D) fourteen that are officially recognized
(E) among whom fourteen have official recognition

The use of *whom* in A and E is incorrect; *whom* refers to people, but the referent of the pronoun in this sentence is *languages*. The pronoun *which* refers to things and is idiomatic as the object of the preposition *of*; *of* helps to indicate that the fourteen officially recognized languages are part of the larger group of the fifty regional languages, and so should be retained. D wrongly uses *that* rather than *of which*. The phrase *have official recognition* in A, B, and E makes those choices unidiomatic: languages are described not as having recognition but rather as being recognized. Choice C, the best answer, is grammatically and idiomatically correct.

20. Wind resistance created by opening windows while driving results in a fuel penalty <u>as great or greater than is incurred by using air conditioning</u>.

(A) as great or greater than is incurred by using air conditioning
(B) that is as great or greater than is incurred using air conditioning
(C) as great as or greater than that of using air conditioning
(D) at least as great as air conditioning's
(E) at least as great as that incurred by using air conditioning

The corrected sentence should compare the fuel penalty incurred by opening windows while driving with the fuel penalty incurred by using air conditioning. Choices A and B are grammatically incomplete: *as great* must be *as great as*. Also, the noun phrase *fuel penalty* must be compared to a noun or pronoun; changing *is incurred* to *that incurred* would supply the missing element. Although C sets up the comparison correctly, *as great as or greater than* is needlessly wordy, and *of using air conditioning* is imprecise. In choices D and E, *at least as great as* expresses the comparison between fuel penalties succinctly. In D, however, *air conditioning's* does not indicate that a fuel penalty results from the *use* of air conditioning. Choice E is best.

21. At the time of the Mexican agrarian revolution, the most radical faction, that of Zapata and his followers, proposed a return to communal ownership of <u>land, to what had been a pre-Columbian form of ownership respected by the Spaniards</u>.

(A) land, to what had been a pre-Columbian form of ownership respected by the Spaniards
(B) land, a form of ownership of the pre-Columbians and respected by the Spaniards
(C) land, respected by the Spaniards and a pre-Columbian form of ownership
(D) land in which a pre-Columbian form of ownership was respected by the Spaniards
(E) land that had been a pre-Columbian form of ownership respected by the Spaniards

Choice A is the best answer. In A, the meaning of *communal ownership of land* is clearly and logically amplified by a parallel noun phrase also introduced by *to*. Choice B contains an ambiguous construction that leaves it unclear whether *form of ownership of the pre-Columbians* means *"form. . .of ownership associated with"* or *"form of owning the pre-Columbians"*; B can also be faulted for an illogical *and* before *respected*. Choices C, D, and E all follow *land* with phrases that can be read either as inappropriately referring to *land* or as awkwardly referring to *ownership*.

22. **Even though Béla Bartók's music has proved less popular than Igor Stravinsky's and less influential than Arnold Schönberg's, it is no less important.**

    (A) Stravinsky's and less influential than Arnold Schönberg's, it
    (B) Stravinsky's and less influential than Arnold Schönberg's, he
    (C) Stravinsky's is and less influential than Arnold Schönberg's is, it
    (D) Stravinsky and not as influential as Arnold Schönberg, he
    (E) Stravinsky and not as influential as Arnold Schönberg, it

Choice A correctly compares the music of the three composers mentioned. In D and E, the music of Bartók is illogically compared to the other two composers themselves. The pronoun *he* in B and D is incorrect because the subject of the sentence the pronoun refers to is Bartók's music, not Bartók. Choice C is wordy and awkward.

23. **According to United States Air Force officials, a cannon shooting dead chickens at airplanes has proved helpful to demonstrate what kind of damage can result when jets fly into a flock of large birds.**

    (A) shooting dead chickens at airplanes has proved helpful to demonstrate
    (B) shooting dead chickens at airplanes has proved itself helpful as a demonstration of
    (C) shooting dead chickens at airplanes proves itself helpful as demonstrating
    (D) that shoots dead chickens at airplanes proves itself helpful to demonstrate
    (E) that shoots dead chickens at airplanes has proved helpful in demonstrating

Choice A is incorrect because *a cannon shooting* imprecisely suggests either an event, the shooting of dead chickens at airplanes, or what appears to be intended, a description of the cannon that specifies its use. Choices B and C also include this error. In addition, choices A, C, and D use unidiomatic constructions, *to demonstrate* and *as demonstrating*, after *helpful*, rather than the correct *in demonstrating*. The phrase *as a demonstration of* in choice B is idiomatic but inappropriate because it suggests a single event rather than a

purpose. Choices B, C, and D all introduce an unnecessary *itself* as well, and C and D wrongly use the present tense *proves* rather than *has proved* to indicate recently completed action. The best answer is choice E.

24. **In his eagerness to find a city worthy of Priam, the German archaeologist Schliemann cut through Troy and uncovered a civilization a thousand years older as was the city Homer's heroes knew.**

    (A) older as was the city Homer's heroes knew
    (B) more ancient than the city known to Homer's heroes
    (C) older than was the city known to Homer's heroes
    (D) more ancient of a city than Homer's heroes knew
    (E) older of a city than was the one known to Homer's heroes

Choice A is incorrect. The correct word following the comparative form of an adjective such as *older* is *than,* not *as.* Because the more ancient civilization continues to be a thousand years more ancient than Troy, it is incorrect to use the past tense *was* as choices A, C, and E do. Choices D and E also include an ungrammatical structure that follows the comparative form of an adjective with *of.* The best answer is B.

25. **To speak habitually of the "truly needy" is gradually instilling the notion that many of those who are just called "needy" actually have adequate resources; such a conclusion is unwarranted.**

    (A) To speak habitually of the "truly needy" is gradually instilling the notion
    (B) To speak habitually of the "truly needy" is instilling the notion gradually
    (C) To speak habitually of the "truly needy" is gradually to instill the notion
    (D) Speaking habitually of the "truly needy" is to instill the gradual notion
    (E) Speaking habitually of the "truly needy" is instilling the gradual notion

The correct form of the sentence requires parallel infinitive phrases in the form "to x is to y." Choices A, B, and D fail to provide one or the other of the *to* structures. Choice E abandons the infinitive parallelism entirely and substitutes a construction that awkwardly and unidiomatically makes *speaking. . ."needy"* the grammatical subject of *instilling.* Both choices D and E use *gradual* instead of *gradually* and position it before *notion* so that it appears that the notion itself, rather than the instilling of the notion, is what is gradual. The best answer is choice C.

SENTENCE CORRECTION SAMPLE TEST SECTION 4

30 Minutes

25 Questions

<u>Directions:</u> In each of the following sentences, some part of the sentence or the entire sentence is underlined. Beneath each sentence you will find five ways of phrasing the underlined part. The first of these repeats the original; the other four are different. If you think the original is better than any of the alternatives, choose answer A; otherwise choose one of the others. Select the best version and fill in the corresponding oval on your answer sheet.

This is a test of correctness and effectiveness of expression. In choosing answers, follow the requirements of standard written English; that is, pay attention to grammar, choice of words, and sentence construction. Choose the answer that expresses most effectively what is presented in the original sentence; this answer should be clear and exact, without awkwardness, ambiguity, or redundancy.

1. During the first one hundred fifty years of the existence of this republic, no one expected the press <u>was</u> fair; newspapers were mostly shrill, scurrilous, and partisan.

   (A) was
   (B) to be
   (C) of being
   (D) should be
   (E) had to be

2. Most victims of infectious mononucleosis recover after a few weeks of listlessness, <u>but an unlucky few may suffer</u> for years.

   (A) but an unlucky few may suffer
   (B) and an unlucky few have suffered
   (C) that an unlucky few might suffer
   (D) that a few being unlucky may suffer
   (E) but a few who, being unlucky, suffered

3. It was the loss of revenue from declines in tourism that in 1935 led the Saudi <u>authorities' granting a concession for oil exploration to the company that would later be known by the name of</u> Aramco.

   (A) authorities' granting a concession for oil exploration to the company that would later be known by the name of
   (B) authorities' granting a concession for oil exploration to the company later to be known as named
   (C) authorities granting a concession for oil exploration to the company that would later be known by the name of
   (D) authorities to grant a concession for oil exploration to the company that later will be known as being
   (E) authorities to grant a concession for oil exploration to the company later to be known as

4. Framed by traitorous colleagues, Alfred Dreyfus was imprisoned for twelve years before <u>there was exoneration and his freedom.</u>

   (A) there was exoneration and his freedom
   (B) he was to be exonerated with freedom
   (C) being exonerated and freed
   (D) exoneration and his freedom
   (E) being freed, having been exonerated

GO ON TO THE NEXT PAGE.

5. By studying the primitive visual systems of single-cell aquatic organisms, biophysicists have discovered a striking similarity between algae and cows, a similarity that indicates the common evolutionary origin of plants and animals: both algae and cows produce a light-sensitive protein called rhodopsin.

   (A) biophysicists have discovered a striking similarity between algae and cows
   (B) a striking similarity between algae and cows has been discovered by biophysicists
   (C) there is a striking similarity that biophysicists have discovered between algae and cows
   (D) the discovery of a striking similarity between algae and cows was made by biophysicists
   (E) algae and cows have a striking similarity that was discovered by biophysicists

6. Because young children do not organize their attention or perceptions systematically, like adults, they may notice and remember details that their elders ignore.

   (A) like adults
   (B) unlike an adult
   (C) as adults
   (D) as adults do
   (E) as an adult

7. As many as 300 of the 720 paintings attributed to Rembrandt may actually be the works of his students or other admirers.

   (A) the 720 paintings attributed to Rembrandt may
   (B) the 720 paintings attributed to be Rembrandt's might
   (C) the 720 paintings that were attributed to be by Rembrandt may
   (D) the 720 Rembrandt paintings that were once attributed to him might
   (E) Rembrandt's paintings, although 720 were once attributed to him, may

8. Studies of the human "sleep-wake cycle" have practical relevance for matters ranging from duty assignments in nuclear submarines and air-traffic control towers to the staff of shifts in 24-hour factories.

   (A) to the staff of
   (B) to those who staff
   (C) to the staffing of
   (D) and staffing
   (E) and the staff of

9. Many psychologists and sociologists now contend that the deliberate and even brutal aggression integral to some forms of competitive athletics increase the likelihood of imitative violence that erupts among crowds of spectators dominated by young adult males.

   (A) increase the likelihood of imitative violence that erupts
   (B) increase the likelihood that there will be an eruption of imitative violence
   (C) increase the likelihood of imitative violence erupting
   (D) increases the likelihood for imitative violence to crupt
   (E) increases the likelihood that imitative violence will erupt

10. More than five thousand years ago, Chinese scholars accurately described the flow of blood as a continuous circle controlled by the heart, but it went unnoticed in the West.

   (A) but it went
   (B) but it was
   (C) although it was
   (D) but the discovery went
   (E) although the discovery was

GO ON TO THE NEXT PAGE.

11. Several studies have found that the coronary patients who exercise most actively have half or less than half the chance of dying of a heart attack as those who are sedentary.

(A) have half or less than half the chance of dying of a heart attack as those who are sedentary
(B) have half the chance, or less, of dying of a heart attack than those who are sedentary do
(C) have half the chance that they will die of a heart attack, or less, than those who are sedentary do
(D) are at least fifty percent less likely to die of a heart attack as those who are sedentary
(E) are at least fifty percent less likely than those who are sedentary to die of a heart attack

12. Most nations regard their airspace as extending upward as high as an aircraft can fly; no specific altitude, however, has been officially recognized as a boundary.

(A) as extending
(B) as the extent
(C) to be an extent
(D) to be an extension
(E) to extend

13. According to scientists at the University of California, the pattern of changes that have occurred in human DNA over the millennia indicate the possibility that everyone alive today might be descended from a single female ancestor who lived in Africa sometime between 140,000 and 280,000 years ago.

(A) indicate the possibility that everyone alive today might be descended from a single female ancestor who
(B) indicate that everyone alive today might possibly be a descendant of a single female ancestor who had
(C) may indicate that everyone alive today has descended from a single female ancestor who had
(D) indicates that everyone alive today may be a descendant of a single female ancestor who
(E) indicates that everyone alive today might be a descendant from a single female ancestor who

14. Several senior officials spoke to the press on condition that they not be named in the story.

(A) that they not be named
(B) that their names will not be used
(C) that their names are not used
(D) of not being named
(E) they will not be named

15. According to his own account, Frédéric-Auguste Bartholdi, the sculptor of the Statue of Liberty, modeled the face of the statue like his mother's and the body like his wife's.

(A) modeled the face of the statue like his mother's and the body like his wife's
(B) modeled the face of the statue after that of his mother and the body after that of his wife
(C) modeled the face of the statue like his mother and the body like his wife
(D) made the face of the statue after his mother and the body after his wife
(E) made the face of the statue look like his mother and the body look like his wife

16. One of Ronald Reagan's first acts as President was to rescind President Carter's directive that any chemical banned on medical grounds in the United States be prohibited from sale to other countries.

(A) that any chemical banned on medical grounds in the United States be prohibited from sale to other countries
(B) that any chemical be prohibited from sale to other countries that was banned on medical grounds in the United States
(C) prohibiting the sale to other countries of any chemical banned on medical grounds in the United States
(D) prohibiting that any chemical banned on medical grounds in the United States is sold to other countries
(E) that any chemical banned in the United States on medical grounds is prohibited from being sold to other countries

17. Although just inside the orbit of Jupiter, amateur astronomers with good telescopes should be able to see the comet within the next few weeks.

(A) Although just inside the orbit of
(B) Although it is just inside the orbit of
(C) Just inside the orbit of
(D) Orbiting just inside
(E) Having orbited just inside

GO ON TO THE NEXT PAGE.

18. Under Napoleon the French were not able to organize an adequate supply system, and it was a major cause of the failure of their invasion of Russia.

(A) Under Napoleon the French were not able to organize an adequate supply system, and it

(B) The French being unable to organize an adequate supply system under Napoleon

(C) For the French under Napoleon, to be unable to organize an adequate supply system

(D) The inability of the French under Napoleon to organize an adequate supply system

(E) The French inability under Napoleon of organizing an adequate supply system

19. To help preserve ancient Egyptian monuments threatened by high water tables, a Swedish engineering firm has proposed installing pumps, perhaps solar powered, to lower the underground water level and dig trenches around the bases of the stone walls.

(A) to lower the underground water level and dig trenches

(B) to lower the underground water level and to dig trenches

(C) to lower the underground water level and digging trenches

(D) that lower the underground water level and that trenches be dug

(E) that lower the underground water level and trench digging

20. When rates were raised in 1985, postal service officials predicted they would make further rate increases unnecessary for at least three years.

(A) they would make further rate increases unnecessary

(B) they would mean that further rate increases would not be needed

(C) that it would not be necessary for further rate increases

(D) that the increase would make further rate increases unnecessary

(E) further rate increases will not be needed

21. With its plan to develop seven and a half acres of shore land, Cleveland is but one of a large number of communities on the Great Lakes that is looking to its waterfront as a way to improve the quality of urban life and attract new businesses.

(A) is looking to its waterfront as a way to improve the quality of urban life and attract

(B) is looking at its waterfront to improve the quality of urban life and attract

(C) are looking to their waterfronts to improve the quality of urban life and attract

(D) are looking to its waterfront as a way of improving the quality of urban life and attracting

(E) are looking at their waterfronts as a way they can improve the quality of urban life and attract

22. A collection of 38 poems by Phillis Wheatley, a slave, was published in the 1770's, the first book by a Black woman and it was only the second published by an American woman.

(A) it was only the second published by an American woman

(B) it was only the second that an American woman published

(C) the second one only published by an American woman

(D) the second one only that an American woman published

(E) only the second published by an American woman

23. A huge flying reptile that died out with the dinosaurs some 65 million years ago, the Quetzalcoatlus had a wingspan of 36 feet, believed to be the largest flying creature the world has ever seen.

(A) believed to be

(B) and that is believed to be

(C) and it is believed to have been

(D) which was, it is believed,

(E) which is believed to be

GO ON TO THE NEXT PAGE.

24. A "calendar stick" carved centuries ago by the Winnebago tribe may provide the first evidence that the North American Indians have developed advanced full-year calendars basing them on systematic astronomical observation.

(A) that the North American Indians have developed advanced full-year calendars basing them

(B) of the North American Indians who have developed advanced full-year calendars and based them

(C) of the development of advanced full-year calendars by North American Indians, basing them

(D) of the North American Indians and their development of advanced full-year calendars based

(E) that the North American Indians developed advanced full-year calendars based

25. Federal incentives now encourage investing capital in commercial office buildings despite vacancy rates in existing structures that are exceptionally high and no demand for new construction.

(A) investing capital in commercial office buildings despite vacancy rates in existing structures that are exceptionally high and

(B) capital investment in commercial office buildings even though vacancy rates in existing structures are exceptionally high and there is

(C) capital to be invested in commercial office buildings even though there are exceptionally high vacancy rates in existing structures with

(D) investing capital in commercial office buildings even though the vacancy rates are exceptionally high in existing structures with

(E) capital investment in commercial office buildings despite vacancy rates in existing structures that are exceptionally high, and although there is

STOP

IF YOU FINISH BEFORE TIME IS CALLED, YOU MAY CHECK YOUR WORK ON THIS SECTION ONLY.
DO NOT TURN TO ANY OTHER SECTION IN THE TEST.

Answer Key for Sample Test Section 4

SENTENCE CORRECTION

1.	B	14.	A
2.	A	15.	B
3.	E	16.	C
4.	C	17.	B
5.	A	18.	D
6.	D	19.	C
7.	A	20.	D
8.	C	21.	C
9.	E	22.	E
10.	D	23.	C
11.	E	24.	E
12.	A	25.	B
13.	D		

Explanatory Material: Sentence Correction Sample Test Section 4

1. **During the first one hundred fifty years of the existence of this republic, no one expected the press <u>was</u> fair; newspapers were mostly shrill, scurrilous, and partisan.**

   (A) was
   (B) to be
   (C) of being
   (D) should be
   (E) had to be

The idiomatic form of expression is either *expected that X would be Y* or *expected X to be Y*. Thus B, which follows the latter form, is the best answer. Each of the other options produces an unidiomatic statement.

2. **Most victims of infectious mononucleosis recover after a few weeks of listlessness, <u>but an unlucky few may suffer</u> for years.**

   (A) but an unlucky few may suffer
   (B) and an unlucky few have suffered
   (C) that an unlucky few might suffer
   (D) that a few being unlucky may suffer
   (E) but a few who, being unlucky, suffered

A is the best choice. The second clause presents a possible exception to the statement made in the first, a contrast that *but* makes clear. B is incorrect because the conjunction *and* fails to show this contrast and because the verb *have suffered* mistakenly presents a possibility as though it were an actual occurrence. *That*, which begins both C and D, is not a coordinating conjunction, which is required to join two independent clauses. D additionally is awkward. Although E begins with *but*, it is not an independent clause; the verb *suffered* takes the relative pronoun *who* as its subject, leaving no verb for the subject *few*. Moreover, E is awkward and, like B, mistakenly presents a possibility as though it were an actual occurrence.

3. **It was the loss of revenue from declines in tourism that in 1935 led the Saudi <u>authorities' granting a concession for oil exploration to the company that would later be known by the name of</u> Aramco.**

   (A) authorities' granting a concession for oil exploration to the company that would later be known by the name of
   (B) authorities' granting a concession for oil exploration to the compnay later to be known as named
   (C) authorities granting a concession for oil exploration to the company that would later be known by the name of
   (D) authorities to grant a concession for oil exploration to the company that later will be known as being
   (E) authorities to grant a concession for oil exploration to the company later to be known as

In this sentence, the verb *led* requires that a person or persons perform an action indicated by the infinitive, or "to ____" form, of the verb, and so choices A, B, and C can be faulted because *led* is completed by *granting*. Choice B is also faulty because the phrase *known as* here requires a noun, and *named* is a past participle. Choice D has *to grant* but inappropriately uses *will* rather than *would* and employs *being* unidiomatically. The best choice is E because it supplies *authorities* for *led*, the infinitive *to grant*, and an idiomatic use of *known as*.

4. Framed by traitorous colleagues, Alfred Dreyfus was imprisoned for twelve years before <u>there was exoneration and his freedom</u>.

   (A) there was exoneration and his freedom
   (B) he was to be exonerated with freedom
   (C) being exonerated and freed
   (D) exoneration and his freedom
   (E) being freed, having been exonerated

This sentence is to be completed with two ideas—exoneration and freedom. Choices A, C, and D connect them with *and* and therefore need parallel words or phrases. In choices A and D, the phrases are not exactly parallel: *freedom* is modified by *his* but *exonerated* is not. Also, choice A uses the wordy and imprecise *there was*. Choice C, the best answer, supplies the parallelism in the past participles *exonerated* and *freed*. Choice B is confusing because the phrase *to be* could imply that the original intention when Dreyfus was imprisoned was to exonerate him in twelve years, and *with* could imply that *freedom* was an attribute of his exoneration. In addition to being awkward, the inappropriate tense shift in E makes it sound as if Dreyfus had been exonerated some period of time before being freed.

5. By studying the primitive visual systems of single-cell aquatic organisms, <u>biophysicists have discovered a striking similarity between algae and cows,</u> a similarity that indicates the common evolutionary origin of plants and animals: both algae and cows produce a light-sensitive protein called rhodopsin.

   (A) biophysicists have discovered a striking similarity between algae and cows
   (B) a striking similarity between algae and cows has been discovered by biophysicists
   (C) there is a striking similarity that biophysicists have discovered between algae and cows
   (D) the discovery of a striking similarity between algae and cows was made by biophysicists
   (E) algae and cows have a striking similarity that was discovered by biophysicists

This question requires that the opening participial phrase modify the subject of the sentence, *biophysicists*. The subject should therefore be placed as close to the phrase as possible. Choice A places the subject next to the phrase and is the best choice. In choice B a *similarity* is doing the studying, in choice D *the discovery* is, and in choice E the *algae and cows* are. By placing *there is* next to the phrase, choice C leaves the participle with nothing to modify.

6. Because young children do not organize their attention or perceptions systematically, <u>like adults</u>, they may notice and remember details that their elders ignore.

   (A) like adults
   (B) unlike an adult
   (C) as adults
   (D) as adults do
   (E) as an adult

The problem in this question concerns like/as. If the underline modified *children*, then *like* would be appropriate; however, if it parallels the clause *children do not organize*, then *as* is appropriate. To modify *children*, the underline should be next to the word, so choices A and B are not correct. Also, choice A states that *children* and *adults* are similar, whereas the rest of the sentence contrasts them. Choice B attempts to contrast them, but it uses the singular *adult*, which does not parallel the plural *children*. Choices C, D, and E use the correct connector, *as*, but choice E, like choice B, uses the singular *adult*, and choice C gives only part of the clause, the subject. Choice D provides the complete parallel clause.

7. As many as 300 of <u>the 720 paintings attributed to Rembrandt may</u> actually be the works of his students or other admirers.

   (A) the 720 paintings attributed to Rembrandt may
   (B) the 720 paintings attributed to be Rembrandt's might
   (C) the 720 paintings that were attributed to be by Rembrandt may
   (D) the 720 Rembrandt paintings that were once attributed to him might
   (E) Rembrandt's paintings, although 720 were once attributed to him, may

Both choices B and C can be faulted for the unidiomatic use of *to be* with *attributed*. Choice D seems contradictory by first calling all 720 paintings Rembrandt's (not just attributing them to the painter) and then saying that 300 of them might not be his. Choice E repeats the seeming contradiction in D and then creates further confusion by the awkward placement of the *although* clause. Choice A uses the correct phrase, *attributed to*, and is the best choice.

8. Studies of the human "sleep-wake cycle" have practical relevance for matters ranging from duty assignments in nuclear submarines and air-traffic control towers <u>to the staff of</u> shifts in 24-hour factories.

   (A) to the staff of
   (B) to those who staff
   (C) to the staffing of
   (D) and staffing
   (E) and the staff of

The best answer for this question must have a phrase parallel to *from duty assignments* — that is, a phrase with the preposition *to* and a word that indicates a thing or an activity. Choices D and E can be faulted for having *and* in place of *to*. Choices A, B, and C supply the proper preposition, but A and B attempt to parallel *duty assignments* with *staff* — that is, with people. Only choice C combines the proper preposition with *the staffing*, a correct parallel to *duty assignments*.

9. Many psychologists and sociologists now contend that the deliberate and even brutal aggression integral to some forms of competitive athletics increase the likelihood of imitative violence that erupts among crowds of spectators dominated by young adult males.

   (A) increase the likelihood of imitative violence that erupts
   (B) increase the likelihood that there will be an eruption of imitative violence
   (C) increase the likelihood of imitative violence erupting
   (D) increases the likelihood for imitative violence to erupt
   (E) increases the likelihood that imitative violence will erupt

Choices A, B, and C are incorrect because they supply a plural form of the verb *increase* for the singular subject *aggression*. Choices D and E supply the correct singular form of the verb, but in D *the likelihood for imitative violence to erupt* is unidiomatic. Choice E is the best choice for this question.

10. More than five thousand years ago, Chinese scholars accurately described the flow of blood as a continuous circle controlled by the heart, but it went unnoticed in the West.

   (A) but it went
   (B) but it was
   (C) although it was
   (D) but the discovery went
   (E) although the discovery was

Choices A, B, and C can be faulted for the lack of any clear antecedent for the pronoun *it*. The nouns that are present — *flow*, *circle*, and *heart* — do not make any sense if substituted for the pronoun. What *it* attempts to refer to is the entire event, and choices D and E, rather than use a pronoun, give that event a name, *the discovery*. In choice E the conjunction *although* implies illogically that the discovery was made in spite of the fact that the West did not notice it. Choice D supplies the correct conjunction, *but,* and is the best choice.

11. Several studies have found that the coronary patients who exercise most actively have half or less than half the chance of dying of a heart attack as those who are sedentary.

   (A) have half or less than half the chance of dying of a heart attack as those who are sedentary
   (B) have half the chance, or less, of dying of a heart attack than those who are sedentary do
   (C) have half the chance that they will die of a heart attack, or less, than those who are sedentary do
   (D) are at least fifty percent less likely to die of a heart attack as those who are sedentary
   (E) are at least fifty percent less likely than those who are sedentary to die of a heart attack

Choice A incorrectly uses *as those who are sedentary* for *that those who are sedentary have* in comparing the chances for survival that active patients have with the chances that sedentary patients have; *that*, a pronoun, is needed to refer to *chance*. Choice B incorrectly substitutes *than* for *that* and is awkward. In choice C, *that they will die* is more wordy and awkward than *of dying*, and the placement of *less* confuses the meaning of the sentence. Choice D incorrectly uses *as* for *than* and separates the elements being compared. Choice E is best.

12. Most nations regard their airspace as extending upward as high as an aircraft can fly; no specific altitude, however, has been offficially recognized as a boundary.

   (A) as extending
   (B) as the extent
   (C) to be an extent
   (D) to be an extension
   (E) to extend

Choice A is best because it is idiomatically correct; *regard*, when its meaning indicates seeing, looking at, or conceiving of something in a particular way, is paired with *as* in the idiomatic construction *regard X as Y*. Choices C, D, and E violate the *regard . . . as* construction. In choices B, C, and D, the nouns *extent* and *extension* cannot be modified by the adverbial phrase that follows: a verb form such as *extending* is needed.

13. According to scientists at the University of California, the pattern of changes that have occurred in human DNA over the millennia indicate the possibility that everyone alive today might be descended from a single female ancestor who lived in Africa sometime between 140,000 and 280,000 years ago.

(A) indicate the possibility that everyone alive today might be descended from a single female ancestor who

(B) indicate that everyone alive today might possibly be a descendant of a single female ancestor who had

(C) may indicate that everyone alive today has descended from a single female ancestor who had

(D) indicates that everyone alive today may be a descendant of a single female ancestor who

(E) indicates that everyone alive today might be a descendant from a single female ancestor who

Choices A, B, and C are incorrect because the plural verb *indicate* does not agree with the singular subject *pattern*. Choices A, B, and E contain *might*, which expresses too much doubt; *may*, which expresses a distinct possibility, is preferable. Given *might*, *possibility* in A and *possibly* in B are redundant. In choices B and C, *had*, the auxiliary of *lived*, should be deleted because the simple past tense is correct; the past perfect is used to refer to action that precedes some other action occurring in the past. In choice C, *may* is misplaced before *indicate*. Also, *descended* would more appropriately take some form of the verb *to be* in place of *has*. Choice D is best. In choice E, *from* should be *of*.

14. Several senior officials spoke to the press on condition that they not be named in the story.

(A) that they not be named
(B) that their names will not be used
(C) that their names are not used
(D) of not being named
(E) they will not be named

Choice A is best; it is the only choice that uses the subjunctive form of the verb, as is appropriate in referring to a conditional circumstance that has not yet been realized as fact. Also, *on condition that* is idiomatic. In addition to failing to use the subjunctive form, choices B and C are wordy. Choices D and E are unidiomatic and, like B and C, fail to use the subjunctive.

15. According to his own account, Frédéric-Auguste Bartholdi, the sculptor of the Statue of Liberty, modeled the face of the statue like his mother's and the body like his wife's.

(A) modeled the face of the statue like his mother's and the body like his wife's

(B) modeled the face of the statue after that of his mother and the body after that of his wife

(C) modeled the face of the statue like his mother and the body like his wife

(D) made the face of the statue after his mother and the body after his wife

(E) made the face of the statue look like his mother and the body look like his wife

In choices A and C, *like* is used inappropriately; as a preposition, it should compare one noun to another, but instead it is used to modify the verb *modeled*. Also, *modeled . . . like* is unidiomatic and awkward. Choice C is also unidiomatic and imprecise. The phrase should indicate that the sculptor modeled the face of the statue after the *face* of his mother and not the entire person; so too, the body of the statue was modeled after only the body of his wife. Choices D and E, like A and C, are imprecise and unidiomatic. Choice B is best; *modeled . . . after* is idiomatic, the prepositional phrases have objects, and each pronoun *that* has an antecedent, *face* and *body*, respectively.

16. One of Ronald Reagan's first acts as President was to rescind President Carter's directive that any chemical banned on medical grounds in the United States be prohibited from sale to other countries.

(A) that any chemical banned on medical grounds in the United States be prohibited from sale to other countries

(B) that any chemical be prohibited from sale to other countries that was banned on medical grounds in the United States

(C) prohibiting the sale to other countries of any chemical banned on medical grounds in the United States

(D) prohibiting that any chemical banned on medical grounds in the United States is sold to other countries

(E) that any chemical banned in the United States on medical grounds is prohibited from being sold to other countries

In choices A, B, and E, *prohibited from sale* and *prohibited from being sold* cannot properly modify *any chemical*: the chemicals are banned, and the *sale* of the chemicals is prohibited. Moreover, in A and B *prohibited from* must be completed by a present participial ("-ing") form, not by a noun such as *sale*. In addition, B clumsily separates modifying phrases, such as *banned on medical grounds*, from the words they modify. Choices D and E, aside from being very awkward, use *is* incorrectly in referring to a situation that did not exist but that President Carter tried to bring about through his directive. Choice C is the best answer.

17. <u>Although just inside the orbit of</u> Jupiter, amateur astronomers with good telescopes should be able to see the comet within the next few weeks.

   (A) Although just inside the orbit of
   (B) Although it is just inside the orbit of
   (C) Just inside the orbit of
   (D) Orbiting just inside
   (E) Having orbited just inside

Initial phrases, which lack a subject and its conjugated verb, attach to the subject of the main clause and modify it. Consequently, the initial phrases represented by choices A and C state absurdly that amateur astronomers with good telescopes are just inside the orbit of Jupiter. D and E worsen their predicament by having them orbit just inside the planet itself. Choice B, the best answer, conveys the intended meaning clearly: the pronoun *it* refers to *the comet* and functions as the subject of a subordinate clause that is grammatically joined to the main clause by *Although*.

18. <u>Under Napoleon the French were not able to organize an adequate supply system, and it</u> was a major cause of the failure of their invasion of Russia.

   (A) Under Napoleon the French were not able to organize an adequate supply system, and it
   (B) The French being unable to organize an adequate supply system under Napoleon
   (C) For the French under Napoleon, to be unable to organize an adequate supply system
   (D) The inability of the French under Napoleon to organize an adequate supply system
   (E) The French inability under Napoleon of organizing an adequate supply system

In choice A, *it* has no logical noun referent; to make complete sense, a noun phrase such as *this inability* would have to replace *it* as the subject of *was*. B also lacks a noun or construction that can be a subject for *was*. The infinitive *to be unable* in C wrongly suggests a permanent or general condition rather than a specific instance of failure. In choice E, *French inability . . . of organizing* is badly worded: *inability* requires *to organize*, and the inability itself was not *French*—it was in this historical circumstance a characteristic *of* the French. Choice D, the best answer, provides idiomatic phrasing and a proper grammatical subject for *was*.

19. To help preserve ancient Egyptian monuments threatened by high water tables, a Swedish engineering firm has proposed installing pumps, perhaps solar powered, <u>to lower the underground water level and dig trenches</u> around the bases of the stone walls.

   (A) to lower the underground water level and dig trenches
   (B) to lower the underground water level and to dig trenches
   (C) to lower the underground water level and digging trenches
   (D) that lower the underground water level and that trenches be dug
   (E) that lower the underground water level and trench digging

Choice C, the best answer, is the only one that achieves parallel verb form by producing the construction *has proposed installing pumps . . . and digging trenches*: *dig trenches* in A, *to dig trenches* in B, *that trenches be dug* in D, and *trench digging* in E do not follow the same grammatical form as *installing pumps*. The false parallels with *to lower* in A and B make it sound as if the pumps were installed in order to dig trenches, and *that lower the underground water level* in D and E seems imprecisely to describe a characteristic of the pumps rather than to identify the purpose for which pumps would be installed.

20. When rates were raised in 1985, postal service officials predicted <u>they would make further rate increases unnecessary</u> for at least three years.

   (A) they would make further rate increases unnecessary
   (B) they would mean that further rate increases would not be needed
   (C) that it would not be necessary for further rate increases
   (D) that the increase would make further rate increases unnecessary
   (E) further rate increases will not be needed

The pronoun *they* is confusing in choices A and B because it seems to refer to *officials*, the nearest plural noun, rather than to *rates*. Choice C is grammatically incomplete: *it would not be necessary* must be completed by an infinitive, such as *to increase rates further*, rather than by the prepositional phrase *for further rate increases*. In choice E, the *will* should be *would* to indicate that what was predicted was only a prediction and not an accomplished fact. Choice D is best.

21. With its plan to develop seven and a half acres of shore land, Cleveland is but one of a large number of communities on the Great Lakes that <u>is looking to its waterfront as a way to improve the quality of urban life and attract</u> new businesses.

(A) is looking to its waterfront as a way to improve the quality of urban life and attract
(B) is looking at its waterfront to improve the quality of urban life and attract
(C) are looking to their waterfronts to improve the quality of urban life and attract
(D) are looking to its waterfront as a way of improving the quality of urban life and attracting
(E) are looking at their waterfronts as a way they can improve the quality of urban life and attract

In choices A and B, the singular *is* does not agree in number with its subject, *that*; *that* is plural here because it refers to the plural noun *communities*, not to *one*. The phrase *looking to* describes not only Cleveland but all of the communities it is grouped with, and so the plural *that are looking to* is required. B and E can be faulted because *looking at* is less idiomatic here than *looking to*: people look *to* something, not *at* something, for a solution. In D, *its* does not agree with the plural subject, the *communities*, and the phrasing is wordy. Choice C, the best answer, is concise and grammatical.

22. A collection of 38 poems by Phillis Wheatley, a slave, was published in the 1770's, the first book by a Black woman and <u>it was only the second published by an American woman</u>.

(A) it was only the second published by an American woman
(B) it was only the second that an American woman published
(C) the second one only published by an American woman
(D) the second one only that an American woman published
(E) only the second published by an American woman

In this question, the phrase that completes the sentence should be grammatically parallel to *the first book by a Black woman*, the phrase it is linked to by *and*. A and B are not parallel because they introduce a new grammatical subject and verb, *it was*, thus producing a clause rather than a parallel phrase. In C and D, *only* is misplaced, and *that an American woman published* in B and D does not parallel *by a Black woman*. Choice E, the best answer, supplies the needed parallel phrase, with the word *book* omitted as being understood.

23. A huge flying reptile that died out with the dinosaurs some 65 million years ago, the Quetzalcoatlus had a wingspan of 36 feet, <u>believed to be</u> the largest flying creature the world has ever seen.

(A) believed to be
(B) and that is believed to be
(C) and it is believed to have been
(D) which was, it is believed,
(E) which is believed to be

In choice A, *believed to be* incorrectly modifies *wingspan*, producing the illogical statement that the wingspan, and not the Quetzalcoatlus, is considered the largest flying creature the world has ever seen. The pronouns *that* and *which* cause the same confusion in B, D, and E by referring grammatically to the noun *wingspan*. Also, the use of *to be* in A, B, and E suggests wrongly that the flying reptile still exists. In choice C, the best answer, *it* refers to the Quetzalcoatlus, and the verb form *is believed to have been* indicates that the belief is current but the creature extinct.

24. A "calendar stick" carved centuries ago by the Winnebago tribe may provide the first evidence <u>that the North American Indians have developed advanced full-year calendars basing them</u> on systematic astronomical observation.

(A) that the North American Indians have developed advanced full-year calendars basing them
(B) of the North American Indians who have developed advanced full-year calendars and based them
(C) of the development of advanced full-year calendars by North American Indians, basing them
(D) of the North American Indians and their development of advanced full-year calendars based
(E) that the North American Indians developed advanced full-year calendars based

Choices A and B contain incorrect verb forms: the present perfect *have developed*, which wrongly suggests a recent accomplishment, should be the simple past form *developed* in order to indicate action that occurred "centuries ago." In A and C, *basing* seems again to describe present action and in C lacks a noun that it can modify grammatically; *based* is needed to describe calendars that were developed in the distant past. In B and D, *(evidence) of the North American Indians* confuses the meaning of the sentence: the issue is not evidence of the Indians' existence, but evidence of their achievement. Concisely and logically phrased, choice E is best.

25. Federal incentives now encourage <u>investing capital in commercial office buildings despite vacancy rates in existing structures that are exceptionally high and</u> no demand for new construction.

(A) investing capital in commercial office buildings despite vacancy rates in existing structures that are exceptionally high and

(B) capital investment in commercial office buildings even though vacancy rates in existing structures are exceptionally high and there is

(C) capital to be invested in commercial office buildings even though there are exceptionally high vacancy rates in existing structures with

(D) investing capital in commercial office buildings even though the vacancy rates are exceptionally high in existing structures with

(E) capital investment in commercial office buildings despite vacancy rates in existing structures that are exceptionally high, and although there is

In choices A, C, and D, *investing capital* and *capital to be invested* are awkward and imprecise; the verb *encourage* more appropriately takes a noun such as *investment* for its object. Moreover, these choices and choice E contain ambiguous wording: *that are exceptionally high* in A and E, and *with (no demand)* in C and D, illogically seem to modify *existing structures*. In A and E, *despite vacancy rates* does not allow for a grammatically complete sentence with parallel construction. Choice B is best: *capital investment* is the proper object for *encourage*, modifying phrases are placed so as to avoid ambiguity, and the construction *even though vacancy rates . . . are . . . high and there is (no demand)* is grammatically parallel.

8 Three Authentic Graduate Management Admission Tests

The tests that follow are Graduate Management Admission Tests that have been slightly modified. Form A was administered in June 1990, Form B in January 1991, and Form C in March 1991. An actual test book contains seven sections, one of which consists of trial questions that are not counted in the scoring. Those trial questions have been omitted from these tests. Also, the total testing time for the tests reproduced here is three hours; the actual test takes about three and a half hours.

Taking these tests will help you become acquainted with testing procedures and requirements and thereby approach the real test with more assurance. Therefore, you should try to take these tests under conditions similar to those in an actual test administration, observing the time limitations, and thinking about each question seriously.

The facsimiles of the response portion of a GMAT answer sheet on pages 307, 381, and 457 may be used for marking your answers to the tests. After you have taken the tests, compare your answers with the correct ones on pages 347, 421, and 497 and determine your scores using the information that follows the answer keys.

Answer Sheet: Form A

Section 1

1 Ⓐ Ⓑ Ⓒ Ⓓ Ⓔ
2 Ⓐ Ⓑ Ⓒ Ⓓ Ⓔ
3 Ⓐ Ⓑ Ⓒ Ⓓ Ⓔ
4 Ⓐ Ⓑ Ⓒ Ⓓ Ⓔ
5 Ⓐ Ⓑ Ⓒ Ⓓ Ⓔ
6 Ⓐ Ⓑ Ⓒ Ⓓ Ⓔ
7 Ⓐ Ⓑ Ⓒ Ⓓ Ⓔ
8 Ⓐ Ⓑ Ⓒ Ⓓ Ⓔ
9 Ⓐ Ⓑ Ⓒ Ⓓ Ⓔ
10 Ⓐ Ⓑ Ⓒ Ⓓ Ⓔ
11 Ⓐ Ⓑ Ⓒ Ⓓ Ⓔ
12 Ⓐ Ⓑ Ⓒ Ⓓ Ⓔ
13 Ⓐ Ⓑ Ⓒ Ⓓ Ⓔ
14 Ⓐ Ⓑ Ⓒ Ⓓ Ⓔ
15 Ⓐ Ⓑ Ⓒ Ⓓ Ⓔ
16 Ⓐ Ⓑ Ⓒ Ⓓ Ⓔ
17 Ⓐ Ⓑ Ⓒ Ⓓ Ⓔ
18 Ⓐ Ⓑ Ⓒ Ⓓ Ⓔ
19 Ⓐ Ⓑ Ⓒ Ⓓ Ⓔ
20 Ⓐ Ⓑ Ⓒ Ⓓ Ⓔ
21 Ⓐ Ⓑ Ⓒ Ⓓ Ⓔ
22 Ⓐ Ⓑ Ⓒ Ⓓ Ⓔ
23 Ⓐ Ⓑ Ⓒ Ⓓ Ⓔ
24 Ⓐ Ⓑ Ⓒ Ⓓ Ⓔ
25 Ⓐ Ⓑ Ⓒ Ⓓ Ⓔ

Section 2

1 Ⓐ Ⓑ Ⓒ Ⓓ Ⓔ
2 Ⓐ Ⓑ Ⓒ Ⓓ Ⓔ
3 Ⓐ Ⓑ Ⓒ Ⓓ Ⓔ
4 Ⓐ Ⓑ Ⓒ Ⓓ Ⓔ
5 Ⓐ Ⓑ Ⓒ Ⓓ Ⓔ
6 Ⓐ Ⓑ Ⓒ Ⓓ Ⓔ
7 Ⓐ Ⓑ Ⓒ Ⓓ Ⓔ
8 Ⓐ Ⓑ Ⓒ Ⓓ Ⓔ
9 Ⓐ Ⓑ Ⓒ Ⓓ Ⓔ
10 Ⓐ Ⓑ Ⓒ Ⓓ Ⓔ
11 Ⓐ Ⓑ Ⓒ Ⓓ Ⓔ
12 Ⓐ Ⓑ Ⓒ Ⓓ Ⓔ
13 Ⓐ Ⓑ Ⓒ Ⓓ Ⓔ
14 Ⓐ Ⓑ Ⓒ Ⓓ Ⓔ
15 Ⓐ Ⓑ Ⓒ Ⓓ Ⓔ
16 Ⓐ Ⓑ Ⓒ Ⓓ Ⓔ
17 Ⓐ Ⓑ Ⓒ Ⓓ Ⓔ
18 Ⓐ Ⓑ Ⓒ Ⓓ Ⓔ
19 Ⓐ Ⓑ Ⓒ Ⓓ Ⓔ
20 Ⓐ Ⓑ Ⓒ Ⓓ Ⓔ
21 Ⓐ Ⓑ Ⓒ Ⓓ Ⓔ
22 Ⓐ Ⓑ Ⓒ Ⓓ Ⓔ
23 Ⓐ Ⓑ Ⓒ Ⓓ Ⓔ
24 Ⓐ Ⓑ Ⓒ Ⓓ Ⓔ
25 Ⓐ Ⓑ Ⓒ Ⓓ Ⓔ

Section 3

1 Ⓐ Ⓑ Ⓒ Ⓓ Ⓔ
2 Ⓐ Ⓑ Ⓒ Ⓓ Ⓔ
3 Ⓐ Ⓑ Ⓒ Ⓓ Ⓔ
4 Ⓐ Ⓑ Ⓒ Ⓓ Ⓔ
5 Ⓐ Ⓑ Ⓒ Ⓓ Ⓔ
6 Ⓐ Ⓑ Ⓒ Ⓓ Ⓔ
7 Ⓐ Ⓑ Ⓒ Ⓓ Ⓔ
8 Ⓐ Ⓑ Ⓒ Ⓓ Ⓔ
9 Ⓐ Ⓑ Ⓒ Ⓓ Ⓔ
10 Ⓐ Ⓑ Ⓒ Ⓓ Ⓔ
11 Ⓐ Ⓑ Ⓒ Ⓓ Ⓔ
12 Ⓐ Ⓑ Ⓒ Ⓓ Ⓔ
13 Ⓐ Ⓑ Ⓒ Ⓓ Ⓔ
14 Ⓐ Ⓑ Ⓒ Ⓓ Ⓔ
15 Ⓐ Ⓑ Ⓒ Ⓓ Ⓔ
16 Ⓐ Ⓑ Ⓒ Ⓓ Ⓔ
17 Ⓐ Ⓑ Ⓒ Ⓓ Ⓔ
18 Ⓐ Ⓑ Ⓒ Ⓓ Ⓔ
19 Ⓐ Ⓑ Ⓒ Ⓓ Ⓔ
20 Ⓐ Ⓑ Ⓒ Ⓓ Ⓔ
21 Ⓐ Ⓑ Ⓒ Ⓓ Ⓔ
22 Ⓐ Ⓑ Ⓒ Ⓓ Ⓔ
23 Ⓐ Ⓑ Ⓒ Ⓓ Ⓔ
24 Ⓐ Ⓑ Ⓒ Ⓓ Ⓔ
25 Ⓐ Ⓑ Ⓒ Ⓓ Ⓔ

Section 4

1 Ⓐ Ⓑ Ⓒ Ⓓ Ⓔ
2 Ⓐ Ⓑ Ⓒ Ⓓ Ⓔ
3 Ⓐ Ⓑ Ⓒ Ⓓ Ⓔ
4 Ⓐ Ⓑ Ⓒ Ⓓ Ⓔ
5 Ⓐ Ⓑ Ⓒ Ⓓ Ⓔ
6 Ⓐ Ⓑ Ⓒ Ⓓ Ⓔ
7 Ⓐ Ⓑ Ⓒ Ⓓ Ⓔ
8 Ⓐ Ⓑ Ⓒ Ⓓ Ⓔ
9 Ⓐ Ⓑ Ⓒ Ⓓ Ⓔ
10 Ⓐ Ⓑ Ⓒ Ⓓ Ⓔ
11 Ⓐ Ⓑ Ⓒ Ⓓ Ⓔ
12 Ⓐ Ⓑ Ⓒ Ⓓ Ⓔ
13 Ⓐ Ⓑ Ⓒ Ⓓ Ⓔ
14 Ⓐ Ⓑ Ⓒ Ⓓ Ⓔ
15 Ⓐ Ⓑ Ⓒ Ⓓ Ⓔ
16 Ⓐ Ⓑ Ⓒ Ⓓ Ⓔ
17 Ⓐ Ⓑ Ⓒ Ⓓ Ⓔ
18 Ⓐ Ⓑ Ⓒ Ⓓ Ⓔ
19 Ⓐ Ⓑ Ⓒ Ⓓ Ⓔ
20 Ⓐ Ⓑ Ⓒ Ⓓ Ⓔ
21 Ⓐ Ⓑ Ⓒ Ⓓ Ⓔ
22 Ⓐ Ⓑ Ⓒ Ⓓ Ⓔ
23 Ⓐ Ⓑ Ⓒ Ⓓ Ⓔ
24 Ⓐ Ⓑ Ⓒ Ⓓ Ⓔ
25 Ⓐ Ⓑ Ⓒ Ⓓ Ⓔ

Section 5

1 Ⓐ Ⓑ Ⓒ Ⓓ Ⓔ
2 Ⓐ Ⓑ Ⓒ Ⓓ Ⓔ
3 Ⓐ Ⓑ Ⓒ Ⓓ Ⓔ
4 Ⓐ Ⓑ Ⓒ Ⓓ Ⓔ
5 Ⓐ Ⓑ Ⓒ Ⓓ Ⓔ
6 Ⓐ Ⓑ Ⓒ Ⓓ Ⓔ
7 Ⓐ Ⓑ Ⓒ Ⓓ Ⓔ
8 Ⓐ Ⓑ Ⓒ Ⓓ Ⓔ
9 Ⓐ Ⓑ Ⓒ Ⓓ Ⓔ
10 Ⓐ Ⓑ Ⓒ Ⓓ Ⓔ
11 Ⓐ Ⓑ Ⓒ Ⓓ Ⓔ
12 Ⓐ Ⓑ Ⓒ Ⓓ Ⓔ
13 Ⓐ Ⓑ Ⓒ Ⓓ Ⓔ
14 Ⓐ Ⓑ Ⓒ Ⓓ Ⓔ
15 Ⓐ Ⓑ Ⓒ Ⓓ Ⓔ
16 Ⓐ Ⓑ Ⓒ Ⓓ Ⓔ
17 Ⓐ Ⓑ Ⓒ Ⓓ Ⓔ
18 Ⓐ Ⓑ Ⓒ Ⓓ Ⓔ
19 Ⓐ Ⓑ Ⓒ Ⓓ Ⓔ
20 Ⓐ Ⓑ Ⓒ Ⓓ Ⓔ
21 Ⓐ Ⓑ Ⓒ Ⓓ Ⓔ
22 Ⓐ Ⓑ Ⓒ Ⓓ Ⓔ
23 Ⓐ Ⓑ Ⓒ Ⓓ Ⓔ
24 Ⓐ Ⓑ Ⓒ Ⓓ Ⓔ
25 Ⓐ Ⓑ Ⓒ Ⓓ Ⓔ

Section 6

1 Ⓐ Ⓑ Ⓒ Ⓓ Ⓔ
2 Ⓐ Ⓑ Ⓒ Ⓓ Ⓔ
3 Ⓐ Ⓑ Ⓒ Ⓓ Ⓔ
4 Ⓐ Ⓑ Ⓒ Ⓓ Ⓔ
5 Ⓐ Ⓑ Ⓒ Ⓓ Ⓔ
6 Ⓐ Ⓑ Ⓒ Ⓓ Ⓔ
7 Ⓐ Ⓑ Ⓒ Ⓓ Ⓔ
8 Ⓐ Ⓑ Ⓒ Ⓓ Ⓔ
9 Ⓐ Ⓑ Ⓒ Ⓓ Ⓔ
10 Ⓐ Ⓑ Ⓒ Ⓓ Ⓔ
11 Ⓐ Ⓑ Ⓒ Ⓓ Ⓔ
12 Ⓐ Ⓑ Ⓒ Ⓓ Ⓔ
13 Ⓐ Ⓑ Ⓒ Ⓓ Ⓔ
14 Ⓐ Ⓑ Ⓒ Ⓓ Ⓔ
15 Ⓐ Ⓑ Ⓒ Ⓓ Ⓔ
16 Ⓐ Ⓑ Ⓒ Ⓓ Ⓔ
17 Ⓐ Ⓑ Ⓒ Ⓓ Ⓔ
18 Ⓐ Ⓑ Ⓒ Ⓓ Ⓔ
19 Ⓐ Ⓑ Ⓒ Ⓓ Ⓔ
20 Ⓐ Ⓑ Ⓒ Ⓓ Ⓔ
21 Ⓐ Ⓑ Ⓒ Ⓓ Ⓔ
22 Ⓐ Ⓑ Ⓒ Ⓓ Ⓔ
23 Ⓐ Ⓑ Ⓒ Ⓓ Ⓔ
24 Ⓐ Ⓑ Ⓒ Ⓓ Ⓔ
25 Ⓐ Ⓑ Ⓒ Ⓓ Ⓔ

Print your full name here: _____
(last)   (first)   (middle)

Graduate Management Admission Test

SECTION 1

Time—30 minutes

20 Questions

Directions: In this section solve each problem, using any available space on the page for scratchwork. Then indicate the best of the answer choices given.

Numbers: All numbers used are real numbers.

Figures: Figures that accompany problems in this test are intended to provide information useful in solving the problems. They are drawn as accurately as possible EXCEPT when it is stated in a specific problem that its figure is not drawn to scale. All figures lie in a plane unless otherwise indicated.

1. If Mario was 32 years old 8 years ago, how old was he x years ago?

(A) $x - 40$
(B) $x - 24$
(C) $40 - x$
(D) $24 - x$
(E) $24 + x$

2. Running at the same constant rate, 6 identical machines can produce a total of 270 bottles per minute. At this rate, how many bottles could 10 such machines produce in 4 minutes?

(A)   648
(B) 1,800
(C) 2,700
(D) 10,800
(E) 64,800

3.   NOT SCORED

4. Three business partners, Q, R, and S, agree to divide their total profit for a certain year in the ratios $2 : 5 : 8$, respectively. If Q's share was \$4,000, what was the total profit of the business partners for the year?

(A) \$26,000
(B) \$30,000
(C) \$52,000
(D) \$60,000
(E) \$300,000

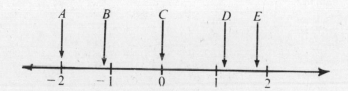

5. Of the five coordinates associated with points A, B, C, D, and E on the number line above, which has the greatest absolute value?

(A) A
(B) B
(C) C
(D) D
(E) E

GO ON TO THE NEXT PAGE.

6. A restaurant meal cost $35.50 and there was no tax. If the tip was more than 10 percent but less than 15 percent of the cost of the meal, then the total amount paid must have been between

(A) $40 and $42
(B) $39 and $41
(C) $38 and $40
(D) $37 and $39
(E) $36 and $37

7. Harriet wants to put up fencing around three sides of her rectangular yard and leave a side of 20 feet unfenced. If the yard has an area of 680 square feet, how many feet of fencing does she need?

(A) 34
(B) 40
(C) 68
(D) 88
(E) 102

8. If $u > t$, $r > q$, $s > t$, and $t > r$, which of the following must be true?

   I. $u > s$
  II. $s > q$
 III. $u > r$

(A) I only
(B) II only
(C) III only
(D) I and II
(E) II and III

9. Increasing the original price of an article by 15 percent and then increasing the new price by 15 percent is equivalent to increasing the original price by

(A) 32.25%
(B) 31.00%
(C) 30.25%
(D) 30.00%
(E) 22.50%

10. If k is an integer and 0.0010101×10^k is greater than 1,000, what is the least possible value of k?

(A) 2
(B) 3
(C) 4
(D) 5
(E) 6

GO ON TO THE NEXT PAGE.

11. If $\left(b - 3\right)\left(4 + \dfrac{2}{b}\right) = 0$ and $b \neq 3$, then $b =$

(A) -8

(B) -2

(C) $-\dfrac{1}{2}$

(D) $\dfrac{1}{2}$

(E) 2

12. In a weight-lifting competition, the total weight of Joe's two lifts was 750 pounds. If twice the weight of his first lift was 300 pounds more than the weight of his second lift, what was the weight, in pounds, of his <u>first</u> lift?

(A) 225
(B) 275
(C) 325
(D) 350
(E) 400

13. One hour after Yolanda started walking from X to Y, a distance of 45 miles, Bob started walking along the same road from Y to X. If Yolanda's walking rate was 3 miles per hour and Bob's was 4 miles per hour, how many miles had Bob walked when they met?

(A) 24
(B) 23
(C) 22
(D) 21
(E) 19.5

14. The average (arithmetic mean) of 6 numbers is 8.5. When one number is discarded, the average of the remaining numbers becomes 7.2. What is the discarded number?

(A) 7.8
(B) 9.8
(C) 10.0
(D) 12.4
(E) 15.0

GO ON TO THE NEXT PAGE.

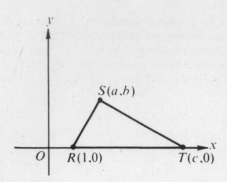

15. In the rectangular coordinate system above, the area of $\triangle RST$ is

(A) $\dfrac{bc}{2}$

(B) $\dfrac{b(c-1)}{2}$

(C) $\dfrac{c(b-1)}{2}$

(D) $\dfrac{a(c-1)}{2}$

(E) $\dfrac{c(a-1)}{2}$

16. Which of the following equations has a root in common with $x^2 - 6x + 5 = 0$?

(A) $x^2 + 1 = 0$
(B) $x^2 - x - 2 = 0$
(C) $x^2 - 10x - 5 = 0$
(D) $2x^2 - 2 = 0$
(E) $x^2 - 2x - 3 = 0$

17. One inlet pipe fills an empty tank in 5 hours. A second inlet pipe fills the same tank in 3 hours. If both pipes are used together, how long will it take to fill $\dfrac{2}{3}$ of the tank?

(A) $\dfrac{8}{15}$ hr

(B) $\dfrac{3}{4}$ hr

(C) $\dfrac{5}{4}$ hr

(D) $\dfrac{15}{8}$ hr

(E) $\dfrac{8}{3}$ hr

GO ON TO THE NEXT PAGE.

18. A total of 40 brand X television sets and 80 brand Y television sets were purchased for a motel chain. If the price of each brand Y set was twice the price of each brand X set, what percent of the total bill was the price of a brand Y set?

(A) 0.25%
(B) 0.5%
(C) 0.625%
(D) 0.833%
(E) 1.0%

19. Ben and Ann are among 7 contestants from which 4 semifinalists are to be selected. Of the different possible selections, how many contain neither Ben nor Ann?

(A) 5
(B) 6
(C) 7
(D) 14
(E) 21

20. How many positive integers k are there such that $100k$ is a factor of $(2^2)(3)(5^3)$?

(A) None
(B) One
(C) Two
(D) Three
(E) Four

STOP

IF YOU FINISH BEFORE TIME IS CALLED, YOU MAY CHECK YOUR WORK ON THIS SECTION ONLY. DO NOT TURN TO ANY OTHER SECTION IN THE TEST.

SECTION 2
Time — 30 minutes

25 Questions

<u>Directions:</u> Each passage in this group is followed by questions based on its content. After reading a passage, choose the best answer to each question and fill in the corresponding oval on the answer sheet. Answer all questions following a passage on the basis of what is <u>stated</u> or <u>implied</u> in that passage.

Caffeine, the stimulant in coffee, has been called "the most widely used psychoactive substance on Earth." Snyder, Daly, and Bruns have recently proposed that caffeine affects behavior by countering the activity in the human brain of a naturally occurring chemical called adenosine. Adenosine normally depresses neuron firing in many areas of the brain. It apparently does this by inhibiting the release of neurotransmitters, chemicals that carry nerve impulses from one neuron to the next. Like many other agents that affect neuron firing, adenosine must first bind to specific receptors on neuronal membranes. There are at least two classes of these receptors, which have been designated A_1 and A_2. Snyder et al propose that caffeine, which is structurally similar to adenosine, is able to bind to both types of receptors, which prevents adenosine from attaching there and allows the neurons to fire more readily than they otherwise would.

For many years, caffeine's effects have been attributed to its inhibition of the production of phosphodiesterase, an enzyme that breaks down the chemical called cyclic AMP. A number of neurotransmitters exert their effects by first increasing cyclic AMP concentrations in target neurons. Therefore, prolonged periods at the elevated concentrations, as might be brought about by a phosphodiesterase inhibitor, could lead to a greater amount of neuron firing and, consequently, to behavioral stimulation. But Snyder et al point out that the caffeine concentrations needed to inhibit the production of phosphodiesterase in the brain are much higher than those that produce stimulation. Moreover, other compounds that block phosphodiesterase's activity are not stimulants.

To buttress their case that caffeine acts instead by preventing adenosine binding, Snyder et al compared the stimulatory effects of a series of caffeine derivatives with their ability to dislodge adenosine from its receptors in the brains of mice. "In general," they reported, "the ability of the compounds to compete at the receptors correlates with their ability to stimulate locomotion in the mouse; i.e., the higher their capacity to bind at the receptors, the higher their ability to stimulate locomotion." Theophylline, a close structural relative of caffeine and the major stimulant in tea, was one of the most effective compounds in both regards.

There were some apparent exceptions to the general correlation observed between adenosine-receptor binding and stimulation. One of these was a compound called 3-isobutyl-1-methylxanthine (IBMX), which bound very well but actually depressed mouse locomotion. Snyder et al suggest that this is not a major stumbling block to their hypothesis. The problem is that the compound has mixed effects in the brain, a not unusual occurrence with psychoactive drugs. Even caffeine, which is generally known only for its stimulatory effects, displays this property, depressing mouse locomotion at very low concentrations and stimulating it at higher ones.

1. The primary purpose of the passage is to

(A) discuss a plan for investigation of a phenomenon that is not yet fully understood
(B) present two explanations of a phenomenon and reconcile the differences between them
(C) summarize two theories and suggest a third theory that overcomes the problems encountered in the first two
(D) describe an alternative hypothesis and provide evidence and arguments that support it
(E) challenge the validity of a theory by exposing the inconsistencies and contradictions in it

2. Which of the following, if true, would most weaken the theory proposed by Snyder et al?

(A) At very low concentrations in the human brain, both caffeine and theophylline tend to have depressive rather than stimulatory effects on human behavior.
(B) The ability of caffeine derivatives at very low concentrations to dislodge adenosine from its receptors in mouse brains correlates well with their ability to stimulate mouse locomotion at these low concentrations.
(C) The concentration of cyclic AMP in target neurons in the human brain that leads to increased neuron firing can be produced by several different phosphodiesterase inhibitors in addition to caffeine.
(D) The concentration of caffeine required to dislodge adenosine from its receptors in the human brain is much greater than the concentration that produces behavioral stimulation in humans.
(E) The concentration of IBMX required to dislodge adenosine from its receptors in mouse brains is much smaller than the concentration that stimulates locomotion in the mouse.

GO ON TO THE NEXT PAGE.

3. According to Snyder et al, caffeine differs from adenosine in that caffeine

(A) stimulates behavior in the mouse and in humans, whereas adenosine stimulates behavior in humans only

(B) has mixed effects in the brain, whereas adenosine has only a stimulatory effect

(C) increases cyclic AMP concentrations in target neurons, whereas adenosine decreases such concentrations

(D) permits release of neurotransmitters when it is bound to adenosine receptors, whereas adenosine inhibits such release

(E) inhibits both neuron firing and the production of phosphodiesterase when there is a sufficient concentration in the brain, whereas adenosine inhibits only neuron firing

4. In response to experimental results concerning IBMX, Snyder et al contended that it is not uncommon for psychoactive drugs to have

(A) mixed effects in the brain

(B) inhibitory effects on enzymes in the brain

(C) close structural relationships with caffeine

(D) depressive effects on mouse locomotion

(E) the ability to dislodge caffeine from receptors in the brain

5. The passage suggests that Snyder et al believe that if the older theory concerning caffeine's effects were correct, which of the following would have to be the case?

I. All neurotransmitters would increase the short-term concentration of cyclic AMP in target neurons.

II. Substances other than caffeine that inhibit the production of phosphodiesterase would be stimulants.

III. All concentration levels of caffeine that are high enough to produce stimulation would also inhibit the production of phosphodiesterase.

(A) I only

(B) I and II only

(C) I and III only

(D) II and III only

(E) I, II, and III

6. According to Snyder et al, all of the following compounds can bind to specific receptors in the brain EXCEPT

(A) IBMX

(B) caffeine

(C) adenosine

(D) theophylline

(E) phosphodiesterase

7. Snyder et al suggest that caffeine's ability to bind to A_1 and A_2 receptors can be at least partially attributed to which of the following?

(A) The chemical relationship between caffeine and phosphodiesterase

(B) The structural relationship between caffeine and adenosine

(C) The structural similarity between caffeine and neurotransmitters

(D) The ability of caffeine to stimulate behavior

(E) The natural occurrence of caffeine and adenosine in the brain

8. The author quotes Snyder et al in lines 38-43 most probably in order to

(A) reveal some of the assumptions underlying their theory

(B) summarize a major finding of their experiments

(C) point out that their experiments were limited to the mouse

(D) indicate that their experiments resulted only in general correlations

(E) refute the objections made by supporters of the older theory

9. The last paragraph of the passage performs which of the following functions?

(A) Describes a disconfirming experimental result and reports the explanation given by Snyder et al in an attempt to reconcile this result with their theory.

(B) Specifies the basis for the correlation observed by Snyder et al and presents an explanation in an attempt to make the correlation consistent with the operation of psychoactive drugs other than caffeine.

(C) Elaborates the description of the correlation observed by Snyder et al and suggests an additional explanation in an attempt to make the correlation consistent with the older theory.

(D) Reports inconsistent experimental data and describes the method Snyder et al will use to reanalyze this data.

(E) Provides an example of the hypothesis proposed by Snyder et al and relates this example to caffeine's properties.

GO ON TO THE NEXT PAGE.

Archaeology as a profession faces two major problems. First, it is the poorest of the poor. Only paltry sums are available for excavating and even less is available for publishing the results and preserving the sites
Line
(5) once excavated. Yet archaeologists deal with priceless objects every day. Second, there is the problem of illegal excavation, resulting in museum-quality pieces being sold to the highest bidder.

I would like to make an outrageous suggestion that
(10) would at one stroke provide funds for archaeology and reduce the amount of illegal digging. I would propose that scientific archaeological expeditions and governmental authorities sell excavated artifacts on the open market. Such sales would provide substantial funds for
(15) the excavation and preservation of archaeological sites and the publication of results. At the same time, they would break the illegal excavator's grip on the market, thereby decreasing the inducement to engage in illegal activities.

(20) You might object that professionals excavate to acquire knowledge, not money. Moreover, ancient artifacts are part of our global cultural heritage, which should be available for all to appreciate, not sold to the highest bidder. I agree. Sell nothing that has unique
(25) artistic merit or scientific value. But, you might reply, everything that comes out of the ground has scientific value. Here we part company. Theoretically, you may be correct in claiming that every artifact has potential scientific value. Practically, you are wrong.

(30) I refer to the thousands of pottery vessels and ancient lamps that are essentially duplicates of one another. In one small excavation in Cyprus, archaeologists recently uncovered 2,000 virtually indistinguishable small jugs in a single courtyard. Even precious royal seal impressions
(35) known as *l'melekh* handles have been found in abundance—more than 4,000 examples so far.

The basements of museums are simply not large enough to store the artifacts that are likely to be discovered in the future. There is not enough money even to
(40) catalogue the finds; as a result, they cannot be found again and become as inaccessible as if they had never been discovered. Indeed, with the help of a computer, sold artifacts could be more accessible than are the pieces stored in bulging museum basements. Prior to
(45) sale, each could be photographed and the list of the purchasers could be maintained on the computer. A purchaser could even be required to agree to return the piece if it should become needed for scientific purposes.

It would be unrealistic to suggest that illegal digging
(50) would stop if artifacts were sold on the open market. But the demand for the clandestine product would be substantially reduced. Who would want an unmarked pot when another was available whose provenance was known, and that was dated stratigraphically by the professional archaeologist who excavated it?

10. The primary purpose of the passage is to propose

(A) an alternative to museum display of artifacts
(B) a way to curb illegal digging while benefiting the archaeological profession
(C) a way to distinguish artifacts with scientific value from those that have no such value
(D) the governmental regulation of archaeological sites
(E) a new system for cataloguing duplicate artifacts

11. The author implies that all of the following statements about duplicate artifacts are true EXCEPT:

(A) A market for such artifacts already exists.
(B) Such artifacts seldom have scientific value.
(C) There is likely to be a continuing supply of such artifacts.
(D) Museums are well supplied with examples of such artifacts.
(E) Such artifacts frequently exceed in quality those already catalogued in museum collections.

12. Which of the following is mentioned in the passage as a disadvantage of storing artifacts in museum basements?

(A) Museum officials rarely allow scholars access to such artifacts.
(B) Space that could be better used for display is taken up for storage.
(C) Artifacts discovered in one excavation often become separated from each other.
(D) Such artifacts are often damaged by variations in temperature and humidity.
(E) Such artifacts often remain uncatalogued and thus cannot be located once they are put in storage.

GO ON TO THE NEXT PAGE.

13. The author mentions the excavation in Cyprus (lines 31-34) to emphasize which of the following points?

    (A) Ancient lamps and pottery vessels are less valuable, although more rare, than royal seal impressions.
    (B) Artifacts that are very similar to each other present cataloguing difficulties to archaeologists.
    (C) Artifacts that are not uniquely valuable, and therefore could be sold, are available in large quantities.
    (D) Cyprus is the most important location for unearthing large quantities of salable artifacts.
    (E) Illegal sales of duplicate artifacts are widespread, particularly on the island of Cyprus.

14. The author's argument concerning the effect of the official sale of duplicate artifacts on illegal excavation is based on which of the following assumptions?

    (A) Prospective purchasers would prefer to buy authenticated artifacts.
    (B) The price of illegally excavated artifacts would rise.
    (C) Computers could be used to trace sold artifacts.
    (D) Illegal excavators would be forced to sell only duplicate artifacts.
    (E) Money gained from selling authenticated artifacts could be used to investigate and prosecute illegal excavators.

15. The author anticipates which of the following initial objections to the adoption of his proposal?

    (A) Museum officials will become unwilling to store artifacts.
    (B) An oversupply of salable artifacts will result and the demand for them will fall.
    (C) Artifacts that would have been displayed in public places will be sold to private collectors.
    (D) Illegal excavators will have an even larger supply of artifacts for resale.
    (E) Counterfeiting of artifacts will become more commonplace.

16. The author implies that which of the following would occur if duplicate artifacts were sold on the open market?

    I. Illegal excavation would eventually cease completely.
    II. Cyprus would become the primary source of marketable duplicate artifacts.
    III. Archaeologists would be able to publish the results of their excavations more frequently than they currently do.

    (A) I only
    (B) III only
    (C) I and II only
    (D) II and III only
    (E) I, II, and III

GO ON TO THE NEXT PAGE.

(This passage is excerpted from material published in 1980.)

Federal efforts to aid minority businesses began in the 1960's when the Small Business Administration (SBA) began making federally guaranteed loans and government-sponsored management and technical assistance
Line
(5) available to minority business enterprises. While this program enabled many minority entrepreneurs to form new businesses, the results were disappointing, since managerial inexperience, unfavorable locations, and capital shortages led to high failure rates. Even 15
(10) years after the program was implemented, minority business receipts were not quite two percent of the national economy's total receipts.

Recently federal policymakers have adopted an approach intended to accelerate development of the
(15) minority business sector by moving away from directly aiding small minority enterprises and toward supporting larger, growth-oriented minority firms through intermediary companies. In this approach, large corporations participate in the development of successful and stable
(20) minority businesses by making use of government-sponsored venture capital. The capital is used by a participating company to establish a Minority Enterprise Small Business Investment Company or MESBIC. The MESBIC then provides capital and guidance to minority
(25) businesses that have potential to become future suppliers or customers of the sponsoring company.

MESBIC's are the result of the belief that providing established firms with easier access to relevant management techniques and more job-specific experience, as
(30) well as substantial amounts of capital, gives those firms a greater opportunity to develop sound business foundations than does simply making general management experience and small amounts of capital available. Further, since potential markets for the minority busi
(35) nesses already exist through the sponsoring companies, the minority businesses face considerably less risk in terms of location and market fluctuation. Following early financial and operating problems, sponsoring corporations began to capitalize MESBIC's far above
(40) the legal minimum of $500,000 in order to generate sufficient income and to sustain the quality of management needed. MESBIC's are now emerging as increasingly important financing sources for minority enterprises.
(45) Ironically, MESBIC staffs, which usually consist of Hispanic and Black professionals, tend to approach investments in minority firms more pragmatically than do many MESBIC directors, who are usually senior managers from sponsoring corporations. The latter
(50) often still think mainly in terms of the "social responsibility approach" and thus seem to prefer deals that are riskier and less attractive than normal investment criteria would warrant. Such differences in viewpoint have produced uneasiness among many minority staff members,

(55) who feel that minority entrepreneurs and businesses should be judged by established business considerations. These staff members believe their point of view is closer to the original philosophy of MESBIC's and they are concerned that, unless a more prudent course is fol
(60) lowed, MESBIC directors may revert to policies likely to re-create the disappointing results of the original SBA approach.

17. Which of the following best states the central idea of the passage?

   (A) The use of MESBIC's for aiding minority entrepreneurs seems to have greater potential for success than does the original SBA approach.
   (B) There is a crucial difference in point of view between the staff and directors of some MESBIC's.
   (C) After initial problems with management and marketing, minority businesses have begun to expand at a steady rate.
   (D) Minority entrepreneurs wishing to form new businesses now have several equally successful federal programs on which to rely.
   (E) For the first time since 1960, large corporations are making significant contributions to the development of minority businesses.

18. According to the passage, the MESBIC approach differs from the SBA approach in that MESBIC's

   (A) seek federal contracts to provide markets for minority businesses
   (B) encourage minority businesses to provide markets for other minority businesses
   (C) attempt to maintain a specified rate of growth in the minority business sector
   (D) rely on the participation of large corporations to finance minority businesses
   (E) select minority businesses on the basis of their location

19. Which of the following does the author cite to support the conclusion that the results of the SBA program were disappointing?

   (A) The small number of new minority enterprises formed as a result of the program
   (B) The small number of minority enterprises that took advantage of the management and technical assistance offered under the program
   (C) The small percentage of the nation's business receipts earned by minority enterprises following the program's implementation
   (D) The small percentage of recipient minority enterprises that were able to repay federally guaranteed loans made under the program
   (E) The small number of minority enterprises that chose to participate in the program

GO ON TO THE NEXT PAGE.

20. Which of the following statements about the SBA program can be inferred from the passage?

   (A) The maximum term for loans made to recipient businesses was 15 years.
   (B) Business loans were considered to be more useful to recipient businesses than was management and technical assistance.
   (C) The anticipated failure rate for recipient businesses was significantly lower than the rate that actually resulted.
   (D) Recipient businesses were encouraged to relocate to areas more favorable for business development.
   (E) The capitalization needs of recipient businesses were assessed and then provided for adequately.

21. Based on information in the passage, which of the following would be indicative of the pragmatism of MESBIC staff members?

   I. A reluctance to invest in minority businesses that show marginal expectations of return on the investments
   II. A desire to invest in minority businesses that produce goods and services likely to be of use to the sponsoring company
   III. A belief that the minority business sector is best served by investing primarily in newly established businesses

   (A) I only
   (B) III only
   (C) I and II only
   (D) II and III only
   (E) I, II, and III

22. The author refers to the "financial and operating problems" (line 38) encountered by MESBIC's primarily in order to

   (A) broaden the scope of the discussion to include the legal considerations of funding MESBIC's through sponsoring companies
   (B) call attention to the fact that MESBIC's must receive adequate funding in order to function effectively
   (C) show that sponsoring companies were willing to invest only $500,000 of government-sponsored venture capital in the original MESBIC's
   (D) compare SBA and MESBIC limits on minimum funding
   (E) refute suggestions that MESBIC's have been only marginally successful

23. The author's primary objective in the passage is to

   (A) disprove the view that federal efforts to aid minority businesses have been ineffective
   (B) explain how federal efforts to aid minority businesses have changed since the 1960's
   (C) establish a direct link between the federal efforts to aid minority businesses made before the 1960's and those made in the 1980's
   (D) analyze the basis for the belief that job-specific experience is more useful to minority businesses than is general management experience
   (E) argue that the "social responsibility approach" to aiding minority businesses is superior to any other approach

24. It can be inferred from the passage that the attitude of some MESBIC staff members toward the investments preferred by some MESBIC directors can best be described as

   (A) defensive
   (B) resigned
   (C) indifferent
   (D) shocked
   (E) disapproving

25. The passage provides information that would answer which of the following questions?

   (A) What was the average annual amount, in dollars, of minority business receipts before the SBA strategy was implemented?
   (B) What locations are considered to be unfavorable for minority businesses?
   (C) What is the current success rate for minority businesses that are capitalized by MESBIC's?
   (D) How has the use of federal funding for minority businesses changed since the 1960's ?
   (E) How do minority businesses apply to participate in a MESBIC program?

STOP

IF YOU FINISH BEFORE TIME IS CALLED, YOU MAY CHECK YOUR WORK ON THIS SECTION ONLY.
DO NOT TURN TO ANY OTHER SECTION IN THE TEST.

SECTION 3

Time—30 minutes

25 Questions

Directions: Each of the data sufficiency problems below consists of a question and two statements, labeled (1) and (2), in which certain data are given. You have to decide whether the data given in the statements are <u>sufficient</u> for answering the question. Using the data given in the statements <u>plus</u> your knowledge of mathematics and everyday facts (such as the number of days in July or the meaning of <u>counterclockwise</u>), you are to fill in oval

    A   if statement (1) ALONE is sufficient, but statement (2) alone is not sufficient to answer the question asked;

    B   if statement (2) ALONE is sufficient, but statement (1) alone is not sufficient to answer the question asked;

    C   if BOTH statements (1) and (2) TOGETHER are sufficient to answer the question asked, but NEITHER statement ALONE is sufficient;

    D   if EACH statement ALONE is sufficient to answer the question asked;

    E   if statements (1) and (2) TOGETHER are NOT sufficient to answer the question asked, and additional data specific to the problem are needed.

Numbers: All numbers used are real numbers.

Figures: A figure in a data sufficiency problem will conform to the information given in the question, but will not necessarily conform to the additional information given in statements (1) and (2).

You may assume that lines shown as straight are straight and that angle measures are greater than zero.

You may assume that the positions of points, angles, regions, etc., exist in the order shown.

All figures lie in a plane unless otherwise indicated.

Example:

In $\triangle PQR$, what is the value of x?

(1) $PQ = PR$

(2) $y = 40$

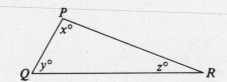

Explanation: According to statement (1), $PQ = PR$; therefore, $\triangle PQR$ is isosceles and $y = z$. Since $x + y + z = 180$, $x + 2y = 180$. Since statement (1) does not give a value for y, you cannot answer the question using statement (1) by itself. According to statement (2), $y = 40$; therefore, $x + z = 140$. Since statement (2) does not give a value for z, you cannot answer the question using statement (2) by itself. Using both statements together, you can find y and z; therefore, you can find x, and the answer to the problem is C.

GO ON TO THE NEXT PAGE.

A   Statement (1) ALONE is sufficient, but statement (2) alone is not sufficient.
B   Statement (2) ALONE is sufficient, but statement (1) alone is not sufficient.
C   BOTH statements TOGETHER are sufficient, but NEITHER statement ALONE is sufficient.
D   EACH statement ALONE is sufficient.
E   Statements (1) and (2) TOGETHER are NOT sufficient.

1. At a certain picnic, each of the guests was served either a single scoop or a double scoop of ice cream. How many of the guests were served a double scoop of ice cream?

(1) At the picnic, 60 percent of the guests were served a double scoop of ice cream.

(2) A total of 120 scoops of ice cream were served to all the guests at the picnic.

2. By what percent was the price of a certain candy bar increased?

(1) The price of the candy bar was increased by 5 cents.

(2) The price of the candy bar after the increase was 45 cents.

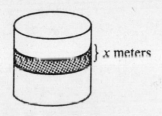
} x meters

3. A circular tub has a band painted around its circumference, as shown above. What is the surface area of this painted band?

(1) $x = 0.5$

(2) The height of the tub is 1 meter.

4. Is it true that $a > b$?

(1) $2a > 2b$

(2) $a + c > b + c$

5. A thoroughly blended biscuit mix includes only flour and baking powder. What is the ratio of the number of grams of baking powder to the number of grams of flour in the mix?

(1) Exactly 9.9 grams of flour is contained in 10 grams of the mix.

(2) Exactly 0.3 gram of baking powder is contained in 30 grams of the mix.

GO ON TO THE NEXT PAGE.

A Statement (1) ALONE is sufficient, but statement (2) alone is not sufficient.
B Statement (2) ALONE is sufficient, but statement (1) alone is not sufficient.
C BOTH statements TOGETHER are sufficient, but NEITHER statement ALONE is sufficient.
D EACH statement ALONE is sufficient.
E Statements (1) and (2) TOGETHER are NOT sufficient.

6. If a real estate agent received a commission of 6 percent of the selling price of a certain house, what was the selling price of the house?

(1) The selling price minus the real estate agent's commission was $84,600.

(2) The selling price was 250 percent of the original purchase price of $36,000.

7. What is the value of $|x|$?

(1) $x = -|x|$
(2) $x^2 = 4$

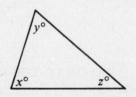

8. What is the value of z in the triangle above?

(1) $x + y = 139$
(2) $y + z = 108$

9. A certain bakery sells rye bread in 16-ounce loaves and 24-ounce loaves, and all loaves of the same size sell for the same price per loaf regardless of the number of loaves purchased. What is the price of a 24-ounce loaf of rye bread in this bakery?

(1) The total price of a 16-ounce loaf and a 24-ounce loaf of this bread is $2.40.

(2) The total price of two 16-ounce loaves and one 24-ounce loaf of this bread is $3.40.

10. If $\dfrac{\sqrt{x}}{y} = n$, what is the value of x ?

(1) $yn = 10$
(2) $y = 40$ and $n = \dfrac{1}{4}$

GO ON TO THE NEXT PAGE.

A   Statement (1) ALONE is sufficient, but statement (2) alone is not sufficient.
B   Statement (2) ALONE is sufficient, but statement (1) alone is not sufficient.
C   BOTH statements TOGETHER are sufficient, but NEITHER statement ALONE is sufficient.
D   EACH statement ALONE is sufficient.
E   Statements (1) and (2) TOGETHER are NOT sufficient.

11. If m and n are consecutive positive integers, is m greater than n?

   (1) $m - 1$ and $n + 1$ are consecutive positive integers.

   (2) m is an even integer.

12. Paula and Sandy were among those people who sold raffle tickets to raise money for Club X. If Paula and Sandy sold a total of 100 of the tickets, how many of the tickets did Paula sell?

   (1) Sandy sold $\frac{2}{3}$ as many of the raffle tickets as Paula did.

   (2) Sandy sold 8 percent of all the raffle tickets sold for Club X.

13. Is the integer n odd?

   (1) n is divisible by 3.

   (2) n is divisible by 5.

$3.2\square\triangle 6$

14. If $\square$ and $\triangle$ each represent single digits in the decimal above, what digit does $\square$ represent?

   (1) When the decimal is rounded to the nearest tenth, 3.2 is the result.

   (2) When the decimal is rounded to the nearest hundredth, 3.24 is the result.

15. A certain company currently has how many employees?

   (1) If 3 additional employees are hired by the company and all of the present employees remain, there will be at least 20 employees in the company.

   (2) If no additional employees are hired by the company and 3 of the present employees resign, there will be fewer than 15 employees in the company.

GO ON TO THE NEXT PAGE.

A   Statement (1) ALONE is sufficient, but statement (2) alone is not sufficient.
B   Statement (2) ALONE is sufficient, but statement (1) alone is not sufficient.
C   BOTH statements TOGETHER are sufficient, but NEITHER statement ALONE is sufficient.
D   EACH statement ALONE is sufficient.
E   Statements (1) and (2) TOGETHER are NOT sufficient.

16. If x is equal to one of the numbers $\frac{1}{4}$, $\frac{3}{8}$, or $\frac{2}{5}$, what is the value of x?

(1) $\frac{1}{4} < x < \frac{1}{2}$

(2) $\frac{1}{3} < x < \frac{3}{5}$

17. If a, b, and c are integers, is $a - b + c$ greater than $a + b - c$?

(1) b is negative.

(2) c is positive.

18. If $x + 2y + 1 = y - x$, what is the value of x?

(1) $y^2 = 9$

(2) $y = 3$

19. If n is an integer, then n is divisible by how many positive integers?

(1) n is the product of two different prime numbers.

(2) n and 2^3 are each divisible by the same number of positive integers.

20. How many miles long is the route from Houghton to Callahan?

(1) It will take 1 hour less time to travel the entire route at an average rate of 55 miles per hour than at an average rate of 50 miles per hour.

(2) It will take 11 hours to travel the first half of the route at an average rate of 25 miles per hour.

GO ON TO THE NEXT PAGE.

A   Statement (1) ALONE is sufficient, but statement (2) alone is not sufficient.
B   Statement (2) ALONE is sufficient, but statement (1) alone is not sufficient.
C   BOTH statements TOGETHER are sufficient, but NEITHER statement ALONE is sufficient.
D   EACH statement ALONE is sufficient.
E   Statements (1) and (2) TOGETHER are NOT sufficient.

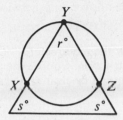

21. What is the circumference of the circle above?

   (1) The length of arc XYZ is 18.

   (2) $r = s$

22. If p, q, r, and s are nonzero numbers, is
    $(p - 1)(q - 2)^2(r - 3)^3(s - 4)^4 \geqq 0$?

   (1) $q > 2$ and $s > 4$

   (2) $p > 1$ and $r > 3$

23. If $\circledast$ denotes a mathematical operation, does
    $x \circledast y = y \circledast x$ for all x and y ?

   (1) For all x and y, $x \circledast y = 2(x^2 + y^2)$.

   (2) For all y, $0 \circledast y = 2y^2$.

24. All trainees in a certain aviator training program
    must take both a written test and a flight test. If
    70 percent of the trainees passed the written test,
    and 80 percent of the trainees passed the flight test,
    what percent of the trainees passed both tests?

   (1) 10 percent of the trainees did not pass either
        test.

   (2) 20 percent of the trainees passed only the flight
        test.

25. If n is an integer, is $\frac{n}{15}$ an integer?

   (1) $\frac{3n}{15}$ is an integer.

   (2) $\frac{8n}{15}$ is an integer.

STOP

IF YOU FINISH BEFORE TIME IS CALLED, YOU MAY CHECK YOUR WORK ON THIS SECTION ONLY.
DO NOT TURN TO ANY OTHER SECTION IN THE TEST.

SECTION 4

Time—30 minutes

25 Questions

<u>Directions:</u> In each of the following sentences, some part of the sentence or the entire sentence is underlined. Beneath each sentence you will find five ways of phrasing the underlined part. The first of these repeats the original; the other four are different. If you think the original is better than any of the alternatives, choose answer A; otherwise, choose one of the others. Select the best version and fill in the corresponding oval on your answer sheet.

This is a test of correctness and effectiveness of expression. In choosing answers, follow the requirements of standard written English; that is, pay attention to grammar, choice of words, and sentence construction. Choose the answer that expresses most effectively what is presented in the original sentence; this answer should be clear and exact, without awkwardness, ambiguity, or redundancy.

1. The Wallerstein study indicates that even after a decade young men and women still experience some of the effects of a divorce <u>occurring when a child</u>.

   (A) occurring when a child
   (B) occurring when children
   (C) that occurred when a child
   (D) that occurred when they were children
   (E) that has occurred as each was a child

2. Since 1981, when the farm depression began, the number of acres overseen by professional farm-management companies <u>have grown from 48 million to nearly 59 million, an area that is about Colorado's size.</u>

   (A) have grown from 48 million to nearly 59 million, an area that is about Colorado's size
   (B) have grown from 48 million to nearly 59 million, about the size of Colorado
   (C) has grown from 48 million to nearly 59 million, an area about the size of Colorado
   (D) has grown from 48 million up to nearly 59 million, an area about the size of Colorado's
   (E) has grown from 48 million up to nearly 59 million, about Colorado's size

3. Some bat caves, like honeybee hives, have residents that take on different duties such as defending the entrance, <u>acting as sentinels and to sound a warning</u> at the approach of danger, and scouting outside the cave for new food and roosting sites.

   (A) acting as sentinels and to sound
   (B) acting as sentinels and sounding
   (C) to act as sentinels and sound
   (D) to act as sentinels and to sound
   (E) to act as a sentinel sounding

4. The only way for growers to salvage frozen citrus is <u>to process them quickly into juice concentrate before they rot when warmer weather returns.</u>

   (A) to process them quickly into juice concentrate before they rot when warmer weather returns
   (B) if they are quickly processed into juice concentrate before warmer weather returns to rot them
   (C) for them to be processed quickly into juice concentrate before the fruit rots when warmer weather returns
   (D) if the fruit is quickly processed into juice concentrate before they rot when warmer weather returns
   (E) to have it quickly processed into juice concentrate before warmer weather returns and rots the fruit

GO ON TO THE NEXT PAGE.

5. Carbon-14 dating reveals that the megalithic monuments in Brittany are nearly 2,000 years <u>as old as any of their supposed</u> Mediterranean predecessors.

(A) as old as any of their supposed
(B) older than any of their supposed
(C) as old as their supposed
(D) older than any of their supposedly
(E) as old as their supposedly

6. In virtually all types of tissue in every animal species, dioxin induces the production of enzymes that are the organism's <u>trying to metabolize, or render harmless, the chemical that is irritating it.</u>

(A) trying to metabolize, or render harmless, the chemical that is irritating it
(B) trying that it metabolize, or render harmless, the chemical irritant
(C) attempt to try to metabolize, or render harmless, such a chemical irritant
(D) attempt to try and metabolize, or render harmless, the chemical irritating it
(E) attempt to metabolize, or render harmless, the chemical irritant

7. Dr. Hakuta's research among Hispanic children in the United States indicates that the more the children use both Spanish and English, <u>their intellectual advantage is greater in skills underlying reading ability and nonverbal logic.</u>

(A) their intellectual advantage is greater in skills underlying reading ability and nonverbal logic
(B) their intellectual advantage is the greater in skills underlaying reading ability and nonverbal logic
(C) the greater their intellectual advantage in skills underlying reading ability and nonverbal logic
(D) in skills that underlay reading ability and nonverbal logic, their intellectual advantage is the greater
(E) in skills underlying reading ability and nonverbal logic, the greater intellectual advantage is theirs

8. Lacking information about energy use, people tend to overestimate the amount of energy used by <u>equipment, such as lights, that are visible and must be turned on and off and underestimate that</u> used by unobtrusive equipment, such as water heaters.

(A) equipment, such as lights, that are visible and must be turned on and off and underestimate that
(B) equipment, such as lights, that are visible and must be turned on and off and underestimate it when
(C) equipment, such as lights, that is visible and must be turned on and off and underestimate it when
(D) visible equipment, such as lights, that must be turned on and off and underestimate that
(E) visible equipment, such as lights, that must be turned on and off and underestimate it when

9. Astronomers at the Palomar Observatory have discovered a distant supernova explosion, one <u>that they believe is</u> a type previously unknown to science.

(A) that they believe is
(B) that they believe it to be
(C) they believe that it is of
(D) they believe that is
(E) they believe to be of

GO ON TO THE NEXT PAGE.

10. However much United States voters may agree that there is waste in government and that the government as a whole spends beyond its means, it is difficult to find broad support for a movement toward a minimal state.

(A) However much United States voters may agree that

(B) Despite the agreement among United States voters to the fact

(C) Although United States voters agree

(D) Even though United States voters may agree

(E) There is agreement among United States voters that

11. Based on accounts of various ancient writers, scholars have painted a sketchy picture of the activities of an all-female cult that, perhaps as early as the sixth century B.C., worshipped a goddess known in Latin as Bona Dea, "the good goddess."

(A) Based on accounts of various ancient writers

(B) Basing it on various ancient writers' accounts

(C) With accounts of various ancient writers used for a basis

(D) By the accounts of various ancient writers they used

(E) Using accounts of various ancient writers

12. Formulas for cash flow and the ratio of debt to equity do not apply to new small businesses in the same way as they do to established big businesses, because they are growing and are seldom in equilibrium.

(A) Formulas for cash flow and the ratio of debt to equity do not apply to new small businesses in the same way as they do to established big businesses, because they are growing and are seldom in equilibrium.

(B) Because they are growing and are seldom in equilibrium, formulas for cash flow and the ratio of debt to equity do not apply to new small businesses in the same way as they do to established big businesses.

(C) Because they are growing and are seldom in equilibrium, new small businesses are not subject to the same applicability of formulas for cash flow and the ratio of debt to equity as established big businesses.

(D) Because new small businesses are growing and are seldom in equilibrium, formulas for cash flow and the ratio of debt to equity do not apply to them in the same way as to established big businesses.

(E) New small businesses are not subject to the applicability of formulas for cash flow and the ratio of debt to equity in the same way as established big businesses, because they are growing and are seldom in equilibrium.

13. State officials report that soaring rates of liability insurance have risen to force cutbacks in the operations of everything from local governments and school districts to day-care centers and recreational facilities.

(A) rates of liability insurance have risen to force

(B) rates of liability insurance are a force for

(C) rates for liability insurance are forcing

(D) rises in liability insurance rates are forcing

(E) liability insurance rates have risen to force

GO ON TO THE NEXT PAGE.

14. Paleontologists believe that fragments of a primate jawbone unearthed in Burma and estimated at 40 to 44 million years old provide evidence of a crucial step along the evolutionary path that led to human beings.

    (A) at 40 to 44 million years old provide evidence of
    (B) as being 40 to 44 million years old provides evidence of
    (C) that it is 40 to 44 million years old provides evidence of what was
    (D) to be 40 to 44 million years old provide evidence of
    (E) as 40 to 44 million years old provides evidence of what was

15. In his research paper, Dr. Frosh, medical director of the Payne Whitney Clinic, distinguishes mood swings, which may be violent without their being grounded in mental disease, from genuine manic-depressive psychosis.

    (A) mood swings, which may be violent without their being grounded in mental disease, from genuine manic-depressive psychosis
    (B) mood swings, perhaps violent without being grounded in mental disease, and genuine manic-depressive psychosis
    (C) between mood swings, which may be violent without being grounded in mental disease, and genuine manic-depressive psychosis
    (D) between mood swings, perhaps violent without being grounded in mental disease, from genuine manic-depressive psychosis
    (E) genuine manic-depressive psychosis and mood swings, which may be violent without being grounded in mental disease

16. Unlike a typical automobile loan, which requires a fifteen- to twenty-percent down payment, the lease-loan buyer is not required to make an initial deposit on the new vehicle.

    (A) the lease-loan buyer is not required to make
    (B) with lease-loan buying there is no requirement of
    (C) lease-loan buyers are not required to make
    (D) for the lease-loan buyer there is no requirement of
    (E) a lease-loan does not require the buyer to make

17. Native American burial sites dating back 5,000 years indicate that the residents of Maine at that time were part of a widespread culture of Algonquian-speaking people.

    (A) were part of a widespread culture of Algonquian-speaking people
    (B) had been part of a widespread culture of people who were Algonquian-speaking
    (C) were people who were part of a widespread culture that was Algonquian-speaking
    (D) had been people who were part of a widespread culture that was Algonquian-speaking
    (E) were a people which had been part of a widespread, Algonquian-speaking culture

18. Each of Hemingway's wives—Hadley Richardson, Pauline Pfeiffer, Martha Gelhorn, and Mary Welsh—were strong and interesting women, very different from the often pallid women who populate his novels.

    (A) Each of Hemingway's wives—Hadley Richardson, Pauline Pfeiffer, Martha Gelhorn, and Mary Welsh—were strong and interesting women,
    (B) Hadley Richardson, Pauline Pfeiffer, Martha Gelhorn, and Mary Welsh—each of them Hemingway's wives—were strong and interesting women,
    (C) Hemingway's wives—Hadley Richardson, Pauline Pfeiffer, Martha Gelhorn, and Mary Welsh—were all strong and interesting women,
    (D) Strong and interesting women—Hadley Richardson, Pauline Pfeiffer, Martha Gelhorn, and Mary Welsh—each a wife of Hemingway, was
    (E) Strong and interesting women—Hadley Richardson, Pauline Pfeiffer, Martha Gelhorn, and Mary Welsh—every one of Hemingway's wives were

GO ON TO THE NEXT PAGE.

19. In addition to having more protein than wheat does, the protein in rice is higher quality than that in wheat, with more of the amino acids essential to the human diet.

    (A) the protein in rice is higher quality than that in
    (B) rice has protein of higher quality than that in
    (C) the protein in rice is higher in quality than it is in
    (D) rice protein is higher in quality than it is in
    (E) rice has a protein higher in quality than

20. An array of tax incentives has led to a boom in the construction of new office buildings; so abundant has capital been for commercial real estate that investors regularly scour the country for areas in which to build.

    (A) so abundant has capital been for commercial real estate that
    (B) capital has been so abundant for commercial real estate, so that
    (C) the abundance of capital for commercial real estate has been such,
    (D) such has the abundance of capital been for commercial real estate that
    (E) such has been an abundance of capital for commercial real estate,

21. Defense attorneys have occasionally argued that their clients' misconduct stemmed from a reaction to something ingested, but in attributing criminal or delinquent behavior to some food allergy, the perpetrators are in effect told that they are not responsible for their actions.

    (A) in attributing criminal or delinquent behavior to some food allergy
    (B) if criminal or delinquent behavior is attributed to an allergy to some food
    (C) in attributing behavior that is criminal or delinquent to an allergy to some food
    (D) if some food allergy is attributed as the cause of criminal or delinquent behavior
    (E) in attributing a food allergy as the cause of criminal or delinquent behavior

22. The voluminous personal papers of Thomas Alva Edison reveal that his inventions typically sprang to life not in a flash of inspiration but evolved slowly from previous works.

    (A) sprang to life not in a flash of inspiration but evolved slowly
    (B) sprang to life not in a flash of inspiration but were slowly evolved
    (C) did not spring to life in a flash of inspiration but evolved slowly
    (D) did not spring to life in a flash of inspiration but had slowly evolved
    (E) did not spring to life in a flash of inspiration but they were slowly evolved

23. As more and more people invest their money in savings certificates or money-market funds in order to earn higher interest, they are abandoning traditional low-interest investment havens such as passbook accounts and life insurance policies.

    (A) As more and more people invest their money
    (B) While people have more and more been investing their money
    (C) As money is more and more invested by people
    (D) More and more, when investors put their money
    (E) While, more and more, investors have been putting their money

GO ON TO THE NEXT PAGE.

24. Margaret Courtney-Clarke has traveled to remote dwellings in the Transvaal to photograph the art of Ndebele women, whose murals are brilliantly colored, their geometrical symmetries embellished with old and new iconography and in a style that varies from woman to woman and house to house.

   (A) whose murals are brilliantly colored, their geometrical symmetries embellished with old and new iconography and in a style that varies from woman to woman and house to house

   (B) whose murals are brilliantly colored, their geometrical symmetries are embellished with old and new iconography, and their style is varying among women and houses

   (C) whose murals are brilliantly colored, their geometrical symmetries are embellished with old and new iconography, and they are in styles that vary from woman to woman and house to house

   (D) with murals brilliantly colored, their geometrical symmetries embellished with old and new iconography, and their style varies among women and houses

   (E) with murals that are brilliantly colored, their geometrical symmetries embellished with old and new iconography, and their styles vary among women and houses

25. Florida will gain another quarter-million jobs this year alone, many of them in high-paying fields like electronics and banking, making the state's economy far more diversified than ten years ago.

   (A) high-paying fields like electronics and banking, making the state's economy far more diversified than

   (B) high-paying fields like electronics and banking, and making the state's economy far more diversified than its economy

   (C) high-paying fields such as electronics and banking, to make the state's economy far more diversified than

   (D) such high-paying fields as electronics and banking, making the state's economy far more diversified than it was

   (E) such high-paying fields as electronics and banking, and make the state's economy far more diversified than it was

STOP

IF YOU FINISH BEFORE TIME IS CALLED, YOU MAY CHECK YOUR WORK ON THIS SECTION ONLY. DO NOT TURN TO ANY OTHER SECTION IN THE TEST.

NO TEST MATERIAL ON THIS PAGE

SECTION 5

Time—30 minutes

25 Questions

Directions: In this section solve each problem, using any available space on the page for scratchwork. Then indicate the best of the answer choices given.

Numbers: All numbers used are real numbers.

Figures: Figures that accompany problems in this test are intended to provide information useful in solving the problems. They are drawn as accurately as possible EXCEPT when it is stated in a specific problem that its figure is not drawn to scale. All figures lie in a plane unless otherwise indicated.

1. During the first week of September, a shoe retailer sold 10 pairs of a certain style of oxfords at $35.00 a pair. If, during the second week of September, 15 pairs were sold at the sale price of $27.50 a pair, by what amount did the revenue from weekly sales of these oxfords increase during the second week?

(A) $62.50
(B) $75.00
(C) $112.50
(D) $137.50
(E) $175.00

2. The number $2 - 0.5$ is how many times the number $1 - 0.5$?

(A) 2
(B) 2.5
(C) 3
(D) 3.5
(E) 4

3. If $x = -1$, then $-(x^4 + x^3 + x^2 + x) =$

(A) -10
(B) -4
(C) 0
(D) 4
(E) 10

4. Coins are dropped into a toll box so that the box is being filled at the rate of approximately 2 cubic feet per hour. If the empty rectangular box is 4 feet long, 4 feet wide, and 3 feet deep, approximately how many hours does it take to fill the box?

(A) 4
(B) 8
(C) 16
(D) 24
(E) 48

5. $\left(\dfrac{1}{5}\right)^2 - \left(\dfrac{1}{5}\right)\left(\dfrac{1}{4}\right) =$

(A) $-\dfrac{1}{20}$

(B) $-\dfrac{1}{100}$

(C) $\dfrac{1}{100}$

(D) $\dfrac{1}{20}$

(E) $\dfrac{1}{5}$

GO ON TO THE NEXT PAGE.

6. A club collected exactly $599 from its members. If each member contributed at least $12, what is the greatest number of members the club could have?

(A) 43
(B) 44
(C) 49
(D) 50
(E) 51

7. A union contract specifies a 6 percent salary increase plus a $450 bonus for each employee. For a certain employee, this is equivalent to an 8 percent salary increase. What was this employee's salary before the new contract?

(A) $21,500
(B) $22,500
(C) $23,500
(D) $24,300
(E) $25,000

8. If n is a positive integer and $k + 2 = 3^n$, which of the following could NOT be a value of k?

(A) 1
(B) 4
(C) 7
(D) 25
(E) 79

9. Elena purchased brand X pens for $4.00 apiece and brand Y pens for $2.80 apiece. If Elena purchased a total of 12 of these pens for $42.00, how many brand X pens did she purchase?

(A) 4
(B) 5
(C) 6
(D) 7
(E) 8

GO ON TO THE NEXT PAGE.

10. If the length and width of a rectangular garden plot were each increased by 20 percent, what would be the percent increase in the area of the plot?

(A) 20%
(B) 24%
(C) 36%
(D) 40%
(E) 44%

11. The population of a bacteria culture doubles every 2 minutes. Approximately how many minutes will it take for the population to grow from 1,000 to 500,000 bacteria?

(A) 10
(B) 12
(C) 14
(D) 16
(E) 18

12. When 10 is divided by the positive integer n, the remainder is $n - 4$. Which of the following could be the value of n?

(A) 3
(B) 4
(C) 7
(D) 8
(E) 12

13. For a light that has an intensity of 60 candles at its source, the intensity in candles, S, of the light at a point d feet from the source is given by the formula $S = \dfrac{60k}{d^2}$, where k is a constant. If the intensity of the light is 30 candles at a distance of 2 feet from the source, what is the intensity of the light at a distance of 20 feet from the source?

(A) $\dfrac{3}{10}$ candle

(B) $\dfrac{1}{2}$ candle

(C) $1\dfrac{1}{3}$ candles

(D) 2 candles

(E) 3 candles

GO ON TO THE NEXT PAGE.

14. If x and y are prime numbers, which of the following CANNOT be the sum of x and y?

   (A) 5
   (B) 9
   (C) 13
   (D) 16
   (E) 23

15. Of the 3,600 employees of Company X, $\frac{1}{3}$ are clerical. If the clerical staff were to be reduced by $\frac{1}{3}$, what percent of the total number of the remaining employees would then be clerical?

   (A) 25%
   (B) 22.2%
   (C) 20%
   (D) 12.5%
   (E) 11.1%

16. In which of the following pairs are the two numbers reciprocals of each other?

   I. 3 and $\frac{1}{3}$

   II. $\frac{1}{17}$ and $\frac{-1}{17}$

   III. $\sqrt{3}$ and $\frac{\sqrt{3}}{3}$

   (A) I only
   (B) II only
   (C) I and II
   (D) I and III
   (E) II and III

17. For a certain performance, x tickets for lower-level seats were sold at $10 each and y tickets for balcony seats were sold at $6 each. If there were no other tickets sold and the number of tickets sold for lower-level seats was 3 times the number of tickets sold for balcony seats, which of the following expresses the total number of dollars from ticket sales in terms of x?

   (A) $12x$
   (B) $16x$
   (C) $28x$
   (D) $32x$
   (E) $36x$

GO ON TO THE NEXT PAGE.

18. If the circumference of a circular region is c, which of the following represents the area of that circular region?

(A) $\dfrac{c^2}{2}$

(B) $\dfrac{c^2}{4}$

(C) $\dfrac{c^2}{2\pi}$

(D) $\dfrac{c^2}{4\pi}$

(E) $\dfrac{c^2}{4\pi^2}$

19. Each of the integers from 0 to 9, inclusive, is written on a separate slip of blank paper and the ten slips are dropped into a hat. If the slips are then drawn one at a time without replacement, how many must be drawn to ensure that the numbers on two of the slips drawn will have a sum of 10 ?

(A) Three
(B) Four
(C) Five
(D) Six
(E) Seven

20. In a certain formula, p is directly proportional to s and inversely proportional to r. If $p = 1$ when $r = 0.5$ and $s = 2$, what is the value of p in terms of r and s ?

(A) $\dfrac{s}{r}$

(B) $\dfrac{r}{4s}$

(C) $\dfrac{s}{4r}$

(D) $\dfrac{r}{s}$

(E) $\dfrac{4r}{s}$

STOP

IF YOU FINISH BEFORE TIME IS CALLED, YOU MAY CHECK YOUR WORK ON THIS SECTION ONLY. DO NOT TURN TO ANY OTHER SECTION IN THE TEST.

SECTION 6

Time—30 minutes

20 Questions

Directions: For each question in this section, select the best of the answer choices given.

1. Which of the following best completes the passage below?

In a survey of job applicants, two-fifths admitted to being at least a little dishonest. However, the survey may underestimate the proportion of job applicants who are dishonest, because -------.

(A) some dishonest people taking the survey might have claimed on the survey to be honest
(B) some generally honest people taking the survey might have claimed on the survey to be dishonest
(C) some people who claimed on the survey to be at least a little dishonest may be very dishonest
(D) some people who claimed on the survey to be dishonest may have been answering honestly
(E) some people who are not job applicants are probably at least a little dishonest

Questions 2-3 are based on the following.

The average life expectancy for the United States population as a whole is 73.9 years, but children born in Hawaii will live an average of 77 years, and those born in Louisiana, 71.7 years. If a newlywed couple from Louisiana were to begin their family in Hawaii, therefore, their children would be expected to live longer than would be the case if the family remained in Louisiana.

2. Which of the following, if true, would most seriously weaken the conclusion drawn in the passage?

(A) Insurance company statisticians do not believe that moving to Hawaii will significantly lengthen the average Louisianian's life.
(B) The governor of Louisiana has falsely alleged that statistics for his state are inaccurate.
(C) The longevity ascribed to Hawaii's current population is attributable mostly to genetically determined factors.
(D) Thirty percent of all Louisianians can expect to live longer than 77 years.
(E) Most of the Hawaiian Islands have levels of air pollution well below the national average for the United States.

3. Which of the following statements, if true, would most significantly strengthen the conclusion drawn in the passage?

(A) As population density increases in Hawaii, life expectancy figures for that state are likely to be revised downward.
(B) Environmental factors tending to favor longevity are abundant in Hawaii and less numerous in Louisiana.
(C) Twenty-five percent of all Louisianians who move to Hawaii live longer than 77 years.
(D) Over the last decade, average life expectancy has risen at a higher rate for Louisianians than for Hawaiians.
(E) Studies show that the average life expectancy for Hawaiians who move permanently to Louisiana is roughly equal to that of Hawaiians who remain in Hawaii.

GO ON TO THE NEXT PAGE.

4. Insurance Company X is considering issuing a new policy to cover services required by elderly people who suffer from diseases that afflict the elderly. Premiums for the policy must be low enough to attract customers. Therefore, Company X is concerned that the income from the policies would not be sufficient to pay for the claims that would be made.

Which of the following strategies would be most likely to minimize Company X's losses on the policies?

(A) Attracting middle-aged customers unlikely to submit claims for benefits for many years
(B) Insuring only those individuals who did not suffer any serious diseases as children
(C) Including a greater number of services in the policy than are included in other policies of lower cost
(D) Insuring only those individuals who were rejected by other companies for similar policies
(E) Insuring only those individuals who are wealthy enough to pay for the medical services

5. A program instituted in a particular state allows parents to prepay their children's future college tuition at current rates. The program then pays the tuition annually for the child at any of the state's public colleges in which the child enrolls. Parents should participate in the program as a means of decreasing the cost for their children's college education.

Which of the following, if true, is the most appropriate reason for parents not to participate in the program?

(A) The parents are unsure about which public college in the state the child will attend.
(B) The amount of money accumulated by putting the prepayment funds in an interest-bearing account today will be greater than the total cost of tuition for any of the public colleges when the child enrolls.
(C) The annual cost of tuition at the state's public colleges is expected to increase at a faster rate than the annual increase in the cost of living.
(D) Some of the state's public colleges are contemplating large increases in tuition next year.
(E) The prepayment plan would not cover the cost of room and board at any of the state's public colleges.

6. Company Alpha buys free-travel coupons from people who are awarded the coupons by Bravo Airlines for flying frequently on Bravo airplanes. The coupons are sold to people who pay less for the coupons than they would pay by purchasing tickets from Bravo. This marketing of coupons results in lost revenue for Bravo.

To discourage the buying and selling of free-travel coupons, it would be best for Bravo Airlines to restrict the

(A) number of coupons that a person can be awarded in a particular year
(B) use of the coupons to those who were awarded the coupons and members of their immediate families
(C) days that the coupons can be used to Monday through Friday
(D) amount of time that the coupons can be used after they are issued
(E) number of routes on which travelers can use the coupons

7. The ice on the front windshield of the car had formed when moisture condensed during the night. The ice melted quickly after the car was warmed up the next morning because the defrosting vent, which blows only on the front windshield, was turned on full force.

Which of the following, if true, most seriously jeopardizes the validity of the explanation for the speed with which the ice melted?

(A) The side windows had no ice condensation on them.
(B) Even though no attempt was made to defrost the back window, the ice there melted at the same rate as did the ice on the front windshield.
(C) The speed at which ice on a window melts increases as the temperature of the air blown on the window increases.
(D) The warm air from the defrosting vent for the front windshield cools rapidly as it dissipates throughout the rest of the car.
(E) The defrosting vent operates efficiently even when the heater, which blows warm air toward the feet or faces of the driver and passengers, is on.

GO ON TO THE NEXT PAGE.

8. To prevent some conflicts of interest, Congress could prohibit high-level government officials from accepting positions as lobbyists for three years after such officials leave government service. One such official concluded, however, that such a prohibition would be unfortunate because it would prevent high-level government officials from earning a livelihood for three years.

The official's conclusion logically depends on which of the following assumptions?

(A) Laws should not restrict the behavior of former government officials.

(B) Lobbyists are typically people who have previously been high-level government officials.

(C) Low-level government officials do not often become lobbyists when they leave government service.

(D) High-level government officials who leave government service are capable of earning a livelihood only as lobbyists.

(E) High-level government officials who leave government service are currently permitted to act as lobbyists for only three years.

9. A conservation group in the United States is trying to change the long-standing image of bats as frightening creatures. The group contends that bats are feared and persecuted solely because they are shy animals that are active only at night.

Which of the following, if true, would cast the most serious doubt on the accuracy of the group's contention?

(A) Bats are steadily losing natural roosting places such as caves and hollow trees and are thus turning to more developed areas for roosting.

(B) Bats are the chief consumers of nocturnal insects and thus can help make their hunting territory more pleasant for humans.

(C) Bats are regarded as frightening creatures not only in the United States but also in Europe, Africa, and South America.

(D) Raccoons and owls are shy and active only at night; yet they are not generally feared and persecuted.

(E) People know more about the behavior of other greatly feared animal species, such as lions, alligators, and snakes, than they do about the behavior of bats.

10. Meteorite explosions in the Earth's atmosphere as large as the one that destroyed forests in Siberia, with approximately the force of a twelve-megaton nuclear blast, occur about once a century.

The response of highly automated systems controlled by complex computer programs to unexpected circumstances is unpredictable.

Which of the following conclusions can most properly be drawn, if the statements above are true, about a highly automated nuclear-missile defense system controlled by a complex computer program?

(A) Within a century after its construction, the system would react inappropriately and might accidentally start a nuclear war.

(B) The system would be destroyed if an explosion of a large meteorite occurred in the Earth's atmosphere.

(C) It would be impossible for the system to distinguish the explosion of a large meteorite from the explosion of a nuclear weapon.

(D) Whether the system would respond inappropriately to the explosion of a large meteorite would depend on the location of the blast.

(E) It is not certain what the system's response to the explosion of a large meteorite would be, if its designers did not plan for such a contingency.

GO ON TO THE NEXT PAGE.

Questions 11-12 are based on the following.

The fewer restrictions there are on the advertising of legal services, the more lawyers there are who advertise their services, and the lawyers who advertise a specific service usually charge less for that service than lawyers who do not advertise. Therefore, if the state removes any of its current restrictions, such as the one against advertisements that do not specify fee arrangements, overall consumer legal costs will be lower than if the state retains its current restrictions.

11. If the statements above are true, which of the following must be true?

(A) Some lawyers who now advertise will charge more for specific services if they do not have to specify fee arrangements in the advertisements.

(B) More consumers will use legal services if there are fewer restrictions on the advertising of legal services.

(C) If the restriction against advertisements that do not specify fee arrangements is removed, more lawyers will advertise their services.

(D) If more lawyers advertise lower prices for specific services, some lawyers who do not advertise will also charge less than they currently charge for those services.

(E) If the only restrictions on the advertising of legal services were those that apply to every type of advertising, most lawyers would advertise their services.

12. Which of the following, if true, would most seriously weaken the argument concerning overall consumer legal costs?

(A) The state has recently removed some other restrictions that had limited the advertising of legal services.

(B) The state is unlikely to remove all of the restrictions that apply solely to the advertising of legal services.

(C) Lawyers who do not advertise generally provide legal services of the same quality as those provided by lawyers who do advertise.

(D) Most lawyers who now specify fee arrangements in their advertisements would continue to do so even if the specification were not required.

(E) Most lawyers who advertise specific services do not lower their fees for those services when they begin to advertise.

13. Defense Department analysts worry that the ability of the United States to wage a prolonged war would be seriously endangered if the machine-tool manufacturing base shrinks further. Before the Defense Department publicly connected this security issue with the import quota issue, however, the machine-tool industry raised the national security issue in its petition for import quotas.

Which of the following, if true, contributes most to an explanation of the machine-tool industry's raising the issue above regarding national security?

(A) When the aircraft industries retooled, they provided a large amount of work for tool builders.

(B) The Defense Department is only marginally concerned with the effects of foreign competition on the machine-tool industry.

(C) The machine-tool industry encountered difficulty in obtaining governmental protection against imports on grounds other than defense.

(D) A few weapons important for defense consist of parts that do not require extensive machining.

(E) Several federal government programs have been designed which will enable domestic machine-tool manufacturing firms to compete successfully with foreign toolmakers.

GO ON TO THE NEXT PAGE.

14. Opponents of laws that require automobile drivers and passengers to wear seat belts argue that in a free society people have the right to take risks as long as the people do not harm others as a result of taking the risks. As a result, they conclude that it should be each person's decision whether or not to wear a seat belt.

Which of the following, if true, most seriously weakens the conclusion drawn above?

(A) Many new cars are built with seat belts that automatically fasten when someone sits in the front seat.

(B) Automobile insurance rates for all automobile owners are higher because of the need to pay for the increased injuries or deaths of people not wearing seat belts.

(C) Passengers in airplanes are required to wear seat belts during takeoffs and landings.

(D) The rate of automobile fatalities in states that do not have mandatory seat-belt laws is greater than the rate of fatalities in states that do have such laws.

(E) In automobile accidents, a greater number of passengers who do not wear seat belts are injured than are passengers who do wear seat belts.

15. The cost of producing radios in Country Q is ten percent less than the cost of producing radios in Country Y. Even after transportation fees and tariff charges are added, it is still cheaper for a company to import radios from Country Q to Country Y than to produce radios in Country Y.

The statements above, if true, best support which of the following assertions?

(A) Labor costs in Country Q are ten percent below those in Country Y.

(B) Importing radios from Country Q to Country Y will eliminate ten percent of the manufacturing jobs in Country Y.

(C) The tariff on a radio imported from Country Q to Country Y is less than ten percent of the cost of manufacturing the radio in Country Y.

(D) The fee for transporting a radio from Country Q to Country Y is more than ten percent of the cost of manufacturing the radio in Country Q.

(E) It takes ten percent less time to manufacture a radio in Country Q than it does in Country Y.

16. During the Second World War, about 375,000 civilians died in the United States and about 408,000 members of the United States armed forces died overseas. On the basis of those figures, it can be concluded that it was not much more dangerous to be overseas in the armed forces during the Second World War than it was to stay at home as a civilian.

Which of the following would reveal most clearly the absurdity of the conclusion drawn above?

(A) Counting deaths among members of the armed forces who served in the United States in addition to deaths among members of the armed forces serving overseas

(B) Expressing the difference between the numbers of deaths among civilians and members of the armed forces as a percentage of the total number of deaths

(C) Separating deaths caused by accidents during service in the armed forces from deaths caused by combat injuries

(D) Comparing death rates per thousand members of each group rather than comparing total numbers of deaths

(E) Comparing deaths caused by accidents in the United States to deaths caused by combat in the armed forces

GO ON TO THE NEXT PAGE.

17. One state adds a 7 percent sales tax to the price of most products purchased within its jurisdiction. This tax, therefore, if viewed as tax on income, has the reverse effect of the federal income tax: the lower the income, the higher the annual percentage rate at which the income is taxed.

The conclusion above would be properly drawn if which of the following were assumed as a premise?

(A) The amount of money citizens spend on products subject to the state tax tends to be equal across income levels.
(B) The federal income tax favors citizens with high incomes, whereas the state sales tax favors citizens with low incomes.
(C) Citizens with low annual incomes can afford to pay a relatively higher percentage of their incomes in state sales tax, since their federal income tax is relatively low.
(D) The lower a state's sales tax, the more it will tend to redistribute income from the more affluent citizens to the rest of society.
(E) Citizens who fail to earn federally taxable income are also exempt from the state sales tax.

18. The average age of chief executive officers (CEO's) in a large sample of companies is 57. The average age of CEO's in those same companies 20 years ago was approximately eight years younger. On the basis of those data, it can be concluded that CEO's in general tend to be older now.

Which of the following casts the most doubt on the conclusion drawn above?

(A) The dates when the CEO's assumed their current positions have not been specified.
(B) No information is given concerning the average number of years that CEO's remain in office.
(C) The information is based only on companies that have been operating for at least 20 years.
(D) Only approximate information is given concerning the average age of the CEO's 20 years ago.
(E) Information concerning the exact number of companies in the sample has not been given.

Questions 19-20 are based on the following.

Surveys show that every year only 10 percent of cigarette smokers switch brands. Yet the manufacturers have been spending an amount equal to 10 percent of their gross receipts on cigarette promotion in magazines. It follows from these figures that inducing cigarette smokers to switch brands did not pay, and that cigarette companies would have been no worse off economically if they had dropped their advertising.

19. Of the following, the best criticism of the conclusion that inducing cigarette smokers to switch brands did not pay is that the conclusion is based on

(A) computing advertising costs as a percentage of gross receipts, not of overall costs
(B) past patterns of smoking and may not carry over to the future
(C) the assumption that each smoker is loyal to a single brand of cigarettes at any one time
(D) the assumption that each manufacturer produces only one brand of cigarettes
(E) figures for the cigarette industry as a whole and may not hold for a particular company

20. Which of the following, if true, most seriously weakens the conclusion that cigarette companies could have dropped advertising without suffering economically?

(A) Cigarette advertisements provide a major proportion of total advertising revenue for numerous magazines.
(B) Cigarette promotion serves to attract first-time smokers to replace those people who have stopped smoking.
(C) There exists no research conclusively demonstrating that increases in cigarette advertising are related to increases in smoking.
(D) Advertising is so firmly established as a major business activity of cigarette manufacturers that they would be unlikely to drop it.
(E) Brand loyalty is typically not very strong among those who smoke inexpensive cigarettes.

STOP

IF YOU FINISH BEFORE TIME IS CALLED, YOU MAY CHECK YOUR WORK ON THIS SECTION ONLY. DO NOT TURN TO ANY OTHER SECTION IN THE TEST.

Section 1

#	Answer
1	C
2	B
3	NOT SCORED
4	B
5	A
6	B
7	D
8	E
9	A
10	E
11	C
12	D
13	A
14	E
15	B
16	E
17	C
18	E
19	A
20	E
21	
22	
23	
24	
25	

Section 2

#	Answer
1	D
2	D
3	D
4	A
5	D
6	E
7	A
8	A
9	A
10	B
11	E
12	E
13	C
14	A
15	C
16	B
17	A
18	D
19	C
20	D
21	C
22	B
23	B
24	E
25	D

Section 3

#	Answer
1	C
2	C
3	E
4	D
5	C
6	D
7	B
8	A
9	C
10	D
11	C
12	A
13	E
14	E
15	C
16	E
17	E
18	B
19	D
20	C
21	C
22	C
23	A
24	D
25	B

Section 4

#	Answer
1	D
2	C
3	B
4	E
5	B
6	E
7	C
8	C
9	E
10	A
11	D
12	D
13	C
14	E
15	C
16	E
17	A
18	C
19	B
20	A
21	B
22	C
23	A
24	A
25	D

Section 5

#	Answer
1	A
2	C
3	C
4	D
5	B
6	C
7	B
8	E
9	D
10	E
11	E
12	C
13	A
14	E
15	A
16	D
17	A
18	C
19	E
20	C
21	
22	
23	
24	
25	

Section 6

#	Answer
1	A
2	C
3	B
4	B
5	B
6	B
7	B
8	D
9	D
10	E
11	C
12	E
13	C
14	B
15	D
16	D
17	A
18	C
19	E
20	B
21	
22	
23	
24	
25	

Explanatory Material:
Problem Solving I, Section 1

1. If Mario was 32 years old 8 years ago, how old was he x years ago?

   (A) $x - 40$
   (B) $x - 24$
   (C) $40 - x$
   (D) $24 - x$
   (E) $24 + x$

Since Mario was 32 years old 8 years ago, his age now is $32 + 8 = 40$. x years ago, Mario was x years younger, so his age then was $40 - x$. Thus, the best answer is C.

2. Running at the same constant rate, 6 identical machines can produce a total of 270 bottles per minute. At this rate, how many bottles could 10 such machines produce in 4 minutes?

   (A) 648
   (B) 1,800
   (C) 2,700
   (D) 10,800
   (E) 64,800

The production rate of each machine is $\frac{270}{6} = 45$ bottles per minute. The production rate for 10 machines is $45(10) = 450$ bottles per minute. Therefore, the 10 machines can produce $450(4) = 1,800$ bottles in 4 minutes. The best answer is B.

3. NOT SCORED

4. Three business partners, Q, R, and S, agree to divide their total profit for a certain year in the ratios $2 : 5 : 8$, respectively. If Q's share was \$4,000, what was the total profit of the business partners for the year?

   (A) \$26,000
   (B) \$30,000
   (C) \$52,000
   (D) \$60,000
   (E) \$300,000

Based on the ratios $2 : 5 : 8$, the total profit T was divided as follows: $\frac{2}{15}T$ was given to Q, $\frac{5}{15}T$ was given to R, and $\frac{8}{15}T$ was given to S. Since $\frac{2}{15}T = \$4,000$, $T = \frac{15}{2}(4,000) = \$30,000$.

Therefore, the best answer is B.

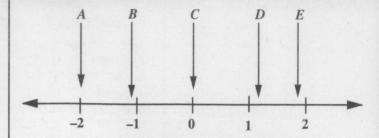

5. Of the five coordinates associated with points A, B, C, D, and E on the number line above, which has the greatest absolute value?

   (A) A
   (B) B
   (C) C
   (D) D
   (E) E

The absolute value of a number x may be thought of as the distance between x and 0 on the number line. By inspection of the five points, the coordinate of point A is farthest from 0 and thus has the greatest absolute value. Therefore, the best answer is A.

6. A restaurant meal cost \$35.50 and there was no tax. If the tip was more than 10 percent but less than 15 percent of the cost of the meal, then the total amount paid must have been between

   (A) \$40 and \$42
   (B) \$39 and \$41
   (C) \$38 and \$40
   (D) \$37 and \$39
   (E) \$36 and \$37

If P is the total amount paid, then P must be greater than $\$35.50(1.1)$ but less than $\$35.50(1.15)$. That is, P is between \$39.05 and \$40.825. It follows that P must be between \$39 and \$41, which is choice B. Each of the other choices excludes a possible value of P. Thus, the best answer is B.

7. Harriet wants to put up fencing around three sides of her rectangular yard and leave a side of 20 feet unfenced. If the yard has an area of 680 square feet, how many feet of fencing does she need?

   (A) 34
   (B) 40
   (C) 68
   (D) 88
   (E) 102

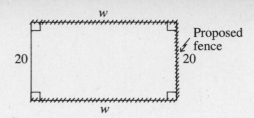

The diagram above shows the rectangular yard with the known dimension, 20 feet, and the unknown dimension, w feet. The area of the yard is $20w = 680$ square feet, so $w = \dfrac{680}{20} = 34$ feet. The length of fencing needed is then $34 + 20 + 34 = 88$ feet. Thus, the best answer is D.

8. If $u > t, r > q, s > t$, and $t > r$, which of the following must be true?

   I. $u > s$
   II. $s > q$
   III. $u > r$

(A) I only
(B) II only
(C) III only
(D) I and II
(E) II and III

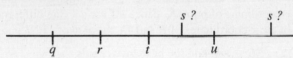

The number line shown above is based on the given inequalities and may be helpful when I, II, and III are considered.

   I. It may be that $q = 0, r = 1, t = 2, u = 3$, and $s = 4$, so that $u > s$ is not necessarily true.

   II. Since $s > t, t > r$, and $r > q$, it follows that $s > q$.

   III. Since $u > t$ and $t > r$, it follows that $u > r$.

Since II and III must be true, the best answer is E.

9. Increasing the original price of an article by 15 percent and then increasing the new price by 15 percent is equivalent to increasing the original price by

(A) 32.25%
(B) 31.00%
(C) 30.25%
(D) 30.00%
(E) 22.50%

If p is the original price, then the 15 percent increase in price results in a price of $1.15p$. The next 15 percent increase in price results in a price of $1.15(1.15p)$, or $1.3225p$. Thus, the price increased by $1.3225p - p = 0.3225p$, or 32.25% of p. The best answer is A.

10. If k is an integer and 0.0010101×10^k is greater than 1,000, what is the least possible value of k ?

(A) 2
(B) 3
(C) 4
(D) 5
(E) 6

Since 0.0010101 is being multiplied by the kth power of 10, k is the number of decimal places that the decimal point in 0.0010101 will move to the right (if k 0) in the product 0.0010101×10^k. By inspection, 6 is the least number of decimal places that the decimal point must move to the right in order for the product to be greater than 1,000. Thus, the best answer is E.

11. If $(b - 3)\left(4 + \dfrac{2}{b}\right) = 0$ and b 3, then $b =$

(A) −8

(B) −2

(C) $-\dfrac{1}{2}$

(D) $\dfrac{1}{2}$

(E) 2

Since $(b - 3)\left(4 + \dfrac{2}{b}\right) = 0$, it follows that either $b - 3 = 0$ or $4 + \dfrac{2}{b} = 0$. That is, either $b = 3$ or $b = -\dfrac{1}{2}$. But b 3 is given, so $b = -\dfrac{1}{2}$, and the best answer is C.

12. In a weight-lifting competition, the total weight of Joe's two lifts was 750 pounds. If twice the weight of his first lift was 300 pounds more than the weight of his second lift, what was the weight, in pounds, of his first lift?

(A) 225
(B) 275
(C) 325
(D) 350
(E) 400

Let F and S be the weights, in pounds, of Joe's first and second lifts, respectively. Then $F + S = 750$ and $2F = S + 300$. The second equation may be written as $S = 2F - 300$, and $2F - 300$ may be substituted for S in the first equation to get $F + (2F - 300) = 750$. Thus, $3F = 1,050$, or $F = 350$ pounds, and the best answer is D.

13. One hour after Yolanda started walking from X to Y, a distance of 45 miles, Bob started walking along the same road from Y to X. If Yolanda's walking rate was 3 miles per hour and Bob's was 4 miles per hour, how many miles had Bob walked when they met?

(A) 24
(B) 23
(C) 22
(D) 21
(E) 19.5

Let t be the number of hours that Bob had walked when he met Yolanda. Then, when they met, Bob had walked $4t$ miles and Yolanda had walked $3(t + 1)$ miles. These distances must sum to 45 miles, so $4t + 3(t + 1) = 45$, which may be solved for t as follows.

$$4t + 3(t + 1) = 45$$
$$4t + 3t + 3 = 45$$
$$7t = 42$$
$$t = 6 \text{ (hours)}$$

Therefore, Bob had walked $4t = 4(6) = 24$ miles when they met. The best answer is A.

14. The average (arithmetic mean) of 6 numbers is 8.5. When one number is discarded, the average of the remaining numbers becomes 7.2. What is the discarded number?

(A)   7.8
(B)   9.8
(C)   10.0
(D)   12.4
(E)   15.0

The sum of the 6 numbers is $6(8.5) = 51.0$; the sum of the 5 remaining numbers is $5(7.2) = 36.0$. Thus, the discarded number must be $51.0 - 36.0 = 15.0$, and the best answer is E.

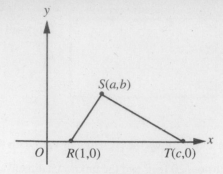

15. In the rectangular coordinate system above, the area of RST is

(A) $\dfrac{bc}{2}$

(B) $\dfrac{b(c - 1)}{2}$

(C) $\dfrac{c(b - 1)}{2}$

(D) $\dfrac{a(c - 1)}{2}$

(E) $\dfrac{c(a - 1)}{2}$

If segment RT is chosen as the base of RST, then the height is b, the y-coordinate of point S. Since $RT = c - 1$ (the difference between the x-coordinates of R and T), the area of RST is $\frac{1}{2}(RT)b = \frac{1}{2}(c - 1)b$, and the best answer is B.

16. Which of the following equations has a root in common with $x^2 - 6x + 5 = 0$?

(A) $x^2 + 1 = 0$
(B) $x^2 - x - 2 = 0$
(C) $x^2 - 10x - 5 = 0$
(D) $2x^2 - 2 = 0$
(E) $x^2 - 2x - 3 = 0$

Since $x^2 - 6x + 5 = (x - 5)(x - 1)$, the roots of $x^2 - 6x + 5 = 0$ are 1 and 5. When these two values are substituted in each of the five choices to determine whether or not they satisfy the equation, only in choice D does a value satisfy the equation, namely, $2(1)^2 - 2 = 0$. Thus, the best answer is D.

17. One inlet pipe fills an empty tank in 5 hours. A second inlet pipe fills the same tank in 3 hours. If both pipes are used together, how long will it take to fill $\frac{2}{3}$ of the tank?

(A) $\frac{8}{15}$ hr

(B) $\frac{3}{4}$ hr

(C) $\frac{5}{4}$ hr

(D) $\frac{15}{8}$ hr

(E) $\frac{8}{3}$ hr

Since the first pipe fills $\frac{1}{5}$ of the tank in one hour and the second pipe fills $\frac{1}{3}$ of the tank in one hour, together they fill $\frac{1}{5} + \frac{1}{3} = \frac{8}{15}$ of the tank in one hour. At this rate, if t is the number of hours needed to fill $\frac{2}{3}$ of the tank, then $\frac{8}{15}t = \frac{2}{3}$, or $t = \frac{2}{3}\left(\frac{15}{8}\right) = \frac{5}{4}$ hours. Thus, the best answer is C.

18. A total of 40 brand X television sets and 80 brand Y television sets were purchased for a motel chain. If the price of each brand Y set was twice the price of each brand X set, what percent of the total bill was the price of a brand Y set?

(A) 0.25%
(B) 0.5%
(C) 0.625%
(D) 0.833%
(E) 1.0%

If P was the price of each brand X set, then $2P$ was the price of each brand Y set, and the total bill was $40P + 80(2P) = 200P$. Therefore, the price of a brand Y set was $\frac{2P}{200P} = \frac{1}{100}$, or 1%, of the total bill. Thus, the best answer is E.

19. Ben and Ann are among 7 contestants from which 4 semifinalists are to be selected. Of the different possible selections, how many contain neither Ben nor Ann?

(A) 5
(B) 6
(C) 7
(D) 14
(E) 21

The number of selections from the 7 contestants that contain neither Ben nor Ann is the same as the number of selections from the 5 remaining contestants. Selecting 4 people from a group of 5 is the same as leaving out 1 person from the selection. Since this may be done in exactly 5 different ways, the number of different possible selections that contain neither Ben nor Ann is 5. Thus, the best answer is A.

20. How many positive integers k are there such that $100k$ is a factor of $(2^2)(3)(5^3)$?

(A) None
(B) One
(C) Two
(D) Three
(E) Four

Since $(2^2)(3)(5^3) = (2^2)(5^2)(3)(5) = 100(15)$, $100k$ is a positive factor of $100(15)$ if and only if k is a positive factor of 15. There are only four such factors of 15: 1, 3, 5, and 15. Thus, the best answer is E.

Explanatory Material:
Reading Comprehension, Section 2

(The passage for questions 1-9 appears on page 316.)

1. The primary purpose of the passage is to

(A) discuss a plan for investigation of a phenomenon that is not yet fully understood
(B) present two explanations of a phenomenon and reconcile the differences between them
(C) summarize two theories and suggest a third theory that overcomes the problems encountered in the first two
(D) describe an alternative hypothesis and provide evidence and arguments that support it
(E) challenge the validity of a theory by exposing the inconsistencies and contradictions in it

The best answer is D. This question requires you to identify the primary concern of the passage as a whole. The first paragraph presents a recent hypothesis about how caffeine affects behavior. The second paragraph describes an earlier and widely accepted hypothesis about how caffeine affects behavior, and then presents evidence that is not consistent with that hypothesis. The third and fourth paragraphs return to the newer hypothesis introduced in the first paragraph and provide "evidence and arguments" that support this alternative hypothesis.

2. Which of the following, if true, would most weaken the theory proposed by Snyder et al?

(A) At very low concentrations in the human brain, both caffeine and theophylline tend to have depressive rather than stimulatory effects on human behavior.

(B) The ability of caffeine derivatives at very low concentrations to dislodge adenosine from its receptors in mouse brains correlates well with their ability to stimulate mouse locomotion at these low concentrations.

(C) The concentration of cyclic AMP in target neurons in the human brain that leads to increased neuron firing can be produced by several different phosphodiesterase inhibitors in addition to caffeine.

(D) The concentration of caffeine required to dislodge adenosine from its receptors in the human brain is much greater than the concentration that produces behavioral stimulation in humans.

(E) The concentration of IBMX required to dislodge adenosine from its receptors in mouse brains is much smaller than the concentration that stimulates locomotion in the mouse.

The best answer is D. To answer this question you must first identify the theory proposed by Snyder et al. Snyder et al propose that caffeine stimulates behavior by successfully competing with adenosine, a chemical that inhibits neuron firing, in binding to specific receptors in the brain; neurons fire more readily when caffeine is bound to the specific receptors. Choices A, C, and E all deal with something other than caffeine's ability to bind to adenosine receptors; B would tend to strengthen the Snyder et al hypothesis. Only D states a fact that, if it were true, would weaken the proposed theory, because D states that the behavior Snyder et al seek to explain can happen without caffeine dislodging adenosine from its receptors.

3. According to Snyder et al, caffeine differs from adenosine in that caffeine

(A) stimulates behavior in the mouse and in humans, whereas adenosine stimulates behavior in humans only

(B) has mixed effects in the brain, whereas adenosine has only a stimulatory effect

(C) increases cyclic AMP concentrations in target neurons, whereas adenosine decreases such concentrations

(D) permits release of neurotransmitters when it is bound to adenosine receptors, whereas adenosine inhibits such release

(E) inhibits both neuron firing and the production of phosphodiesterase when there is a sufficient concentration in the brain, whereas adenosine inhibits only neuron firing

The best answer is D. Lines 6-12 state that adenosine "depresses neuron firing" by binding to specific receptors on neuronal membranes, which in turn inhibits the release of neurotransmitters. Lines 14-18 describe Snyder et al's hypothesis about caffeine. They propose that caffeine binds to specific receptors on neuronal membranes, which prevents adenosine from binding to those receptors and "allows the neurons to fire more readily than they otherwise would." Therefore, according to Snyder et al, caffeine differs from adenosine in that caffeine permits neurotransmitter release when it is bound to adenosine receptors, whereas adenosine inhibits neurotransmitter release.

4. In response to experimental results concerning IBMX, Snyder et al contended that it is not uncommon for psychoactive drugs to have

(A) mixed effects in the brain
(B) inhibitory effects on enzymes in the brain
(C) close structural relationships with caffeine
(D) depressive effects on mouse locomotion
(E) the ability to dislodge caffeine from receptors in the brain

The best answer is A. The effects of IBMX are discussed in the last paragraph of the passage. IBMX apparently binds to adenosine-specific receptors on neuronal membranes, but, in contrast to the other caffeine derivatives that Snyder et al experimented with, IBMX depresses rather than stimulates mouse locomotion. Snyder et al respond to this experimental result by stating that IBMX has "mixed effects in the brain, a not unusual occurrence with psychoactive drugs" (lines 53-54).

5. The passage suggests that Snyder et al believe that if the older theory concerning caffeine's effects were correct, which of the following would have to be the case?

I. All neurotransmitters would increase the short-term concentration of cyclic AMP in target neurons.

II. Substances other than caffeine that inhibit the production of phosphodiesterase would be stimulants.

III. All concentration levels of caffeine that are high enough to produce stimulation would also inhibit the production of phosphodiesterase.

(A) I only
(B) I and II only
(C) I and III only
(D) II and III only
(E) I, II, and III

The best answer is D. The older theory is discussed in the second paragraph of the passage. Snyder et al raise two objections to that theory. They point out that the concentrations of caffeine needed to inhibit the production of phosphodiesterase are higher than the concentrations of caffeine that normally cause stimulation. Thus, to address this objection, statement III would have to be true. Snyder et al also state that phosphodiesterase's activity is blocked by other compounds that are not stimulants. To address this objection, statement II would have to be true. Neither of these objections to the older theory is addressed by statement I. Thus, the passage suggests that Snyder et al believe that if the older theory were true, statements II and III would also have to be true.

6. According to Snyder et al, all of the following compounds can bind to specific receptors in the brain EXCEPT

 (A) IBMX
 (B) caffeine
 (C) adenosine
 (D) theophylline
 (E) phosphodiesterase

The best answer is E. This question asks you to identify which compound, according to Snyder et al, does NOT bind to specific receptors in the brain. The last paragraph describes IBMX (A) as a compound that binds to specific receptors in the brain. Lines 14-18 describe Snyder et al's proposal that caffeine (B) can bind to specific receptors in the brain. Lines 6-12 state that adenosine (C) inhibits neuron firing by binding to specific receptors in the brain. Lines 43-45 mention theophylline (D) as an example of a caffeine derivative that binds to specific receptors in the brain. Phosphodiesterase (E), identified as an "enzyme that breaks down the chemical called cyclic AMP" (lines 21-22), is the only compound that is not identified as one that binds to specific receptors in the brain.

7. Snyder et al suggest that caffeine's ability to bind to A_1 and A_2 receptors can be at least partially attributed to which of the following?

 (A) The chemical relationship between caffeine and phosphodiesterase
 (B) The structural relationship between caffeine and adenosine
 (C) The structural similarity between caffeine and neurotransmitters
 (D) The ability of caffeine to stimulate behavior
 (E) The natural occurrence of caffeine and adenosine in the brain

The best answer is B. This question asks you to identify information that is suggested rather than directly stated in the passage. To answer it, first look for the location in the passage of the information specified in the question. The A_1 and A_2 receptors are mentioned in lines 12-14. Lines 14-18 go on to describe Snyder et al's hypothesis about the effects of caffeine on behavior. They propose that caffeine, "which is structurally similar to adenosine," is able to bind to A_1 and A_2 receptors in the brain, the same receptors that adenosine normally binds to. Thus, the passage suggests that the structural relationship between caffeine and adenosine may be partially responsible for caffeine's ability to bind to A_1 and A_2 receptors.

8. The author quotes Snyder et al in lines 38-43 most probably in order to

 (A) reveal some of the assumptions underlying their theory
 (B) summarize a major finding of their experiments
 (C) point out that their experiments were limited to the mouse
 (D) indicate that their experiments resulted only in general correlations
 (E) refute the objections made by supporters of the older theory

The best answer is B. This question asks you to identify the function of a quotation in the third paragraph of the passage. The third paragraph provides evidence for Snyder et al's hypothesis by discussing experiments they conducted on mice. The quotation in lines 38-43 "summarizes" the findings of these experiments. Snyder et al found that a number of caffeine derivatives are able to bind to specific receptors in the brains of mice just as adenosine does, and that the derivatives that are most successful at stimulating locomotion are also the most successful in competing with adenosine in binding at the receptors. This finding is "major" in that it supports their hypothesis that the stimulative effects of caffeine are a result of its ability to compete with adenosine.

9. The last paragraph of the passage performs which of the following functions?

 (A) Describes a disconfirming experimental result and reports the explanation given by Snyder et al in an attempt to reconcile this result with their theory.
 (B) Specifies the basis for the correlation observed by Snyder et al and presents an explanation in an attempt to make the correlation consistent with the operation of psychoactive drugs other than caffeine.
 (C) Elaborates the description of the correlation observed by Snyder et al and suggests an additional explanation in an attempt to make the correlation consistent with the older theory.
 (D) Reports inconsistent experimental data and describes the method Snyder et al will use to reanalyze this data.
 (E) Provides an example of the hypothesis proposed by Snyder et al and relates this example to caffeine's properties.

The best answer is A. This question asks you to identify the function of the last paragraph in the context of the passage. The last paragraph describes an exception to the experimental results discussed in the third paragraph. The caffeine derivatives that stimulated locomotion in mice were successful at binding to specific receptors in the brain, thus supporting Snyder et al's theory that caffeine stimulates behavior by competing with adenosine in binding to specific receptors. However, although the compound IBMX bound very well to specific receptors, it did not stimulate mouse locomotion as the compounds discussed in the third paragraph did. Snyder et al attempt to "reconcile" this result by stating that psycho-active drugs such as IBMX often have "mixed effects in the brain" (line 53) depending on their concentration.

(The passage for questions 10-16 appears on page 318.)

10. The primary purpose of the passage is to propose

   (A) an alternative to museum display of artifacts
   (B) a way to curb illegal digging while benefiting the archaeological profession
   (C) a way to distinguish artifacts with scientific value from those that have no such value
   (D) the governmental regulation of archaeological sites
   (E) a new system for cataloguing duplicate artifacts

The best answer is B. The first paragraph identifies two major problems faced by the archaeological profession: inadequate funding and illegal digging. Lines 9-11 indicate that the author is going to suggest how to remedy both problems, thereby benefiting the archaeological profession. The author proceeds to propose allowing the sale of excavated artifacts (lines 11-14) and to explain how this would solve both problems (lines 14-19). The author then supports the proposal by countering possible objections to it, and in the last paragraph explains how the proposal would curb illegal digging (lines 51-55). Thus, the way information is organized in the passage indicates that the author's purpose is to suggest that allowing the sale of excavated artifacts would provide funds for the archaeological profession and curb illegal digging.

11. The author implies that all of the following statements about duplicate artifacts are true EXCEPT:

   (A) A market for such artifacts already exists.
   (B) Such artifacts seldom have scientific value.
   (C) There is likely to be a continuing supply of such artifacts.
   (D) Museums are well supplied with examples of such artifacts.
   (E) Such artifacts frequently exceed in quality those already catalogued in museum collections.

The best answer is E. The question requires you to identify the answer choice that CANNOT be inferred from the passage. Choice A asserts that potential purchasers for duplicate artifacts exist; this is implied in lines 51-55, which suggest that purchasers would prefer legally acquired duplicate artifacts, thereby reducing demand for clandestine products. Choice B is implied in lines 25-31, which deny the practical scientific value of duplicate artifacts. Choice C is implied in lines 37-39, which express doubt about storing all the artifacts that "are likely to be discovered in the future." Choice D is implied by the reference to "pieces stored in bulging museum basements" (line 44). Nothing in the passage implies that duplicate artifacts exceed museum objects in quality (choice E).

12. Which of the following is mentioned in the passage as a disadvantage of storing artifacts in museum basements?

   (A) Museum officials rarely allow scholars access to such artifacts.
   (B) Space that could be better used for display is taken up for storage.
   (C) Artifacts discovered in one excavation often become separated from each other.
   (D) Such artifacts are often damaged by variations in temperature and humidity.
   (E) Such artifacts often remain uncatalogued and thus cannot be located once they are put in storage.

The best answer is E. The disadvantages of storing artifacts in museum basements are discussed in the fifth paragraph. Lines 39-42 state that "There is not enough money . . . to catalogue the finds" and declare that as a result stored objects cannot be located. The fact that such objects become "inaccessible" (line 41) is clearly connected to the problems in cataloguing, not to museum policy toward scholars, as choice A states. No mention is made of the situations discussed in choices B, C, and D.

13. The author mentions the excavation in Cyprus (lines 31-34) to emphasize which of the following points?

   (A) Ancient lamps and pottery vessels are less valuable, although more rare, than royal seal impressions.
   (B) Artifacts that are very similar to each other present cataloguing difficulties to archaeologists.
   (C) Artifacts that are not uniquely valuable, and therefore could be sold, are available in large quantities.
   (D) Cyprus is the most important location for unearthing large quantities of salable artifacts.
   (E) Illegal sales of duplicate artifacts are widespread, particularly on the island of Cyprus.

The best answer is C. In lines 27-29, the author refutes the assertion that every object excavated has potential scientific value and therefore should not be sold. In lines 30-31, the author defines those objects that do not have scientific value: "the thousands of pottery vessels . . . that are essentially duplicates of one another." The Cyprus excavation appears in the next sentence as an example of one location in which such duplicate artifacts have been found in large quantities. The reference to "2,000 virtually indistinguishable small jugs" highlights the profusion and uniformity of the Cyprus finds. Thus, the excavation is mentioned in order to emphasize the ready availability of objects that lack unique value and therefore could be sold.

14. The author's argument concerning the effect of the official sale of duplicate artifacts on illegal excavation is based on which of the following assumptions?

(A) Prospective purchasers would prefer to buy authenticated artifacts.
(B) The price of illegally excavated artifacts would rise.
(C) Computers could be used to trace sold artifacts.
(D) Illegal excavators would be forced to sell only duplicate artifacts.
(E) Money gained from selling authenticated artifacts could be used to investigate and prosecute illegal excavators.

The best answer is A. The author's argument concerning the effect of the official sale of duplicate artifacts on illegal excavation appears in lines 51-52, in which the author predicts that such official sale would reduce demand for "the clandestine product." The rhetorical question that follows (lines 52-55) indicates that the author finds it unlikely that any purchaser would prefer objects of unknown provenance to objects of known origin, or, to rephrase, the author assumes that most people would prefer to purchase objects of authenticated provenance, as choice A states. The author's argument concerning the effect of such sales on illegal excavation does not assume any of the other answer choices.

15. The author anticipates which of the following initial objections to the adoption of his proposal?

(A) Museum officials will become unwilling to store artifacts.
(B) An oversupply of salable artifacts will result and the demand for them will fall.
(C) Artifacts that would have been displayed in public places will be sold to private collectors.
(D) Illegal excavators will have an even larger supply of artifacts for resale.
(E) Counterfeiting of artifacts will become more commonplace.

The best answer is C. The author begins the third paragraph by saying "You might object . . ." in order to anticipate possible objections to the adoption of his proposal. In the next sentence the author asserts that "ancient artifacts . . . should be available for all to appreciate, not sold to the highest bidder" (lines 21-24), acknowledging an opponent's fear that individuals might be allowed to purchase objects that ought to be displayed in public institutions. This objection is paraphrased in choice C. Choice A alludes to a situation that shows the benefits, not the drawbacks, of the author's proposal; B, D, and E describe situations that are not discussed in the passage.

16. The author implies that which of the following would occur if duplicate artifacts were sold on the open market?

I. Illegal excavation would eventually cease completely.
II. Cyprus would become the primary source of marketable duplicate artifacts.
III. Archaeologists would be able to publish the results of their excavations more frequently than they currently do.

(A) I only
(B) III only
(C) I and II only
(D) II and III only
(E) I, II, and III

The best answer is B. The question asks you to identify one or more consequences that the author implies would result from the sale of duplicate artifacts on the open market. Statement I is explicitly contradicted by the author's admission that it "would be unrealistic to suggest that illegal digging would stop if artifacts were sold on the open market" (lines 49-50). Statement II cannot be inferred from any information given in the passage. The author implies (lines 3-4) that the lack of available funds restricts publication of excavation results; the fact that duplicate sales "would provide substantial funds . . . for . . . publication" (lines 14-16) suggests that more frequent publication would occur if duplicate artifacts were sold. Therefore, statement III alone is an implied consequence of such sales.

(The passage for questions 17-25 appears on page 320.)

17. Which of the following best states the central idea of the passage?

(A) The use of MESBIC's for aiding minority entrepreneurs seems to have greater potential for success than does the original SBA approach.
(B) There is a crucial difference in point of view between the staff and directors of some MESBIC's.
(C) After initial problems with management and marketing, minority businesses have begun to expand at a steady rate.
(D) Minority entrepreneurs wishing to form new businesses now have several equally successful federal programs on which to rely.
(E) For the first time since 1960, large corporations are making significant contributions to the development of minority businesses.

The best answer is A. The passage begins by indicating that the results of the SBA approach to aiding minority entrepreneurs "were disappointing" (line 7). Lines 42-44 state that "MESBIC's are now emerging as increasingly important financing sources for minority enterprises." Much of the passage is devoted to supporting the author's view that MESBIC's have the greater potential for success, and the last sentence in the passage confirms this view. Choice B accurately restates a point made by the author, that differences exist between staff and directors of MESBIC's, but the point is not central to the author's discussion. The statements in C, D, and E are not supported by information in the passage.

18. According to the passage, the MESBIC approach differs from the SBA approach in that MESBIC's

(A) seek federal contracts to provide markets for minority businesses

(B) encourage minority businesses to provide markets for other minority businesses

(C) attempt to maintain a specified rate of growth in the minority business sector

(D) rely on the participation of large corporations to finance minority businesses

(E) select minority businesses on the basis of their location

The best answer is D. In the second paragraph, the author describes the MESBIC approach as one in which "large corporations participate in the development of successful and stable minority businesses by making use of government-sponsored venture capital" (lines 18-21). There is no indication in the passage that the SBA approach relies on the participation of large corporations. Although any of the other answer choices might actually be true of MESBIC's, there is no information in the passage that confirms that these statements are correct.

19. Which of the following does the author cite to support the conclusion that the results of the SBA program were disappointing?

(A) The small number of new minority enterprises formed as a result of the program

(B) The small number of minority enterprises that took advantage of the management and technical assistance offered under the program

(C) The small percentage of the nation's business receipts earned by minority enterprises following the program's implementation

(D) The small percentage of recipient minority enterprises that were able to repay federally guaranteed loans made under the program

(E) The small number of minority enterprises that chose to participate in the program

The best answer is C. The author concludes that the results of the SBA approach "were disappointing" (line 7) and then supports the conclusion by citing the fact that "Even 15 years

after the program was implemented, minority business receipts were not quite two percent of the national economy's total receipts" (lines 9-12). The statements in A, B, D, and E are not supported by the information in the passage.

20. Which of the following statements about the SBA program can be inferred from the passage?

(A) The maximum term for loans made to recipient businesses was 15 years.

(B) Business loans were considered to be more useful to recipient businesses than was management and technical assistance.

(C) The anticipated failure rate for recipient businesses was significantly lower than the rate that actually resulted.

(D) Recipient businesses were encouraged to relocate to areas more favorable for business development.

(E) The capitalization needs of recipient businesses were assessed and then provided for adequately.

The best answer is C. This question asks you to draw an inference about the SBA program. Although the passage does not actually state that the failure rate for SBA recipient businesses was higher than anticipated, in the first paragraph the author does state that the results of the SBA program were disappointing, in part because of the high failure rate among SBA-sponsored businesses. From this it can be inferred that the anticipated failure rate was lower than the actual rate. There is no information in the passage to suggest that A, B, D, and E could be true.

21. Based on information in the passage, which of the following would be indicative of the pragmatism of MESBIC staff members?

I. A reluctance to invest in minority businesses that show marginal expectations of return on the investments

II. A desire to invest in minority businesses that produce goods and services likely to be of use to the sponsoring company

III. A belief that the minority business sector is best served by investing primarily in newly established businesses

(A) I only

(B) III only

(C) I and II only

(D) II and III only

(E) I, II, and III

The best answer is C. In this question, you are asked to determine which of statements I, II, and III would indicate pragmatism on the part of MESBIC staff members. The author discusses the pragmatism of MESBIC staff members at the beginning of the fourth paragraph. The information in lines 45-53 makes clear that statement I would indicate staff members' pragmatism: staff members prefer investments involving less risk than investments preferred by MESBIC directors. Lines 34-37 indicate that, because sponsoring companies provide markets for the minority businesses they sponsor, these businesses face "considerably less risk" than they would otherwise. Thus, statement II would also indicate the pragmatism of MESBIC staff members. The information in the passage does not suggest that the investment mentioned in statement III would be risk-free.

22. The author refers to the "financial and operating problems" (line 38) encountered by MESBIC's primarily in order to

   (A) broaden the scope of the discussion to include the legal considerations of funding MESBIC's through sponsoring companies
   (B) call attention to the fact that MESBIC's must receive adequate funding in order to function effectively
   (C) show that sponsoring companies were willing to invest only $500,000 of government-sponsored venture capital in the original MESBIC's
   (D) compare SBA and MESBIC limits on minimum funding
   (E) refute suggestions that MESBIC's have been only marginally successful

The best answer is B. The reference in line 38 to "financial and operating problems" appears in the context of a discussion of why corporations came to capitalize MESBIC's "far above the legal minimum of $500,000." The problems are cited to illustrate the reasons that MESBIC's need more than the minimum funding required by law, and thus call attention to this need. The reference is not primarily concerned with legal considerations as suggested in A, or with a comparison with SBA funding limits as suggested in D. The $500,000 mentioned in the passage is the *minimum* level of funding required, not a maximum as suggested in C. There is no suggestion in the passage that MESBIC's have been only marginally successful; thus, choice E is not correct.

23. The author's primary objective in the passage is to

   (A) disprove the view that federal efforts to aid minority businesses have been ineffective
   (B) explain how federal efforts to aid minority businesses have changed since the 1960's
   (C) establish a direct link between the federal efforts to aid minority businesses made before the 1960's and those made in the 1980's
   (D) analyze the basis for the belief that job-specific experience is more useful to minority businesses than is general management experience
   (E) argue that the "social responsibility approach" to aiding minority businesses is superior to any other approach

The best answer is B. The passage describes efforts undertaken in the 1960's to aid minority businesses and then describes MESBIC's, a newer approach to such efforts. Choice A is not correct because, although the author does suggest that MESBIC's have been effective in aiding minority businesses, there is no indication in the passage that the author's purpose is to disprove the view that federal efforts have been ineffective. Because the passage does not discuss efforts undertaken during the 1980's to aid minority businesses, C cannot be correct. The passage neither attempts to analyze the basis for the belief mentioned in D nor argues that the "social responsibility approach" is the most effective. Therefore, neither D nor E can be correct.

24. It can be inferred from the passage that the attitude of some MESBIC staff members toward the investments preferred by some MESBIC directors can best be described as

   (A) defensive
   (B) resigned
   (C) indifferent
   (D) shocked
   (E) disapproving

The best answer is E. According to the last paragraph of the passage, MESBIC staff members feel that the directors' preference for riskier investments may lead the MESBIC's to "re-create the disappointing results of the original SBA approach" (lines 61-62). D is not correct because, though the staff members would prefer that the directors choose different investments, there is no indication that the staff members are shocked by the directors' investment preferences. The staff members are not defensive in their attitude toward the investments, nor are they resigned or indifferent to the situation.

25. The passage provides information that would answer which of the following questions?

   (A) What was the average annual amount, in dollars, of minority business receipts before the SBA strategy was implemented?
   (B) What locations are considered to be unfavorable for minority businesses?
   (C) What is the current success rate for minority businesses that are capitalized by MESBIC's?
   (D) How has the use of federal funding for minority businesses changed since the 1960's?
   (E) How do minority businesses apply to participate in a MESBIC program?

The best answer is D. The passage provides a general discussion of the way in which the use of federal funding for minority businesses changed between the 1960's and 1980, when the material from which the passage is excerpted was written. Although the other choices ask questions that might be of interest to readers of the passage, none of them can be answered using the information provided.

Explanatory Material: Data Sufficiency, Section 3

1. **At a certain picnic, each of the guests was served either a single scoop or a double scoop of ice cream. How many of the guests were served a double scoop of ice cream?**

   (1) At the picnic, 60 percent of the guests were served a double scoop of ice cream.

   (2) A total of 120 scoops of ice cream were served to all the guests at the picnic.

Statement (1) alone is not sufficient because the total number of guests is unknown. Thus, the answer must be B, C, or E. Statement (2) alone is not sufficient since there is no information indicating how the 120 scoops were divided into single-scoop and double-scoop servings. Thus, the answer must be C or E. From (1) the ratio of the number of guests who were served a single scoop to the number of guests who were served a double scoop can be determined and can be used with (2) to determine the number of guests who were served a double scoop. Thus, the best answer is C. (It may be helpful to set up equations to determine whether there is sufficient information given in (1) and (2) for answering the question, but it is not actually necessary to solve the equations.)

2. **By what percent was the price of a certain candy bar increased?**

   (1) The price of the candy bar was increased by 5 cents.

   (2) The price of the candy bar after the increase was 45 cents.

In (1), only the increase in price is given, and both the original and final prices are unknown. Thus, the percent increase cannot be determined from (1) alone, and the answer must be B, C, or E. In (2), only the final price is given, so the percent increase cannot be determined from (2) alone, and the answer must be C or E. From (1) and (2) together, the amount of the increase is known and the price before the increase can be computed. Therefore, the percent increase can be determined, and the best answer is C.

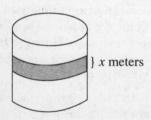

} x meters

3. **A circular tub has a band painted around its circumference, as shown above. What is the surface area of this painted band?**

   (1) $x = 0.5$
   (2) The height of the tub is 1 meter.

The surface area of the band is the product of the circumference of the band and the width of the band. In (1) the width of the band is given, but the circumference is unknown, so the surface area cannot be determined. Therefore, (1) alone is not sufficient, and the answer must be B, C, or E. In (2) the height of the tub is given, which has no relation to the circumference or the width of the band. Thus, (2) is not sufficient, with or without (1), so the best answer is E.

4. **Is it true that $a > b$?**

   (1) $2a > 2b$
   (2) $a + c > b + c$

In (1), when both sides of $2a > 2b$ are divided by 2, the result is $a > b$. Thus, (1) alone is sufficient, and the answer must be A or D. In (2), when c is subtracted from both sides of $a + c > b + c$, the result is $a > b$. Thus, (2) alone is also sufficient, and the best answer is D.

5. **A thoroughly blended biscuit mix includes only flour and baking powder. What is the ratio of the number of grams of baking powder to the number of grams of flour in the mix?**

   (1) Exactly 9.9 grams of flour is contained in 10 grams of the mix.

   (2) Exactly 0.3 gram of baking powder is contained in 30 grams of the mix.

In any amount of the mix, once both ingredient amounts are known, their ratio can be determined. (This ratio must be the same in any amount of the mix since the mix is thoroughly blended.) Each of statements (1) and (2) alone gives the amount of one ingredient in some amount of the mix, so the amount of the other ingredient can be determined. Thus, each of (1) and (2) alone is sufficient, and the best answer is D.

6. **If a real estate agent received a commission of 6 percent of the selling price of a certain house, what was the selling price of the house?**

   (1) The selling price minus the real estate agent's commission was $84,600.

   (2) The selling price was 250 percent of the original purchase price of $36,000.

From (1) it follows that $84,600 is 94% (100% − 6%) of the selling price, and thus the selling price, $\frac{\$84,600}{0.94}$, can be determined. Therefore, (1) alone is sufficient, and the answer must be A or D. From (2) it follows that the selling price is 2.5($36,000). Thus, (2) alone is also sufficient, and the best answer is D.

7. **What is the value of $|x|$?**

(1) $x = -|x|$

(2) $x^2 = 4$

From (1) all that can be determined is that x is negative (or 0) since $|x|$, the absolute value of x, is always positive (or 0). Thus, (1) alone is not sufficient, and the answer must be B, C, or E. From (2) it can be determined that $x = \pm 2$; in either case $|x| = 2$. Since (2) alone is sufficient to determine the value of $|x|$, the best answer is B.

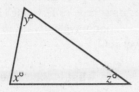

8. **What is the value of z in the triangle above?**

(1) $x + y = 139$

(2) $y + z = 108$

Note that, as in any triangle, $x + y + z = 180$. Using (1), the value 139 can be substituted for $x + y$ in $x + y + z = 180$ to obtain the value of z. Thus, (1) alone is sufficient, and the answer must be A or D. When the equation in (2) is combined with $x + y + z = 180$, all that can be deduced is the value of x. Thus, (2) alone is not sufficient, and the best answer is A.

9. **A certain bakery sells rye bread in 16-ounce loaves and 24-ounce loaves, and all loaves of the same size sell for the same price per loaf regardless of the number of loaves purchased. What is the price of a 24-ounce loaf of rye bread in this bakery?**

(1) **The total price of a 16-ounce loaf and a 24-ounce loaf of this bread is $2.40.**

(2) **The total price of two 16-ounce loaves and one 24-ounce loaf of this bread is $3.40.**

Let s and t be the prices of a 16-ounce loaf and a 24-ounce loaf, respectively. According to (1), $s + t = \$2.40$. Since t cannot be determined without knowing s, statement (1) alone is not sufficient, and the answer must be B, C, or E. Similarly, according to (2), $2s + t = \$3.40$, so t cannot be determined. Therefore, (2) alone is not sufficient, and the answer must be C or E. Using both equations from (1) and (2), $t = \$2.40 - s = \$3.40 - 2s$, from which s, and thus t, can be determined. The best answer is therefore C.

10. **If $\dfrac{\sqrt{x}}{y} = n$, what is the value of x ?**

(1) $yn = 10$

(2) $y = 40$ and $n = \dfrac{1}{4}$

Note that $\dfrac{\sqrt{x}}{y} = n$ is equivalent to $\sqrt{x} = yn$ (if $y \neq 0$). From this information and (1), $\sqrt{x} = yn = 10$, and x can be deter-

mined. Therefore, the answer must be A or D. From (2), $yn = (40)\left(\dfrac{1}{4}\right) = 10$, as in (1). Therefore, (2) alone is also sufficient and the best answer is D.

11. **If m and n are consecutive positive integers, is m greater than n ?**

(1) **$m - 1$ and $n + 1$ are consecutive positive integers.**

(2) **m is an even integer.**

Note that for two consecutive integers the larger must be 1 more than the smaller. That (1) alone is sufficient can probably be seen most easily by considering particular values for m and n. For example, if $m = 4$, then $n = 3$ or 5 since m and n are consecutive. Then $m - 1 = 3$ and $n + 1 = 4$ or 6. Since $m - 1$ and $n + 1$ are consecutive, $n = 3$ and $m > n$. More generally, since m and n are consecutive, either $m = n + 1$ or $n = m + 1$. But, if $n = m + 1$, then $n + 1 = m + 2$, which is 3 more than $m - 1$, contradicting the fact that $m - 1$ and $n + 1$ are consecutive integers. Thus, $m = n + 1$, or $m > n$, and the answer must be A or D. Because the fact given in (2) that m is even is irrelevant, the best answer is A.

12. **Paula and Sandy were among those people who sold raffle tickets to raise money for Club X. If Paula and Sandy sold a total of 100 of the tickets, how many of the tickets did Paula sell?**

(1) **Sandy sold $\dfrac{2}{3}$ as many of the raffle tickets as Paula did.**

(2) **Sandy sold 8 percent of all the raffle tickets sold for Club X.**

If Paula sold p tickets and Sandy sold s tickets, then $p + s = 100$. According to (1), $s = \dfrac{2}{3}p$. The value of p can be determined by solving both equations simultaneously. Therefore, the answer must be A or D. From (2) the number of raffle tickets that Sandy (and thus Paula) sold cannot be determined since the total number of raffle tickets sold is unknown. Thus, (2) alone is not sufficient, and the best answer is A.

13. **Is the integer n odd?**

(1) **n is divisible by 3.**

(2) **n is divisible by 5.**

In statement (1), n is divisible by 3, but n may be even or odd as the examples $n = 6$ and $n = 9$ show. Similarly, in statement (2), n is divisible by 5, but it may be even or odd as the examples $n = 10$ and $n = 15$ show. Since neither statement alone is sufficient, the answer must be C or E. From (1) and (2) together, n must be divisible by 15, and the examples $n = 30$ and $n = 45$ show that n may be even or odd. Thus, the best answer is E.

14. If □ and   each represent single digits in the decimal above, what digit does□ represent?

(1) When the decimal is rounded to the nearest tenth, 3.2 is the result.

(2) When the decimal is rounded to the nearest hundredth, 3.24 is the result.

From (1) the decimal must have been rounded down since the tenths digit is 2 in both 3.2□ 6 and 3.2. Hence, □ represents 0, 1, 2, 3, or 4. Since it cannot be determined from (1) alone what digit □ represents, the answer must be B, C, or E. From (2), □ can represent 3 or 4, depending upon the value of . For example, both 3.2376 and 3.2416, when rounded to the nearest hundredth, are 3.24. Since (2) alone is not sufficient, the answer must be C or E, and since the numbers 3.2376 and 3.2416 also satisfy (1) and (2) together, the best answer is E.

15. A certain company currently has how many employees?

(1) If 3 additional employees are hired by the company and all of the present employees remain, there will be at least 20 employees in the company.

(2) If no additional employees are hired by the company and 3 of the present employees resign, there will be fewer than 15 employees in the company.

Let n be the current number of employees. According to (1), $n + 3 \geq 20$, or $n \geq 17$, which gives a range of possible values of n. Thus, (1) alone is not sufficient, and the answer must be B, C, or E. According to (2), $n - 3 < 15$, or $n < 18$, which also gives a range for n. Thus, (2) alone is not sufficient, and the answer must be C or E. From (1) and (2) together, the value of n can be determined to be 17. Therefore, the best answer is C.

16. If x is equal to one of the numbers $\frac{1}{4}$, $\frac{3}{8}$, or $\frac{2}{5}$, what is the value of x ?

(1) $\frac{1}{4} < x < \frac{1}{2}$

(2) $\frac{1}{3} < x < \frac{3}{5}$

In decimal form, $\frac{1}{4} = 0.25$, $\frac{3}{8} = 0.375$, and $\frac{2}{5} = 0.4$, and statement (1) can be written as $0.25 < x < 0.5$, so that both $\frac{3}{8}$ and $\frac{2}{5}$ are possible values of x. Thus, (1) alone is not sufficient, and the answer must be B, C, or E. Statement (2) can be written as $0.333 \ldots < x < 0.6$, so that both $\frac{3}{8}$ and $\frac{2}{5}$ are possible values of x. Thus, (2) alone is not sufficient, and the answer must be C or E. When both (1) and (2) are considered, it follows that $0.333 \ldots < x < 0.5$, so that, again, $\frac{3}{8}$ and $\frac{2}{5}$ are both possible values of x. Therefore, the best answer is E.

17. If a, b, and c are integers, is $a - b + c$ greater than $a + b - c$?

(1) b is negative.

(2) c is positive.

The inequality, $a - b + c > a + b - c$, is equivalent to $-b + c > b - c$, which is equivalent to $2c > 2b$, or $c > b$. Thus, the simpler inequality, $c > b$, may be considered. In (1), $b < 0$ is not sufficient to determine whether $c > b$ since no information is given about c. Hence, the answer must be B, C, or E. Similarly, in (2), $c > 0$ is not sufficient since no information is given about b, and so the answer must be C or E. Using (1) and (2) together, $b < 0 < c$, so that $c > b$, or equivalently, $a - b + c > a + b - c$. Thus, the best answer is C.

18. If $x + 2y + 1 = y - x$, what is the value of x ?

(1) $y^2 = 9$

(2) $y = 3$

The equation $x + 2y + 1 = y - x$ is equivalent to $2x = -y - 1$, or $x = -\frac{1}{2}(y + 1)$. Thus, the value of x can be determined if and only if the value of y is known. From (1) it follows that $y = 3$ or $y = -3$, so that x has two possible values as well. Thus, (1) alone is not sufficient, and the answer must be B, C, or E. In (2) the value of y is given; therefore, the value of x can be determined. Thus, (2) alone is sufficient, and the best answer is B.

19. If n is an integer, then n is divisible by how many positive integers?

(1) n is the product of two different prime numbers.

(2) n and 2^3 are each divisible by the same number of positive integers.

According to (1), $n = pq$, where both p and q are prime numbers and $p \neq q$. Thus, n is divisible by the positive integers $1, p, q, pq$, and no others. Statement (1) alone is therefore sufficient to determine the number of positive divisors of n, and the answer must be A or D. Since $2^3 = 8$ and the number of positive divisors of 8 can be determined, statement (2) alone is also sufficient, and the best answer is D.

20. How many miles long is the route from Houghton to Callahan?

(1) It will take 1 hour less time to travel the entire route at an average rate of 55 miles per hour than at an average rate of 50 miles per hour.

(2) It will take 11 hours to travel the first half of the route at an average rate of 25 miles per hour.

Using the standard formula rate $\times$ time = distance, or $rt = d$, it can be determined from (1) that $d = 50t$ and $d = 55(t - 1)$, where t is the time it takes to travel the entire route at an average rate of 50 miles per hour. These equations can be solved simultaneously for t, and then d can be determined. Therefore, (1) alone is sufficient, and the answer must be A or

D. Statement (2) can be expressed as $\frac{d}{2} = 25(11)$, which can be solved for d. Thus, statement (2) alone is also sufficient, and the best answer is D.

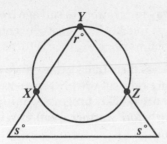

21. What is the circumference of the circle above?

   (1) The length of arc XYZ is 18.

   (2) $r = s$

Statement (1) gives only part of the circumference. Since r can be any positive number less than 180, arc XZ can be any given length. Consequently, the circumference can be any length and the answer must be B, C, or E. From (2) it follows that the triangle is equilateral and that $r = 60$. However, since no lengths are given in the figure, (2) alone is not sufficient, and the answer must be C or E. Statements (1) and (2) together are sufficient because the ratio of the length of arc XYZ to the circumference is determined and thus the circumference is determined. In particular, $\angle XYZ$ cuts off a 120° arc of the circle, so the length of arc XYZ (which is 18) is $\frac{2}{3}$ of the circumference of the circle. Therefore, the best answer is C.

22. If $p, q, r,$ and s are nonzero numbers, is
$(p-1)(q-2)^2(r-3)^3(s-4)^4 \geqq 0$?

   (1) $q > 2$ and $s > 4$

   (2) $p > 1$ and $r > 3$

Because it is always the case that $(q-2)^2 \geq 0$ and $(s-4)^4 \geq 0$, the question hinges on whether or not $p-1 \geq 0$ and $(r-3)^3 \geq 0$. Statement (1) alone is not sufficient since it gives information about q and s only. Thus, the answer must be B, C, or E. From (2), $p - 1 > 0$ and $r - 3 > 0$ (so that $(r-3)^3 > 0$) and the product is greater than or equal to 0. Thus, (2) alone is sufficient, and the best answer is B.

23. If ⊛ denotes a mathematical operation, does
$x \circledast y = y \circledast x$ **for all x and y ?**

   (1) For all x and y, $x \circledast y = 2(x^2 + y^2)$.

   (2) For all y, $0 \circledast y = 2y^2$.

According to (1), $x \circledast y = 2(x^2 + y^2)$ for all x and y, so $y \circledast x = 2(y^2 + x^2)$. Since $x^2 + y^2 = y^2 + x^2$, it follows that $x \circledast y = y \circledast x$ for all x and y. Hence, (1) alone is sufficient, and the answer must be A or D. Statement (2) is a specific case of $x \circledast y$ in which $x = 0$. There are many possible

definitions of $x \circledast y$ for which $0 \circledast y = 2y^2$ — for example, $x \circledast y = x + 2y^2$ or $x \circledast y = (x + 1)(2y^2)$. If we consider $x \circledast y = x + 2y^2$, then $y \circledast x = y + 2x^2$. But it is not true that $x + 2y^2 = y + 2x^2$ for all x and y. Thus, (2) alone is not sufficient, and the best answer is A.

24. All trainees in a certain aviator training program must take both a written test and a flight test. If 70 percent of the trainees passed the written test, and 80 percent of the trainees passed the flight test, what percent of the trainees passed both tests?

   (1) 10 percent of the trainees did not pass either test.

   (2) 20 percent of the trainees passed only the flight test.

It follows from (1) that 90 percent of the trainees passed at least one of the tests. Since 80 percent passed the flight test, 10 percent (90 – 80) passed only the written test. Thus, among those who passed the written test (70 percent), 60 percent (70 – 10) passed both tests. Therefore, (1) alone is sufficient, and the answer must be A or D. It follows from (2) that, among those who passed the flight test (80 percent), 20 percent passed only the flight test, so the remaining 60 percent passed both tests. Because statement (2) alone is also sufficient, the best answer is D.

25. If n is an integer, is $\frac{n}{15}$ an integer?

   (1) $\frac{3n}{15}$ is an integer.

   (2) $\frac{8n}{15}$ is an integer.

In (1), since $\frac{3n}{15} = \frac{n}{5}$, n must be a multiple of 5. Though some multiples of 5 are also multiples of 15 (e.g., $n = 30$), others are not (e.g., $n = 10$). Hence, (1) alone is not sufficient, and the answer must be B, C, or E. In (2), since $\frac{8n}{15}$ reduces to an integer but 8 and 15 have no common factors greater than 1, n must be divisible by 15; that is, $\frac{n}{15}$ must be an integer. Thus, (2) alone is sufficient, and the best answer is B.

Explanatory Material:
Sentence Correction, Section 4

1. The Wallerstein study indicates that even after a decade young men and women still experience some of the effects of a divorce <u>occurring when a child</u>.

   (A) occurring when a child
   (B) occurring when children
   (C) that occurred when a child
   (D) that occurred when they were children
   (E) that has occurred as each was a child

Choice D is best. The phrasing *a divorce that occurred when they were children* correctly uses the relative clause *that occurred* to modify *a divorce* and includes a pronoun and verb (*they were*) that refer unambiguously to their antecedent, *men and women*. Choice A incorrectly introduces the *when . . .* phrase with *occur-ring*, thus illogically making *divorce* the grammatical referent of *when a child*; furthermore, the singular *child* does not agree with the plural *men and women*. B replaces *child* with *children* but otherwise fails to correct A's errors of structure and logic, and C corrects only the error created by *occurring*. Choice E includes an incorrect verb tense (*has occurred*) and wrongly replaces *when* with *as*. Also, *each was* does not properly refer to *men and women*.

2. **Since 1981, when the farm depression began, the number of acres overseen by professional farm-management companies have grown from 48 million to nearly 59 million, an area that is about Colorado's size.**

   (A) have grown from 48 million to nearly 59 million, an area that is about Colorado's size
   (B) have grown from 48 million to nearly 59 million, about the size of Colorado
   (C) has grown from 48 million to nearly 59 million, an area about the size of Colorado
   (D) has grown from 48 million up to nearly 59 million, an area about the size of Colorado's
   (E) has grown from 48 million up to nearly 59 million, about Colorado's size

In choice C, the best answer, *an area about the size of Colorado* clearly describes a rough equivalence between the area of Colorado and the area overseen by the companies. In A and B, the plural verb *have* does not agree with the singular subject *number*. Choice A is also wordy, since *that is* can be deleted without loss of clarity. The absence of *an area* in B and E impairs clarity: the phrase beginning with *about* must modify a noun such as *area* that is logically equivalent to the number of acres given. In D and E *up to* is unidiomatic; the correct expression is *from x to y*. In D, *the size of Colorado's* is unidiomatic, since *of Colorado* forms a complete possessive.

3. **Some bat caves, like honeybee hives, have residents that take on different duties such as defending the entrance, acting as sentinels and to sound a warning at the approach of danger, and scouting outside the cave for new food and roosting sites.**

   (A) acting as sentinels and to sound
   (B) acting as sentinels and sounding
   (C) to act as sentinels and sound
   (D) to act as sentinels and to sound
   (E) to act as a sentinel sounding

Because the verb phrases used to describe the bats' duties are governed by the phrase *different duties such as*, they should each be expressed in the present participial (or "-ing") form to parallel *defending* and *scouting*. Choices A, C, D, and E all violate parallelism by employing infinitives (*to . . .*) in place of participial phrases. In E the singular *sentinel* is not consistent with *residents*, and the omission of *and* distorts the meaning of the original. Only B, the best answer, preserves the sense of the original, uses the correct idiom, and observes the parallelism required among and within the three main verb phrases.

4. **The only way for growers to salvage frozen citrus is to process them quickly into juice concentrate before they rot when warmer weather returns.**

   (A) to process them quickly into juice concentrate before they rot when warmer weather returns
   (B) if they are quickly processsed into juice concentrate before warmer weather returns to rot them
   (C) for them to be processed quickly into juice concentrate before the fruit rots when warmer weather returns
   (D) if the fruit is quickly processed into juice concentrate before they rot when warmer weather returns
   (E) to have it quickly processed into juice concentrate before warmer weather returns and rots the fruit

For parallelism, the linking verb *is* should link two infinitives: *The only way to salvage . . . is to process*. Choice A begins with an infinitive, but the plural pronouns *them* and *they* do not agree with the singular noun *citrus*. Choices B, C, and D do not begin with an infinitive, and all present pronoun errors: the plural pronouns cannot grammatically refer to *citrus* or *fruit*, nor can they refer to *farmers* without absurdity. The best choice, E, has parallel infinitives and uses *fruit* to refer unambiguously to *citrus*. E also expresses the cause-and-effect relationship between the return of warmer weather and the rotting of the fruit; A, C, and E merely describe these events as contemporaneous.

5. **Carbon-14 dating reveals that the megalithic monuments in Brittany are nearly 2,000 years as old as any of their supposed Mediterranean predecessors.**

   (A) as old as any of their supposed
   (B) older than any of their supposed
   (C) as old as their supposed
   (D) older than any of their supposedly
   (E) as old as their supposedly

Choices A, C, and E do not state the comparison logically. The expression *as old as* indicates equality of age, but the sentence indicates that the Brittany monuments predate the Mediterranean monuments by 2,000 years. In B, the best choice, *older than* makes this point of comparison clear. B also correctly uses the adjective *supposed*, rather than the adverb *supposedly* used in D and E, to modify the noun phrase *Mediterranean predecessors*.

6. In virtually all types of tissue in every animal species, dioxin induces the production of enzymes that are the organism's trying to metabolize, or render harmless, the chemical that is irritating it.

   (A) trying to metabolize, or render harmless, the chemical that is irritating it
   (B) trying that it metabolize, or render harmless, the chemical irritant
   (C) attempt to try to metabolize, or render harmless, such a chemical irritant
   (D) attempt to try and metabolize, or render harmless, the chemical irritating it
   (E) attempt to metabolize, or render harmless, the chemical irritant

Although an "-ing" verb such as *trying* can sometimes be used as a noun, the phrase *the organism's trying to metabolize* in A is unidiomatic because *trying* is used as the object of *organism's*. In B, *trying that it metabolize* is ungrammatical. The noun *attempt* could follow *organism's*; also, it would parallel the noun *enzymes*, and parallelism is needed here because the sentence uses the linking verb *are* to equate *enzymes* and *attempt*. In C and D, however, *attempt to try* is redundant. Choice E, which says *attempt to metabolize*, is best. The phrase *the chemical irritant* is also the most concise and precise conclusion for the sentence because it clearly refers to the *dioxin* mentioned earlier.

7. Dr. Hakuta's research among Hispanic children in the United States indicates that the more the children use both Spanish and English, their intellectual advantage is greater in skills underlying reading ability and nonverbal logic.

   (A) their intellectual advantage is greater in skills underlying reading ability and nonverbal logic
   (B) their intellectual advantage is the greater in skills underlaying reading ability and nonverbal logic
   (C) the greater their intellectual advantage in skills underlying reading ability and nonverbal logic
   (D) in skills that underlay reading ability and nonverbal logic, their intellectual advantage is the greater
   (E) in skills underlying reading ability and nonverbal logic, the greater intellectual advantage is theirs

The best choice is C. The phrase *the more the children* should be completed by a parallel phrase that begins with a comparative adjective and a noun phrase, as in *the greater their . . . advantage*. Only C correctly completes the structure with a parallel phrase. Choices A, B, D, and E present structures that are unwieldy and awkward in addition to being nonparallel, and that state the relationship between language use and skills development less clearly than C does. Also, *underlaying* in B and *underlay* in D are incorrect; the meaning of this sentence requires the present participle of "underlie," *underlying,* as a modifier of *skills*.

8. Lacking information about energy use, people tend to overestimate the amount of energy used by equipment, such as lights, that are visible and must be turned on and off and underestimate that used by unobtrusive equipment, such as water heaters.

   (A) equipment, such as lights, that are visible and must be turned on and off and underestimate that
   (B) equipment, such as lights, that are visible and must be turned on and off and underestimate it when
   (C) equipment, such as lights, that is visible and must be turned on and off and underestimate it when
   (D) visible equipment, such as lights, that must be turned on and off and underestimate that
   (E) visible equipment, such as lights, that must be turned on and off and underestimate it when

Choices A and B incorrectly use the plural verb *are* with the singular noun *equipment*. In B, C, and E, *when used by* does not parallel *amount . . . used by* and nonsensically suggests that the people are used by the equipment. D, the best choice, correctly parallels *the amount . . . used by* with *that used by*, in which *that* is the pronoun substitute for *amount*. Moreover, D solves the agreement problem of A and B by omitting the *to be* verb used with *visible* and placing *visible* before *equipment*; the phrase *visible equipment* is also parallel with *unobtrusive equipment*.

9. Astronomers at the Palomar Observatory have discovered a distant supernova explosion, one that they believe is a type previously unknown to science.

   (A) that they believe is
   (B) that they believe it to be
   (C) they believe that it is of
   (D) they believe that is
   (E) they believe to be of

Choice E is best. The relative pronoun *that*, which follows *one* in A and B, should be deleted, since the pronoun *one* is sufficient to introduce the modifier and the sentence is more fluid without *that*. The verb form *to be* is needed in place of *is* here because *one* is the object of *they believe* and thus cannot serve as the subject of a conjugated verb. In B and C, *it* and *that it* are intrusive and ungrammatical: the idiom is "believe x to be y." Also, A, B, and D lack *of* and so illogically equate this particular explosion with the whole class of explosions to which it belongs: it is not *a type* but possibly one *of a type*.

10. However much United States voters may agree that there is waste in government and that the government as a whole spends beyond its means, it is difficult to find broad support for a movement toward a minimal state.

    (A) However much United States voters may agree that
    (B) Despite the agreement among United States voters to the fact
    (C) Although United States voters agree
    (D) Even though United States voters may agree
    (E) There is agreement among United States voters that

A is the best choice. Choices B, C, and D incorrectly omit *that* after *agree*; *that* is needed to create the parallel construction *agree that there is waste . . . and that the government . . . spends*. Choice E, though it retains *that*, is grammatically incorrect: because E starts with an independent rather than a subordinate clause and separates its two independent clauses with a comma, it creates a run-on sentence with no logical connection established between the halves. In B, *the agreement . . . to the fact* is unidiomatic, and B, C, and E alter the sense of the original sentence by saying that voters *agree* rather than that they *may agree*.

11. Based on accounts of various ancient writers, scholars have painted a sketchy picture of the activities of an all-female cult that, perhaps as early as the sixth century B.C., worshipped a goddess known in Latin as Bona Dea, "the good goddess."

    (A) Based on accounts of various ancient writers
    (B) Basing it on various ancient writers' accounts
    (C) With accounts of various ancient writers used for a basis
    (D) By the accounts of various ancient writers they used
    (E) Using accounts of various ancient writers

In choice A, the introductory clause beginning *Based on* modifies *scholars*, the noun that immediately follows it: in other words, A says that *scholars* were *based on the accounts of various ancient writers*. Choice B is awkward and imprecise in that the referent for the pronoun *it* is not immediately clear. C and D are also wordy and awkward, and in D *By the accounts . . . they used* is an unidiomatic and roundabout way of saying that scholars used the accounts. E, the best choice, is clear and concise; it correctly uses a present participle (or "-ing" verb) to introduce the modifier describing how the scholars worked.

12. Formulas for cash flow and the ratio of debt to equity do not apply to new small businesses in the same way as they do to established big businesses, because they are growing and are seldom in equilibrium.

    (A) Formulas for cash flow and the ratio of debt to equity do not apply to new small businesses in the same way as they do to established big businesses, because they are growing and are seldom in equilibrium.
    (B) Because they are growing and are seldom in equilibrium, formulas for cash flow and the ratio of debt to equity do not apply to new small businesses in the same way as they do to established big businesses.
    (C) Because they are growing and are seldom in equilibrium, new small businesses are not subject to the same applicability of formulas for cash flow and the ratio of debt to equity as established big businesses.
    (D) Because new small businesses are growing and are seldom in equilibrium, formulas for cash flow and the ratio of debt to equity do not apply to them in the same way as to established big businesses.
    (E) New small businesses are not subject to the applicability of formulas for cash flow and the ratio of debt to equity in the same way as established big businesses, because they are growing and are seldom in equilibrium.

In A, the *they* after *because* is ambiguous; it seems illogically to refer to *Formulas* because *they* and *Formulas* are each the grammatical subject of a clause and because the previous *they* refers to *Formulas*. In A and B, *do not apply to . . . in the same way as they do to* is wordy and awkward. D, the best choice, says more concisely *in the same way as to*. Also in B, because *they* refers to *formulas*, the introductory clause states confusedly that the formulas are growing. In C and E, *subject to the [same] applicability of . . .* is wordy, awkward, and imprecise; furthermore, *are* is preferable either before or after *established big businesses* to complete the comparison. Finally, the referent of *they* is not immediately clear in E.

13. State officials report that soaring rates of liability insurance have risen to force cutbacks in the operations of everything from local governments and school districts to day-care centers and recreational facilities.

    (A) rates of liability insurance have risen to force
    (B) rates of liability insurance are a force for
    (C) rates for liability insurance are forcing
    (D) rises in liability insurance rates are forcing
    (E) liability insurance rates have risen to force

In choices A and B, *rates of* is incorrect; when *rates* means "prices charged," it should be followed by *for*. Also in B, *are a force for* does not accurately convey the meaning that the soaring rates are actually forcing cutbacks in the present. In A and E, it is redundant to say that soaring rates *have risen*. Similarly, the word *rises* makes D redundant. C, the best choice, is idiomatic and concise, and it correctly uses the progressive verb form *are forcing* to indicate an ongoing situation.

14. **Paleontologists believe that fragments of a primate jawbone unearthed in Burma and estimated <u>at 40 to 44 million years old provide evidence of</u> a crucial step along the evolutionary path that led to human beings.**

   (A) at 40 to 44 million years old provide evidence of
   (B) as being 40 to 44 million years old provides evidence of
   (C) that it is 40 to 44 million years old provides evidence of what was
   (D) to be 40 to 44 million years old provide evidence of
   (E) as 40 to 44 million years old provides evidence of what was

D, the best choice, correctly follows *estimated* with *to be*. The other choices present structures that are not idiomatic when used in conjunction with *estimated*. Choices B, C, and E all mismatch the singular verb *provides* with its plural subject, *fragments*, and in choices C and E, *what was* is unnecessary and wordy. In choice C, the use of the verb phrase *estimated that it is* produces an ungrammatical sentence.

15. **In his research paper, Dr. Frosh, medical director of the Payne Whitney Clinic, distinguishes <u>mood swings, which may be violent without their being grounded in mental disease, from genuine manic-depressive psychosis</u>.**

   (A) mood swings, which may be violent without their being grounded in mental disease, from genuine manic-depressive psychosis
   (B) mood swings, perhaps violent without being grounded in mental disease, and genuine manic-depressive psychosis
   (C) between mood swings, which may be violent without being grounded in mental disease, and genuine manic-depressive psychosis
   (D) between mood swings, perhaps violent without being grounded in mental disease, from genuine manic-depressive psychosis
   (E) genuine manic-depressive psychosis and mood swings, which may be violent without being grounded in mental disease

The best choice is C because it uses the idiomatically correct expression *distinguishes between* x *and* y and because it provides a structure in which the relative clause beginning *which may be violent* clearly modifies *mood swings*. The other choices use *distinguishes* in unidiomatic constructions. Additionally, *their* in A is intrusive and unnecessary, and the modifier of *mood swings* in B and D (*perhaps violent*) is awkward and less clear than the more developed clause *which may be violent*.

16. **Unlike a typical automobile loan, which requires a fifteen- to twenty-percent down payment, <u>the lease-loan buyer is not required to make</u> an initial deposit on the new vehicle.**

   (A) the lease-loan buyer is not required to make
   (B) with lease-loan buying there is no requirement of
   (C) lease-loan buyers are not required to make
   (D) for the lease-loan buyer there is no requirement of
   (E) a lease-loan does not require the buyer to make

Choice E, the best answer, correctly uses a parallel construction to draw a logical comparison: *Unlike a typical automobile loan, . . . a lease-loan . . . .* Choice A illogically compares an *automobile loan*, an inanimate thing, with a *lease-loan buyer*, a person. In choice C, *buyers* makes the comparison inconsistent in number as well as illogical. Choices B and D are syntactically and logically flawed because each attempts to compare the noun *loan* and a prepositional phrase: *with lease-loan buying* in B and *for the lease-loan buyer* in D. Choices B and D are also imprecise and awkward. Finally, choice E is the only option that supplies an active verb form, *does not require*, to parallel *requires*.

17. **Native American burial sites dating back 5,000 years indicate that the residents of Maine at that time <u>were part of a widespread culture of Algonquian-speaking people</u>.**

   (A) were part of a widespread culture of Algonquian-speaking people
   (B) had been part of a widespread culture of people who were Algonquian-speaking
   (C) were people who were part of a widespread culture that was Algonquian-speaking
   (D) had been people who were part of a widespread culture that was Algonquian-speaking
   (E) were a people which had been part of a widespread, Algonquian-speaking culture

Choice A is best because it correctly uses the simple past tense, *the residents . . . at that time were*, and because it is the most concise. In B and D, the replacement of *were* with the past perfect *had been* needlessly changes the original meaning by suggesting that the Native Americans had previously ceased to be part of the widespread culture. All of the choices but A are wordy, and in C, D, and E the word *people* redundantly describes *the residents* rather than the larger group to which the residents belonged. These choices are also imprecise because they state that the *culture*, rather than *people*, spoke the Algonquian language. Choice E displays inconsistent tenses and an error of pronoun reference, *people which*.

18. Each of Hemingway's wives — Hadley Richardson, Pauline Pfeiffer, Martha Gelhorn, and Mary Welsh — were strong and interesting women, very different from the often pallid women who populate his novels.

(A) Each of Hemingway's wives — Hadley Richardson, Pauline Pfeiffer, Martha Gelhorn, and Mary Welsh — were strong and interesting women,

(B) Hadley Richardson, Pauline Pfeiffer, Martha Gelhorn, and Mary Welsh — each of them Hemingway's wives — were strong and interesting women,

(C) Hemingway's wives — Hadley Richardson, Pauline Pfeiffer, Martha Gelhorn, and Mary Welsh — were all strong and interesting women,

(D) Strong and interesting women — Hadley Richardson, Pauline Pfeiffer, Martha Gelhorn, and Mary Welsh — each a wife of Hemingway, was

(E) Strong and interesting women — Hadley Richardson, Pauline Pfeiffer, Martha Gelhorn, and Mary Welsh — every one of Hemingway's wives were

Each choice but C contains errors of agreement. In both A and E, the singular subject (*each* in A, *every one* in E) does not agree with the plural verb *were*, while in D, the plural subject *women* is mismatched with the singular verb *was*. In B, the subject and verb agree, but the descriptive phrase placed between them creates an illogical statement because *each* cannot be *wives*; *each* can be one of the wives, or a wife. The pronoun constructions in A, B, D, and E are wordy; also, B, D, and E are very awkwardly structured and do not convey the point about Hemingway's wives clearly. Choice C correctly links *wives* with *were*, eliminates the unnecessary pronouns, and provides a clearer structure.

19. In addition to having more protein than wheat does, the protein in rice is higher quality than that in wheat, with more of the amino acids essential to the human diet.

(A) the protein in rice is higher quality than that in
(B) rice has protein of higher quality than that in
(C) the protein in rice is higher in quality than it is in
(D) rice protein is higher in quality than it is in
(E) rice has a protein higher in quality than

In this sentence, the initial clause modifies the nearest noun, identifying it as the thing being compared with *wheat*. By making *protein* the noun modified, choices A, C, and D illogically compare *wheat* with *protein* and claim that the protein in rice has more protein than wheat does. In C and D, the comparative structure *higher in quality than it is in wheat* absurdly suggests that rice protein contains wheat. B, the best choice, logically compares *wheat* to *rice* by placing the noun *rice* immediately after the initial clause. B also uses *that* to refer to *protein* in making the comparison between the proteins of rice and wheat. Choice E needs either *that in* or *does* after *wheat* to make a complete and logical comparison.

20. An array of tax incentives has led to a boom in the construction of new office buildings; so abundant has capital been for commercial real estate that investors regularly scour the country for areas in which to build.

(A) so abundant has capital been for commercial real estate that
(B) capital has been so abundant for commercial real estate, so that
(C) the abundance of capital for commercial real estate has been such,
(D) such has the abundance of capital been for commercial real estate that
(E) such has been an abundance of capital for commercial real estate,

Choice A is best. The construction *so abundant has capital been . . . that* correctly and clearly expresses the relationship between the abundance and the investors' response. In choice B, the repetition of *so* is illogical and unidiomatic. Choices C, D, and E alter somewhat the intended meaning of the sentence; because of its position in these statements, *such* functions to mean "of a kind" rather than to intensify *abundant*. Choice D awkwardly separates *has* and *been*, and the omission of *that* from C and E makes those choices ungrammatical.

21. Defense attorneys have occasionally argued that their clients' misconduct stemmed from a reaction to something ingested, but in attributing criminal or delinquent behavior to some food allergy, the perpetrators are in effect told that they are not responsible for their actions.

(A) in attributing criminal or delinquent behavior to some food allergy
(B) if criminal or delinquent behavior is attributed to an allergy to some food
(C) in attributing behavior that is criminal or delinquent to an allergy to some food
(D) if some food allergy is attributed as the cause of criminal or delinquent behavior
(E) in attributing a food allergy as the cause of criminal or delinquent behavior

In choices A, C, and E, *in attributing . . . behavior* modifies *the perpetrators*, producing the illogical statement that the perpetrators rather than the defense attorneys are attributing behavior to food allergies. Choice C is also wordy, and *attributing . . . as* is unidiomatic in E. In the correct form of the expression, one *attributes* x, an effect, *to* y, a cause; or, if a passive construction is used, x *is attributed to* y. D avoids the initial modification error by using a passive construction (in which the attributors are not identified), but *attributed* x *as the cause of* y is unidiomatic. Choice B is best.

22. The voluminous personal papers of Thomas Alva Edison reveal that his inventions typically <u>sprang to life not in a flash of inspiration but evolved slowly</u> from previous works.

- (A) sprang to life not in a flash of inspiration but evolved slowly
- (B) sprang to life not in a flash of inspiration but were slowly evolved
- (C) did not spring to life in a flash of inspiration but evolved slowly
- (D) did not spring to life in a flash of inspiration but had slowly evolved
- (E) did not spring to life in a flash of inspiration but they were slowly evolved

C, the best choice, places *not* and *but* in such a way that the distinction between springing to life in a flash of inspiration and evolving slowly is logically and idiomatically expressed. A and B are faulty because, for grammatical parallelism, *not in a flash . . .* must be followed by *but in . . .*, not by a conjugated form of the verb. Moreover, *were slowly evolved* is incorrect in B because *evolve*, in this sense of the word, cannot be made passive. Choices C, D, and E all correctly place *not* before *spring*. D, however, contains inconsistent verb tenses; E contains the faulty passive and an intrusive *they*.

23. <u>As more and more people invest their money</u> in savings certificates or money-market funds in order to earn higher interest, they are abandoning traditional low-interest investment havens such as passbook accounts and life insurance policies.

- (A) As more and more people invest their money
- (B) While people have more and more been investing their money
- (C) As money is more and more invested by people
- (D) More and more, when investors put their money
- (E) While, more and more, investors have been putting their money

A, the best choice, most precisely establishes that the action of the main clause is a consequence of the action of the introductory clause, and that the two actions are continuing contemporaneously. *While* in B and E is less clear than *as* because *while* can indicate contrast or concession rather than contemporaneity. The present perfect tense in these choices is also inappropriate; contemporaneous actions should be expressed by verbs of the same tense. C contains an awkward use of the passive. B, C, D, and E alter the original meaning by changing *more and more* from an adjectival to an awkwardly placed adverbial phrase: that is, *more and more* no longer modifies *people* but loosely describes the action of investing money in savings certificates.

24. Margaret Courtney-Clark has traveled to remote dwellings in the Transvaal to photograph the art of Ndebele women, <u>whose murals are brilliantly colored, their geometrical symmetries embellished with old and new iconography and in a style that varies from woman to woman and house to house</u>.

- (A) whose murals are brilliantly colored, their geometrical symmetries embellished with old and new iconography and in a style that varies from woman to woman and house to house
- (B) whose murals are brilliantly colored, their geometrical symmetries are embellished with old and new iconography, and their style is varying among women and houses
- (C) whose murals are brilliantly colored, their geometrical symmetries are embellished with old and new iconography, and they are in styles that vary from woman to woman and house to house
- (D) with murals brilliantly colored, their geometrical symmetries embellished with old and new iconography, and their style varies among women and houses
- (E) with murals that are brilliantly colored, their geometrical symmetries embellished with old and new iconography, and their styles vary among women and houses

By inserting *are* before *established*, B and C turn the modifier of *murals* into an independent clause (one containing a subject and a conjugated verb) and thus create run-on sentences. All the choices but A also incorrectly create independent clauses by including both a pronoun subject and a conjugated form of the verb "to vary" after *and*. In B, the replacement of the present tense *varies* with the present progressive *is varying* is also unnecessary and awkward. The phrase *among women and houses*, which appears in B, D, and E, is imprecise and awkward. In D and E, *with* does not indicate *whose* murals are being described. Choice A, the best answer, provides the appropriate structures for the various modifiers, and it is clear.

25. Florida will gain another quarter-million jobs this year alone, many of them in <u>high-paying fields like electronics and banking, making the state's economy far more diversified than</u> ten years ago.

(A) high-paying fields like electronics and banking, making the state's economy far more diversified than

(B) high-paying fields like electronics and banking, and making the state's economy far more diversified than its economy

(C) high-paying fields such as electronics and banking, to make the state's economy far more diversified than

(D) such high-paying fields as electronics and banking, making the state's economy far more diversified than it was

(E) such high-paying fields as electronics and banking, and make the state's economy far more diversified than it was

Choice D is best because it employs the expression *such . . . as* to list examples, correctly introduces the subordinate modifier with the present participle *making*, and logically completes the intended comparison by using the construction *than it was*. A and B are faulty because *like* is properly used to express similarity rather than to present instances. In A and C, the intended comparison of economic conditions now and ten years ago is incomplete because those choices fail to include *it was*, with *it* referring to *the state's economy*. Choices B and C have improperly formed subordinate modifiers after *banking*; *and* is wrong in B and E because the constructions it introduces cannot be logically compounded with any other grammatical structure in the sentence.

Explanatory Material: Problem Solving II, Section 5

1. During the first week of September, a shoe retailer sold 10 pairs of a certain style of oxfords at $35.00 a pair. If, during the second week of September, 15 pairs were sold at the sale price of $27.50 a pair, by what amount did the revenue from weekly sales of these oxfords increase during the second week?

(A) $62.50
(B) $75.00
(C) $112.50
(D) $137.50
(E) $175.00

The total sales revenue from the oxfords during the first week was 10($35.00) = $350.00, and during the second week it was 15($27.50) = $412.50. Thus, the increase in sales revenue was $412.50 – $350.00 = $62.50, and the best answer is A.

2. The number 2 – 0.5 is how many times the number 1 – 0.5 ?

(A) 2
(B) 2.5
(C) 3
(D) 3.5
(E) 4

Since 2 – 0.5 = 1.5 and 1 – 0.5 = 0.5, the number 2 – 0.5 is $\frac{1.5}{0.5} = 3$ times the number 1 – 0.5. Thus, the best answer is C.

3. If $x = -1$, then $-(x^4 + x^3 + x^2 + x) =$

(A) –10
(B) –4
(C) 0
(D) 4
(E) 10

$-((-1)^4 + (-1)^3 + (-1)^2 + (-1)) = -(1 - 1 + 1 - 1) = -0 = 0$. The best answer is C.

4. Coins are dropped into a toll box so that the box is being filled at the rate of approximately 2 cubic feet per hour. If the empty rectangular box is 4 feet long, 4 feet wide, and 3 feet deep, approximately how many hours does it take to fill the box?

(A) 4
(B) 8
(C) 16
(D) 24
(E) 48

The volume of the toll box is (4)(4)(3) = 48 cubic feet. Since the box is filled at the rate of 2 cubic feet per hour, it takes $\frac{48}{2} = 24$ hours to fill the box. Thus, the best answer is D.

5. $\left(\frac{1}{5}\right)^2 - \left(\frac{1}{5}\right)\left(\frac{1}{4}\right) =$

(A) $-\frac{1}{20}$

(B) $-\frac{1}{100}$

(C) $\frac{1}{100}$

(D) $\frac{1}{20}$

(E) $\frac{1}{5}$

$\left(\frac{1}{5}\right)^2 - \left(\frac{1}{5}\right)\left(\frac{1}{4}\right) = \frac{1}{25} - \frac{1}{20} = \frac{4}{100} - \frac{5}{100} = -\frac{1}{100}$. Thus, the best answer is B.

6. A club collected exactly $599 from its members. If each member contributed at least $12, what is the greatest number of members the club could have?

   (A) 43
   (B) 44
   (C) 49
   (D) 50
   (E) 51

If n is the number of members in the club, then at least $12n$ dollars, but perhaps more, was contributed. Thus, $12n \leq 599$, or $n \leq \frac{599}{12} = 49\frac{11}{12}$. Since n is a whole number, the greatest possible value of n is 49. Therefore, the best answer is C.

7. A union contract specifies a 6 percent salary increase plus a $450 bonus for each employee. For a certain employee, this is equivalent to an 8 percent salary increase. What was this employee's salary before the new contract?

   (A) $21,500
   (B) $22,500
   (C) $23,500
   (D) $24,300
   (E) $25,000

If S is the employee's salary before the new contract, then the increase in the employee's earnings is $450 plus 6 percent of S, or $450 + 0.06S$. Since this increase is 8 percent of S, it follows that $450 + 0.06S = 0.08S$, or $0.02S = 450, so that $S = \frac{\$450}{0.02} = \$22,500$. Thus, the best answer is B.

8. If n is a positive integer and $k + 2 = 3^n$, which of the following could NOT be a value of k ?

   (A) 1
   (B) 4
   (C) 7
   (D) 25
   (E) 79

As each of the choices is substituted for k, the sum $k + 2$ can be examined to determine whether or not it is a power of 3. The sums corresponding to A-E are 3, 6, 9, 27, and 81, respectively. Note that $3 = 3^1$, $9 = 3^2$, $27 = 3^3$, and $81 = 3^4$, but 6 is not a power of 3. So 4 cannot be a value of k, whereas 1, 7, 25, and 79 can be values of k. Thus, the best answer is B.

   Alternatively, since any power of 3 must be odd, $k = 3^n - 2$ must also be odd and $k = 4$ is not possible.

9. Elena purchased brand X pens for $4.00 apiece and brand Y pens for $2.80 apiece. If Elena purchased a total of 12 of these pens for $42.00, how many brand X pens did she purchase?

   (A) 4
   (B) 5
   (C) 6
   (D) 7
   (E) 8

Let x denote the number of brand X pens Elena purchased. Then the number of brand Y pens she purchased was $12 - x$ and the total cost of the pens was $4x + 2.80(12 - x) = 42.00$ dollars. This equation can be solved as follows.

$$4x + 2.80(12 - x) = 42.00$$
$$4x + 33.60 - 2.80x = 42.00$$
$$1.20x = 8.40$$
$$x = 7$$

Thus, the best answer is D.

10. If the length and width of a rectangular garden plot were each increased by 20 percent, what would be the percent increase in the area of the plot?

   (A) 20%
   (B) 24%
   (C) 36%
   (D) 40%
   (E) 44%

If the length and width are L and W, respectively, then the increased length and width are $1.2L$ and $1.2W$, respectively. Thus, the increased area is $(1.2L)(1.2W) = 1.44LW$, and the percent increase in area is 44%. The best answer is therefore E.

11. The population of a bacteria culture doubles every 2 minutes. Approximately how many minutes will it take for the population to grow from 1,000 to 500,000 bacteria?

   (A) 10
   (B) 12
   (C) 14
   (D) 16
   (E) 18

After each successive 2-minute period, the bacteria population is 2,000, 4,000, 8,000, 16,000, 32,000, 64,000, 128,000, 256,000, and then 512,000. Therefore, after eight 2-minute periods, or 16 minutes, the population is only 256,000; and after nine 2-minute periods, or 18 minutes, the population is just over 500,000. Thus, the best answer is E.

   Alternatively, if n denotes the number of 2-minute periods it takes for the population to grow from 1,000 to 500,000, then $2^n(1,000) = 500,000$, or $2^n = 500$. Since $2^4 = 16$, $2^8 = 16^2 = 256$, and $2^9 = 2(256) = 512$, the value of n is approximately 9. Thus, the approximate time is $2(9) = 18$ minutes.

12. When 10 is divided by the positive integer n, the remainder is $n - 4$. Which of the following could be the value of n ?

   (A) 3
   (B) 4
   (C) 7
   (D) 8
   (E) 12

One way to answer the question is to examine each option to see which one satisfies the specified divisibility conditions. A: If $n = 3$, then $n - 4 = -1$; but 10 divided by 3 has remainder 1. B: If $n = 4$, then $n - 4 = 0$; but 10 divided by 4 has remainder 2. C: If $n = 7$, then $n - 4 = 3$, which does equal the remainder when 10 is divided by 7. That neither D nor E gives a possible value of n can be shown in the manner used for A and B. Thus, the best answer is C.

   An alternative solution, which does not involve extensive checking of each option, is to first write the divisibility condition as the equation $10 = nq + (n - 4)$, where q denotes the quotient. Then,
$$14 = nq + n = n(q + 1),$$
so n must be a divisor of 14. Also, $n - 4 \geq 0$, or $n \geq 4$. Thus, $n = 7$ or $n = 14$.

13. For a light that has an intensity of 60 candles at its source, the intensity in candles, S, of the light at a point d feet from the source is given by the formula $S = \dfrac{60k}{d^2}$, where k is a constant. If the intensity of the light is 30 candles at a distance of 2 feet from the source, what is the intensity of the light at a distance of 20 feet from the source?

   (A) $\dfrac{3}{10}$ candle

   (B) $\dfrac{1}{2}$ candle

   (C) $1\dfrac{1}{3}$ candles

   (D) 2 candles

   (E) 3 candles

In order to compute $S = \dfrac{60k}{d^2}$ when $d = 20$, the value of the constant k must be determined. Since $S = 30$ candles when $d = 2$ feet, substituting these values into the formula yields $30 = \dfrac{60k}{2^2}$, or $k = 2$. Therefore, when $d = 20$ feet, the intensity is $S = \dfrac{60(2)}{20^2} = \dfrac{120}{400} = \dfrac{3}{10}$ candle. Thus, the best answer is A.

14. If x and y are prime numbers, which of the following CANNOT be the sum of x and y ?

   (A) 5
   (B) 9
   (C) 13
   (D) 16
   (E) 23

Note that $5 = 2 + 3$, $9 = 2 + 7$, $13 = 2 + 11$, and $16 = 5 + 11$, so that each of choices A-D may be expressed as a sum of two prime numbers. However, if $23 = x + y$, then either x or y (but not both) must be even. Since 2 is the only even prime number, either $x = 2$ and $y = 21$, or $x = 21$ and $y = 2$. Since 21 is not prime, 23 cannot be expressed as the sum of two prime numbers, and the best answer is E.

15. Of the 3,600 employees of Company X, $\dfrac{1}{3}$ are clerical. If the clerical staff were to be reduced by $\dfrac{1}{3}$, what percent of the total number of the remaining employees would then be clerical?

   (A) 25%
   (B) 22.2%
   (C) 20%
   (D) 12.5%
   (E) 11.1%

The number of clerical employees is $\dfrac{1}{3}(3,600) = 1,200$. As a result of the proposed reduction, the number of clerical employees would be reduced by $\dfrac{1}{3}(1,200) = 400$ and consequently would equal $1,200 - 400 = 800$. The total number of employees would then be $3,600 - 400 = 3,200$. Hence, the percent of clerical employees would then be $\dfrac{800}{1,200} = \dfrac{1}{4} = 25\%$. Thus, the best answer is A.

16. In which of the following pairs are the two numbers reciprocals of each other?

   I. 3 and $\dfrac{1}{3}$

   II. $\dfrac{1}{17}$ and $\dfrac{-1}{17}$

   III. $\sqrt{3}$ and $\dfrac{\sqrt{3}}{3}$

   (A) I only
   (B) II only
   (C) I and II
   (D) I and III
   (E) II and III

Two numbers are reciprocals of each other if and only if their product is 1. Since $3\left(\dfrac{1}{3}\right) = 1$, $\left(\dfrac{1}{17}\right)\left(-\dfrac{1}{17}\right) = -\dfrac{1}{289} \neq 1$, and $\sqrt{3}\left(\dfrac{\sqrt{3}}{3}\right) = \dfrac{3}{3} = 1$, only in I and III are the two numbers reciprocals of each other. Thus, the best answer is D.

17. For a certain performance, x tickets for lower-level seats were sold at \$10 each and y tickets for balcony seats were sold at \$6 each. If there were no other tickets sold and the number of tickets sold for lower-level seats was 3 times the number of tickets sold for balcony seats, which of the following expresses the total number of dollars from ticket sales in terms of x ?

(A) $12x$
(B) $16x$
(C) $28x$
(D) $32x$
(E) $36x$

The total number of dollars from ticket sales is $10x + 6y$. In addition, we know that $x = 3y$, or $y = \dfrac{x}{3}$. Therefore, by substituting $\dfrac{x}{3}$ for y, the ticket sales in terms of x is

$10x + 6\left(\dfrac{x}{3}\right) = 10x + 2x = 12x$ dollars. Thus, the best answer is A.

18. If the circumference of a circular region is c, which of the following represents the area of that circular region?

(A) $\dfrac{c^2}{2}$

(B) $\dfrac{c^2}{4}$

(C) $\dfrac{c^2}{2\pi}$

(D) $\dfrac{c^2}{4\pi}$

(E) $\dfrac{c^2}{4\pi^2}$

If r is the radius of the circle, then $c = 2\pi r$, so that $r = \dfrac{c}{2\pi}$. Hence, the area of the circular region is

$$\pi r^2 = \pi\left(\dfrac{c}{2\pi}\right)^2 = \pi\left(\dfrac{c^2}{4\pi^2}\right) = \dfrac{c^2}{4\pi},$$

and the best answer is D.

19. Each of the integers from 0 to 9, inclusive, is written on a separate slip of blank paper and the ten slips are dropped into a hat. If the slips are then drawn one at a time without replacement, how many must be drawn to ensure that the numbers on two of the slips drawn will have a sum of 10 ?

(A) Three
(B) Four
(C) Five
(D) Six
(E) Seven

There are four pairs of numbers, each having a sum equal to 10: $1 + 9$, $2 + 8$, $3 + 7$, and $4 + 6$. Drawing any five of these eight numbers will ensure that at least one of the four pairs is included. Two extra drawings are necessary in case both 0 and 5 are drawn in the first five drawings. Thus, seven drawings will ensure that a sum of two of the drawn numbers is 10. (To see that six drawings are not sufficient, consider the possibility of drawing 0, 1, 2, 3, 4, and 5.) The best answer is E.

20. In a certain formula, p is directly proportional to s and inversely proportional to r. If $p = 1$ when $r = 0.5$ and $s = 2$, what is the value of p in terms of r and s ?

(A) $\dfrac{s}{r}$

(B) $\dfrac{r}{4s}$

(C) $\dfrac{s}{4r}$

(D) $\dfrac{r}{s}$

(E) $\dfrac{4r}{s}$

According to the question, $p = k\left(\dfrac{s}{r}\right)$, where k is the proportionality constant to be determined. Since $p = 1$ when $r = 0.5$ and $s = 2$, it follows that $1 = k\left(\dfrac{2}{0.5}\right) = 4k$, or $k = \dfrac{1}{4}$. Therefore, $p = \dfrac{1}{4}\left(\dfrac{s}{r}\right) = \dfrac{s}{4r}$, and the best answer is C.

Explanatory Material: Critical Reasoning, Section 6

1. Which of the following best completes the passage below?

   In a survey of job applicants, two-fifths admitted to being at least a little dishonest. However, the survey may underestimate the proportion of job applicants who are dishonest, because -----.

   (A) some dishonest people taking the survey might have claimed on the survey to be honest
   (B) some generally honest people taking the survey might have claimed on the survey to be dishonest
   (C) some people who claimed on the survey to be at least a little dishonest may be very dishonest
   (D) some people who claimed on the survey to be dishonest may have been answering honestly
   (E) some people who are not job applicants are probably at least a little dishonest

If applicants who are in fact dishonest claimed to be honest, the survey results would show a smaller proportion of dishonest applicants than actually exists. Therefore, A is the best answer.

Choice B is inappropriate because generally honest applicants who claimed to be dishonest could contribute to the overestimation, but not to the underestimation, of dishonest applicants. Choice D is inappropriate because applicants who admitted their dishonesty would not contribute to an underestimation of the proportion of dishonest applicants. Choices C and E are inappropriate because the argument is concerned neither with degrees of dishonesty nor with the honesty of nonapplicants.

Questions 2-3 are based on the following.

The average life expectancy for the United States population as a whole is 73.9 years, but children born in Hawaii will live an average of 77 years, and those born in Louisiana, 71.7 years. If a newlywed couple from Louisiana were to begin their family in Hawaii, therefore, their children would be expected to live longer than would be the case if the family remained in Louisiana.

2. Which of the following, if true, would most seriously weaken the conclusion drawn in the passage?

   (A) Insurance company statisticians do not believe that moving to Hawaii will significantly lengthen the average Louisianian's life.
   (B) The governor of Louisiana has falsely alleged that statistics for his state are inaccurate.
   (C) The longevity ascribed to Hawaii's current population is attributable mostly to genetically determined factors.
   (D) Thirty percent of all Louisianians can expect to live longer than 77 years.
   (E) Most of the Hawaiian Islands have levels of air pollution well below the national average for the United States.

Choice C suggests that a significant proportion of Hawaii's population is genetically predisposed to be long-lived. Since Louisianians are not necessarily so predisposed, and since the Louisianians' children will acquire their genetic characteristics from their parents, not from their birthplace, choice C presents a reason to doubt that Hawaiian-born children of native Louisianians will have an increased life expectancy. Therefore, C is the best answer.

Because the conclusion concerns people born in Hawaii, not the average Louisianian, A does not weaken the conclusion. Because the governor's allegation is false (choice B), it cannot affect the conclusion. Choice D fails to weaken the conclusion because it is consistent with the information given and the conclusion about life expectancy. By suggesting that Hawaii's environment is in one respect particularly healthy, E supports the conclusion.

3. **Which of the following statements, if true, would most significantly strengthen the conclusion drawn in the passage?**

   (A) As population density increases in Hawaii, life expectancy figures for that state are likely to be revised downward.
   (B) Environmental factors tending to favor longevity are abundant in Hawaii and less numerous in Louisiana.
   (C) Twenty-five percent of all Louisianians who move to Hawaii live longer than 77 years.
   (D) Over the last decade, average life expectancy has risen at a higher rate for Louisianians than for Hawaiians.
   (E) Studies show that the average life expectancy for Hawaiians who move permanently to Louisiana is roughly equal to that of Hawaiians who remain in Hawaii.

If B is true, the greater abundance of longevity-promoting environmental factors it mentions is probably at least partly responsible for the higher life expectancy in Hawaii. Children born in Hawaii benefit from these factors from birth, and thus Louisianians who have children in Hawaii increase their children's chances of living longer. Therefore, B is the best answer.

If life expectancy in Hawaii is likely to be falling, as A says, the argument is weakened rather than strengthened. Choices C and E, in the absence of other relevant information, have no bearing on the conclusion; thus, C and E are inappropriate. Choice D is irrelevant, because the information it mentions about rates would already have been incorporated into the statistics cited in the passage.

4. Insurance Company X is considering issuing a new policy to cover services required by elderly people who suffer from diseases that afflict the elderly. Premiums for the policy must be low enough to attract customers. Therefore, Company X is concerned that the income from the policies would not be sufficient to pay for the claims that would be made.

   Which of the following strategies would be most likely to minimize Company X's losses on the policies?

   (A) Attracting middle-aged customers unlikely to submit claims for benefits for many years
   (B) Insuring only those individuals who did not suffer any serious diseases as children
   (C) Including a greater number of services in the policy than are included in other policies of lower cost
   (D) Insuring only those individuals who were rejected by other companies for similar policies
   (E) Insuring only those individuals who are wealthy enough to pay for the medical services

Insurance companies can improve the ratio of revenues to claims paid, thus minimizing losses, if they insure as many people belonging to low-risk groups as they can. Because the strategy described in A adds a low-risk group to the pool of policyholders, A is the best answer.

Choice B is irrelevant, since no link is established between childhood diseases and diseases affecting the elderly. Choice C is inappropriate, since increasing the number of services covered is unlikely to minimize losses. Choice D is inappropriate, since it would increase the likelihood that claims against the policy will be made. Because policyholders will file claims against the policy for services covered rather than pay for the cost of the services themselves, E is irrelevant.

5. A program instituted in a particular state allows parents to prepay their children's future college tuition at current rates. The program then pays the tuition annually for the child at any of the state's public colleges in which the child enrolls. Parents should participate in the program as a means of decreasing the cost for their children's college education.

   Which of the following, if true, is the most appropriate reason for parents not to participate in the program?

   (A) The parents are unsure about which public college in the state the child will attend.
   (B) The amount of money accumulated by putting the prepayment funds in an interest-bearing account today will be greater than the total cost of tuition for any of the public colleges when the child enrolls.
   (C) The annual cost of tuition at the state's public colleges is expected to increase at a faster rate than the annual increase in the cost of living.
   (D) Some of the state's public colleges are contemplating large increases in tuition next year.
   (E) The prepayment plan would not cover the cost of room and board at any of the state's public colleges.

The passage recommends that parents participate in a tuition prepayment program as a means of decreasing the cost of their children's future college education. If B were true, placing the funds in an interest-bearing account would be more cost-effective than participating in the prepayment program. Therefore B would be a reason for *not* participating and is the best answer.

Neither A nor E is clearly relevant to deciding whether to participate. Since the program applies to whatever public college the child might choose to attend, contingency A is covered by the plan. Regardless of whether the parents participate, the expenses E mentions would not be included in the cost of tuition. Choices C and D, by stating that tuition will increase, provide support for participating in the program.

6. Company Alpha buys free-travel coupons from people who are awarded the coupons by Bravo Airlines for flying frequently on Bravo airplanes. The coupons are sold to people who pay less for the coupons than they would pay by purchasing tickets from Bravo. This marketing of coupons results in lost revenue for Bravo.

To discourage the buying and selling of free-travel coupons, it would be best for Bravo Airlines to restrict the

(A) number of coupons that a person can be awarded in a particular year
(B) use of the coupons to those who were awarded the coupons and members of their immediate families
(C) days that the coupons can be used to Monday through Friday
(D) amount of time that the coupons can be used after they are issued
(E) number of routes on which travelers can use the coupons

Restricting use of the coupons to the immediate families of those awarded them, as B suggests, would make the coupons valueless for anyone else, so that marketing the coupons would no longer be possible. The coupons, however, would still allow the people to whom Bravo gives them to enjoy free travel. Thus, awarding coupons would remain a strong incentive to frequent travel on Bravo. Therefore, B is the best answer.

Choice A, conversely, would do nothing to reduce the resale value of the coupons. Choices C, D, and E all not only fail to prevent Alpha's coupon sales from competing with Bravo's own ticket sales, but also potentially reduce the usefulness of the coupons to the people to whom they are awarded.

7. The ice on the front windshield of the car had formed when moisture condensed during the night. The ice melted quickly after the car was warmed up the next morning because the defrosting vent, which blows only on the front windshield, was turned on full force.

Which of the following, if true, most seriously jeopardizes the validity of the explanation for the speed with which the ice melted?

(A) The side windows had no ice condensation on them.
(B) Even though no attempt was made to defrost the back window, the ice there melted at the same rate as did the ice on the front windshield.
(C) The speed at which ice on a window melts increases as the temperature of the air blown on the window increases.
(D) The warm air from the defrosting vent for the front windshield cools rapidly as it dissipates throughout the rest of the car.
(E) The defrosting vent operates efficiently even when the heater, which blows warm air toward the feet or faces of the driver and passengers, is on.

The speed with which the ice on the windshield melted is attributed to the air blowing full force from the defrosting vent onto the front windshield. This explanation is undermined if, as B states, no attempt was made to defrost the back window and the ice on the back window melted as quickly as did the ice on the windshield. Therefore, B is the best answer.

In the absence of other information, the lack of ice condensation on the side windows that is mentioned in A is irrelevant to the validity of the explanation. Choice C might support the explanation, since the air from the defrosting vent was warm. Neither D nor E gives a reason to doubt that air from the vent caused the ice's melting, and thus neither jeopardizes the explanation's validity.

8. To prevent some conflicts of interest, Congress could prohibit high-level government officials from accepting positions as lobbyists for three years after such officials leave government service. One such official concluded, however, that such a prohibition would be unfortunate because it would prevent high-level government officials from earning a livelihood for three years.

The official's conclusion logically depends on which of the following assumptions?

(A) Laws should not restrict the behavior of former government officials.

(B) Lobbyists are typically people who have previously been high-level government officials.

(C) Low-level government officials do not often become lobbyists when they leave government service.

(D) High-level government officials who leave government service are capable of earning a livelihood only as lobbyists.

(E) High-level government officials who leave government service are currently permitted to act as lobbyists for only three years.

The official argues that prohibiting high-level government officials from accepting positions as lobbyists for three years would prevent the officials from earning a livelihood for that period. This reasoning tacitly excludes the possibility of such officials earning a living through work other than lobbying. Therefore, D, which expresses this tacit assumption, is the best answer.

The official's argument does not depend on assumption A, B, C, or E, since the argument would not be invalidated if some restrictions on the behavior of government officials were desirable (A), or if lobbyists were not typically former high-level government officials (B), or if former low-level government officials did often become lobbyists (C), or if former high-level government officials could act as lobbyists indefinitely (E).

9. A conservation group in the United States is trying to change the long-standing image of bats as frightening creatures. The group contends that bats are feared and persecuted solely because they are shy animals that are active only at night.

Which of the following, if true, would cast the most serious doubt on the accuracy of the group's contention?

(A) Bats are steadily losing natural roosting places such as caves and hollow trees and are thus turning to more developed areas for roosting.

(B) Bats are the chief consumers of nocturnal insects and thus can help make their hunting territory more pleasant for humans.

(C) Bats are regarded as frightening creatures not only in the United States but also in Europe, Africa, and South America.

(D) Raccoons and owls are shy and active only at night; yet they are not generally feared and persecuted.

(E) People know more about the behavior of other greatly feared animal species, such as lions, alligators, and snakes, than they do about the behavior of bats.

The group's contention suggests that animals that are shy and active at night are feared and persecuted for that reason. Choice D establishes that raccoons and owls are shy and active at night, but that they are neither feared nor persecuted. Therefore, D is the best answer.

Although an increasing prevalence of bats might explain the importance of addressing people's fear of bats, A does not address the original causes of that fear. Choices B and E, while relevant to the rationality of people's fear of bats, do not affect the assessment of the accuracy of the group's contention. That bats are feared outside the United States, as C states, does not conflict with the group's explanation for fear of bats in the United States.

10. Meteorite explosions in the Earth's atmosphere as large as the one that destroyed forests in Siberia, with approximately the force of a twelve-megaton nuclear blast, occur about once a century.

The response of highly automated systems controlled by complex computer programs to unexpected circumstances is unpredictable.

Which of the following conclusions can most properly be drawn, if the statements above are true, about a highly automated nuclear-missile defense system controlled by a complex computer program?

(A) Within a century after its construction, the system would react inappropriately and might accidentally start a nuclear war.

(B) The system would be destroyed if an explosion of a large meteorite occurred in the Earth's atmosphere.

(C) It would be impossible for the system to distinguish the explosion of a large meteorite from the explosion of a nuclear weapon.

(D) Whether the system would respond inappropriately to the explosion of a large meteorite would depend on the location of the blast.

(E) It is not certain what the system's response to the explosion of a large meteorite would be, if its designers did not plan for such a contingency.

If the defense system designers did not plan for the contingency of large meteorite explosions, such explosions would, from the system's perspective, be unexpected. The system's response to such explosions is consequently unpredictable. Choice E expresses this inference and is thus the best answer.

Choices A and C cannot be inferred since it is consistent with the stated information that no meteorite explosion will occur within a century and that an appropriately designed nuclear defense system might be able to distinguish nuclear from meteorite explosions. Choices B and D cannot be inferred since there is no information to suggest either that meteorite explosions in the atmosphere would destroy the system or that the location of blasts would determine the appropriateness of the defense system's response.

Questions 11-12 are based on the following.

The fewer restrictions there are on the advertising of legal services, the more lawyers there are who advertise their services, and the lawyers who advertise a specific service usually charge less for that service than lawyers who do not advertise. Therefore, if the state removes any of its current restrictions, such as the one against advertisements that do not specify fee arrangements, overall consumer legal costs will be lower than if the state retains its current restrictions.

11. If the statements above are true, which of the following must be true?

(A) Some lawyers who now advertise will charge more for specific services if they do not have to specify fee arrangements in the advertisements.

(B) More consumers will use legal services if there are fewer restrictions on the advertising of legal services.

(C) If the restriction against advertisements that do not specify fee arrangements is removed, more lawyers will advertise their services.

(D) If more lawyers advertise lower prices for specific services, some lawyers who do not advertise will also charge less than they currently charge for those services.

(E) If the only restrictions on the advertising of legal services were those that apply to every type of advertising, most lawyers would advertise their services.

The supposition in C involves reducing by one the number of restrictions on the advertising of legal services. Any such reduction will, if the stated correlation exists, be accompanied by an increase in the number of lawyers advertising their services, as C predicts. Therefore, C is the best answer.

Choices A, B, D, and E do not follow from the stated information since it is still possible that no lawyers would raise their fees (contrary to A); there would be no increase in the number of consumers using legal services (contrary to B); none of the lawyers who do not advertise would decide to lower their prices (contrary to D); and few lawyers would advertise their legal services (contrary to E).

12. Which of the following, if true, would most seriously weaken the argument concerning overall consumer legal costs?

(A) The state has recently removed some other restrictions that had limited the advertising of legal services.

(B) The state is unlikely to remove all of the restrictions that apply solely to the advertising of legal services.

(C) Lawyers who do not advertise generally provide legal services of the same quality as those provided by lawyers who do advertise.

(D) Most lawyers who now specify fee arrangements in their advertisements would continue to do so even if the specification were not required.

(E) Most lawyers who advertise specific services do not lower their fees for those services when they begin to advertise.

If E is true, the lawyers who begin advertising when the restriction is removed might all be among those who do not lower their fees on beginning to advertise, in which case no decrease in consumer legal costs will occur. Therefore, E weakens the argument and is the best answer.

Since A does not relate the recent removal of restrictions to changes in consumer legal costs, A alone does not weaken the argument. Since the argument is unconcerned with whatever restrictions remain in effect but focuses only on those that will be removed, B does not weaken the argument. Choices C and D are irrelevant to an evaluation of the argument, which is concerned with cost considerations, not with the quality of legal services or the content of lawyers' advertisements.

13. Defense Department analysts worry that the ability of the United States to wage a prolonged war would be seriously endangered if the machine-tool manufacturing base shrinks further. Before the Defense Department publicly connected this security issue with the import quota issue, however, the machine-tool industry raised the national security issue in its petition for import quotas.

Which of the following, if true, contributes most to an explanation of the machine-tool industry's raising the issue above regarding national security?

(A) When the aircraft industries retooled, they provided a large amount of work for tool builders.

(B) The Defense Department is only marginally concerned with the effects of foreign competition on the machine-tool industry.

(C) The machine-tool industry encountered difficulty in obtaining governmental protection against imports on grounds other than defense.

(D) A few weapons important for defense consist of parts that do not require extensive machining.

(E) Several federal government programs have been designed which will enable domestic machine-tool manufacturing firms to compete successfully with foreign toolmakers.

Since the size of the machine-tool manufacturing base presumably has implications in areas beyond national security, one might find it surprising that the industry raised the security issue in its petition. Choice C, the best answer, explains that the industry turned to this issue because others tended to be ineffective in efforts to obtain governmental protection.

Choices A and B, on the other hand, merely explain why the industry might *not* raise the security issue. Choice A suggests that the industry might have raised the issue of jobs instead. Choice B suggests that the part of the government concerned with security is not concerned enough with the industry's import problem to take action. Neither D nor E is relevant to the industry's choice of strategy for securing import quotas.

14. Opponents of laws that require automobile drivers and passengers to wear seat belts argue that in a free society people have the right to take risks as long as the people do not harm others as a result of taking the risks. As a result, they conclude that it should be each person's decision whether or not to wear a seat belt.

Which of the following, if true, most seriously weakens the conclusion drawn above?

(A) Many new cars are built with seat belts that automatically fasten when someone sits in the front seat.

(B) Automobile insurance rates for all automobile owners are higher because of the need to pay for the increased injuries or deaths of people not wearing seat belts.

(C) Passengers in airplanes are required to wear seat belts during takeoffs and landings.

(D) The rate of automobile fatalities in states that do not have mandatory seat-belt laws is greater than the rate of fatalities in states that do have such laws.

(E) In automobile accidents, a greater number of passengers who do not wear seat belts are injured than are passengers who do wear seat belts.

The principle that people are entitled to risk injury provided they do not thereby harm others fails to justify the individual's right to decide not to wear seat belts if it can be shown, as B shows, that that decision does harm others. Therefore, B is the best answer.

The argument implicitly concedes that individuals take risks by not wearing seat belts; therefore, D and E, which simply confirm this concession, do not weaken the conclusion. Choice C cites a requirement analogous to the one at issue, but its existence alone does not bear on the legitimacy of the one at issue. Choice A suggests that the law may be irrelevant in some cases, but it does not address the issue of the law's legitimacy.

15. The cost of producing radios in Country Q is ten percent less than the cost of producing radios in Country Y. Even after transportation fees and tariff charges are added, it is still cheaper for a company to import radios from Country Q to Country Y than to produce radios in Country Y.

The statements above, if true, best support which of the following assertions?

(A) Labor costs in Country Q are ten percent below those in Country Y.

(B) Importing radios from Country Q to Country Y will eliminate ten percent of the manufacturing jobs in Country Y.

(C) The tariff on a radio imported from Country Q to Country Y is less than ten percent of the cost of manufacturing the radio in Country Y.

(D) The fee for transporting a radio from Country Q to Country Y is more than ten percent of the cost of manufacturing the radio in Country Q.

(E) It takes ten percent less time to manufacture a radio in Country Q than it does in Country Y.

If the tariff on importing radios from Country Q to Country Y were as high as ten percent or more of the cost of producing radios in Y, then, contrary to what the passage says, the cost of importing radios from Q to Y would be equal to or more than the cost of producing radios in Y. Thus, the tariff cannot be that high, and C is the best answer.

Choices A and E give possible partial explanations for the cost difference, but neither is supported by the passage because the cost advantage in Q might be attributable to other factors. Choices B and D are both consistent with the information in the passage, but the passage provides no evidence to support them.

16. During the Second World War, about 375,000 civilians died in the United States and about 408,000 members of the United States armed forces died overseas. On the basis of those figures, it can be concluded that it was not much more dangerous to be overseas in the armed forces during the Second World War than it was to stay at home as a civilian.

Which of the following would reveal most clearly the absurdity of the conclusion drawn above?

(A) Counting deaths among members of the armed forces who served in the United States in addition to deaths among members of the armed forces serving overseas

(B) Expressing the difference between the numbers of deaths among civilians and members of the armed forces as a percentage of the total number of deaths

(C) Separating deaths caused by accidents during service in the armed forces from deaths caused by combat injuries

(D) Comparing death rates per thousand members of each group rather than comparing total numbers of deaths

(E) Comparing deaths caused by accidents in the United States to deaths caused by combat in the armed forces

Concluding from the similar numbers of deaths in two groups that the relative danger of death was similar for both groups is absurd if, as here, one group was far smaller. Choice D exposes this absurdity by pointing out the need to compare death rates of the two groups, which would reveal the higher death rate for the smaller group. Therefore, D is the best answer.

Since the conclusion acknowledges the difference between the number of civilian and armed forces deaths, expressing this difference as a percentage, as suggested by B, is beside the point. Choice A is inappropriate because it simply adds a third group to the two being compared. Because cause of death is not at issue, C and E are irrelevant.

17. One state adds a 7 percent sales tax to the price of most products purchased within its jurisdiction. This tax, therefore, if viewed as tax on income, has the reverse effect of the federal income tax: the lower the income, the higher the annual percentage rate at which the income is taxed.

The conclusion above would be properly drawn if which of the following were assumed as a premise?

(A) The amount of money citizens spend on products subject to the state tax tends to be equal across income levels.

(B) The federal income tax favors citizens with high incomes, whereas the state sales tax favors citizens with low incomes.

(C) Citizens with low annual incomes can afford to pay a relatively higher percentage of their incomes in state sales tax, since their federal income tax is relatively low.

(D) The lower a state's sales tax, the more it will tend to redistribute income from the more affluent citizens to the rest of society.

(E) Citizens who fail to earn federally taxable income are also exempt from the state sales tax.

Given that there is a single sales tax rate, if the amount of money citizens spend on products subject to sales tax tends to be constant across income levels, the amount of money paid in sales tax will be virtually equal regardless of income. Hence this tax will generate roughly the same amount of money from each citizen, an amount that represents a greater percentage of a lower income than of a higher income. Thus, if A is assumed the conclusion follows.

Choice B contradicts the conclusion by asserting that the state sales tax favors citizens with low incomes. Choices C, D, and E are all irrelevant to the conclusion since they fail to establish a relation between the sales-tax rate and income.

18. The average age of chief executive officers (CEO's) in a large sample of companies is 57. The average age of CEO's in those same companies 20 years ago was approximately eight years younger. On the basis of those data, it can be concluded that CEO's in general tend to be older now.

Which of the following casts the most doubt on the conclusion drawn above?

(A) The dates when the CEO's assumed their current positions have not been specified.
(B) No information is given concerning the average number of years that CEO's remain in office.
(C) The information is based only on companies that have been operating for at least 20 years.
(D) Only approximate information is given concerning the average age of the CEO's 20 years ago.
(E) Information concerning the exact number of companies in the sample has not been given.

If the sample of companies is not representative, what is true of the sample need not be true in general. Unlike the sample, companies in general are not necessarily at least 20 years old. Since it is possible that recently established companies have relatively younger CEO's, C indicates that the sample may not be representative and casts doubt on the conclusion. Therefore, C is the best answer.

The absence of additional data noted in A and B does not undermine the conclusion: if the sample had been representative, the absence of these data would not have precluded the generalization. The conclusion is affected by neither D nor E, since it relies neither on exact information concerning the age of the CEO's nor on the exact number of companies in the study.

Questions 19-20 are based on the following.

Surveys show that every year only 10 percent of cigarette smokers switch brands. Yet the manufacturers have been spending an amount equal to 10 percent of their gross receipts on cigarette promotion in magazines. It follows from these figures that inducing cigarette smokers to switch brands did not pay, and that cigarette companies would have been no worse off economically if they had dropped their advertising.

19. Of the following, the best criticism of the conclusion that inducing cigarette smokers to switch brands did not pay is that the conclusion is based on

(A) computing advertising costs as a percentage of gross receipts, not of overall costs
(B) past patterns of smoking and may not carry over to the future
(C) the assumption that each smoker is loyal to a single brand of cigarettes at any one time
(D) the assumption that each manufacturer produces only one brand of cigarettes
(E) figures for the cigarette industry as a whole and may not hold for a particular company

Since brand switching cannot benefit the industry as a whole but only particular manufacturers, the question of whether it paid off to induce smokers to switch brands cannot be answered by using industry-wide statistics. Choice E criticizes the conclusion along these lines and is thus the best answer.

Although the argument does do what A and B describe, neither A nor B is a criticism of the conclusion. The argument assumes neither that each smoker is loyal to a single brand (contrary to C), nor that each manufacturer produces only a single brand (contrary to D).

20. Which of the following, if true, most seriously weakens the conclusion that cigarette companies could have dropped advertising without suffering economically?

(A) Cigarette advertisements provide a major proportion of total advertising revenue for numerous magazines.
(B) Cigarette promotion serves to attract first-time smokers to replace those people who have stopped smoking.
(C) There exists no research conclusively demonstrating that increases in cigarette advertising are related to increases in smoking.
(D) Advertising is so firmly established as a major business activity of cigarette manufacturers that they would be unlikely to drop it.
(E) Brand loyalty is typically not very strong among those who smoke inexpensive cigarettes.

The argument considers only one purpose of cigarette advertising: its attempt to induce smokers to switch brands. If cigarette promotion also served to attract first-time smokers, as B indicates, then manufacturers might indeed have lost by dropping advertising. Thus, B is the best answer.

Choice A addresses the economic interest of magazines, not of manufacturers. Choice C is irrelevant, since the argument concerns the effect of decreasing, not increasing, cigarette advertising. That cigarette manufacturers would be unlikely to cease advertising (choice D) is irrelevant to determining whether it is in their economic interest to advertise. Choice E is consistent with the possibility that exploiting the weak brand loyalty is not worth the cost of the advertising involved, so E does not weaken the conclusion.

Answer Sheet: Form B

Section 1

1. Ⓐ Ⓑ Ⓒ Ⓓ Ⓔ
2. Ⓐ Ⓑ Ⓒ Ⓓ Ⓔ
3. Ⓐ Ⓑ Ⓒ Ⓓ Ⓔ
4. Ⓐ Ⓑ Ⓒ Ⓓ Ⓔ
5. Ⓐ Ⓑ Ⓒ Ⓓ Ⓔ
6. Ⓐ Ⓑ Ⓒ Ⓓ Ⓔ
7. Ⓐ Ⓑ Ⓒ Ⓓ Ⓔ
8. Ⓐ Ⓑ Ⓒ Ⓓ Ⓔ
9. Ⓐ Ⓑ Ⓒ Ⓓ Ⓔ
10. Ⓐ Ⓑ Ⓒ Ⓓ Ⓔ
11. Ⓐ Ⓑ Ⓒ Ⓓ Ⓔ
12. Ⓐ Ⓑ Ⓒ Ⓓ Ⓔ
13. Ⓐ Ⓑ Ⓒ Ⓓ Ⓔ
14. Ⓐ Ⓑ Ⓒ Ⓓ Ⓔ
15. Ⓐ Ⓑ Ⓒ Ⓓ Ⓔ
16. Ⓐ Ⓑ Ⓒ Ⓓ Ⓔ
17. Ⓐ Ⓑ Ⓒ Ⓓ Ⓔ
18. Ⓐ Ⓑ Ⓒ Ⓓ Ⓔ
19. Ⓐ Ⓑ Ⓒ Ⓓ Ⓔ
20. Ⓐ Ⓑ Ⓒ Ⓓ Ⓔ
21. Ⓐ Ⓑ Ⓒ Ⓓ Ⓔ
22. Ⓐ Ⓑ Ⓒ Ⓓ Ⓔ
23. Ⓐ Ⓑ Ⓒ Ⓓ Ⓔ
24. Ⓐ Ⓑ Ⓒ Ⓓ Ⓔ
25. Ⓐ Ⓑ Ⓒ Ⓓ Ⓔ

Section 2

1. Ⓐ Ⓑ Ⓒ Ⓓ Ⓔ
2. Ⓐ Ⓑ Ⓒ Ⓓ Ⓔ
3. Ⓐ Ⓑ Ⓒ Ⓓ Ⓔ
4. Ⓐ Ⓑ Ⓒ Ⓓ Ⓔ
5. Ⓐ Ⓑ Ⓒ Ⓓ Ⓔ
6. Ⓐ Ⓑ Ⓒ Ⓓ Ⓔ
7. Ⓐ Ⓑ Ⓒ Ⓓ Ⓔ
8. Ⓐ Ⓑ Ⓒ Ⓓ Ⓔ
9. Ⓐ Ⓑ Ⓒ Ⓓ Ⓔ
10. Ⓐ Ⓑ Ⓒ Ⓓ Ⓔ
11. Ⓐ Ⓑ Ⓒ Ⓓ Ⓔ
12. Ⓐ Ⓑ Ⓒ Ⓓ Ⓔ
13. Ⓐ Ⓑ Ⓒ Ⓓ Ⓔ
14. Ⓐ Ⓑ Ⓒ Ⓓ Ⓔ
15. Ⓐ Ⓑ Ⓒ Ⓓ Ⓔ
16. Ⓐ Ⓑ Ⓒ Ⓓ Ⓔ
17. Ⓐ Ⓑ Ⓒ Ⓓ Ⓔ
18. Ⓐ Ⓑ Ⓒ Ⓓ Ⓔ
19. Ⓐ Ⓑ Ⓒ Ⓓ Ⓔ
20. Ⓐ Ⓑ Ⓒ Ⓓ Ⓔ
21. Ⓐ Ⓑ Ⓒ Ⓓ Ⓔ
22. Ⓐ Ⓑ Ⓒ Ⓓ Ⓔ
23. Ⓐ Ⓑ Ⓒ Ⓓ Ⓔ
24. Ⓐ Ⓑ Ⓒ Ⓓ Ⓔ
25. Ⓐ Ⓑ Ⓒ Ⓓ Ⓔ

Section 3

1. Ⓐ Ⓑ Ⓒ Ⓓ Ⓔ
2. Ⓐ Ⓑ Ⓒ Ⓓ Ⓔ
3. Ⓐ Ⓑ Ⓒ Ⓓ Ⓔ
4. Ⓐ Ⓑ Ⓒ Ⓓ Ⓔ
5. Ⓐ Ⓑ Ⓒ Ⓓ Ⓔ
6. Ⓐ Ⓑ Ⓒ Ⓓ Ⓔ
7. Ⓐ Ⓑ Ⓒ Ⓓ Ⓔ
8. Ⓐ Ⓑ Ⓒ Ⓓ Ⓔ
9. Ⓐ Ⓑ Ⓒ Ⓓ Ⓔ
10. Ⓐ Ⓑ Ⓒ Ⓓ Ⓔ
11. Ⓐ Ⓑ Ⓒ Ⓓ Ⓔ
12. Ⓐ Ⓑ Ⓒ Ⓓ Ⓔ
13. Ⓐ Ⓑ Ⓒ Ⓓ Ⓔ
14. Ⓐ Ⓑ Ⓒ Ⓓ Ⓔ
15. Ⓐ Ⓑ Ⓒ Ⓓ Ⓔ
16. Ⓐ Ⓑ Ⓒ Ⓓ Ⓔ
17. Ⓐ Ⓑ Ⓒ Ⓓ Ⓔ
18. Ⓐ Ⓑ Ⓒ Ⓓ Ⓔ
19. Ⓐ Ⓑ Ⓒ Ⓓ Ⓔ
20. Ⓐ Ⓑ Ⓒ Ⓓ Ⓔ
21. Ⓐ Ⓑ Ⓒ Ⓓ Ⓔ
22. Ⓐ Ⓑ Ⓒ Ⓓ Ⓔ
23. Ⓐ Ⓑ Ⓒ Ⓓ Ⓔ
24. Ⓐ Ⓑ Ⓒ Ⓓ Ⓔ
25. Ⓐ Ⓑ Ⓒ Ⓓ Ⓔ

Section 4

1. Ⓐ Ⓑ Ⓒ Ⓓ Ⓔ
2. Ⓐ Ⓑ Ⓒ Ⓓ Ⓔ
3. Ⓐ Ⓑ Ⓒ Ⓓ Ⓔ
4. Ⓐ Ⓑ Ⓒ Ⓓ Ⓔ
5. Ⓐ Ⓑ Ⓒ Ⓓ Ⓔ
6. Ⓐ Ⓑ Ⓒ Ⓓ Ⓔ
7. Ⓐ Ⓑ Ⓒ Ⓓ Ⓔ
8. Ⓐ Ⓑ Ⓒ Ⓓ Ⓔ
9. Ⓐ Ⓑ Ⓒ Ⓓ Ⓔ
10. Ⓐ Ⓑ Ⓒ Ⓓ Ⓔ
11. Ⓐ Ⓑ Ⓒ Ⓓ Ⓔ
12. Ⓐ Ⓑ Ⓒ Ⓓ Ⓔ
13. Ⓐ Ⓑ Ⓒ Ⓓ Ⓔ
14. Ⓐ Ⓑ Ⓒ Ⓓ Ⓔ
15. Ⓐ Ⓑ Ⓒ Ⓓ Ⓔ
16. Ⓐ Ⓑ Ⓒ Ⓓ Ⓔ
17. Ⓐ Ⓑ Ⓒ Ⓓ Ⓔ
18. Ⓐ Ⓑ Ⓒ Ⓓ Ⓔ
19. Ⓐ Ⓑ Ⓒ Ⓓ Ⓔ
20. Ⓐ Ⓑ Ⓒ Ⓓ Ⓔ
21. Ⓐ Ⓑ Ⓒ Ⓓ Ⓔ
22. Ⓐ Ⓑ Ⓒ Ⓓ Ⓔ
23. Ⓐ Ⓑ Ⓒ Ⓓ Ⓔ
24. Ⓐ Ⓑ Ⓒ Ⓓ Ⓔ
25. Ⓐ Ⓑ Ⓒ Ⓓ Ⓔ

Section 5

1. Ⓐ Ⓑ Ⓒ Ⓓ Ⓔ
2. Ⓐ Ⓑ Ⓒ Ⓓ Ⓔ
3. Ⓐ Ⓑ Ⓒ Ⓓ Ⓔ
4. Ⓐ Ⓑ Ⓒ Ⓓ Ⓔ
5. Ⓐ Ⓑ Ⓒ Ⓓ Ⓔ
6. Ⓐ Ⓑ Ⓒ Ⓓ Ⓔ
7. Ⓐ Ⓑ Ⓒ Ⓓ Ⓔ
8. Ⓐ Ⓑ Ⓒ Ⓓ Ⓔ
9. Ⓐ Ⓑ Ⓒ Ⓓ Ⓔ
10. Ⓐ Ⓑ Ⓒ Ⓓ Ⓔ
11. Ⓐ Ⓑ Ⓒ Ⓓ Ⓔ
12. Ⓐ Ⓑ Ⓒ Ⓓ Ⓔ
13. Ⓐ Ⓑ Ⓒ Ⓓ Ⓔ
14. Ⓐ Ⓑ Ⓒ Ⓓ Ⓔ
15. Ⓐ Ⓑ Ⓒ Ⓓ Ⓔ
16. Ⓐ Ⓑ Ⓒ Ⓓ Ⓔ
17. Ⓐ Ⓑ Ⓒ Ⓓ Ⓔ
18. Ⓐ Ⓑ Ⓒ Ⓓ Ⓔ
19. Ⓐ Ⓑ Ⓒ Ⓓ Ⓔ
20. Ⓐ Ⓑ Ⓒ Ⓓ Ⓔ
21. Ⓐ Ⓑ Ⓒ Ⓓ Ⓔ
22. Ⓐ Ⓑ Ⓒ Ⓓ Ⓔ
23. Ⓐ Ⓑ Ⓒ Ⓓ Ⓔ
24. Ⓐ Ⓑ Ⓒ Ⓓ Ⓔ
25. Ⓐ Ⓑ Ⓒ Ⓓ Ⓔ

Section 6

1. Ⓐ Ⓑ Ⓒ Ⓓ Ⓔ
2. Ⓐ Ⓑ Ⓒ Ⓓ Ⓔ
3. Ⓐ Ⓑ Ⓒ Ⓓ Ⓔ
4. Ⓐ Ⓑ Ⓒ Ⓓ Ⓔ
5. Ⓐ Ⓑ Ⓒ Ⓓ Ⓔ
6. Ⓐ Ⓑ Ⓒ Ⓓ Ⓔ
7. Ⓐ Ⓑ Ⓒ Ⓓ Ⓔ
8. Ⓐ Ⓑ Ⓒ Ⓓ Ⓔ
9. Ⓐ Ⓑ Ⓒ Ⓓ Ⓔ
10. Ⓐ Ⓑ Ⓒ Ⓓ Ⓔ
11. Ⓐ Ⓑ Ⓒ Ⓓ Ⓔ
12. Ⓐ Ⓑ Ⓒ Ⓓ Ⓔ
13. Ⓐ Ⓑ Ⓒ Ⓓ Ⓔ
14. Ⓐ Ⓑ Ⓒ Ⓓ Ⓔ
15. Ⓐ Ⓑ Ⓒ Ⓓ Ⓔ
16. Ⓐ Ⓑ Ⓒ Ⓓ Ⓔ
17. Ⓐ Ⓑ Ⓒ Ⓓ Ⓔ
18. Ⓐ Ⓑ Ⓒ Ⓓ Ⓔ
19. Ⓐ Ⓑ Ⓒ Ⓓ Ⓔ
20. Ⓐ Ⓑ Ⓒ Ⓓ Ⓔ
21. Ⓐ Ⓑ Ⓒ Ⓓ Ⓔ
22. Ⓐ Ⓑ Ⓒ Ⓓ Ⓔ
23. Ⓐ Ⓑ Ⓒ Ⓓ Ⓔ
24. Ⓐ Ⓑ Ⓒ Ⓓ Ⓔ
25. Ⓐ Ⓑ Ⓒ Ⓓ Ⓔ

Print your full name here: _____
(last)   (first)   (middle)

Graduate Management Admission Test

SECTION 1

Time—30 minutes

20 Questions

Directions: For each question in this section, select the best of the answer choices given.

1. Toughened hiring standards have not been the primary cause of the present staffing shortage in public schools. The shortage of teachers is primarily caused by the fact that in recent years teachers have not experienced any improvements in working conditions and their salaries have not kept pace with salaries in other professions.

Which of the following, if true, would most support the claims above?

(A) Many teachers already in the profession would not have been hired under the new hiring standards.

(B) Today more teachers are entering the profession with a higher educational level than in the past.

(C) Some teachers have cited higher standards for hiring as a reason for the current staffing shortage.

(D) Many teachers have cited low pay and lack of professional freedom as reasons for their leaving the profession.

(E) Many prospective teachers have cited the new hiring standards as a reason for not entering the profession.

2. A proposed ordinance requires the installation in new homes of sprinklers automatically triggered by the presence of a fire. However, a home builder argued that because more than ninety percent of residential fires are extinguished by a household member, residential sprinklers would only marginally decrease property damage caused by residential fires.

Which of the following, if true, would most seriously weaken the home builder's argument?

(A) Most individuals have no formal training in how to extinguish fires.

(B) Since new homes are only a tiny percentage of available housing in the city, the new ordinance would be extremely narrow in scope.

(C) The installation of smoke detectors in new residences costs significantly less than the installation of sprinklers.

(D) In the city where the ordinance was proposed, the average time required by the fire department to respond to a fire was less than the national average.

(E) The largest proportion of property damage that results from residential fires is caused by fires that start when no household member is present.

3. Even though most universities retain the royalties from faculty members' inventions, the faculty members retain the royalties from books and articles they write. Therefore, faculty members should retain the royalties from the educational computer software they develop.

The conclusion above would be more reasonably drawn if which of the following were inserted into the argument as an additional premise?

(A) Royalties from inventions are higher than royalties from educational software programs.

(B) Faculty members are more likely to produce educational software programs than inventions.

(C) Inventions bring more prestige to universities than do books and articles.

(D) In the experience of most universities, educational software programs are more marketable than are books and articles.

(E) In terms of the criteria used to award royalties, educational software programs are more nearly comparable to books and articles than to inventions.

GO ON TO THE NEXT PAGE.

-384-

4. Increases in the level of high-density lipoprotein (HDL) in the human bloodstream lower bloodstream-cholesterol levels by increasing the body's capacity to rid itself of excess cholesterol. Levels of HDL in the bloodstream of some individuals are significantly increased by a program of regular exercise and weight reduction.

Which of the following can be correctly inferred from the statements above?

(A) Individuals who are underweight do not run any risk of developing high levels of cholesterol in the bloodstream.

(B) Individuals who do not exercise regularly have a high risk of developing high levels of cholesterol in the bloodstream late in life.

(C) Exercise and weight reduction are the most effective methods of lowering bloodstream cholesterol levels in humans.

(D) A program of regular exercise and weight reduction lowers cholesterol levels in the bloodstream of some individuals.

(E) Only regular exercise is necessary to decrease cholesterol levels in the bloodstream of individuals of average weight.

5. When limitations were in effect on nuclear-arms testing, people tended to save more of their money, but when nuclear-arms testing increased, people tended to spend more of their money. The perceived threat of nuclear catastrophe, therefore, decreases the willingness of people to postpone consumption for the sake of saving money.

The argument above assumes that

(A) the perceived threat of nuclear catastrophe has increased over the years

(B) most people supported the development of nuclear arms

(C) people's perception of the threat of nuclear catastrophe depends on the amount of nuclear-arms testing being done

(D) the people who saved the most money when nuclear-arms testing was limited were the ones who supported such limitations

(E) there are more consumer goods available when nuclear-arms testing increases

6. Which of the following best completes the passage below?

People buy prestige when they buy a premium product. They want to be associated with something special. Mass-marketing techniques and price-reduction strategies should not be used because _____ .

(A) affluent purchasers currently represent a shrinking portion of the population of all purchasers

(B) continued sales depend directly on the maintenance of an aura of exclusivity

(C) purchasers of premium products are concerned with the quality as well as with the price of the products

(D) expansion of the market niche to include a broader spectrum of consumers will increase profits

(E) manufacturing a premium brand is not necessarily more costly than manufacturing a standard brand of the same product

7. A cost-effective solution to the problem of airport congestion is to provide high-speed ground transportation between major cities lying 200 to 500 miles apart. The successful implementation of this plan would cost far less than expanding existing airports and would also reduce the number of airplanes clogging both airports and airways.

Which of the following, if true, could proponents of the plan above most appropriately cite as a piece of evidence for the soundness of their plan?

(A) An effective high-speed ground-transportation system would require major repairs to many highways and mass-transit improvements.

(B) One-half of all departing flights in the nation's busiest airport head for a destination in a major city 225 miles away.

(C) The majority of travelers departing from rural airports are flying to destinations in cities over 600 miles away.

(D) Many new airports are being built in areas that are presently served by high-speed ground-transportation systems.

(E) A large proportion of air travelers are vacationers who are taking long-distance flights.

GO ON TO THE NEXT PAGE.

Questions 8-9 are based on the following.

If there is an oil-supply disruption resulting in higher international oil prices, domestic oil prices in open-market countries such as the United States will rise as well, whether such countries import all or none of their oil.

8. If the statement above concerning oil-supply disruptions is true, which of the following policies in an open-market nation is most likely to reduce the long-term economic impact on that nation of sharp and unexpected increases in international oil prices?

(A) Maintaining the quantity of oil imported at constant yearly levels
(B) Increasing the number of oil tankers in its fleet
(C) Suspending diplomatic relations with major oil-producing nations
(D) Decreasing oil consumption through conservation
(E) Decreasing domestic production of oil

9. Which of the following conclusions is best supported by the statement above?

(A) Domestic producers of oil in open-market countries are excluded from the international oil market when there is a disruption in the international oil supply.
(B) International oil-supply disruptions have little, if any, effect on the price of domestic oil as long as an open-market country has domestic supplies capable of meeting domestic demand.
(C) The oil market in an open-market country is actually part of the international oil market, even if most of that country's domestic oil is usually sold to consumers within its borders.
(D) Open-market countries that export little or none of their oil can maintain stable domestic oil prices even when international oil prices rise sharply.
(E) If international oil prices rise, domestic distributors of oil in open-market countries will begin to import more oil than they export.

10. The average normal infant born in the United States weighs between twelve and fourteen pounds at the age of three months. Therefore, if a three-month-old child weighs only ten pounds, its weight gain has been below the United States average.

Which of the following indicates a flaw in the reasoning above?

(A) Weight is only one measure of normal infant development.
(B) Some three-month-old children weigh as much as seventeen pounds.
(C) It is possible for a normal child to weigh ten pounds at birth.
(D) The phrase "below average" does not necessarily mean insufficient.
(E) Average weight gain is not the same as average weight.

11. Red blood cells in which the malarial-fever parasite resides are eliminated from a person's body after 120 days. Because the parasite cannot travel to a new generation of red blood cells, any fever that develops in a person more than 120 days after that person has moved to a malaria-free region is not due to the malarial parasite.

Which of the following, if true, most seriously weakens the conclusion above?

(A) The fever caused by the malarial parasite may resemble the fever caused by flu viruses.
(B) The anopheles mosquito, which is the principal insect carrier of the malarial parasite, has been eradicated in many parts of the world.
(C) Many malarial symptoms other than the fever, which can be suppressed with antimalarial medication, can reappear within 120 days after the medication is discontinued.
(D) In some cases, the parasite that causes malarial fever travels to cells of the spleen, which are less frequently eliminated from a person's body than are red blood cells.
(E) In any region infested with malaria-carrying mosquitoes, there are individuals who appear to be immune to malaria.

GO ON TO THE NEXT PAGE.

12. Fact 1: Television advertising is becoming less effective: the proportion of brand names promoted on television that viewers of the advertising can recall is slowly decreasing.

Fact 2: Television viewers recall commercials aired first or last in a cluster of consecutive commercials far better than they recall commercials aired somewhere in the middle.

Fact 2 would be most likely to contribute to an explanation of fact 1 if which of the following were also true?

(A) The average television viewer currently recalls fewer than half the brand names promoted in commercials he or she saw.
(B) The total time allotted to the average cluster of consecutive television commercials is decreasing.
(C) The average number of hours per day that people spend watching television is decreasing.
(D) The average number of clusters of consecutive commercials per hour of television is increasing.
(E) The average number of television commercials in a cluster of consecutive commercials is increasing.

13. The number of people diagnosed as having a certain intestinal disease has dropped significantly in a rural county this year, as compared to last year. Health officials attribute this decrease entirely to improved sanitary conditions at water-treatment plants, which made for cleaner water this year and thus reduced the incidence of the disease.

Which of the following, if true, would most seriously weaken the health officials' explanation for the lower incidence of the disease?

(A) Many new water-treatment plants have been built in the last five years in the rural county.
(B) Bottled spring water has not been consumed in significantly different quantities by people diagnosed as having the intestinal disease, as compared to people who did not contract the disease.
(C) Because of a new diagnostic technique, many people who until this year would have been diagnosed as having the intestinal disease are now correctly diagnosed as suffering from intestinal ulcers.
(D) Because of medical advances this year, far fewer people who contract the intestinal disease will develop severe cases of the disease.
(E) The water in the rural county was brought up to the sanitary standards of the water in neighboring counties ten years ago.

14. The price the government pays for standard weapons purchased from military contractors is determined by a pricing method called "historical costing." Historical costing allows contractors to protect their profits by adding a percentage increase, based on the current rate of inflation, to the previous year's contractual price.

Which of the following statements, if true, is the best basis for a criticism of historical costing as an economically sound pricing method for military contracts?

(A) The government might continue to pay for past inefficient use of funds.
(B) The rate of inflation has varied considerably over the past twenty years.
(C) The contractual price will be greatly affected by the cost of materials used for the products.
(D) Many taxpayers question the amount of money the government spends on military contracts.
(E) The pricing method based on historical costing might not encourage the development of innovative weapons.

GO ON TO THE NEXT PAGE.

15. Some who favor putting governmental enterprises into private hands suggest that conservation objectives would in general be better served if private environmental groups were put in charge of operating and financing the national park system, which is now run by the government.

Which of the following, assuming that it is a realistic possibility, argues most strongly against the suggestion above?

(A) Those seeking to abolish all restrictions on exploiting the natural resources of the parks might join the private environmental groups as members and eventually take over their leadership.

(B) Private environmental groups might not always agree on the best ways to achieve conservation objectives.

(C) If they wished to extend the park system, the private environmental groups might have to seek contributions from major donors and the general public.

(D) There might be competition among private environmental groups for control of certain park areas.

(E) Some endangered species, such as the California condor, might die out despite the best efforts of the private environmental groups, even if those groups are not hampered by insufficient resources.

16. A recent spate of launching and operating mishaps with television satellites led to a corresponding surge in claims against companies underwriting satellite insurance. As a result, insurance premiums shot up, making satellites more expensive to launch and operate. This, in turn, has added to the pressure to squeeze more performance out of currently operating satellites.

Which of the following, if true, taken together with the information above, best supports the conclusion that the cost of television satellites will continue to increase?

(A) Since the risk to insurers of satellites is spread over relatively few units, insurance premiums are necessarily very high.

(B) When satellites reach orbit and then fail, the causes of failure are generally impossible to pinpoint with confidence.

(C) The greater the performance demands placed on satellites, the more frequently those satellites break down.

(D) Most satellites are produced in such small numbers that no economies of scale can be realized.

(E) Since many satellites are built by unwieldy international consortia, inefficiencies are inevitable.

17. Tocqueville, a nineteenth-century writer known for his study of democracy in the United States, believed that a government that centralizes power in one individual or institution is dangerous to its citizens. Biographers claim that Tocqueville disliked centralized government because he blamed Napoleon's rule for the poverty of his childhood in Normandy.

Which of the following, if true, would cast the most serious doubt on the biographers' claim?

(A) Although Napoleon was popularly blamed at the time for the terrible living conditions in Normandy, historians now know that bad harvests were really to blame for the poor economic conditions.

(B) Napoleon was notorious for refusing to share power with any of his political associates.

(C) Tocqueville said he knew that if his father had not suffered ill health, his family would have had a steady income and a comfortable standard of living.

(D) Although Tocqueville asserted that United States political life was democratic, the United States of the nineteenth century allowed political power to be concentrated in a few institutions.

(E) Tocqueville once wrote in a letter that, although his childhood was terribly impoverished, it was not different from the experience of his friends and neighbors in Normandy.

GO ON TO THE NEXT PAGE.

18. Radio interferometry is a technique for studying details of celestial objects that combines signals intercepted by widely spaced radio telescopes. This technique requires ultraprecise timing, exact knowledge of the locations of the telescopes, and sophisticated computer programs. The successful interferometric linking of an Earth-based radio telescope with a radio telescope on an orbiting satellite was therefore a significant technological accomplishment.

Which of the following can be correctly inferred from the statements above?

(A) Special care was taken in the launching of the satellite so that the calculations of its orbit would be facilitated.
(B) The signals received on the satellite are stronger than those received by a terrestrial telescope.
(C) The resolution of detail achieved by the satellite-Earth interferometer system is inferior to that achieved by exclusively terrestrial systems.
(D) The computer programs required for making use of the signals received by the satellite required a long time for development.
(E) The location of an orbiting satellite relative to locations on Earth can be well enough known for interferometric purposes.

19. Recent estimates predict that between 1982 and 1995 the greatest increase in the number of people employed will be in the category of low-paying service occupations. This category, however, will not increase its share of total employment, whereas the category of high-paying service occupations will increase its share.

If the estimates above are accurate, which of the following conclusions can be drawn?

(A) In 1982 more people were working in low-paying service occupations than were working in high-paying service occupations.
(B) In 1995 more people will be working in high-paying service occupations than will be working in low-paying service occupations.
(C) Nonservice occupations will account for the same share of total employment in 1995 as in 1982.
(D) Many of the people who were working in low-paying service occupations in 1982 will be working in high-paying service occupations by 1995.
(E) The rate of growth for low-paying service occupations will be greater than the overall rate of employment growth between 1982 and 1995.

20. For a local government to outlaw all strikes by its workers is a costly mistake, because all its labor disputes must then be settled by binding arbitration, without any negotiated public-sector labor settlements guiding the arbitrators. Strikes should be outlawed only for categories of public-sector workers for whose services no acceptable substitute exists.

The statements above best support which of the following conclusions?

(A) Where public-service workers are permitted to strike, contract negotiations with those workers are typically settled without a strike.
(B) Where strikes by all categories of public-sector workers are outlawed, no acceptable substitutes for the services provided by any of those workers are available.
(C) Binding arbitration tends to be more advantageous for public-service workers where it is the only available means of settling labor disputes with such workers.
(D) Most categories of public-sector workers have no counterparts in the private sector.
(E) A strike by workers in a local government is unlikely to be settled without help from an arbitrator.

STOP

IF YOU FINISH BEFORE TIME IS CALLED, YOU MAY CHECK YOUR WORK ON THIS SECTION ONLY. DO NOT TURN TO ANY OTHER SECTION IN THE TEST.

SECTION 2

Time—30 minutes

25 Questions

Directions: Each of the data sufficiency problems below consists of a question and two statements, labeled (1) and (2), in which certain data are given. You have to decide whether the data given in the statements are <u>sufficient</u> for answering the question. Using the data given in the statements <u>plus</u> your knowledge of mathematics and everyday facts (such as the number of days in July or the meaning of <u>counterclockwise</u>), you are to fill in oval

  A if statement (1) ALONE is sufficient, but statement (2) alone is not sufficient to answer the question asked;

  B if statement (2) ALONE is sufficient, but statement (1) alone is not sufficient to answer the question asked;

  C if BOTH statements (1) and (2) TOGETHER are sufficient to answer the question asked, but NEITHER statement ALONE is sufficient;

  D if EACH statement ALONE is sufficient to answer the question asked;

  E if statements (1) and (2) TOGETHER are NOT sufficient to answer the question asked, and additional data specific to the problem are needed.

Numbers: All numbers used are real numbers.

Figures: A figure in a data sufficiency problem will conform to the information given in the question, but will not necessarily conform to the additional information given in statements (1) and (2).

  You may assume that lines shown as straight are straight and that angle measures are greater than zero.

  You may assume that the positions of points, angles, regions, etc., exist in the order shown.

  All figures lie in a plane unless otherwise indicated.

Example:

In $\triangle PQR$, what is the value of x ?

(1) $PQ = PR$

(2) $y = 40$

Explanation: According to statement (1), $PQ = PR$; therefore, $\triangle PQR$ is isosceles and $y = z$. Since $x + y + z = 180$, $x + 2y = 180$. Since statement (1) does not give a value for y, you cannot answer the question using statement (1) by itself. According to statement (2), $y = 40$; therefore, $x + z = 140$. Since statement (2) does not give a value for z, you cannot answer the question using statement (2) by itself. Using both statements together, you can find y and z; therefore, you can find x, and the answer to the problem is C.

GO ON TO THE NEXT PAGE.

A Statement (1) ALONE is sufficient, but statement (2) alone is not sufficient.
B Statement (2) ALONE is sufficient, but statement (1) alone is not sufficient.
C BOTH statements TOGETHER are sufficient, but NEITHER statement ALONE is sufficient.
D EACH statement ALONE is sufficient.
E Statements (1) and (2) TOGETHER are NOT sufficient.

1. If x and y are positive, what is the value of x?

   (1) $x = 3.927y$
   (2) $y = 2.279$

2. John and David each received a salary increase. Which one received the greater dollar increase?

   (1) John's salary increased 8 percent.
   (2) David's salary increased 5 percent.

3. Carlotta can drive from her home to her office by one of two possible routes. If she must also return by one of these routes, what is the distance of the shorter route?

   (1) When she drives from her home to her office by the shorter route and returns by the longer route, she drives a total of 42 kilometers.

   (2) When she drives both ways, from her home to her office and back, by the longer route, she drives a total of 46 kilometers.

4. If r and s are positive integers, r is what percent of s?

   (1) $r = \dfrac{3}{4}s$

   (2) $r \div s = \dfrac{75}{100}$

5. A shirt and a pair of gloves cost a total of $41.70. How much does the pair of gloves cost?

   (1) The shirt costs twice as much as the gloves.

   (2) The shirt costs $27.80.

GO ON TO THE NEXT PAGE.

A Statement (1) ALONE is sufficient, but statement (2) alone is not sufficient.
B Statement (2) ALONE is sufficient, but statement (1) alone is not sufficient.
C BOTH statements TOGETHER are sufficient, but NEITHER statement ALONE is sufficient.
D EACH statement ALONE is sufficient.
E Statements (1) and (2) TOGETHER are NOT sufficient.

6. What is the number of 360-degree rotations that a bicycle wheel made while rolling 100 meters in a straight line without slipping?

(1) The diameter of the bicycle wheel, including the tire, was 0.5 meter.

(2) The wheel made twenty 360-degree rotations per minute.

7. What is the value of the sum of a list of n odd integers?

(1) $n = 8$

(2) The square of the number of integers on the list is 64.

8. If a certain animated cartoon consists of a total of 17,280 frames on film, how many minutes will it take to run the cartoon?

(1) The cartoon runs without interruption at the rate of 24 frames per second.

(2) It takes 6 times as long to run the cartoon as it takes to rewind the film, and it takes a total of 14 minutes to do both.

9. What was the average number of miles per gallon of gasoline for a car during a certain trip?

(1) The total cost of the gasoline used by the car for the 180-mile trip was $12.00.

(2) The cost of the gasoline used by the car for the trip was $1.20 per gallon.

10. If x and y are positive, is $\frac{x}{y}$ greater than 1 ?

(1) $xy > 1$

(2) $x - y > 0$

GO ON TO THE NEXT PAGE.

A   Statement (1) ALONE is sufficient, but statement (2) alone is not sufficient.
B   Statement (2) ALONE is sufficient, but statement (1) alone is not sufficient.
C   BOTH statements TOGETHER are sufficient, but NEITHER statement ALONE is sufficient.
D   EACH statement ALONE is sufficient.
E   Statements (1) and (2) TOGETHER are NOT sufficient.

11. In $\triangle PQR$, if $PQ = x$, $QR = x + 2$, and $PR = y$, which of the three angles of $\triangle PQR$ has the greatest degree measure?

(1) $y = x + 3$

(2) $x = 2$

12. Is the prime number p equal to 37 ?

(1) $p = n^2 + 1$, where n is an integer.

(2) p^2 is greater than 200.

13. The only contents of a parcel are 25 photographs and 30 negatives. What is the total weight, in ounces, of the parcel's contents?

(1) The weight of each photograph is 3 times the weight of each negative.

(2) The total weight of 1 of the photographs and 2 of the negatives is $\frac{1}{3}$ ounce.

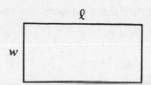

14. If ℓ and w represent the length and width, respectively, of the rectangle above, what is the perimeter?

(1) $2\ell + w = 40$

(2) $\ell + w = 25$

15. What is the ratio of x to y ?

(1) x is 4 more than twice y.

(2) The ratio of $0.5x$ to $2y$ is 3 to 5.

GO ON TO THE NEXT PAGE.

A   Statement (1) ALONE is sufficient, but statement (2) alone is not sufficient.
B   Statement (2) ALONE is sufficient, but statement (1) alone is not sufficient.
C   BOTH statements TOGETHER are sufficient, but NEITHER statement ALONE is sufficient.
D   EACH statement ALONE is sufficient.
E   Statements (1) and (2) TOGETHER are NOT sufficient.

16. If x, y, and z are three integers, are they consecutive integers?

(1) $z - x = 2$

(2) $x < y < z$

17. What is the value of x?

(1) $-(x + y) = x - y$

(2) $x + y = 2$

18. A sum of $200,000 from a certain estate was divided among a spouse and three children. How much of the estate did the youngest child receive?

(1) The spouse received $\frac{1}{2}$ of the sum from the estate, and the oldest child received $\frac{1}{4}$ of the remainder.

(2) Each of the two younger children received $12,500 more than the oldest child and $62,500 less than the spouse.

19. If the Lincoln Library's total expenditure for books, periodicals, and newspapers last year was $35,000, how much of the expenditure was for books?

(1) The expenditure for newspapers was 40 percent greater than the expenditure for periodicals.

(2) The total of the expenditure for periodicals and newspapers was 25 percent less than the expenditure for books.

20. The symbol ∇ represents one of the following operations: addition, subtraction, multiplication, or division. What is the value of $3 \nabla 2$?

(1) $0 \nabla 1 = 1$

(2) $1 \nabla 0 = 1$

GO ON TO THE NEXT PAGE.

-394-

A   Statement (1) ALONE is sufficient, but statement (2) alone is not sufficient.
B   Statement (2) ALONE is sufficient, but statement (1) alone is not sufficient.
C   BOTH statements TOGETHER are sufficient, but NEITHER statement ALONE is sufficient.
D   EACH statement ALONE is sufficient.
E   Statements (1) and (2) TOGETHER are NOT sufficient.

21. Are the numbers $\frac{k}{4}$, $\frac{z}{3}$, and $\frac{r}{2}$ in increasing order?

    (1) $3 < z < 4$
    (2) $r < z < k$

22. In a certain group of people, the average (arithmetic mean) weight of the males is 180 pounds and of the females, 120 pounds. What is the average weight of the people in the group?

    (1) The group contains twice as many females as males.
    (2) The group contains 10 more females than males.

23. If $n = p + r$, where n, p, and r are positive integers and n is odd, does p equal 2 ?

    (1) p and r are prime numbers.
    (2) $r \neq 2$

24. If $y = 2^{x+1}$, what is the value of $y - x$?

    (1) $2^{2x+2} = 64$
    (2) $y = 2^{2x-1}$

25. If $x \neq 1$, is y equal to $x + 1$?

    (1) $\frac{y - 2}{x - 1} = 1$
    (2) $y^2 = (x + 1)^2$

STOP

**IF YOU FINISH BEFORE TIME IS CALLED, YOU MAY CHECK YOUR WORK ON THIS SECTION ONLY.
DO NOT TURN TO ANY OTHER SECTION IN THE TEST.**

SECTION 3

Time—30 minutes

25 Questions

Directions: In this section solve each problem, using any available space on the page for scratchwork. Then indicate the best of the answer choices given.

Numbers: All numbers used are real numbers.

Figures: Figures that accompany problems in this section are intended to provide information useful in solving the problems. They are drawn as accurately as possible EXCEPT when it is stated in a specific problem that its figure is not drawn to scale. All figures lie in a plane unless otherwise indicated.

1. What is 45 percent of $\frac{7}{12}$ of 240 ?

   (A) 63
   (B) 90
   (C) 108
   (D) 140
   (E) 311

2. NOT SCORED

3. If x books cost \$5 each and y books cost \$8 each, then the average (arithmetic mean) cost, in dollars per book, is equal to

   (A) $\dfrac{5x + 8y}{x + y}$

   (B) $\dfrac{5x + 8y}{xy}$

   (C) $\dfrac{5x + 8y}{13}$

   (D) $\dfrac{40xy}{x + y}$

   (E) $\dfrac{40xy}{13}$

GO ON TO THE NEXT PAGE.

4. If $\frac{1}{2}$ of the money in a certain trust fund was invested in stocks, $\frac{1}{4}$ in bonds, $\frac{1}{5}$ in a mutual fund, and the remaining $10,000 in a government certificate, what was the total amount of the trust fund?

(A) $100,000
(B) $150,000
(C) $200,000
(D) $500,000
(E) $2,000,000

5. Marion rented a car for $18.00 plus $0.10 per mile driven. Craig rented a car for $25.00 plus $0.05 per mile driven. If each drove d miles and each was charged exactly the same amount for the rental, then d equals

(A) 100
(B) 120
(C) 135
(D) 140
(E) 150

6. Machine A produces bolts at a uniform rate of 120 every 40 seconds, and machine B produces bolts at a uniform rate of 100 every 20 seconds. If the two machines run simultaneously, how many seconds will it take for them to produce a total of 200 bolts?

(A) 22
(B) 25
(C) 28
(D) 32
(E) 56

7. $\dfrac{3.003}{2.002} =$

(A) 1.05
(B) 1.50015
(C) 1.501
(D) 1.5015
(E) 1.5

GO ON TO THE NEXT PAGE.

Questions 8-10 refer to the following graph.

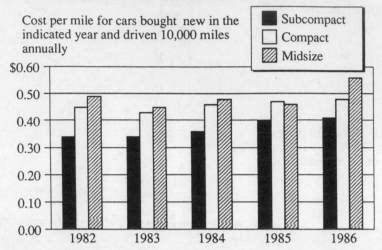

AVERAGE COSTS OF OPERATING SUBCOMPACT, COMPACT, AND
MIDSIZE CARS IN THE UNITED STATES, 1982–1986

8. In 1982 the approximate average cost of operating
a subcompact car for 10,000 miles was

   (A) $360
   (B) $3,400
   (C) $4,100
   (D) $4,500
   (E) $4,900

9. In 1984 the average cost of operating a subcompact
car was approximately what percent less than the
average cost of operating a midsized car?

   (A) 12%
   (B) 20%
   (C) 25%
   (D) 33%
   (E) 48%

10. For each of the years shown, the average cost per
mile of operating a compact car minus the average
cost per mile of operating a subcompact car was
between

   (A) $0.12 and $0.18
   (B) $0.10 and $0.15
   (C) $0.09 and $0.13
   (D) $0.06 and $0.12
   (E) $0.05 and $0.08

GO ON TO THE NEXT PAGE.

11. What is the decimal equivalent of $\left(\dfrac{1}{5}\right)^5$?

(A) 0.00032
(B) 0.0016
(C) 0.00625
(D) 0.008
(E) 0.03125

12. Two hundred gallons of fuel oil are purchased at \$0.91 per gallon and are consumed at a rate of \$0.70 worth of fuel per hour. At this rate, how many hours are required to consume the 200 gallons of fuel oil?

(A) 140
(B) 220
(C) 260
(D) 322
(E) 330

13. If $\dfrac{4 - x}{2 + x} = x$, what is the value of $x^2 + 3x - 4$?

(A) −4
(B) −1
(C) 0
(D) 1
(E) 2

14. If $b < 2$ and $2x - 3b = 0$, which of the following must be true?

(A) $x > -3$
(B) $x < 2$
(C) $x = 3$
(D) $x < 3$
(E) $x > 3$

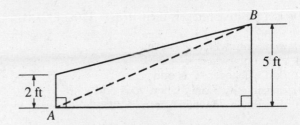

15. The trapezoid shown in the figure above represents a cross section of the rudder of a ship. If the distance from A to B is 13 feet, what is the area of the cross section of the rudder in square feet?

(A) 39
(B) 40
(C) 42
(D) 45
(E) 46.5

GO ON TO THE NEXT PAGE.

16. $\dfrac{(-1.5)(1.2) - (4.5)(0.4)}{30} =$

(A) −1.2
(B) −0.12
(C)   0
(D)   0.12
(E)   1.2

17. If n is a positive integer, then $n(n + 1)(n + 2)$ is

(A) even only when n is even
(B) even only when n is odd
(C) odd whenever n is odd
(D) divisible by 3 only when n is odd
(E) divisible by 4 whenever n is even

18. The figure above is composed of 6 squares, each
with side s centimeters. If the number of centimeters in the perimeter of the figure is equal to the
number of square centimeters in its area, what is
the value of s ?

(A) 1

(B) $\dfrac{5}{3}$

(C) 2

(D) $\dfrac{5}{2}$

(E) $\dfrac{7}{3}$

19. If $\dfrac{s}{t} = 2,$ then the value of which of the following
can be determined?

I. $\dfrac{2t}{s}$

II. $\dfrac{s - t}{t}$

III. $\dfrac{t - 1}{s - 1}$

(A) I only
(B) III only
(C) I and II only
(D) II and III only
(E) I, II, and III

GO ON TO THE NEXT PAGE.

NET INCOME FOR CORPORATIONS *A* and *B*

	Corporation *A*	Corporation *B*
Net Income in 1987	$2.9 million	$0.87 million
Percent Decrease in Net Income from 1986 to 1987	8.8%	13.3%

20. The net income of Corporation *B* in 1986 was approximately what percent of the net income of Corporation *A* in 1987 ?

(A) 35%
(B) 30%
(C) 25%
(D) 20%
(E) 15%

STOP

IF YOU FINISH BEFORE TIME IS CALLED, YOU MAY CHECK YOUR WORK ON THIS SECTION ONLY. DO NOT TURN TO ANY OTHER SECTION IN THE TEST.

SECTION 4

Time—30 minutes

25 Questions

Directions: Each passage in this group is followed by questions based on its content. After reading a passage, choose the best answer to each question and fill in the corresponding oval on the answer sheet. Answer all questions following a passage on the basis of what is stated or implied in that passage.

The majority of successful senior managers do not closely follow the classical rational model of first clarifying goals, assessing the problem, formulating options, estimating likelihoods of success, making a decision,
(5) and only then taking action to implement the decision. Rather, in their day-by-day tactical maneuvers, these senior executives rely on what is vaguely termed "intuition" to manage a network of interrelated problems that require them to deal with ambiguity, inconsistency,
(10) novelty, and surprise; and to integrate action into the process of thinking.

Generations of writers on management have recognized that some practicing managers rely heavily on intuition. In general, however, such writers display a
(15) poor grasp of what intuition is. Some see it as the opposite of rationality; others view it as an excuse for capriciousness.

Isenberg's recent research on the cognitive processes of senior managers reveals that managers' intuition is
(20) neither of these. Rather, senior managers use intuition in at least five distinct ways. First, they intuitively sense when a problem exists. Second, managers rely on intuition to perform well-learned behavior patterns rapidly. This intuition is not arbitrary or irrational, but is based
(25) on years of painstaking practice and hands-on experience that build skills. A third function of intuition is to synthesize isolated bits of data and practice into an integrated picture, often in an "Aha!" experience. Fourth, some managers use intuition as a check on the results
(30) of more rational analysis. Most senior executives are familiar with the formal decision analysis models and tools, and those who use such systematic methods for reaching decisions are occasionally leery of solutions suggested by these methods which run counter to their
(35) sense of the correct course of action. Finally, managers can use intuition to bypass in-depth analysis and move rapidly to engender a plausible solution. Used in this way, intuition is an almost instantaneous cognitive process in which a manager recognizes familiar patterns.
(40) One of the implications of the intuitive style of executive management is that "thinking" is inseparable from acting. Since managers often "know" what is right before they can analyze and explain it, they frequently act first and explain later. Analysis is inextricably tied
(45) to action in thinking/acting cycles, in which managers develop thoughts about their companies and organizations not by analyzing a problematic situation and then

acting, but by acting and analyzing in close concert.

Given the great uncertainty of many of the manage-
(50) ment issues that they face, senior managers often instigate a course of action simply to learn more about an issue. They then use the results of the action to develop a more complete understanding of the issue. One implication of thinking/acting cycles is that action is often
(55) part of defining the problem, not just of implementing the solution.

1. According to the passage, senior managers use intuition in all of the following ways EXCEPT to

(A) speed up the creation of a solution to a problem
(B) identify a problem
(C) bring together disparate facts
(D) stipulate clear goals
(E) evaluate possible solutions to a problem

2. The passage suggests which of the following about the "writers on management" mentioned in line 12 ?

(A) They have criticized managers for not following the classical rational model of decision analysis.
(B) They have not based their analyses on a sufficiently large sample of actual managers.
(C) They have relied in drawing their conclusions on what managers say rather than on what managers do.
(D) They have misunderstood how managers use intuition in making business decisions.
(E) They have not acknowledged the role of intuition in managerial practice.

GO ON TO THE NEXT PAGE.

3. Which of the following best exemplifies "an 'Aha!' experience" (line 28) as it is presented in the passage?

(A) A manager risks taking an action whose outcome is unpredictable to discover whether the action changes the problem at hand.

(B) A manager performs well-learned and familiar behavior patterns in creative and uncharacteristic ways to solve a problem.

(C) A manager suddenly connects seemingly unrelated facts and experiences to create a pattern relevant to the problem at hand.

(D) A manager rapidly identifies the methodology used to compile data yielded by systematic analysis.

(E) A manager swiftly decides which of several sets of tactics to implement in order to deal with the contingencies suggested by a problem.

4. According to the passage, the classical model of decision analysis includes all of the following EXCEPT

(A) evaluation of a problem

(B) creation of possible solutions to a problem

(C) establishment of clear goals to be reached by the decision

(D) action undertaken in order to discover more information about a problem

(E) comparison of the probable effects of different solutions to a problem

5. It can be inferred from the passage that which of the following would most probably be one major difference in behavior between Manager X, who uses intuition to reach decisions, and Manager Y, who uses only formal decision analysis?

(A) Manager X analyzes first and then acts; Manager Y does not.

(B) Manager X checks possible solutions to a problem by systematic analysis; Manager Y does not.

(C) Manager X takes action in order to arrive at the solution to a problem; Manager Y does not.

(D) Manager Y draws on years of hands-on experience in creating a solution to a problem; Manager X does not.

(E) Manager Y depends on day-to-day tactical maneuvering; Manager X does not.

6. It can be inferred from the passage that "thinking/ acting cycles" (line 45) in managerial practice would be likely to result in which of the following?

   I. A manager analyzes a network of problems and then acts on the basis of that analysis.
   II. A manager gathers data by acting and observing the effects of action.
   III. A manager takes action without being able to articulate reasons for that particular action.

(A) I only

(B) II only

(C) I and II only

(D) II and III only

(E) I, II, and III

7. The passage provides support for which of the following statements?

(A) Managers who rely on intuition are more successful than those who rely on formal decision analysis.

(B) Managers cannot justify their intuitive decisions.

(C) Managers' intuition works contrary to their rational and analytical skills.

(D) Logical analysis of a problem increases the number of possible solutions.

(E) Intuition enables managers to employ their practical experience more efficiently.

8. Which of the following best describes the organization of the first paragraph of the passage?

(A) An assertion is made and a specific supporting example is given.

(B) A conventional model is dismissed and an alternative introduced.

(C) The results of recent research are introduced and summarized.

(D) Two opposing points of view are presented and evaluated.

(E) A widely accepted definition is presented and qualified.

GO ON TO THE NEXT PAGE.

Nearly a century ago, biologists found that if they separated an invertebrate animal embryo into two parts at an early stage of its life, it would survive and develop
Line
(5) as two normal embryos. This led them to believe that the cells in the early embryo are undetermined in the sense that each cell has the potential to develop in a variety of different ways. Later biologists found that the situation was not so simple. It matters in which plane the embryo is cut. If it is cut in a plane different from the one used
(10) by the early investigators, it will not form two whole embryos.

A debate arose over what exactly was happening. Which embryo cells are determined, just when do they become irreversibly committed to their fates, and what
(15) are the "morphogenetic determinants" that tell a cell what to become? But the debate could not be resolved because no one was able to ask the crucial questions in a form in which they could be pursued productively. Recent discoveries in molecular biology, however, have
(20) opened up prospects for a resolution of the debate. Now investigators think they know at least some of the molecules that act as morphogenetic determinants in early development. They have been able to show that, in a sense, cell determination begins even before an egg
(25) is fertilized.

Studying sea urchins, biologist Paul Gross found that an unfertilized egg contains substances that function as morphogenetic determinants. They are located in the cytoplasm of the egg cell; i.e., in that part of the
(30) cell's protoplasm that lies outside of the nucleus. In the unfertilized egg, the substances are inactive and are not distributed homogeneously. When the egg is fertilized, the substances become active and, presumably, govern the behavior of the genes they interact with. Since the
(35) substances are unevenly distributed in the egg, when the fertilized egg divides, the resulting cells are different from the start and so can be qualitatively different in their own gene activity.

The substances that Gross studied are maternal
(40) messenger RNA's—products of certain of the maternal genes. He and other biologists studying a wide variety of organisms have found that these particular RNA's direct, in large part, the synthesis of histones, a class of proteins that bind to DNA. Once synthesized, the
(45) histones move into the cell nucleus, where sections of DNA wrap around them to form a structure that resembles beads, or knots, on a string. The beads are DNA segments wrapped around the histones; the string is the intervening DNA. And it is the structure of these beaded
(50) DNA strings that guides the fate of the cells in which they are located.

9. The passage is most probably directed at which kind of audience?

(A) State legislators deciding about funding levels for a state-funded biological laboratory
(B) Scientists specializing in molecular genetics
(C) Readers of an alumni newsletter published by the college that Paul Gross attended
(D) Marine biologists studying the processes that give rise to new species
(E) Undergraduate biology majors in a molecular biology course

10. It can be inferred from the passage that the morphogenetic determinants present in the early embryo are

(A) located in the nucleus of the embryo cells
(B) evenly distributed unless the embryo is not developing normally
(C) inactive until the embryo cells become irreversibly committed to their final function
(D) identical to those that were already present in the unfertilized egg
(E) present in larger quantities than is necessary for the development of a single individual

11. The main topic of the passage is

(A) the early development of embryos of lower marine organisms
(B) the main contribution of modern embryology to molecular biology
(C) the role of molecular biology in disproving older theories of embryonic development
(D) cell determination as an issue in the study of embryonic development
(E) scientific dogma as a factor in the recent debate over the value of molecular biology

GO ON TO THE NEXT PAGE.

12. According to the passage, when biologists believed that the cells in the early embryo were undetermined, they made which of the following mistakes?

   (A) They did not attempt to replicate the original experiment of separating an embryo into two parts.
   (B) They did not realize that there was a connection between the issue of cell determination and the outcome of the separation experiment.
   (C) They assumed that the results of experiments on embryos did not depend on the particular animal species used for such experiments.
   (D) They assumed that it was crucial to perform the separation experiment at an early stage in the embryo's life.
   (E) They assumed that different ways of separating an embryo into two parts would be equivalent as far as the fate of the two parts was concerned.

13. It can be inferred from the passage that the initial production of histones after an egg is fertilized takes place

   (A) in the cytoplasm
   (B) in the maternal genes
   (C) throughout the protoplasm
   (D) in the beaded portions of the DNA strings
   (E) in certain sections of the cell nucleus

14. It can be inferred from the passage that which of the following is dependent on the fertilization of an egg?

   (A) Copying of maternal genes to produce maternal messenger RNA's
   (B) Synthesis of proteins called histones
   (C) Division of a cell into its nucleus and the cytoplasm
   (D) Determination of the egg cell's potential for division
   (E) Generation of all of a cell's morphogenetic determinants

15. According to the passage, the morphogenetic determinants present in the unfertilized egg cell are which of the following?

   (A) Proteins bound to the nucleus
   (B) Histones
   (C) Maternal messenger RNA's
   (D) Cytoplasm
   (E) Nonbeaded intervening DNA

16. The passage suggests that which of the following plays a role in determining whether an embryo separated into two parts will develop as two normal embryos?

   I. The stage in the embryo's life at which the separation occurs
   II. The instrument with which the separation is accomplished
   III. The plane in which the cut is made that separates the embryo

   (A) I only
   (B) II only
   (C) I and II only
   (D) I and III only
   (E) I, II, and III

17. Which of the following circumstances is most comparable to the impasse biologists encountered in trying to resolve the debate about cell determination (lines 12-18) ?

   (A) The problems faced by a literary scholar who wishes to use original source materials that are written in an unfamiliar foreign language
   (B) The situation of a mathematician who in preparing a proof of a theorem for publication detects a reasoning error in the proof
   (C) The difficulties of a space engineer who has to design equipment to function in an environment in which it cannot first be tested
   (D) The predicament of a linguist trying to develop a theory of language acquisition when knowledge of the structure of language itself is rudimentary at best
   (E) The dilemma confronting a foundation when the funds available to it are sufficient to support one of two equally deserving scientific projects but not both

GO ON TO THE NEXT PAGE.

In the two decades between 1910 and 1930, over ten percent of the Black population of the United States left the South, where the preponderance of the Black population had been located, and migrated to northern states, with the largest number moving, it is claimed, between 1916 and 1918. It has been frequently assumed, but not proved, that the majority of the migrants in what has come to be called the Great Migration came from rural areas and were motivated by two concurrent factors: the collapse of the cotton industry following the boll weevil infestation, which began in 1898, and increased demand in the North for labor following the cessation of European immigration caused by the outbreak of the First World War in 1914. This assumption has led to the conclusion that the migrants' subsequent lack of economic mobility in the North is tied to rural background, a background that implies unfamiliarity with urban living and a lack of industrial skills.

But the question of who actually left the South has never been rigorously investigated. Although numerous investigations document an exodus from rural southern areas to southern cities prior to the Great Migration, no one has considered whether the same migrants then moved on to northern cities. In 1910 over 600,000 Black workers, or ten percent of the Black work force, reported themselves to be engaged in "manufacturing and mechanical pursuits," the federal census category roughly encompassing the entire industrial sector. The Great Migration could easily have been made up entirely of this group and their families. It is perhaps surprising to argue that an employed population could be enticed to move, but an explanation lies in the labor conditions then prevalent in the South.

About thirty-five percent of the urban Black population in the South was engaged in skilled trades. Some were from the old artisan class of slavery—blacksmiths, masons, carpenters—which had had a monopoly of certain trades, but they were gradually being pushed out by competition, mechanization, and obsolescence. The remaining sixty-five percent, more recently urbanized, worked in newly developed industries—tobacco, lumber, coal and iron manufacture, and railroads. Wages in the South, however, were low, and Black workers were aware, through labor recruiters and the Black press, that they could earn more even as unskilled workers in the North than they could as artisans in the South. After the boll weevil infestation, urban Black workers faced competition from the continuing influx of both Black and White rural workers, who were driven to undercut the wages formerly paid for industrial jobs. Thus, a move north would be seen as advantageous to a group that was already urbanized and steadily employed, and the easy conclusion tying their subsequent economic problems in the North to their rural background comes into question.

18. The author indicates explicitly that which of the following records has been a source of information in her investigation?

(A) United States Immigration Service reports from 1914 to 1930
(B) Payrolls of southern manufacturing firms between 1910 and 1930
(C) The volume of cotton exports between 1898 and 1910
(D) The federal census of 1910
(E) Advertisements of labor recruiters appearing in southern newspapers after 1910

19. In the passage, the author anticipates which of the following as a possible objection to her argument?

(A) It is uncertain how many people actually migrated during the Great Migration.
(B) The eventual economic status of the Great Migration migrants has not been adequately traced.
(C) It is not likely that people with steady jobs would have reason to move to another area of the country.
(D) It is not true that the term "manufacturing and mechanical pursuits" actually encompasses the entire industrial sector.
(E) Of the Black workers living in southern cities, only those in a small number of trades were threatened by obsolescence.

20. According to the passage, which of the following is true of wages in southern cities in 1910?

(A) They were being pushed lower as a result of increased competition.
(B) They had begun to rise so that southern industry could attract rural workers.
(C) They had increased for skilled workers but decreased for unskilled workers.
(D) They had increased in large southern cities but decreased in small southern cities.
(E) They had increased in newly developed industries but decreased in the older trades.

GO ON TO THE NEXT PAGE.

21. The author cites each of the following as possible influences in a Black worker's decision to migrate north in the Great Migration EXCEPT

   (A) wage levels in northern cities
   (B) labor recruiters
   (C) competition from rural workers
   (D) voting rights in northern states
   (E) the Black press

22. It can be inferred from the passage that the "easy conclusion" mentioned in line 53 is based on which of the following assumptions?

   (A) People who migrate from rural areas to large cities usually do so for economic reasons.
   (B) Most people who leave rural areas to take jobs in cities return to rural areas as soon as it is financially possible for them to do so.
   (C) People with rural backgrounds are less likely to succeed economically in cities than are those with urban backgrounds.
   (D) Most people who were once skilled workers are not willing to work as unskilled workers.
   (E) People who migrate from their birthplaces to other regions of a country seldom undertake a second migration.

23. The primary purpose of the passage is to

   (A) support an alternative to an accepted methodology
   (B) present evidence that resolves a contradiction
   (C) introduce a recently discovered source of information
   (D) challenge a widely accepted explanation
   (E) argue that a discarded theory deserves new attention

24. According to information in the passage, which of the following is a correct sequence of groups of workers, from highest paid to lowest paid, in the period between 1910 and 1930 ?

   (A) Artisans in the North; artisans in the South; unskilled workers in the North; unskilled workers in the South
   (B) Artisans in the North and South; unskilled workers in the North; unskilled workers in the South
   (C) Artisans in the North; unskilled workers in the North; artisans in the South
   (D) Artisans in the North and South; unskilled urban workers in the North; unskilled rural workers in the South
   (E) Artisans in the North and South; unskilled rural workers in the North and South; unskilled urban workers in the North and South

25. The material in the passage would be most relevant to a long discussion of which of the following topics?

   (A) The reasons for the subsequent economic difficulties of those who participated in the Great Migration
   (B) The effect of migration on the regional economies of the United States following the First World War
   (C) The transition from a rural to an urban existence for those who migrated in the Great Migration
   (D) The transformation of the agricultural South following the boll weevil infestation
   (E) The disappearance of the artisan class in the United States as a consequence of mechanization in the early twentieth century

STOP

**IF YOU FINISH BEFORE TIME IS CALLED, YOU MAY CHECK YOUR WORK ON THIS SECTION ONLY.
DO NOT TURN TO ANY OTHER SECTION IN THE TEST.**

NO TEST MATERIAL ON THIS PAGE

SECTION 5

Time—30 minutes

20 Questions

<u>Directions:</u> In this section solve each problem, using any available space on the page for scratchwork. Then indicate the best of the answer choices given.

<u>Numbers:</u> All numbers used are real numbers.

<u>Figures:</u> Figures that accompany problems in this section are intended to provide information useful in solving the problems. They are drawn as accurately as possible EXCEPT when it is stated in a specific problem that its figure is not drawn to scale. All figures lie in a plane unless otherwise indicated.

1. If Jack had twice the amount of money that he has, he would have exactly the amount necessary to buy 3 hamburgers at $0.96 apiece and 2 milk shakes at $1.28 apiece. How much money does Jack have?

(A) $1.60
(B) $2.24
(C) $2.72
(D) $3.36
(E) $5.44

2. If a photocopier makes 2 copies in $\frac{1}{3}$ second, then, at the same rate, how many copies does it make in 4 minutes?

(A)   360
(B)   480
(C)   576
(D)   720
(E) 1,440

3. The price of a certain television set is discounted by 10 percent, and the reduced price is then discounted by 10 percent. This series of successive discounts is equivalent to a single discount of

(A) 20%
(B) 19%
(C) 18%
(D) 11%
(E) 10%

4. If $\dfrac{2}{1 + \dfrac{2}{y}} = 1$, then $y =$

(A) -2

(B) $-\dfrac{1}{2}$

(C) $\dfrac{1}{2}$

(D) 2

(E) 3

GO ON TO THE NEXT PAGE.

5. If a rectangular photograph that is 10 inches wide by 15 inches long is to be enlarged so that the width will be 22 inches and the ratio of width to length will be unchanged, then the length, in inches, of the enlarged photograph will be

(A) 33
(B) 32
(C) 30
(D) 27
(E) 25

6. If m is an integer such that $(-2)^{2m} = 2^{9-m}$, then $m =$

(A) 1
(B) 2
(C) 3
(D) 4
(E) 6

7. If $0 \leq x \leq 4$ and $y < 12$, which of the following CANNOT be the value of xy?

(A) -2
(B) 0
(C) 6
(D) 24
(E) 48

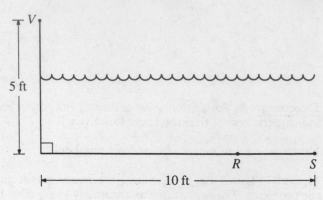

8. In the figure above, V represents an observation point at one end of a pool. From V, an object that is actually located on the bottom of the pool at point R appears to be at point S. If $VR = 10$ feet, what is the distance RS, in feet, between the actual position and the perceived position of the object?

(A) $10 - 5\sqrt{3}$

(B) $10 - 5\sqrt{2}$

(C) 2

(D) $2\frac{1}{2}$

(E) 4

GO ON TO THE NEXT PAGE.

9. If the total payroll expense of a certain business in year Y was \$84,000, which was 20 percent more than in year X, what was the total payroll expense in year X?

(A) \$70,000
(B) \$68,320
(C) \$64,000
(D) \$60,000
(E) \$52,320

10. If a, b, and c are consecutive positive integers and $a < b < c$, which of the following must be true?

   I. $c - a = 2$

   II. abc is an even integer.

   III. $\dfrac{a + b + c}{3}$ is an integer.

(A) I only
(B) II only
(C) I and II only
(D) II and III only
(E) I, II, and III

11. A straight pipe 1 yard in length was marked off in fourths and also in thirds. If the pipe was then cut into separate pieces at each of these markings, which of the following gives all the different lengths of the pieces, in fractions of a yard?

(A) $\dfrac{1}{6}$ and $\dfrac{1}{4}$ only

(B) $\dfrac{1}{4}$ and $\dfrac{1}{3}$ only

(C) $\dfrac{1}{6}$, $\dfrac{1}{4}$, and $\dfrac{1}{3}$

(D) $\dfrac{1}{12}$, $\dfrac{1}{6}$, and $\dfrac{1}{4}$

(E) $\dfrac{1}{12}$, $\dfrac{1}{6}$, and $\dfrac{1}{3}$

12. What is the least integer that is a sum of three different primes each greater than 20 ?

(A) 69
(B) 73
(C) 75
(D) 79
(E) 83

13. A tourist purchased a total of \$1,500 worth of traveler's checks in \$10 and \$50 denominations. During the trip the tourist cashed 7 checks and then lost all of the rest. If the number of \$10 checks cashed was one more or one less than the number of \$50 checks cashed, what is the minimum possible value of the checks that were lost?

(A) \$1,430
(B) \$1,310
(C) \$1,290
(D) \$1,270
(E) \$1,150

GO ON TO THE NEXT PAGE.

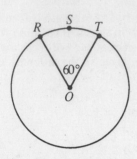

14. If the circle above has center O and circumference 18π, then the perimeter of sector $RSTO$ is

(A) $3\pi + 9$
(B) $3\pi + 18$
(C) $6\pi + 9$
(D) $6\pi + 18$
(E) $6\pi + 24$

15. If each of the following fractions were written as a repeating decimal, which would have the longest sequence of different digits?

(A) $\dfrac{2}{11}$

(B) $\dfrac{1}{3}$

(C) $\dfrac{41}{99}$

(D) $\dfrac{2}{3}$

(E) $\dfrac{23}{37}$

16. Today Rose is twice as old as Sam and Sam is 3 years younger than Tina. If Rose, Sam, and Tina are all alive 4 years from today, which of the following must be true on that day?

   I. Rose is twice as old as Sam.
  II. Sam is 3 years younger than Tina.
 III. Rose is older than Tina.

(A) I only
(B) II only
(C) III only
(D) I and II
(E) II and III

17. If k and w are the dimensions of a rectangle that has area 42, and if k and w are integers such that $k > w$, what is the total number of possible values of k?

(A) Two
(B) Three
(C) Four
(D) Five
(E) Six

18. R campers fished for 3 hours. If m of the campers caught 2 fish apiece and the rest caught a combined total of n fish, how many fish did the R campers catch per hour?

(A) $2m + n(R - m)$

(B) $\dfrac{2m + n(R - m)}{3}$

(C) $\dfrac{2m + n(m - R)}{3}$

(D) $\dfrac{2m + n}{3}$

(E) $\dfrac{2m + n}{R}$

GO ON TO THE NEXT PAGE.

19. Last year the annual premium on a certain hospitalization insurance policy was $408, and the policy paid 80 percent of any hospital expenses incurred. If the amount paid by the insurance policy last year was equal to the annual premium plus the amount of hospital expenses not paid by the policy, what was the total amount of hospital expenses last year?

(A) $850.00
(B) $680.00
(C) $640.00
(D) $510.00
(E) $326.40

20. The average (arithmetic mean) of three numbers is $3x + 2$. If one of the numbers is x, what is the average of the other two numbers?

(A) $x + 1$
(B) $2x + 2$
(C) $4x + 1$
(D) $4x + 3$
(E) $8x + 6$

STOP

IF YOU FINISH BEFORE TIME IS CALLED, YOU MAY CHECK YOUR WORK ON THIS SECTION ONLY.
DO NOT TURN TO ANY OTHER SECTION IN THE TEST.

NO TEST MATERIAL ON THIS PAGE

SECTION 6

Time—30 minutes

25 Questions

Directions: In each of the following sentences, some part of the sentence or the entire sentence is underlined. Beneath each sentence you will find five ways of phrasing the underlined part. The first of these repeats the original; the other four are different. If you think the original is better than any of the alternatives, choose answer A; otherwise, choose one of the others. Select the best version and fill in the corresponding oval on your answer sheet.

This is a test of correctness and effectiveness of expression. In choosing answers, follow the requirements of standard written English; that is, pay attention to grammar, choice of words, and sentence construction. Choose the answer that expresses most effectively what is presented in the original sentence; this answer should be clear and exact, without awkwardness, ambiguity, or redundancy.

1. A Labor Department study states that the <u>numbers of women employed outside the home grew by more than a thirty-five percent increase</u> in the past decade and accounted for more than sixty-two percent of the total growth in the civilian work force.

    (A) numbers of women employed outside the home grew by more than a thirty-five percent increase
    (B) numbers of women employed outside the home grew more than thirty-five percent
    (C) numbers of women employed outside the home were raised by more than thirty-five percent
    (D) number of women employed outside the home increased by more than thirty-five percent
    (E) number of women employed outside the home was raised by more than a thirty-five percent increase

2. The first decision for most tenants living in a building undergoing <u>being converted to cooperative ownership is if to sign</u> a no-buy pledge with the other tenants.

    (A) being converted to cooperative ownership is if to sign
    (B) being converted to cooperative ownership is whether they should be signing
    (C) being converted to cooperative ownership is whether or not they sign
    (D) conversion to cooperative ownership is if to sign
    (E) conversion to cooperative ownership is whether to sign

3. The end of the eighteenth century saw the emergence of prize-stock breeding, with individual bulls and cows receiving awards, fetching unprecedented prices, and <u>excited</u> enormous interest whenever they were put on show.

    (A) excited
    (B) it excited
    (C) exciting
    (D) would excite
    (E) it had excited

4. Of all the possible disasters that threaten American agriculture, the possibility of an adverse change in climate <u>is maybe the more difficult for analysis</u>.

    (A) is maybe the more difficult for analysis
    (B) is probably the most difficult to analyze
    (C) is maybe the most difficult for analysis
    (D) is probably the more difficult to analyze
    (E) is, it may be, the analysis that is most difficult

GO ON TO THE NEXT PAGE.

-415-

5. Published in Harlem, the owner and editor of the *Messenger* were two young journalists, Chandler Owen and A. Philip Randolph, who would later make his reputation as a labor leader.

(A) Published in Harlem, the owner and editor of the *Messenger* were two young journalists, Chandler Owen and A. Philip Randolph, who would later make his reputation as a labor leader.

(B) Published in Harlem, two young journalists, Chandler Owen and A. Philip Randolph, who would later make his reputation as a labor leader, were the owner and editor of the *Messenger*.

(C) Published in Harlem, the *Messenger* was owned and edited by two young journalists, A. Philip Randolph, who would later make his reputation as a labor leader, and Chandler Owen.

(D) The *Messenger* was owned and edited by two young journalists, Chandler Owen and A. Philip Randolph, who would later make his reputation as a labor leader, and published in Harlem.

(E) The owner and editor being two young journalists, Chandler Owen and A. Philip Randolph, who would later make his reputation as a labor leader, the *Messenger* was published in Harlem.

6. The rise in the Commerce Department's index of leading economic indicators suggest that the economy should continue its expansion into the coming months, but that the mixed performance of the index's individual components indicates that economic growth will proceed at a more moderate pace than in the first quarter of this year.

(A) suggest that the economy should continue its expansion into the coming months, but that

(B) suggest that the economy is to continue expansion in the coming months, but

(C) suggests that the economy will continue its expanding in the coming months, but that

(D) suggests that the economy is continuing to expand into the coming months, but that

(E) suggests that the economy will continue to expand in the coming months, but

7. In three centuries—from 1050 to 1350—several million tons of stone were quarried in France for the building of eighty cathedrals, five hundred large churches, and some tens of thousands of parish churches.

(A) for the building of eighty cathedrals, five hundred large churches, and some

(B) in order that they might build eighty cathedrals, five hundred large churches, and some

(C) so as they might build eighty cathedrals, five hundred large churches, and some

(D) so that there could be built eighty cathedrals, five hundred large churches, and

(E) such that they could build eighty cathedrals, five hundred large churches, and

8. What was as remarkable as the development of the compact disc has been the use of the new technology to revitalize, in better sound than was ever before possible, some of the classic recorded performances of the pre-LP era.

(A) What was as remarkable as the development of the compact disc

(B) The thing that was as remarkable as developing the compact disc

(C) No less remarkable than the development of the compact disc

(D) Developing the compact disc has been none the less remarkable than

(E) Development of the compact disc has been no less remarkable as

9. Unlike computer skills or other technical skills, there is a disinclination on the part of many people to recognize the degree to which their analytical skills are weak.

(A) Unlike computer skills or other technical skills, there is a disinclination on the part of many people to recognize the degree to which their analytical skills are weak.

(B) Unlike computer skills or other technical skills, which they admit they lack, many people are disinclined to recognize that their analytical skills are weak.

(C) Unlike computer skills or other technical skills, analytical skills bring out a disinclination in many people to recognize that they are weak to a degree.

(D) Many people, willing to admit that they lack computer skills or other technical skills, are disinclined to recognize that their analytical skills are weak.

(E) Many people have a disinclination to recognize the weakness of their analytical skills while willing to admit their lack of computer skills or other technical skills.

GO ON TO THE NEXT PAGE.

10. Some buildings that were destroyed and heavily damaged in the earthquake last year were constructed in violation of the city's building code.

(A) Some buildings that were destroyed and heavily damaged in the earthquake last year were

(B) Some buildings that were destroyed or heavily damaged in the earthquake last year had been

(C) Some buildings that the earthquake destroyed and heavily damaged last year have been

(D) Last year the earthquake destroyed or heavily damaged some buildings that have been

(E) Last year some of the buildings that were destroyed or heavily damaged in the earthquake had been

11. From the earliest days of the tribe, kinship determined the way in which the Ojibwa society organized its labor, provided access to its resources, and defined rights and obligations involved in the distribution and consumption of those resources.

(A) and defined rights and obligations involved in the distribution and consumption of those resources

(B) defining rights and obligations involved in their distribution and consumption

(C) and defined rights and obligations as they were involved in its distribution and consumption

(D) whose rights and obligations were defined in their distribution and consumption

(E) the distribution and consumption of them defined by rights and obligations

12. A report by the American Academy for the Advancement of Science has concluded that much of the currently uncontrolled dioxins to which North Americans are exposed comes from the incineration of wastes.

(A) much of the currently uncontrolled dioxins to which North Americans are exposed comes

(B) much of the currently uncontrolled dioxins that North Americans are exposed to come

(C) much of the dioxins that are currently uncontrolled and that North Americans are exposed to comes

(D) many of the dioxins that are currently uncontrolled and North Americans are exposed to come

(E) many of the currently uncontrolled dioxins to which North Americans are exposed come

13. In June of 1987, *The Bridge of Trinquetaille*, Vincent van Gogh's view of an iron bridge over the Rhone sold for $20.2 million and it was the second highest price ever paid for a painting at auction.

(A) Rhone sold for $20.2 million and it was

(B) Rhone, which sold for $20.2 million, was

(C) Rhone, was sold for $20.2 million,

(D) Rhone was sold for $20.2 million, being

(E) Rhone, sold for $20.2 million, and was

14. *Bufo marinus* toads, fierce predators that will eat frogs, lizards, and even small birds, are native to South America but were introduced into Florida during the 1930's in an attempt to control pests in the state's vast sugarcane fields.

(A) are native to South America but were introduced into Florida during the 1930's in an attempt to control

(B) are native in South America but were introduced into Florida during the 1930's as attempts to control

(C) are natives of South America but were introduced into Florida during the 1930's in an attempt at controlling

(D) had been native to South America but were introduced to Florida during the 1930's as an attempt at controlling

(E) had been natives of South America but were introduced to Florida during the 1930's as attempts at controlling

15. While some academicians believe that business ethics should be integrated into every business course, others say that students will take ethics seriously only if it would be taught as a separately required course.

(A) only if it would be taught as a separately required course

(B) only if it is taught as a separate, required course

(C) if it is taught only as a course required separately

(D) if it was taught only as a separate and required course

(E) if it would only be taught as a required course, separately

GO ON TO THE NEXT PAGE.

16. Scientists have observed large concentrations of heavy-metal deposits in the upper twenty centimeters of Baltic Sea sediments, which are consistent with the growth of industrial activity there.

(A) Baltic Sea sediments, which are consistent with the growth of industrial activity there
(B) Baltic Sea sediments, where the growth of industrial activity is consistent with these findings
(C) Baltic Sea sediments, findings consistent with its growth of industrial activity
(D) sediments from the Baltic Sea, findings consistent with the growth of industrial activity in the area
(E) sediments from the Baltic Sea, consistent with the growth of industrial activity there

17. For members of the seventeenth-century Ashanti nation in Africa, animal-hide shields with wooden frames were essential items of military equipment, a method to protect warriors against enemy arrows and spears.

(A) a method to protect
(B) as a method protecting
(C) protecting
(D) as a protection of
(E) to protect

18. In metalwork one advantage of adhesive-bonding over spot-welding is that the contact, and hence the bonding, is effected continuously over a broad surface instead of a series of regularly spaced points with no bonding in between.

(A) instead of
(B) as opposed to
(C) in contrast with
(D) rather than at
(E) as against being at

19. Under a provision of the Constitution that was never applied, Congress has been required to call a convention for considering possible amendments to the document when formally asked to do it by the legislatures of two-thirds of the states.

(A) was never applied, Congress has been required to call a convention for considering possible amendments to the document when formally asked to do it
(B) was never applied, there has been a requirement that Congress call a convention for consideration of possible amendments to the document when asked to do it formally
(C) was never applied, whereby Congress is required to call a convention for considering possible amendments to the document when asked to do it formally
(D) has never been applied, whereby Congress is required to call a convention to consider possible amendments to the document when formally asked to do so
(E) has never been applied, Congress is required to call a convention to consider possible amendments to the document when formally asked to do so

20. The current administration, being worried over some foreign trade barriers being removed and our exports failing to increase as a result of deep cuts in the value of the dollar, has formed a group to study ways to sharpen our competitiveness.

(A) being worried over some foreign trade barriers being removed and our exports failing
(B) worrying over some foreign trade barriers being removed, also over the failure of our exports
(C) worried about the removal of some foreign trade barriers and the failure of our exports
(D) in that they were worried about the removal of some foreign trade barriers and also about the failure of our exports
(E) because of its worry concerning the removal of some foreign trade barriers, also concerning the failure of our exports

21. In the minds of many people living in England, before Australia was Australia, it was the antipodes, the opposite pole to civilization, an obscure and unimaginable place that was considered the end of the world.

(A) before Australia was Australia, it was the antipodes
(B) before there was Australia, it was the antipodes
(C) it was the antipodes that was Australia
(D) Australia was what was the antipodes
(E) Australia was what had been known as the antipodes

GO ON TO THE NEXT PAGE.

22. Using a Doppler ultrasound device, fetal heartbeats can be detected by the twelfth week of pregnancy.

   (A) Using a Doppler ultrasound device, fetal heartbeats can be detected by the twelfth week of pregnancy.
   (B) Fetal heartbeats can be detected by the twelfth week of pregnancy, using a Doppler ultrasound device.
   (C) Detecting fetal heartbeats by the twelfth week of pregnancy, a physician can use a Doppler ultrasound device.
   (D) By the twelfth week of pregnancy, fetal heartbeats can be detected using a Doppler ultrasound device by a physician.
   (E) Using a Doppler ultrasound device, a physician can detect fetal heartbeats by the twelfth week of pregnancy.

23. Constance Horner, chief of the United States government's personnel agency, has recommended that the use of any dangerous or illegal drug in the five years prior to application for a job be grounds for not hiring an applicant.

   (A) the use of any dangerous or illegal drug in the five years prior to application for a job be grounds for not hiring an applicant
   (B) any dangerous or illegal drug, if used in the five years prior to applying for a job, should be grounds not to hire the applicant
   (C) an applicant's use of any dangerous or illegal drug in the five years prior to application for a job be grounds not to hire them
   (D) an applicant's use of any dangerous or illegal drug in the five years prior to applying for a job are grounds that they not be hired
   (E) for five years prior to applying for a job, an applicant's use of any dangerous or illegal drug be grounds for not hiring them

24. Inflation in medical costs slowed in 1986 for the fifth consecutive year but were still about 50 percent greater than the rate of price increases for other items included in the consumer price index.

   (A) Inflation in medical costs slowed in 1986 for the fifth consecutive year but were
   (B) Inflation in medical costs slowed for the fifth consecutive year in 1986 but was
   (C) In 1986 inflation in medical costs were slowed for the fifth consecutive year but were
   (D) 1986 was the fifth consecutive year in which inflation in medical costs slowed but was
   (E) 1986 was the fifth consecutive year that inflation in medical costs were slowed, but they were

25. The most common reasons for an employee's unwillingness to accept a transfer are that mortgage rates are high, housing in the new location costs more, and the difficulty of selling the old home.

   (A) that mortgage rates are high, housing in the new location costs more, and the difficulty of selling the old home
   (B) that mortgage rates are high, housing in the new location costs more, and that it is difficult to sell the old home
   (C) high mortgage rates, the greater cost of housing in the new location, and that the old home is difficult to sell
   (D) high mortgage rates, the greater cost of housing in the new location, and it is difficult to sell the old home
   (E) high mortgage rates, the greater cost of housing in the new location, and the difficulty of selling the old home

STOP

IF YOU FINISH BEFORE TIME IS CALLED, YOU MAY CHECK YOUR WORK ON THIS SECTION ONLY.
DO NOT TURN TO ANY OTHER SECTION IN THE TEST.

Answer Sheet

B

Section 1

1. A B C ● E
2. A B C D ●
3. A B C D ●
4. A B C ● E
5. A B ● D E
6. A ● C D E
7. A ● C D E
8. A B ● D E
9. A B ● D E
10. A B C D ●
11. A B C ● E
12. A B C D ●
13. A B ● D E
14. ● B C D E
15. ● B C D E
16. A B C ● E
17. A B ● D E
18. A B C D ●
19. ● B C D E
20. A B ● D E
21. A B C D E
22. A B C D E
23. A B C D E
24. A B C D E
25. A B C D E

Section 2

1. A B ● D E
2. A B C D ●
3. A B ● D E
4. A B C ● E
5. A B ● D E
6. ● B C D E
7. A B C D ●
8. A B ● D E
9. A B ● D E
10. A ● C D E
11. ● B C D E
12. A B C D ●
13. A B ● D E
14. A ● C D E
15. A ● C D E
16. A B ● D E
17. ● B C D E
18. A ● C D E
19. A ● C D E
20. ● B C D E
21. A B C D ●
22. ● B C D E
23. A B ● D E
24. A B C ● E
25. ● B C D E

Section 3

1. ● B C D E
2. NOT SCORED
3. ● B C D E
4. A B ● D E
5. A B C ● E
6. A ● C D E
7. A B C D ●
8. A ● C D E
9. A B C ● E
10. A B ● D E
11. ● B C D E
12. A B ● D E
13. A B ● D E
14. A B C ● E
15. A ● C D E
16. A ● C D E
17. A B C D ●
18. A B C D ●
19. A B ● D E
20. ● B C D E
21. A B C D E
22. A B C D E
23. A B C D E
24. A B C D E
25. A B C D E

Section 4

1. A B C ● E
2. A B C ● E
3. A B ● D E
4. A B C ● E
5. A B ● D E
6. A B C ● E
7. A B C D ●
8. A ● C D E
9. A B C D ●
10. A B C D ●
11. A B C ● E
12. A B C D ●
13. ● B C D E
14. A ● C D E
15. A B ● D E
16. A B C ● E
17. A B C ● E
18. A B C ● E
19. A B ● D E
20. ● B C D E
21. A B C ● E
22. A B ● D E
23. A B C ● E
24. A B ● D E
25. ● B C D E

Section 5

1. A B ● D E
2. A B C D ●
3. A ● C D E
4. A B C ● E
5. ● B C D E
6. A ● C D E
7. A B C D ●
8. ● B C D E
9. A ● C D E
10. A B C D ●
11. A B C ● E
12. A B C D ●
13. A B C ● E
14. A ● C D E
15. A B ● D E
16. A ● C D E
17. A B ● D E
18. A B C ● E
19. A ● C D E
20. A B C ● E
21. A B C ● E
22. A ● C D E
23. A ● C D E
24. A ● C D E
25. A B C D E

Section 6

1. A B C ● E
2. A B C D ●
3. A B ● D E
4. A ● C D E
5. A B ● D E
6. A B C D ●
7. ● B C D E
8. A ● C D E
9. A B C ● E
10. A ● C D E
11. ● B C D E
12. A B C D ●
13. A B ● D E
14. ● B C D E
15. A ● C D E
16. A B C ● E
17. A B C D ●
18. A B C ● E
19. A B C D ●
20. A B C ● E
21. ● B C D E
22. A B C D ●
23. ● B C D E
24. A ● C D E
25. A B C D ●

Explanatory Material: Critical Reasoning, Section 1

1. Toughened hiring standards have not been the primary cause of the present staffing shortage in public schools. The shortage of teachers is primarily caused by the fact that in recent years teachers have not experienced any improvements in working conditions and their salaries have not kept pace with salaries in other professions.

   Which of the following, if true, would most support the claims above?

   (A) Many teachers already in the profession would not have been hired under the new hiring standards.
   (B) Today more teachers are entering the profession with a higher educational level than in the past.
   (C) Some teachers have cited higher standards for hiring as a reason for the current staffing shortage.
   (D) Many teachers have cited low pay and lack of professional freedom as reasons for their leaving the profession.
   (E) Many prospective teachers have cited the new hiring standards as a reason for not entering the profession.

The passage rejects one explanation of the shortage of teachers — that it results from toughened hiring standards — and advances an alternative — that it results from deficiencies in pay and working conditions. Choice D provides corroborative evidence for the latter explanation by suggesting that, for many former teachers, poor pay and working conditions were reasons for their quitting the profession. Therefore, D is the best answer.

Choices A, C, and E provide evidence that tends to implicate new hiring standards in the staffing shortage, and thus support the explanation that the passage rejects. Choice B describes what may be a result of the new hiring standards, but it provides no evidence favoring one explanation of the staffing shortage over the other.

2. A proposed ordinance requires the installation in new homes of sprinklers automatically triggered by the presence of a fire. However, a home builder argued that because more than ninety percent of residential fires are extinguished by a household member, residential sprinklers would only marginally decrease property damage caused by residential fires.

   Which of the following, if true, would most seriously weaken the home builder's argument?

   (A) Most individuals have no formal training in how to extinguish fires.
   (B) Since new homes are only a tiny percentage of available housing in the city, the new ordinance would be extremely narrow in scope.
   (C) The installation of smoke detectors in new residences costs significantly less than the installation of sprinklers.
   (D) In the city where the ordinance was proposed, the average time required by the fire department to respond to a fire was less than the national average.
   (E) The largest proportion of property damage that results from residential fires is caused by fires that start when no household member is present.

The home builder reasons from evidence about most residential fires to a conclusion about the effectiveness of sprinklers in preventing property damage. But this reasoning is faulty because of the possibility that most of the property damage results from the minority of fires excluded from the builder's evidence. This possibility is realized if E is true. Thus, E is the best answer.

Because the builder's argument concerns neither the cost of installing sprinklers nor a comparison with fire department performance in other locations, choices C and D are irrelevant. The evidence the home builder cites suggests that formal training (choice A) is not needed in order to extinguish fires. Choice B supports the builder's view that requiring sprinklers would have a limited effect.

3. Even though most universities retain the royalties from faculty members' inventions, the faculty members retain the royalties from books and articles they write. Therefore, faculty members should retain the royalties from the educational computer software they develop.

The conclusion above would be more reasonably drawn if which of the following were inserted into the argument as an additional premise?

(A) Royalties from inventions are higher than royalties from educational software programs.
(B) Faculty members are more likely to produce educational software programs than inventions.
(C) Inventions bring more prestige to universities than do books and articles.
(D) In the experience of most universities, educational software programs are more marketable than are books and articles.
(E) In terms of the criteria used to award royalties, educational software programs are more nearly comparable to books and articles than to inventions.

The passage concludes that, where royalty retention of faculty members' works is concerned, software should be treated as books and articles are, not as inventions are. The conclusion requires an additional premise establishing that software is, in relevant respects, more comparable to books and articles than to inventions. Choice E provides this kind of premise and is therefore the best answer.

Choices A, B, C, and D, conversely, each describe some difference between software and inventions (choices A and B), or between inventions and books and articles (choice C), or between software and books and articles (choice D), but none establishes the required relationship among inventions, software, and books and articles.

4. Increases in the level of high-density lipoprotein (HDL) in the human bloodstream lower bloodstream-cholesterol levels by increasing the body's capacity to rid itself of excess cholesterol. Levels of HDL in the bloodstream of some individuals are significantly increased by a program of regular exercise and weight reduction.

Which of the following can be correctly inferred from the statements above?

(A) Individuals who are underweight do not run any risk of developing high levels of cholesterol in the bloodstream.
(B) Individuals who do not exercise regularly have a high risk of developing high levels of cholesterol in the bloodstream late in life.
(C) Exercise and weight reduction are the most effective methods of lowering bloodstream cholesterol levels in humans.
(D) A program of regular exercise and weight reduction lowers cholesterol levels in the bloodstream of some individuals.
(E) Only regular exercise is necessary to decrease cholesterol levels in the bloodstream of individuals of average weight.

If increased HDL levels cause reduced cholesterol levels and if a certain program increases HDL levels in some individuals, it follows that some individuals who undertake that program achieve reduced cholesterol levels. Choice D is thus correctly inferable and the best answer.

Choice A cannot be correctly inferred because the statements do not establish any connection between being underweight and levels of cholesterol. Neither B nor E is inferable, since there is no indication that exercise alone is either necessary or sufficient to increase HDL levels or to decrease cholesterol levels. Choice C is inappropriate because other methods of cholesterol reduction are not addressed.

5. When limitations were in effect on nuclear-arms testing, people tended to save more of their money, but when nuclear-arms testing increased, people tended to spend more of their money. The perceived threat of nuclear catastrophe, therefore, decreases the willingness of people to postpone consumption for the sake of saving money.

The argument above assumes that

(A) the perceived threat of nuclear catastrophe has increased over the years
(B) most people supported the development of nuclear arms
(C) people's perception of the threat of nuclear catastrophe depends on the amount of nuclear-arms testing being done
(D) the people who saved the most money when nuclear-arms testing was limited were the ones who supported such limitations
(E) there are more consumer goods available when nuclear-arms testing increases

On the basis of an observed correlation between arms testing and people's tendency to save money, the argument concludes that there is a causal connection between a perception of threat and the tendency not to save. That connection cannot be made unless C, linking the perception of threat to the amount of testing being done, is assumed to be true. Therefore, C is the best answer.

The conclusion does not depend on there having been an increase in the perceived threat over time or on how many people supported the development of nuclear arms. Hence, neither A nor B is assumed. Furthermore, the argument does not deal with those who supported arms limitations or with the availability of consumer goods. Thus, D and E are not assumed.

6. Which of the following best completes the passage below?

People buy prestige when they buy a premium product. They want to be associated with something special. Mass-marketing techniques and price-reduction strategies should not be used because _____.

(A) affluent purchasers currently represent a shrinking portion of the population of all purchasers
(B) continued sales depend directly on the maintenance of an aura of exclusivity
(C) purchasers of premium products are concerned with the quality as well as with the price of the products
(D) expansion of the market niche to include a broader spectrum of consumers will increase profits
(E) manufacturing a premium brand is not necessarily more costly than manufacturing a standard brand of the same product

The incomplete passage calls for an explanation of why price-reduction and mass-marketing methods should not be used for premium products. Choice B, which states that sales of these products require that they appear special, provides such an explanation. Therefore, B is the best answer.

No other choice offers an appropriate explanation. Choice C suggests that purchasers of premium products find reduced prices attractive, and it has not been established that the methods affect quality or perception of quality. The diminishing proportion of affluent buyers cited in A argues for using price reductions to attract buyers of lesser means, while D argues for, rather than against, using mass marketing. Choice E is inappropriate, since there is no indication that manufacturing costs are relevant.

7. A cost-effective solution to the problem of airport congestion is to provide high-speed ground transportation between major cities lying 200 to 500 miles apart. The successful implementation of this plan would cost far less than expanding existing airports and would also reduce the number of airplanes clogging both airports and airways.

Which of the following, if true, could proponents of the plan above most appropriately cite as a piece of evidence for the soundness of their plan?

(A) An effective high-speed ground-transportation system would require major repairs to many highways and mass-transit improvements.
(B) One-half of all departing flights in the nation's busiest airport head for a destination in a major city 225 miles away.
(C) The majority of travelers departing from rural airports are flying to destinations in cities over 600 miles away.
(D) Many new airports are being built in areas that are presently served by high-speed ground-transportation systems.
(E) A large proportion of air travelers are vacationers who are taking long-distance flights.

The plan proposes that high-speed ground transportation would be a less expensive solution to airport congestion than would airport expansion. Choice B indicates that between the cities to be served by the plan there is substantial air travel to which ground transportation would represent an alternative. Therefore, B is the best answer.

No other choice could be cited appropriately. Choices A and D both provide some evidence against the plan, A by emphasizing the likely costs of providing high-speed ground transportation, and D by indicating that such an alternative is not by itself a solution to airport congestion. Choices C and E say that there are many travelers for whom the proposed system would actually provide no alternative.

Questions 8-9 are based on the following.

If there is an oil-supply disruption resulting in higher international oil prices, domestic oil prices in open-market countries such as the United States will rise as well, whether such countries import all or none of their oil.

8. **If the statement above concerning oil-supply disruptions is true, which of the following policies in an open-market nation is most likely to reduce the long-term economic impact on that nation of sharp and unexpected increases in international oil prices?**

    (A) **Maintaining the quantity of oil imported at constant yearly levels**
    (B) **Increasing the number of oil tankers in its fleet**
    (C) **Suspending diplomatic relations with major oil-producing nations**
    (D) **Decreasing oil consumption through conservation**
    (E) **Decreasing domestic production of oil**

If the statement about oil-supply disruption is true, domestic oil prices in an open-market country will rise when an oil-supply disruption causes increased international oil prices. A reduction in the amount of oil an open-market country consumes could reduce the economic impact of these increases. Choice D gives a way to reduce oil consumption and is thus the best answer.

None of the other choices is appropriate. Choices A and E describe policies that could actually increase the long-term impact of increases in international oil prices. No relationship is established between the economic impact and either the number of oil tankers (choice B) or diplomatic relations (choice C).

9. **Which of the following conclusions is best supported by the statement above?**

    (A) **Domestic producers of oil in open-market countries are excluded from the international oil market when there is a disruption in the international oil supply.**
    (B) **International oil-supply disruptions have little, if any, effect on the price of domestic oil as long as an open-market country has domestic supplies capable of meeting domestic demand.**
    (C) **The oil market in an open-market country is actually part of the international oil market, even if most of that country's domestic oil is usually sold to consumers within its borders.**
    (D) **Open-market countries that export little or none of their oil can maintain stable domestic oil prices even when international oil prices rise sharply.**
    (E) **If international oil prices rise, domestic distributors of oil in open-market countries will begin to import more oil than they export.**

If the oil market in an open-market country were independent, fluctuations in international oil prices would not affect domestic oil prices. However, if the statement about oil-supply disruption is true, it is evidence that domestic oil prices are dependent on the international market and hence that the domestic oil market is a part of the international oil market. Therefore, C is the best answer.

Choices B and D are not supported, since each contradicts the claim that an international oil-supply disruption will lead to rising oil prices in an open-market nation. Neither are A and E supported, since the statement provides information only about the effect of disruption on oil prices, not domestic producers or distributors.

10. **The average normal infant born in the United States weighs between twelve and fourteen pounds at the age of three months. Therefore, if a three-month-old child weighs only ten pounds, its weight gain has been below the United States average.**

     Which of the following indicates a flaw in the reasoning above?

     (A) **Weight is only one measure of normal infant development.**
     (B) **Some three-month-old children weigh as much as seventeen pounds.**
     (C) **It is possible for a normal child to weigh ten pounds at birth.**
     (D) **The phrase "below average" does not necessarily mean insufficient.**
     (E) **Average weight gain is not the same as average weight.**

The evidence on which the conclusion is based concerns only average weight, but the conclusion concerns average weight gain. Because there is not necessarily a connection between an absolute measurement — such as weight — and a rate of increase — such as weight gain — this argument is flawed. The relevant reasoning error is described in E, which is the best answer.

Neither A nor D identifies a reasoning error in the passage, since the passage makes no claim that weight is the only relevant measure of infant development in general (choice A), and no claim about sufficiency (choice D). Both B and C are consistent with the claims in the passage, and neither identifies a flaw in the argument.

11. Red blood cells in which the malarial-fever parasite resides are eliminated from a person's body after 120 days. Because the parasite cannot travel to a new generation of red blood cells, any fever that develops in a person more than 120 days after that person has moved to a malaria-free region is not due to the malarial parasite.

Which of the following, if true, most seriously weakens the conclusion above?

(A) The fever caused by the malarial parasite may resemble the fever caused by flu viruses.

(B) The anopheles mosquito, which is the principal insect carrier of the malarial parasite, has been eradicated in many parts of the world.

(C) Many malarial symptoms other than the fever, which can be suppressed with antimalarial medication, can reappear within 120 days after the medication is discontinued.

(D) In some cases, the parasite that causes malarial fever travels to cells of the spleen, which are less frequently eliminated from a person's body than are red blood cells.

(E) In any region infested with malaria-carrying mosquitoes, there are individuals who appear to be immune to malaria.

The passage concludes that, because the malarial parasite cannot reside in red blood cells for more than 120 days, the malarial parasite cannot cause fever more than 120 days after infection. However, according to D, there is a site in the body where the parasite could reside for more than 120 days after infection. Therefore, D weakens the conclusion and is the best answer.

The resemblance between malarial-fever symptoms and those of other diseases (choice A), the existence of other malarial symptoms (choice C), and the possibility of immunity to malaria (choice E) are irrelevant to the issue of the conditions under which malarial fever can occur. Choice B provides confirmation for the existence of malaria-free regions but does not otherwise bear on the conclusion.

12. Fact 1: Television advertising is becoming less effective: the proportion of brand names promoted on television that viewers of the advertising can recall is slowly decreasing.

Fact 2: Television viewers recall commercials aired first or last in a cluster of consecutive commercials far better than they recall commercials aired somewhere in the middle.

Fact 2 would be most likely to contribute to an explanation of fact 1 if which of the following were also true?

(A) The average television viewer currently recalls fewer than half the brand names promoted in commercials he or she saw.

(B) The total time allotted to the average cluster of consecutive television commercials is decreasing.

(C) The average number of hours per day that people spend watching television is decreasing.

(D) The average number of clusters of consecutive commercials per hour of television is increasing.

(E) The average number of television commercials in a cluster of consecutive commercials is increasing.

Because E indicates that the number of commercials in a cluster is increasing, E entails that proportionally more commercials are aired in intermediate positions. Hence, E helps fact 2 explain fact 1 by showing that increasingly more commercials are aired in positions in which viewers find them difficult to recall. E is the best answer.

Choice A testifies to the ineffectiveness of television advertising but does not help fact 2 explain fact 1. Choice B indicates that fact 2 contradicts rather than explains fact 1, since it suggests that the number of commercials per cluster is decreasing. Choices C and D help to explain fact 1 — C by describing a change in viewing habits and D by describing a change in programming — but neither relates fact 2 to fact 1.

13. The number of people diagnosed as having a certain intestinal disease has dropped significantly in a rural county this year, as compared to last year. Health officials attribute this decrease entirely to improved sanitary conditions at water-treatment plants, which made for cleaner water this year and thus reduced the incidence of the disease.

Which of the following, if true, would most seriously weaken the health officials' explanation for the lower incidence of the disease?

(A) Many new water-treatment plants have been built in the last five years in the rural county.
(B) Bottled spring water has not been consumed in significantly different quantities by people diagnosed as having the intestinal disease, as compared to people who did not contract the disease.
(C) Because of a new diagnostic technique, many people who until this year would have been diagnosed as having the intestinal disease are now correctly diagnosed as suffering from intestinal ulcers.
(D) Because of medical advances this year, far fewer people who contract the intestinal disease will develop severe cases of the disease.
(E) The water in the rural county was brought up to the sanitary standards of the water in neighboring counties ten years ago.

The health officials' explanation assumes that the decrease in the number of people diagnosed with the disease accurately reflects a diminution in cases of the disease. By pointing out that this assumption is false, C undermines the officials' explanation and thus is the best answer.

Since A supports the view that sanitary conditions have been improving, it tends to support the officials' explanation. So does B, which eliminates a factor that might have differentiated between those contracting and those not contracting the disease and thus rules out an alternative explanation. The reduction of the severity of the diagnosed cases (choice D) does not bear on the officials' explanation. Since the standards in neighboring counties might themselves have been inadequate, E does not weaken the officials' explanation.

14. The price the government pays for standard weapons purchased from military contractors is determined by a pricing method called "historical costing." Historical costing allows contractors to protect their profits by adding a percentage increase, based on the current rate of inflation, to the previous year's contractual price.

Which of the following statements, if true, is the best basis for a criticism of historical costing as an economically sound pricing method for military contracts?

(A) The government might continue to pay for past inefficient use of funds.
(B) The rate of inflation has varied considerably over the past twenty years.
(C) The contractual price will be greatly affected by the cost of materials used for the products.
(D) Many taxpayers question the amount of money the government spends on military contracts.
(E) The pricing method based on historical costing might not encourage the development of innovative weapons.

If the original contractual price for the weapons purchased incorporated an inefficient use of funds, then, since historical costing merely adds to the original price, it preserves these inefficiencies. An economically sound pricing method should at least allow the possibility of reductions in price as such inefficiencies are removed. Hence, A is the best answer.

Because historical costing responds to inflation, both B and C are consistent with the economic soundness of historical costing — B because it refers to the rate of inflation and C because it refers to costs that are reflected in inflation. Choice D offers no grounds for questioning the economic soundness of historical costing in particular. Historical costing applies to standard weapons only, not to the innovative weapons that are mentioned in E.

15. Some who favor putting governmental enterprises into private hands suggest that conservation objectives would in general be better served if private environmental groups were put in charge of operating and financing the national park system, which is now run by the government.

Which of the following, assuming that it is a realistic possibility, argues most strongly against the suggestion above?

(A) Those seeking to abolish all restrictions on exploiting the natural resources of the parks might join the private environmental groups as members and eventually take over their leadership.

(B) Private environmental groups might not always agree on the best ways to achieve conservation objectives.

(C) If they wished to extend the park system, the private environmental groups might have to seek contributions from major donors and the general public.

(D) There might be competition among private environmental groups for control of certain park areas.

(E) Some endangered species, such as the California condor, might die out despite the best efforts of the private environmental groups, even if those groups are not hampered by insufficient resources.

If those seeking to abolish restrictions on exploiting the natural resources of the parks assumed the leadership of a group that was placed in charge of operating the park system, conservation objectives would not be better served. Choice A suggests that such a scenario might result from the proposed policy and is thus the best answer.

Choices C, D, and E list problems that might confront private environmental groups in charge of parks, but they do not give reason to believe that such groups would not be better able to pursue conservation objectives than is the current administration of the park system. Choice B indicates the potential for disagreement among various private environmental groups, but it does not suggest that disagreements could not be resolved.

16. A recent spate of launching and operating mishaps with television satellites led to a corresponding surge in claims against companies underwriting satellite insurance. As a result, insurance premiums shot up, making satellites more expensive to launch and operate. This, in turn, had added to the pressure to squeeze more performance out of currently operating satellites.

Which of the following, if true, taken together with the information above, best supports the conclusion that the cost of television satellites will continue to increase?

(A) Since the risk to insurers of satellites is spread over relatively few units, insurance premiums are necessarily very high.

(B) When satellites reach orbit and then fail, the causes of failure are generally impossible to pinpoint with confidence.

(C) The greater the performance demands placed on satellites, the more frequently those satellites break down.

(D) Most satellites are produced in such small numbers that no economies of scale can be realized.

(E) Since many satellites are built by unwieldy international consortia, inefficiencies are inevitable.

According to the passage, satellite mishaps caused a surge in insurance claims, which, in turn, caused increased insurance premiums. Higher premiums made the satellites more costly, resulting in increased performance demands. If C is true, the greater demands on performance will lead to further increases in costs by increasing the number of mishaps, and thus pushing insurance premiums still higher. Thus, C is the best answer.

Choices A, D, and E all describe factors relevant to costs, but there is no reason to think that the situation described in the passage will cause the costs resulting from these factors to increase. Similarly, the impossibility of pinpointing the causes of failure, mentioned in B, is consistent with the cost of satellites remaining stable.

17. Tocqueville, a nineteenth-century writer known for his study of democracy in the United States, believed that a government that centralizes power in one individual or institution is dangerous to its citizens. Biographers claim that Tocqueville disliked centralized government because he blamed Napoleon's rule for the poverty of his childhood in Normandy.

Which of the following, if true, would cast the most serious doubt on the biographers' claim?

(A) Although Napoleon was popularly blamed at the time for the terrible living conditions in Normandy, historians now know that bad harvests were really to blame for the poor economic conditions.

(B) Napoleon was notorious for refusing to share power with any of his political associates.

(C) Tocqueville said he knew that if his father had not suffered ill health, his family would have had a steady income and a comfortable standard of living.

(D) Although Tocqueville asserted that United States political life was democratic, the United States of the nineteenth century allowed political power to be concentrated in a few institutions.

(E) Tocqueville once wrote in a letter that, although his childhood was terribly impoverished, it was not different from the experience of his friends and neighbors in Normandy.

If Tocqueville held the view that C reports, then he blamed the poverty of his childhood on something other than Napoleon's rule, contrary to the biographers' claim. So C casts serious doubt on the biographers' claim and is the best answer.

If, as A states, Napoleon was popularly blamed for the poverty in Normandy, the claim is more plausible. Choice B merely confirms that Napoleon's government was highly centralized, as is implicit in the biographers' claim. The accuracy of Tocqueville's assertion about United States political life does not bear directly on his reason for disliking centralized government, so D is incorrect. The biographers' claim could be true whether or not, as E states, Tocqueville and his friends and neighbors in Normandy experienced similar misfortunes.

18. Radio interferometry is a technique for studying details of celestial objects that combines signals intercepted by widely spaced radio telescopes. This technique requires ultraprecise timing, exact knowledge of the locations of the telescopes, and sophisticated computer programs. The successful interferometric linking of an Earth-based radio telescope with a radio telescope on an orbiting satellite was therefore a significant technological accomplishment.

Which of the following can be correctly inferred from the statements above?

(A) Special care was taken in the launching of the satellite so that the calculations of its orbit would be facilitated.

(B) The signals received on the satellite are stronger than those received by a terrestrial telescope.

(C) The resolution of detail achieved by the satellite-Earth interferometer system is inferior to that achieved by exclusively terrestrial systems.

(D) The computer programs required for making use of the signals received by the satellite required a long time for development.

(E) The location of an orbiting satellite relative to locations on Earth can be well enough known for interferometric purposes.

Because the technique of radio interferometry requires exact knowledge of the locations of the telescopes, it follows that the successful interferometric linking of an Earth-based radio telescope with a radio telescope on a satellite would require exact knowledge of the locations of the telescopes relative to each other. Thus E, which expresses this inference, is the best answer.

Choices A and D cannot be inferred because the passage provides no concrete information regarding the implementation of the successful interferometric linking. Nor does the passage provide any information about differences in operational performance between a linking that is wholly terrestrial and a linking of an Earth-based telescope with a satellite-based telescope. Thus, neither B nor C can be inferred.

19. Recent estimates predict that between 1982 and 1995 the greatest increase in the number of people employed will be in the category of low-paying service occupations. This category, however, will not increase its share of total employment, whereas the category of high-paying service occupations will increase its share.

If the estimates above are accurate, which of the following conclusions can be drawn?

(A) In 1982 more people were working in low-paying service occupations than were working in high-paying service occupations.

(B) In 1995 more people will be working in high-paying service occupations than will be working in low-paying service occupations.

(C) Nonservice occupations will account for the same share of total employment in 1995 as in 1982.

(D) Many of the people who were working in low-paying service occupations in 1982 will be working in high-paying service occupations by 1995.

(E) The rate of growth for low-paying service occupations will be greater than the overall rate of employment growth between 1982 and 1995.

The passage states that the percentage of high-paying service occupations will increase, but the percentage of low-paying occupations will not. Thus if in 1982, contrary to A, at least as many people were working in high-paying service occupations as in low-paying ones, the projected increase in number of people employed would be greater for high-paying service occupations. Since this contradicts the estimates, A is the best answer.

By similar reasoning, B must be false if the estimates are true. The passage does not address nonservice occupations or the overall rate of employment growth, so neither C nor E can be concluded. Similarly for D: the statements provide no information about people changing occupations.

20. For a local government to outlaw all strikes by its workers is a costly mistake, because all its labor disputes must then be settled by binding arbitration, without any negotiated public-sector labor settlements guiding the arbitrators. Strikes should be outlawed only for categories of public-sector workers for whose services no acceptable substitute exists.

The statements above best support which of the following conclusions?

(A) Where public-service workers are permitted to strike, contract negotiations with those workers are typically settled without a strike.

(B) Where strikes by all categories of public-sector workers are outlawed, no acceptable substitutes for the services provided by any of those workers are available.

(C) Binding arbitration tends to be more advantageous for public-service workers where it is the only available means of settling labor disputes with such workers.

(D) Most categories of public-sector workers have no counterparts in the private sector.

(E) A strike by workers in a local government is unlikely to be settled without help from an arbitrator.

The passage recommends a partial ban as an alternative to outlawing strikes, which it says is too costly. Thus the partial strike ban must be less costly, and, since the reason given for the costliness of outlawing all strikes is the necessity of settling *all* labor disputes by binding arbitration, one can infer that binding arbitration is more costly for local governments when it is the only means of settling labor disputes. Therefore, since what costs employers in labor settlements is advantageous for employees, C is supported by the passage and is the best answer.

None of the other choices can be inferred because, given only the statements in the passage, they could as easily be false as true.

Explanatory Material: Data Sufficiency, Section 2

1. If x and y are positive, what is the value of x ?

(1) $x = 3.927y$
(2) $y = 2.279$

Statement (1) indicates that the value of x is 3.927 times the value of y, and statement (2) gives the value of y. Therefore, (1) and (2) together are sufficient to determine the value of x, but neither statement alone is sufficient, and so the best answer is C.

2. **John and David each received a salary increase. Which one received the greater dollar increase?**

   (1) John's salary increased 8 percent.
   (2) David's salary increased 5 percent.

In (1) there is no information about David's salary and in (2) there is no information about John's salary; thus, neither statement alone is sufficient, and the answer must be C or E. Since (1) and (2) together give only the percentage increases in salary, it cannot be determined which person received the greater dollar increase. For example, if John's salary was the larger salary, then his salary increase would evidently be the greater amount; however, if David's salary was more than $\frac{8}{5}$ times John's salary, then David's salary increase would be the greater amount. Therefore, (1) and (2) together are not sufficient, and the best answer is E.

3. **Carlotta can drive from her home to her office by one of two possible routes. If she must also return by one of these routes, what is the distance of the shorter route?**

   (1) When she drives from her home to her office by the shorter route and returns by the longer route, she drives a total of 42 kilometers.
   (2) When she drives both ways, from her home to her office and back, by the longer route, she drives a total of 46 kilometers.

Statement (1) alone is not sufficient because only the sum of the distances of the two routes is given and there are infinitely many pairs of numbers with a given sum. Thus, the answer must be B, C, or E. From (2) the distance of the longer route can be found, but there is no information about the distance of the shorter route. Statement (2) alone is therefore not sufficient, so the answer must be C or E. From (1) and (2) together, the distance of the shorter route can be determined $(42 - \frac{46}{2})$, and the best answer is C.

4. **If r and s are positive integers, r is what percent of s ?**

   (1) $r = \frac{3}{4}s$
   (2) $r \div s = \frac{75}{100}$

To determine r as a percent of s it suffices to know the ratio of r to s, since any ratio can be converted to an equivalent ratio with denominator 100. Since (1) and (2) both give the ratio of r to s, each alone is sufficient, and the best answer is D.

5. **A shirt and a pair of gloves cost a total of $41.70. How much does the pair of gloves cost?**

   (1) The shirt costs twice as much as the gloves.
   (2) The shirt costs $27.80.

From (1) it can be determined that the total cost of the shirt and gloves is three times the cost of the gloves alone; in other words, the gloves cost one third as much as the shirt and gloves together. Thus, (1) alone is sufficient, and the answer must be A or D. Since the cost of the gloves is the difference between the total cost, $41.70, and the cost of the shirt, statement (2) alone is also sufficient. The best answer is therefore D.

6. **What is the number of 360-degree rotations that a bicycle wheel made while rolling 100 meters in a straight line without slipping?**

   (1) The diameter of the bicycle wheel, including the tire, was 0.5 meter.
   (2) The wheel made twenty 360-degree rotations per minute.

For each 360-degree rotation, the wheel has traveled a distance equal to its circumference. Thus, the number of 360-degree rotations is equal to the number of times the circumference of the wheel can be laid out along the straight-line path that is 100 meters long; so it suffices to know the size of the wheel. From (1) the circumference of the wheel can be determined. Thus, (1) alone is sufficient, and the answer must be A or D. Statement (2) gives the speed at which the wheel is traveling; however, the size of the wheel cannot be determined, and (2) alone is not sufficient. Therefore, the best answer is A.

7. **What is the value of the sum of a list of n odd integers?**

   (1) $n = 8$
   (2) The square of the number of integers on the list is 64.

Statements (1) and (2) give only the number of integers in the list. Since additional information is needed to determine the sum of the integers (for example, their average), the best answer is E.

8. **If a certain animated cartoon consists of a total of 17,280 frames on film, how many minutes will it take to run the cartoon?**

   (1) The cartoon runs without interruption at the rate of 24 frames per second.
   (2) It takes 6 times as long to run the cartoon as it takes to rewind the film, and it takes a total of 14 minutes to do both.

From (1) it can be determined that it takes $\frac{17,280}{24 \times 60}$ minutes to run the cartoon. Thus, (1) alone is sufficient, and the answer must be A or D. From (2) it can be determined that the time it takes to run the cartoon is $\frac{6}{7}$ of the 14 minutes it takes both to run the cartoon and to rewind the film, and so (2) alone is also sufficient. The best answer is therefore D.

9. What was the average number of miles per gallon of gasoline for a car during a certain trip?

(1) The total cost of the gasoline used by the car for the 180-mile trip was $12.00.

(2) The cost of the gasoline used by the car for the trip was $1.20 per gallon.

Statement (1) gives the number of miles the car traveled; however, the number of gallons of gasoline used cannot be determined, since only the total cost of the gasoline used is given. Thus, (1) alone is not sufficient, and the answer must be B, C, or E. Statement (2) alone is obviously not sufficient, but it gives the additional information needed in (1) to determine the number of gallons of gasoline used. Once the number of miles traveled and the number of gallons used are known, the average number of miles per gallon can be determined. Therefore, (1) and (2) together are sufficient, and the best answer is C.

10. If x and y are positive, is $\frac{x}{y}$ greater than 1 ?

(1) $xy > 1$

(2) $x - y > 0$

Since $y > 0$, it follows that $\frac{x}{y} > 1$ if and only if $x > y$. Thus, to answer the question it suffices to determine whether $x > y$. In (1) there are innumerable pairs of different numbers x and y whose product xy is greater than 1, and the larger number in each such pair can be either x or y. Thus, (1) alone is not sufficient, and the answer must be B, C, or E. In (2), $x - y > 0$ is equivalent to $x > y$, so (2) alone is sufficient. The best answer is B.

11. In $\triangle PQR$, if $PQ = x$, $QR = x + 2$, and $PR = y$, which of the three angles of $\triangle PQR$ has the greatest degree measure?

(1) $y = x + 3$

(2) $x = 2$

In any triangle, the largest angle is opposite the longest side. To determine the longest side it suffices to determine whether $y > x + 2$. Since $x + 3 > x + 2$, it follows from (1) that $y > x + 2$. Statement (1) alone is therefore sufficient, and the answer must be A or D. From (2) it follows that $PQ = 2$ and $QR = 4$. Thus, y can be any value between 2 and 6; it follows that $y > x$, but it cannot be concluded that $y > x + 2$. Statement (2) alone is therefore not sufficient, so the best answer is A.

12. Is the prime number p equal to 37 ?

(1) $p = n^2 + 1$, where n is an integer.

(2) p^2 is greater than 200.

In (1) the expression $n^2 + 1$ can represent a prime number less than 37, equal to 37, or greater than 37, depending on the value of n. For example, if $n = 4$, then $4^2 + 1 = 17$; if $n = 6$, then $6^2 + 1 = 37$; if $n = 10$, then $10^2 + 1 = 101$; and 17, 37, and

101 are all prime numbers. Thus, (1) alone is not sufficient, and the answer must be B, C, or E. Since $14^2 = 196$ and $15^2 = 225$, it follows from (2) that $p > 14$, so that p might or might not equal 37. Thus, (2) alone is not sufficient, and the answer must be C or E. The values of p for $n = 4$ and for $n = 6$ given above show that (1) and (2) together are not sufficient, and the best answer is E.

13. The only contents of a parcel are 25 photographs and 30 negatives. What is the total weight, in ounces, of the parcel's contents?

(1) The weight of each photograph is 3 times the weight of each negative.

(2) The total weight of 1 of the photographs and 2 of the negatives is $\frac{1}{3}$ ounce.

Let p and n denote the weight, in ounces, of a photograph and a negative, respectively. Then the total weight of the parcel's contents can be written as $25p + 30n$. The information in (1) can be written as $p = 3n$. By substituting $3n$ for p in the expression $25p + 30n$, it can be seen that the resulting expression depends on n. Thus, (1) alone is not sufficient, and the answer must be B, C, or E. The information in (2) can be written as $p + 2n = \frac{1}{3}$ and is, similarly, not sufficient. Thus, the answer must be C or E. The two linear equations summarizing the information in (1) and (2) can be solved simultaneously for p and n, so that statements (1) and (2) together are sufficient. The best answer is therefore C.

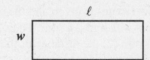

14. If ℓ and w represent the length and width, respectively, of the rectangle above, what is the perimeter?

(1) $2\ell + w = 40$

(2) $\ell + w = 25$

The formula for the perimeter of a rectangle is $P = 2\ell + 2w = 2(\ell + w)$, where ℓ and w represent the length and width, respectively. The perimeter can therefore be determined once $\ell + w$ is known. The value of $\ell + w$ cannot be determined from (1), since $2\ell + w = 40$ is equivalent to $\ell + w = 40 - \ell$, which depends on ℓ. Thus, (1) alone is not sufficient, and the answer must be B, C, or E. However, (2) alone is sufficient because $\ell + w$ is known, and the best answer is B.

15. What is the ratio of x to y ?

(1) x is 4 more than twice y.

(2) The ratio of $0.5x$ to $2y$ is 3 to 5.

-432-

Statement (1) can be expressed as $x = 2y + 4$, which is not sufficient since $\frac{x}{y} = 2 + \frac{4}{y}$, showing that $\frac{x}{y}$ depends on y.

Thus, the answer must be B, C, or E. Statement (2) can be expressed as $\frac{0.5x}{2y} = \frac{3}{5}$; so $\frac{x}{y} = \frac{3}{5} \div \frac{0.5}{2}$. Therefore, (2) alone is sufficient, and the best answer is B.

16. If x, y, and z are three integers, are they consecutive integers?

(1) $z - x = 2$

(2) $x < y < z$

From (1) it follows that there is exactly one integer between x and z, but there is no information about y. Thus, (1) alone is not sufficient, and the answer must be B, C, or E. Statement (2) alone is not sufficient because there could be other integers between x and z besides y, so the answer must be C or E. From (1) and (2) together, it follows that y is the unique integer between x and z; that is, $y = x + 1$ and $z = y + 1$, and the integers are consecutive. The best answer is therefore C.

17. What is the value of x ?

(1) $-(x + y) = x - y$

(2) $x + y = 2$

In (1) the equation $-(x + y) = x - y$ can be written as $-x - y = x - y$, which reduces to $-x = x$. The expression $-x$ denotes the additive inverse of x. Because 0 is the only number that is equal to its additive inverse, it follows that $x = 0$, and (1) alone is sufficient. Alternatively, $-x = x$ can be written as $2x = 0$ so that $x = 0$. Thus, the answer must be A or D. In (2) the value of x depends on the value of y, so (2) alone is not sufficient. The best answer is therefore A.

18. A sum of $200,000 from a certain estate was divided among a spouse and three children. How much of the estate did the youngest child receive?

(1) The spouse received $\frac{1}{2}$ of the sum from the estate, and the oldest child received $\frac{1}{4}$ of the remainder.

(2) Each of the two younger children received $12,500 more than the oldest child and $62,500 less than the spouse.

From (1) the combined amount of the estate that the two younger children received can be determined, but not the individual amount received by either of them. Thus, (1) alone is not sufficient, and the answer must be B, C, or E. In (2) the amount of the estate received by the oldest child and by the spouse can each be expressed in terms of the amount, x, received by each of the two younger children. An equation expressing the sum of $200,000 in terms of x can then be set up and solved for x. It follows that (2) alone is sufficient, so the best answer is B.

19. If the Lincoln Library's total expenditure for books, periodicals, and newspapers last year was $35,000, how much of the expenditure was for books?

(1) The expenditure for newspapers was 40 percent greater than the expenditure for periodicals.

(2) The total of the expenditure for periodicals and newspapers was 25 percent less than the expenditure for books.

Let b, p, and n denote the expenditure, in dollars, for books, periodicals, and newspapers, respectively. Then $b + p + n = 35{,}000$. In (1) it follows that $n = 1.4p$, so $b + 2.4p = 35{,}000$. Since the value of b cannot be determined, (1) alone is not sufficient, and the answer must be B, C, or E. In (2) it follows that $p + n = 0.75b$. Then $0.75b$ can be substituted for $p + n$ in the equation $b + p + n = 35{,}000$, resulting in an equation involving b alone. Since the value of b can be determined by solving this equation, (2) alone is sufficient, and the best answer is B.

20. The symbol $\triangledown$ represents one of the following operations: addition, subtraction, multiplication, or division. What is the value of $3 \triangledown 2$?

(1) $0 \triangledown 1 = 1$

(2) $1 \triangledown 0 = 1$

Since $0 + 1 = 1$, $0 - 1 = -1$, $0 \times 1 = 0$, and $0 : 1 = 0$, it follows from (1) that $\triangledown$ represents addition, so the value of $3 \triangledown 2$ can be determined. Thus, (1) alone is sufficient, and the answer must be A or D. Since $1 + 0 = 1$, $1 - 0 = 1$, $1 \times 0 = 0$, and $1 \div 0$ is undefined, it follows from (2) that $\triangledown$ could represent either addition or subtraction, so $3 \triangledown 2$ could equal 5 or 1. Thus, (2) alone is not sufficient, and the best answer is A.

21. Are the numbers $\frac{k}{4}$, $\frac{z}{3}$, and $\frac{r}{2}$ in increasing order?

(1) $3 < z < 4$

(2) $r < z < k$

One way to approach this problem is to construct examples and counterexamples by trial and error, although such an approach can be tedious. An alternative approach is to observe that $\frac{k}{4} < \frac{z}{3} < \frac{r}{2}$ is equivalent to $\frac{k}{4} < \frac{z}{3}$ and $\frac{z}{3} < \frac{r}{2}$, or $k < \frac{4}{3}z$ and $r > \frac{2}{3}z$. Since not even one of these latter two inequalities must hold from the information given in (1) and (2), it follows that (1) and (2) together are not sufficient, and the best answer is E.

-433-

22. In a certain group of people, the average (arithmetic mean) weight of the males is 180 pounds and of the females, 120 pounds. What is the average weight of the people in the group?

   (1) The group contains twice as many females as males.

   (2) The group contains 10 more females than males.

If m, f, and t denote the number of males, the number of females, and the total number of people in the group, respectively, then the average weight of the people in the group can be expressed by $\dfrac{180m + 120f}{t} = 180\left(\dfrac{m}{t}\right) + 120\left(\dfrac{f}{t}\right)$. Thus, the average can be determined provided that $\dfrac{f}{t}$, the proportion of females in the group, can be determined, since $m = t - f$ or $\dfrac{m}{t} = 1 - \dfrac{f}{t}$. From (1) it can be concluded that $\dfrac{f}{t} = \dfrac{2}{3}$, so (1) alone is sufficient. The answer must therefore be A or D.

From (2) the value of $\dfrac{f}{t}$ cannot be determined. For example, if $m = 5$, then $\dfrac{f}{t} = \dfrac{3}{4}$; whereas if $m = 10$, then $\dfrac{f}{t} = \dfrac{2}{3}$. Thus, (2) alone is not sufficient, and the best answer is A.

23. If $n = p + r$, where n, p, and r are positive integers and n is odd, does p equal 2 ?

   (1) p and r are prime numbers.

   (2) r 2

Since n is odd, it follows that either p is odd and r is even or p is even and r is odd. From (1) together with the fact that 2 is the only even prime number, it can be concluded that $p = 2$ or $r = 2$; but additional information is needed to decide which one of these two alternatives holds. Thus, (1) alone is not sufficient, and the answer must be B, C, or E. Since (2) supplies this additional information, but alone is not sufficient, the best answer is C.

24. If $y = 2^{x+1}$, what is the value of $y - x$?

   (1) $2^{2x+2} = 64$

   (2) $y = 2^{2x-1}$

The equation in (1) can be written as $2^{2x+2} = 2^6$ because $64 = 2^6$. It follows that $2x + 2 = 6$, from which the value of x can be determined. Since the value of y depends only on x, the value of y can also be determined. Therefore, from (1) alone the value of $y - x$ can be determined, so the answer must be A or D. From (2) together with the fact that $y = 2^{x+1}$, it follows that $2^{2x-1} = 2^{x+1}$, or $2x - 1 = x + 1$; the value of x, and hence the value of y, can be determined, so (2) alone is also sufficient. The best answer is D.

25. If x 1, is y equal to $x + 1$?

   (1) $\dfrac{y - 2}{x - 1} = 1$

   (2) $y^2 = (x + 1)^2$

Since $x - 1$ 0, both sides of the equation in (1) can be multiplied by $x - 1$, yielding the equation $y - 2 = x - 1$, from which it follows that $y = x + 1$. Thus, (1) alone is sufficient, and the answer must be A or D. In (2) it can only be concluded that either $y = x + 1$ or $y = -(x + 1)$, and additional information is needed to decide which of these two alternatives holds. Thus, (2) alone is not sufficient, and the best answer is A.

Explanatory Material: Problem Solving I, Section 3

1. What is 45 percent of $\dfrac{7}{12}$ of 240 ?

   (A) 63
   (B) 90
   (C) 108
   (D) 140
   (E) 311

Since 45 percent is $\dfrac{45}{100} = \dfrac{9}{20}$, 45 percent of $\dfrac{7}{12}$ of 240 is $\left(\dfrac{9}{20}\right)\left(\dfrac{7}{12}\right)(240) = 63$. The best answer is A.

2. NOT SCORED

3. If x books cost \$5 each and y books cost \$8 each, then the average (arithmetic mean) cost, in dollars per book, is equal to

(A) $\dfrac{5x + 8y}{x + y}$

(B) $\dfrac{5x + 8y}{xy}$

(C) $\dfrac{5x + 8y}{13}$

(D) $\dfrac{40xy}{x + y}$

(E) $\dfrac{40xy}{13}$

The total number of books is $x + y$, and their total cost is $5x + 8y$ dollars. Therefore, the average cost per book is $\dfrac{5x + 8y}{x + y}$ dollars. The best answer is A.

4. If $\dfrac{1}{2}$ of the money in a certain trust fund was invested in stocks, $\dfrac{1}{4}$ in bonds, $\dfrac{1}{5}$ in a mutual fund, and the remaining \$10,000 in a government certificate, what was the total amount of the trust fund?

(A) \$100,000
(B) \$150,000
(C) \$200,000
(D) \$500,000
(E) \$2,000,000

Since $\dfrac{1}{2} + \dfrac{1}{4} + \dfrac{1}{5} = \dfrac{19}{20}$, then $\dfrac{19}{20}$ of the trust fund was invested in stocks, bonds, and a mutual fund. Thus, if F is the dollar amount of the trust fund, the remaining $\dfrac{1}{20}$ of F is \$10,000. That is, $\dfrac{1}{20}F = \$10,000$, or $F = \$200,000$. The best answer is therefore C.

5. Marion rented a car for \$18.00 plus \$0.10 per mile driven. Craig rented a car for \$25.00 plus \$0.05 per mile driven. If each drove d miles and each was charged exactly the same amount for the rental, then d equals

(A) 100
(B) 120
(C) 135
(D) 140
(E) 150

Marion's total rental charge was $18.00 + 0.10d$ dollars, and Craig's total rental charge was $25.00 + 0.05d$ dollars. Since these amounts are the same, $18.00 + 0.10d = 25.00 + 0.05d$, which implies $0.05d = 7.00$, or $d = \dfrac{7.00}{0.05} = 140$ miles. Thus, the best answer is D.

6. Machine A produces bolts at a uniform rate of 120 every 40 seconds, and machine B produces bolts at a uniform rate of 100 every 20 seconds. If the two machines run simultaneously, how many seconds will it take for them to produce a total of 200 bolts?

(A) 22
(B) 25
(C) 28
(D) 32
(E) 56

Machine A produces $\dfrac{120}{40} = 3$ bolts per second and machine B produces $\dfrac{100}{20} = 5$ bolts per second. Running simultaneously, they produce 8 bolts per second. At this rate, they will produce 200 bolts in $\dfrac{200}{8} = 25$ seconds. The best answer is therefore B.

7. $\dfrac{3.003}{2.002} =$

(A) 1.05
(B) 1.50015
(C) 1.501
(D) 1.5015
(E) 1.5

$\dfrac{3.003}{2.002} = \dfrac{3(1.001)}{2(1.001)} = \dfrac{3}{2} = 1.5$

The best answer is E.

AVERAGE COSTS OF OPERATING SUBCOMPACT, COMPACT,
AND MIDSIZE CARS IN THE UNITED STATES, 1982–1986

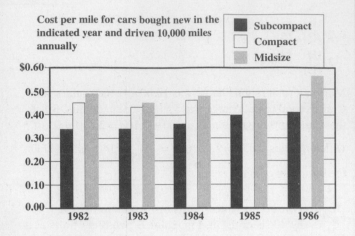

8. In 1982 the approximate average cost of operating a
   subcompact car for 10,000 miles was

   (A) $360
   (B) $3,400
   (C) $4,100
   (D) $4,500
   (E) $4,900

According to the bar graph, the average cost per mile of
operating a subcompact car in 1982 was about $0.34. Thus,
the cost of operating the car for 10,000 miles was approximately $0.34(10,000) = $3,400. The best answer is B.

9. In 1984 the average cost of operating a subcompact
   car was approximately what percent less than the
   average cost of operating a midsized car?

   (A)   12%
   (B)   20%
   (C)   25%
   (D)   33%
   (E)   48%

According to the bars shown for 1984, the average operating
cost per mile for a subcompact car was approximately $0.36,
or $0.12 less than the $0.48 per mile for a midsized car. Thus,
in 1984 the operating cost for a subcompact car was approximately $\frac{0.12}{0.48} = 25\%$ less than the operating cost for a
midsized car. The best answer is C.

10. For each of the years shown, the average cost per mile
    of operating a compact car minus the average cost per
    mile of operating a subcompact car was between

    (A) $0.12 and $0.18
    (B) $0.10 and $0.15
    (C) $0.09 and $0.13
    (D) $0.06 and $0.12
    (E) $0.05 and $0.08

The differences in the average operating cost per mile between
a subcompact car and a compact car may be estimated from
the bar graph. For the consecutive years 1982-1986, the
differences were approximately $0.11, $0.09, $0.10, $0.07,
and $0.07, respectively. Only choice D gives a range that
includes all of these amounts. Thus, the best answer is D.
   Alternatively, inspection of the bar graph reveals that the
largest difference was about $0.11 (in 1982) and the smallest
difference was about $0.07 (in 1985 or 1986). Only choice D
gives a range that includes these extreme values, and thus the
differences for all five years.

11. What is the decimal equivalent of $\left(\frac{1}{5}\right)^5$?

    (A)   0.00032
    (B)   0.0016
    (C)   0.00625
    (D)   0.008
    (E)   0.03125

$$\left(\frac{1}{5}\right)^5 = (0.2)^5 = (0.2)(0.2)(0.2)(0.2)(0.2) = 0.00032$$
The best answer is A.

12. Two hundred gallons of fuel oil are purchased at $0.91
    per gallon and are consumed at a rate of $0.70 worth
    of fuel per hour. At this rate, how many hours are
    required to consume the 200 gallons of fuel oil?

    (A)   140
    (B)   220
    (C)   260
    (D)   322
    (E)   330

The total worth of the 200 gallons of fuel oil is
$0.91(200) = $182.00. The time required to consume the
$182.00 worth of fuel at a rate of $0.70 worth of fuel per hour
is $\frac{\$182.00}{\$0.70} = 260$ hours. Therefore, the best answer is C.

13. If $\dfrac{4-x}{2+x} = x$, what is the value of $x^2 + 3x - 4$?

   (A) −4
   (B) −1
   (C) 0
   (D) 1
   (E) 2

Multiplying both sides of $\dfrac{4-x}{2+x} = x$ by $2 + x$ yields
$4 - x = x(2 + x) = 2x + x^2$, or $x^2 + 3x - 4 = 0$. Thus, the value of
$x^2 + 3x - 4$ is 0, and the best answer is C.

14. If $b < 2$ and $2x - 3b = 0$, which of the following must be true?

   (A) $x > -3$
   (B) $x < 2$
   (C) $x = 3$
   (D) $x < 3$
   (E) $x > 3$

It follows from $2x - 3b = 0$ that $b = \dfrac{2}{3}x$. So $b < 2$ implies
$\dfrac{2}{3}x < 2$, or $x < 2\left(\dfrac{3}{2}\right)$, which means $x < 3$ (choice D). Since
none of the other choices must be true (although $x > -3$ and
$x < 2$ could be true), the best answer is D.

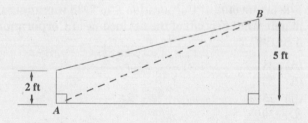

15. The trapezoid shown in the figure above represents a cross section of the rudder of a ship. If the distance from A to B is 13 feet, what is the area of the cross section of the rudder in square feet?

   (A) 39
   (B) 40
   (C) 42
   (D) 45
   (E) 46.5

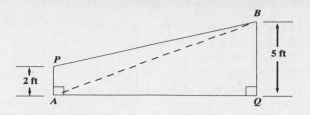

From the figure above, the area of the trapezoidal cross section
is $\dfrac{1}{2}(AP + BQ)(AQ) = \dfrac{1}{2}(2 + 5)(AQ) = \dfrac{7}{2}(AQ)$. Since
$AB = 13$ feet, using the Pythagorean theorem,
$AQ = \sqrt{13^2 - 5^2} = \sqrt{144} = 12$ feet. Thus, the area is
$\dfrac{7}{2}(12) = 42$ square feet, and the best answer is C.

   Alternatively, the areas of the two triangles may be added
together. If AP is taken as the base of $\triangle APB$ and BQ is
taken as the base of $\triangle BQA$, then the height of both
triangles is AQ. Thus, the area of the trapezoid is
$\dfrac{1}{2}(AP)(AQ) + \dfrac{1}{2}(BQ)(AQ) = \dfrac{1}{2}(2)(12) + \dfrac{1}{2}(5)(12) = 42$
square feet.

16. $\dfrac{(-1.5)(1.2) - (4.5)(0.4)}{30} =$

   (A) −1.2
   (B) −0.12
   (C) 0
   (D) 0.12
   (E) 1.2

One way to reduce the expression is
$$\dfrac{(-1.5)(1.2) - (4.5)(0.4)}{30} = \dfrac{-1.80 - 1.80}{30} = \dfrac{-3.60}{30} = -0.12.$$

Another way is
$$\dfrac{(-1.5)(1.2) - (4.5)(0.4)}{30} = -\dfrac{15(12) + 45(4)}{3,000} = -\dfrac{12 + 3(4)}{200}$$
$$= -\dfrac{24}{200} = -\dfrac{12}{100} = -0.12.$$

The best answer is B.

17. If n is a positive integer, then $n(n + 1)(n + 2)$ is

   (A) even only when n is even
   (B) even only when n is odd
   (C) odd whenever n is odd
   (D) divisible by 3 only when n is odd
   (E) divisible by 4 whenever n is even

If n is a positive integer, then either n is even or n is odd (and thus $n + 1$ is even). In either case, the product $n(n + 1)(n + 2)$ is even. Thus, each of choices A, B, and C is false. Since $n(n + 1)(n + 2)$ is divisible by 3 when n is 6 (or any even multiple of 3), choice D is false. If n is even, then $n + 2$ is even as well; thus, $n(n + 1)(n + 2)$ is divisible by 4 since even numbers are divisible by 2. The best answer is therefore E.

18. The figure above is composed of 6 squares, each with side s centimeters. If the number of centimeters in the perimeter of the figure is equal to the number of square centimeters in its area, what is the value of s ?

   (A) 1

   (B) $\dfrac{5}{3}$

   (C) 2

   (D) $\dfrac{5}{2}$

   (E) $\dfrac{7}{3}$

The area of the figure is $6s^2$ square centimeters, and the perimeter of the figure is $14s$ centimeters. If these values are equal, then $6s^2 = 14s$. Dividing through by s (since $s \neq 0$), $6s = 14$, or $s = \dfrac{14}{6} = \dfrac{7}{3}$. Thus, the best answer is E.

19. If $\dfrac{s}{t} = 2$, then the value of which of the following can be determined?

   I. $\dfrac{2t}{s}$

   II. $\dfrac{s - t}{t}$

   III. $\dfrac{t - 1}{s - 1}$

   (A) I only
   (B) III only
   (C) I and II only
   (D) II and III only
   (E) I, II, and III

Note that $\dfrac{s}{t} = 2$ implies $s = 2t$. In I, $\dfrac{2t}{s} = \dfrac{2t}{2t} = 1$. In II, $\dfrac{s - t}{t} = \dfrac{2t - t}{t} = \dfrac{t}{t} = 1$. However, in III, $\dfrac{t - 1}{s - 1} = \dfrac{t - 1}{2t - 1}$, which cannot be evaluated since the variable t cannot be eliminated. Since only the value of the expressions in I and II can be determined, the best answer is C.

Alternatively, $\dfrac{s}{t} = 2$ implies $\dfrac{t}{s} = \dfrac{1}{2}$. Then, in I, $\dfrac{2t}{s} = 2\left(\dfrac{t}{s}\right)$ can be determined. Also, $\dfrac{s - t}{t} = \dfrac{s}{t} - \dfrac{t}{t} = \dfrac{s}{t} - 1$ is another way of showing that the value of the expression in II can be determined.

NET INCOME FOR CORPORATIONS A and B

	Corporation A	Corporation B
Net Income in 1987	\$2.9 million	\$0.87 million
Percent Decrease in Net Income from 1986 to 1987	8.8%	13.3%

20. The net income of Corporation B in 1986 was approximately what percent of the net income of Corporation A in 1987 ?

   (A) 35%
   (B) 30%
   (C) 25%
   (D) 20%
   (E) 15%

Let x be the net income, in millions, of Corporation B in 1986. Then the net income of Corporation B in 1987 was 86.7% (100% − 13.3%) of x; that is, $0.87 = 0.867x$. So $x = \dfrac{0.87}{0.867}$ million dollars, or approximately \$1 million. Therefore, the ratio of x to the net income of Corporation A in 1987 was approximately $\dfrac{\$1 \text{ million}}{\$2.9 \text{ million}} \approx 0.34$, or 34%. The best answer is therefore A.

Explanatory Material:
Reading Comprehension, Section 4

(The passage for questions 1-8 appears on page 402.)

1. According to the passage, senior managers use intuition in all of the following ways EXCEPT to

   (A) speed up the creation of a solution to a problem
   (B) identify a problem
   (C) bring together disparate facts
   (D) stipulate clear goals
   (E) evaluate possible solutions to a problem

The best answer is D. The question requires you to recognize which of the choices is NOT mentioned in the passage as a way in which senior managers use intuition. Choice A, speeding up the creation of a solution, is mentioned in lines 36-37, which describe intuition as enabling managers to "move rapidly to engender a plausible solution." B appears in lines 21-22: "they intuitively sense when a problem exists." C is a restatement of the sentence in lines 26-28. E may be gathered from lines 29-30, which state that intuition is used "as a check on the results of more rational analysis"; those results are identified in the next sentence as "solutions." The passage does not mention stipulating goals (choice D).

2. The passage suggests which of the following about the "writers on management" mentioned in line 12 ?

   (A) They have criticized managers for not following the classical rational model of decision analysis.
   (B) They have not based their analyses on a sufficiently large sample of actual managers.
   (C) They have relied in drawing their conclusions on what managers say rather than on what managers do.
   (D) They have misunderstood how managers use intuition in making business decisions.
   (E) They have not acknowledged the role of intuition in managerial practice.

The best answer is D. The author asserts that the writers in question "display a poor grasp of what intuition is" (lines 14-15). The next paragraph presents a view that, according to the author of the passage, characterizes intuition more accurately than the writers on management do. Isenberg's research is specifically described as showing the ways in which managers use intuition (lines 20-21). Therefore, what Isenberg correctly comprehends, and the writers in question misunderstand, is how managers use intuition, as D states.

3. Which of the following best exemplifies "an 'Aha!' experience" (line 28) as it is presented in the passage?

   (A) A manager risks taking an action whose outcome is unpredictable to discover whether the action changes the problem at hand.
   (B) A manager performs well-learned and familiar behavior patterns in creative and uncharacteristic ways to solve a problem.
   (C) A manager suddenly connects seemingly unrelated facts and experiences to create a pattern relevant to the problem at hand.
   (D) A manager rapidly identifies the methodology used to compile data yielded by systematic analysis.
   (E) A manager swiftly decides which of several sets of tactics to implement in order to deal with the contingencies suggested by a problem.

The best answer is C. An "Aha! experience" is said in lines 26-28 to result from the synthesizing of "isolated bits of data and practice into an integrated picture." C is the best example of this kind of process. The connecting of seemingly unrelated facts and experiences mentioned in the answer choice is equivalent to synthesizing "isolated bits of data and practice," and the pattern referred to is comparable to an "integrated picture."

4. According to the passage, the classical model of decision analysis includes all of the following EXCEPT

   (A) evaluation of a problem
   (B) creation of possible solutions to a problem
   (C) establishment of clear goals to be reached by the decision
   (D) action undertaken in order to discover more information about a problem
   (E) comparison of the probable effects of different solutions to a problem

The best answer is D. The question requires you to recognize which of the choices is NOT mentioned in the passage as a component of the classical model of decision analysis. Four of the answer choices are mentioned in the first sentence of the passage, which describes the classical model of analysis: "clarifying goals" (C), "assessing the problem" (A), "formulating options" (B), and "estimating likelihoods of success" (E). Only D, "action undertaken in order to discover more information about a problem," does not appear in the passage.

5. It can be inferred from the passage that which of the following would most probably be one major difference in behavior between Manager X, who uses intuition to reach decisions, and Manager Y, who uses only formal decision analysis?

(A) Manager X analyzes first and then acts; Manager Y does not.
(B) Manager X checks possible solutions to a problem by systematic analysis; Manager Y does not.
(C) Manager X takes action in order to arrive at the solution to a problem; Manager Y does not.
(D) Manager Y draws on years of hands-on experience in creating a solution to a problem; Manager X does not.
(E) Manager Y depends on day-to-day tactical maneuvering; Manager X does not.

The best answer is C. The question requires you to compare behavior based on intuition with behavior based on formal decision analysis. Choice C specifies that the manager who uses intuition incorporates action into the decision-making process, but the manager who uses formal analysis does not. This distinction is made in several places in the passage. Lines 4-5 emphasize that decision-making and action-taking are separate steps in formal decision analysis: "making a decision, and only then taking action." On the other hand, those who use intuition "integrate action into the process of thinking" (lines 10-11). Again, the author mentions that in the intuitive style of management, " 'thinking' is inseparable from acting" (lines 41-42), and "action is often part of defining the problem" (lines 54-55).

6. It can be inferred from the passage that "thinking/acting cycles" (line 45) in managerial practice would be likely to result in which of the following?

I. A manager analyzes a network of problems and then acts on the basis of that analysis.
II. A manager gathers data by acting and observing the effects of action.
III. A manager takes action without being able to articulate reasons for that particular action.

(A) I only
(B) II only
(C) I and II only
(D) II and III only
(E) I, II, and III

The best answer is D. The question asks you to identify one or more consequences that the author implies would result from "thinking/acting cycles" in managerial practice. Statement I, which describes a manager as analyzing first and then acting, is explicitly contradicted by lines 44-48, which state that in thinking/acting cycles managers do *not* analyze first and act later. The author implies statement II in lines 50-52: "managers often instigate a course of action simply to learn more

about an issue." Statement III is implied in lines 42-44, which suggest that managers are able to explain their actions only after the actions are complete. Therefore, statements II and III only are implied in the passage.

7. The passage provides support for which of the following statements?

(A) Managers who rely on intuition are more successful than those who rely on formal decision analysis.
(B) Managers cannot justify their intuitive decisions.
(C) Managers' intuition works contrary to their rational and analytical skills.
(D) Logical analysis of a problem increases the number of possible solutions.
(E) Intuition enables managers to employ their practical experience more efficiently.

The best answer is E. The question requires you to identify a statement that can be inferred from information in the passage but is not explicitly stated. The author asserts that intuitive managers can "move rapidly to engender a plausible solution" (lines 36-37) and that their intuition is based on "experience that builds skills" (lines 25-26). This implies that the combination of skill and rapidity enables managers to employ their practical experience more efficiently, as E states. Choice A cannot be inferred from the passage, which states only that a majority of successful managers are intuitive (lines 1-11), not that their degree of success is greater. B and C are directly contradicted by the passage, and the passage provides no support for D.

8. Which of the following best describes the organization of the first paragraph of the passage?

(A) An assertion is made and a specific supporting example is given.
(B) A conventional model is dismissed and an alternative introduced.
(C) The results of recent research are introduced and summarized.
(D) Two opposing points of view are presented and evaluated.
(E) A widely accepted definition is presented and qualified.

The best answer is B. In the first paragraph, the author dismisses the idea that most successful senior managers follow the classical (or conventional) model of decision analysis (lines 1-5). The author then proceeds to introduce an alternative model to explain the behavior of most successful senior managers: reliance on intuition (lines 6-11).

(The passage for questions 9-17 appears on page 404.)

9. The passage is most probably directed at which kind of audience?

    (A) State legislators deciding about funding levels for a state-funded biological laboratory
    (B) Scientists specializing in molecular genetics
    (C) Readers of an alumni newsletter published by the college that Paul Gross attended
    (D) Marine biologists studying the processes that give rise to new species
    (E) Undergraduate biology majors in a molecular biology course

The best answer is E. The style of the passage and the information it contains are most consistent with the needs of an audience of undergraduate biology majors. Choice A is incorrect because the passage does not contain the kind of financial information legislators would need to determine funding levels for a laboratory. B and D are incorrect because the author's definitions of "morphogenetic determinants" (line 15) and "cytoplasm" (lines 29-30) suggest that the passage is directed at an audience with a less specialized knowledge of biology than scientists mentioned in B and D could reasonably be expected to have. C can be eliminated because the passage is primarily concerned with biological issues, not the kind of biographical information that would be of interest to readers of an alumni newsletter.

10. It can be inferred from the passage that the morphogenetic determinants present in the early embryo are

    (A) located in the nucleus of the embryo cells
    (B) evenly distributed unless the embryo is not developing normally
    (C) inactive until the embryo cells become irreversibly committed to their final function
    (D) identical to those that were already present in the unfertilized egg
    (E) present in larger quantities than is necessary for the development of a single individual

The best answer is E. The second and third paragraphs of the passage indicate that morphogenetic determinants are substances in the embryo that are activated after the egg has been fertilized and that "tell a cell what to become" (lines 15-16). If, as the author asserts in the first paragraph, biologists have succeeded in dividing an embryo into two parts, each of which survives and develops into a normal embryo, it can be concluded that the quantity of morphogenetic determinants in the early embryo is greater than that required for the development of a single individual. Choices A, B, and C are directly contradicted by information in the passage, and D makes an assertion that cannot be inferred from the passage.

11. The main topic of the passage is

    (A) the early development of embryos of lower marine organisms
    (B) the main contribution of modern embryology to molecular biology
    (C) the role of molecular biology in disproving older theories of embryonic development
    (D) cell determination as an issue in the study of embryonic development
    (E) scientific dogma as a factor in the recent debate over the value of molecular biology

The best answer is D. In identifying the main topic of the passage, you must consider the passage as a whole. In the first paragraph, the author provides a historical context for the debate described in the second paragraph, concerning when and how the determination of embryo cells takes place. The third and fourth paragraphs provide a specific example of the "Recent discoveries in molecular biology" (line 19) that may lead to the resolution of that debate. C is incorrect because although the passage does indicate that biologists revised their initial belief that early embryo cells are undetermined, this revision is seen as having taken place prior to the "Recent discoveries in molecular biology." Choices A, B, and E do not accurately reflect the content of the passage.

12. According to the passage, when biologists believed that the cells in the early embryo were undetermined, they made which of the following mistakes?

    (A) They did not attempt to replicate the original experiment of separating an embryo into two parts.
    (B) They did not realize that there was a connection between the issue of cell determination and the outcome of the separation experiment.
    (C) They assumed that the results of experiments on embryos did not depend on the particular animal species used for such experiments.
    (D) They assumed that it was crucial to perform the separation experiment at an early stage in the embryo's life.
    (E) They assumed that different ways of separating an embryo into two parts would be equivalent as far as the fate of the two parts was concerned.

The best answer is E. According to the author, early investigators arrived at the conclusion that the cells of the embryo are undetermined because they "found that if they separated an invertebrate animal embryo into two parts at an early stage of its life, it would survive and develop as two normal embryos" (lines 1-4). However, later biologists discovered that when an embryo was cut in planes different from the one used by the early investigators, it did not form two whole embryos. Because the earlier biologists apparently arrived at their conclusion without attempting to cut an embryo in different planes, it would appear that they assumed, erroneously, that different ways of separating the embryos would not affect the fate of the two embryo parts.

13. It can be inferred from the passage that the initial production of histones after an egg is fertilized takes place

    (A) in the cytoplasm
    (B) in the maternal genes
    (C) throughout the protoplasm
    (D) in the beaded portions of the DNA strings
    (E) in certain sections of the cell nucleus

The best answer is A. In the third paragraph, the author asserts that substances that function as morphogenetic determinants are located in the cytoplasm of the cell and become active after the cell is fertilized. In the fourth paragraph we learn that these substances are "maternal messenger RNA's" and that they "direct, in large part, the synthesis of histones," which, after being synthesized, "move into the cell nucleus" (lines 39-45). Thus, it can be inferred that after the egg is fertilized, the initial production of histones occurs in the cytoplasm.

14. It can be inferred from the passage that which of the following is dependent on the fertilization of an egg?

    (A) Copying of maternal genes to produce maternal messenger RNA's
    (B) Synthesis of proteins called histones
    (C) Division of a cell into its nucleus and the cytoplasm
    (D) Determination of the egg cell's potential for division
    (E) Generation of all of a cell's morphogenetic determinants

The best answer is B. Lines 30-34 indicate that substances that function as morphogenetic determinants are inactive in the unfertilized egg and that when the egg is fertilized, they "become active and, presumably, govern the behavior of the genes they interact with." In the fourth paragraph, we learn that these substances exert their control over the fate of the cell by directing "the synthesis of histones." Because these histones cannot be synthesized until the substances that function as morphogenetic determinants become active, and because these substances do not become active until the egg is fertilized, it can be inferred that the synthesis of the histones is dependent on the fertilization of the egg.

15. According to the passage, the morphogenetic determinants present in the unfertilized egg cell are which of the following?

    (A) Proteins bound to the nucleus
    (B) Histones
    (C) Maternal messenger RNA's
    (D) Cytoplasm
    (E) Nonbeaded intervening DNA

The best answer is C. Lines 26-28 inform us that in his study of sea urchins, Gross "found that an unfertilized egg contains substances that function as morphogenetic determinants." Lines 39-40 assert that the "substances that Gross studied are maternal messenger RNA's," and in lines 41-42 we learn that

these maternal messenger RNA's can be found in "a wide variety of organisms." B is incorrect. Although after becoming active these messenger RNA's are said to direct the synthesis of histones, the synthesis of the histones is said to occur after, not before, the egg has been fertilized.

16. The passage suggests that which of the following plays a role in determining whether an embryo separated into two parts will develop as two normal embryos?

    I. The stage in the embryo's life at which the separation occurs
    II. The instrument with which the separation is accomplished
    III. The plane in which the cut is made that separates the embryo

    (A) I only
    (B) II only
    (C) I and II only
    (D) I and III only
    (E) I, II, and III

The best answer is D. Statement I is correct because lines 1-3 indicate that biologists nearly a century ago found that the divided embryo will survive and develop into two embryos if it is divided "at an early stage of its life." Statement III is correct because lines 8-11 assert that when the embryo is "cut in a plane different from the one used by the early investigators, it will not form two whole embryos." Statement II is incorrect because nowhere in the passage is it suggested that the instrument used to separate the embryo into parts has an effect on their development. Therefore, statements I and III only are implied in the passage.

17. Which of the following circumstances is most comparable to the impasse biologists encountered in trying to resolve the debate about cell determination (lines 12-18) ?

    (A) The problems faced by a literary scholar who wishes to use original source materials that are written in an unfamiliar foreign language
    (B) The situation of a mathematician who in preparing a proof of a theorem for publication detects a reasoning error in the proof
    (C) The difficulties of a space engineer who has to design equipment to function in an environment in which it cannot first be tested
    (D) The predicament of a linguist trying to develop a theory of language acquisition when knowledge of the structure of language itself is rudimentary at best
    (E) The dilemma confronting a foundation when the funds available to it are sufficient to support one of two equally deserving scientific projects but not both

The best answer is D. The impasse biologists encountered in trying to resolve the debate about cell determination was caused in part by the lack of fundamental knowledge about the mechanism by which cells are determined. Resolution of the debate is possible only with the help of the recent discovery of "at least some of the molecules that act as morphogenetic determinants" (lines 21-22). This is comparable to D because, just as the biologists attempted to formulate a theory of cell determination without fully understanding crucial cellular processes, so the linguist attempts to understand the process by which language is acquired without fully understanding the structure of language. Both the linguist and the biologists lack crucial information concerning the phenomena they attempt to explain.

(The passage for questions 18-25 appears on page 406.)

18. The author indicates explicitly that which of the following records has been a source of information in her investigation?

(A) United States Immigration Service reports from 1914 to 1930
(B) Payrolls of southern manufacturing firms between 1910 and 1930
(C) The volume of cotton exports between 1898 and 1910
(D) The federal census of 1910
(E) Advertisements of labor recruiters appearing in southern newspapers after 1910

The best answer is D. In lines 24-28, the author states that ten percent of the Black workers in the South were employed in "manufacturing and mechanical pursuits" and then identifies "manufacturing and mechanical pursuits" as the general federal census category for industrial occupations in 1910. Thus, she indicates that she used the federal census as a source of information. Although the author discusses information that may have been included in the records mentioned in A, B, C, and E, she does not "explicitly" identify any of those records as sources used in her investigation.

19. In the passage, the author anticipates which of the following as a possible objection to her argument?

(A) It is uncertain how many people actually migrated during the Great Migration.
(B) The eventual economic status of the Great Migration migrants has not been adequately traced.
(C) It is not likely that people with steady jobs would have reason to move to another area of the country.
(D) It is not true that the term "manufacturing and mechanical pursuits" actually encompasses the entire industrial sector.
(E) Of the Black workers living in southern cities, only those in a small number of trades were threatened by obsolescence.

The best answer is C. To answer this question, you must first identify the author's argument. The author argues that it is possible that Black migrants to the North were living and working in urban areas of the South rather than in rural areas, as researchers had previously assumed. In lines 30-33, the author states that it may be "surprising" that an employed population would relocate. Thus, the author anticipates an objection to her argument on the grounds that Black urban workers in the South would have been unlikely to leave an economically secure existence. She meets that objection by stating that "an explanation lies in the labor conditions then prevalent in the South" (lines 32-33), and discusses the low wages that may have motivated Black workers to migrate north for higher pay.

20. According to the passage, which of the following is true of wages in southern cities in 1910?

(A) They were being pushed lower as a result of increased competition.
(B) They had begun to rise so that southern industry could attract rural workers.
(C) They had increased for skilled workers but decreased for unskilled workers.
(D) They had increased in large southern cities but decreased in small southern cities.
(E) They had increased in newly developed industries but decreased in the older trades.

The best answer is A. The author discusses wages in southern cities in the third paragraph. Lines 47-50 state that an increase in the number of rural workers who migrated to southern cities after the collapse of the cotton industry led to increased competition for jobs and resulted in wages being pushed lower. There is no indication in the passage that B, C, D, or E was true.

21. The author cites each of the following as possible influences in a Black worker's decision to migrate north in the Great Migration EXCEPT

(A) wage levels in northern cities
(B) labor recruiters
(C) competition from rural workers
(D) voting rights in northern states
(E) the Black press

The best answer is D. This question asks you to identify the possible influences that motivated Black workers in their decision to migrate north, and then to recognize which of the choices is NOT mentioned as an influence on Black workers. Choices A, B, C, and E are all discussed in the third paragraph. Lines 48-50 state that "competition from . . . rural workers" (C) resulted in even lower wages in the South. Lines 43-47 state that Black workers were aware through "labor recruiters" (B) and the "Black press" (E) that "wage levels in northern cities" (A) were higher than they were in the South. D — "voting rights in northern states" — is the only option not mentioned in the passage as an influence that may have motivated southern Black workers to move north.

22. It can be inferred from the passage that the "easy conclusion" mentioned in line 53 is based on which of the following assumptions?

(A) People who migrate from rural areas to large cities usually do so for economic reasons.

(B) Most people who leave rural areas to take jobs in cities return to rural areas as soon as it is financially possible for them to do so.

(C) People with rural backgrounds are less likely to succeed economically in cities than are those with urban backgrounds.

(D) Most people who were once skilled workers are not willing to work as unskilled workers.

(E) People who migrate from their birthplaces to other regions of a country seldom undertake a second migration.

The best answer is C. To answer this question, you must first identify the "easy conclusion" mentioned in line 53, which ties Black migrants' "subsequent economic problems in the North to their rural background." This linkage of rural background to economic difficulty after migration to the North is first mentioned in lines 14-18. Here, the author points out that researchers have assumed that Black migrants encountered economic difficulties in northern cities because they were from rural rather than urban backgrounds, and that rural backgrounds imply "unfamiliarity with urban living and a lack of industrial skills." Choice C provides an assumption about the relationship between rural backgrounds and economic difficulty that underlies this conclusion. It states that people with rural backgrounds are more likely to have economic difficulty in urban areas than are people with urban backgrounds. A, B, D, and E can be eliminated because they do not deal with the connection between economic difficulties and rural backgrounds.

23. The primary purpose of the passage is to

(A) support an alternative to an accepted methodology
(B) present evidence that resolves a contradiction
(C) introduce a recently discovered source of information
(D) challenge a widely accepted explanation
(E) argue that a discarded theory deserves new attention

The best answer is D. The first paragraph describes a common assumption about the Great Migration, that the majority of migrants came from rural areas. It also restates the conclusion that is based on this assumption, that the subsequent economic difficulties of Black migrants in the North were a result of their unfamiliarity with urban life. In the second paragraph, the author states that the "question of who actually left the South" (line 19) has never been adequately researched. She goes on to argue that Black migrants may actually have been from urban areas rather than rural areas, and thus that their subsequent economic problems in northern cities were not caused by their rural background. In making this argument, the author is challenging the "widely accepted explanation" presented in the first paragraph.

24. According to information in the passage, which of the following is a correct sequence of groups of workers, from highest paid to lowest paid, in the period between 1910 and 1930?

(A) Artisans in the North; artisans in the South; unskilled workers in the North; unskilled workers in the South

(B) Artisans in the North and South; unskilled workers in the North; unskilled workers in the South

(C) Artisans in the North; unskilled workers in the North; artisans in the South

(D) Artisans in the North and South; unskilled urban workers in the North; unskilled rural workers in the South

(E) Artisans in the North and South; unskilled rural workers in the North and South; unskilled urban workers in the North and South

The best answer is C. Lines 43-47 state that Black workers were aware that they could earn more as unskilled workers in the North than as artisans in the South. It can be inferred from this that artisans in the North — highly skilled workers — would earn even higher wages. Thus, according to information in the passage, the correct sequence of groups of workers from highest paid to lowest paid is artisans in the North, unskilled workers in the North, artisans in the South.

25. The material in the passage would be most relevant to a long discussion of which of the following topics?

(A) The reasons for the subsequent economic difficulties of those who participated in the Great Migration

(B) The effect of migration on the regional economies of the United States following the First World War

(C) The transition from a rural to an urban existence for those who migrated in the Great Migration

(D) The transformation of the agricultural South following the boll weevil infestation

(E) The disappearance of the artisan class in the United States as a consequence of mechanization in the early twentieth century

The best answer is A. The passage presents a common explanation for the economic difficulties encountered by Black migrants to northern cities. It then proposes that that explanation is based on inadequate data about who actually left the South. The author suggests that the migrants were primarily urban rather than rural, and thus that their economic problems cannot be attributed to their unfamiliarity with urban living. Therefore, the material in the passage is most relevant to a discussion of "the reasons for the subsequent economic difficulties of those who participated in the Great Migration." Choice C can be eliminated because the author argues that Black migrants were urban, and so would have no need to make a transition. B, D, and E can be eliminated because they mention topics not relevant to the passage.

Explanatory Material:
Problem Solving II, Section 5

1. If Jack had twice the amount of money that he has, he would have exactly the amount necessary to buy 3 hamburgers at $0.96 apiece and 2 milk shakes at $1.28 apiece. How much money does Jack have?

   (A) $1.60
   (B) $2.24
   (C) $2.72
   (D) $3.36
   (E) $5.44

Let J be the amount of money Jack has. Then

$2J = 3(\$0.96) + 2(\$1.28) = \$5.44$. So $J = \dfrac{1}{2}(\$5.44) = \$2.72$,

and the best answer is C.

2. If a photocopier makes 2 copies in $\dfrac{1}{3}$ second, then, at the same rate, how many copies does it make in 4 minutes?

   (A) 360
   (B) 480
   (C) 576
   (D) 720
   (E) 1,440

The photocopier makes copies at the rate of 2 copies in $\dfrac{1}{3}$ second, or 6 copies per second. Since 4 minutes equals 240 seconds, the photocopier makes $6(240) = 1,440$ copies in 4 minutes. Therefore, the best answer is E.

3. The price of a certain television set is discounted by 10 percent, and the reduced price is then discounted by 10 percent. This series of successive discounts is equivalent to a single discount of

   (A) 20%
   (B) 19%
   (C) 18%
   (D) 11%
   (E) 10%

If P is the original price of the television set, then $0.9P$ is the price after the first discount, and $0.9(0.9P) = 0.81P$ is the price after the second discount. Thus, the original price is discounted by 19% $(100\% - 81\%)$, and the best answer is B.

4. If $\dfrac{2}{1 + \dfrac{2}{y}} = 1$, then $y =$

   (A) -2
   (B) $-\dfrac{1}{2}$
   (C) $\dfrac{1}{2}$
   (D) 2
   (E) 3

Since $\dfrac{2}{1 + \dfrac{2}{y}} = 1$, $1 + \dfrac{2}{y} = 2$. Thus, $\dfrac{2}{y} = 1$, or $y = 2$, and the best answer is D.

5. If a rectangular photograph that is 10 inches wide by 15 inches long is to be enlarged so that the width will be 22 inches and the ratio of width to length will be unchanged, then the length, in inches, of the enlarged photograph will be

   (A) 33
   (B) 32
   (C) 30
   (D) 27
   (E) 25

The ratio of width to length of the original photograph is

$\dfrac{10}{15} = \dfrac{2}{3}$. If x is the length of the enlarged photograph, in

inches, then $\dfrac{2}{3} = \dfrac{22}{x}$ since the ratio of width to length will be

unchanged. Thus, $x = 33$ inches, and the best answer is A.

6. If m is an integer such that $(-2)^{2m} = 2^{9-m}$, then $m =$

   (A) 1
   (B) 2
   (C) 3
   (D) 4
   (E) 6

Since $(-2)^{2m} = ((-2)^2)^m = 4^m = 2^{2m}$, it follows that $2^{2m} = 2^{9-m}$. The exponents must be equal, so that $2m = 9 - m$, or $m = 3$. The best answer is therefore C.

7. If $0 \leq x \leq 4$ and $y < 12$, which of the following CANNOT be the value of xy ?

(A) −2
(B) 0
(C) 6
(D) 24
(E) 48

Each of choices A, B, and C can be a value of xy. For if $x = 1$, then $xy = y$, and each of these choices is less than 12. If $x = 4$ and $y = 6$, then $xy = 24$, so that choice D also gives a possible value of xy. In choice E, if $xy = 48$, then for all values of x such that $0 \ x \ 4$, it follows that $y \ 12$, which contradicts $y < 12$. Thus, 48 cannot be the value of xy, and the best answer is E.

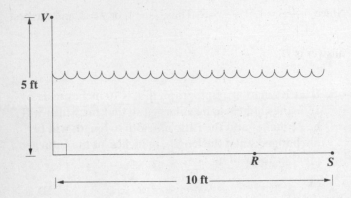

8. In the figure above, V represents an observation point at one end of a pool. From V, an object that is actually located on the bottom of the pool at point R appears to be at point S. If $VR = 10$ feet, what is the distance RS, in feet, between the actual position and the perceived position of the object?

(A) $10 - 5\sqrt{3}$

(B) $10 - 5\sqrt{2}$

(C) 2

(D) $2\frac{1}{2}$

(E) 4

Let P be the point 5 feet directly below V. P is the vertex of the right angle indicated in the figure, and $\triangle VPR$ is thus a right triangle. Then, by the Pythagorean theorem,
$PR = \sqrt{10^2 - 5^2} = \sqrt{75} = 5\sqrt{3}$. Thus,
$RS = PS - PR = 10 - 5\sqrt{3}$, and the best answer is A.

9. If the total payroll expense of a certain business in year Y was \$84,000, which was 20 percent more than in year X, what was the total payroll expense in year X ?

(A) \$70,000
(B) \$68,320
(C) \$64,000
(D) \$60,000
(E) \$52,320

If p is the total payroll expense in year X, then $1.2p = \$84,000$, so that $p = \dfrac{\$84,000}{1.2} = \$70,000$. Thus, the best answer is A.

10. If a, b, and c are consecutive positive integers and $a < b < c$, which of the following must be true?

I. $c - a = 2$

II. abc is an even integer.

III. $\dfrac{a \ | \ b \ | \ c}{3}$ is an integer.

(A) I only
(B) II only
(C) I and II only
(D) II and III only
(E) I, II, and III

Since a, b, and c are consecutive integers and $a < b < c$, it follows that $b = a + 1$ and $c = a + 2$. Statement I follows from $c = a + 2$. Concerning statement II, if a is even, then abc is even; if a is odd, then b is even so that abc is even. In either case, abc is even, so statement II must be true. In statement III, $\dfrac{a + b + c}{3} = \dfrac{a + (a + 1) + (a + 2)}{3} = \dfrac{3a + 3}{3} = a + 1 = b$, which is an integer. Therefore, statement III must be true, and the best answer is E.

11. A straight pipe 1 yard in length was marked off in fourths and also in thirds. If the pipe was then cut into separate pieces at each of these markings, which of the following gives all the different lengths of the pieces, in fractions of a yard?

(A) $\dfrac{1}{6}$ and $\dfrac{1}{4}$ only

(B) $\dfrac{1}{4}$ and $\dfrac{1}{3}$ only

(C) $\dfrac{1}{6}, \dfrac{1}{4}$, and $\dfrac{1}{3}$

(D) $\dfrac{1}{12}, \dfrac{1}{6}$, and $\dfrac{1}{4}$

(E) $\dfrac{1}{12}, \dfrac{1}{6}$, and $\dfrac{1}{3}$

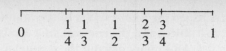

The number line above illustrates the markings on the pipe.

Since the pipe is cut at the five markings, six pieces of pipe

are produced having lengths, in yards,

$$\frac{1}{4} - 0 = \frac{1}{4}, \quad \frac{1}{3} - \frac{1}{4} = \frac{1}{12}, \quad \frac{1}{2} - \frac{1}{3} = \frac{1}{6}, \quad \frac{2}{3} - \frac{1}{2} = \frac{1}{6},$$

$\frac{3}{4} - \frac{2}{3} = \frac{1}{12}$, and $1 - \frac{3}{4} = \frac{1}{4}$. The different lengths of the

pieces are therefore $\frac{1}{12}$, $\frac{1}{6}$, and $\frac{1}{4}$ yard, and the best answer

is D.

12. **What is the least integer that is a sum of three different primes each greater than 20?**

(A) 69
(B) 73
(C) 75
(D) 79
(E) 83

The three smallest primes that are each greater than 20 are 23, 29, and 31, and their sum is 83. Since any other set of three primes, each greater than 20, would include a prime greater than 31 but no prime less than 23, the corresponding sum would be greater than 83. Thus, 83 is the least such sum, and the best answer is E.

13. **A tourist purchased a total of $1,500 worth of traveler's checks in $10 and $50 denominations. During the trip the tourist cashed 7 checks and then lost all of the rest. If the number of $10 checks cashed was one more or one less than the number of $50 checks cashed, what is the minimum possible value of the checks that were lost?**

(A) $1,430
(B) $1,310
(C) $1,290
(D) $1,270
(E) $1,150

Let t be the number of $10 traveler's checks that were cashed and let f be the number of $50 traveler's checks that were cashed. Then $t + f = 7$, and either $t = f + 1$ or $t = f - 1$. Thus, either $t = 4$ and $f = 3$, or $t = 3$ and $f = 4$. In the first case, the value of the lost checks would have been
$1,500 - t(\$10) - f(\$50) = \$1,500 - \$40 - \$150 = \$1,310$;
whereas, in the second case, the value would have been
$1,500 - \$30 - \$200 = \$1,270$. Since the lesser of these amounts is $1,270, the best answer is D.

Alternatively, note that the minimum possible value of the lost checks corresponds to the maximum possible value of the checks that were cashed. Thus, $t = 3$ and $f = 4$, and the minimum possible value of the lost checks is
$$\$1,500 - \$30 - \$200 = \$1,270.$$

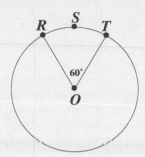

14. **If the circle above has center O and circumference 18, then the perimeter of sector $RSTO$ is**

(A) $3 + 9$
(B) $3 + 18$
(C) $6 + 9$
(D) $6 + 18$
(E) $6 + 24$

If r is the radius of the circle, then the circumference is

$2\pi r = 18$, so that $r = 9$. The ratio of the length of arc RST to

the circumference is the same as the ratio of 60° to 360°. Thus,

the length of arc RST is $\frac{60}{360}(18) = 3$, and, consequently,

the perimeter of sector $RSTO$ is $3 + r + r = 3 + 18$. The best

answer is therefore B.

15. **If each of the following fractions were written as a repeating decimal, which would have the longest sequence of different digits?**

(A) $\frac{2}{11}$

(B) $\frac{1}{3}$

(C) $\frac{41}{99}$

(D) $\frac{2}{3}$

(E) $\frac{23}{37}$

As repeating decimals, choices A-E are $\frac{2}{11} = 0.181818\ldots$,

$\frac{1}{3} = 0.333\ldots$, $\frac{41}{99} = 0.414141\ldots$, $\frac{2}{3} = 0.666\ldots$,

and $\frac{23}{37} = 0.621621621\ldots$, respectively. The longest

sequence of different digits appears in the last decimal, so the

best answer is E.

16. Today Rose is twice as old as Sam and Sam is 3 years younger than Tina. If Rose, Sam, and Tina are all alive 4 years from today, which of the following must be true on that day?

    I. Rose is twice as old as Sam.
   II. Sam is 3 years younger than Tina.
  III. Rose is older than Tina.

    (A) I only
    (B) II only
    (C) III only
    (D) I and II
    (E) II and III

When considering the relationships between people's ages, it may be helpful to keep in mind the fact that the difference between two ages remains constant from one year to the next, but their ratio does not. Thus, statement I need not be true, whereas statement II must be true. For statement III, if R, S, and T denote the respective ages of Rose, Sam, and Tina today, then $R = 2S$ and $S = T - 3$, so that $R = 2(T - 3)$. Thus, $R > T$ if and only if $2(T - 3) > T$, or $T > 6$. Therefore, statement III need not be true, and the best answer is B.

17. If k and w are the dimensions of a rectangle that has area 42, and if k and w are integers such that $k > w$, what is the total number of possible values of k ?

    (A) Two
    (B) Three
    (C) Four
    (D) Five
    (E) Six

The area 42 may be factored into two positive integers in four different ways: $42 = (1)(42) = (2)(21) = (3)(14) = (6)(7)$. Since k and w are positive integers such that $kw = 42$ and $k > w$, the possible values of k are 42, 21, 14, and 7. Thus, the best answer is C.

18. R campers fished for 3 hours. If m of the campers caught 2 fish apiece and the rest caught a combined total of n fish, how many fish did the R campers catch per hour?

    (A) $2m + n(R - m)$

    (B) $\dfrac{2m + n(R - m)}{3}$

    (C) $\dfrac{2m + n(m - R)}{3}$

    (D) $\dfrac{2m + n}{3}$

    (E) $\dfrac{2m + n}{R}$

The m campers who caught 2 fish apiece caught a total of $2m$ fish. The other campers caught a total of n fish. Thus, the total number of fish caught by the R campers in 3 hours was $2m + n$. The number of fish caught per hour was therefore $\dfrac{2m + n}{3}$, and the best answer is D.

19. Last year the annual premium on a certain hospitalization insurance policy was $408, and the policy paid 80 percent of any hospital expenses incurred. If the amount paid by the insurance policy last year was equal to the annual premium plus the amount of hospital expenses not paid by the policy, what was the total amount of hospital expenses last year?

    (A) $850.00
    (B) $680.00
    (C) $640.00
    (D) $510.00
    (E) $326.40

If x is the total amount of last year's hospital expenses, then $0.8x$ is the amount paid by the insurance policy and $0.2x$ is the amount not paid by the policy. According to the information given in the question, $0.8x = \$408 + 0.2x$, which implies $0.6x = \$408$, or $x = \dfrac{\$408}{0.6} = \$680$. The best answer is therefore B.

20. The average (arithmetic mean) of three numbers is $3x + 2$. If one of the numbers is x, what is the average of the other two numbers?

(A) $x + 1$
(B) $2x + 2$
(C) $4x + 1$
(D) $4x + 3$
(E) $8x + 6$

Note that the average of the three numbers is the sum of the numbers divided by 3. It follows that the sum of the three numbers is 3 times the average, or $3(3x + 2) = 9x + 6$. Thus, the sum of the other two numbers is $9x + 6 - x = 8x + 6$, and their average is $\dfrac{8x + 6}{2} = 4x + 3$. The best answer is therefore D.

Alternatively, if y and z are the other two numbers, the average of all three numbers is $\dfrac{x + y + z}{3}$, so that $\dfrac{x + y + z}{3} = 3x + 2$. This equation may be solved for the sum $y + z$ in terms of x, so that the average $\dfrac{y + z}{2}$ can be found.

$$\frac{x + y + z}{3} = 3x + 2$$
$$x + y + z = 9x + 6$$
$$y + z = 8x + 6$$
$$\frac{y + z}{2} = 4x + 3$$

Explanatory Material: Sentence Correction, Section 6

1. A Labor Department study states that the <u>numbers of women employed outside the home grew by more than a thirty-five percent increase</u> in the past decade and accounted for more than sixty-two percent of the total growth in the civilian work force.

(A) numbers of women employed outside the home grew by more than a thirty-five percent increase
(B) numbers of women employed outside the home grew more than thirty-five percent
(C) numbers of women employed outside the home were raised by more than thirty-five percent
(D) number of women employed outside the home increased by more than thirty-five percent
(E) number of women employed outside the home was raised by more than a thirty-five percent increase

Because a count of women employed outside the home at any given time will be expressed by a single number, the use of the plural noun *numbers* in choices A, B, and C is illogical. In A, the phrase *grew by more than a thirty-five percent increase* is redundant and wordy, since the sense of *increase* is implicit in the verb *grew*. In C and E, the passive verb forms *were raised* and *was raised* are inappropriate because there is no identifiable agent responsible for the raising of the number of women employed. In choice E, *was raised by . . . increase* is redundant. Choice D, which presents the comparison logically and idiomatically, is the best answer.

2. The first decision for most tenants living in a building undergoing <u>being converted to cooperative ownership is if to sign</u> a no-buy pledge with the other tenants.

(A) being converted to cooperative ownership is if to sign
(B) being converted to cooperative ownership is whether they should be signing
(C) being converted to cooperative ownership is whether or not they sign
(D) conversion to cooperative ownership is if to sign
(E) conversion to cooperative ownership is whether to sign

In A, B, and C, the phrase *being converted* is awkward and redundant, since the sense of process indicated by *being* has already been conveyed by *undergoing*. A and D can be faulted for saying *if* rather than *whether*, since the sentence poses alternative possibilities, to sign or not to sign. Only E, the best choice, idiomatically completes *whether* with an infinitive, *to sign*, that functions as a noun equivalent of *decision*. Choice E also uses the noun *conversion*, which grammatically completes the phrase begun by *undergoing*.

3. The end of the eighteenth century saw the emergence of prize-stock breeding, with individual bulls and cows receiving awards, fetching unprecedented prices, and <u>excited</u> enormous interest whenever they were put on show.

(A) excited
(B) it excited
(C) exciting
(D) would excite
(E) it had excited

Choice C is best. The third verb phrase in the series describing *bulls and cows* should have the same grammatical form as the first two. Only choice C has a present participle (or "-ing" form) that is parallel with the two preceding verbs, *receiving* and *fetching*. Instead of the present participle, choices A and B use the past tense (*excited*), choice D uses an auxiliary verb (*would excite*), and choice E uses the past perfect tense (*had excited*). Additionally, the incorrect verb tenses in B and E are introduced by a pronoun, *it*, that lacks a logical noun referent.

4. Of all the possible disasters that threaten American agriculture, the possibility of an adverse change in climate <u>is maybe the more difficult for analysis</u>.

   (A) is maybe the more difficult for analysis
   (B) is probably the most difficult to analyze
   (C) is maybe the most difficult for analysis
   (D) is probably the more difficult to analyze
   (E) is, it may be, the analysis that is most difficult

Choice B is the best answer. The sentence compares one thing, *an adverse change in climate*, to all other things in its class — that is, to *all the possible disasters that threaten American agriculture*; therefore, the sentence requires the superlative form of the adjective, *most difficult*, rather than the comparative form, *more difficult*, which appears in choices A and D. In A and C, the use of *maybe* is unidiomatic, and *difficult* should be completed by the infinitive *to analyze*. Choice E is awkwardly phrased and, when inserted into the sentence, produces an illogical structure: *the possibility . . . is . . . the analysis that.*

5. <u>Published in Harlem, the owner and editor of the *Messenger* were two young journalists, Chandler Owen and A. Philip Randolph, who would later make his reputation as a labor leader.</u>

   (A) Published in Harlem, the owner and editor of the *Messenger* were two young journalists, Chandler Owen and A. Philip Randolph, who would later make his reputation as a labor leader.
   (B) Published in Harlem, two young journalists, Chandler Owen and A. Philip Randolph, who would later make his reputation as a labor leader, were the owner and editor of the *Messenger*.
   (C) Published in Harlem, the *Messenger* was owned and edited by two young journalists, A. Philip Randolph, who would later make his reputation as a labor leader, and Chandler Owen.
   (D) The *Messenger* was owned and edited by two young journalists, Chandler Owen and A. Philip Randolph, who would later make his reputation as a labor leader, and published in Harlem.
   (E) The owner and editor being two young journalists, Chandler Owen and A. Philip Randolph, who would later make his reputation as a labor leader, the *Messenger* was published in Harlem.

Choices A and B present dangling modifiers that illogically suggest that Owen and Randolph, rather than the *Messenger*, were published in Harlem. In D, the phrase *and published in Harlem* is too remote from *the Messenger* to modify it effectively. In E, *being* produces an awkward construction, and the placement of the main clause at the end of the sentence is confusing. Only in C, the best answer, is *Published in Harlem* followed immediately by *the Messenger*. Also, C makes it clear that the clause beginning *who* refers to Randolph.

6. The rise in the Commerce Department's index of leading economic indicators <u>suggest that the economy should continue its expansion into the coming months, but that</u> the mixed performance of the index's individual components indicates that economic growth will proceed at a more moderate pace than in the first quarter of this year.

   (A) suggest that the economy should continue its expansion into the coming months, but that
   (B) suggest that the economy is to continue expansion in the coming months, but
   (C) suggests that the economy will continue its expanding in the coming months, but that
   (D) suggests that the economy is continuing to expand into the coming months, but that
   (E) suggests that the economy will continue to expand in the coming months, but

In choices A and B, the verb *suggest* does not agree with its singular subject, *rise*. In context, the phrase *into the coming months* in A and D is not idiomatic; *in the coming months* is preferable. In A, C, and D, the *that* appearing after *but* creates a subordinate clause where an independent clause is needed for the new subject, *mixed performance*. Choice E includes the correct verb form, *suggests*, eliminates *that*, and properly employs the future tense, *will continue to expand*. That this tense is called for is indicated both by the future time to which *the coming months* refers and by the parallel verb form *will proceed* in the nonunderlined part of the sentence. Choice E is best.

7. In three centuries — from 1050 to 1350 — several million tons of stone were quarried in France <u>for the building of eighty cathedrals, five hundred large churches, and some</u> tens of thousands of parish churches.

   (A) for the building of eighty cathedrals, five hundred large churches, and some
   (B) in order that they might build eighty cathedrals, five hundred large churches, and some
   (C) so as they might build eighty cathedrals, five hundred large churches, and some
   (D) so that there could be built eighty cathedrals, five hundred large churches, and
   (E) such that they could build eighty cathedrals, five hundred large churches, and

Choice A is best. The other choices are unidiomatic or unnecessarily wordy, and the pronoun *they*, which appears in B, C, and E, has no grammatical referent.

8. <u>What was as remarkable as the development of the compact disc</u> has been the use of the new technology to revitalize, in better sound than was ever before possible, some of the classic recorded performances of the pre-LP era.

(A) What was as remarkable as the development of the compact disc
(B) The thing that was as remarkable as developing the compact disc
(C) No less remarkable than the development of the compact disc
(D) Developing the compact disc has been none the less remarkable than
(E) Development of the compact disc has been no less remarkable as

Besides being wordy, the clauses beginning *What was* in A and *The thing that was* in B cause inconsistencies in verb tense: *the use of the new technology* cannot logically be described by both the present perfect *has been* and the past *was*. In B and D, *developing the compact disc* is not parallel to *the use of new technology to revitalize . . . performances*; in C, the best answer, the noun *development* is parallel to *use*. The phrases *none the less . . . than* in D and *no less . . . as* in E are unidiomatic; the correct form of expression, *no less . . . than*, appears in C, the best choice.

9. <u>Unlike computer skills or other technical skills, there is a disinclination on the part of many people to recognize the degree to which their analytical skills are weak.</u>

(A) Unlike computer skills or other technical skills, there is a disinclination on the part of many people to recognize the degree to which their analytical skills are weak.
(B) Unlike computer skills or other technical skills, which they admit they lack, many people are disinclined to recognize that their analytical skills are weak.
(C) Unlike computer skills or other technical skills, analytical skills bring out a disinclination in many people to recognize that they are weak to a degree.
(D) Many people, willing to admit that they lack computer skills or other technical skills, are disinclined to recognize that their analytical skills are weak.
(E) Many people have a disinclination to recognize the weakness of their analytical skills while willing to admit their lack of computer skills or other technical skills.

Choice D is best. Choice A illogically compares *skills* to *a disinclination*; choice B compares *skills* to *many people*. Choice C makes the comparison logical by casting *analytical skills* as the subject of the sentence, but it is awkward and unidiomatic to say *skills bring out a disinclination*. Also in C, the referent of *they* is unclear, and *weak to a degree* changes the meaning of the

original statement. In E, *have a disinclination . . . while willing* is grammatically incomplete, and *admit their lack* should be *admit to their lack*. By making *people* the subject of the sentence, D best expresses the intended contrast, which pertains not so much to skills as to people's willingness to recognize different areas of weakness.

10. <u>Some buildings that were destroyed and heavily damaged in the earthquake last year were</u> constructed in violation of the city's building code.

(A) Some buildings that were destroyed and heavily damaged in the earthquake last year were
(B) Some buildings that were destroyed or heavily damaged in the earthquake last year had been
(C) Some buildings that the earthquake destroyed and heavily damaged last year have been
(D) Last year the earthquake destroyed or heavily damaged some buildings that have been
(E) Last year some of the buildings that were destroyed or heavily damaged in the earthquake had been

Choice B is best. Choices A and C illogically state that some buildings were both destroyed *and* damaged; *or* is needed to indicate that each of the buildings suffered either one fate or the other. In using only one verb tense, *were*, A fails to indicate that the buildings were constructed before the earthquake occurred. Choices C and D use the present perfect tense incorrectly, saying in effect that the buildings *have been constructed* after they were destroyed last year. Choice E suggests that the construction of the buildings, rather than the earthquake, occurred last year, thus making the sequence of events unclear. Only B uses verb tenses correctly to indicate that construction of the buildings was completed prior to the earthquake.

11. From the earliest days of the tribe, kinship determined the way in which the Ojibwa society organized its labor, provided access to its resources, <u>and defined rights and obligations involved in the distribution and consumption of those resources.</u>

(A) and defined rights and obligations involved in the distribution and consumption of those resources
(B) defining rights and obligations involved in their distribution and consumption
(C) and defined rights and obligations as they were involved in its distribution and consumption
(D) whose rights and obligations were defined in their distribution and consumption
(E) the distribution and consumption of them defined by rights and obligations

Choice A is best. The activities listed are presented as parallel ideas and should thus be expressed in grammatically parallel structures. Choice A correctly uses the simple past tense *defined* to parallel *organized* and *provided*. Choice A also correctly joins the last two parallel phrases with *and* and clearly expresses the relationship of *rights and obligations* to *resources*. Choice C preserves parallelism but is wordy, and *its* has no logical referent. Choices B, D, and E each replace the verb phrase with a subordinate modifier, violating parallelism and making the statements ungrammatical. Furthermore, it is unclear what *defining . . . consumption* in B is intended to modify; in D, *whose* incorrectly attributes *rights and obligations* to *resources*; and E presents *rights and obligations* as defining, rather than as being defined.

12. A report by the American Academy for the Advancement of Science has concluded that <u>much of the currently uncontrolled dioxins to which North Americans are exposed comes</u> from the incineration of wastes.

   (A) much of the currently uncontrolled dioxins to which North Americans are exposed comes
   (B) much of the currently uncontrolled dioxins that North Americans are exposed to come
   (C) much of the dioxins that are currently uncontrolled and that North Americans are exposed to comes
   (D) many of the dioxins that are currently uncontrolled and North Americans are exposed to come
   (E) many of the currently uncontrolled dioxins to which North Americans are exposed come

Choices A, B, and C are flawed because the countable noun *dioxins* should be modified by *many* rather than *much*, which is used with uncountable nouns such as "work" or "happiness." In addition, both A and C incorrectly use the singular verb *comes* with the plural noun *dioxins*. Choices C and D are needlessly wordy, and D requires *that* before *North Americans* to be grammatically complete. Choice E, the best answer, is both grammatically correct and concise.

13. In June of 1987, *The Bridge of Trinquetaille,* Vincent van Gogh's view of an iron bridge over the <u>Rhone sold for $20.2 million and it was</u> the second highest price ever paid for a painting at auction.

   (A) Rhone sold for $20.2 million and it was
   (B) Rhone, which sold for $20.2 million, was
   (C) Rhone, was sold for $20.2 million,
   (D) Rhone was sold for $20.2 million, being
   (E) Rhone, sold for $20.2 million, and was

A comma is needed after *Rhone* in choices A and D to set off the modifying phrase that begins *Vincent . . .*; without the comma, the phrase appears to be part of the main clause, and it is thus unclear what noun should govern the verb *sold*. Furthermore, *it* in A has no logical referent, and *being* in D is not idiomatic. Choices B and E produce the illogical statement that the painting *was the second highest price*. Choice C, the best answer, avoids this problem by using a noun phrase in which *price* clearly refers to *$20.2 million*. And by using a comma after *Rhone* to set off the phrase that modifies *The Bridge of Trinquetaille*, C makes the painting the subject of *was sold*.

14. *Bufo marinus* toads, fierce predators that will eat frogs, lizards, and even small birds, <u>are native to South America but were introduced into Florida during the 1930's in an attempt to control</u> pests in the state's vast sugarcane fields.

   (A) are native to South America but were introduced into Florida during the 1930's in an attempt to control
   (B) are native in South America but were introduced into Florida during the 1930's as attempts to control
   (C) are natives of South America but were introduced into Florida during the 1930's in an attempt at controlling
   (D) had been native to South America but were introduced to Florida during the 1930's as an attempt at controlling
   (E) had been natives of South America but were introduced to Florida during the 1930's as attempts at controlling

Choice A is best. The phrasing *are native to* correctly suggests that the toad species is indigenous to, and still exists in, South America. In B, *native in* is unidiomatic; in C and E, *natives of* illogically suggests that each toad now in Florida hails from South America. In D and E, *had been* inaccurately implies that the toads are no longer native, or indigenous, to South America, and *introduced to Florida* is unidiomatic. Both *as attempts* in B and E and *as an attempt* in D are wrong because the attempt consists not of the toads themselves, but of their introduction into the environment. The correct phrase, *in an attempt*, should be completed by an infinitive (here, *to control*), as in A.

15. While some academicians believe that business ethics should be integrated into every business course, others say that students will take ethics seriously <u>only if it would be taught as a separately required course</u>.

   (A) only if it would be taught as a separately required course
   (B) only if it is taught as a separate, required course
   (C) if it is taught only as a course required separately
   (D) if it was taught only as a separate and required course
   (E) if it would only be taught as a required course, separately

Choice B is best: in sentences expressing a conditional result (*x will happen if y happens*), the verb of the main clause should be in the future tense and the verb of the *if* clause should be in the present indicative. Thus, *is taught* (in B) is consistent with *will take*, whereas *would be taught* (in A and E) and *was taught* (in D) are not. For clarity, *only* in C, D, and E should immediately precede the entire *if* clause that it is meant to modify. Also, the intended meaning is distorted when the adverb *separately* is used to modify *required*, as in A and C, or *taught*, as in E; B correctly uses the adjective *separate* to modify *course*.

16. Scientists have observed large concentrations of heavy-metal deposits in the upper twenty centimeters of Baltic Sea sediments, which are consistent with the growth of industrial activity there.

    (A) Baltic Sea sediments, which are consistent with the growth of industrial activity there
    (B) Baltic Sea sediments, where the growth of industrial activity is consistent with these findings
    (C) Baltic Sea sediments, findings consistent with its growth of industrial activity
    (D) sediments from the Baltic Sea, findings consistent with the growth of industrial activity in the area
    (E) sediments from the Baltic Sea, consistent with the growth of industrial activity there

All of the choices but D contain ambiguities. In A and B the words *which* and *where* appear to refer to *sediments*, and in E it is not clear what *consistent* describes. In A, C, and E, there is no logical place to which *there* or *its* could refer. In D, the best choice, the phrase *sediments from the Baltic Sea* tells where the sediments originate, *findings* provides a noun for *consistent* to modify, and *in the area* clearly identifies where the industrial activity is growing.

17. For members of the seventeenth-century Ashanti nation in Africa, animal-hide shields with wooden frames were essential items of military equipment, a method to protect warriors against enemy arrows and spears.

    (A) a method to protect
    (B) as a method protecting
    (C) protecting
    (D) as a protection of
    (E) to protect

Choice C is best because the participle *protecting* begins a phrase that explains what the shields did. Choices A and B awkwardly use the singular word *method* to refer to *items of military equipment* rather than to the use of such items. Also, *a method of protecting* would be more idiomatic than *a method to protect* in A or *a method protecting* in B. In B and D, *as* is incorrect; also, *a protection* in D has no noun for which it can logically substitute. Choice E is incomplete; *used to protect* would have been acceptable.

18. In metalwork one advantage of adhesive-bonding over spot-welding is that the contact, and hence the bonding, is effected continuously over a broad surface instead of a series of regularly spaced points with no bonding in between.

    (A) instead of
    (B) as opposed to
    (C) in contrast with
    (D) rather than at
    (E) as against being at

The corrected sentence must contrast an effect of spot-welding with an effect of adhesive-bonding. To do so logically and grammatically, it must describe the effects in parallel terms. When inserted into the sentence, D produces the parallel construction *over a broad surface rather than at a series*. Having no word such as *over* or *at* to indicate location, choices A, B, and C fail to complete the parallel and so illogically draw a contrast between *surface* and *series*. In E, *as against being* is a wordy and unidiomatic way to establish the intended contrast. Choice D is best.

19. Under a provision of the Constitution that was never applied, Congress has been required to call a convention for considering possible amendments to the document when formally asked to do it by the legislatures of two-thirds of the states.

    (A) was never applied, Congress has been required to call a convention for considering possible amendments to the document when formally asked to do it
    (B) was never applied, there has been a requirement that Congress call a convention for consideration of possible amendments to the document when asked to do it formally
    (C) was never applied, whereby Congress is required to call a convention for considering possible amendments to the document when asked to do it formally
    (D) has never been applied, whereby Congress is required to call a convention to consider possible amendments to the document when formally asked to do so
    (E) has never been applied, Congress is required to call a convention to consider possible amendments to the document when formally asked to do so

Choices A, B, C, and D contain tense errors (the use of *was never applied* with *has been required* in A, for example), unidiomatic expressions (*call . . . for considering*), and uses of a pronoun (*it*) with no noun referent. By introducing the subordinating conjunction *whereby*, C and D produce sentence fragments. Only E, the best choice, corrects all of these problems. The predicate *has never been applied* refers to a span of time, from the writing of the Constitution to the present, rather than to a past event (as *was* does), and the phrase *is required* indicates that the provision still applies. The phrase *call . . . to consider* is idiomatic, and *to do so* can substitute grammatically for it.

20. The current administration, <u>being worried over some foreign trade barriers being removed and our exports failing</u> to increase as a result of deep cuts in the value of the dollar, has formed a group to study ways to sharpen our competitiveness.

    (A) being worried over some foreign trade barriers being removed and our exports failing

    (B) worrying over some foreign trade barriers being removed, also over the failure of our exports

    (C) worried about the removal of some foreign trade barriers and the failure of our exports

    (D) in that they were worried about the removal of some foreign trade barriers and also about the failure of our exports

    (E) because of its worry concerning the removal of some foreign trade barriers, also concerning the failure of our exports

Choice C is best because its phrasing is parallel and concise. A, D, and E begin with unnecessarily wordy phrases. Choice C also uses the idiomatic expression *worried about* rather than *worried over* (as in A) or *worrying over* (as in B); *worried about* is preferable when describing a condition rather than an action. Whereas C uses compact and parallel noun phrases such as *the removal . . . and the failure . . .* , the other choices employ phrases that are wordy, awkward, or nonparallel. D is also flawed in that the plural pronoun *they* does not agree with the singular noun *administration*.

21. In the minds of many people living in England, <u>before Australia was Australia, it was the antipodes</u>, the opposite pole to civilization, an obscure and unimaginable place that was considered the end of the world.

    (A) before Australia was Australia, it was the antipodes

    (B) before there was Australia, it was the antipodes

    (C) it was the antipodes that was Australia

    (D) Australia was what was the antipodes

    (E) Australia was what had been known as the antipodes

Choice A is best, for A alone makes clear that the land now known as Australia was considered the antipodes before it was developed. In B, *it* has no logical referent, because the previous clause describes a time when there was no Australia. Nor does *it* have a referent in C: substituting *Australia* for *it* produces a nonsensical statement. D is wordy, with the unnecessary *what was*, and imprecise in suggesting that Australia was considered the antipodes after it became Australia. E similarly distorts the original meaning, and the past perfect *had been* is inconsistent with the past tense used to establish a time frame for the rest of the sentence.

22. <u>Using a Doppler ultrasound device, fetal heartbeats can be detected by the twelfth week of pregnancy.</u>

    (A) Using a Doppler ultrasound device, fetal heartbeats can be detected by the twelfth week of pregnancy.

    (B) Fetal heartbeats can be detected by the twelfth week of pregnancy, using a Doppler ultrasound device.

    (C) Detecting fetal heartbeats by the twelfth week of pregnancy, a physician can use a Doppler ultrasound device.

    (D) By the twelfth week of pregnancy, fetal heartbeats can be detected using a Doppler ultrasound device by a physician.

    (E) Using a Doppler ultrasound device, a physician can detect fetal heartbeats by the twelfth week of pregnancy.

Choice A presents a dangling modifier. The phrase beginning the sentence has no noun that it can logically modify and hence cannot fit anywhere in the sentence and make sense. Coming first, it modifies *heartbeats*, the nearest free noun in the main clause; that is, choice A says that the heartbeats are using the Doppler ultrasound device. Choice B contains the same main clause and dangling modifier, now at the end. Contrary to intent, the wording in choice C suggests that physicians can use a Doppler ultrasound device after they detect fetal heartbeats. In choice D the phrase *using . . . device* should follow *physician*, the noun it modifies. Choice E is best.

23. Constance Horner, chief of the United States government's personnel agency, has recommended that <u>the use of any dangerous or illegal drug in the five years prior to application for a job be grounds for not hiring an applicant</u>.

    (A) the use of any dangerous or illegal drug in the five years prior to application for a job be grounds for not hiring an applicant

    (B) any dangerous or illegal drug, if used in the five years prior to applying for a job, should be grounds not to hire the applicant

    (C) an applicant's use of any dangerous or illegal drug in the five years prior to application for a job be grounds not to hire them

    (D) an applicant's use of any dangerous or illegal drug in the five years prior to applying for a job are grounds that they not be hired

    (E) for five years prior to applying for a job, an applicant's use of any dangerous or illegal drug be grounds for not hiring them

Choice A is best. The wording of choice B is imprecise, suggesting that any dangerous or illegal drug — not the use of such a substance — should be grounds for not hiring an applicant. In choice C, the pronoun *them* cannot logically refer to *applicant's use*; also, the plural *them* does not agree with the singular noun. Similarly, in choice D the pronoun *they* cannot logically or grammatically refer to *applicant's use*. Choice E can be faulted for using *them*; moreover, E says that the *applicant's use* rather than the applicant is applying for a job, and *for five years prior* illogically modifies *grounds* rather than the use of drugs.

24. <u>Inflation in medical costs slowed in 1986 for the fifth consecutive year but were</u> still about 50 percent greater than the rate of price increases for other items included in the consumer price index.

    (A) Inflation in medical costs slowed in 1986 for the fifth consecutive year but were
    (B) Inflation in medical costs slowed for the fifth consecutive year in 1986 but was
    (C) In 1986 inflation in medical costs were slowed for the fifth consecutive year but were
    (D) 1986 was the fifth consecutive year in which inflation in medical costs slowed but was
    (E) 1986 was the fifth consecutive year that inflation in medical costs were slowed, but they were

Choices A, C, and E are incorrect because in each the verb *were* does not agree in number with *inflation*, the grammatical subject of the clause. Also, the passive construction *were slowed* in C and E wrongly suggests that some external agent is slowing the rate of inflation. Choice D changes the meaning of the original sentence by stating that the inflation in medical costs was greater than the rate of price increases for five consecutive years. In choice E, the plural pronoun *they* suggests that *medical costs* rather than the *inflation in medical costs* are being compared to the rate of price increases. Choice B is best.

25. The most common reasons for an employee's unwillingness to accept a transfer are <u>that mortgage rates are high, housing in the new location costs more, and the difficulty of selling the old home</u>.

    (A) that mortgage rates are high, housing in the new location costs more, and the difficulty of selling the old home
    (B) that mortgage rates are high, housing in the new location costs more, and that it is difficult to sell the old home
    (C) high mortgage rates, the greater cost of housing in the new location, and that the old home is difficult to sell
    (D) high mortgage rates, the greater cost of housing in the new location, and it is difficult to sell the old home
    (E) high mortgage rates, the greater cost of housing in the new location, and the difficulty of selling the old home

Choice A is incorrect because the noun phrase *the difficulty of selling the old home* cannot grammatically complete the structure begun by *that*. Clauses, such as those explaining the first two reasons, are needed after *that*. The corrected sentence will have all three reasons listed in grammatically parallel form. The phrasing of the third reason in choices B, C, and D departs from the parallel wording of the first two by introducing a *that . . .* or an *it . . .* construction. Choice E is best.

Answer Sheet: Form C

Section 1

	A	B	C	D	E
1	Ⓐ	Ⓑ	Ⓒ	Ⓓ	Ⓔ
2	Ⓐ	Ⓑ	Ⓒ	Ⓓ	Ⓔ
3	Ⓐ	Ⓑ	Ⓒ	Ⓓ	Ⓔ
4	Ⓐ	Ⓑ	Ⓒ	Ⓓ	Ⓔ
5	Ⓐ	Ⓑ	Ⓒ	Ⓓ	Ⓔ
6	Ⓐ	Ⓑ	Ⓒ	Ⓓ	Ⓔ
7	Ⓐ	Ⓑ	Ⓒ	Ⓓ	Ⓔ
8	Ⓐ	Ⓑ	Ⓒ	Ⓓ	Ⓔ
9	Ⓐ	Ⓑ	Ⓒ	Ⓓ	Ⓔ
10	Ⓐ	Ⓑ	Ⓒ	Ⓓ	Ⓔ
11	Ⓐ	Ⓑ	Ⓒ	Ⓓ	Ⓔ
12	Ⓐ	Ⓑ	Ⓒ	Ⓓ	Ⓔ
13	Ⓐ	Ⓑ	Ⓒ	Ⓓ	Ⓔ
14	Ⓐ	Ⓑ	Ⓒ	Ⓓ	Ⓔ
15	Ⓐ	Ⓑ	Ⓒ	Ⓓ	Ⓔ
16	Ⓐ	Ⓑ	Ⓒ	Ⓓ	Ⓔ
17	Ⓐ	Ⓑ	Ⓒ	Ⓓ	Ⓔ
18	Ⓐ	Ⓑ	Ⓒ	Ⓓ	Ⓔ
19	Ⓐ	Ⓑ	Ⓒ	Ⓓ	Ⓔ
20	Ⓐ	Ⓑ	Ⓒ	Ⓓ	Ⓔ
21	Ⓐ	Ⓑ	Ⓒ	Ⓓ	Ⓔ
22	Ⓐ	Ⓑ	Ⓒ	Ⓓ	Ⓔ
23	Ⓐ	Ⓑ	Ⓒ	Ⓓ	Ⓔ
24	Ⓐ	Ⓑ	Ⓒ	Ⓓ	Ⓔ
25	Ⓐ	Ⓑ	Ⓒ	Ⓓ	Ⓔ

Section 2

	A	B	C	D	E
1	Ⓐ	Ⓑ	Ⓒ	Ⓓ	Ⓔ
2	Ⓐ	Ⓑ	Ⓒ	Ⓓ	Ⓔ
3	Ⓐ	Ⓑ	Ⓒ	Ⓓ	Ⓔ
4	Ⓐ	Ⓑ	Ⓒ	Ⓓ	Ⓔ
5	Ⓐ	Ⓑ	Ⓒ	Ⓓ	Ⓔ
6	Ⓐ	Ⓑ	Ⓒ	Ⓓ	Ⓔ
7	Ⓐ	Ⓑ	Ⓒ	Ⓓ	Ⓔ
8	Ⓐ	Ⓑ	Ⓒ	Ⓓ	Ⓔ
9	Ⓐ	Ⓑ	Ⓒ	Ⓓ	Ⓔ
10	Ⓐ	Ⓑ	Ⓒ	Ⓓ	Ⓔ
11	Ⓐ	Ⓑ	Ⓒ	Ⓓ	Ⓔ
12	Ⓐ	Ⓑ	Ⓒ	Ⓓ	Ⓔ
13	Ⓐ	Ⓑ	Ⓒ	Ⓓ	Ⓔ
14	Ⓐ	Ⓑ	Ⓒ	Ⓓ	Ⓔ
15	Ⓐ	Ⓑ	Ⓒ	Ⓓ	Ⓔ
16	Ⓐ	Ⓑ	Ⓒ	Ⓓ	Ⓔ
17	Ⓐ	Ⓑ	Ⓒ	Ⓓ	Ⓔ
18	Ⓐ	Ⓑ	Ⓒ	Ⓓ	Ⓔ
19	Ⓐ	Ⓑ	Ⓒ	Ⓓ	Ⓔ
20	Ⓐ	Ⓑ	Ⓒ	Ⓓ	Ⓔ
21	Ⓐ	Ⓑ	Ⓒ	Ⓓ	Ⓔ
22	Ⓐ	Ⓑ	Ⓒ	Ⓓ	Ⓔ
23	Ⓐ	Ⓑ	Ⓒ	Ⓓ	Ⓔ
24	Ⓐ	Ⓑ	Ⓒ	Ⓓ	Ⓔ
25	Ⓐ	Ⓑ	Ⓒ	Ⓓ	Ⓔ

Section 3

	A	B	C	D	E
1	Ⓐ	Ⓑ	Ⓒ	Ⓓ	Ⓔ
2	Ⓐ	Ⓑ	Ⓒ	Ⓓ	Ⓔ
3	Ⓐ	Ⓑ	Ⓒ	Ⓓ	Ⓔ
4	Ⓐ	Ⓑ	Ⓒ	Ⓓ	Ⓔ
5	Ⓐ	Ⓑ	Ⓒ	Ⓓ	Ⓔ
6	Ⓐ	Ⓑ	Ⓒ	Ⓓ	Ⓔ
7	Ⓐ	Ⓑ	Ⓒ	Ⓓ	Ⓔ
8	Ⓐ	Ⓑ	Ⓒ	Ⓓ	Ⓔ
9	Ⓐ	Ⓑ	Ⓒ	Ⓓ	Ⓔ
10	Ⓐ	Ⓑ	Ⓒ	Ⓓ	Ⓔ
11	Ⓐ	Ⓑ	Ⓒ	Ⓓ	Ⓔ
12	Ⓐ	Ⓑ	Ⓒ	Ⓓ	Ⓔ
13	Ⓐ	Ⓑ	Ⓒ	Ⓓ	Ⓔ
14	Ⓐ	Ⓑ	Ⓒ	Ⓓ	Ⓔ
15	Ⓐ	Ⓑ	Ⓒ	Ⓓ	Ⓔ
16	Ⓐ	Ⓑ	Ⓒ	Ⓓ	Ⓔ
17	Ⓐ	Ⓑ	Ⓒ	Ⓓ	Ⓔ
18	Ⓐ	Ⓑ	Ⓒ	Ⓓ	Ⓔ
19	Ⓐ	Ⓑ	Ⓒ	Ⓓ	Ⓔ
20	Ⓐ	Ⓑ	Ⓒ	Ⓓ	Ⓔ
21	Ⓐ	Ⓐ	Ⓒ	Ⓓ	Ⓔ
22	Ⓐ	Ⓑ	Ⓒ	Ⓓ	Ⓔ
23	Ⓐ	Ⓑ	Ⓒ	Ⓓ	Ⓔ
24	Ⓐ	Ⓑ	Ⓒ	Ⓓ	Ⓔ
25	Ⓐ	Ⓑ	Ⓒ	Ⓓ	Ⓔ

Section 4

	A	B	C	D	E
1	Ⓐ	Ⓑ	Ⓒ	Ⓓ	Ⓔ
2	Ⓐ	Ⓑ	Ⓒ	Ⓓ	Ⓔ
3	Ⓐ	Ⓑ	Ⓒ	Ⓓ	Ⓔ
4	Ⓐ	Ⓑ	Ⓒ	Ⓓ	Ⓔ
5	Ⓐ	Ⓑ	Ⓒ	Ⓓ	Ⓔ
6	Ⓐ	Ⓑ	Ⓒ	Ⓓ	Ⓔ
7	Ⓐ	Ⓑ	Ⓒ	Ⓓ	Ⓔ
8	Ⓐ	Ⓑ	Ⓒ	Ⓓ	Ⓔ
9	Ⓐ	Ⓑ	Ⓒ	Ⓓ	Ⓔ
10	Ⓐ	Ⓑ	Ⓒ	Ⓓ	Ⓔ
11	Ⓐ	Ⓑ	Ⓒ	Ⓓ	Ⓔ
12	Ⓐ	Ⓑ	Ⓒ	Ⓓ	Ⓔ
13	Ⓐ	Ⓑ	Ⓒ	Ⓓ	Ⓔ
14	Ⓐ	Ⓑ	Ⓒ	Ⓓ	Ⓔ
15	Ⓐ	Ⓑ	Ⓒ	Ⓓ	Ⓔ
16	Ⓐ	Ⓑ	Ⓒ	Ⓓ	Ⓔ
17	Ⓐ	Ⓑ	Ⓒ	Ⓓ	Ⓔ
18	Ⓐ	Ⓑ	Ⓒ	Ⓓ	Ⓔ
19	Ⓐ	Ⓑ	Ⓒ	Ⓓ	Ⓔ
20	Ⓐ	Ⓑ	Ⓒ	Ⓓ	Ⓔ
21	Ⓐ	Ⓑ	Ⓒ	Ⓓ	Ⓔ
22	Ⓐ	Ⓑ	Ⓒ	Ⓓ	Ⓔ
23	Ⓐ	Ⓑ	Ⓒ	Ⓓ	Ⓔ
24	Ⓐ	Ⓑ	Ⓒ	Ⓓ	Ⓔ
25	Ⓐ	Ⓑ	Ⓒ	Ⓓ	Ⓔ

Section 5

	A	B	C	D	E
1	Ⓐ	Ⓑ	Ⓒ	Ⓓ	Ⓔ
2	Ⓐ	Ⓑ	Ⓒ	Ⓓ	Ⓔ
3	Ⓐ	Ⓑ	Ⓒ	Ⓓ	Ⓔ
4	Ⓐ	Ⓑ	Ⓒ	Ⓓ	Ⓔ
5	Ⓐ	Ⓑ	Ⓒ	Ⓓ	Ⓔ
6	Ⓐ	Ⓑ	Ⓒ	Ⓓ	Ⓔ
7	Ⓐ	Ⓑ	Ⓒ	Ⓓ	Ⓔ
8	Ⓐ	Ⓑ	Ⓒ	Ⓓ	Ⓔ
9	Ⓐ	Ⓑ	Ⓒ	Ⓓ	Ⓔ
10	Ⓐ	Ⓑ	Ⓒ	Ⓓ	Ⓔ
11	Ⓐ	Ⓑ	Ⓒ	Ⓓ	Ⓔ
12	Ⓐ	Ⓑ	Ⓒ	Ⓓ	Ⓔ
13	Ⓐ	Ⓑ	Ⓒ	Ⓓ	Ⓔ
14	Ⓐ	Ⓑ	Ⓒ	Ⓓ	Ⓔ
15	Ⓐ	Ⓑ	Ⓒ	Ⓓ	Ⓔ
16	Ⓐ	Ⓑ	Ⓒ	Ⓓ	Ⓔ
17	Ⓐ	Ⓑ	Ⓒ	Ⓓ	Ⓔ
18	Ⓐ	Ⓑ	Ⓒ	Ⓓ	Ⓔ
19	Ⓐ	Ⓑ	Ⓒ	Ⓓ	Ⓔ
20	Ⓐ	Ⓑ	Ⓒ	Ⓓ	Ⓔ
21	Ⓐ	Ⓑ	Ⓒ	Ⓓ	Ⓔ
22	Ⓐ	Ⓑ	Ⓒ	Ⓓ	Ⓔ
23	Ⓐ	Ⓑ	Ⓒ	Ⓓ	Ⓔ
24	Ⓐ	Ⓑ	Ⓒ	Ⓓ	Ⓔ
25	Ⓐ	Ⓑ	Ⓒ	Ⓓ	Ⓔ

Section 6

	A	B	C	D	E
1	Ⓐ	Ⓑ	Ⓒ	Ⓓ	Ⓔ
2	Ⓐ	Ⓑ	Ⓒ	Ⓓ	Ⓔ
3	Ⓐ	Ⓑ	Ⓒ	Ⓓ	Ⓔ
4	Ⓐ	Ⓑ	Ⓒ	Ⓓ	Ⓔ
5	Ⓐ	Ⓑ	Ⓒ	Ⓓ	Ⓔ
6	Ⓐ	Ⓑ	Ⓒ	Ⓓ	Ⓔ
7	Ⓐ	Ⓑ	Ⓒ	Ⓓ	Ⓔ
8	Ⓐ	Ⓑ	Ⓒ	Ⓓ	Ⓔ
9	Ⓐ	Ⓑ	Ⓒ	Ⓓ	Ⓔ
10	Ⓐ	Ⓑ	Ⓒ	Ⓓ	Ⓔ
11	Ⓐ	Ⓑ	Ⓒ	Ⓓ	Ⓔ
12	Ⓐ	Ⓑ	Ⓒ	Ⓓ	Ⓔ
13	Ⓐ	Ⓑ	Ⓒ	Ⓓ	Ⓔ
14	Ⓐ	Ⓑ	Ⓒ	Ⓓ	Ⓔ
15	Ⓐ	Ⓑ	Ⓒ	Ⓓ	Ⓔ
16	Ⓐ	Ⓑ	Ⓒ	Ⓓ	Ⓔ
17	Ⓐ	Ⓑ	Ⓒ	Ⓓ	Ⓔ
18	Ⓐ	Ⓑ	Ⓒ	Ⓓ	Ⓔ
19	Ⓐ	Ⓑ	Ⓒ	Ⓓ	Ⓔ
20	Ⓐ	Ⓑ	Ⓒ	Ⓓ	Ⓔ
21	Ⓐ	Ⓑ	Ⓒ	Ⓓ	Ⓔ
22	Ⓐ	Ⓑ	Ⓒ	Ⓓ	Ⓔ
23	Ⓐ	Ⓑ	Ⓒ	Ⓓ	Ⓔ
24	Ⓐ	Ⓑ	Ⓒ	Ⓓ	Ⓔ
25	Ⓐ	Ⓑ	Ⓒ	Ⓓ	Ⓔ

Print your full name here: _____
    (last)   (first)   (middle)

Graduate Management Admission Test

SECTION 1

Time—30 minutes

25 Questions

Directions: Each of the data sufficiency problems below consists of a question and two statements, labeled (1) and (2), in which certain data are given. You have to decide whether the data given in the statements are <u>sufficient</u> for answering the question. Using the data given in the statements <u>plus</u> your knowledge of mathematics and everyday facts (such as the number of days in July or the meaning of <u>counterclockwise</u>), you are to fill in oval

   A   if statement (1) ALONE is sufficient, but statement (2) alone is not sufficient to answer the question asked;

   B   if statement (2) ALONE is sufficient, but statement (1) alone is not sufficient to answer the question asked;

   C   if BOTH statements (1) and (2) TOGETHER are sufficient to answer the question asked, but NEITHER statement ALONE is sufficient;

   D   if EACH statement ALONE is sufficient to answer the question asked;

   E   if statements (1) and (2) TOGETHER are NOT sufficient to answer the question asked, and additional data specific to the problem are needed.

Numbers: All numbers used are real numbers.

Figures: A figure in a data sufficiency problem will conform to the information given in the question, but will not necessarily conform to the additional information given in statements (1) and (2).

You may assume that lines shown as straight are straight and that angle measures are greater than zero.

You may assume that the positions of points, angles, regions, etc., exist in the order shown.

All figures lie in a plane unless otherwise indicated.

Example:

In $\triangle PQR$, what is the value of x ?

(1) $PQ = PR$

(2) $y = 40$

Explanation: According to statement (1), $PQ = PR$; therefore, $\triangle PQR$ is isosceles and $y = z$. Since $x + y + z = 180$, $x + 2y = 180$. Since statement (1) does not give a value for y, you cannot answer the question using statement (1) by itself. According to statement (2), $y = 40$; therefore, $x + z = 140$. Since statement (2) does not give a value for z, you cannot answer the question using statement (2) by itself. Using both statements together, you can find y and z; therefore, you can find x, and the answer to the problem is C.

GO ON TO THE NEXT PAGE.

A   Statement (1) ALONE is sufficient, but statement (2) alone is not sufficient.
B   Statement (2) ALONE is sufficient, but statement (1) alone is not sufficient.
C   BOTH statements TOGETHER are sufficient, but NEITHER statement ALONE is sufficient.
D   EACH statement ALONE is sufficient.
E   Statements (1) and (2) TOGETHER are NOT sufficient.

1. The regular price for canned soup was reduced during a sale. How much money could one have saved by purchasing a dozen 7-ounce cans of soup at the reduced price rather than at the regular price?

   (1)   The regular price for the 7-ounce cans was 3 for a dollar.

   (2)   The reduced price for the 7-ounce cans was 4 for a dollar.

2. If on a fishing trip Jim and Tom each caught some fish, which one caught more fish?

   (1)   Jim caught $\frac{2}{3}$ as many fish as Tom.

   (2)   After Tom stopped fishing, Jim continued fishing until he had caught 12 fish.

3. If $5x + 3y = 17$, what is the value of x?

   (1) x is a positive integer.

   (2) $y = 4x$

4. Yesterday Nan parked her car at a certain parking garage that charges more for the first hour than for each additional hour. If Nan's total parking charge at the garage yesterday was $3.75, for how many hours of parking was she charged?

   (1)   Parking charges at the garage are $0.75 for the first hour and $0.50 for each additional hour or fraction of an hour.

   (2)   If the charge for the first hour had been $1.00, Nan's total parking charge would have been $4.00.

5. If r and s are integers, is $r + s$ divisible by 3 ?

   (1) s is divisible by 3.

   (2) r is divisible by 3.

GO ON TO THE NEXT PAGE.

A Statement (1) ALONE is sufficient, but statement (2) alone is not sufficient.
B Statement (2) ALONE is sufficient, but statement (1) alone is not sufficient.
C BOTH statements TOGETHER are sufficient, but NEITHER statement ALONE is sufficient.
D EACH statement ALONE is sufficient.
E Statements (1) and (2) TOGETHER are NOT sufficient.

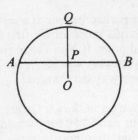

6. What is the radius of the circle above with center O?

   (1) The ratio of OP to PQ is 1 to 2.

   (2) P is the midpoint of chord AB.

7. A certain 4-liter solution of vinegar and water consists of x liters of vinegar and y liters of water. How many liters of vinegar does the solution contain?

   (1) $\frac{x}{4} = \frac{3}{8}$

   (2) $\frac{y}{4} = \frac{5}{8}$

8. Is $x < 0$?

   (1) $-2x > 0$

   (2) $x^3 < 0$

9. Of the 230 single-family homes built in City X last year, how many were occupied at the end of the year?

   (1) Of all single-family homes in City X, 90 percent were occupied at the end of last year.

   (2) A total of 7,200 single-family homes in City X were occupied at the end of last year.

10. Does the product $jkmn$ equal 1?

   (1) $\frac{jk}{mn} = 1$

   (2) $j = \frac{1}{k}$ and $m = \frac{1}{n}$

GO ON TO THE NEXT PAGE.

A Statement (1) ALONE is sufficient, but statement (2) alone is not sufficient.
B Statement (2) ALONE is sufficient, but statement (1) alone is not sufficient.
C BOTH statements TOGETHER are sufficient, but NEITHER statement ALONE is sufficient.
D EACH statement ALONE is sufficient.
E Statements (1) and (2) TOGETHER are NOT sufficient.

11. How many of the boys in a group of 100 children have brown hair?

   (1) Of the children in the group, 60 percent have brown hair.

   (2) Of the children in the group, 40 are boys.

12. Is the perimeter of square S greater than the perimeter of equilateral triangle T?

   (1) The ratio of the length of a side of S to the length of a side of T is $4 : 5$.

   (2) The sum of the lengths of a side of S and a side of T is 18.

13. If p and q are positive integers and $pq = 24$, what is the value of p?

   (1) $\frac{q}{6}$ is an integer.

   (2) $\frac{p}{2}$ is an integer.

14. If $x \neq 0$, what is the value of $\left(\frac{x^p}{x^q}\right)^4$?

   (1) $p = q$

   (2) $x = 3$

15. From May 1, 1960 to May 1, 1975, the closing price of a share of stock X doubled. What was the closing price of a share of stock X on May 1, 1960?

   (1) From May 1, 1975, to May 1, 1984, the closing price of a share of stock X doubled.

   (2) From May 1, 1975, to May 1, 1984, the closing price of a share of stock X increased by $4.50.

GO ON TO THE NEXT PAGE.

A Statement (1) ALONE is sufficient, but statement (2) alone is not sufficient.
B Statement (2) ALONE is sufficient, but statement (1) alone is not sufficient.
C BOTH statements TOGETHER are sufficient, but NEITHER statement ALONE is sufficient.
D EACH statement ALONE is sufficient.
E Statements (1) and (2) TOGETHER are NOT sufficient.

16. If d is a positive integer, is $\sqrt{d}$ an integer?

(1) d is the square of an integer.

(2) $\sqrt{d}$ is the square of an integer.

17. If Q is an integer between 10 and 100, what is the value of Q ?

(1) One of Q's digits is 3 more than the other, and the sum of its digits is 9.

(2) $Q < 50$

18. If digit h is the hundredths' digit in the decimal $d = 0.2h6$, what is the value of d, rounded to the nearest tenth?

(1) $d < \frac{1}{4}$

(2) $h < 5$

19. What is the value of $x^2 - y^2$?

(1) $x - y = y + 2$

(2) $x - y = \dfrac{1}{x + y}$

20. If $\circ$ represents one of the operations $+$, $-$, and $\times$, is $k \circ (\ell + m) = (k \circ \ell) + (k \circ m)$ for all numbers k, ℓ, and m?

(1) $k \circ 1$ is not equal to $1 \circ k$ for some numbers k.

(2) $\circ$ represents subtraction.

21. What was Janet's score on the fourth physics test she took?

(1) Her score on the fourth test was 12 points higher than her average (arithmetic mean) score on the first three tests she took.

(2) Her score on the fourth test raised her average (arithmetic mean) test score from 87 to 90.

GO ON TO THE NEXT PAGE.

A Statement (1) ALONE is sufficient, but statement (2) alone is not sufficient.
B Statement (2) ALONE is sufficient, but statement (1) alone is not sufficient.
C BOTH statements TOGETHER are sufficient, but NEITHER statement ALONE is sufficient.
D EACH statement ALONE is sufficient.
E Statements (1) and (2) TOGETHER are NOT sufficient.

22. If $x + y > 0$, is $x > |y|$?

(1) $x > y$

(2) $y < 0$

23. If x is an integer, is $(x + p)(x + q)$ an even integer?

(1) q is an even integer.

(2) p is an even integer.

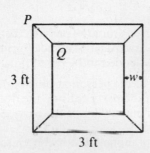

3 ft

←w→

3 ft

24. The figure above shows the dimensions of a square picture frame that was constructed using four pieces of frame as shown. If w is the width of each piece of the frame, what is the area of each piece?

(1) $w = 3$ inches

(2) $PQ = \sqrt{18}$ inches

25. A total of 774 doctorates in mathematics were granted to United States citizens by American universities in the 1972-1973 school year, and W of these doctorates were granted to women. The total of such doctorates in the 1986-1987 school year was 362, and w of these were granted to women. If the number of doctorates in mathematics granted to female citizens of the United States by American universities decreased from the 1972-1973 school year to the 1986-1987 school year, was the decrease less than 10 percent?

(1) $\dfrac{1}{10} < \dfrac{W}{774} < \dfrac{1}{9}$

(2) $W = w + 5$

STOP

IF YOU FINISH BEFORE TIME IS CALLED, YOU MAY CHECK YOUR WORK ON THIS SECTION ONLY.
DO NOT TURN TO ANY OTHER SECTION IN THE TEST.

SECTION 2

Time — 30 minutes

25 Questions

Directions: Each passage in this group is followed by questions based on its content. After reading a passage, choose the best answer to each question and fill in the corresponding oval on the answer sheet. Answer all questions following a passage on the basis of what is <u>stated</u> or <u>implied</u> in that passage.

In 1896 a Georgia couple suing for damages in the accidental death of their two year old was told that since the child had made no real economic contribution to the
Line family, there was no liability for damages. In contrast,
(5) less than a century later, in 1979, the parents of a three year old sued in New York for accidental-death damages and won an award of $750,000.

The transformation in social values implicit in juxtaposing these two incidents is the subject of Viviana
(10) Zelizer's excellent book, *Pricing the Priceless Child*. During the nineteenth century, she argues, the concept of the "useful" child who contributed to the family economy gave way gradually to the present-day notion of the "useless" child who, though producing no income
(15) for, and indeed extremely costly to, its parents, is yet considered emotionally "priceless." Well established among segments of the middle and upper classes by the mid-1800's, this new view of childhood spread throughout society in the late-nineteenth and early-twentieth
(20) centuries as reformers introduced child-labor regulations and compulsory education laws predicated in part on the assumption that a child's emotional value made child labor taboo.

For Zelizer the origins of this transformation were
(25) many and complex. The gradual erosion of children's productive value in a maturing industrial economy, the decline in birth and death rates, especially in child mortality, and the development of the companionate family (a family in which members were united by
(30) explicit bonds of love rather than duty) were all factors critical in changing the assessment of children's worth. Yet "expulsion of children from the 'cash nexus,' . . . although clearly shaped by profound changes in the economic, occupational, and family structures," Zelizer
(35) maintains, "was also part of a cultural process of 'sacralization' of children's lives." Protecting children from the crass business world became enormously important for late-nineteenth-century middle-class Americans, she suggests; this sacralization was a way of resisting what
(40) they perceived as the relentless corruption of human values by the marketplace.

In stressing the cultural determinants of a child's worth, Zelizer takes issue with practitioners of the new "sociological economics," who have analyzed such tradi-
(45) tionally sociological topics as crime, marriage, education, and health solely in terms of their economic determinants. Allowing only a small role for cultural forces

in the form of individual "preferences," these sociologists tend to view all human behavior as directed primarily by
(50) the principle of maximizing economic gain. Zelizer is highly critical of this approach, and emphasizes instead the opposite phenomenon: the power of social values to transform price. As children became more valuable in emotional terms, she argues, their "exchange" or "sur-
(55) render" value on the market, that is, the conversion of their intangible worth into cash terms, became much greater.

1. It can be inferred from the passage that accidental-death damage awards in America during the nineteenth century tended to be based principally on the

(A) earnings of the person at time of death
(B) wealth of the party causing the death
(C) degree of culpability of the party causing the death
(D) amount of money that had been spent on the person killed
(E) amount of suffering endured by the family of the person killed

2. It can be inferred from the passage that in the early 1800's children were generally regarded by their families as individuals who

(A) needed enormous amounts of security and affection
(B) required constant supervision while working
(C) were important to the economic well-being of a family
(D) were unsuited to spending long hours in school
(E) were financial burdens assumed for the good of society

GO ON TO THE NEXT PAGE.

3. Which of the following alternative explanations of the change in the cash value of children would be most likely to be put forward by sociological economists as they are described in the passage?

(A) The cash value of children rose during the nineteenth century because parents began to increase their emotional investment in the upbringing of their children.

(B) The cash value of children rose during the nineteenth century because their expected earnings over the course of a lifetime increased greatly.

(C) The cash value of children rose during the nineteenth century because the spread of humanitarian ideals resulted in a wholesale reappraisal of the worth of an individual.

(D) The cash value of children rose during the nineteenth century because compulsory education laws reduced the supply, and thus raised the costs, of available child labor.

(E) The cash value of children rose during the nineteenth century because of changes in the way negligence law assessed damages in accidental-death cases.

4. The primary purpose of the passage is to

(A) review the literature in a new academic subfield
(B) present the central thesis of a recent book
(C) contrast two approaches to analyzing historical change
(D) refute a traditional explanation of a social phenomenon
(E) encourage further work on a neglected historical topic

5. It can be inferred from the passage that which of the following statements was true of American families over the course of the nineteenth century?

(A) The average size of families grew considerably.
(B) The percentage of families involved in industrial work declined dramatically.
(C) Family members became more emotionally bonded to one another.
(D) Family members spent an increasing amount of time working with each other.
(E) Family members became more economically dependent on each other.

6. Zelizer refers to all of the following as important influences in changing the assessment of children's worth EXCEPT changes in

(A) the mortality rate
(B) the nature of industry
(C) the nature of the family
(D) attitudes toward reform movements
(E) attitudes toward the marketplace

7. Which of the following would be most consistent with the practices of sociological economics as these practices are described in the passage?

(A) Arguing that most health-care professionals enter the field because they believe it to be the most socially useful of any occupation

(B) Arguing that most college students choose majors that they believe will lead to the most highly paid jobs available to them

(C) Arguing that most decisions about marriage and divorce are based on rational assessments of the likelihood that each partner will remain committed to the relationship

(D) Analyzing changes in the number of people enrolled in colleges and universities as a function of changes in the economic health of these institutions

(E) Analyzing changes in the ages at which people get married as a function of a change in the average number of years that young people have lived away from their parents

GO ON TO THE NEXT PAGE.

Prior to 1975, union efforts to organize public-sector clerical workers, most of whom are women, were somewhat limited. The factors favoring unionization drives
Line
(5) seem to have been either the presence of large numbers of workers, as in New York City, to make it worth the effort, or the concentration of small numbers in one or two locations, such as a hospital, to make it relatively easy. Receptivity to unionization on the workers' part was also a consideration, but when there were large
(10) numbers involved or the clerical workers were the only unorganized group in a jurisdiction, the multioccupational unions would often try to organize them regardless of the workers' initial receptivity. The strategic reasoning was based, first, on the concern that politi-
(15) cians and administrators might play off unionized against nonunionized workers, and, second, on the conviction that a fully unionized public work force meant power, both at the bargaining table and in the legislature. In localities where clerical workers were few
(20) in number, were scattered in several workplaces, and expressed no interest in being organized, unions more often than not ignored them in the pre-1975 period.

But since the mid-1970's, a different strategy has emerged. In 1977, 34 percent of government clerical
(25) workers were represented by a labor organization, compared with 46 percent of government professionals, 44 percent of government blue-collar workers, and 41 percent of government service workers. Since then, however, the biggest increases in public-sector unioniza-
(30) tion have been among clerical workers. Between 1977 and 1980, the number of unionized government workers in blue-collar and service occupations increased only about 1.5 percent, while in the white-collar occupations the increase was 20 percent and among clerical workers
(35) in particular, the increase was 22 percent.

What accounts for this upsurge in unionization among clerical workers? First, more women have entered the work force in the past few years, and more of them plan to remain working until retirement age. Conse-
(40) quently, they are probably more concerned than their predecessors were about job security and economic benefits. Also, the women's movement has succeeded in legitimizing the economic and political activism of women on their own behalf, thereby producing a more positive atti-
(45) tude toward unions. The absence of any comparable increase in unionization among private-sector clerical workers, however, identifies the primary catalyst—the structural change in the multioccupational public-sector unions themselves. Over the past twenty years, the occu-
(50) pational distribution in these unions has been steadily shifting from predominantly blue-collar to predominantly white-collar. Because there are far more women in white-collar jobs, an increase in the proportion of female members has accompanied the occupational shift
(55) and has altered union policy-making in favor of organizing women and addressing women's issues.

8. According to the passage, the public-sector workers who were most likely to belong to unions in 1977 were

(A) professionals
(B) managers
(C) clerical workers
(D) service workers
(E) blue-collar workers

9. The author cites union efforts to achieve a fully unionized work force (lines 13-19) in order to account for why

(A) politicians might try to oppose public-sector union organizing
(B) public-sector unions have recently focused on organizing women
(C) early organizing efforts often focused on areas where there were large numbers of workers
(D) union efforts with regard to public-sector clerical workers increased dramatically after 1975
(E) unions sometimes tried to organize workers regardless of the workers' initial interest in unionization

10. The author's claim that, since the mid-1970's, a new strategy has emerged in the unionization of public-sector clerical workers (line 23) would be strengthened if the author

(A) described more fully the attitudes of clerical workers toward labor unions
(B) compared the organizing strategies employed by private-sector unions with those of public-sector unions
(C) explained why politicians and administrators sometimes oppose unionization of clerical workers
(D) indicated that the number of unionized public-sector clerical workers was increasing even before the mid-1970's
(E) showed that the factors that favored unionization drives among these workers prior to 1975 have decreased in importance

GO ON TO THE NEXT PAGE.

11. According to the passage, in the period prior to 1975, each of the following considerations helped determine whether a union would attempt to organize a certain group of clerical workers EXCEPT

(A) the number of clerical workers in that group
(B) the number of women among the clerical workers in that group
(C) whether the clerical workers in that area were concentrated in one workplace or scattered over several workplaces
(D) the degree to which the clerical workers in that group were interested in unionization
(E) whether all the other workers in the same jurisdiction as that group of clerical workers were unionized

12. The author states that which of the following is a consequence of the women's movement of recent years?

(A) An increase in the number of women entering the work force
(B) A structural change in multioccupational public-sector unions
(C) A more positive attitude on the part of women toward unions
(D) An increase in the proportion of clerical workers that are women
(E) An increase in the number of women in administrative positions

13. The main concern of the passage is to

(A) advocate particular strategies for future efforts to organize certain workers into labor unions
(B) explain differences in the unionized proportions of various groups of public-sector workers
(C) evaluate the effectiveness of certain kinds of labor unions that represent public-sector workers
(D) analyze and explain an increase in unionization among a certain category of workers
(E) describe and distinguish strategies appropriate to organizing different categories of workers

14. The author implies that if the increase in the number of women in the work force and the impact of the women's movement were the main causes of the rise in unionization of public-sector clerical workers, then

(A) more women would hold administrative positions in unions
(B) more women who hold political offices would have positive attitudes toward labor unions
(C) there would be an equivalent rise in unionization of private-sector clerical workers
(D) unions would have shown more interest than they have in organizing women
(E) the increase in the number of unionized public-sector clerical workers would have been greater than it has been

15. The author suggests that it would be disadvantageous to a union if

(A) many workers in the locality were not unionized
(B) the union contributed to political campaigns
(C) the union included only public-sector workers
(D) the union included workers from several jurisdictions
(E) the union included members from only a few occupations

16. The author implies that, in comparison with working women today, women working in the years prior to the mid-1970's showed a greater tendency to

(A) prefer smaller workplaces
(B) express a positive attitude toward labor unions
(C) maximize job security and economic benefits
(D) side with administrators in labor disputes
(E) quit working prior to retirement age

GO ON TO THE NEXT PAGE.

Milankovitch proposed in the early twentieth century that the ice ages were caused by variations in the Earth's orbit around the Sun. For sometime this theory was considered untestable, largely because there was no suffi-
Line
(5) ciently precise chronology of the ice ages with which the orbital variations could be matched.

To establish such a chronology it is necessary to determine the relative amounts of land ice that existed at various times in the Earth's past. A recent discovery
(10) makes such a determination possible: relative land-ice volume for a given period can be deduced from the ratio of two oxygen isotopes, 16 and 18, found in ocean sediments. Almost all the oxygen in water is oxygen 16, but a few molecules out of every thousand incorporate the
(15) heavier isotope 18. When an ice age begins, the continental ice sheets grow, steadily reducing the amount of water evaporated from the ocean that will eventually return to it. Because heavier isotopes tend to be left behind when water evaporates from the ocean surfaces,
(20) the remaining ocean water becomes progressively enriched in oxygen 18. The degree of enrichment can be determined by analyzing ocean sediments of the period, because these sediments are composed of calcium carbonate shells of marine organisms, shells that were
(25) constructed with oxygen atoms drawn from the surrounding ocean. The higher the ratio of oxygen 18 to oxygen 16 in a sedimentary specimen, the more land ice there was when the sediment was laid down.

As an indicator of shifts in the Earth's climate, the
(30) isotope record has two advantages. First, it is a global record: there is remarkably little variation in isotope ratios in sedimentary specimens taken from different continental locations. Second, it is a more continuous record than that taken from rocks on land. Because of
(35) these advantages, sedimentary evidence can be dated with sufficient accuracy by radiometric methods to establish a precise chronology of the ice ages. The dated isotope record shows that the fluctuations in global ice volume over the past several hundred thousand years
(40) have a pattern: an ice age occurs roughly once every 100,000 years. These data have established a strong connection between variations in the Earth's orbit and the periodicity of the ice ages.

However, it is important to note that other factors,
(45) such as volcanic particulates or variations in the amount of sunlight received by the Earth, could potentially have affected the climate. The advantage of the Milankovitch theory is that it is testable; changes in the Earth's orbit can be calculated and dated by applying Newton's laws
(50) of gravity to progressively earlier configurations of the bodies in the solar system. Yet the lack of information about other possible factors affecting global climate does not make them unimportant.

17. In the passage, the author is primarily interested in

(A) suggesting an alternative to an outdated research method
(B) introducing a new research method that calls an accepted theory into question
(C) emphasizing the instability of data gathered from the application of a new scientific method
(D) presenting a theory and describing a new method to test that theory
(E) initiating a debate about a widely accepted theory

18. The author of the passage would be most likely to agree with which of the following statements about the Milankovitch theory?

(A) It is the only possible explanation for the ice ages.
(B) It is too limited to provide a plausible explanation for the ice ages, despite recent research findings.
(C) It cannot be tested and confirmed until further research on volcanic activity is done.
(D) It is one plausible explanation, though not the only one, for the ice ages.
(E) It is not a plausible explanation for the ice ages, although it has opened up promising possibilities for future research.

19. It can be inferred from the passage that the isotope record taken from ocean sediments would be less useful to researchers if which of the following were true?

(A) It indicated that lighter isotopes of oxygen predominated at certain times.
(B) It had far more gaps in its sequence than the record taken from rocks on land.
(C) It indicated that climate shifts did not occur every 100,000 years.
(D) It indicated that the ratios of oxygen 16 and oxygen 18 in ocean water were not consistent with those found in fresh water.
(E) It stretched back for only a million years.

GO ON TO THE NEXT PAGE.

20. According to the passage, which of the following is true of the ratios of oxygen isotopes in ocean sediments?

    (A) They indicate that sediments found during an ice age contain more calcium carbonate than sediments formed at other times.
    (B) They are less reliable than the evidence from rocks on land in determining the volume of land ice.
    (C) They can be used to deduce the relative volume of land ice that was present when the sediment was laid down.
    (D) They are more unpredictable during an ice age than in other climatic conditions.
    (E) They can be used to determine atmospheric conditions at various times in the past.

21. It can be inferred from the passage that precipitation formed from evaporated ocean water has

    (A) the same isotopic ratio as ocean water
    (B) less oxygen 18 than does ocean water
    (C) less oxygen 18 than has the ice contained in continental ice sheets
    (D) a different isotopic composition than has precipitation formed from water on land
    (E) more oxygen 16 than has precipitation formed from fresh water

22. According to the passage, which of the following is (are) true of the ice ages?

    I. The last ice age occurred about 25,000 years ago.
    II. Ice ages have lasted about 10,000 years for at least the last several hundred thousand years.
    III. Ice ages have occurred about every 100,000 years for at least the last several hundred thousand years.

    (A) I only
    (B) II only
    (C) III only
    (D) I and III only
    (E) I, II, and III

23. It can be inferred from the passage that calcium carbonate shells

    (A) are not as susceptible to deterioration as rocks
    (B) are less common in sediments formed during an ice age
    (C) are found only in areas that were once covered by land ice
    (D) contain radioactive material that can be used to determine a sediment's isotopic composition
    (E) reflect the isotopic composition of the water at the time the shells were formed

24. The purpose of the last paragraph of the passage is to

    (A) offer a note of caution
    (B) introduce new evidence
    (C) present two recent discoveries
    (D) summarize material in the preceding paragraphs
    (E) offer two explanations for a phenomenon

25. According to the passage, one advantage of studying the isotope record of ocean sediments is that it

    (A) corresponds with the record of ice volume taken from rocks on land
    (B) shows little variation in isotope ratios when samples are taken from different continental locations
    (C) corresponds with predictions already made by climatologists and experts in other fields
    (D) confirms the record of ice volume initially established by analyzing variations in volcanic emissions
    (E) provides data that can be used to substantiate records concerning variations in the amount of sunlight received by the Earth

STOP

IF YOU FINISH BEFORE TIME IS CALLED, YOU MAY CHECK YOUR WORK ON THIS SECTION ONLY. DO NOT TURN TO ANY OTHER SECTION IN THE TEST.

NO TEST MATERIAL ON THIS PAGE

SECTION 3

Time—30 minutes

20 Questions

Directions: In this section solve each problem, using any available space on the page for scratchwork. Then indicate the best of the answer choices given.

Numbers: All numbers used are real numbers.

Figures: Figures that accompany problems in this section are intended to provide information useful in solving the problems. They are drawn as accurately as possible EXCEPT when it is stated in a specific problem that its figure is not drawn to scale. All figures lie in a plane unless otherwise indicated.

1. The average (arithmetic mean) of 6, 8, and 10 equals the average of 7, 9, and

(A) 5
(B) 7
(C) 8
(D) 9
(E) 11

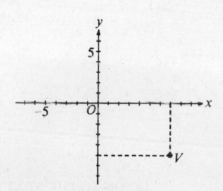

2. In the figure above, the coordinates of point V are

(A) $(-7, 5)$
(B) $(-5, 7)$
(C) $(5, 7)$
(D) $(7, 5)$
(E) $(7, -5)$

3. Tickets for all but 100 seats in a 10,000-seat stadium were sold. Of the tickets sold, 20 percent were sold at half price and the remaining tickets were sold at the full price of $2. What was the total revenue from ticket sales?

(A) $15,840
(B) $17,820
(C) $18,000
(D) $19,800
(E) $21,780

4. In a mayoral election, Candidate X received $\frac{1}{3}$ more votes than Candidate Y, and Candidate Y received $\frac{1}{4}$ fewer votes than Candidate Z. If Candidate Z received 24,000 votes, how many votes did Candidate X receive?

(A) 18,000
(B) 22,000
(C) 24,000
(D) 26,000
(E) 32,000

GO ON TO THE NEXT PAGE.

5. René earns $8.50 per hour on days other than Sundays and twice that rate on Sundays. Last week she worked a total of 40 hours, including 8 hours on Sunday. What were her earnings for the week?

(A) $272
(B) $340
(C) $398
(D) $408
(E) $476

6. In a shipment of 120 machine parts, 5 percent were defective. In a shipment of 80 machine parts, 10 percent were defective. For the two shipments combined, what percent of the machine parts were defective?

(A) 6.5%
(B) 7.0%
(C) 7.5%
(D) 8.0%
(E) 8.5%

7. $\dfrac{2\frac{3}{5} - 1\frac{2}{3}}{\frac{2}{3} - \frac{3}{5}} =$

(A) 16
(B) 14
(C) 3
(D) 1
(E) −1

8. If $x = -1$, then $\dfrac{x^4 - x^3 + x^2}{x - 1} =$

(A) $-\dfrac{3}{2}$

(B) $-\dfrac{1}{2}$

(C) 0

(D) $\dfrac{1}{2}$

(E) $\dfrac{3}{2}$

9. Which of the following equations is NOT equivalent to $25x^2 = y^2 - 4$?

(A) $25x^2 + 4 = y^2$

(B) $75x^2 = 3y^2 - 12$

(C) $25x^2 = (y + 2)(y - 2)$

(D) $5x = y - 2$

(E) $x^2 = \dfrac{y^2 - 4}{25}$

GO ON TO THE NEXT PAGE.

10. A toy store regularly sells all stock at a discount of 20 percent to 40 percent. If an additional 25 percent were deducted from the discount price during a special sale, what would be the lowest possible price of a toy costing $16 before any discount?

    (A) $5.60
    (B) $7.20
    (C) $8.80
    (D) $9.60
    (E) $15.20

11. If there are 664,579 prime numbers among the first 10 million positive integers, approximately what percent of the first 10 million positive integers are prime numbers?

    (A) 0.0066%
    (B) 0.066%
    (C) 0.66%
    (D) 6.6%
    (E) 66%

12. A bank customer borrowed $10,000, but received y dollars less than this due to discounting. If there was a separate $25 service charge, then, in terms of y, the service charge was what fraction of the amount that the customer received?

    (A) $\dfrac{25}{10,000 - y}$

    (B) $\dfrac{25}{10,000 - 25y}$

    (C) $\dfrac{25y}{10,000 - y}$

    (D) $\dfrac{y - 25}{10,000 - y}$

    (E) $\dfrac{25}{10,000 - (y - 25)}$

13. An airline passenger is planning a trip that involves three connecting flights that leave from Airports A, B, and C, respectively. The first flight leaves Airport A every hour, beginning at 8:00 a.m., and arrives at Airport B $2\frac{1}{2}$ hours later. The second flight leaves Airport B every 20 minutes, beginning at 8:00 a.m., and arrives at Airport C $1\frac{1}{6}$ hours later. The third flight leaves Airport C every hour, beginning at 8:45 a.m. What is the least total amount of time the passenger must spend between flights if all flights keep to their schedules?

    (A) 25 min
    (B) 1 hr 5 min
    (C) 1 hr 15 min
    (D) 2 hr 20 min
    (E) 3 hr 40 min

GO ON TO THE NEXT PAGE.

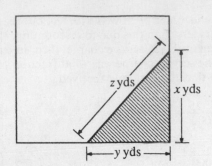

14. The shaded portion of the rectangular lot shown above represents a flower bed. If the area of the bed is 24 square yards and $x = y + 2$, then z equals

(A) $\sqrt{13}$

(B) $2\sqrt{13}$

(C) 6

(D) 8

(E) 10

15. How many multiples of 4 are there between 12 and 96, inclusive?

(A) 21
(B) 22
(C) 23
(D) 24
(E) 25

16. Jack is now 14 years older than Bill. If in 10 years Jack will be twice as old as Bill, how old will Jack be in 5 years?

(A) 9
(B) 19
(C) 21
(D) 23
(E) 33

17. In Township K, $\frac{1}{5}$ of the housing units are equipped with cable television. If $\frac{1}{10}$ of the housing units, including $\frac{1}{3}$ of those that are equipped with cable television, are equipped with videocassette recorders, what fraction of the housing units have neither cable television nor videocassette recorders?

(A) $\frac{23}{30}$

(B) $\frac{11}{15}$

(C) $\frac{7}{10}$

(D) $\frac{1}{6}$

(E) $\frac{2}{15}$

GO ON TO THE NEXT PAGE.

18. Set S consists of n distinct positive integers, none of which is greater than 12. What is the greatest possible value of n if no two integers in S have a common factor greater than 1 ?

(A) 4
(B) 5
(C) 6
(D) 7
(E) 11

19. In a certain contest, Fred must select any 3 of 5 different gifts offered by the sponsor. From how many different combinations of 3 gifts can Fred make his selection?

(A) 10
(B) 15
(C) 20
(D) 30
(E) 60

20. If the number of square units in the area of circle C is twice the number of linear units in the circumference of C, what is the number of square units in the area?

(A) 4
(B) 8
(C) 4π
(D) 8π
(E) 16π

STOP

IF YOU FINISH BEFORE TIME IS CALLED, YOU MAY CHECK YOUR WORK ON THIS SECTION ONLY.
DO NOT TURN TO ANY OTHER SECTION IN THE TEST.

NO TEST MATERIAL ON THIS PAGE

SECTION 4

Time—30 minutes

25 Questions

<u>Directions:</u> In each of the following sentences, some part of the sentence or the entire sentence is underlined. Beneath each sentence you will find five ways of phrasing the underlined part. The first of these repeats the original: the other four are different. If you think the original is better than any of the alternatives, choose answer A; otherwise choose one of the others. Select the best version and fill in the corresponding oval on your answer sheet.

This is a test of correctness and effectiveness of expression. In choosing answers, follow the requirements of standard written English; that is, pay attention to grammar, choice of words, and sentence construction. Choose the answer that expresses most effectively what is presented in the original sentence; this answer should be clear and exact, without awkwardness, ambiguity, or redundancy.

1. Delighted by the reported earnings for the first quarter of the fiscal year, <u>it was decided by the company manager to give her staff a raise.</u>

   (A) it was decided by the company manager to give her staff a raise
   (B) the decision of the company manager was to give her staff a raise
   (C) the company manager decided to give her staff a raise
   (D) the staff was given a raise by the company manager
   (E) a raise was given to the staff by the company manager

2. A study commissioned by the Department of Agriculture showed that if calves exercise and <u>associated with other calves, they will require less medication and gain weight quicker than do</u> those raised in confinement.

   (A) associated with other calves, they will require less medication and gain weight quicker than do
   (B) associated with other calves, they require less medication and gain weight quicker than
   (C) associate with other calves, they required less medication and will gain weight quicker than do
   (D) associate with other calves, they have required less medication and will gain weight more quickly than do
   (E) associate with other calves, they require less medication and gain weight more quickly than

3. Displays of the aurora borealis, or "northern lights," can heat the atmosphere over the arctic enough <u>to affect the trajectories of ballistic missiles, induce</u> electric currents that can cause blackouts in some areas and corrosion in north-south pipelines.

   (A) to affect the trajectories of ballistic missiles, induce
   (B) that the trajectories of ballistic missiles are affected, induce
   (C) that it affects the trajectories of ballistic missiles, induces
   (D) that the trajectories of ballistic missiles are affected and induces
   (E) to affect the trajectories of ballistic missiles and induce

4. The golden crab of the Gulf of Mexico has not been fished commercially in great numbers, primarily <u>on account of living</u> at great depths—2,500 to 3,000 feet down.

   (A) on account of living
   (B) on account of their living
   (C) because it lives
   (D) because of living
   (E) because they live

GO ON TO THE NEXT PAGE.

5. The cameras of the Voyager II spacecraft detected six small, previously unseen moons circling Uranus, which doubles to twelve the number of satellites now known as orbiting the distant planet.

(A) which doubles to twelve the number of satellites now known as orbiting
(B) doubling to twelve the number of satellites now known to orbit
(C) which doubles to twelve the number of satellites now known in orbit around
(D) doubling to twelve the number of satellites now known as orbiting
(E) which doubles to twelve the number of satellites now known that orbit

6. As a baby emerges from the darkness of the womb with a rudimentary sense of vision, it would be rated about 20/500, or legally blind if it were an adult with such vision.

(A) As a baby emerges from the darkness of the womb with a rudimentary sense of vision, it would be rated about 20/500, or legally blind if it were an adult with such vision.
(B) A baby emerges from the darkness of the womb with a rudimentary sense of vision that would be rated about 20/500, or legally blind as an adult.
(C) As a baby emerges from the darkness of the womb, its rudimentary sense of vision would be rated about 20/500; qualifying it to be legally blind if an adult.
(D) A baby emerges from the darkness of the womb with a rudimentary sense of vision that would be rated about 20/500; an adult with such vision would be deemed legally blind.
(E) As a baby emerges from the darkness of the womb, its rudimentary sense of vision, which would be deemed legally blind for an adult, would be rated about 20/500.

7. While Jackie Robinson was a Brooklyn Dodger, his courage in the face of physical threats and verbal attacks was not unlike that of Rosa Parks, who refused to move to the back of a bus in Montgomery, Alabama.

(A) not unlike that of Rosa Parks, who refused
(B) not unlike Rosa Parks, who refused
(C) like Rosa Parks and her refusal
(D) like that of Rosa Parks for refusing
(E) as that of Rosa Parks, who refused

8. The rising of costs of data-processing operations at many financial institutions has created a growing opportunity for independent companies to provide these services more efficiently and at lower cost.

(A) The rising of costs
(B) Rising costs
(C) The rising cost
(D) Because the rising cost
(E) Because of rising costs

9. There is no consensus on what role, if any, is played by acid rain in slowing the growth or damaging forests in the eastern United States.

(A) slowing the growth or damaging
(B) the damage or the slowing of the growth of
(C) the damage to or the slowness of the growth of
(D) damaged or slowed growth of
(E) damaging or slowing the growth of

10. Galileo was convinced that natural phenomena, as manifestations of the laws of physics, would appear the same to someone on the deck of a ship moving smoothly and uniformly through the water as a person standing on land.

(A) water as a
(B) water as to a
(C) water; just as it would to a
(D) water, as it would to the
(E) water; just as to the

11. A recent study has found that within the past few years, many doctors had elected early retirement rather than face the threats of lawsuits and the rising costs of malpractice insurance.

(A) had elected early retirement rather than face
(B) had elected early retirement instead of facing
(C) have elected retiring early instead of facing
(D) have elected to retire early rather than facing
(E) have elected to retire early rather than face

GO ON TO THE NEXT PAGE.

12. Architects and stonemasons, <u>huge palace and temple clusters were built by the Maya without benefit of the wheel or animal transport</u>.

   (A) huge palace and temple clusters were built by the Maya without benefit of the wheel or animal transport
   (B) without the benefits of animal transport or the wheel, huge palace and temple clusters were built by the Maya
   (C) the Maya built huge palace and temple clusters without the benefit of animal transport or the wheel
   (D) there were built, without the benefit of the wheel or animal transport, huge palace and temple clusters by the Maya
   (E) were the Maya who, without the benefit of the wheel or animal transport, built huge palace and temple clusters

13. In astronomy the term "red shift" denotes the extent <u>to which light from a distant galaxy has been shifted</u> toward the red, or long-wave, end of the light spectrum by the rapid motion of the galaxy away from the Earth.

   (A) to which light from a distant galaxy has been shifted
   (B) to which light from a distant galaxy has shifted
   (C) that light from a distant galaxy has been shifted
   (D) of light from a distant galaxy shifting
   (E) of the shift of light from a distant galaxy

14. William H. Johnson's artistic debt to Scandinavia is evident in paintings that range from sensitive portraits of citizens in his wife's Danish home, Kerteminde, <u>and</u> awe-inspiring views of fjords and mountain peaks in the western and northern regions of Norway.

   (A) and
   (B) to
   (C) and to
   (D) with
   (E) in addition to

15. In 1978 only half the women granted child support by a court received the amount awarded; <u>at least as much as a million and more others had not any</u> support agreements whatsoever.

   (A) at least as much as a million and more others had not any
   (B) at least as much as more than a million others had no
   (C) more than a million others had not any
   (D) more than a million others had no
   (E) there was at least a million or more others without any

16. According to a recent poll, owning and living in a freestanding house on its own land is still a goal of a majority of young adults, <u>like that of earlier generations</u>.

   (A) like that of earlier generations
   (B) as that for earlier generations
   (C) just as earlier generations did
   (D) as have earlier generations
   (E) as it was of earlier generations

17. The Gorton-Dodd bill requires <u>that a bank disclose to their customers how long they will delay access to funds from deposited checks</u>.

   (A) that a bank disclose to their customers how long they will delay access to funds from deposited checks
   (B) a bank to disclose to their customers how long they will delay access to funds from a deposited check
   (C) that a bank disclose to its customers how long it will delay access to funds from deposited checks
   (D) a bank that it should disclose to its customers how long it will delay access to funds from a deposited check
   (E) that banks disclose to customers how long access to funds from their deposited check is to be delayed

GO ON TO THE NEXT PAGE.

18. Geologists believe that the warning signs for a major earthquake may include sudden fluctuations in local seismic activity, tilting and other deformations of the Earth's crust, changing the measured strain across a fault zone, and varying the electrical properties of underground rocks.

    (A) changing the measured strain across a fault zone, and varying
    (B) changing measurements of the strain across a fault zone, and varying
    (C) changing the strain as measured across a fault zone, and variations of
    (D) changes in the measured strain across a fault zone, and variations in
    (E) changes in measurements of the strain across a fault zone, and variations among

19. Health officials estimate that 35 million Africans are in danger of contracting trypanosomiasis, or "African sleeping sickness," a parasitic disease spread by the bites of tsetse flies.

    (A) are in danger of contracting
    (B) are in danger to contract
    (C) have a danger of contracting
    (D) are endangered by contraction
    (E) have a danger that they will contract

20. Unlike a funded pension system, in which contributions are invested to pay future beneficiaries, a pay-as-you-go approach is the foundation of Social Security.

    (A) a pay-as-you-go approach is the foundation of Social Security
    (B) the foundation of Social Security is a pay-as-you-go approach
    (C) the approach of Social Security is pay-as-you-go
    (D) Social Security's approach is pay-as-you-go
    (E) Social Security is founded on a pay-as-you-go approach

21. Critics of the trend toward privately operated prisons consider corrections facilities to be an integral part of the criminal justice system and question if profits should be made from incarceration.

    (A) to be an integral part of the criminal justice system and question if
    (B) as an integral part of the criminal justice system and they question if
    (C) as being an integral part of the criminal justice system and question whether
    (D) an integral part of the criminal justice system and question whether
    (E) are an integral part of the criminal justice system, and they question whether

22. The Federal Reserve Board's reduction of interest rates on loans to financial institutions is both an acknowledgement of past economic trends and an effort to influence their future direction.

    (A) reduction of interest rates on loans to financial institutions is both an acknowledgement of past economic trends and an effort
    (B) reduction of interest rates on loans to financial institutions is an acknowledgement both of past economic trends as well as an effort
    (C) reduction of interest rates on loans to financial institutions both acknowledge past economic trends and attempt
    (D) reducing interest rates on loans to financial institutions is an acknowledgement both of past economic trends and an effort
    (E) reducing interest rates on loans to financial institutions both acknowledge past economic trends as well as attempt

GO ON TO THE NEXT PAGE.

23. Tiny quantities of more than thirty rare gases, most of them industrial by-products, threaten to warm the Earth's atmosphere even more rapidly than carbon dioxide during the next fifty years.

(A) to warm the Earth's atmosphere even more rapidly than carbon dioxide during the next fifty years

(B) to warm the Earth's atmosphere even more rapidly over the next fifty years than carbon dioxide will

(C) during the next fifty years to warm the Earth's atmosphere even more rapidly than carbon dioxide

(D) a warming of the Earth's atmosphere during the next fifty years even more rapid than carbon dioxide's

(E) a warming of the Earth's atmosphere even more rapid than carbon dioxide's will be over the next fifty years

24. Several years ago the diet industry introduced a variety of appetite suppressants, but some of these drugs caused stomach disorders severe enough to have them banned by the Food and Drug Administration.

(A) stomach disorders severe enough to have them

(B) stomach disorders that were severe enough so they were

(C) stomach disorders of such severity so as to be

(D) such severe stomach disorders that they were

(E) such severe stomach disorders as to be

25. Some analysts contend that true capitalism exists only when the ownership of both property and the means of production is regarded as an inalienable right of an individual's, and it is not a license granted by government and revokable at whim.

(A) is regarded as an inalienable right of an individual's, and it is not

(B) are regarded as individuals' inalienable rights, and that it not be

(C) is regarded as an individual's inalienable right, not as

(D) are regarded as an individual's inalienable rights, not when they are

(E) is regarded as the inalienable rights of an individual, not when it is

STOP

IF YOU FINISH BEFORE TIME IS CALLED, YOU MAY CHECK YOUR WORK ON THIS SECTION ONLY.
DO NOT TURN TO ANY OTHER SECTION IN THE TEST.

NO TEST MATERIAL ON THIS PAGE

SECTION 5

Time—30 minutes

20 Questions

Directions: In this section solve each problem, using any available space on the page for scratchwork. Then indicate the best of the answer choices given.

Numbers: All numbers used are real numbers.

Figures: Figures that accompany problems in this section are intended to provide information useful in solving the problems. They are drawn as accurately as possible EXCEPT when it is stated in a specific problem that its figure is not drawn to scale. All figures lie in a plane unless otherwise indicated.

1. In Country X a returning tourist may import goods with a total value of $500 or less tax free, but must pay an 8 percent tax on the portion of the total value in excess of $500. What tax must be paid by a returning tourist who imports goods with a total value of $730 ?

(A) $58.40
(B) $40.00
(C) $24.60
(D) $18.40
(E) $16.00

2. Which of the following is greater than $\frac{2}{3}$?

(A) $\frac{33}{50}$

(B) $\frac{8}{11}$

(C) $\frac{3}{5}$

(D) $\frac{13}{27}$

(E) $\frac{5}{8}$

3. A rope 40 feet long is cut into two pieces. If one piece is 18 feet longer than the other, what is the length, in feet, of the shorter piece?

(A) 9
(B) 11
(C) 18
(D) 22
(E) 29

4. If 60 percent of a rectangular floor is covered by a rectangular rug that is 9 feet by 12 feet, what is the area, in square feet, of the floor?

(A) 65
(B) 108
(C) 180
(D) 270
(E) 300

GO ON TO THE NEXT PAGE.

5. The Earth travels around the Sun at a speed of approximately 18.5 miles per second. This approximate speed is how many miles per hour?

   (A)   1,080
   (B)   1,160
   (C)   64,800
   (D)   66,600
   (E) 3,996,000

6. A collection of books went on sale, and $\frac{2}{3}$ of them were sold for $2.50 each. If none of the 36 remaining books were sold, what was the total amount received for the books that were sold?

   (A) $180
   (B) $135
   (C) $90
   (D) $60
   (E) $54

7. If "basis points" are defined so that 1 percent is equal to 100 basis points, then 82.5 percent is how many basis points greater than 62.5 percent?

   (A)   0.02
   (B)   0.2
   (C) 20
   (D) 200
   (E) 2,000

8. The amounts of time that three secretaries worked on a special project are in the ratio of 1 to 2 to 5. If they worked a combined total of 112 hours, how many hours did the secretary who worked the longest spend on the project?

   (A) 80
   (B) 70
   (C) 56
   (D) 16
   (E) 14

GO ON TO THE NEXT PAGE.

9. If the quotient $\frac{a}{b}$ is positive, which of the following must be true?

(A) $a > 0$

(B) $b > 0$

(C) $ab > 0$

(D) $a - b > 0$

(E) $a + b > 0$

10. If $8^{2x+3} = 2^{3x+6}$, then $x =$

(A) -3
(B) -1
(C) 0
(D) 1
(E) 3

11. Of the following, the closest approximation to

$$\sqrt{\frac{5.98(601.5)}{15.79}} \text{ is}$$

(A) 5
(B) 15
(C) 20
(D) 25
(E) 225

12. Which of the following CANNOT be the greatest common divisor of two positive integers x and y?

(A) 1
(B) x
(C) y
(D) $x - y$
(E) $x + y$

13. An empty pool being filled with water at a constant rate takes 8 hours to fill to $\frac{3}{5}$ of its capacity. How much more time will it take to finish filling the pool?

(A) 5 hr 30 min
(B) 5 hr 20 min
(C) 4 hr 48 min
(D) 3 hr 12 min
(E) 2 hr 40 min

GO ON TO THE NEXT PAGE.

14. A positive number x is multiplied by 2, and this product is then divided by 3. If the positive square root of the result of these two operations equals x, what is the value of x?

(A) $\dfrac{9}{4}$

(B) $\dfrac{3}{2}$

(C) $\dfrac{4}{3}$

(D) $\dfrac{2}{3}$

(E) $\dfrac{1}{2}$

15. A tank contains 10,000 gallons of a solution that is 5 percent sodium chloride by volume. If 2,500 gallons of water evaporate from the tank, the remaining solution will be approximately what percent sodium chloride?

(A) 1.25%
(B) 3.75%
(C) 6.25%
(D) 6.67%
(E) 11.7%

16. A certain grocery purchased x pounds of produce for p dollars per pound. If y pounds of the produce had to be discarded due to spoilage and the grocery sold the rest for s dollars per pound, which of the following represents the gross profit on the sale of the produce?

(A) $(x - y)s - xp$

(B) $(x - y)p - ys$

(C) $(s - p)y - xp$

(D) $xp - ys$

(E) $(x - y)(s - p)$

17. NOT SCORED

GO ON TO THE NEXT PAGE.

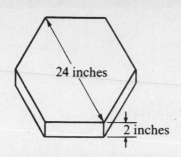

24 inches

2 inches

Note: Figure not drawn to scale.

18. The hexagonal face of the block shown in the figure above has sides of equal length and angles of equal measure. If each lateral face is rectangular, what is the area, in square inches, of one lateral face?

(A) $2\sqrt{10}$

(B) 12

(C) 20

(D) $12\sqrt{3}$

(E) 24

19. If w, x, y, and z are non-negative integers, each less than 3, and $w(3^3) + x(3^2) + y(3) + z = 34$, then $w + z =$

(A) 0
(B) 1
(C) 2
(D) 3
(E) 4

20. Cars X and Y were traveling together on a straight road at a constant speed of 55 miles per hour when car X stopped for 5 minutes. If car Y continued to travel at 55 miles per hour, how many minutes from the time that car X resumed traveling did it take car X traveling at 60 miles per hour to catch up with car Y? (Assume that the time for car X to slow down and speed up was negligible.)

(A) 5
(B) 30
(C) 45
(D) 55
(E) 60

STOP

IF YOU FINISH BEFORE TIME IS CALLED, YOU MAY CHECK YOUR WORK ON THIS SECTION ONLY.
DO NOT TURN TO ANY OTHER SECTION IN THE TEST.

SECTION 6
Time—30 minutes

20 Questions

Directions: For each question in this section, select the best of the answer choices given.

1. Rural households have more purchasing power than do urban or suburban households at the same income level, since some of the income urban and suburban households use for food and shelter can be used by rural households for other needs.

Which of the following inferences is best supported by the statement made above?

(A) The average rural household includes more people than does the average urban or suburban household.

(B) Rural households have lower food and housing costs than do either urban or suburban households.

(C) Suburban households generally have more purchasing power than do either rural or urban households.

(D) The median income of urban and suburban households is generally higher than that of rural households.

(E) All three types of households spend more of their income on food and housing than on all other purchases combined.

2. In 1985 state border colleges in Texas lost the enrollment of more than half, on average, of the Mexican nationals they had previously served each year. Teaching faculties have alleged that this extreme drop resulted from a rise in tuition for international and out-of-state students from $40 to $120 per credit hour.

Which of the following, if feasible, offers the best prospects for alleviating the problem of the drop in enrollment of Mexican nationals as the teaching faculties assessed it?

(A) Providing grants-in-aid to Mexican nationals to study in Mexican universities

(B) Allowing Mexican nationals to study in Texas border colleges and to pay in-state tuition rates, which are the same as the previous international rate

(C) Reemphasizing the goals and mission of the Texas state border colleges as serving both in-state students and Mexican nationals

(D) Increasing the financial resources of Texas colleges by raising the tuition for in-state students attending state institutions

(E) Offering career counseling for those Mexican nationals who graduate from state border colleges and intend to return to Mexico

3. Affirmative action is good business. So asserted the National Association of Manufacturers while urging retention of an executive order requiring some federal contractors to set numerical goals for hiring minorities and women. "Diversity in work force participation has produced new ideas in management, product development, and marketing," the association claimed.

The association's argument as it is presented in the passage above would be most strengthened if which of the following were true?

(A) The percentage of minority and women workers in business has increased more slowly than many minority and women's groups would prefer.

(B) Those businesses with the highest percentages of minority and women workers are those that have been the most innovative and profitable.

(C) Disposable income has been rising as fast among minorities and women as among the population as a whole.

(D) The biggest growth in sales in the manufacturing sector has come in industries that market the most innovative products.

(E) Recent improvements in management practices have allowed many manufacturers to experience enormous gains in worker productivity.

GO ON TO THE NEXT PAGE.

Questions 4-5 refer to the following.

If the airspace around centrally located airports were restricted to commercial airliners and only those private planes equipped with radar, most of the private-plane traffic would be forced to use outlying airfields. Such a reduction in the amount of private-plane traffic would reduce the risk of midair collision around the centrally located airports.

4. The conclusion drawn in the first sentence depends on which of the following assumptions?

(A) Outlying airfields would be as convenient as centrally located airports for most pilots of private planes.
(B) Most outlying airfields are not equipped to handle commercial-airline traffic.
(C) Most private planes that use centrally located airports are not equipped with radar.
(D) Commercial airliners are at greater risk of becoming involved in midair collisions than are private planes.
(E) A reduction in the risk of midair collision would eventually lead to increases in commercial-airline traffic.

5. Which of the following, if true, would most strengthen the conclusion drawn in the second sentence?

(A) Commercial airliners are already required by law to be equipped with extremely sophisticated radar systems.
(B) Centrally located airports are experiencing over-crowded airspace primarily because of sharp increases in commercial-airline traffic.
(C) Many pilots of private planes would rather buy radar equipment than be excluded from centrally located airports.
(D) The number of midair collisions that occur near centrally located airports has decreased in recent years.
(E) Private planes not equipped with radar systems cause a disproportionately large number of midair collisions around centrally located airports.

6. Which of the following best completes the passage below?

Established companies concentrate on defending what they already have. Consequently, they tend not to be innovative themselves and tend to underestimate the effects of the innovations of others. The clearest example of this defensive strategy is the fact that -------.

(A) ballpoint pens and soft-tip markers have eliminated the traditional market for fountain pens, clearing the way for the marketing of fountain pens as luxury or prestige items
(B) a highly successful automobile was introduced by the same company that had earlier introduced a model that had been a dismal failure
(C) a once-successful manufacturer of slide rules reacted to the introduction of electronic calculators by trying to make better slide rules
(D) one of the first models of modern accounting machines, designed for use in the banking industry, was purchased by a public library as well as by banks
(E) the inventor of a commonly used anesthetic did not intend the product to be used by dentists, who currently account for almost the entire market for that drug

GO ON TO THE NEXT PAGE.

7. Most archaeologists have held that people first reached the Americas less than 20,000 years ago by crossing a land bridge into North America. But recent discoveries of human shelters in South America dating from 32,000 years ago have led researchers to speculate that people arrived in South America first, after voyaging across the Pacific, and then spread northward.

Which of the following, if it were discovered, would be pertinent evidence against the speculation above?

(A) A rock shelter near Pittsburgh, Pennsylvania, contains evidence of use by human beings 19,000 years ago.

(B) Some North American sites of human habitation predate any sites found in South America.

(C) The climate is warmer at the 32,000-year-old South American site than at the oldest known North American site.

(D) The site in South America that was occupied 32,000 years ago was continuously occupied until 6,000 years ago.

(E) The last Ice Age, between 11,500 and 20,000 years ago, considerably lowered worldwide sea levels.

8. In Asia, where palm trees are non-native, the trees' flowers have traditionally been pollinated by hand, which has kept palm fruit productivity unnaturally low. When weevils known to be efficient pollinators of palm flowers were introduced into Asia in 1980, palm fruit productivity increased—by up to fifty percent in some areas—but then decreased sharply in 1984.

Which of the following statements, if true, would best explain the 1984 decrease in productivity?

(A) Prices for palm fruit fell between 1980 and 1984 following the rise in production and a concurrent fall in demand.

(B) Imported trees are often more productive than native trees because the imported ones have left behind their pests and diseases in their native lands.

(C) Rapid increases in productivity tend to deplete trees of nutrients needed for the development of the fruit-producing female flowers.

(D) The weevil population in Asia remained at approximately the same level between 1980 and 1984.

(E) Prior to 1980 another species of insect pollinated the Asian palm trees, but not as efficiently as the species of weevil that was introduced in 1980.

9. Since the mayor's publicity campaign for Greenville's bus service began six months ago, morning automobile traffic into the midtown area of the city has decreased seven percent. During the same period, there has been an equivalent rise in the number of persons riding buses into the midtown area. Obviously, the mayor's publicity campaign has convinced many people to leave their cars at home and ride the bus to work.

Which of the following, if true, casts the most serious doubt on the conclusion drawn above?

(A) Fares for all bus routes in Greenville have risen an average of five percent during the past six months.

(B) The mayor of Greenville rides the bus to City Hall in the city's midtown area.

(C) Road reconstruction has greatly reduced the number of lanes available to commuters in major streets leading to the midtown area during the past six months.

(D) The number of buses entering the midtown area of Greenville during the morning hours is exactly the same now as it was one year ago.

(E) Surveys show that longtime bus riders are no more satisfied with the Greenville bus service than they were before the mayor's publicity campaign began.

GO ON TO THE NEXT PAGE.

10. In the aftermath of a worldwide stock-market crash, Country T claimed that the severity of the stock-market crash it experienced resulted from the accelerated process of denationalization many of its industries underwent shortly before the crash.

Which of the following, if it could be carried out, would be most useful in an evaluation of Country T's assessment of the causes of the severity of its stock-market crash?

(A) Calculating the average loss experienced by individual traders in Country T during the crash

(B) Using economic theory to predict the most likely date of the next crash in Country T

(C) Comparing the total number of shares sold during the worst days of the crash in Country T to the total number of shares sold in Country T just prior to the crash

(D) Comparing the severity of the crash in Country T to the severity of the crash in countries otherwise economically similar to Country T that have not experienced recent denationalization

(E) Comparing the long-term effects of the crash on the purchasing power of the currency of Country T to the immediate, more severe short-term effects of the crash on the purchasing power of the currency of Country T

11. With the emergence of biotechnology companies, it was feared that they would impose silence about proprietary results on their in-house researchers and their academic consultants. This constraint, in turn, would slow the development of biological science and engineering.

Which of the following, if true, would tend to weaken most seriously the prediction of scientific secrecy described above?

(A) Biotechnological research funded by industry has reached some conclusions that are of major scientific importance.

(B) When the results of scientific research are kept secret, independent researchers are unable to build on those results.

(C) Since the research priorities of biotechnology companies are not the same as those of academic institutions, the financial support of research by such companies distorts the research agenda.

(D) To enhance the companies' standing in the scientific community, the biotechnology companies encourage employees to publish their results, especially results that are important.

(E) Biotechnology companies devote some of their research resources to problems that are of fundamental scientific importance and that are not expected to produce immediate practical applications.

12. Some people have questioned the judge's objectivity in cases of sex discrimination against women. But the record shows that in sixty percent of such cases, the judge has decided in favor of the women. This record demonstrates that the judge has not discriminated against women in cases of sex discrimination against women.

The argument above is flawed in that it ignores the possibility that

(A) a large number of the judge's cases arose out of allegations of sex discrimination against women

(B) many judges find it difficult to be objective in cases of sex discrimination against women

(C) the judge is biased against women defendants or plaintiffs in cases that do not involve sex discrimination

(D) the majority of the cases of sex discrimination against women that have reached the judge's court have been appealed from a lower court

(E) the evidence shows that the women should have won in more than sixty percent of the judge's cases involving sex discrimination against women

13. The tobacco industry is still profitable and projections are that it will remain so. In the United States this year, the total amount of tobacco sold by tobacco-farmers has increased, even though the number of adults who smoke has decreased.

Each of the following, if true, could explain the simultaneous increase in tobacco sales and decrease in the number of adults who smoke EXCEPT:

(A) During this year, the number of women who have begun to smoke is greater than the number of men who have quit smoking.

(B) The number of teen-age children who have begun to smoke this year is greater than the number of adults who have quit smoking during the same period.

(C) During this year, the number of nonsmokers who have begun to use chewing tobacco or snuff is greater than the number of people who have quit smoking.

(D) The people who have continued to smoke consume more tobacco per person than they did in the past.

(E) More of the cigarettes made in the United States this year were exported to other countries than was the case last year.

GO ON TO THE NEXT PAGE.

-493-

14. Kale has more nutritional value than spinach. But since collard greens have more nutritional value than lettuce, it follows that kale has more nutritional value than lettuce.

Any of the following, if introduced into the argument as an additional premise, makes the argument above logically correct EXCEPT:

(A) Collard greens have more nutritional value than kale.
(B) Spinach has more nutritional value than lettuce.
(C) Spinach has more nutritional value than collard greens.
(D) Spinach and collard greens have the same nutritional value.
(E) Kale and collard greens have the same nutritional value.

15. On the basis of a decrease in the college-age population, many colleges now anticipate increasingly smaller freshman classes each year. Surprised by a 40 percent increase in qualified applicants over the previous year, however, administrators at Nice College now plan to hire more faculty for courses taken by all freshmen.

Which of the following statements about Nice College's current qualified applicants, if true, would strongly suggest that the administrators' plan is flawed?

(A) A substantially higher percentage than usual plan to study for advanced degrees after graduation from college.
(B) According to their applications, their level of participation in extracurricular activities and varsity sports is unusually high.
(C) According to their applications, none of them lives in a foreign country.
(D) A substantially lower percentage than usual rate Nice College as their first choice among the colleges to which they are applying.
(E) A substantially lower percentage than usual list mathematics as their intended major.

Questions 16-17 are based on the following.

A researcher discovered that people who have low levels of immune-system activity tend to score much lower on tests of mental health than do people with normal or high immune-system activity. The researcher concluded from this experiment that the immune system protects against mental illness as well as against physical disease.

16. The researcher's conclusion depends on which of the following assumptions?

(A) High immune-system activity protects against mental illness better than normal immune-system activity does.
(B) Mental illness is similar to physical disease in its effects on body systems.
(C) People with high immune-system activity cannot develop mental illness.
(D) Mental illness does not cause people's immune-system activity to decrease.
(E) Psychological treatment of mental illness is not as effective as is medical treatment.

17. The researcher's conclusion would be most seriously weakened if it were true that

(A) there was a one-year delay between the completion of a pilot study for the experiment and the initiation of the experiment itself
(B) people's levels of immune-system activity are not affected by their use of medications
(C) a few people with high immune-system activity had scores on the test of mental health that were similar to the scores of people who had normal immune-system activity
(D) people who have low immune-system activity tend to contract more viral infections than do people with normal or high immune-system activity
(E) high levels of stress first cause mental illness and then cause decreased immune-system activity in normal individuals

GO ON TO THE NEXT PAGE.

18. The value of a product is determined by the ratio of its quality to its price. The higher the value of a product, the better will be its competitive position. Therefore, either increasing the quality or lowering the price of a given product will increase the likelihood that a consumer will select that product rather than a competing one.

Which of the following, if true, would most strengthen the conclusion drawn above?

(A) It is possible to increase both the quality and the price of a product without changing its competitive position.

(B) For certain segments of the population of consumers, higher-priced brands of some product lines are preferred to the lower-priced brands.

(C) Competing products often try to appeal to different segments of the population of consumers.

(D) The competitive position of a product can be affected by such factors as advertising and brand loyalty.

(E) Consumers' perceptions of the quality of a product are based on the actual quality of the product.

19. In January there was a large drop in the number of new houses sold, because interest rates for mortgages were falling and many consumers were waiting to see how low the rates would go. This large sales drop was accompanied by a sharp rise in the average price of new houses sold.

Which of the following, if true, best explains the sharp rise in the average price of new houses?

(A) Sales of higher-priced houses were unaffected by the sales drop because their purchasers have fewer constraints limiting the total amount they pay.

(B) Labor agreements of builders with construction unions are not due to expire until the next January.

(C) The prices of new houses have been rising slowly over the past three years because there is an increasing shortage of housing.

(D) There was a greater amount of moderate-priced housing available for resale by owners during January than in the preceding three months.

(E) Interest rates for home mortgages are expected to rise sharply later in the year if predictions of increased business activity in general prove to be accurate.

20. Seven countries signed a treaty binding each of them to perform specified actions on a certain fixed date, with the actions of each conditional on simultaneous action taken by the other countries. Each country was also to notify the six other countries when it had completed its action.

The simultaneous-action provision of the treaty leaves open the possibility that

(A) the compliance date was subject to postponement, according to the terms of the treaty

(B) one of the countries might not be required to make any changes or take any steps in order to comply with the treaty, whereas all the other countries are so required

(C) each country might have a well-founded excuse, based on the provision, for its own lack of compliance

(D) the treaty specified that the signal for one of the countries to initiate action was notification by the other countries that they had completed action

(E) there was ambiguity with respect to the date after which all actions contemplated in the treaty are to be complete

STOP

IF YOU FINISH BEFORE TIME IS CALLED, YOU MAY CHECK YOUR WORK ON THIS SECTION ONLY. DO NOT TURN TO ANY OTHER SECTION IN THE TEST.

-495-

Section 1

	A	B	C	D	E
1	○	○	●	○	○
2	●	○	○	○	○
3	○	●	○	○	○
4	●	○	○	○	○
5	○	○	●	○	○
6	○	○	○	○	●
7	○	○	○	●	○
8	○	○	○	●	○
9	○	○	○	○	●
10	○	●	○	○	○
11	○	○	○	○	●
12	●	○	○	○	○
13	○	○	○	○	●
14	●	○	○	○	○
15	○	○	●	○	○
16	○	○	○	●	○
17	○	○	●	○	○
18	○	○	○	●	○
19	○	●	○	○	○
20	○	○	○	●	○
21	○	●	○	○	○
22	○	○	○	●	○
23	○	○	○	○	●
24	○	○	○	●	○
25	○	○	●	○	○

Section 2

	A	B	C	D	E
1	●	○	○	○	○
2	○	○	●	○	○
3	○	●	○	○	○
4	○	●	○	○	○
5	○	●	○	○	○
6	○	○	○	●	○
7	○	●	○	○	○
8	●	○	○	○	○
9	○	○	○	○	●
10	○	○	○	○	●
11	○	○	●	○	○
12	○	○	○	●	○
13	○	○	○	●	○
14	○	○	○	●	○
15	●	○	○	○	○
16	○	○	○	○	●
17	○	○	○	●	○
18	○	○	○	●	○
19	○	●	○	○	○
20	○	○	●	○	○
21	●	○	○	○	○
22	○	○	●	○	○
23	○	○	○	○	●
24	●	○	○	○	○
25	○	●	○	○	○

Section 3

	A	B	C	D	E
1	○	○	●	○	○
2	○	○	○	○	●
3	○	●	○	○	○
4	○	○	●	○	○
5	○	○	○	●	○
6	○	●	○	○	○
7	●	○	○	○	○
8	●	○	○	○	○
9	○	○	●	○	○
10	○	●	○	○	○
11	○	○	○	●	○
12	●	○	○	○	○
13	○	○	○	●	○
14	○	○	○	○	●
15	○	●	○	○	○
16	○	○	○	●	○
17	●	○	○	○	○
18	○	○	●	○	○
19	●	○	○	○	○
20	○	○	○	○	●
21	○	●	○	○	○
22	○	○	●	○	○
23	○	○	○	●	○
24	○	○	○	●	○
25	○	○	○	○	○

Section 4

	A	B	C	D	E
1	○	○	●	○	○
2	○	○	○	○	●
3	○	○	○	○	●
4	○	○	●	○	○
5	○	●	○	○	○
6	○	○	○	●	○
7	●	○	○	○	○
8	○	○	●	○	○
9	○	○	○	○	●
10	○	●	○	○	○
11	○	○	○	○	●
12	○	○	●	○	○
13	●	○	○	○	○
14	○	●	○	○	○
15	○	○	○	●	○
16	○	○	○	○	●
17	○	○	●	○	○
18	○	○	○	●	○
19	●	○	○	○	○
20	○	○	○	●	○
21	○	○	○	●	○
22	●	○	○	○	○
23	○	●	○	○	○
24	○	○	○	●	○
25	○	○	●	○	○

Section 5

	A	B	C	D	E
1	○	○	○	●	○
2	○	●	○	○	○
3	○	●	○	○	○
4	○	○	●	○	○
5	●	○	○	○	○
6	●	○	○	○	○
7	○	○	○	○	●
8	●	○	○	○	○
9	○	○	●	○	○
10	○	●	○	○	○
11	●	○	○	○	○
12	○	○	○	●	○
13	○	●	○	○	○
14	○	○	○	●	○
15	○	○	○	●	○
16	●	○	○	○	○
17	NOT SCORED				
18	○	○	○	○	●
19	○	○	●	○	○
20	○	○	○	○	●
21	○	○	●	○	○
22	○	○	●	○	○
23	○	○	○	●	○
24	○	○	●	○	○
25	○	○	○	○	○

Section 6

	A	B	C	D	E
1	○	●	○	○	○
2	○	●	○	○	○
3	○	●	○	○	○
4	○	○	●	○	○
5	○	○	○	○	●
6	○	○	○	●	○
7	○	●	○	○	○
8	○	○	○	●	○
9	○	○	○	●	○
10	○	○	○	●	○
11	○	○	○	○	●
12	○	○	○	○	●
13	●	○	○	○	○
14	●	○	○	○	○
15	○	○	○	●	○
16	○	○	○	●	○
17	○	○	○	○	●
18	○	○	○	○	●
19	●	○	○	○	○
20	○	○	●	○	○
21	○	○	●	○	○
22	○	○	○	○	○
23	○	○	○	○	○
24	○	○	○	○	●
25	○	○	○	○	●

Explanatory Material: Data Sufficiency, Section 1

1. **The regular price for canned soup was reduced during a sale. How much money could one have saved by purchasing a dozen 7-ounce cans of soup at the reduced price rather than at the regular price?**

    (1) **The regular price for the 7-ounce cans was 3 for a dollar.**

    (2) **The reduced price for the 7-ounce cans was 4 for a dollar.**

The saving is the difference between the regular price of a dozen cans and their reduced price. Since (1) gives no information about the reduced price, (1) alone is not sufficient to determine the saving, and the answer must be B, C, or E. Statement (2) alone gives no information about the regular price. Therefore, (2) alone is not sufficient, and the answer must be C or E. From (1) and (2) together, both prices can be computed, and the saving can be determined. Therefore, the best answer is C.

2. **If on a fishing trip Jim and Tom each caught some fish, which one caught more fish?**

    (1) **Jim caught $\frac{2}{3}$ as many fish as Tom.**

    (2) **After Tom stopped fishing, Jim continued fishing until he had caught 12 fish.**

Statement (1) indicates that Jim caught fewer fish than Tom. Therefore, (1) alone is sufficient to answer the question, and the answer must be A or D. Statement (2) gives no information about the number of fish Tom caught. Therefore, (2) alone is not sufficient, and the best answer is A.

3. **If $5x + 3y = 17$, what is the value of x ?**

    (1) **x is a positive integer.**

    (2) **$y = 4x$**

Statement (1) alone is not sufficient because it gives no information about the value of y. Thus, the answer must be B, C, or E. From (2) it follows that $5x + 3(4x) = 17$, which can be solved for x. Therefore, the best answer is B.

4. **Yesterday Nan parked her car at a certain parking garage that charges more for the first hour than for each additional hour. If Nan's total parking charge at the garage yesterday was $3.75, for how many hours of parking was she charged?**

    (1) **Parking charges at the garage are $0.75 for the first hour and $0.50 for each additional hour or fraction of an hour.**

    (2) **If the charge for the first hour had been $1.00, Nan's total parking charge would have been $4.00.**

Statement (1) gives the charge for the first hour and for subsequent hours. From this information, together with the total charge that is given, the number of hours after the first hour can be computed. Thus, the answer must be A or D. From statement (2) the charge for the first hour can be determined; however, there is no information about charges after the first hour. Therefore, (2) alone is not sufficient, and the best answer is A.

5. **If r and s are integers, is $r + s$ divisible by 3 ?**

    (1) **s is divisible by 3.**

    (2) **r is divisible by 3.**

One approach to answering this question is to choose values for r and s. In statement (1), for example, let $s = 6$, which is divisible by 3. Then, $r + s$ is divisible by 3 if $r = 9$ but not if $r = 10$, and similarly for statement (2). In more general terms, $r + s$ is divisible by 3 if both r and s are divisible by 3. If either r or s is not divisible by 3, then $r + s$ might or might not be divisible by 3. Since neither (1) alone nor (2) alone gives information about both r and s, neither statement alone is sufficient, and the answer must be C or E. Statements (1) and (2) together state that both r and s are divisible by 3, however, so the best answer is C.

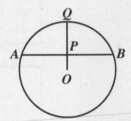

6. **What is the radius of the circle above with center O ?**

    (1) **The ratio of OP to PQ is 1 to 2.**

    (2) **P is the midpoint of chord AB.**

From statement (1) it can be concluded only that the radius is 3 times the length of OP. Since there are many possible lengths of OP and PQ that would have a ratio of 1 to 2, statement (1) alone is not sufficient, and the answer must be B, C, or E. Similarly, knowing that P is the midpoint of chord AB is of no help in determining the radius, so (2) alone is not sufficient. Therefore, the answer must be C or E. Statements (1) and (2) together do not give the length of any line segment shown in the circle, so they are not sufficient to determine the radius. Thus, the best answer is E.

7. **A certain 4-liter solution of vinegar and water consists of x liters of vinegar and y liters of water. How many liters of vinegar does the solution contain?**

    (1) $\dfrac{x}{4} = \dfrac{3}{8}$

    (2) $\dfrac{y}{4} = \dfrac{5}{8}$

Statement (1) can be solved for x, so (1) alone is sufficient. Therefore, the answer must be A or D. Statement (2) can be solved for y. Since $x + y = 4$, substituting the value of y in the equation will give the value of x. Thus, statement (2) alone is also sufficient, and the best answer is D.

8. Is $x < 0$?

(1) $-2x > 0$
(2) $x^3 < 0$

A negative number times a positive number is negative, whereas a negative number times a negative number is positive. Thus, from statement (1) it can be determined that x must be negative, since -2 times x is positive. Therefore, (1) alone is sufficient, and the answer must be A or D. Statement (2) alone is also sufficient, since the cube of a positive number is positive and the cube of a negative number is negative. Therefore, each statement alone is sufficient, and the best answer is D.

9. Of the 230 single-family homes built in City X last year, how many were occupied at the end of the year?

(1) Of all single-family homes in City X, 90 percent were occupied at the end of last year.
(2) A total of 7,200 single-family homes in City X were occupied at the end of last year.

Statement (1) does not give the percentage of homes built last year that were occupied. Any number of the 230 homes could be included in the 90 percent of the total. Therefore, the answer must be B, C, or E. Similarly, any number of the 230 homes could be included in the total, and (2) alone is not sufficient. Therefore, the answer must be C or E. From (1) and (2) together, only the total number of single-family homes can be determined. Thus, the best answer is E.

10. Does the product $jkmn$ equal 1 ?

(1) $\dfrac{jk}{mn} = 1$
(2) $j = \dfrac{1}{k}$ and $m = \dfrac{1}{n}$

From statement (1) it can be determined only that $jk = mn$. Since this information is not sufficient, the answer must be B, C, or E. From (2) alone, it can be determined that $jk = 1$ and $mn = 1$, so $jkmn = 1$. Thus, (2) alone is sufficient, and the best answer is B.

11. How many of the boys in a group of 100 children have brown hair?

(1) Of the children in the group, 60 percent have brown hair.
(2) Of the children in the group, 40 are boys.

From statement (1), only the total number of children who have brown hair can be determined, so (1) alone is not sufficient. Therefore, the answer must be B, C, or E. Clearly

(2) alone is not sufficient because nothing is said about brown hair. Therefore, the answer must be C or E. From statements (1) and (2) together, only the total number of children who have brown hair and the number of boys in the group are known. Thus, (1) and (2) together are not sufficient, and the best answer is E.

12. Is the perimeter of square S greater than the perimeter of equilateral triangle T ?

(1) The ratio of the length of a side of S to the length of a side of T is 4 : 5.
(2) The sum of the lengths of a side of S and a side of T is 18.

In considering (1), let the length of each side of S be $4x$ and the length of each side of T be $5x$, which is consistent with the ratio given. Thus, the perimeter of S is $4(4x)$ and the perimeter of T is $3(5x)$, and statement (1) alone is sufficient. Thus, the answer must be A or D. Statement (2) alone is not sufficient because there are many pairs of numbers whose sum is 18, and for some of these pairs the perimeter of S is less than that of T, while for other pairs it is greater. The best answer is A.

13. If p and q are positive integers and $pq = 24$, what is the value of p ?

(1) $\dfrac{q}{6}$ is an integer.
(2) $\dfrac{p}{2}$ is an integer.

There are four pairs of positive integers whose product is 24: 1 and 24, 2 and 12, 3 and 8, and 4 and 6. From statement (1) the possible values of q are 24, 12, and 6, and there is a value of p corresponding to each of these three values. Thus, statement (1) alone is not sufficient, and the answer must be B, C, or E. From (2), the possible values of p are 2, 4, 6, 8, 12, and 24. Thus, (2) alone is not sufficient, and the answer must be C or E. From (1) and (2) together, it can be determined only that q can be either 12 or 6, so p can be either 2 or 4. Thus, (1) and (2) together are not sufficient, and the best answer is E.

14. If $x\ 0$, what is the value of $\left(\dfrac{x^p}{x^q}\right)^4$?

(1) $p = q$
(2) $x = 3$

From statement (1) it follows, by substitution, that $\dfrac{x^p}{x^q} = 1$, and thus (1) alone is sufficient to determine the value of $\left(\dfrac{x^p}{x^q}\right)^4$. Therefore, the answer must be A or D. Statement (2) alone is not sufficient because it gives no information about the values of p and q. Thus, the best answer is A.

15. From May 1, 1960 to May 1, 1975, the closing price of a share of stock X doubled. What was the closing price of a share of stock X on May 1, 1960 ?

 (1) From May 1, 1975, to May 1, 1984, the closing price of a share of stock X doubled.
 (2) From May 1, 1975, to May 1, 1984, the closing price of a share of stock X increased by $4.50.

Neither statement (1) alone nor statement (2) alone gives any information about the price from 1960 to 1975. Thus, the answer must be C or E. From statements (1) and (2) together, the closing price of a share of the stock on May 1, 1975, can be determined ($4.50) and the closing price on May 1, 1960, can be determined (half of $4.50). Therefore, (1) and (2) together are sufficient, and the best answer is C.

16. If d is a positive integer, is $\sqrt{d}$ an integer?

 (1) d is the square of an integer.
 (2) $\sqrt{d}$ is the square of an integer.

Statement (1) can be expressed as $d = x^2$, where x is a nonzero integer. Then $\sqrt{d} = \sqrt{x^2}$ equals x or –x, depending on whether x is positive or negative, respectively. In either case, $\sqrt{d}$ is an integer. For example, $\sqrt{10^2} = 10$ and $\sqrt{(-4)^2} = \sqrt{16} = 4 = -(-4)$. Therefore, (1) alone is sufficient, and the answer must be A or D. In (2) the square of an integer must also be an integer. Thus, (2) alone is also sufficient, and the best answer is D.

17. If Q is an integer between 10 and 100, what is the value of Q ?

 (1) One of Q's digits is 3 more than the other, and the sum of its digits is 9.
 (2) Q < 50

If x and y are the digits of Q, statement (1) can be expressed as $x = y + 3$ and $x + y = 9$, which can be solved for x and y. It is also possible to see that only the numbers 36 and 63 satisfy (1) without actually setting up equations, but the order of the digits is not known regardless of the method used. Thus, (1) alone is not sufficient, and the answer must be B, C, or E. Clearly, (2) alone is not sufficient because it only narrows the range of possible values of Q. Therefore, the answer must be C or E. When the two possible values of Q are considered and it is noted that only one of the values is less than 50, it can be seen that (1) and (2) together are sufficient to determine the value of Q, and the best answer is C.

18. If digit h is the hundredths' digit in the decimal $d = 0.2h6$, what is the value of d, rounded to the nearest tenth?

 (1) $d < \frac{1}{4}$
 (2) $h < 5$

The value of d, rounded to the nearest tenth, is 0.3 for $h \geq 5$ and 0.2 for $h < 5$. Statement (1) can be written $d < 0.250$, so $h < 5$. Thus, (1) alone is sufficient, and the answer must be A or D. Statement (2) gives the information that $h < 5$ directly, so (2) alone is also sufficient. The best answer is D.

19. What is the value of $x^2 - y^2$?

 (1) $x - y = y + 2$
 (2) $x - y = \frac{1}{x + y}$

From statement (1) it can be determined only that $x = 2y + 2$ and that $x^2 - y^2 = (2y + 2)^2 - y^2$, which depends on the value of y. Thus, (1) alone is not sufficient to determine the value of $x^2 - y^2$, and the answer must be B, C, or E. Statement (2) can be rewritten $(x - y)(x + y) = 1$, or $x^2 - y^2 = 1$. Therefore, (2) alone is sufficient, and the best answer is B.

20. If ∘ represents one of the operations +, –, and ×, is $k \circ (\ell + m) = (k \circ \ell) + (k \circ m)$ for all numbers k, ℓ, and m ?

 (1) $k \circ 1$ is not equal to $1 \circ k$ for some numbers k.
 (2) ∘ represents subtraction.

Since $k \circ 1 = 1 \circ k$ for both + and × (i.e., $k + 1 = 1 + k$ and $k \times 1 = 1 \times k$ for all values of k), according to statement (1), ∘ must represent subtraction. Thus, it can be determined whether $k - (\ell + m) = (k - \ell) + (k - m)$ holds for all k, ℓ, and m. Note, however, that it is not actually necessary to answer this question, only to see that the answer can be determined. Thus, (1) alone is sufficient, and the answer must be A or D. Because statement (2) gives the information directly that ∘ represents subtraction, (2) alone is also sufficient, and the best answer is D.

21. What was Janet's score on the fourth physics test she took?

 (1) Her score on the fourth test was 12 points higher than her average (arithmetic mean) score on the first three tests she took.
 (2) Her score on the fourth test raised her average (arithmetic mean) test score from 87 to 90.

Because statement (1) does not give her average score on the first three tests, her score on the fourth test cannot be determined from (1) alone, and the answer must be B, C, or E. From statement (2), her score on the fourth test can be determined as the sum of her scores on the four tests (4×90) minus the sum of her scores on the first three tests (3×87). Thus, (2) alone is sufficient, and the best answer is B.

22. If $x + y > 0$, is $x > |y|$?

    (1) $x > y$

    (2) $y < 0$

The absolute value of a number y, denoted by $|y|$, is defined to be y if y is positive or zero and $-y$ if y is negative. For example, if $y = 8$, then $|y| = |8| = 8 = y$; but if $y = -8$, then $|y| = |-8| = 8 = -(-8) = -y$. It is given that $x + y > 0$, or $x > -y$. Thus, statement (1) alone is sufficient to determine that $x > |y|$, since $x > -y$ and $x > y$, and the answer must be A or D. From (2), y is negative, and so by definition $|y| = -y$. Since $x > -y$ is given, it follows that $x > |y|$. Thus, (2) alone is sufficient, and the best answer is D.

23. If x is an integer, is $(x + p)(x + q)$ an even integer?

    (1) q is an even integer.

    (2) p is an even integer.

From statement (1) alone it can be determined that $x + q$ is an integer, but not whether it is even or odd, and nothing is known about the value of $x + p$. Similarly, (2) alone is not sufficient, so the answer must be C or E. From (1) and (2) together, it is known that $x + p$ and $x + q$ are both integers. If x is even, then both $x + p$ and $x + q$ are even, and the product is even; but if x is odd, then both $x + p$ and $x + q$ are odd, and the product is odd. Therefore, (1) and (2) together are not sufficient, and the best answer is E.

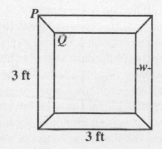

24. The figure above shows the dimensions of a square picture frame that was constructed using four pieces of frame as shown. If w is the width of each piece of the frame, what is the area of each piece?

    (1) $w = 3$ inches

    (2) $PQ = \sqrt{18}$ inches

Each of the pieces of the frame is a trapezoid whose area is $\frac{1}{2}(a + b)h$, where a and b are the lengths of the parallel sides $(a < b)$ and h is the altitude. Although statement (1) appears to give only the value of h (i.e., w), it also is sufficient to determine the length of the shorter parallel side. The following redrawing of the figure illustrates this.

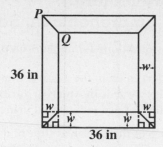

From statement (1), $a = (36 - 3 - 3)$ inches (using the fact that 12 inches = 1 foot), $b = 36$ inches, and $h = 3$ inches, and the area of each piece can be found. Therefore, (1) alone is sufficient, and the answer must be A or D. Statement (2) gives the length of the diagonal (PQ) of the square of side w inches that can be drawn at the top left corner of the figure, and the Pythagorean theorem can be used to determine the value of w, which has been shown to be sufficient to answer the question. Thus, (2) alone is sufficient, and the best answer is D.

Alternatively, the area of the picture frame is the area of the large square minus the area of the small square. In square inches, the large square has area $(3 \times 12)^2 = 36^2$ and the small square has area $(36 - 2w)^2$. Thus, the area of each of the 4 pieces of frame is $\frac{1}{4}(36^2 - (36 - 2w)^2)$ square inches, which can be determined once the value of w is known. Statements (1) and (2) alone are each sufficient since the value of w is given directly in (1) and follows from (2) together with the Pythagorean theorem.

25. A total of 774 doctorates in mathematics were granted to United States citizens by American universities in the 1972-1973 school year, and W of these doctorates were granted to women. The total of such doctorates in the 1986-1987 school year was 362, and w of these were granted to women. If the number of doctorates in mathematics granted to female citizens of the United States by American universities decreased from the 1972-1973 school year to the 1986-1987 school year, was the decrease less than 10 percent?

    (1) $\dfrac{1}{10} < \dfrac{W}{774} < \dfrac{1}{9}$

    (2) $W = w + 5$

From statement (1) only the possible values of W can be determined. Thus, (1) alone is not sufficient, and the answer must be B, C, or E. Statement (2) gives only the decrease in the number of doctorates granted to women and is not sufficient. Thus, the answer must be C or E. Statement (1) indicates that $77.4 < W < 86$, and (2) indicates that $W - w = 5$. Since 5 is less than 10 percent of any possible value of W, both (1) and (2) together are sufficient, and the best answer is C.

Explanatory Material:
Reading Comprehension, Section 2

(The passage for questions 1-7 appears on page 466.)

1. It can be inferred from the passage that accidental-death damage awards in America during the nineteenth century tended to be based principally on the

   (A) earnings of the person at time of death
   (B) wealth of the party causing the death
   (C) degree of culpability of the party causing the death
   (D) amount of money that had been spent on the person killed
   (E) amount of suffering endured by the family of the person killed

The best answer is A. In the first paragraph, the author cites an accidental-death case from nineteenth-century America in which the absence of economic contribution on the part of a deceased child was ruled sufficient grounds to deny the awarding of damages to the child's parents. The author goes on to discuss how this case typified attitudes that persisted even into the twentieth century. It can be inferred from this that in nineteenth-century America the chief consideration in determining damages in an accidental-death case was the deceased person's earnings. There is no evidence in the passage to suggest that the factors cited in B, C, D, and E were of primary concern in determining accidental-death damages in nineteenth-century America.

2. It can be inferred from the passage that in the early 1800's children were generally regarded by their families as individuals who

   (A) needed enormous amounts of security and affection
   (B) required constant supervision while working
   (C) were important to the economic well-being of a family
   (D) were unsuited to spending long hours in school
   (E) were financial burdens assumed for the good of society

The best answer is C. In the second paragraph, the author describes how during the nineteenth century the concept of the "'useful' child who contributed to the family economy" (lines 12-13) gradually gave way to the present-day notion of the economically "useless" but emotionally "priceless" child; this new view of childhood was "Well established among segments of the middle and upper classes by the mid-1800's" and "spread throughout society in the late-nineteenth and early-twentieth centuries" (lines 16-20). Thus in the early 1800's, prior to the shift in the valuation of children, families valued the role children had to play in the family's economic well-being. Choices A and E describe attitudes more in accord with the present-day view of childhood, and B and D address issues that are not raised in the passage.

3. Which of the following alternative explanations of the change in the cash value of children would be most likely to be put forward by sociological economists as they are described in the passage?

   (A) The cash value of children rose during the nineteenth century because parents began to increase their emotional investment in the upbringing of their children.
   (B) The cash value of children rose during the nineteenth century because their expected earnings over the course of a lifetime increased greatly.
   (C) The cash value of children rose during the nineteenth century because the spread of humanitarian ideals resulted in a wholesale reappraisal of the worth of an individual.
   (D) The cash value of children rose during the nineteenth century because compulsory education laws reduced the supply, and thus raised the costs, of available child labor.
   (E) The cash value of children rose during the nineteenth century because of changes in the way negligence law assessed damages in accidental-death cases.

The best answer is B. According to the author, practitioners of the new "sociological economics" explain sociological phenomena "solely in terms of their economic determinants" and "tend to view all human behavior as directed primarily by the principle of maximizing economic gain" (lines 46-50). Choice B provides just such an economic explanation for the nineteenth-century rise in the cash value of children. A paraphrases Zelizer's own explanation, which is at odds with that of the sociological economists, and C uses social values and emotional factors to explain an even broader revaluation of individual worth. D uses an economic argument to explain the change, but here the economic factors at work are the result of a change in social values. E provides a legal explanation for the change.

4. The primary purpose of the passage is to

   (A) review the literature in a new academic subfield
   (B) present the central thesis of a recent book
   (C) contrast two approaches to analyzing historical change
   (D) refute a traditional explanation of a social phenomenon
   (E) encourage further work on a neglected historical topic

The best answer is B. In the first paragraph, the author contrasts two incidents that are said to exemplify the transformation in social values that forms the subject of Zelizer's book. The second and third paragraphs consist of a brief history of that transformation, as Zelizer presents it, and an account of the factors she considers important in bringing it about. In the last paragraph, the author explains how Zelizer's thesis differs from that of sociological economists. Thus, the passage serves primarily to present the central thesis of Zelizer's book. Choice C is incorrect because although the passage does contrast two approaches, this contrast takes place only in the final paragraph. The other answer choices misrepresent either the author's approach or the subject matter of the passage.

5. It can be inferred from the passage that which of the following statements was true of American families over the course of the nineteenth century?

   (A) The average size of families grew considerably.
   (B) The percentage of families involved in industrial work declined dramatically.
   (C) Family members became more emotionally bonded to one another.
   (D) Family members spent an increasing amount of time working with each other.
   (E) Family members became more economically dependent on each other.

The best answer is C. In the third paragraph, the author cites Zelizer's contention that the new view of childhood that developed in nineteenth-century America was due in part to "the development of the companionate family (a family in which members were united by explicit bonds of love rather than duty)" (lines 28-30). From this it can be inferred that the emotional bonds between family members became increasingly important during this period. There is no information in the passage to support the other answer choices.

6. Zelizer refers to all of the following as important influences in changing the assessment of children's worth EXCEPT changes in

   (A) the mortality rate
   (B) the nature of industry
   (C) the nature of the family
   (D) attitudes toward reform movements
   (E) attitudes toward the marketplace

The best answer is D. Choices A, B, and C are mentioned in lines 25-31 as factors Zelizer regards as "critical in changing the assessment of children's worth"; E is mentioned in lines 36-41, which describe how the "sacralization" of children's lives represented "a way of resisting what they [middle-class Americans] perceived as the relentless corruption of human values by the marketplace." Although reform movements are mentioned in lines 20-23, the passage does not discuss attitudes or changes in attitudes toward those movements. D is therefore *not* among the influences Zelizer is said to regard as important in changing the assessment of children's worth.

7. Which of the following would be most consistent with the practices of sociological economics as these practices are described in the passage?

   (A) Arguing that most health-care professionals enter the field because they believe it to be the most socially useful of any occupation
   (B) Arguing that most college students choose majors that they believe will lead to the most highly paid jobs available to them
   (C) Arguing that most decisions about marriage and divorce are based on rational assessments of the likelihood that each partner will remain committed to the relationship
   (D) Analyzing changes in the number of people enrolled in colleges and universities as a function of changes in the economic health of these institutions
   (E) Analyzing changes in the ages at which people get married as a function of a change in the average number of years that young people have lived away from their parents

The best answer is B. The arguments and analyses described in A, C, and E stress social values, emotional commitment, and cultural forces, respectively; according to the passage, these are factors Zelizer finds important, whereas the practitioners of sociological economics are said to analyze traditional sociological topics "solely in terms of their economic determinants" while "Allowing only a small role for cultural forces" (lines 46-47). D describes the analysis of circumstances involving economic factors, but purely economic motivations are not attributed to the individuals described. According to the passage, sociological economists "tend to view all human behavior as directed primarily by the principle of maximizing economic gain" (lines 49-50); only B describes an argument that explains behavior in terms of this principle.

(The passage for questions 8-16 appears on page 468.)

8. According to the passage, the public-sector workers who were most likely to belong to unions in 1977 were

   (A) professionals
   (B) managers
   (C) clerical workers
   (D) service workers
   (E) blue-collar workers

The best answer is A. In the second paragraph, the author gives the percentages of workers who were unionized in different categories of the public sector in 1977. Forty-six percent of government professionals were unionized; this is greater than the percentage for any of the other categories of unionized workers from among the listed categories of public-sector workers. Therefore, professionals were more likely to belong to unions than were other public-sector workers.

9. The author cites union efforts to achieve a fully union-ized work force (lines 13-19) in order to account for why

(A) politicians might try to oppose public-sector union organizing
(B) public-sector unions have recently focused on organizing women
(C) early organizing efforts often focused on areas where there were large numbers of workers
(D) union efforts with regard to public-sector clerical workers increased dramatically after 1975
(E) unions sometimes tried to organize workers regardless of the workers' initial interest in unionization

The best answer is E. In lines 13-19, the author describes the reasoning behind the multioccupational unions' attempt to achieve a fully unionized workplace. This reasoning is provided to explain why "the multioccupational unions would often try to organize them [clerical workers] regardless of the workers' initial receptivity" (lines 11-13). Choice A helps to explain, but is not explained by, the attempt to achieve a fully unionized work force. An explanation for C is given in lines 3-6; B and D are explained in the second and third paragraphs of the passage.

10. The author's claim that, since the mid-1970's, a new strategy has emerged in the unionization of public-sector clerical workers (line 23) would be strengthened if the author

(A) described more fully the attitudes of clerical workers toward labor unions
(B) compared the organizing strategies employed by private-sector unions with those of public-sector unions
(C) explained why politicians and administrators sometimes oppose unionization of clerical workers
(D) indicated that the number of unionized public-sector clerical workers was increasing even before the mid-1970's
(E) showed that the factors that favored unionization drives among these workers prior to 1975 have decreased in importance

The best answer is E. The question asks what would strengthen the author's claim that a new strategy for unioniza-tion has emerged since the mid-1970's. Line 23 cites the appearance of the new strategy. The paragraphs that follow describe the changed circumstances that provided a context for such new strategies, and lines 52-56 explain precisely how these changed circumstances created a reason for new unioniz-ing strategies. The author's claim would be strengthened if it could be shown not only that there are such new circum-stances, but that the old circumstances discussed in the first paragraph have become less important, further necessitating the adoption of a new strategy in place of an old strategy suitable to those older circumstances.

11. According to the passage, in the period prior to 1975, each of the following considerations helped determine whether a union would attempt to organize a certain group of clerical workers EXCEPT

(A) the number of clerical workers in that group
(B) the number of women among the clerical workers in that group
(C) whether the clerical workers in that area were concentrated in one workplace or scattered over several workplaces
(D) the degree to which the clerical workers in that group were interested in unionization
(E) whether all the other workers in the same jurisdiction as that group of clerical workers were unionized

The best answer is B. In the first paragraph, the author describes the considerations relevant to a union's attempt to organize a certain group of clerical workers prior to 1975. Choices A, C, D, and E are all cited as important consider-ations. In line 2, the author notes the fact that most of these clerical workers were women, but does not suggest that this was an important consideration for unionizers.

12. The author states that which of the following is a consequence of the women's movement of recent years?

(A) An increase in the number of women entering the work force
(B) A structural change in multioccupational public-sector unions
(C) A more positive attitude on the part of women toward unions
(D) An increase in the proportion of clerical workers that are women
(E) An increase in the number of women in adminis-trative positions

The best answer is C. According to the author, "the women's movement has succeeded in legitimizing the economic and political activism of women on their own behalf," and this in turn has produced in women "a more positive attitude toward unions" (lines 42-45). Although A, B, D, and E describe developments mentioned in the passage, none of these are said to have been a consequence of the women's movement.

13. The main concern of the passage is to

(A) advocate particular strategies for future efforts to organize certain workers into labor unions
(B) explain differences in the unionized proportions of various groups of public-sector workers
(C) evaluate the effectiveness of certain kinds of labor unions that represent public-sector workers
(D) analyze and explain an increase in unionization among a certain category of workers
(E) describe and distinguish strategies appropriate to organizing different categories of workers

The best answer is D. In the first paragraph of the passage, the author asserts that efforts to unionize public-sector clerical workers prior to 1975 were limited and then goes on to describe these limited efforts. In the second paragraph, the author asserts that a new strategy developed after 1975 and cites an increase in union membership among public-sector clerical workers. The author begins the last paragraph by asking what can explain this increase in union membership, and then proceeds to provide an explanation. Thus, the passage is primarily concerned with analyzing and explaining the increase in unionization among public-sector clerical workers.

14. **The author implies that if the increase in the number of women in the work force and the impact of the women's movement were the main causes of the rise in unionization of public-sector clerical workers, then**

(A) more women would hold administrative positions in unions
(B) more women who hold political offices would have positive attitudes toward labor unions
(C) there would be an equivalent rise in unionization of private-sector clerical workers
(D) unions would have shown more interest than they have in organizing women
(E) the increase in the number of unionized public-sector clerical workers would have been greater than it has been

The best answer is C. After describing the increase in unionization among public-sector clerical workers and attributing this increase in part to the increased number of women in the work force and to the impact of the women's movement, the author goes on to say that the "absence of any comparable increase in unionization among private-sector clerical workers, however, identifies the primary catalyst" as something other than these two factors (lines 45-49). From this it can be inferred that if these two factors had, in fact, been the main causes of the rise in unionization among public-sector clerical workers, the same factors ought to have led to a comparable increase among private-sector clerical workers.

15. **The author suggests that it would be disadvantageous to a union if**

(A) many workers in the locality were not unionized
(B) the union contributed to political campaigns
(C) the union included only public-sector workers
(D) the union included workers from several jurisdictions
(E) the union included members from only a few occupations

The best answer is A. The author explains that the reasoning behind attempts to organize workers regardless of their receptivity to unionization "was based, first, on the concern that politicians and administrators might play off unionized against nonunionized workers, and, second, on the conviction that a fully unionized public work force meant power, both at the bargaining table and in the legislature" (lines 14-19). This suggests that having many nonunionized workers in a locality would be disadvantageous to a union.

16. **The author implies that, in comparison with working women today, women working in the years prior to the mid-1970's showed a greater tendency to**

(A) prefer smaller workplaces
(B) express a positive attitude toward labor unions
(C) maximize job security and economic benefits
(D) side with administrators in labor disputes
(E) quit working prior to retirement age

The best answer is E. In the last paragraph, the author describes the changed circumstances of working women since the mid-1970's. The author describes how more women have entered the work force, and also how "more of them plan to remain working until retirement age" (lines 38-39). Therefore, by implication, prior to the mid-1970's women were less likely to work until retirement age.

(The passage for questions 17-25 appears on page 470.)

17. **In the passage, the author is primarily interested in**

(A) suggesting an alternative to an outdated research method
(B) introducing a new research method that calls an accepted theory into question
(C) emphasizing the instability of data gathered from the application of a new scientific method
(D) presenting a theory and describing a new method to test that theory
(E) initiating a debate about a widely accepted theory

The best answer is D. In the first paragraph, the author describes Milankovitch's theory and explains why the theory previously had been considered untestable. In the second and third paragraphs, the author describes a scientific breakthrough that has made it possible to test and provide support for Milankovitch's theory. Although the author also mentions other factors that potentially could have affected the Earth's climate, the passage as a whole is concerned primarily with Milankovitch's theory and the scientific method that has been used to test that theory. Choices A, C, and E do not accurately reflect the content of the passage, and, although the passage does describe a new research method as B suggests, this method supports rather than casts doubt on Milankovitch's theory.

18. The author of the passage would be most likely to agree with which of the following statements about the Milankovitch theory?

(A) It is the only possible explanation for the ice ages.
(B) It is too limited to provide a plausible explanation for the ice ages, despite recent research findings.
(C) It cannot be tested and confirmed until further research on volcanic activity is done.
(D) It is one plausible explanation, though not the only one, for the ice ages.
(E) It is not a plausible explanation for the ice ages, although it has opened up promising possibilities for future research.

The best answer is D. In lines 7-13, the author states that a recent discovery has made it possible to establish a precise chronology of the Earth's ice ages. Scientists have used this discovery to test the basic premise of Milankovitch's theory — that the ice ages were caused by variations in the Earth's orbit around the Sun. The author notes in lines 41-43 that the data have established a "strong connection" between orbital variation and ice ages, which confirms the plausibility of Milankovitch's theory. However, one can infer from the last paragraph that the author believes factors other than variations in the Earth's orbit could provide plausible explanations for global climate change.

19. It can be inferred from the passage that the isotope record taken from ocean sediments would be less useful to researchers if which of the following were true?

(A) It indicated that lighter isotopes of oxygen predominated at certain times.
(B) It had far more gaps in its sequence than the record taken from rocks on land.
(C) It indicated that climate shifts did not occur every 100,000 years.
(D) It indicated that the ratios of oxygen 16 and oxygen 18 in ocean water were not consistent with those found in fresh water.
(E) It stretched back for only a million years.

The best answer is B. The author states that one advantage of obtaining an isotopic record from ocean sediment is that the ocean's isotopic record is "a more continuous record than that taken from rocks on land" (lines 33-34). Because a continuous record can indicate more precisely when shifts in the Earth's climate have occurred, the ocean's isotopic record would be less useful if it had more gaps in it than the record taken from rocks. Choice A describes a circumstance that is in fact true, since oxygen 16 is the lighter isotope and, according to the passage, "Almost all the oxygen in water is oxygen 16" (line 13); but this fact clearly has not compromised the usefulness of the ocean's isotopic record as an indicator of climatic shifts. Likewise, E would not diminish its usefulness, since isotopic records showing "flunctuations in global ice volume over the past several hundred thousand years" have been sufficient to determine a meaningful pattern (lines 37-41). If C were shown to be true, Milankovitch's theory would be weakened, but this would not diminish the value of the isotopic record. If D were true, researchers would need to accommodate the inconsistency described in evaluating the isotopic record, but, again, this would not compromise the usefulness of the record itself.

20. According to the passage, which of the following is true of the ratios of oxygen isotopes in ocean sediments?

(A) They indicate that sediments found during an ice age contain more calcium carbonate than sediments formed at other times.
(B) They are less reliable than the evidence from rocks on land in determining the volume of land ice.
(C) They can be used to deduce the relative volume of land ice that was present when the sediment was laid down.
(D) They are more unpredictable during an ice age than in other climatic conditions.
(E) They can be used to determine atmospheric conditions at various times in the past.

The best answer is C. Lines 10-13 state that the relative volume of land ice can be deduced from the ratio of oxygen 18 to oxygen 16 in ocean sediments. Choices A, D, and E are incorrect because there is no information in the passage to support these statements. B is incorrect because it contradicts lines 33-34, in which the author states that ocean sediment provides "a more continuous record than that taken from rocks on land."

21. It can be inferred from the passage that precipitation formed from evaporated ocean water has

(A) the same isotopic ratio as ocean water
(B) less oxygen 18 than does ocean water
(C) less oxygen 18 than has the ice contained in continental ice sheets
(D) a different isotopic composition than has precipitation formed from water on land
(E) more oxygen 16 than has precipitation formed from fresh water

The best answer is B. Lines 18-21 state that when water evaporates from the ocean surface, oxygen 18, a heavier isotope than oxygen 16, tends to be left behind in the remaining ocean water. Thus, one can infer that evaporated ocean water would contain less oxygen 18 than would the remaining ocean water. Choice A is incorrect because it contradicts information stated in lines 15-21. C is incorrect because the passage suggests that the water evaporated from the ocean contributes to the growth of continental ice sheets, which should therefore have an isotopic composition similar to that of the precipitation formed from evaporated ocean water. Choices D and E describe information that cannot be inferred from the passage.

22. According to the passage, which of the following is (are) true of the ice ages?

    I. The last ice age occurred about 25,000 years ago.
   II. Ice ages have lasted about 10,000 years for at least the last several hundred thousand years.
  III. Ice ages have occurred about every 100,000 years for at least the last several hundred thousand years.

  (A) I only
  (B) II only
  (C) III only
  (D) I and III only
  (E) I, II, and III

The best answer is C. To answer this question, it is necessary to determine whether or not each of the three statements is supported by information in the passage. In this instance, there is no information in the passage to support either statement I or statement II. However, lines 40-41 of the passage state that over the past several hundred thousand years, ice ages have occurred "roughly once every 100,000 years." Thus, from the information in the passage, statement III is the only true statement.

23. It can be inferred from the passage that calcium carbonate shells

  (A) are not as susceptible to deterioration as rocks
  (B) are less common in sediments formed during an ice age
  (C) are found only in areas that were once covered by land ice
  (D) contain radioactive material that can be used to determine a sediment's isotopic composition
  (E) reflect the isotopic composition of the water at the time the shells were formed

The best answer is E. Lines 23-26 of the passage state that the calcium carbonate shells of marine organisms are constructed with "oxygen atoms drawn from the surrounding ocean." This water contains varying proportions of oxygen 16 and oxygen 18 and, according to the passage, "becomes progressively enriched in oxygen 18" with the onset of an ice age (lines 15-21). The author states that "The degree of enrichment can be determined by analyzing ocean sediments . . . composed of calcium carbonate shells of marine animals "(lines 21-24). Thus, it can be inferred that the shells of marine organisms would reflect the isotopic composition of the surrounding ocean water at the time when the shells were formed.

24. The purpose of the last paragraph of the passage is to

  (A) offer a note of caution
  (B) introduce new evidence
  (C) present two recent discoveries
  (D) summarize material in the preceding paragraphs
  (E) offer two explanations for a phenomenon

The best answer is A. In the last paragraph of the passage, the author states that "it is important to note" that factors other than variations in the Earth's orbit (Milankovitch's theory) could have caused the ice ages. The author further notes that the lack of information about the possible influence of these factors on the Earth's climate does not reduce their importance. Thus, the author's primary purpose in this paragraph is to caution readers to take note of factors other than variations in the Earth's orbit that may have played a role in global climate change.

25. According to the passage, one advantage of studying the isotope record of ocean sediments is that it

  (A) corresponds with the record of ice volume taken from rocks on land
  (B) shows little variation in isotope ratios when samples are taken from different continental locations
  (C) corresponds with predictions already made by climatologists and experts in other fields
  (D) confirms the record of ice volume initially established by analyzing variations in volcanic emissions
  (E) provides data that can be used to substantiate records concerning variations in the amount of sunlight received by the Earth

The best answer is B. In lines 30-33, the author states that one advantage of using the isotope record of ocean sediment is that it provides a global record; that is, there is "little variation" in isotope ratios taken from samples in different locations around the world. None of the other answer choices describes what the passage presents as an advantage of studying the ocean's isotope record.

Explanatory Material: Problem Solving I, Section 3

1. The average (arithmetic mean) of 6, 8, and 10 equals the average of 7, 9, and

  (A) 5
  (B) 7
  (C) 8
  (D) 9
  (E) 11

The average of 6, 8, and 10 is $\dfrac{6+8+10}{3} = 8$, which equals the average of 7, 9, and x. Thus, $\dfrac{7+9+x}{3} = 8$, $16 + x = 24$, and $x = 8$. The best answer is therefore C.

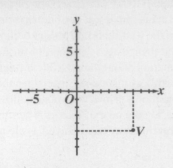

2. In the figure above, the coordinates of point V are

(A) (−7, 5)
(B) (−5, 7)
(C) (5, 7)
(D) (7, 5)
(E) (7, −5)

The x-coordinate of V is 7 and the y-coordinate of V is −5. Thus, the coordinates, (x,y), of V are (7, −5), and the best answer is E. Alternatively, since point V lies in quadrant IV, the x-coordinate of V is positive, and the y-coordinate of V is negative. Only choice E meets these conditions and is, therefore, the best answer.

3. Tickets for all but 100 seats in a 10,000-seat stadium were sold. Of the tickets sold, 20 percent were sold at half price and the remaining tickets were sold at the full price of $2. What was the total revenue from ticket sales?

(A) $15,840
(B) $17,820
(C) $18,000
(D) $19,800
(E) $21,780

The number of tickets sold was 10,000 − 100 = 9,900. If 20 percent of the tickets were sold at half price, then 80 percent were sold at full price. Total revenue was therefore 0.2(9,900)($1.00) + 0.8(9,900)($2.00) = $17,820. The best answer is B.

4. In a mayoral election, Candidate X received $\frac{1}{3}$ more votes than Candidate Y, and Candidate Y received $\frac{1}{4}$ fewer votes than Candidate Z. If Candidate Z received 24,000 votes, how many votes did Candidate X receive?

(A) 18,000
(B) 22,000
(C) 24,000
(D) 26,000
(E) 32,000

If x, y, and z are the number of votes received by candidates X, Y, and Z, respectively, then $x = \frac{4}{3}\,y$, $y = \frac{3}{4}\,z$, and z = 24,000. By substitution, $y = \left(\frac{3}{4}\right)(24,000) = 18,000$ and $x = \left(\frac{4}{3}\right)(18,000) = 24,000$. Candidate X received a total of 24,000 votes, and the best answer is C. Alternatively, and more directly, $x = \left(\frac{4}{3}\right)\left(\frac{3}{4}\right)z = z = 24,000$.

5. René earns $8.50 per hour on days other than Sundays and twice that rate on Sundays. Last week she worked a total of 40 hours, including 8 hours on Sunday. What were her earnings for the week?

(A) $272
(B) $340
(C) $398
(D) $408
(E) $476

René worked a total of 32 hours at $8.50 per hour during the week, and 8 hours on Sunday at $17.00 per hour. Her total earnings for the week were 32($8.50) + 8($17) = $408. The best answer is D.

6. In a shipment of 120 machine parts, 5 percent were defective. In a shipment of 80 machine parts, 10 percent were defective. For the two shipments combined, what percent of the machine parts were defective?

(A) 6.5%
(B) 7.0%
(C) 7.5%
(D) 8.0%
(E) 8.5%

In the combined shipments, there was a total of 200 machine parts, of which 0.05(120) + 0.1(80) = 6 + 8 = 14 were defective. The percent of machine parts that were defective in the two shipments combined was $\frac{14}{200} = \frac{7}{100} = 7\%$. The best answer is therefore B.

7. $\dfrac{2\frac{3}{5} - 1\frac{2}{3}}{\frac{2}{3} - \frac{3}{5}} =$

(A) 16
(B) 14
(C) 3
(D) 1
(E) −1

$$\frac{2\frac{3}{5} - 1\frac{2}{3}}{\frac{2}{3} - \frac{3}{5}} = \frac{\frac{13}{5} - \frac{5}{3}}{\frac{2}{3} - \frac{3}{5}} = \frac{\frac{39-25}{15}}{\frac{10-9}{15}} = \frac{\frac{14}{15}}{\frac{1}{15}} = \frac{14}{15} \times \frac{15}{1} = 14.$$

The best answer is B.

8. If $x = -1$, then $\dfrac{x^4 - x^3 + x^2}{x-1} =$

(A) $-\dfrac{3}{2}$

(B) $-\dfrac{1}{2}$

(C) 0

(D) $\dfrac{1}{2}$

(E) $\dfrac{3}{2}$

Substituting the value -1 for x in the expression results in
$$\frac{(-1)^4 - (-1)^3 + (-1)^2}{-1-1} = \frac{1 - (-1) + 1}{-2} = -\frac{3}{2}.$$
The best answer is A.

9. Which of the following equations is NOT equivalent to $25x^2 = y^2 - 4$?

(A) $25x^2 + 4 = y^2$
(B) $75x^2 = 3y^2 - 12$
(C) $25x^2 = (y+2)(y-2)$
(D) $5x = y - 2$
(E) $x^2 = \dfrac{y^2 - 4}{25}$

Choice A is obtained by adding 4 to both sides of the equation $25x^2 = y^2 - 4$. Choice B is obtained by multiplying both sides of the original equation by 3, while choice C is equivalent because $y^2 - 4 = (y+2)(y-2)$. Choice E is obtained by dividing both sides of the original equation by 25. By the process of elimination, the answer must be D. Squaring both sides of $5x = y - 2$, choice D, gives $25x^2 = y^2 - 4y + 4$, which is NOT equivalent to the original equation. Therefore, the best answer is D.

10. A toy store regularly sells all stock at a discount of 20 percent to 40 percent. If an additional 25 percent were deducted from the discount price during a special sale, what would be the lowest possible price of a toy costing $16 before any discount?

(A) $5.60
(B) $7.20
(C) $8.80
(D) $9.60
(E) $15.20

The lowest possible price is paid when the maximum discount is received, so the lowest possible regular price is $16 - 0.40(\$16) = \$9.60$. With an additional 25 percent discount, the lowest possible price is $\$9.60 - 0.25(\$9.60) = \$7.20$. The best answer is B.

Alternatively, the lowest possible price to be paid for the item can be calculated by realizing that if you are being given a discount of 40 percent you are paying 60 percent of the listed price of the item. If an additional 25 percent discount is offered on the item, the price of the item becomes $(0.75)(0.60)(\$16) = \$7.20$.

11. If there are 664,579 prime numbers among the first 10 million positive integers, approximately what percent of the first 10 million positive integers are prime numbers?

(A) 0.0066%
(B) 0.066%
(C) 0.66%
(D) 6.6%
(E) 66%

The ratio of 664,579 to 10 million is approximately 660,000 to 10,000,000 or $\dfrac{66}{1,000} = 0.066 = 6.6\%$. The best answer is therefore D.

12. A bank customer borrowed $10,000, but received y dollars less than this due to discounting. If there was a separate $25 service charge, then, in terms of y, the service charge was what fraction of the amount that the customer received?

(A) $\dfrac{25}{10,000 - y}$

(B) $\dfrac{25}{10,000 - 25y}$

(C) $\dfrac{25y}{10,000 - y}$

(D) $\dfrac{y - 25}{10,000 - y}$

(E) $\dfrac{25}{10,000 - (y - 25)}$

The amount of money the customer received was $(10,000 - y)$ dollars. The $25 service charge as a fraction of the amount received was, therefore, $\dfrac{25}{10,000 - y}$. The best answer is A.

13. An airline passenger is planning a trip that involves three connecting flights that leave from Airports *A*, *B*, and *C*, respectively. The first flight leaves Airport *A* every hour, beginning at 8:00 a.m., and arrives at Airport *B* $2\frac{1}{2}$ hours later. The second flight leaves Airport *B* every 20 minutes, beginning at 8:00 a.m., and arrives at Airport *C* $1\frac{1}{6}$ hours later. The third flight leaves Airport *C* every hour, beginning at 8:45 a.m. What is the <u>least</u> total amount of time the passenger must spend between flights if all flights keep to their schedules?

(A) 25 min
(B) 1 hr 5 min
(C) 1 hr 15 min
(D) 2 hr 20 min
(E) 3 hr 40 min

Regardless of the time of departure from Airport *A*, arrival at Airport *B* will be at 30 minutes past the hour. Flights leave Airport *B* on the hour, and at either 20 or 40 minutes past the hour. Therefore, the earliest a passenger from Airport *A* could leave Airport *B* would be at 40 minutes past the hour with a 10-minute wait between flights. The flight from Airport *B* to Airport *C* takes $1\frac{1}{6}$ hours or 1 hour 10 minutes. A flight taken at 40 minutes past the hour would arrive at Airport *C* at 50 minutes past the hour, causing the passenger to have missed the flight from Airport *C* by 5 minutes. The passenger therefore has a 55-minute wait, and the least total amount of time the passenger must spend between flights is $10 + 55 = 65$ minutes, or 1 hour 5 minutes. The best answer is B.

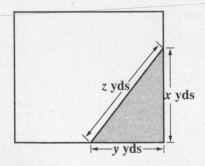

14. The shaded portion of the rectangular lot shown above represents a flower bed. If the area of the bed is 24 square yards and $x = y + 2$, then z equals

(A) $\sqrt{13}$
(B) $2\sqrt{13}$
(C) 6
(D) 8
(E) 10

The area of the triangular flower bed can be found by the formula $A = \frac{1}{2}$ (altitude)(base) or $24 = \frac{1}{2}(x)(y) = \frac{1}{2}(y+2)(y)$. Thus, $y^2 + 2y = 48$ or $y^2 + 2y - 48 = 0$. Factoring yields $(y + 8)(y - 6) = 0$, and $y = 6$ since the length must be positive. The altitude *x* of the region is $6 + 2 = 8$, and the flower bed is a 6-8-10 right triangle. The hypotenuse, *z*, can be found by using the Pythagorean theorem. The best answer is therefore E.

15. How many multiples of 4 are there between 12 and 96, inclusive?

(A) 21
(B) 22
(C) 23
(D) 24
(E) 25

The most direct way to find the number of multiples of 4 between 12 and 96, inclusive, would be to write every multiple of 4 starting with 12 (i.e., 12, 16, 20, 24,. . . , 96), but this is very time-consuming and leaves many opportunities for error. Another approach would be to note that in each group of 4 consecutive integers there is one multiple of 4. Between 12 and 96, inclusive, there are 85 numbers that, when divided by 4, yield 21 groups of 4 with 1 number remaining that must be considered independently. In the 21 groups of 4, there are 21 multiples of 4 and the remaining number, 96, is also a multiple of 4. The total number of multiples of 4 between 12 and 96, inclusive, is thus $21 + 1 = 22$. The best answer is B.

Alternatively, since $12 = 3 \times 4$ and $96 = 24 \times 4$, the number of multiples of 4 between 12 and 96, inclusive, is the same as the number of integers between 3 and 24, inclusive, namely, 22.

16. Jack is now 14 years older than Bill. If in 10 years Jack will be twice as old as Bill, how old will Jack be in 5 years?

(A) 9
(B) 19
(C) 21
(D) 23
(E) 33

Let *j* and *b* be Jack's and Bill's current ages. Then $j = b + 14$ and $j + 10 = 2(b + 10)$. By substitution, $b + 14 + 10 = 2(b + 10)$, and $b + 24 = 2b + 20$. Therefore, $b = 4$ and $j = 18$, and Jack's age in 5 years is $18 + 5 = 23$. The best answer is D.

17. In Township K, $\frac{1}{5}$ of the housing units are equipped with cable television. If $\frac{1}{10}$ of the housing units, including $\frac{1}{3}$ of those that are equipped with cable television, are equipped with videocassette recorders, what fraction of the housing units have neither cable television nor videocassette recorders?

(A) $\frac{23}{30}$

(B) $\frac{11}{15}$

(C) $\frac{7}{10}$

(D) $\frac{1}{6}$

(E) $\frac{2}{15}$

Let x denote the total number of housing units in Township K.

The portion of those units having neither cable television nor a videocassette recorder (VCR) can therefore be expressed as x minus the number of units with cable or a VCR or both, that is, $x - \left[\left(\frac{1}{5}x + \frac{1}{10}x \right) - \frac{1}{15}x \right]$. Simplifying yields $x - \frac{7}{30}x$ or $\frac{23}{30}x$. The best answer, therefore, is A.

Alternatively, let x be the number of housing units in Township K. Then $\frac{1}{5}x$ have cable, $\frac{1}{10}x$ have videocassette recorders (VCR's), $\frac{9}{10}x$ do not have VCR's, and $\left(\frac{1}{3} \right)\left(\frac{1}{5}x \right)$ have both cable and VCR's. The number of units with cable but not VCR's, therefore, is

$$\frac{1}{5}x - \left(\frac{1}{3} \right)\left(\frac{1}{5} \right)x = \left(\frac{1}{5}x \right) - \frac{1}{15}x = \frac{2}{15}x,$$

and the number of units with neither cable nor a VCR is $\frac{9}{10}x - \frac{2}{15}x$. The fraction of units with neither cable nor a VCR is $\frac{9}{10} - \frac{2}{15} = \frac{135 - 20}{150} = \frac{115}{150} = \frac{23}{30}$.

18. Set S consists of n distinct positive integers, none of which is greater than 12. What is the greatest possible value of n if no two integers in S have a common factor greater than 1 ?

(A) 4
(B) 5
(C) 6
(D) 7
(E) 11

If no two integers in S have a common factor greater than 1, then the integers in S other than 1 must have no prime divisors in common. But there are only five prime numbers less than 12: 2, 3, 5, 7 and 11. Thus, set S can contain at most six integers, including 1. For example, S can consist of 1, 2, 3, 5, 7, and 11, or S can consist of 1, 4, 5, 7, 9, and 11. The best answer is therefore C.

19. In a certain contest, Fred must select any 3 of 5 different gifts offered by the sponsor. From how many different combinations of 3 gifts can Fred make his selection?

(A) 10
(B) 15
(C) 20
(D) 30
(E) 60

The formula for the number of combinations, C, of n things taken p at a time is $C = \dfrac{n!}{p!(n-p)!}$. Therefore, the number of possible combinations of 5 gifts taken 3 at a time is

$$\frac{5!}{3!(5-3)!} = \frac{5!}{3!2!} = \frac{(5)(4)(3)(2)(1)}{(3)(2)(1)(2)(1)} = 10.$$

Alternatively, consider the 5 gifts as labeled A through E. Fred could choose any of the following possible combinations of 3: ABC, ABD, ABE, ACD, ACE, ADE, BCD, BCE, BDE, and CDE. The best answer is A.

20. If the number of square units in the area of circle C is twice the number of linear units in the circumference of C, what is the number of square units in the area?

(A) 4
(B) 8
(C) 4
(D) 8
(E) 16

For a circle with radius r, the area is πr^2 square units and the circumference is $2\pi r$ linear units. Thus, $\pi r^2 = 2(2\pi r) = 4\pi r$. Dividing both sides of the equation by πr gives $r = 4$. The number of square units in the area then is $\pi (4)^2 = 16\pi$, and the best answer is E.

Explanatory Material:
Sentence Correction, Section 4

1. **Delighted by the reported earnings for the first quarter of the fiscal year, _it was decided by the company manager to give her staff a raise_.**

   (A) it was decided by the company manager to give her staff a raise
   (B) the decision of the company manager was to give her staff a raise
   (C) the company manager decided to give her staff a raise
   (D) the staff was given a raise by the company manager
   (E) a raise was given to the staff by the company manager

Grammatically, the participial phrase beginning _delighted_ must modify the subject of the main clause. Because it is the manager who was delighted, choice C, in which _the company manager_ appears as the subject, is the best answer. Choices A, B, D, and E create illogical statements by using _it, the decision, the staff,_ and _a raise,_ respectively, as the sentence subject. Use of the passive voice in A, D, and E produces unnecessary wordiness, as does the construction _the decision of the company manager was to_ in B.

2. **A study commissioned by the Department of Agriculture showed that if calves exercise and _associated with other calves, they will require less medication and gain weight quicker than do_ those raised in confinement.**

   (A) associated with other calves, they will require less medication and gain weight quicker than do
   (B) associated with other calves, they require less medication and gain weight quicker than
   (C) associate with other calves, they required less medication and will gain weight quicker than do
   (D) associate with other calves, they have required less medication and will gain weight more quickly than do
   (E) associate with other calves, they require less medication and gain weight more quickly than

Choice E, the best answer, uses the adverbial phrase _more quickly than_ to modify the verb phrase _gain weight_. In A, B, and C, _quicker than_ is incorrect because an adjective should not be used to modify a verb phrase. E is also the only choice with consistent verb tenses. The first verb in the clauses introduced by _showed that_ is _exercise_. A and B incorrectly compound that present tense verb with a past tense verb, _associated_. C and D correctly use _associate_, but C follows with the past tense _required_ and D with the present perfect _have required_. Both C and D incorrectly conclude with the future tense _will gain_.

3. **Displays of the aurora borealis, or "northern lights," can heat the atmosphere over the arctic enough <u>to affect the trajectories of ballistic missiles, induce</u> electric currents that can cause blackouts in some areas and corrosion in north-south pipelines.**

   (A) to affect the trajectories of ballistic missiles, induce
   (B) that the trajectories of ballistic missiles are affected, induce
   (C) that it affects the trajectories of ballistic missiles, induces
   (D) that the trajectories of ballistic missiles are affected and induces
   (E) to affect the trajectories of ballistic missiles and induce

The use of the phrasing _can heat . . . enough to affect_ in A and E is more idiomatic than the use of the subordinate clause beginning with _that_ in B, C, and D. Also, B produces an illogical and ungrammatical statement by making _induce_ parallel with the verb _heat_ rather than with the appropriate form of the verb _affect_; C lacks agreement in using the singular pronoun _it_ to refer to the plural noun _displays_; and D is faulty because _induces_ cannot fit grammatically with any noun in the sentence. Choice A incorrectly separates the two infinitives _to affect_ and _[to] induce_ with a comma when it should compound them with _and_, as does E, the best choice.

4. **The golden crab of the Gulf of Mexico has not been fished commercially in great numbers, primarily <u>on account of living</u> at great depths — 2,500 to 3,000 feet down.**

   (A) on account of living
   (B) on account of their living
   (C) because it lives
   (D) because of living
   (E) being they live

As used in choices A, B, and D, the phrases _on account of_ and _because of_ are unidiomatic; _because_, which appears in C and E, is preferable here since _because_ can introduce a complete subordinate clause explaining the reason why the golden crab has not been fished extensively. B and E also produce agreement errors by using the plural pronouns _their_ and _they_ to refer to the singular noun _crab_. Choice D, like A, fails to provide a noun or pronoun to perform the action of _living_, but even with _its_ the phrases would be more awkward and less clear than _it lives_. C, which uses _because_ and _it_ as the singular subject of a clause, is the best choice.

5. The cameras of the Voyager II spacecraft detected six small, previously unseen moons circling Uranus, <u>which doubles to twelve the number of satellites now known as orbiting</u> the distant planet.

(A) which doubles to twelve the number of satellites now known as orbiting

(B) doubling to twelve the number of satellites now known to orbit

(C) which doubles to twelve the number of satellites now known in orbit around

(D) doubling to twelve the number of satellites now known as orbiting

(E) which doubles to twelve the number of satellites now known that orbit

The pronoun *which* should be used to refer to a previously mentioned noun, not to the idea expressed in an entire clause. In A, C, and E, *which* seems to refer to a vague concept involving the detection of moons, but there is no specific noun, such as *detection*, to which it can refer. Also in E, the use of the phrasing *the number . . . now known that orbit* is ungrammatical and unclear. B and D use the correct participial form, *doubling*, to modify the preceding clause, but D, like A, uses *known as orbiting* rather than *known to orbit*, a phrase that is more idiomatic in context. B, therefore, is the best answer.

6. <u>As a baby emerges from the darkness of the womb with a rudimentary sense of vision, it would be rated about 20/500, or legally blind if it were an adult with such vision.</u>

(A) As a baby emerges from the darkness of the womb with a rudimentary sense of vision, it would be rated about 20/500, or legally blind if it were an adult with such vision.

(B) A baby emerges from the darkness of the womb with a rudimentary sense of vision that would be rated about 20/500, or legally blind as an adult.

(C) As a baby emerges from the darkness of the womb, its rudimentary sense of vision would be rated about 20/500; qualifying it to be legally blind if an adult.

(D) A baby emerges from the darkness of the womb with a rudimentary sense of vision that would be rated about 20/500; an adult with such vision would be deemed legally blind.

(E) As a baby emerges from the darkness of the womb, its rudimentary sense of vision, which would deemed legally blind for an adult, would be rated about 20/500.

In choice A, *it*, the subject of the main clause, seems to refer to *baby*, the subject of the subordinate clause; thus, A seems to state that the newborn baby, rather than its sense of vision, would be rated 20/500. Similarly, choices B and E use awkward and ambiguous phrasing that suggests that the *sense of vision*, rather than an adult with 20/500 vision, would be considered legally blind. C incorrectly uses the semicolon, which should separate independent clauses, to set off a verb phrase. The phrase *if an adult* in C is also illogical, since it states that a baby could also be an adult. D is the best choice.

7. While Jackie Robinson was a Brooklyn Dodger, his courage in the face of physical threats and verbal attacks was <u>not unlike that of Rosa Parks, who refused</u> to move to the back of a bus in Montgomery, Alabama.

(A) not unlike that of Rosa Parks, who refused

(B) not unlike Rosa Parks, who refused

(C) like Rosa Parks and her refusal

(D) like that of Rosa Parks for refusing

(E) as that of Rosa Parks, who refused

Choices B and C present faulty comparisons: in B, Jackie Robinson's courage is compared to Rosa Parks herself, not to her courage, and in C it is compared to both Rosa Parks and her refusal. Choice D does not make clear whether it was Jackie Robinson or Rosa Parks who showed courage in refusing to move to the back of the bus; in fact, saying *for refusing* rather than *who refused* makes it sound as if *courage* moved to the back of the bus. Choice E incorrectly uses *as* rather than *like* to compare two noun phrases. Choice A is best.

8. <u>The rising of costs</u> of data-processing operations at many financial institutions has created a growing opportunity for independent companies to provide these services more efficiently and at lower cost.

(A) The rising of costs

(B) Rising costs

(C) The rising cost

(D) Because the rising cost

(E) Because of rising costs

C is the best choice. In choice A, *The rising of costs* is unidiomatic, and in B *costs . . . has* lacks subject-verb agreement. Choices D and E produce sentence fragments since *Because* makes the clause subordinate rather than independent.

9. There is no consensus on what role, if any, is played by acid rain in <u>slowing the growth or damaging</u> forests in the eastern United States.

(A) slowing the growth or damaging

(B) the damage or the slowing of the growth of

(C) the damage to or the slowness of the growth of

(D) damaged or slowed growth of

(E) damaging or slowing the growth of

The corrected sentence must make clear that both *damaging* and *slowing the growth of* refer to *forests*. E is the only choice that does so without introducing errors. In choice A, *of* is required after *growth*. In choices B and C, the use of *the damage* instead of *damaging* produces awkward and wordy constructions, and without *to* after *damage*, B is grammatically incomplete. In C, *the slowness of* does not convey the original sense that the rate of growth has been slowed by acid rain. Choice D also changes the meaning of the sentence by making both *damaged* and *slowed* refer to *growth*.

10. Galileo was convinced that natural phenomena, as manifestations of the laws of physics, would appear the same to someone on the deck of a ship moving smoothly and uniformly through the <u>water as a</u> person standing on land.

   (A) water as a
   (B) water as to a
   (C) water; just as it would to a
   (D) water, as it would to the
   (E) water; just as to the

B, the best choice, uses the idiomatic and grammatically parallel form *the same to X as to Y*. Because A lacks the preposition *to*, it seems to compare the appearance of natural phenomena to that of a person standing on land. C and D unnecessarily repeat *would* and wrongly use the singular *it* to refer to the plural *phenomena*. C and E each contain a faulty semicolon and produce errors in idiom, *the same to X just as [it would] to*. D and E use the definite article *the* where the indefinite article *a* is needed to refer to an unspecified person.

11. A recent study has found that within the past few years, many doctors <u>had elected early retirement rather than face</u> the threats of lawsuits and the rising costs of malpractice insurance.

   (A) had elected early retirement rather than face
   (B) had elected early retirement instead of facing
   (C) have elected retiring early instead of facing
   (D) have elected to retire early rather than facing
   (E) have elected to retire early rather than face

Because the sentence describes a situation that continues into the present, choices A and B are incorrect in using the past perfect *had elected*, which denotes an action completed at a specific time in the past. Also, alternatives presented in the expressions *x rather than y* and *x instead of y* should be parallel in form, but A and B mismatch the noun *retirement* with the verb forms *face* and *facing*. C is faulty because *have elected*, which is correct in tense, cannot idiomatically be followed by a participle such as *retiring*. D correctly follows *have elected* with an infinitive, *to retire*, but, like A and B, fails to maintain parallelism. Only E, the best choice, uses the correct tense, observes parallelism, and is idiomatic.

12. Architects and stonemasons, <u>huge palace and temple clusters were built by the Maya without benefit of the wheel or animal transport</u>.

   (A) huge palace and temple clusters were built by the Maya without benefit of the wheel or animal transport
   (B) without the benefits of animal transport or the wheel, huge palace and temple clusters were built by the Maya
   (C) the Maya built huge palace and temple clusters without the benefit of animal transport or the wheel
   (D) there were built, without the benefit of the wheel or animal transport, huge palace and temple clusters by the Maya
   (E) were the Maya who, without the benefit of the wheel or animal transport, built huge palace and temple clusters

A, B, and D illogically suggest that the *palace and temple clusters* were architects and stonemasons. For the modification to be logical, *Architects and stonemasons* must immediately precede *the Maya*, the noun phrase it is meant to modify. A, B, and D also use the passive verb form *were built*, which produces unnecessary awkwardness and wordiness. E is awkwardly phrased and produces a sentence fragment, because the appositive noun phrase *Architects and stonemasons* cannot serve as the subject of *were the Maya*. C, the best answer, places *the Maya* immediately after its modifier and uses the active verb form *built*.

13. In astronomy the term "red shift" denotes the extent <u>to which light from a distant galaxy has been shifted</u> toward the red, or long-wave, end of the light spectrum by the rapid motion of the galaxy away from the Earth.

   (A) to which light from a distant galaxy has been shifted
   (B) to which light from a distant galaxy has shifted
   (C) that light from a distant galaxy has been shifted
   (D) of light from a distant galaxy shifting
   (E) of the shift of light from a distant galaxy

Choice A is best because it is idiomatic and because its passive verb construction, *has been shifted*, clearly indicates that the *light* has been acted upon *by the rapid motion*. In B, the active verb *has shifted* suggests that the light, not the motion, is the agency of action, but such a construction leaves the phrase *by the rapid motion of the galaxy away from the Earth* without any logical or grammatical function. In C, the construction *the extent that light* is ungrammatical; *denotes the extent* must be completed by *to which*. D incorrectly employs an active verb, *shifting*, and *extent of light* is imprecise and awkward. E is faulty because it contains no verb to express the action performed by the *rapid motion*.

14. William H. Johnson's artistic debt to Scandinavia is evident in paintings that range from sensitive portraits of citizens in his wife's Danish home, Kerteminde, <u>and</u> awe-inspiring views of fjords and mountain peaks in the western and northern regions of Norway.

   (A) and
   (B) to
   (C) and to
   (D) with
   (E) in addition to

The construction *range from x* must be completed by *to y*, as in choice B, the best answer: Johnson's paintings *range from . . . portraits . . . to . . . views*. Each of the other choices produces an unidiomatic construction.

15. In 1978 only half the women granted child support by a court received the amount awarded; <u>at least as much as a million and more others had not any</u> support agreements whatsoever.

   (A) at least as much as a million and more others had not any
   (B) at least as much as more than a million others had no
   (C) more than a million others had not any
   (D) more than a million others had no
   (E) there was at least a million or more others without any

D, the best choice, is idiomatic, clear, and concise. Both A and B incorrectly use *much* rather than *many* to describe the countable noun *others*; *much* should be used with uncountable nouns such as "joy" or "labor." Even if this error were corrected, though, A and B would still be wrong. Because *more than x* necessarily includes the sense of *at least as many as x*, it is redundant and confusing to use elements of both expressions to refer to the same number of women. In A and C, *not any support agreements* is wordy and awkward. Like A and B, E redundantly uses both *at least* and *more*, and it incorrectly links the singular verb *was* with the plural subject *others*.

16. According to a recent poll, owning and living in a freestanding house on its own land is still a goal of a majority of young adults, <u>like that of earlier generations</u>.

   (A) like that of earlier generations
   (B) as that for earlier generations
   (C) just as earlier generations did
   (D) as have earlier generations
   (E) as it was of earlier generations

The intended comparison should be completed by a clause beginning with *as* and containing a subject and verb that correspond to the subject and verb of the main clause. In E, the best choice, *it* refers unambiguously to the phrasal subject *owning . . . land*, the verb *was* corresponds to *is*, and today's *young adults* are appropriately compared to *earlier generations*. Choices A and B lack a verb corresponding to *is* and a clear referent for *that*. Choices C and D are confusing and illogical because their verbs, *did* and *have*, cannot substitute for *is* in the main clause.

17. The Gorton-Dodd bill requires <u>that a bank disclose to their customers how long they will delay access to funds from deposited checks</u>.

   (A) that a bank disclose to their customers how long they will delay access to funds from deposited checks
   (B) a bank to disclose to their customers how long they will delay access to funds from a deposited check
   (C) that a bank disclose to its customers how long it will delay access to funds from deposited checks
   (D) a bank that it should disclose to its customers how long it will delay access to funds from a deposited check
   (E) that banks disclose to customers how long access to funds from their deposited check is to be delayed

Choice C is best. In A and B, the plural pronouns *their* and *they* do not agree with the singular noun *bank*. B, like D and E, illogically shifts from the plural *customers* and *funds* to the singular *check*, as if the customers were jointly depositing only one check. In D, *requires a bank that it should* is ungrammatical; *requires that a bank* is the appropriate idiom. In E, the use of the passive construction *is to be delayed* is less informative than the active voice because the passive does not explicitly identify the bank as the agent responsible for the delay.

18. Geologists believe that the warning signs for a major earthquake may include sudden fluctuations in local seismic activity, tilting and other deformations of the Earth's crust, <u>changing the measured strain across a fault zone, and varying</u> the electrical properties of underground rocks.

   (A) changing the measured strain across a fault zone, and varying
   (B) changing measurements of the strain across a fault zone, and varying
   (C) changing the strain as measured across a fault zone, and variations of
   (D) changes in the measured strain across a fault zone, and variations in
   (E) changes in measurements of the strain across a fault zone, and variations among

D, the best choice, describes *the warning signs* in parallel phrases. Despite surface appearances, the nouns *changes* and *variations* are parallel with *tilting*, but the verbal forms *changing* and *varying* in A, B, and C are not: *tilting*, one of the *deformations of the Earth's crust*, is used here as a noun that is parallel to *fluctuations*, whereas *changing* and *varying* are used as verbs indicating some action undertaken. Moreover, these verbs are used incorrectly because the sentence mentions no subject that is performing these actions. B and E illogically state that it is not the *strain* but the *measurements* that portend danger, and *among* in E wrongly suggests a comparison of different electrical properties rather than of different behaviors of the same properties.

19. Health officials estimate that 35 million Africans <u>are in danger of contracting</u> trypanosomiasis, or "African sleeping sickness," a parasitic disease spread by the bites of tsetse flies.

    (A) are in danger of contracting
    (B) are in danger to contract
    (C) have a danger of contracting
    (D) are endangered by contraction
    (E) have a danger that they will contract

Choice A, which is both idiomatic and concise, is best. In choice B, *to contract* is wrong because the phrase *are in danger* must be followed by *of*, not by an infinitive. The phrase *have a danger* is unidiomatic in C. In D, the phrase *by contraction trypanosomiasis* requires *of* after *contraction*; even if this correction were made, though, the passive construction in D would be unnecessarily wordy and also imprecise, because it is the disease more than the act of contracting it that poses the danger. In E, *have a danger* is again unidiomatic, and the *that* clause following the phrase is, within the structure of the sentence, ungrammatical and awkward.

20. Unlike a funded pension system, in which contributions are invested to pay future beneficiaries, <u>a pay-as-you-go approach is the foundation of Social Security</u>.

    (A) a pay-as-you-go approach is the foundation of Social Security
    (B) the foundation of Social Security is a pay-as-you-go approach
    (C) the approach of Social Security is pay-as-you-go
    (D) Social Security's approach is pay-as-you-go
    (E) Social Security is founded on a pay-as-you-go approach

In this sentence, the first noun of the main clause grammatically identifies what is being compared with *a funded pension system*; to be logical, the comparison must be made between comparable things. Only E, the best choice, compares one kind of system of providing for retirees, the *funded pension system*, with another such system, *Social Security*. Choices A, C, and D all illogically compare the pension system with the *approach* taken by Social Security itself. In B, the comparison of *pension system* with *foundation* is similarly flawed.

21. Critics of the trend toward privately operated prisons consider corrections facilities <u>to be an integral part of the criminal justice system and question if</u> profits should be made from incarceration.

    (A) to be an integral part of the criminal justice system and question if
    (B) as an integral part of the criminal justice system and they question if
    (C) as being an integral part of the criminal justice system and question whether
    (D) an integral part of the criminal justice system and question whether
    (E) are an integral part of the criminal justice system, and they question whether

When *consider* means "regard as," as it does in this sentence, its object should be followed immediately by the phrase that identifies or describes that object. Thus, *to be* in A, *as* in B, and *as being* in C produce unidiomatic constructions in the context of the sentence. Also, although *if* and *whether* can be used interchangeably after some verbs, *question if*, which appears in A and B, is unidiomatic, and *they* in B is unnecessary. E also contains the unnecessary *they*, and it uses the ungrammatical construction *consider . . . facilities are*. Grammatically and idiomatically sound, D is the best choice.

22. The Federal Reserve Board's <u>reduction of interest rates on loans to financial institutions is both an acknowledgment of past economic trends and an effort</u> to influence their future direction.

    (A) reduction of interest rates on loans to financial institutions is both an acknowledgment of past economic trends and an effort
    (B) reduction of interest rates on loans to financial institutions is an acknowledgment both of past economic trends as well as an effort
    (C) reduction of interest rates on loans to financial institutions both acknowledge past economic trends and attempt
    (D) reducing interest rates on loans to financial institutions is an acknowledgment both of past economic trends and an effort
    (E) reducing interest rates on loans to financial institutions both acknowledge past economic trends as well as attempt

Choice A is best. In B, *both* must come before *acknowledgment* if it is to link *acknowledgment* and *effort*; as misplaced here, it creates the unfulfilled expectation that the *reduction of interest rates* will be an acknowledgment of two different things. Moreover, *both . . . as well as . . .* is redundant: the correct idiom is *both x and y*. In C, the plural verbs *acknowledge* and *attempt* do not agree with their singular subject, *reduction*; also, it is imprecise to characterize a *reduction* as performing actions such as acknowledging or attempting. In both D and E, the use of the participle *reducing* rather than the noun *reduction* is awkward. Like B, D misplaces *both*, while E repeats both the redundancy of B and the agreement error of C.

23. **Tiny quantities of more than thirty rare gases, most of them industrial by-products, threaten to warm the Earth's atmosphere even more rapidly than carbon dioxide during the next fifty years.**

    (A) to warm the Earth's atmosphere even more rapidly than carbon dioxide during the next fifty years
    (B) to warm the Earth's atmosphere even more rapidly over the next fifty years than carbon dioxide will
    (C) during the next fifty years to warm the Earth's atmosphere even more rapidly than carbon dioxide
    (D) a warming of the Earth's atmosphere during the next fifty years even more rapid than carbon dioxide's
    (E) a warming of the Earth's atmosphere even more rapid than carbon dioxide's will be over the next fifty years

B, the best choice, uses the verb *will* to substitute for *warm* in completing the comparison between *rare gases* and *carbon dioxide*. Because they lack *will*, A and C are ambiguous and awkward: *carbon dioxide* could be considered the object of the verb *warm*. In A, C, and D, *during* does not establish that the warming described will occur over the entire fifty-year period, and in C *during* illogically modifies *threaten*. Choices D and E eliminate the need for *will* by awkwardly converting the infinitive *to warm* into *warming,* a participle that functions as a noun; the idiomatic form of expression, however, is *threaten to x.*

24. **Several years ago the diet industry introduced a variety of appetite suppressants, but some of these drugs caused stomach disorders severe enough to have them banned by the Food and Drug Administration.**

    (A) stomach disorders severe enough to have them
    (B) stomach disorders that were severe enough so they were
    (C) stomach disorders of such severity so as to be
    (D) such severe stomach disorders that they were
    (E) such severe stomach disorders as to be

Choice D, the best answer, employs the idiomatic construction *such x that y* in which *x* describes a condition and *y* the result of that condition. In A and B, *severe enough*, which suggests a condition that makes something possible rather than one leading to a particular result, is awkward and imprecise; also, it cannot grammatically be followed by *so they*, as it is in B. In addition, *to have them banned* in A and *so they were banned* in B suggest illogically that the *stomach disorders* rather than the *drugs* were banned. In C and E, *(so) as to be banned* produces the same ambiguity and cannot correctly complete the construction begun by *such*.

25. **Some analysts contend that true capitalism exists only when the ownership of both property and the means of production is regarded as an inalienable right of an individual's, and it is not a license granted by government and revokable at whim.**

    (A) is regarded as an inalienable right of an individual's, and it is not
    (B) are regarded as individuals' inalienable rights, and that it not be
    (C) is regarded as an individual's inalienable right, not as
    (D) are regarded as an individual's inalienable rights, not when they are
    (E) is regarded as the inalienable rights of an individual, not when it is

The best choice, C, correctly matches the singular subject *ownership* with the singular verb *is* and uses the parallel construction *regarded as x, not as y* to express the contrast between the two conceptions of *ownership*. Choice A incorrectly uses both *of* and *'s* to indicate the possessive, B mismatches *ownership* with *are*, D mismatches *ownership* with *are* and *they*, and both D and E incorrectly use the plural *rights* to refer to *ownership*. In addition, all choices but C fail to use *not as* after the comma to complete a parallel construction; the nonparallel constructions thus do not continue to describe ownership in terms of how it is regarded.

Explanatory Material: Problem Solving II, Section 5

1. **In Country X a returning tourist may import goods with a total value of $500 or less tax free, but must pay an 8 percent tax on the portion of the total value in excess of $500. What tax must be paid by a returning tourist who imports goods with a total value of $730 ?**

    (A) $58.40
    (B) $40.00
    (C) $24.60
    (D) $18.40
    (E) $16.00

The tourist must pay tax on $730 - $500 = $230. The amount of the tax is 0.08($230) = $18.40. The best answer is therefore D.

2. Which of the following is greater than $\frac{2}{3}$?

(A) $\frac{33}{50}$

(B) $\frac{8}{11}$

(C) $\frac{3}{5}$

(D) $\frac{13}{27}$

(E) $\frac{5}{8}$

One way to determine which of the options given is a value greater than $\frac{2}{3}$ is to establish equivalent fractions. In choice A, $\frac{33}{50} < \frac{2}{3}$ because $\frac{99}{150} < \frac{100}{150}$. In B, $\frac{8}{11} > \frac{2}{3}$ because $\frac{24}{33} > \frac{22}{33}$. In C, $\frac{3}{5} < \frac{2}{3}$ because $\frac{9}{15} < \frac{10}{15}$; in D, $\frac{13}{27} < \frac{2}{3}$ because $\frac{13}{27} < \frac{18}{27}$; and in E, $\frac{5}{8} < \frac{2}{3}$ because $\frac{15}{24} < \frac{16}{24}$. Therefore, the best answer is B.

Alternatively, convert the fractions to decimal form:
$\frac{2}{3} = 0.666666\ldots$, $\frac{33}{50} = 0.66$, $\frac{8}{11} = 0.727272\ldots$, $\frac{3}{5} = 0.6$, $\frac{13}{27} = 0.481481\ldots$, and $\frac{5}{8} = 0.625$. Thus, by comparing decimal equivalents, only $\frac{8}{11}$ is greater than $\frac{2}{3}$.

3. A rope 40 feet long is cut into two pieces. If one piece is 18 feet longer than the other, what is the length, in feet, of the shorter piece?

(A) 9
(B) 11
(C) 18
(D) 22
(E) 29

Let x be the length of the shorter piece of rope, and let $x + 18$ be the length of the longer piece. Then $x + (x + 18) = 40$, which yields $2x + 18 = 40$, and $x = 11$. The best answer is B.

4. If 60 percent of a rectangular floor is covered by a rectangular rug that is 9 feet by 12 feet, what is the area, in square feet, of the floor?

(A) 65
(B) 108
(C) 180
(D) 270
(E) 300

The area of the rug is $(9)(12) = 108$ square feet, which is 60 percent of x, the total area of the floor. Thus, $108 = 0.6x$, or $x = \frac{108}{0.6} = 180$. The best answer is therefore C.

5. The Earth travels around the Sun at a speed of approximately 18.5 miles per second. This approximate speed is how many miles per hour?

(A) 1,080
(B) 1,160
(C) 64,800
(D) 66,600
(E) 3,996,000

There are 60 seconds in one minute, and 60 minutes in one hour. In one hour the Earth travels $18.5 \times 60 \times 60 = 66,600$ miles, and the best answer is D.

6. A collection of books went on sale, and $\frac{2}{3}$ of them were sold for $2.50 each. If none of the 36 remaining books were sold, what was the total amount received for the books that were sold?

(A) $180
(B) $135
(C) $90
(D) $60
(E) $54

Since $\frac{2}{3}$ of the books in the collection were sold, $\frac{1}{3}$ were not sold. The 36 unsold books represent $\frac{1}{3}$ of the total number of books in the collection, and $\frac{2}{3}$ of the total number of books equals 2(36) or 72. The total proceeds of the sale was 72($2.50) or $180. The best answer is therefore A.

7. If "basis points" are defined so that 1 percent is equal to 100 basis points, then 82.5 percent is how many basis points greater than 62.5 percent?

(A) 0.02
(B) 0.2
(C) 20
(D) 200
(E) 2,000

There is a difference of 20 percent between 82.5 percent and 62.5 percent. If 1 percent equals 100 basis points, then 20 percent equals 20(100) or 2,000 basis points. The best answer is E.

8. The amounts of time that three secretaries worked on a special project are in the ratio of 1 to 2 to 5. If they worked a combined total of 112 hours, how many hours did the secretary who worked the longest spend on the project?

   (A) 80
   (B) 70
   (C) 56
   (D) 16
   (E) 14

Since the ratio of hours worked by the secretaries on the project is 1 to 2 to 5, the third secretary spent the longest time on the project, that is, $\frac{5}{8}(112)$ or 70 hours. The best answer is therefore B.

9. If the quotient $\frac{a}{b}$ is positive, which of the following must be true?

   (A) $a > 0$
   (B) $b > 0$
   (C) $ab > 0$
   (D) $a - b > 0$
   (E) $a + b > 0$

If the quotient $\frac{a}{b}$ is positive, then either $a > 0$ and $b > 0$, or $a < 0$ and $b < 0$. It follows that answer choices A and B need not be true. Choice C must be true, because the product of two positive or two negative numbers is positive. Finally, $2 \cdot 3 = -1$ and $-2 + (-1) = -3$ show that choices D and E, respectively, need not be true. The best answer is therefore C.

10. If $8^{2x+3} = 2^{3x+6}$, then $x =$

   (A) -3
   (B) -1
   (C) 0
   (D) 1
   (E) 3

Since $8^{2x+3} = (2^3)^{2x+3} = 2^{6x+9}$, it follows, by equating exponents, that $6x + 9 = 3x + 6$, or $x = -1$. The best answer is therefore B.

11. Of the following, the closest approximation to

   $\sqrt{\dfrac{5.98(601.5)}{15.79}}$ is

   (A) 5
   (B) 15
   (C) 20
   (D) 25
   (E) 225

The value of the expression under the square root sign is approximately $\frac{6(600)}{16} = 225$. Since $225 = 15^2$, $\sqrt{225} = 15$, and the best answer is B.

12. Which of the following CANNOT be the greatest common divisor of two positive integers x and y ?

   (A) 1
   (B) x
   (C) y
   (D) $x - y$
   (E) $x + y$

Each answer choice except E can be the greatest common divisor (g.c.d.) of two positive integers. For example, if $x = 3$ and $y = 2$, then x and y have g.c.d. 1, which equals $x - y$, eliminating A and D. If the two numbers are 2 and 4, then the g.c.d. is 2, which can be x or y, eliminating B and C. However, the greatest common divisor of two positive integers cannot be greater than either one of the integers individually, so the best answer is E.

13. An empty pool being filled with water at a constant rate takes 8 hours to fill to $\frac{3}{5}$ of its capacity. How much more time will it take to finish filling the pool?

   (A) 5 hr 30 min
   (B) 5 hr 20 min
   (C) 4 hr 48 min
   (D) 3 hr 12 min
   (E) 2 hr 40 min

If t is the total time required to fill the entire pool, then $\frac{3}{5}t = 8$. Thus, $t = \frac{40}{3} = 13\frac{1}{3}$ hours, or 13 hours 20 minutes. It will therefore take 13 hours 20 minutes $-$ 8 hours $=$ 5 hours 20 minutes to finish filling the pool, and the best answer is B.

14. A positive number x is multiplied by 2, and this product is then divided by 3. If the positive square root of the result of these two operations equals x, what is the value of x ?

   (A) $\dfrac{9}{4}$
   (B) $\dfrac{3}{2}$
   (C) $\dfrac{4}{3}$
   (D) $\dfrac{2}{3}$
   (E) $\dfrac{1}{2}$

The value of x must satisfy the equation $\sqrt{\dfrac{2x}{3}} = x$. Squaring both sides of the equation and multiplying by 3 yields $2x = 3x^2$, and, since $x > 0$, it follows that $x = \dfrac{2}{3}$. The best answer is therefore D.

15. A tank contains 10,000 gallons of a solution that is 5 percent sodium chloride by volume. If 2,500 gallons of water evaporate from the tank, the remaining solution will be approximately what percent sodium chloride?

   (A)   1.25%
   (B)   3.75%
   (C)   6.25%
   (D)   6.67%
   (E)   11.7%

The amount of sodium chloride in the tank is $0.05 \times 10,000$ or 500 gallons. After the evaporation of the water, the total amount of solution is $10,000 - 2,500 = 7,500$ gallons, and 500 gallons of sodium chloride remain. The percent of sodium chloride is thus $\dfrac{500}{7,500} = 6.67$ percent. The best answer is D.

   Alternatively, this problem can be approached as an inverse proportion. The original solution contains 5 percent sodium chloride by volume in 10,000 gallons. As water evaporates from the tank, the concentration of sodium chloride in the solution will increase. If x is the fraction of sodium chloride in the remaining solution, then $\dfrac{10,000}{7,500} = \dfrac{x}{0.05}$. Solving for x gives $\dfrac{(0.05)(10,000)}{7,500} = 0.0667,$ which equals 6.67 percent.

16. A certain grocery purchased x pounds of produce for p dollars per pound. If y pounds of the produce had to be discarded due to spoilage and the grocery sold the rest for s dollars per pound, which of the following represents the gross profit on the sale of the produce?

   (A) $(x - y)s - xp$
   (B) $(x - y)p - ys$
   (C) $(s - p)y - xp$
   (D) $xp - ys$
   (E) $(x - y)(s - p)$

The grocery paid xp dollars for the produce. The grocery sold $(x - y)$ pounds of the produce for s dollars per pound, and so the total income was $(x - y)s$ dollars. The gross profit, or income minus cost, was therefore $(x - y)s - xp$. The best answer is A.

17. **NOT SCORED**

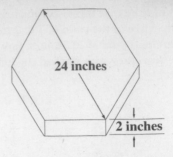

Note: Figure not drawn to scale.

18. The hexagonal face of the block shown in the figure above has sides of equal length and angles of equal measure. If each lateral face is rectangular, what is the area, in square inches, of one lateral face?

   (A) $2\sqrt{10}$
   (B) 12
   (C) 20
   (D) $12\sqrt{3}$
   (E) 24

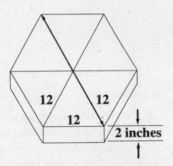

As shown in the figure, the hexagonal face can be divided into 6 equilateral triangles, each with sides of length $\dfrac{1}{2}(24) = 12$ inches. The area of each rectangular lateral face is length times width, which is $(12)(2) = 24$ square inches. The best answer is therefore E.

19. If $w, x, y,$ and z are non-negative integers, each less than 3, and $w(3^3) + x(3^2) + y(3) + z = 34$, then $w + z =$

   (A) 0
   (B) 1
   (C) 2
   (D) 3
   (E) 4

The values of $w, x, y,$ and z must be either 0, 1, or 2. Since $2(3^3) = 54$, which is greater than 34, it follows that $w < 2$, and since $0(3^3) + 2(3^2) + 2(3) + 2 = 26$, which is less than 34, it follows that $w > 0$. Therefore, $w = 1$. Then $x(3^2) + y(3) + z = 7$, so $x = 0, y = 2,$ and $z = 1$. Thus, $w + z = 1 + 1 = 2$, and the best answer is C.

20. Cars X and Y were traveling together on a straight road at a constant speed of 55 miles per hour when car X stopped for 5 minutes. If car Y continued to travel at 55 miles per hour, how many minutes from the time that car X resumed traveling did it take car X traveling at 60 miles per hour to catch up with car Y? (Assume that the time for car X to slow down and speed up was negligible.)

(A) 5
(B) 30
(C) 45
(D) 55
(E) 60

If car X traveled for t minutes, or $\frac{t}{60}$ hour, at 60 miles per hour until it caught up with car Y, then car X traveled a distance of $60\left(\frac{t}{60}\right)$ miles. Since car Y traveled for 5 additional minutes, car Y traveled for $t + 5$ minutes, or $\frac{t+5}{60}$ hour, at 55 miles per hour. Thus, car Y traveled a distance of $55\left(\frac{t+5}{60}\right)$ miles. Since both cars traveled the same distance, $60\left(\frac{t}{60}\right) = 55\left(\frac{t+5}{60}\right)$, and so $t = 55$ minutes. The best answer is therefore D.

Explanatory Material: Critical Reasoning, Section 6

1. Rural households have more purchasing power than do urban or suburban households at the same income level, since some of the income urban and suburban households use for food and shelter can be used by rural households for other needs.

Which of the following inferences is best supported by the statement made above?

(A) The average rural household includes more people than does the average urban or suburban household.
(B) Rural households have lower food and housing costs than do either urban or suburban households.
(C) Suburban households generally have more purchasing power than do either rural or urban households.
(D) The median income of urban and suburban households is generally higher than that of rural households.
(E) All three types of households spend more of their income on housing than on all other purchases combined.

If the greater purchasing power of rural households results from their having more money left over after meeting basic expenses, it follows, as B says, that those expenses are lower for those households than they are for suburban or urban households at the same income level. Consequently, B is the best answer.

Choice A is not a supported inference, since there is no information to suggest that larger households are not more likely to have either more purchasing power or lower food and shelter expenses. Choices C and D are not supported, since the passage compares only households that share the same income level. Because the relative amounts spent on different types of expenditures are not specified for any of the categories of households, E is not supported.

2. In 1985 state border colleges in Texas lost the enrollment of more than half, on average, of the Mexican nationals they had previously served each year. Teaching faculties have alleged that this extreme drop resulted from a rise in tuition for international and out-of-state students from $40 to $120 per credit hour.

Which of the following, if feasible, offers the best prospects for alleviating the problem of the drop in enrollment of Mexican nationals as the teaching faculties assessed it?

(A) Providing grants-in-aid to Mexican nationals to study in Mexican universities

(B) Allowing Mexican nationals to study in Texas border colleges and to pay in-state tuition rates, which are the same as the previous international rate

(C) Reemphasizing the goals and mission of the Texas state border colleges as serving both in-state students and Mexican nationals

(D) Increasing the financial resources of Texas colleges by raising the tuition for in-state students attending state institutions

(E) Offering career counseling for those Mexican nationals who graduate from state border colleges and intend to return to Mexico

The teaching faculties attribute the drop in enrollment of Mexican nationals to an increase in tuition costs. If the faculties are correct, reducing these costs should halt the drop in enrollment. Choice B offers a plan for reducing these costs and so is the best answer.

Neither C nor D nor E offers a plan that would reduce the costs taken to be responsible for the drop in enrollment. Nor does A offer such a plan: because the problem to be addressed is a drop in enrollment of Mexican nationals at Texas border colleges, providing financial incentive for Mexican nationals to study at Mexican universities, as A suggests, would offer no prospect of alleviating the problem.

3. Affirmative action is good business. So asserted the National Association of Manufacturers while urging retention of an executive order requiring some federal contractors to set numerical goals for hiring minorities and women. "Diversity in work force participation has produced new ideas in management, product development, and marketing," the association claimed.

The association's argument as it is presented in the passage above would be most strengthened if which of the following were true?

(A) The percentage of minority and women workers in business has increased more slowly than many minority and women's groups would prefer.

(B) Those businesses with the highest percentages of minority and women workers are those that have been the most innovative and profitable.

(C) Disposable income has been rising as fast among minorities and women as among the population as a whole.

(D) The biggest growth in sales in the manufacturing sector has come in industries that market the most innovative products.

(E) Recent improvements in management practices have allowed many manufacturers to experience enormous gains in worker productivity.

If, as B says, businesses with the highest percentages of minorities and women have been the most profitable, there is reason to believe that, because it increases the level of participation of women and minorities in the work force, affirmative action is good business. Thus, B is the best answer.

Choice A suggests that minority and women's groups have reason to support affirmative action, but it does not indicate that affirmative action is good business. Because there is no indication that the improvement in disposable income noted in C is due to affirmative action, C does not strengthen the argument given for affirmative action. Choice D addresses growth in sales and E addresses improvements in management; neither, however, asserts that these benefits are due to affirmative action.

Questions 4-5 refer to the following.

If the airspace around centrally located airports were restricted to commercial airliners and only those private planes equipped with radar, most of the private-plane traffic would be forced to use outlying airfields. Such a reduction in the amount of private-plane traffic would reduce the risk of midair collision around the centrally located airports.

4. The conclusion drawn in the first sentence depends on which of the following assumptions?

   (A) Outlying airfields would be as convenient as centrally located airports for most pilots of private planes.
   (B) Most outlying airfields are not equipped to handle commercial-airline traffic.
   (C) Most private planes that use centrally located airports are not equipped with radar.
   (D) Commercial airliners are at greater risk of becoming involved in midair collisions than are private planes.
   (E) A reduction in the risk of midair collision would eventually lead to increases in commercial-airline traffic.

The first sentence concludes that prohibiting private planes that are not radar-equipped from centrally located airports would force most private planes away from those airports. This conclusion cannnot be true unless it is true that, as choice C says, most private planes that use these airports are not radar-equipped. Therefore the first sentence's conclusion assumes choice C, which is thus the best answer.

The conclusion need not assume that outlying airfields are convenient for private planes (choice A), since the restrictions would give planes that are not radar equipped no choice. The conclusion concerns only how the radar requirement would affect the volume of private plane traffic, so choice B, which deals with commercial planes, and choices D and E, which deal with risk of midair collision, need not be assumed.

5. Which of the following, if true, would most strengthen the conclusion drawn in the second sentence?

   (A) Commercial airliners are already required by law to be equipped with extremely sophisticated radar systems.
   (B) Centrally located airports are experiencing overcrowded airspace primarily because of sharp increases in commercial-airline traffic.
   (C) Many pilots of private planes would rather buy radar equipment than be excluded from centrally located airports.
   (D) The number of midair collisions that occur near centrally located airports has decreased in recent years.
   (E) Private planes not equipped with radar systems cause a disproportionately large number of midair collisions around centrally located airports.

The second sentence concludes that the reduction described in the first sentence would reduce the risk of midair collisions around centrally located airports. According to E, such a reduction would remove precisely the kind of plane that causes a disproportionate number of midair collisions. Thus E is the best answer.

Choices B and C concern the question of whether or not the proposed restrictions would reduce plane traffic, but not the question of whether any resulting reductions would reduce the risk of midair collisions. Because A does not address the question of whether reducing private-plane traffic would reduce the risk of midair collisions, A is inappropriate. That the number of midair collisions has recently decreased is irrelevant to whether the proposed reduction would further reduce collisions, so D is inappropriate.

6. Which of the following best completes the passage below?

Established companies concentrate on defending what they already have. Consequently, they tend not to be innovative themselves and tend to underestimate the effects of the innovations of others. The clearest example of this defensive strategy is the fact that ------.

(A) ballpoint pens and soft-tip markers have eliminated the traditional market for fountain pens, clearing the way for the marketing of fountain pens as luxury or prestige items

(B) a highly successful automobile was introduced by the same company that had earlier introduced a model that had been a dismal failure

(C) a once-successful manufacturer of slide rules reacted to the introduction of electronic calculators by trying to make better slide rules

(D) one of the first models of modern accounting machines, designed for use in the banking industry, was purchased by a public library as well as by banks

(E) the inventor of a commonly used anesthetic did not intend the product to be used by dentists, who currently account for almost the entire market for that drug

Choice C is a clear example of a defensive, noninnovative strategy that underestimates the effects of others' innovations: the slide-rule manufacturer acted as though any advantages offered by the newer and fundamentally different technology of a competing product, the electronic calculator, could be matched by improving the older, more familiar product. Choice C is thus the best answer.

The other choices are not examples of the defensive strategy the author cites. Choices D and E are cases of new products finding unintended users, not of responses to innovations of others; nor does B describe such a response. Choice A presents a case in which innovative products displaced an older product from its traditional market but in so doing made possible a new marketing strategy for the older product.

7. Most archaeologists have held that people first reached the Americas less than 20,000 years ago by crossing a land bridge into North America. But recent discoveries of human shelters in South America dating from 32,000 years ago have led researchers to speculate that people arrived in South America first, after voyaging across the Pacific, and then spread northward.

Which of the following, if it were discovered, would be pertinent evidence against the speculation above?

(A) A rock shelter near Pittsburgh, Pennsylvania, contains evidence of use by human beings 19,000 years ago.

(B) Some North American sites of human habitation predate any sites found in South America.

(C) The climate is warmer at the 32,000-year-old South American site than at the oldest known North American site.

(D) The site in South America that was occupied 32,000 years ago was continuously occupied until 6,000 years ago.

(E) The last Ice Age, between 11,500 and 20,000 years ago, considerably lowered worldwide sea levels.

The reasoning behind the researchers' speculation that people first arrived in South America is that there is no evidence of North American sites that predate the human shelters discovered in South America. If it were discovered that, as B states, some North American sites predate those in South America, the reasoning behind the speculation would no longer hold. Thus, B is the best answer.

The facts related in A and E both involve time periods occurring after those discussed in the passage, and so create no conflict with the speculation. Although C and D describe discoveries about the South American site, neither the relative climates mentioned in C nor the duration of occupation mentioned in D provides evidence against the speculation.

8. In Asia, where palm trees are non-native, the trees' flowers have traditionally been pollinated by hand, which has kept palm fruit productivity unnaturally low. When weevils known to be efficient pollinators of palm flowers were introduced into Asia in 1980, palm fruit productivity increased — by up to fifty percent in some areas — but then decreased sharply in 1984.

Which of the following statements, if true, would best explain the 1984 decrease in productivity?

(A) Prices for palm fruit fell between 1980 and 1984 following the rise in production and a concurrent fall in demand.

(B) Imported trees are often more productive than native trees because the imported ones have left behind their pests and diseases in their native lands.

(C) Rapid increases in productivity tend to deplete trees of nutrients needed for the development of the fruit-producing female flowers.

(D) The weevil population in Asia remained at approximately the same level between 1980 and 1984.

(E) Prior to 1980 another species of insect pollinated the Asian palm trees, but not as efficiently as the species of weevil that was introduced in 1980.

If C is true, the rapid increase in productivity among Asian palm trees after 1980 probably depleted nutrients needed for the development of fruit-producing flowers. Thus C explains why the palms' productivity could subsequently decline, and is the best answer.

Choice A relates a drop in the price of palm fruit to a rise in production and a fall in demand, but it does not explain the subsequent drop in the trees' productivity. Choice B gives no reason for the decrease in productivity of the trees introduced to Asia. Nor does D, since the stability of the weevil population described in D would support stability of palm fruit productivity between 1980 and 1984 rather than a decrease. Because E describes the pollination of the trees prior to 1980, it cannot explain a change occurring in 1984.

9. Since the mayor's publicity campaign for Greenville's bus service began six months ago, morning automobile traffic into the midtown area of the city has decreased seven percent. During the same period, there has been an equivalent rise in the number of persons riding buses into the midtown area. Obviously, the mayor's publicity campaign has convinced many people to leave their cars at home and ride the bus to work.

Which of the following, if true, casts the most serious doubt on the conclusion drawn above?

(A) Fares for all bus routes in Greenville have risen an average of five percent during the past six months.

(B) The mayor of Greenville rides the bus to City Hall in the city's midtown area.

(C) Road reconstruction has greatly reduced the number of lanes available to commuters in major streets leading to the midtown area during the past six months.

(D) The number of buses entering the midtown area of Greenville during the morning hours is exactly the same now as it was one year ago.

(E) Surveys show that longtime bus riders are no more satisfied with the Greenville bus service than they were before the mayor's publicity campaign began.

The passage concludes that the mayor's publicity campaign has persuaded people to ride the bus to work instead of driving, and it cites as evidence the decreased morning automobile traffic and increased bus ridership into the midtown area. But the road reconstruction described in C provides an alternative explanation for this evidence, so C is the best answer.

Choice A eliminates decreased fares as a possible explanation for the increased ridership, so it supports rather than casts doubt on the conclusion. Similarly, (D) and (E) each eliminate a possible explanation: the unchanged number of buses cited in D, and longtime bus riders' attitudes cited in E suggest that the increased ridership is not explained by improved service. The fact that the mayor rides the bus, cited in B, may contribute to the effectiveness of the publicity campaign, but it is irrelevant to assessing whether the campaign caused the increased ridership.

10. In the aftermath of a worldwide stock-market crash, Country T claimed that the severity of the stock market crash it experienced resulted from the accelerated process of denationalization many of its industries underwent shortly before the crash.

Which of the following, if it could be carried out, would be most useful in an evaluation of Country T's assessment of the causes of the severity of its stock-market crash?

(A) Calculating the average loss experienced by individual traders in Country T during the crash

(B) Using economic theory to predict the most likely date of the next crash in Country T

(C) Comparing the total number of shares sold during the worst days of the crash in Country T to the total number of shares sold in Country T just prior to the crash

(D) Comparing the severity of the crash in Country T to the severity of the crash in countries otherwise economically similar to Country T that have not experienced recent denationalization

(E) Comparing the long-term effects of the crash on the purchasing power of the currency of Country T to the immediate, more severe short-term effects of the crash on the purchasing power of the currency of Country T

The comparison suggested in D would be useful in evaluating Country T's assessment of the causes of the severity of its stock market crash. If the severity of the crash is at least as great in the countries that are, except for recent nationalization, economically similar to Country T, Country T's assessment is undermined. If the severity of the crash is not as great in these countries as in Country T, however, the assessment is supported. Thus, D is the best answer.

Choices A, C, and E are not good answers because each concerns only determining the severity of the crash in Country T, not assessing a hypothesis about the causes of the crash. Nor is the date of Country T's next crash relevant to assessing such a hypothesis; thus, B is inappropriate.

11. With the emergence of biotechnology companies, it was feared that they would impose silence about proprietary results on their in-house researchers and their academic consultants. This constraint, in turn, would slow the development of biological science and engineering.

Which of the following, if true, would tend to weaken most seriously the prediction of scientific secrecy described above?

(A) Biotechnological research funded by industry has reached some conclusions that are of major scientific importance.

(B) When the results of scientific research are kept secret, independent researchers are unable to build on those results.

(C) Since the research priorities of biotechnology companies are not the same as those of academic institutions, the financial support of research by such companies distorts the research agenda.

(D) To enhance the companies' standing in the scientific community, the biotechnology companies encourage employees to publish their results, especially results that are important.

(E) Biotechnology companies devote some of their research resources to problems that are of fundamental scientific importance and that are not expected to produce immediate practical applications.

Choice D weakens the prediction of secrecy by establishing that biotechnology companies have a strong motive to encourage their researchers to publicize results. Therefore, D is the best answer.

Neither A nor B nor E provides any reason to expect that the prediction will be or will not be fulfilled. Choices A and B support the argument that developments in biological science and engineering would be slowed if the prediction of secrecy were fulfilled. Choice E, which says that biotechnology companies devote some resources to fundamental problems without immediate practical benefits, is merely consistent with that argument and so does not weaken the prediction. The distortion of the research agenda asserted in C is not relevant to the question of scientific secrecy.

12. Some people have questioned the judge's objectivity in cases of sex discrimination against women. But the record shows that in sixty percent of such cases, the judge has decided in favor of the women. This record demonstrates that the judge has not discriminated against women in cases of sex discrimination against women.

The argument above is flawed in that it ignores the possibility that

(A) a large number of the judge's cases arose out of allegations of sex discrimination against women
(B) many judges find it difficult to be objective in cases of sex discrimination against women
(C) the judge is biased against women defendants or plaintiffs in cases that do not involve sex discrimination
(D) the majority of the cases of sex discrimination against women that have reached the judge's court have been appealed from a lower court
(E) the evidence shows that the women should have won in more than sixty percent of the judge's cases involving sex discrimination against women

The flaw in the argument is that it assumes erroneously that a majority of decisions favorable to women in sex discrimination cases demonstrates absence of discriminatory behavior against women on the part of the judge who made those decisions. Choice E exposes this flaw by pointing out that the judge may well have failed to decide in favor of women in cases where evidence shows that the women should have won. Therefore, E is the best answer.

Choices B and C introduce considerations with no bearing on the reasoning of the argument. Because the argument concerns a particular judge, B is inappropriate; because it concerns cases of a particular type, C is inappropriate. Choices A and D also have no bearing, because the origin of these cases is not at issue in the argument.

13. The tobacco industry is still profitable and projections are that it will remain so. In the United States this year, the total amount of tobacco sold by tobacco-farmers has increased, even though the number of adults who smoke has decreased.

Each of the following, if true, could explain the simultaneous increase in tobacco sales and decrease in the number of adults who smoke EXCEPT:

(A) During this year, the number of women who have begun to smoke is greater than the number of men who have quit smoking.
(B) The number of teen-age children who have begun to smoke this year is greater than the number of adults who have quit smoking during the same period.
(C) During this year, the number of nonsmokers who have begun to use chewing tobacco or snuff is greater than the number of people who have quit smoking.
(D) The people who have continued to smoke consume more tobacco per person than they did in the past.
(E) More of the cigarettes made in the United States this year were exported to other countries than was the case last year.

If the number of men beginning to smoke and the number of women quitting smoking during the year are equal, choice A would result in an increase, not a decrease, in the number of adults who smoke. Hence, A does *not* explain the facts cited and is the best answer.

Given the decrease in the number of adults who smoke, the increase in tobacco sales could be explained by a proportionally greater increase in the nonadults who smoke or the nonsmokers who use tobacco. An increase in total tobacco use by smokers or in the sales of United States tobacco abroad would also explain the facts cited. Thus, because B, C, D, and E could explain the facts cited, none of them can be the best answer.

14. Kale has more nutritional value than spinach. But since collard greens have more nutritional value than lettuce, it follows that kale has more nutritional value than lettuce.

Any of the following, if introduced into the argument as an additional premise, makes the argument above logically correct EXCEPT:

(A) Collard greens have more nutritional value than kale.
(B) Spinach has more nutritional value than lettuce.
(C) Spinach has more nutritional value than collard greens.
(D) Spinach and collard greens have the same nutritional value.
(E) Kale and collard greens have the same nutritional value.

The question asks for an additional premise that does *not* make the argument logically correct. Adding choice A to the information given in the passage leaves open the possibility that, in order of nutritional value, the vegetables rank: collard greens, lettuce, kale, spinach. Because this order is contrary to the conclusion of the argument, A leaves open the possibility that the conclusion of the argument is false; A is thus the best answer.

By contrast, any of choices B, C, D, and E, when added to the information that the nutritional value of kale is greater than that of spinach and that the nutritional value of collard greens is greater than that of lettuce, makes the conclusion — that kale has more nutritional value than lettuce — follow logically.

15. **On the basis of a decrease in the college-age population, many colleges now anticipate increasingly smaller freshman classes each year. Surprised by a 40 percent increase in qualified applicants over the previous year, however, administrators at Nice College now plan to hire more faculty for courses taken by all freshmen.**

   Which of the following statements about Nice College's current qualified applicants, if true, would strongly suggest that the administrators' plan is flawed?

   (A) **A substantially higher percentage than usual plan to study for advanced degrees after graduation from college.**
   (B) **According to their applications, their level of participation in extracurricular activities and varsity sports is unusually high.**
   (C) **According to their applications, none of them lives in a foreign country.**
   (D) **A substantially lower percentage than usual rate Nice College as their first choice among the colleges to which they are applying.**
   (E) **A substantially lower percentage than usual list mathematics as their intended major.**

If, as D states, a substantial percentage of the qualified applicants do not rate Nice College as their first choice, then, provided many of these applicants are accepted at and enroll in the colleges that are their first choices, the increase in applications to Nice College might not result in any increase in the size of its freshman class. So D is the best answer.

Nothing can be determined from A, B, C, or E about the size of the freshman class, so none of these choices is relevant to the question of whether Nice College should hire more faculty to teach courses taken by all freshmen. Thus, these choices are inappropriate.

Questions 16-17 are based on the following.

   A researcher discovered that people who have low levels of immune-system activity tend to score much lower on tests of mental health than do people with normal or high immune-system activity. The researcher concluded from this experiment that the immune system protects against mental illness as well as against physical disease.

16. **The researcher's conclusion depends on which of the following assumptions?**

   (A) **High immune-system activity protects against mental illness better than normal immune-system activity does.**
   (B) **Mental illness is similar to physical disease in its effects on body systems.**
   (C) **People with high immune-system activity cannot develop mental illness.**
   (D) **Mental illness does not cause people's immune-system activity to decrease.**
   (E) **Psychological treatment of mental illness is not as effective as is medical treatment.**

The researcher concludes from the association of low immune-system activity with low mental-health scores that, in effect, immune system activity can inhibit mental illness. If, contrary to D, mental illness can depress immune-system activity, the association mentioned does not support the researcher's conclusion. So D must be assumed.

Normal immune-system activity could protect against mental illness without high-immune system activity offering increased protection, contrary to what A states, or prevention, contrary to what C states, so neither A nor C is assumed. The conclusion does not depend on there being a similarity between mental and physical illness, so B is not assumed; nor does it depend on there being a difference in treatments, so E is not assumed.

17. **The researcher's conclusion would be most seriously weakened if it were true that**

   (A) **there was a one-year delay between the completion of a pilot study for the experiment and the initiation of the experiment itself**
   (B) **people's levels of immune-system activity are not affected by their use of medications**
   (C) **a few people with high immune-system activity had scores on the test of mental health that were similar to the scores of people who had normal immune-system activity**
   (D) **people who have low immune-system activity tend to contract more viral infections than do people with normal or high immune-system activity**
   (E) **high levels of stress first cause mental illness and then cause decreased immune-system activity in normal individuals**

If the association between low immune-system activity and mental illness is due to a third factor that, as E states, causes first mental illness and then decreased immune-system activity, a conclusion that immune-system activity affects mental health is seriously weakened. Thus, E is the best answer.

There is no reason to think the delay cited in A should have compromised the results of the experiment; therefore, A does not weaken the conclusion. The conclusion does not assume that people with high immune-system activity score higher on tests of mental health than do people with normal immune-system activity, so C does not weaken the conclusion. The considerations addressed in B and D are consistent with the researcher's conclusion and so do not weaken it.

18. The value of a product is determined by the ratio of its quality to its price. The higher the value of a product, the better will be its competitive position. Therefore, either increasing the quality or lowering the price of a given product will increase the likelihood that a consumer will select that product rather than a competing one.

Which of the following, if true, would most strengthen the conclusion drawn above?

(A) It is possible to increase both the quality and the price of a product without changing its competitive position.
(B) For certain segments of the population of consumers, higher-priced brands of some product lines are preferred to the lower-priced brands.
(C) Competing products often try to appeal to different segments of the population of consumers.
(D) The competitive position of a product can be affected by such factors as advertising and brand loyalty.
(E) Consumers' perceptions of the quality of a product are based on the actual quality of the product.

The conclusion as stated is vulnerable to the criticism that changes in quality cannot affect consumer behavior if consumers are unaware of those changes. Choice E, which disposes of this objection, thereby strengthens the conclusion and is the best answer.

Choice A concerns a circumstance in which competitive position remains unchanged and thus offers no evidence about conditions that could change that position. Because D states that the competitive position of a product can be affected by factors other than its value, it tends to weaken the conclusion. Choices B and C deal with particular segments of the consumer population and offer no considerations that strengthen the general link being established between a product's value and consumer behavior.

19. In January there was a large drop in the number of new houses sold, because interest rates for mortgages were falling and many consumers were waiting to see how low the rates would go. This large sales drop was accompanied by a sharp rise in the average price of new houses sold.

Which of the following, if true, best explains the sharp rise in the average price of new houses?

(A) Sales of higher-priced houses were unaffected by the sales drop because their purchasers have fewer constraints limiting the total amount they pay.
(B) Labor agreements of builders with construction unions are not due to expire until the next January.
(C) The prices of new houses have been rising slowly over the past three years because there is an increasing shortage of housing.
(D) There was a greater amount of moderate-priced housing available for resale by owners during January than in the preceding three months.
(E) Interest rates for home mortgages are expected to rise sharply later in the year if predictions of increased business activity in general prove to be accurate.

Choice A implies that the fall in new-house sales was confined to medium- and lower-priced houses, and thus that higher-priced houses accounted for a greater proportion of new-house sales after the sales drop. The average sale price of new houses would consequently rise. Therefore, A explains the price rise and is the best answer.

Choice B does not explain the sharp rise in new-house prices, since it suggests that labor costs are currently stable. Choice C might explain the rise, if the housing shortage had become exacerbated; so might E, if consumers were buying houses to escape rising mortgage rates. However, neither of these circumstances obtains. Because buyers might regard houses for resale as substitutes for new houses, D suggests that prices would fall.

20. Seven countries signed a treaty binding each of them to perform specified actions on a certain fixed date, with the actions of each conditional on simultaneous action taken by the other countries. Each country was also to notify the six other countries when it had completed its action.

The simultaneous-action provision of the treaty leaves open the possibility that

(A) the compliance date was subject to postponement, according to the terms of the treaty

(B) one of the countries might not be required to make any changes to take any steps in order to comply with the treaty, whereas all the other countries are so required.

(C) each country might have a well-founded excuse, based on the provision, for its own lack of compliance

(D) the treaty specified that the signal for one of the countries to initiate action was notification by the other countries that they had completed action

(E) there was ambiguity with respect to the date after which all actions contemplated in the treaty are to be complete

If for any reason one of the countries fails to perform its specified actions on the designated date, the provision would give each country a well-founded excuse for its own nonperformance. Thus C, which describes this possibility, is the best answer.

The provision specifies that the actions, if undertaken, must be undertaken on a certain fixed date, so it does not allow postponement (choice A). Nor does the provision consider date of completion (choice E), so the provision cannot be ambiguous about that date. Because the provision requires that six of the countries could not be required to act unless the seventh also acted, B is inappropriate. Choice D is inappropriate since actions are not simultaneous if one is initiated when the others are completed.

Scoring Information

How to Calculate Your Scores: Form A

Your Verbal Raw Score

Step 1:	Using the answer key, mark your answer sheet as follows: put a C next to each question that you answered correctly; put an I next to each question that you answered incorrectly. Cross out any questions that you did not answer or for which you marked more than one answer; these will not be counted in the scoring.
Step 2:	Sections 2, 4, and 6 are used to determine your verbal score. In these sections only, count the number of correct answers (marked C) and enter this number here . . . . _____
Step 3:	In these same sections (2, 4, and 6), count the number of questions that you answered incorrectly (marked I). Enter the number here . . . . _____
Step 4:	Count the number of questions in sections 2, 4, and 6 that you crossed out because you did not answer them or marked more than one answer. Enter this number here. . . . . _____
Step 5:	Add the numbers in Steps 2, 3, and 4. Enter the number here. . . . . _____ (This number should be 70, the total number of verbal questions. If it is not, check your work for Steps 2, 3, and 4.)
Step 6:	Enter the number from Step 2 here. . . . . _____
Step 7:	Enter the number from Step 3 here $\dfrac{\text{_____}}{4}$; divide it by 4. (This is the correction for guessing.) Write the resulting number here . . . . − _____
Step 8:	Subtract the number in Step 7 from the number in Step 6; enter the result here . . . . _____
	+ _____.5_____
Step 9:	Add .5 to the number in Step 8. Enter the result here. . . . . _____
Step 10:	Drop all the digits to the right of the decimal point and write the result here. . . . . _____
	This is your verbal raw score corrected for guessing. Instructions for converting this score to a scaled score are on page 540.

Your Quantitative Raw Score

Step 1:	Sections 1, 3, and 5 are used to determine your quantitative score. In these sections only, count the number of correct answers (marked C) and enter this number here	———————
Step 2:	In these same sections (1, 3, and 5), count the number of questions that you answered incorrectly (marked I). Enter the number here	———————
Step 3:	Count the number of questions in sections 2, 4, and 5 that you crossed out because you did not answer them or marked more than one answer. Enter this number here.	———————
Step 4:	Add the numbers in Steps 1, 2, and 3. Enter the total here . . . . (This number should be 64, the total number of quantitative questions. If it is not, check your work for Steps 1, 2, and 3.)	———————
Step 5:	Enter the number from Step 1 here.	———————
Step 6:	Enter the number from Step 2 here ————— ; divide $\frac{}{4}$ it by 4. (This is the correction for guessing.) Write the resulting number here	− ———————
Step 7:	Subtract the number in Step 6 from the number in Step 5; enter the result here	———————
		+ ——————.5——————
Step 8:	Add .5 to the number in Step 7. Enter the result here.	———————
Step 9:	Drop all the digits to the right of the decimal point and write the result here.	———————
This is your quantitative raw score corrected for guessing. Instructions for converting this score to a scaled score are on page 540.		

Your Total Raw Score

Step 1:	Using all the sections of the test, count the number of correct answers (marked C) and enter this number here.	_____
Step 2:	Count the number of questions in all the sections that you answered incorrectly (marked I). Enter the number here.	_____
Step 3:	Count the number of questions in all sections that you crossed out because you did not answer them or marked more than one answer. Enter this number here.	_____
Step 4:	Add the numbers in Steps 1, 2, and 3. Enter the total here . . . . (This number should be 134, the total number of questions in the test. If it is not, check your work for Steps 1, 2, and 3.)	_____
Step 5:	Enter the number from Step 1 here.	_____
Step 6:	Enter the number from Step 2 here_____; divide it by 4. (This is the correction for guessing.) Write the resulting number here	− _____
Setp 7:	Subtract the number in Step 6 from the number in Step 5; enter the result here	_____
Step 8:	Add .5 to the number in Step 7. Enter the result here.	+ _____.5_____ _____
Step 9:	Drop all the digits to the right of the decimal point and write the result here.	_____

This is your total raw score corrected for guessing. It is possible that the sum of your verbal and quantitative raw scores may be one point higher or lower than the total raw score due to the rounding procedures for each score. Instructions for converting this score—along with your verbal and quantitative raw scores corrected for guessing—to scaled scores are on page 540.

How to Calculate Your Scores: Form B

Your Verbal Raw Score

Step 1:	Using the answer key, mark your answer sheet as follows: put a C next to each question that you answered correctly; put an I next to each question that you answered incorrectly. Cross out any questions that you did not answer or for which you marked more than one answer; these will not be counted in the scoring.
Step 2:	Sections 1, 4, and 6 are used to determine your verbal score. In these sections only, count the number of correct answers (marked C) and enter this number here . . . . _____
Step 3:	In these same sections (1, 4, and 6), count the number of questions that you answered incorrectly (marked I). Enter the number here . . . . _____
Step 4:	Count the number of questions in sections 1, 4, and 6 that you crossed out because you did not answer them or marked more than one answer. Enter this number here. . . . . _____
Step 5:	Add the numbers in Steps 2, 3, and 4. Enter the number here. . . . . _____ (This number should be 70, the total number of verbal questions. If it is not, check your work for Steps 2, 3, and 4.)
Step 6:	Enter the number from Step 2 here. . . . . _____
Step 7:	Enter the number from Step 3 here _____ ; divide it by 4. (This is the correction for guessing.) Write the resulting number here . . . . − _____
Step 8:	Subtract the number in Step 7 from the number in Step 6; enter the result here . . . . _____
Step 9:	Add .5 to the number in Step 8. Enter the result here. . . . . + ____.5____ _____
Step 10:	Drop all the digits to the right of the decimal point and write the result here. . . . . _____

This is your verbal raw score corrected for guessing. Instructions for converting this score to a scaled score are on page 540.

Your Quantitative Raw Score

Step 1:	Sections 2, 3, and 5 are used to determine your quantitative score. In these sections only, count the number of correct answers (marked C) and enter this number here	_____
Step 2:	In these same sections (2, 3, and 5), count the number of questions that you answered incorrectly (marked I). Enter the number here	_____
Step 3:	Count the number of questions in sections 2, 3, and 5 that you crossed out because you did not answer them or marked more than one answer. Enter this number here.	_____
Step 4:	Add the numbers in Steps 1, 2, and 3. Enter the total here . . . . (This number should be 64, the total number of quantitative questions. If it is not, check your work for Steps 1, 2, and 3.)	_____
Step 5:	Enter the number from Step 1 here.	_____
Step 6:	Enter the number from Step 2 here _____ ; divide it by 4. (This is the correction for guessing.) Write the resulting number here	− _____
Step 7:	Subtract the number in Step 6 from the number in Step 5; enter the result here	_____
		+ _____.5_____
Step 8:	Add .5 to the number in Step 7. Enter the result here.	_____
Step 9:	Drop all the digits to the right of the decimal point and write the result here.	_____
This is your quantitative raw score corrected for guessing. Instructions for converting this score to a scaled score are on page 540.		

Your Total Raw Score

Step 1:	Using all the sections of the test, count the number of correct answers (marked C) and enter this number here....................................	_____
Step 2:	Count the number of questions in all the sections that you answered incorrectly (marked I). Enter the number here....................................	_____
Step 3:	Count the number of questions in all sections that you crossed out because you did not answer them or marked more than one answer. Enter this number here..	_____
Step 4:	Add the numbers in Steps 1, 2, and 3. Enter the total here .... (This number should be 134, the total number of questions in the test. If it is not, check your work for Steps 1, 2, and 3.)	_____

Step 5:	Enter the number from Step 1 here.................		_____
Step 6:	Enter the number from Step 2 here_____; divide $\dfrac{}{4}$ it by 4. (This is the correction for guessing.) Write the resulting number here	−	_____
Setp 7:	Subtract the number in Step 6 from the number in Step 5; enter the result here		_____
		+	.5 _____
Step 8:	Add .5 to the number in Step 7. Enter the result here...		_____
Step 9:	Drop all the digits to the right of the decimal point and write the result here........................		_____

This is your total raw score corrected for guessing. It is possible that the sum of your verbal and quantitative raw scores may be one point higher or lower than the total raw score due to the rounding procedures for each score. Instructions for converting this score—along with your verbal and quantitative raw scores corrected for guessing—to scaled scores are on page 540.

How to Calculate Your Scores: Form C

Your Verbal Raw Score

Step 1:	Using the answer key, mark your answer sheet as follows: put a C next to each question that you answered correctly; put an I next to each question that you answered incorrectly. Cross out any questions that you did not answer or for which you marked more than one answer; these will not be counted in the scoring.
Step 2:	Sections 2, 4, and 6 are used to determine your verbal score. In these sections only, count the number of correct answers (marked C) and enter this number here . . . . : _____
Step 3:	In these same sections (2, 4, and 6), count the number of questions that you answered incorrectly (marked I). Enter the number here . . . . _____
Step 4:	Count the number of questions in sections 2, 4, and 6 that you crossed out because you did not answer them or marked more than one answer. Enter this number here . . . . _____
Step 5:	Add the numbers in Steps 2, 3, and 4. Enter the number here . . . . _____ (This number should be 70, the total number of verbal questions. If it is not, check your work for Steps 2, 3, and 4.)
Step 6:	Enter the number from Step 2 here . . . . _____
Step 7:	Enter the number from Step 3 here $\frac{_____}{4}$; divide it by 4. (This is the correction for guessing.) Write the resulting number here . . . . − _____
Step 8:	Subtract the number in Step 7 from the number in Step 6; enter the result here . . . . _____
	+ _____.5_____
Step 9:	Add .5 to the number in Step 8. Enter the result here . . . . _____
Step 10:	Drop all the digits to the right of the decimal point and write the result here . . . . _____
This is your verbal raw score corrected for guessing. Instructions for converting this score to a scaled score are on page 540.	

Your Quantitative Raw Score

Step 1:	Sections 1, 3, and 5 are used to determine your quantitative score. In these sections only, count the number of correct answers (marked C) and enter this number here	_____
Step 2:	In these same sections (1, 3, and 5), count the number of questions that you answered incorrectly (marked I). Enter the number here	_____
Step 3:	Count the number of questions in sections 1, 3, and 5 that you crossed out because you did not answer them or marked more than one answer. Enter this number here.	_____
Step 4:	Add the numbers in Steps 1, 2, and 3. Enter the total here . . . . (This number should be 64, the total number of quantitative questions. If it is not, check your work for Steps 1, 2, and 3.)	_____
Step 5:	Enter the number from Step 1 here.	_____
Step 6:	Enter the number from Step 2 here $\frac{\rule{1cm}{0.4pt}}{4}$; divide it by 4. (This is the correction for guessing.) Write the resulting number here	− _____
Step 7:	Subtract the number in Step 6 from the number in Step 5; enter the result here	_____
		+ _____.5_____
Step 8:	Add .5 to the number in Step 7. Enter the result here.	_____
Step 9:	Drop all the digits to the right of the decimal point and write the result here	_____
This is your quantitative raw score corrected for guessing. Instructions for converting this score to a scaled score are on page 540.		

Your Total Raw Score

Step 1:	Using all the sections of the test, count the number of correct answers (marked C) and enter this number here....................................	_____
Step 2:	Count the number of questions in all the sections that you answered incorrectly (marked I). Enter the number here....................................	_____
Step 3:	Count the number of questions in all sections that you crossed out because you did not answer them or marked more than one answer. Enter this number here....................................	_____
Step 4:	Add the numbers in Steps 1, 2, and 3. Enter the total here .... (This number should be 134, the total number of questions in the test. If it is not, check your work for Steps 1, 2, and 3.)	_____
Step 5:	Enter the number from Step 1 here..................	_____
Step 6:	Enter the number from Step 2 here_____; divide it by 4. (This is the correction for guessing.) Write the resulting number here .... −	_____
Setp 7:	Subtract the number in Step 6 from the number in Step 5; enter the result here	_____
	+	.5
Step 8:	Add .5 to the number in Step 7. Enter the result here..	_____
Step 9:	Drop all the digits to the right of the decimal point and write the result here........................	_____
This is your total raw score corrected for guessing. It is possible that the sum of your verbal and quantitative raw scores may be one point higher or lower than the total raw score due to the rounding procedures for each score. Instructions for converting this score—along with your verbal and quantitative raw scores corrected for guessing—to scaled scores follow.		

Converting Your Raw Scores to Scaled Scores

The raw scores corrected for guessing that you have obtained (last step in each worksheet) may be converted to scaled scores using the conversion tables on the following pages. Raw scores are converted to scaled scores to ensure that a score earned on any one form of the GMAT is directly comparable to the same scaled score earned (within a five-year period) on any other form of the test. Scaled scores are "standard scores" with understood and accepted meanings. The scores reported to schools when you take the actual GMAT will be scaled scores.

Using the conversion tables, for each form of the test that you took (A, B, C), find the GMAT scaled scores that correspond to your three raw scores (verbal, quantitative, total), corrected for guessing. For example, a verbal raw score of 44 on Form A would correspond to a scaled score of 34; a quantitative raw score of 44 on Form A would correspond to a scaled score of 38. A total raw score of 88 on Form A would correspond to a scaled score of 590.

When you take the GMAT at an actual administration, one or more of your scores will probably differ from the scaled scores you obtained on these representative GMAT tests. Even the same student performs at different levels at different times—for a variety of reasons unrelated to the test itself. In addition, your test scores may differ because the conditions under which you took these tests could not be exactly the same as those at an actual test administration.

After you have scored your tests, analyze the results with a view to improving your performance when you take the actual GMAT.

■ Did the time you spent reading directions make serious inroads on the time you had available for answering questions? If you become thoroughly familiar with the directions given in this book (in Chapter 1, Chapters 3-7, and the representative tests), you may need to spend less time reading directions in the actual test.

■ Did you run out of time before you reached the end of a section? If so, could you pace yourself better in the actual test? Remember, not everyone finishes all sections; accuracy is also important.

■ Look at the specific questions you missed. In which ones did you suffer from lack of knowledge? Faulty reasoning? Faulty reading of the questions? Being aware of the causes of your errors may enable you to avoid some errors when you actually take the GMAT.

What Your Scaled Scores Mean

The tables on page 544 contain information that will be of help in understanding your scaled scores. Each table consists of a column marked "Scaled Score" and a column indicating the percentage of test takers in the time period specified who scored below the scores listed. For example, if you earned a total scaled score of about 600 on a representative test and you are able to achieve the same score on an actual GMAT, the 83 opposite 600 tells you that 83 percent of the 694,061 people taking the test in the 1988-1991 period earned scores lower than that; the remainder earned the same or a higher score. Also given in each table is the average score of the group tested in the 1988-1991 time period.

Graduate school admissions officers understand the statistical meaning of GMAT scores, but each institution uses and interprets the scores according to the needs of its own programs. You should, therefore, consult the schools to which you are applying to learn how they will interpret and use your scores.

Some Cautions about Score Interpretation

1. The GMAT is designed to yield only the reported verbal, quantitative, and total scaled scores. One should not calculate raw scores for individual test sections and infer specific strengths or weaknesses from a comparison of the raw score results by section. There are two reasons for this.

   First, different sections have different numbers of questions and, even if the numbers were the same or if percentages were used to make the numbers comparable, the sections might not be equally difficult. For illustrative purposes only, suppose that one section had 20 items and another had 25. Furthermore, suppose you received a corrected raw score of 10 on the first and 10 on the second. It would be inappropriate to conclude that you had equal ability in the two sections because the corrected raw scores were equal, as you really obtained 50 percent on the first section and only 40 percent on the second. It could be equally inappropriate, however, to conclude from the percentages that you were better on the first section than on the second. Suppose the first section was relatively easy for most candidates (say, an average corrected raw score percentage across candidates of 55 percent) and the second was relatively difficult (an average corrected raw score percentage of 35 percent). Now you might conclude that you were worse than average on the first section and better than average on the second.

   Differences in difficulty level between editions are accounted for in the procedure for converting the verbal, quantitative, and total corrected raw scores to scaled scores. Since the raw scores for individual sections are not converted to produce scaled scores by section, performance on individual sections of the test cannot be compared.

   Second, corrected raw scores by section are not converted to scaled scores by section because the GMAT is not designed to reliably measure specific strengths and weaknesses beyond the general verbal and quantitative abilities for which separate scaled scores are reported. Reliability is dependent, in part, on the number of questions in the test—the more questions, the higher the reliability. The relatively few questions in each section, taken alone, are not sufficient to produce a reliable result for each section. Only the reported verbal, quantitative, and total scaled scores (which include questions across several sections) have sufficient reliability to permit their use in counseling and predicting graduate school performance.

2. It is possible, if you repeat the test, that your second raw scores corrected for guessing could be higher than on the first test, but your scaled scores could be lower and vice versa. This is a result of the slight differences in difficulty level between editions of the test, which are taken into account when corrected raw scores are converted to the GMAT scaled scores. That is, for a given scaled score, a more difficult edition requires a lower corrected raw score and an easier edition requires a higher corrected raw score.

Verbal Converted (Scaled) Scores Corresponding to Corrected Raw Scores for Three Forms of the GMAT

Corrected Raw Scores	Form A	Form B	Form C	Corrected Raw Scores	Form A	Form B	Form C	Corrected Raw Scores	Form A	Form B	Form C
70	51	51	51	45	34	34	34	20	19	19	19
69	50	50	50	44	34	33	33	19	18	18	18
68	49	49	49	43	33	33	33	18	17	17	18
67	48	47	48	42	32	32	32	17	17	17	17
66	48	47	47	41	32	31	32	16	16	16	16
65	47	46	46	40	31	31	31	15	15	16	16
64	46	45	45	39	31	30	30	14	15	15	15
63	46	45	45	38	30	30	30	13	14	14	15
62	45	44	44	37	29	29	29	12	13	14	14
61	45	43	44	36	29	28	29	11	13	13	13
60	44	43	43	35	28	28	28	10	12	13	13
59	43	42	42	34	27	27	27	9	12	12	12
58	43	42	42	33	27	27	27	8	11	11	12
57	42	41	41	32	26	26	26	7	10	11	11
56	41	40	41	31	26	25	26	6	10	10	10
55	41	40	40	30	25	25	25	5	9	10	10
54	40	39	39	29	24	24	24	4	8	9	9
53	39	39	39	28	24	23	24	3	8	8	9
52	39	38	38	27	23	23	23	2	7	8	8
51	38	37	38	26	22	22	23	1	7	7	7
50	38	37	37	25	22	22	22	0	6	7	7
49	37	36	36	24	21	21	21				
48	36	36	36	23	20	20	21				
47	36	35	35	22	20	20	20				
46	35	34	35	21	19	19	20				

Quantitative Converted (Scaled) Scores Corresponding to Corrected Raw Scores
for Three Forms of the GMAT

Corrected Raw Scores	Scaled Scores			Corrected Raw Scores	Scaled Scores			Corrected Raw Scores	Scaled Scores		
	Form A	Form B	Form C		Form A	Form B	Form C		Form A	Form B	Form C
				45	38	39	38	20	22	23	22
				44	38	38	38	19	22	23	22
				43	37	38	37	18	21	22	21
				42	36	37	36	17	20	21	20
				41	36	36	36	16	20	21	20
64	51	51	51	40	35	36	35	15	19	20	19
63	50	50	51	39	35	35	35	14	19	20	18
62	49	49	50	38	34	34	34	13	18	19	18
61	49	49	49	37	33	34	33	12	17	18	17
				36	33	33	33	11	17	18	16
60	48	48	49	35	32	33	32	10	16	17	16
59	47	47	48	34	31	32	31	9	15	17	15
58	47	47	47	33	31	31	31	8	15	16	14
57	46	46	46	32	30	31	30	7	14	15	14
56	45	46	46	31	29	30	29	6	13	15	13
55	45	45	45	30	29	30	29	5	13	14	12
54	44	44	44	29	28	29	28	4	12	13	12
53	43	44	44	28	27	28	27	3	12	13	11
52	43	43	43	27	27	28	27	2	11	12	10
51	42	42	42	26	26	27	26	1	10	11	10
50	42	42	42	25	26	26	25	0	10	10	9
49	41	41	41	24	25	26	25				
48	40	41	40	23	24	25	24				
47	40	40	40	22	24	25	24				
46	39	39	39	21	23	24	23				

Total Converted (Scaled) Scores Corresponding to Corrected Raw Scores
for Three Forms of the GMAT

Corrected Raw Scores	Form A	Form B	Form C	Corrected Raw Scores	Form A	Form B	Form C	Corrected Raw Scores	Form A	Form B	Form C
134	800	800	800	85	580	580	570	35	360	360	360
133	790	790	790	84	570	570	570	34	350	360	350
132	780	780	780	83	570	570	570	33	350	350	350
131	780	780	770	82	560	560	560	32	340	350	340
				81	560	560	560	31	340	340	340
130	770	770	770	80	550	560	550	30	330	340	330
129	770	770	770	79	550	550	550	29	330	340	330
128	760	760	760	78	540	550	540	28	330	330	330
127	760	760	760	77	540	540	540	27	320	330	320
126	760	750	750	76	540	540	530	26	320	320	320
125	750	750	750	75	530	530	530	25	310	320	310
124	750	740	740	74	530	530	530	24	310	310	310
123	740	740	740	73	520	520	520	23	300	310	300
122	740	740	740	72	520	520	520	22	300	310	300
121	730	730	730	71	510	520	510	21	300	300	300
120	730	730	730	70	510	510	510	20	290	300	290
119	720	720	720	69	510	510	500	19	290	290	290
118	720	720	720	68	500	500	500	18	280	290	280
117	720	710	710	67	500	500	500	17	280	280	280
116	710	710	710	66	490	490	490	16	270	280	270
115	710	710	700	65	490	490	490	15	270	280	270
114	700	700	700	64	480	490	480	14	260	270	260
113	700	700	700	63	480	480	480	13	260	270	260
112	690	690	690	62	470	480	470	12	260	260	260
111	690	690	690	61	470	470	470	11	250	260	250
110	690	680	680	60	470	470	470	10	250	250	250
109	680	680	680	59	460	460	460	9	240	250	240
108	680	680	670	58	460	460	460	8	240	250	240
107	670	670	670	57	450	460	450	7	230	240	230
106	670	670	670	56	450	450	450	6	230	240	230
105	660	660	660	55	440	450	440	5	230	230	230
104	660	660	660	54	440	440	440	4	220	220	220
103	650	650	650	53	440	440	430	3	220	220	220
102	650	650	650	52	430	430	430	2	210	210	210
101	650	650	640	51	430	430	430	1	210	210	210
100	640	640	640	50	420	430	420	0	200	200	200
99	640	640	640	49	420	420	420				
98	630	630	630	48	410	420	410				
97	630	630	630	47	410	410	410				
96	620	620	620	46	400	410	400				
95	620	620	620	45	400	400	400				
94	620	620	610	44	400	400	400				
93	610	610	610	43	390	400	390				
92	610	610	600	42	390	390	390				
91	600	600	600	41	380	390	380				
90	600	600	600	40	380	380	380				
89	590	590	590	39	370	380	370				
88	590	590	590	38	370	370	370				
87	580	590	580	37	370	370	360				
86	580	580	580	36	360	370	360				

Test Content

If you have questions about specific items in the representative tests or in any of the sample tests included in Chapters 3-7, please write to School and Higher Education Test Development, Educational Testing Service, P.O. Box 6656, Princeton, NJ 08541-6656. Please include in your letter the page number on which the item appears and the number of the question, along with specifics of your inquiry or comment. If you have a question about a particular item or items in an actual GMAT, please write to the same address and include in your letter your name, address, sex, date of birth, the date on which you took the test, the test center name, the section number(s) and number(s) of the questions involved. This information is necessary for ETS to retrieve your answer sheet and determine the particular form of the GMAT you took.

Table 1		
Percentages of Candidates Tested from June 1988 through March 1991 (including repeaters) Who Scored below Selected Verbal and Quantitative Scores		
	Percentage Below	
Scaled Score	*Verbal*	*Quantitative*
50-60	>99	>99
48	>99	98
46	99	96
44	98	93
42	95	88
40	92	83
38	87	77
36	81	70
34	74	63
32	66	55
30	58	47
28	50	39
26	41	31
24	33	23
22	25	17
20	19	11
18	14	7
16	10	4
14	6	2
12	3	1
10	1	0
0-8	0	0
Number of Candidates	694,061	694,061
Mean	27	30
Standard Deviation	9	9

Table 2	
Percentages of Candidates Tested from June 1988 through March 1991 (including repeaters) Who Scored below Selected Total Scores	
Scaled Score	*Percentage Below*
740	>99
720	99
700	98
680	96
660	94
640	91
620	87
600	83
580	78
560	71
540	65
520	57
500	50
480	43
460	35
440	29
420	23
400	17
380	13
360	9
340	6
320	4
300	3
280	1
260	1
240	0
Number of Candidates	694,061
Mean	494
Standard Deviation	103

Guidelines for Use of Graduate Management Admission Test Scores

Introduction

These guidelines have been prepared to provide information about appropriate score use for those who interpret scores and set criteria for admission and to protect students from unfair decisions based on inappropriate use of scores.

The guidelines are based on several policy and psychometric considerations.

- The Graduate Management Admission Council has an obligation to inform users of the scores' strengths and limitations and the users have a concomitant obligation to use the scores in an appropriate, rather than the most convenient, manner.

- The purpose of any testing instrument, including the Graduate Management Admission Test, is to provide information to *assist* in making decisions; the test alone should not be presumed to be a decision maker.

- GMAT test scores are but one of a number of sources of information and should be used, whenever possible, in combination with other information and, in every case, with full recognition of what the test can and cannot do.

The primary asset of the GMAT is that it provides a common measure, administered under standard conditions, with known reliability, validity, and other psychometric qualities, for evaluating the academic skills of many individuals. The GMAT has two primary limitations: (1) it cannot and does not measure all the qualities important for graduate study in management and other pursuits, whether in education, career, or other areas of experience; (2) there are psychometric limitations to the test —for example, only score differences of certain magnitudes are reliable indicators of real differences in performance. Such limits should be taken into consideration as GMAT scores are used.

These guidelines consist of general standards and recommended appropriate uses of GMAT scores as well as a listing of inappropriate uses.

Specific Guidelines

1. **In recognition of the test's limitations, use multiple criteria.** Multiple sources of information should be used when evaluating an applicant for graduate management study. The GMAT itself does not measure every discipline-related skill necessary for academic work, nor does it measure subjective factors important to academic and career success, such as motivation, creativity, and interpersonal skills. Therefore, all available pertinent information about an applicant must be considered before a selection decision is made, with GMAT scores being *only one* of these several criteria. The test's limitations are discussed clearly in the GMAT *Bulletin of Information* and in the *GMAT Technical Report*.

2. **Establish the relationship between GMAT scores and performance in your graduate management school.** It is incumbent on any institution using GMAT scores in the admissions process that it demonstrate empirically the relationship between test scores and measures of performance in its academic program. Data should be collected and analyzed to provide information about the predictive validity of GMAT scores and their appropriateness for the particular use and in the particular circumstances at the score-using school. In addition, any formula used in the admissions process that combines test scores with other criteria should be validated to determine whether the weights attached to the particular measures are appropriate for optimizing the prediction of performance in the program. Once set, these weights should be reviewed regularly through the considered deliberation of qualified experts.

3. **Avoid the use of cutoff scores.** The use of arbitrary cutoff scores (below which no applicant will be considered for admission) is strongly discouraged, primarily for the reasons cited in the introduction to these guidelines. Distinctions based on score differences not substantial enough to be reliable should be avoided. (For information about reliability, see the GMAT *Examinee Score Interpretation Guide*.) Cutoff scores should be used only if there is clear empirical evidence that a large proportion of the applicants scoring below the cutoff scores have substantial difficulty doing satisfactory graduate work. In addition, it is incumbent on the school to demonstrate that the use of cutoff scores does not result in the systematic exclusion of members of either sex, of any age or ethnic groups, or of any other relevant groups in the face of other evidence that would indicate their competence or predict their success.

4. **Do not compare GMAT scores with those on other tests.** GMAT scores cannot be derived from scores on other tests. While minor differences among different editions of the GMAT that have been constructed to be parallel can be compensated for by the statistical process of score equating, the GMAT is not intended to be parallel to graduate admission tests offered by other testing programs.

5. **Interpret the scores of disabled persons cautiously.** The GMAT is offered with special arrangements to accommodate the needs of candidates with visual, physical, and learning disabilities. However, no studies have been performed to validate GMAT scores earned under nonstandard conditions. Therefore, test scores earned under nonstandard conditions are reported with a special notice that disabled persons may be at a disadvantage when taking standardized tests such as the GMAT, even when the test is administered in a manner chosen by the candidate to minimize any adverse effect of his or her disability on test performance. In using these scores, admissions officers should note the usual caution that GMAT scores be considered as only one part of an applicant's record.

Normally Appropriate Uses of GMAT Scores

1. **For selection of applicants for graduate study in management.** A person's GMAT scores tell how the person performed on a test designed to measure general verbal and quantitative abilities that are associated with success in the first year of study at graduate schools of management and that have been developed over a long period of time. The scores can be used in conjunction with other information to help estimate performance in a graduate management program.

2. **For selection of applicants for financial aid based on academic potential.**

3. **For counseling and guidance.** Undergraduate counselors, if they maintain appropriate records, such as the test scores and undergraduate grade-point averages of their students accepted by various graduate management programs, may be able to help students estimate their chances of acceptance at given graduate management schools.

Normally Inappropriate Uses of GMAT Scores

1. **As a requisite for awarding a degree.** The GMAT is designed to measure broadly defined verbal and quantitative skills and is primarily useful for predicting success in graduate management schools. The use of the test for anything other than selection for graduate management study, financial aid awards, or counseling and guidance is to be avoided.

2. **As a requirement for employment, for licensing or certification to perform a job, or for job-related rewards (raises, promotions, etc.).** For the reasons listed in #1 above, the use of the GMAT for these purposes is inappropriate. Further, approved score-receiving institutions are not permitted to make score reports available for any of these purposes.

3. **As an achievement test.** The GMAT is not designed to assess an applicant's achievement or knowledge in specific subject areas.

4. **As a diagnostic test.** Beyond general statements about verbal and quantitative ability, the GMAT does not provide diagnostic information about relative strengths of a person's academic abilities.

Order Form for Official GMAC Publications

My payment of $ _____ is enclosed for:

		U.S. Delivery*	Foreign Delivery**
• *The Official Guide for GMAT Review*	(238407)	☐ $ 11.95	☐ $ 21.95
• *The Official Guide to MBA Programs*	(238325)	☐ $ 13.95	☐ $ 28.95
• *The Official Guide to Financing Your MBA*	(238326)	☐ $ 10.95	☐ $ 20.95
• **Special Savings** — All three books	(238327)	☐ $ 32.00	☐ $ 52.00
• *The Official Software for GMAT Review*†	(299654)	☐ $ 59.95	☐ $ 79.95
• **Best Value!** — Software and all three books†	(299653)	☐ $ 80.00	☐ $110.00

*Books sent to the United States, Guam, Puerto Rico, U.S. Virgin Islands, and U.S. territories are shipped by priority mail (first class); software is sent via UPS, and a <u>street address is required</u>. Allow three to four weeks from time of order receipt for delivery.

**Airmail delivery to Canada and all other countries; allow six to eight weeks from time of order receipt for delivery.

† IMPORTANT: See hardware requirements on reverse side.

Reminder: If you order any of the above *Guides* when registering for the GMAT, be sure to enter the amount of your payment in item 32 of the registration form.

This is your mailing label. Type or print clearly.

TO _____

GRADUATE MANAGEMENT ADMISSION TEST
EDUCATIONAL TESTING SERVICE
P.O. BOX 6108
PRINCETON, NJ 08541-6108

692-38
GMAC
GUIDES
G-96

Order Form for Official GMAC Publications

My payment of $ _____ is enclosed for:

		U.S. Delivery*	Foreign Delivery**
• *The Official Guide for GMAT Review*	(238407)	☐ $ 11.95	☐ $ 21.95
• *The Official Guide to MBA Programs*	(238325)	☐ $ 13.95	☐ $ 28.95
• *The Official Guide to Financing Your MBA*	(238326)	☐ $ 10.95	☐ $ 20.95
• **Special Savings** — All three books	(238327)	☐ $ 32.00	☐ $ 52.00
• *The Official Software for GMAT Review*†	(299654)	☐ $ 59.95	☐ $ 79.95
• **Best Value!** — Software and all three books†	(299653)	☐ $ 80.00	☐ $110.00

*Books sent to the United States, Guam, Puerto Rico, U.S. Virgin Islands, and U.S. territories are shipped by priority mail (first class); software is sent via UPS, and a <u>street address is required</u>. Allow three to four weeks from time of order receipt for delivery.

**Airmail delivery to Canada and all other countries; allow six to eight weeks from time of order receipt for delivery.

† IMPORTANT: See hardware requirements on reverse side.

Reminder: If you order any of the above *Guides* when registering for the GMAT, be sure to enter the amount of your payment in item 32 of the registration form.

This is your mailing label. Type or print clearly.

TO _____

GRADUATE MANAGEMENT ADMISSION TEST
EDUCATIONAL TESTING SERVICE
P.O. BOX 6108
PRINCETON, NJ 08541-6108

692-38
GMAC
GUIDES
G-96

Order Form for Official GMAC Publications

My payment of $ _____ is enclosed for:

		U.S. Delivery*	Foreign Delivery**
• *The Official Guide for GMAT Review*	(238407)	☐ $ 11.95	☐ $ 21.95
• *The Official Guide to MBA Programs*	(238325)	☐ $ 13.95	☐ $ 28.95
• *The Official Guide to Financing Your MBA*	(238326)	☐ $ 10.95	☐ $ 20.95
• **Special Savings** — All three books	(238327)	☐ $ 32.00	☐ $ 52.00
• *The Official Software for GMAT Review*†	(299654)	☐ $ 59.95	☐ $ 79.95
• **Best Value!** — Software and all three books†	(299653)	☐ $ 80.00	☐ $110.00

*Books sent to the United States, Guam, Puerto Rico, U.S. Virgin Islands, and U.S. territories are shipped by priority mail (first class); software is sent via UPS, and a <u>street address is required</u>. Allow three to four weeks from time of order receipt for delivery.

**Airmail delivery to Canada and all other countries; allow six to eight weeks from time of order receipt for delivery.

† IMPORTANT: See hardware requirements on reverse side.

Reminder: If you order any of the above *Guides* when registering for the GMAT, be sure to enter the amount of your payment in item 32 of the registration form.

This is your mailing label. Type or print clearly.

TO _____

GRADUATE MANAGEMENT ADMISSION TEST
EDUCATIONAL TESTING SERVICE
P.O. BOX 6108
PRINCETON, NJ 08541-6108

692-38
GMAC
GUIDES
G-96

Before You Take Our Test, Take Our Advice.

The Official Guide for GMAT Review, 1992-94 Edition
- contains three *actual* tests plus samples of each question type — 900 questions in all!
- gives answers and explanations by GMAT test authors
- includes comprehensive math review

The Official Software for GMAT Review, 1992-94 Edition
- interactive tutorials with examples of each question type and step-by-step explanations
- one *actual* test (different from those in the *GMAT Review* book) with on-screen timer and automatic scoring
- individualized feedback on your test performance
- includes two sets of disks (four 5¼″ and two 3½″) plus user's manual
- **Hardware requirements:** IBM PC, XT, AT, PS/2 or 100% compatible computer; hard disk with 2.5 megabytes of free space; 512K; DOS 2.0 through 5.0; CGA, EGA, VGA, Hercules Graphics, or 100% compatible graphics card and monitor (A printer is optional.)

The Official Guide to MBA Programs, 1992-94 Edition
- profiles and compares more than 550 graduate management programs worldwide
- offers advice on choosing a school and handling the application process
- examines management careers and gives sources for more information

Available September 1, 1992:
The Official Guide to Financing Your MBA, 1992-94 Edition
- suggests ways to pay for your MBA
- includes information on loans, scholarships, work-study, etc.
- compares financial aid packages
- provides information on specific schools
- analyzes total costs and benefits of attendance

Ordering Information

The books are sold in many bookstores or can be ordered by mail from Educational Testing Service (ETS). The software is only available by mail. Send the completed order form and mailing label on the reverse side with the appropriate payment to Graduate Management Admission Test, Educational Testing Service, P.O. Box 6108, Princeton, NJ 08541-6108. *Make checks payable to ETS-GMAT.*

Before You Take Our Test, Take Our Advice.

The Official Guide for GMAT Review, 1992-94 Edition
- contains three *actual* tests plus samples of each question type — 900 questions in all!
- gives answers and explanations by GMAT test authors
- includes comprehensive math review

The Official Software for GMAT Review, 1992-94 Edition
- interactive tutorials with examples of each question type and step-by-step explanations
- one *actual* test (different from those in the *GMAT Review* book) with on-screen timer and automatic scoring
- individualized feedback on your test performance
- includes two sets of disks (four 5¼″ and two 3½″) plus user's manual
- **Hardware requirements:** IBM PC, XT, AT, PS/2 or 100% compatible computer; hard disk with 2.5 megabytes of free space; 512K; DOS 2.0 through 5.0; CGA, EGA, VGA, Hercules Graphics, or 100% compatible graphics card and monitor (A printer is optional.)

The Official Guide to MBA Programs, 1992-94 Edition
- profiles and compares more than 550 graduate management programs worldwide
- offers advice on choosing a school and handling the application process
- examines management careers and gives sources for more information

Available September 1, 1992:
The Official Guide to Financing Your MBA, 1992-94 Edition
- suggests ways to pay for your MBA
- includes information on loans, scholarships, work-study, etc.
- compares financial aid packages
- provides information on specific schools
- analyzes total costs and benefits of attendance

Ordering Information

The books are sold in many bookstores or can be ordered by mail from Educational Testing Service (ETS). The software is only available by mail. Send the completed order form and mailing label on the reverse side with the appropriate payment to Graduate Management Admission Test, Educational Testing Service, P.O. Box 6108, Princeton, NJ 08541-6108. *Make checks payable to ETS-GMAT.*

Before You Take Our Test, Take Our Advice.

The Official Guide for GMAT Review, 1992-94 Edition
- contains three *actual* tests plus samples of each question type — 900 questions in all!
- gives answers and explanations by GMAT test authors
- includes comprehensive math review

The Official Software for GMAT Review, 1992-94 Edition
- interactive tutorials with examples of each question type and step-by-step explanations
- one *actual* test (different from those in the *GMAT Review* book) with on-screen timer and automatic scoring
- individualized feedback on your test performance
- includes two sets of disks (four 5¼″ and two 3½″) plus user's manual
- **Hardware requirements:** IBM PC, XT, AT, PS/2 or 100% compatible computer; hard disk with 2.5 megabytes of free space; 512K; DOS 2.0 through 5.0; CGA, EGA, VGA, Hercules Graphics, or 100% compatible graphics card and monitor (A printer is optional.)

The Official Guide to MBA Programs, 1992-94 Edition
- profiles and compares more than 550 graduate management programs worldwide
- offers advice on choosing a school and handling the application process
- examines management careers and gives sources for more information

Available September 1, 1992:
The Official Guide to Financing Your MBA, 1992-94 Edition
- suggests ways to pay for your MBA
- includes information on loans, scholarships, work-study, etc.
- compares financial aid packages
- provides information on specific schools
- analyzes total costs and benefits of attendance

Ordering Information

The books are sold in many bookstores or can be ordered by mail from Educational Testing Service (ETS). The software is only available by mail. Send the completed order form and mailing label on the reverse side with the appropriate payment to Graduate Management Admission Test, Educational Testing Service, P.O. Box 6108, Princeton, NJ 08541-6108. *Make checks payable to ETS-GMAT.*

Order Form for GMAT Bulletin of Information

Applicants to schools requiring the Graduate Management Admission Test (GMAT) may arrange with Educational Testing Service (ETS) to take the test on one of four dates. If you wish to receive free of charge a *Bulletin of Information* describing arrangements for taking the test, the nature of the exam, and scoring procedures, complete the address label at the right and mail it to:

**Graduate Management Admission Test
Educational Testing Service
P.O. Box 6101
Princeton, NJ 08541-6101**

To order a *GMAT Bulletin of Information* by telephone, call (609) 771-7330.

A registration form and return envelope accompany each *Bulletin of Information*.

Depending on where and when you want to take the test, your completed registration form and fee must be received by the date indicated on the Registration Calendar (see reverse side) for the test date you select (requests for supplementary and Sabbath observer centers have earlier deadlines). It is to your advantage to send for your *Bulletin* and complete your registration form as early as possible. (Processing of registrations for 1992-93 will begin in late August 1992.)

Please note that, although you may receive order forms from several schools, you need only one **Bulletin** *and registration form.*

This is your mailing label. Type or print clearly.

TO

GRADUATE MANAGEMENT ADMISSION TEST   666-17
EDUCATIONAL TESTING SERVICE   GMAT
P.O. BOX 6101   BULLETIN
PRINCETON, NJ 08541-6101

Order Form for GMAT Bulletin of Information

Applicants to schools requiring the Graduate Management Admission Test (GMAT) may arrange with Educational Testing Service (ETS) to take the test on one of four dates. If you wish to receive free of charge a *Bulletin of Information* describing arrangements for taking the test, the nature of the exam, and scoring procedures, complete the address label at the right and mail it to:

**Graduate Management Admission Test
Educational Testing Service
P.O. Box 6101
Princeton, NJ 08541-6101**

To order a *GMAT Bulletin of Information* by telephone, call (609) 771-7330.

A registration form and return envelope accompany each *Bulletin of Information*.

Depending on where and when you want to take the test, your completed registration form and fee must be received by the date indicated on the Registration Calendar (see reverse side) for the test date you select (requests for supplementary and Sabbath observer centers have earlier deadlines). It is to your advantage to send for your *Bulletin* and complete your registration form as early as possible. (Processing of registrations for 1992-93 will begin in late August 1992.)

Please note that, although you may receive order forms from several schools, you need only one **Bulletin** *and registration form.*

This is your mailing label. Type or print clearly.

TO

GRADUATE MANAGEMENT ADMISSION TEST   666-17
EDUCATIONAL TESTING SERVICE   GMAT
P.O. BOX 6101   BULLETIN
PRINCETON, NJ 08541-6101

Order Form for GMAT Bulletin of Information

Applicants to schools requiring the Graduate Management Admission Test (GMAT) may arrange with Educational Testing Service (ETS) to take the test on one of four dates. If you wish to receive free of charge a *Bulletin of Information* describing arrangements for taking the test, the nature of the exam, and scoring procedures, complete the address label at the right and mail it to:

**Graduate Management Admission Test
Educational Testing Service
P.O. Box 6101
Princeton, NJ 08541-6101**

To order a *GMAT Bulletin of Information* by telephone, call (609) 771-7330.

A registration form and return envelope accompany each *Bulletin of Information*.

Depending on where and when you want to take the test, your completed registration form and fee must be received by the date indicated on the Registration Calendar (see reverse side) for the test date you select (requests for supplementary and Sabbath observer centers have earlier deadlines). It is to your advantage to send for your *Bulletin* and complete your registration form as early as possible. (Processing of registrations for 1992-93 will begin in late August 1992.)

Please note that, although you may receive order forms from several schools, you need only one **Bulletin** *and registration form.*

This is your mailing label. Type or print clearly.

TO

GRADUATE MANAGEMENT ADMISSION TEST   666-17
EDUCATIONAL TESTING SERVICE   GMAT
P.O. BOX 6101   BULLETIN
PRINCETON, NJ 08541-6101

Registration Calendar

Test Dates	DOMESTIC REGISTRATION GMAT administrations in the U.S., Guam, Puerto Rico, U.S. Virgin Islands, and U.S. Territories			FOREIGN REGISTRATION GMAT administrations in all other countries (including Canada)	
	REGULAR REGISTRATION	LATE REGISTRATION & CENTER CHANGE	SPECIAL REQUESTS	FINAL REGISTRATION & CENTER CHANGE	SPECIAL REQUESTS
	Registration forms **received** after this date must be accompanied by the late registration fee.	Add the late registration fee. Registration forms **received** after this period will be returned.	Last **receipt** date for supplementary centers and Saturday-Sabbath observer administrations*	Registration forms received after this date will be returned.	Last date for receipt of requests for supplementary centers† and Saturday-Sabbath observer administrations.*
	Deadline Dates				
Oct. 17, 1992*†	Sept. 18	Sept. 19-25	Sept. 1	Sept. 4	Aug. 21
Jan. 16, 1993*	Dec. 18	Dec. 19-25	Dec. 1	Dec. 4	Nov. 20
Mar. 20, 1993*	Feb. 19	Feb. 20-26	Feb. 2	Feb. 5	Jan. 22
June 19, 1993*	May 21	May 22-28	May 4	May 7	April 23

*Administration dates for observers of the Saturday Sabbath are Monday, October 19, 1992; Tuesday, January 19, 1993; Monday, March 22, 1993; and Monday, June 21, 1993.
†No supplementary centers will be established for foreign registration for the October 1992 test date.

Scores are reported approximately *five* weeks after the test date.

Registration Calendar

Test Dates	DOMESTIC REGISTRATION GMAT administrations in the U.S., Guam, Puerto Rico, U.S. Virgin Islands, and U.S. Territories			FOREIGN REGISTRATION GMAT administrations in all other countries (including Canada)	
	REGULAR REGISTRATION	LATE REGISTRATION & CENTER CHANGE	SPECIAL REQUESTS	FINAL REGISTRATION & CENTER CHANGE	SPECIAL REQUESTS
	Registration forms **received** after this date must be accompanied by the late registration fee.	Add the late registration fee. Registration forms **received** after this period will be returned.	Last **receipt** date for supplementary centers and Saturday-Sabbath observer administrations*	Registration forms received after this date will be returned.	Last date for receipt of requests for supplementary centers† and Saturday-Sabbath observer administrations.*
	Deadline Dates				
Oct. 17, 1992*†	Sept. 18	Sept. 19-25	Sept. 1	Sept. 4	Aug. 21
Jan. 16, 1993*	Dec. 18	Dec. 19-25	Dec. 1	Dec. 4	Nov. 20
Mar. 20, 1993*	Feb. 19	Feb. 20-26	Feb. 2	Feb. 5	Jan. 22
June 19, 1993*	May 21	May 22-28	May 4	May 7	April 23

*Administration dates for observers of the Saturday Sabbath are Monday, October 19, 1992; Tuesday, January 19, 1993; Monday, March 22, 1993; and Monday, June 21, 1993.
†No supplementary centers will be established for foreign registration for the October 1992 test date.

Scores are reported approximately *five* weeks after the test date.

Registration Calendar

Test Dates	DOMESTIC REGISTRATION GMAT administrations in the U.S., Guam, Puerto Rico, U.S. Virgin Islands, and U.S. Territories			FOREIGN REGISTRATION GMAT administrations in all other countries (including Canada)	
	REGULAR REGISTRATION	LATE REGISTRATION & CENTER CHANGE	SPECIAL REQUESTS	FINAL REGISTRATION & CENTER CHANGE	SPECIAL REQUESTS
	Registration forms **received** after this date must be accompanied by the late registration fee.	Add the late registration fee. Registration forms **received** after this period will be returned.	Last **receipt** date for supplementary centers and Saturday-Sabbath observer administrations*	Registration forms received after this date will be returned.	Last date for receipt of requests for supplementary centers† and Saturday-Sabbath observer administrations.*
	Deadline Dates				
Oct. 17, 1992*†	Sept. 18	Sept. 19-25	Sept. 1	Sept. 4	Aug. 21
Jan. 16, 1993*	Dec. 18	Dec. 19-25	Dec. 1	Dec. 4	Nov. 20
Mar. 20, 1993*	Feb. 19	Feb. 20-26	Feb. 2	Feb. 5	Jan. 22
June 19, 1993*	May 21	May 22-28	May 4	May 7	April 23

*Administration dates for observers of the Saturday Sabbath are Monday, October 19, 1992; Tuesday, January 19, 1993; Monday, March 22, 1993; and Monday, June 21, 1993.
†No supplementary centers will be established for foreign registration for the October 1992 test date.

Scores are reported approximately *five* weeks after the test date.